PENGUIN BOOKS

THE WAY OF A BOY

'A meticulous and astonishingly vivid re-creation of one child's journey from a kind of paradise – life among the white-skinned "plantocracy" of Dutch-ruled Java – into a kind of hell ... At times sad, yet never the least bit sentimental' – *Globe and Mail*

'It seems to me a striking achievement that the adult telling the story had the strength to allow out the voice of the boy ... As story-telling it is faultless, as witness it is undeniable' – Neil Bissoondath

'The reader is left in awe of the bravery, endurance and solidarity of which humans are capable, as well as the brutality, evil and divisiveness they can inflict' – *South China Morning Post*

'[Hillen's] account of what they ... endured so calmly, so without hysteria and so without complaint, is to me something which is essential if the record of the immense suffering imposed by the Japanese in south-east Asia is to be complete' – Sir Laurens van der Post

'Moving and horrifying as they are, sometimes unbearably so, the gentleness and innocent freshness of these recollections is what stays in the mind ... entrancing' – Christopher Wordsworth in the *Sunday Telegraph*

ABOUT THE AUTHOR

Ernest Hillen was born in Holland and moved to Indonesia when he was three. He emigrated to Canada in 1952 and is currently an associate editor with *Saturday Night* magazine.

ERNEST HILLEN

THE WAY OF A BOY

A MEMOIR OF JAVA

PENGUIN BOOKS

To Anna Cadwallader Watson-Hillen

PENGUIN BOOKS

Published by the Penguin Group
Penguin Books Ltd, 27 Wrights Lane, London W8 5TZ, England
Penguin Books USA Inc., 375 Hudson Street, New York, New York 10014, USA
Penguin Books Australia Ltd, Ringwood, Victoria, Australia
Penguin Books Canada Ltd, 10 Alcorn Avenue, Toronto, Ontario, Canada M4V 3B2
Penguin Books (NZ) Ltd, 182–190 Wairau Road, Auckland 10, New Zealand

Penguin Books Ltd, Registered Offices: Harmondsworth, Middlesex, England

First published in Canada by Viking 1993
First published in Great Britain by Viking 1994
Published in Penguin Books 1995
13 5 7 9 10 8 6 4 2

Printed in England by Clays Ltd, St Ives plc

Acknowledgments

Thank you to:
Marta Tomins for every day and every page, for providing serenity and the finest editorial skill I know; Maia Hillen for patience and inspiration — in the time it took to write this book, she wrote *and* illustrated half a dozen.

Jerry Hillen, John Hillen, Ankie Sonius-Crone, Zuseke Crone, Hanneke Staal, and Ineke Staal-Wondergem for sharing memory.

Jan Whitford of the Lucinda Vardey Agency for good counsel and care.

Cynthia Good, Publisher of Penguin Books Canada, for understanding and editorial guidance; Mary Adachi for meticulous copy editing.

John Fraser, Editor of *Saturday Night* magazine, for encouragement and for providing a "home" at *SN*; Dianne de Gayardon de Fenoyl and Dianna Symonds for enthusiasm and early reading of the MS; Barbara Moon for abiding interest; Hibo Abdalla and Karen Norell for first-rate printing labours; everyone at *SN* for their good will.

Ian Brown, Danielle Crittenden, Kildare Dobbs, George Galt, William Lowther, Candida van Rees Vellinga, and Peter Worthington for their support.

Rita Davidson, William Davidson, Anita Tomins, and Thomas Eva for forgiving absences.

The Toronto Arts Council and the Ontario Arts Council for writing grants.

Segments of this book have appeared in *Saturday Night*, *The Idler*, *The Wall Street Journal* and *Weekend Magazine*.

Contents

1

The Plantation

Something making soft sounds underneath the plank floor woke me. Very quietly, so as not to rouse Jerry next door, I climbed out of bed and pressed my ear to the boards — and heard breathing. It would be completely black down there now. Even during the day it was a dark place because of the spider webs that hung from the edges of the small raised house; to wriggle underneath I had to lift the webs aside with a stick. But I liked crawling around in the cool sand, especially after midday when the sun turned white and banana trees lost their shade.

The breathing was coming in slurps. It was looking for something to eat, of course, but nothing lived there; I'd never even seen a snake. The little house, called the "pavilion" for some reason, stood behind our main house on the plantation. Jerry and I had our own bedrooms and in front was a long room lined with so many windows it got boiling hot during the day if the shutters were left open. Lying underneath the pavilion, I knew just where everything was — Jerry's bed, my bed, the cabin trunk holding my harmonica wrapped in a

1

white handkerchief, and my iron collection. Down there, I sometimes listened to Jerry, who was eleven, and our mother doing his lessons; he correcting her Dutch because he spoke it better. And I lay there in the shadows when Jerry was punished, usually for lying, and locked in with the shutters closed so he couldn't even read. I would tell him stories through the floor; he was four years older so I don't know if he liked them but there was nothing else he could do. Some of the stories were about a Chinese girl who roamed in high red boots over hills and through valleys. She had adventures and because she liked to stop and pick unripe mangoes to eat with salt she often had diarrhea.

With my ear still to the plank floor, I heard a snort then and knew what was beneath me — a wild boar. I'd never seen one because they live so deep in the jungle, but Manang, our gardener, said that they were as fast as locomotives and sometimes went crazy and would run you down and rip you to pieces. If they strayed onto the plantation, usually at night, they could hurt young tea bushes or people, and they had to be killed. Lately, Mr Otten had shot three of them. Mr Otten, the plantation's mechanic, was the only white man left; the other eight, my father too, all Dutch, had been taken away by Japanese soldiers in a truck a few weeks earlier. This had happened on all the plantations. It was 1942; there was a war on and, for now, the Japanese had won. We were living in the mountains on the island of Java in the Dutch East Indies (Indonesia). Mr Otten was a short, kind, half-Dutch, half-Indonesian man with a tiny moustache who had been allowed to stay behind to take care of the factory, and to keep his rifle. He hunted the wild boars together with Indonesians carrying spears with real steel points. Whenever Jerry and I asked if we could come along on a hunt Mr Otten said "Absolutely!" but never kept his word; Manang cut bamboo spears for us anyway, just in case.

I lay unmoving on the floor and it snorted again. I wasn't scared: it didn't sound mad. Imagine having one as a pet! Another snort, and a grunt, but not so close now; it was wandering away. With great speed and terrible strength I threw my spear into the boar's side — no, into its eye — and black-red blood spurted out. I climbed back into bed.

Manang smelled of different kinds of smoke. He never hurried and I liked being near him: it was restful. My father and the other men used to return from the tea gardens in shirts dark with sweat, their faces wet. Not Manang. He never looked hot. Manang wore faded khaki shorts that used to be my father's, no shirt, and a straw hat that hid his eyes. His large flat feet had spaces between the toes because he didn't have to wear shoes. I had felt the bottoms of those feet and they were hard and covered with deep, dry, criss-cross cuts which he said didn't hurt. I wanted feet like that, and his shiny brown skin, and I tried to walk bow-legged like him. Manang usually worked squatting, slowly moving along in the quiet warm air like a duck. That's how he chopped at the lawn with a long knife, that's how he weeded or dug or planted. That's how, from bamboo and from a certain soft wood, he would carve guns, knives, arrows, whatever we needed; we had only to ask. And that's how, from half peanut shells, splinters of wood, and bits of banana leaf, he built boats to sail on a puddle; you lay on your stomach and blew the boat from shore to shore. Manang almost never seemed to need to stand. He didn't often say much, and I don't know if he had a wife or children or where he lived, but he let me stay near him.

When it rained, Manang would squat on the edge of the covered walkway behind the house along which were ranged the tool shed, kitchen, bathroom, and garage; he would smoke the thin cigarettes he rolled and watch the rain, watch it from the distance racing nearer, watch it shake the bushes and drench the grass. He could wait, he had time. When the sun was out you could see far across the hills that glimmered in every shade of green, and the clouds moved high in the sky. But in the drumming, clattering rain the world grew small. Manang stared ahead, smoking, not moving. It was safe near him. There were others like Manang, old men who couldn't work any more, who stayed up all night around the plantation, cigarettes glowing in the dark, guarding us whites, our homes, our trucks, the tea factory. It was good to know they were out there, smoking, watching.

But it has to be said that Manang was not brave; at least he had some cowardly spirits inside him. He himself had told me about spirits — spirits inside people and animals, in the air, on mountains, and in trees where during storms the souls of children cried. Spirits everywhere, and clearly some that could undo Manang. Jerry and I sometimes built war planes from upside-down garden chairs and invited "the girls," who were visible only to us, into our cockpits and made calm, joking remarks as we turned loops and strafed enemy soldiers. That was brave.

And Jerry was brave after our father left. Our father had a bull terrier called Leo, white with brown spots, who listened to no one but him. If the dog didn't obey quickly he'd be shouted at or slapped; if he did, there was no praise because, of course, he was behaving as he should. This, my father said, was how Leo learned "discipline"; Jerry and I were taught discipline as well. When my father was home it was safe to unchain the dog and let him run around and Manang would feed him. But after the soldiers took my father away, Leo wasn't set free at all — and it drove him wild. If he saw someone, anyone, he ran forward so fast his chain jerked him upright and there he danced, snarling and barking. Manang was not brave, because once my father was gone, he never went near Leo again.

It was Jerry who pushed water and food to the angry dog with a broom — and afterwards sometimes vomited. I, of course, was too little to do it, and Jerry would have stopped our mother. This was probably because of what our father had said to us on the day he left. He said it while the truck holding the other white men waited with the motor running and soldiers stood on guard, the bayonets on their long rifles glittering in the sun. He had shaken Jerry's hand and then mine and let his blue-grey eyes burn into our brown ones. His dark blond hair was combed flat back, freeing his forehead and highlighting his eyes. They could see inside your head. If you did something wrong he would shoot you his look, even when there were visitors. It was foolish to lie to him; Jerry tried and nearly always tripped up. On that last day, standing on the stone front steps, our father had said to us, slowly: "Take care of your mother." Well, maybe Jerry knew what he meant, but I had no idea. It was a strange thing to say. How could a little kid take care of his mom? Make her laugh? Bring her tea? It didn't make sense. She was there to take care of *me*.

That day we had been told at breakfast that our father was going down the mountains to a "camp" for men only. Our parents talked in tight voices, in English so we wouldn't understand. My father needed all my mother's attention; they hardly noticed us. There was tea and porridge and we could have one slice of bread with sweetened condensed milk. For months we had watched adults listening to the radio, chewing their lips, smoking a lot. We had heard bombs fall far away and seen planes painted with the red ball fly over. Sitting at the table, we understood that it was a serious time — a camp was really a jail; our father didn't know where it was or how long he'd be there. Since dawn he'd been packing and repacking the one suitcase he could take. During those moments, as our parents prepared for parting, Jerry and I cleaned out the can of condensed milk.

When Manang pretended Leo didn't exist, my mother told him this had to stop, that my father was counting on him. Manang agreed, asked forgiveness, and avoided the dog. And then Leo broke loose — and Manang slipped away. My mother and Jerry and I escaped into the house, and the cook, who in her tight sarong would squat over the coal fire on the kitchen floor, locked herself in along with the washerwoman. Leo trotted back and forth in front of the beds of pink and red oleanders beneath the windows, watching for a face to show; if he saw one of us he'd stand very still and bare his teeth. We were prisoners. Left alone with two children and a mad dog, our mother, her face a little pale under her freckles, told us Leo was Daddy's dog, Daddy loved him, and Daddy wouldn't want him hurt. Thirty-five years old, slim and straight, she paced the living room, her long fingers touching a vase, a tablecloth, her swept-up dark red hair; I always thought her hands moved like a queen's. Her serious brown eyes stared out over the waves of tea bushes broken only by patches of jungle. A decision was needed. What would Daddy do? she asked. It wasn't like her at all. She was proud of her "common sense," inherited, she said, from Grandpa Watson, her father in Canada. "Maybe I'm not as smart as so-and-so," she might say to my father, "but I've got more common sense." Finally, though, she phoned Mr Otten to come with his rifle. She told us that Mr Otten had wondered how he could get a good shot with Leo on the loose. How could he even get out of his car?

Without saying a word, my brother Jerry got a tin of corned beef from the dining-room cupboard where dry goods were kept, opened it with its little key, and shook out the beef. Clutching the fatty meat, he ran out the back door to the tool shed calling, "Leo! Leo!" The dog came storming around the corner just as Jerry pulled open the shed door. He held up the corned beef for Leo to see and threw it inside, but before Leo dove after it he bit Jerry's hand. Then Jerry slammed the door shut.

That was brave action by Jerry, and unusual: what he really liked was to be alone and read. Sometimes he would sit in the front pavilion room late at night and read by moonlight. He almost never yelled, grabbed things away, or beat me up, although he could have because I liked fighting and he was stronger; he didn't enjoy fighting though. Sometimes he teased, but not for long. And when we played, I forgot he was older. Jerry was caught lying — and then got it with my father's thin leather slipper on his bare bum and was locked up for whole days in his room — because he couldn't keep his eyes steady; he never learned to hide what was inside him very well. He wasn't quick to smile, so that by the time he did, it often didn't seem sincere.

One day when I was about four and we were alone at home playing cowboys and Indians, which Jerry knew about from books, he shot me in the eye with a bamboo arrow. The eyelid had shut in time and as I jumped and yelled the arrow was swinging from the eyelid without harm. What Jerry did was just pull the arrow out, sit me on a sofa, put his arm around me, and read out loud from one of his books without pictures until I fell asleep. That's how our parents found us when they came home from playing bridge; the eyelid showed only a tiny red mark. On the evening before I turned seven, after I'd gone to bed, he was allowed to work through the night cleaning his bicycle and then painting it pale grey; he wrapped the saddle in blue ribbon. It was my big present of the day; sitting on the crossbar I could just reach the pedals. It had to be the finest thing Jerry owned but I wasn't so surprised when he gave it to me.

Mr Otten was phoned back and when he drove up it had begun to rain hard. From inside the house the three of us watched him march to the tool shed, part a bunch of strands in the bamboo matting of the door, and stick the rifle through. The gun jumped twice.

Jerry and I took off our shirts and in our short pants we went out and dug the dog's grave by the purple bougainvillaea near the front-door steps where our father had said goodbye. It was always okay for us to be out in that warm rain; our mother watched from a window and let us be. Water half covered Leo after we lowered him into the hole: he really wasn't very big. Mr Otten had shot him in the head and in the throat but the rain had washed the little holes clean. We shovelled the wet red earth on him, stamped and slid about on the grave to flatten it, found some rocks and pressed them in on top. Looking down with clasped hands we said things we thought our father might have said to Leo and we cried; then we thought of more things to say so we could cry more. Manang didn't come back that day.

The morning after the snorting under the floor I went to see Mrs Plomp. The houses on the plantation were near each other and I enjoyed making short visits, to tell a story or to hear one. Mrs Plomp was the youngest woman and the most beautiful. All around us in villages and hamlets tucked away in the bush lived thousands of Indonesians, unhurried people with dark eyes, liking laughter, loving children, kindly but able to turn suddenly *mateklap*, mad with anger. The women in their tight sarongs walked with tiny, swaying steps, never a hair out of place. Most of the people worked

9

in the tea gardens and the factory, a few in our homes. At night through the trees you could see points of light from their oil lamps; they had no electricity. I knew many and visited them in their smoky, dark, bamboo huts where often a picture of Queen Wilhelmina in a huge dress with wide shoulders hung on the wall. They were poor, ate with their fingers, didn't speak Dutch, and I never saw one in the swimming pool except to clean it. So Mrs Plomp was the youngest, most beautiful, *white* woman. She had long red nails, thin arms, and blonde hair that trembled on her neck.

Once I had knocked on their door and Mr Plomp, a big man, also blond, had answered, his face as red as a beet. He told me softly to come around another time. I ran home — they lived across the road from us on a hill of grass and flowers — and my mother told me that Mr Plomp that morning had received a telegram from Holland saying his father had died. After Mr Plomp was picked up by the soldiers with the truck, Mrs Plomp would wander around her house in short pants and shirts that were much too big for her; the pantlegs and the spaces between the shirt buttons were so wide I could see her underwear. Maybe they were Mr Plomp's clothes and she wore them because she missed him.

On top of a high carved cupboard in Mrs Plomp's dining room stood a glass jar filled with red candies. As soon as I spotted it, I didn't look at it again. I told Mrs Plomp that food was important, and she agreed. I said that to stay healthy you should always try to eat healthy. I asked her what were the things she enjoyed eating most, and she named some. Then I mentioned a few of mine: fried bananas, soup with *balletjes,* cucumbers, red candy, peanut butter, fruit salad. "Red candy?" Mrs Plomp said, astonished. "Look!" she pointed to the jar.

When I told Mrs Plomp what I'd heard the night before under the floor her eyes widened and she shivered — and I don't think she was pretending. Her house was very near ours; she lived alone and I was, after all, talking about a real live wild boar poking around in the night. I was sure that's what I'd heard. Mean, hairy, dangerous things with big teeth curling up out of their mouths. Killers. At breakfast I had mentioned the spurting blood and Jerry and my mother had stayed calm. After she gave me my red candy, Mrs Plomp said that perhaps I should warn Mr Otten. I was happy she believed me, and I promised I would — after swimming.

Every morning, before lunch, all the white families strolled up to the swimming pool. It was the choice spot on the plantation: from it you could see all our houses, the soccer field, the factory, the main road. On weekends we took picnic baskets and spent almost entire days there. Jerry and I had few toys, but every day held the certainty of play in the pool. It was never denied (except to Jerry on lock-up days). On birthdays we were allowed to jump in with our clothes on. If it rained, my mother said that was all the more reason to go. In bed I planned amazing jumps and tricks for the next day.

With the men gone, except for Mr Otten, it wasn't as much fun at the pool. The men knew how to be rough and throw kids around. There were cabins to

11

change in for girls and women and for boys and men. The walls were made of the bamboo matting, *bilik*, and it wasn't hard to pull a few strands aside and peek through. Jerry said he once saw two breasts but couldn't tell whose they were.

I liked the water. Whatever fear I might have had I lost when my father picked me up one day, carried me to a corner of the deep end and told me to make it across that corner where he would wait for me — and dropped me in. I was about four. Scary, yes, but it also meant that while I thrashed towards him he was interested in me. And when my father was interested his attention was total. With his hands he could make or repair or draw anything; he read a lot and seemed to know everything in the world. It felt wonderful inside his attention. In a book he showed us pictures of the gloomy-looking men whose music he turned up loud; pianos, violins, flutes; some pieces he could whistle from start to finish. A few times he let us listen to his gramophone records. We had to sit still and terrible itches would begin; Jerry and I never looked at each other — one giggle and you were out. Lessons in discipline, but we didn't mind. We watched the little beige lizards called *tjik-tjaks* flit about the walls after insects. Manang once cut the tail off one to show it didn't bleed and that the tail went on wiggling by itself; he promised that a new tail always grew back on. My father listened to his music with eyes staring or closed, frowning, humming, dipping and shaking his head. When it ended he would say *that* was music, the *only* music. We were happy to have been near him.

I wasn't five yet when I dog-paddled the pool's

length, eyes wide open beneath the surface lit by the sun. When I came up for air adults clapped their hands. A year later I made the length under water back and forth. Even the best swimmer on the plantation, Mr Witte, the chief administrator, had a hard time doing that, and would burst up out of the water gasping. Mr Witte, who was mostly bald, had a deep voice, and powerful, hairy forearms. He laughed a lot and hard, and let no one forget who was boss; even at picnics he gave orders. His wife wasn't like that. Mrs Witte was a small woman, erect and proud, polite even to children. She wore yellow and pink starched dresses and she limped a little because one leg was shorter than the other and a high shoe held its foot. In a bathing suit, barefoot, she had to hop, but then she'd dive into the pool and smoothly breast-stroke lap after lap, eyes ahead, chin up, never wetting her hair. Mr Witte's eyes followed her into the water then followed other women, walking, sitting, easing themselves into the pool; my mother, too, when she took off her bathing cap and her long red hair fell loose. Some women felt his eyes and glanced up and then his eyes would lock on theirs until they looked away. I saw this — everybody did. Chief administrators were kings on their plantations, I heard my father say once. I think he liked Mr Witte, liked his discipline.

I went to see Mr Otten at work after lunch. The factory hummed and puffed out the dry smell of tea; inside, machines shuddered and roared. Everywhere on the plantation it was quiet, the littlest sound carried and hung. Wind breathed on leaves, on high grass; for long moments it was utterly silent. It was only in the factory that you couldn't hear the birds or thunder. Mr Otten wore oily overalls left unbuttoned to the crotch to keep cool. He was now the only boss and very busy but he too believed me about the boar and said he would send a man to check its tracks. As usual he said "Absolutely" when I asked if Jerry and I could come along on the hunt. When I argued that this boar was a little bit mine, Mr Otten stroked his moustache but didn't answer. So I asked if I might go look in his machine shop if I didn't touch the tools, and he let me.

Everywhere I walked in that time it was with my eyes to the ground — scanning for nuts, bolts, nails, pieces of wire, anything metal. The cabin trunk in my bedroom already held a large-size Blue Band margarine can full of metal. I picked up bits around the plantation and when we had gone to the city, Bandung, I had found lots in the streets. From the machine-shop floor I crammed steel filings into my pockets. No one knew why I collected metal. Jerry had asked, and so had my mother, and I'd said it was just something to do.

But I had lied. There was a huge plan. I dreamt about it. When I was three we had come to Indonesia from Holland on a marvellous steamship with one funnel. My goal was this: when I had enough metal I would melt it all down and then build just such a ship — except mine would have two funnels. More metal was needed, much more — it would take years — and meantime it was best to keep the scheme secret. Drawings I had made I pinned up in my room, but of course nobody knew they were of the plan. People would have laughed. For many months in the city and on the plantation, I carefully gathered small metal things and stored them in the cabin trunk. I had patience; lots of it. One day everybody's mouth would fall open.

Everybody also meant Ineke and Hanneke, their baby brother Erik, and their mother and father, *Tante* Ina and *Oom* Fred Staal — "aunt" and "uncle" because they were our parents' best friends. Uncle Fred was the administrator on another, a rubber, plantation some distance away; Ineke was Jerry's age, Hanneke about two years older than I. There were no schools in the mountains so for more than a year our two families had rented a house down in Bandung; when school was on, the mothers took turns every other month staying up at the plantations with their husbands and looking after the kids in the city. Aunt Ina, like my father, was much sterner than my mother, or Uncle Fred; she could be fussy and was hardly interested in my stories. I had known Ineke and Hanneke since I was three. They were like sisters; all four of us had brown eyes. Ineke wore long pigtails and when I was younger she let me use them as reins; Hanneke allowed me to keep some of the lifelike horses and dogs she drew. Mostly, though, Jerry and I were on our own, had only each other to play with. Sometimes we joined Indonesian kids on the soccer field and kicked around a coconut husk tied together with string; nobody owned a real ball.

One morning a few days after I had seen him at the factory, Mr Otten drove up to our house in a small truck and when he shut off the motor he called my name. From the back of the truck he and a helper lifted something heavy wrapped in a sack. I came running up

15

and Mr Otten whipped back the cloth. There was the cut-off head of a wild boar covered in black-red blood and flies. He had shot it the night before and was sure this was the animal I had heard under the floor. Its small yellowish eyes stared up at me. Mr Otten said he hadn't been able to take me on the hunt but here was the head. A present. If I buried it in the ground and let worms eat the hairy skin and the meat, they would leave a beautiful, clean, white, wild boar's skull to put in my room. The boar had roamed around in my mind a lot and for a moment I felt sorry it was dead — but I could *see* the clean white skull.

Jerry and I got shovels and dragged the head up into the garden which rose behind the house. Manang grew sweet potatoes there, and peas, beans, papayas, and pineapples. We began to dig in an open space among the pineapples. It was the spot where we smoked and from which we could see the road on which our father drove home on his motorcycle. We stole his American cigarettes, not often, from a little latched cupboard in the living room that also held Bols gin, cheese biscuits from our Dutch grandmother just for him, and playing cards; in the evenings adults played bridge a lot at each other's houses. One day our father came home on foot and must have seen the smoke from the road. When we noticed him he was already running. We threw the cigarettes into the sharp pineapple leaves and started running ourselves. I looked back to see if my father was gaining, and he was, but smiling a little, so I just let myself drop, and Jerry did too. His back to the sun, our father towered over us, a black giant with legs spread and hands on his hips. Even though we couldn't read his face, we rolled on the ground, kicking and laughing. No punishment that time; he only made us promise to stop smoking because it was bad for us, and we knew that.

Jerry and I looked for Manang to help us dig but he had made himself invisible. Dig deep, Mr Otten had warned, because in the heat the meat would quickly start to smell. He was right. Two days later in the afternoon we found the hole pawed open. Up close the stink from the rotting head already crawling with tiny white worms made our eyes water. We had to dig deeper. Jerry helped pull the thing out but then left me alone. I tied a teatowel over my nose and mouth, breathed in deeply as I did at the pool, ran to the hole, dug, then hurried away for fresh air. Back and forth, back and forth. It was the hottest time of day, very still, and it seemed hours passed with the hole hardly changing. My knees hurt; I cried. My mother watched from a window. Finally the hole was so deep I could stand up in it. I tumbled the head in, shovelled down the loose earth, and piled big rocks on top. Now I would wait.

Time passed, wheeling about on Jerry's bike, swimming and diving, searching for metal, sitting near Manang. When you woke up most mornings everything was hidden in mist; then the burning sun would slowly undress bushes, trees, houses, and the rolling green hills stretching as far as you could see. The quiet on the plantation sometimes made you drowsy and you lay down in the grass below whispering leaves. We listened to tree frogs whistling and the swelling and fading of cricket song. Jerry and I had our hair cut very short in a chair on the lawn by a village *tukang tjukur,* barber, who also massaged our heads, tapping sharply with his fingers until we felt it down to our feet and almost fainted. We boxed wearing Jerry's thick socks from Holland on our fists — and somehow I always won. Through high grass sharp as knives we chased snakes. One slid into a hole and Jerry yanked it out by the tail: that was brave. And with our spears, we hunted down many wild boars and panthers. We pretended to be horses, like the Indonesians did on their New Year's, when they ran around on the soccer field with glassy eyes eating grass and bucking. That was a great feast, alive with spirits. Everybody dressed in new or carefully ironed sarongs and blouses and shirts; they prepared huge meals of roasted meat, fish, spiced rice, and fried bananas; they put on shadow-puppet shows; on a dozen differently shaped gongs they played music that long after hummed on inside you; they danced, telling long, old stories of battles, love, demons, and wicked kings where every slow twist and turn, even of a little finger, had meaning.

The days wore on, with meals, usually Indonesian food, at a certain hour, bedtime always the same; my mother sat alone then and wrote letters to family in Canada and Holland. In the afternoon heat, I still sometimes sat beside her as she rested on her bed, brushed her long hair and told Chinese-girl adventures until she fell asleep; I had done it often when I was small. And every day at four tea was served with a biscuit — a must, no exceptions; my mother said she wouldn't "be herself" without it. First, though, Jerry and I had to splash water on our bodies with a bucket from a bricked-in tub in the bathroom so we could drink tea "fresh and clean." Calm days, safe days. Then one night at supper our mother said quietly, "Boys, I have something to tell you." And our world changed.

She began, "This is serious . . ." and in the times to follow she would never need to say that again: we would know. She brushed us with her fingertips, looking from one face to the other, and took a little breath. "Tomorrow it's our turn to go on a truck," she said. "The Japanese are coming to pick up all the women and children. They'll be here early. We're going to a camp, like Daddy." Then she smiled, "And I've got presents for us!" She brought out three new backpacks made of khaki cloth by a tailor in the village, the smallest one for me. Besides mattresses, the Japanese had said we could take what we could carry, she explained; so a rucksack and a suitcase each. Jerry and I could stay up late and make piles on our beds of what we wanted to take; later she'd come and check it out and add mosquito nets, towels, bed linen, and so on. Should she pack knives and spoons and forks? Soap? Medicine? She talked to us, I noticed, as if she really wanted to know what we thought. We should concentrate on clothes, she said, and use our common sense. And as she would now often say, "This is an adventure, boys."

It was long past our bedtime when she came to the pavilion. Jerry had to put back most of the books he wanted to take. I had lifted the margarine can with iron stuff onto my bed. "Ernest, little love," she said, eyes soft, putting her hands on either side of my face, "that's too heavy." She said I could take my little harmonica wrapped in the white handkerchief. It was a present from my father on my sixth birthday; I could play a bit from "Silent Night, Holy Night" on it.

She wasn't a mother who touched a lot. She sat down on my bed and pulled me on her lap, and Jerry came and leaned against her. "This'll be over one day, you know," she said. "Nobody knows how long we'll be, or even where we're going, and we have to leave everything behind, but one day this'll be over." Her hands stroked us, our hair, our arms. She rocked herself a little bit. Looking at us but not really talking to us she dreamily said things in English that we didn't understand, but we didn't mind. Outside a bird shrieked in grief; spirits sat very still in the dark trees and probably on the roof. That was all right. We were her children and the night wouldn't harm us. It was the last time, I think, that I didn't feel at all grown-up.

2

Bloemenkamp

All of us had to stand in the back of the two old open trucks bumping and jolting out of the plantation next day. The soldiers with the rifles had yelled and pushed — *Lekas! Lekas!* meaning "Hurry! Hurry!" one of the few words they knew in Indonesian — until all the white women and children from the area plus their baggage and mattresses were crowded on; they should have brought three trucks. The drive down from the mountains lasted many hours and it got hotter and hotter; no breeze reached me. Pressed together we swayed around corners and didn't speak because the jarring could make you bite your tongue. The sides of our truck hid everything from me except the sun, sometimes the crown of a bowing coconut tree, and the cloud of red dust from the truck ahead.

Halfway through the day we stopped in a village for water for the radiators, not for us; no food either. We were told to stay on the trucks. I stood on a suitcase to see over the side. The soldiers had jumped to the ground and were yelling orders at the villagers. I needed to pee and my nose and mouth were full of sand. Across the road I saw a girl sitting on a low white-washed stone wall by a holy banyan tree. She wore a brown and gold sarong knotted under an armpit and her long black hair hung loose and wet; she must have just had a bath. She was twelve or thirteen years old, a woman already, and looked so cool and clean and rested. She watched the shouting soldiers and the heads of the white women sticking up out of the trucks, their hair wild from the wind. And then her eyes met mine — and a warmth went through me that I hadn't felt before. I looked and looked and wanted terribly to go to her. She was pulling me to herself. Her mouth once moved a little; it could have been a smile or maybe she said a word. Then the truck jerked forward and we were off again. For many months I kept her inside me: she would flare up in my mind and I would feel that warmth and miss her. She had looked so free.

It was the hottest time of day and my mother shoved our backpacks together so I could lie down; Jerry and she went on standing. We were going to a camp in Bandung one of the soldiers had told a woman who spoke a little Japanese. I shut my eyes against the sun. There were swimming pools and soccer fields in Bandung, there was a restaurant that offered many kinds of ice cream, and on the sidewalks Indonesians cooked spicy food wrapped in banana leaf for one cent a portion. Jerry and I used to buy it whenever we had a cent; it was forbidden, of course, because it might be dirty and give you diarrhea. There were good hilly streets in Bandung for roller-skating; my father had promised I would get roller skates one day. My father had been away six weeks already — how long would we be gone? In a month the boar's head would be clean and white and beautiful. Would Ineke and Hanneke be in the camp? In Bandung there was plenty of metal stuff on the streets, but it would be too heavy to lug around. Would somebody steal my margarine can?

When I couldn't hold any longer I peed in my pants on the rucksacks. I could smell the dried sweat on the silent women bouncing above me.

After the long ride down from the mountains, the soldiers stopped the trucks outside Bandung at a girls school because the camp wasn't ready yet. The classrooms had broken windows and were full of flies. In some corners there were brown messes on the floor; people must have been locked in because the school did have outside toilets. Desks lay scattered about the yard in high grass. The air was much warmer than on the plantation. The guards, none of whom was taller than the tired, sweaty women, at once began barking orders. I would almost never hear the Japanese simply speaking, not even to each other. Their strange words exploded out of their mouths in short bursts and hit you, they heated your skin, and made you feel your heart thud. The soldiers stomped around, restless, angry, their small black eyes showing nothing.

They shouted at the woman who understood a bit of Japanese. She said she was told, first, that we were stupid and lazy, and then that we must clean the floors of two of the rooms and carry in our mattresses from the trucks. She said she had asked for food but was told no, maybe tomorrow. When our three mattresses were

23

down, two next to each other and one across at the end, my mother went outside with a tin cup. She came back with small yellow flowers in the cup, laid down a suitcase in the centre of the mattresses and set the cup on it — we had a table. The other suitcases and the backpacks she placed around us on the edges of the mattresses — and we had our own room.

Darkness came suddenly, as happens in hot countries. There was no electricity but some women had brought candles. The air hung thick, our shadows dragged along the walls, we whispered. For hundreds and hundreds of nights, this was how it would be: people, strangers, all around you. Then we heard voices outside, Indonesian women's singsong voices and the guards' harsh ones. The women's voices, soft and sweet and warm, were begging, begging to see us, please, the white women and their poor little children. There was a soldier's grunt — and they flitted in, barefoot, sarongs rustling, carrying baskets and pots wrapped in cloth with roasted meat, fish, soup, rice, fruit, tea. The smells breezed ahead. They knelt down among us, serving, giggling and clucking and moaning, urging us to eat, to eat more. Oh these were bad times, and Allah knew it. Fragrant brown women with tiny quick hands and tight buns of black hair glinting in the candlelight. They had seen us arrive from their village, and they knew there was no food. Eat more, please.

We were there a few days and the women fed us. Then trucks came that drove us into Bandung, into our first camp, a section of the city that had been closed off by an eight-foot-high fence of plaited and split bamboo rimmed with barbed wire. It was called Bloe-menkamp, which means Camp of Flowers. Its single gate was guarded day and night by soldiers who would let you through only if you were extremely sick or dead. In time, Bloemenkamp held five thousand women and children. We didn't know it was to be just our first camp; adults were certain the Japanese would lose the war soon. There were always rumours of Japanese defeats and victories for our side. Far away, cool and calm American pilots dropped bombs with a smile. The rumours came from hidden radios and from women who read the future in the cards.

With five other families we were crammed into a bungalow on a short street with a church; the only fur-niture in the house was an upright piano in the hallway. Mrs Witte and her daughter Mieke lived there, too. I believe Mieke, who was thirteen, and her older brother, Piet, who had been picked up with the men, had paid little attention to us on the plantation because their father was chief administrator. That was proba-bly also why Mrs Witte and Mieke moved into the front room with the big windows. Soon it wouldn't matter who you had been; no one would care. The three of us got a small storage room without a window, in the back.

Once the mattresses were down, my mother went out for flowers. Wherever we lived there would be flowers, or leafy twigs at least, in cups or jars or bottles. From an old magazine she cut pictures and let us pin them up; she draped a shawl across two nails already in the door. With twine she hung a sheet across the room: we slept on one side, she slept on the other,

25

always staying up late reading by a light bulb shaded with black cloth. She was reading *How Green Was My Valley*. In the beginning she and Jerry were able to get hold of books, which would later be forbidden. The last book she would have was called *The Hermit*, about a wise old Swedish man who lived on a mountain and gave advice to people. My mother liked it so much she copied it entirely, late at night in tiny writing in an old exercise book, until that, too, was confiscated. Her side of the room was also the "living room" and where we ate. We settled on her bed and she told us, keeping her voice low, that to get through this time all we needed were three things: shelter, food, and hygiene. Well, here we were in our room, the camp had a communal kitchen, and there was good pressure in the water taps.

Dirk stood watching us from the sidewalk the first day. About my age, he wore dark blue short pants, a starched white shirt, and socks and shoes. He had black hair and blue eyes, wasn't tanned, and spat often. He had a smart way of tossing back his hair which kept falling forward. His father, now in a men's camp, had been pastor of the church down the street. We would become friends, for a while, and, as I tended to do with some people, I aped him a bit. Not in dress. That was his mother's doing; the socks and shoes were just silly. But I was soon flipping my head back, too, although my hair was short as a brush. And I began to spit.

There was a small split between my two upper front teeth and with a mouthful of water I could spit a fine long squirt; but mostly I relied on saliva. I spat and I spat, left and right and in the air, at a fly, a tree, a smudge on a wall. If I missed I spat again — the target had to be hit. Dirk's spitting was a habit; mine was something I felt I could learn to do better, like swimming. I practised when I was alone outside, and inside, sitting on the toilet. One day my mother and two other women were visiting Mrs Witte in the front room and I was on the sidewalk spitting steadily. The women watched through the big window and laughed. Mrs Witte did feel though that she had to mention the traces of spit on the bathroom walls and ceiling. My mother didn't order me to stop all spitting, just to quit it in the bathroom.

What I liked especially about Dirk were his lead soldiers. He had a shoebox full of them, standing, kneeling, lying down, all shooting, all in Dutch uniform. He let me play with them but I was usually the Japanese or Germans and he was the Americans, British, or Dutch. He also had first choice of troops and picked the battleground, his yard — he and his mother had to share their home next to the church with other families, but, as Dirk said, it was still his house and his furniture. Sometimes he would choose my yard because our garden had a patch of plain earth good for digging tunnels and trenches and, after a rain, building forts.

Dirk and I were alone a lot because, of course, there was no school of any kind, and adults and older children were at work. Prisoners had to run the camp: keep it clean, the above-ground sewers too, cook the food, take care of the sick. We new arrivals were told this by the camp's commandant on the second day, standing at attention on a soccer field. We had waited for him in the sun for two hours with babies crying, people fainting, and not even children or old women allowed

27

to sit down. There would be many such waits in the camps on fields in the sun. When he and some of his staff marched up, I noticed officers wore neat, brownish uniforms as compared with the scruffy, yellowish ones of ordinary soldiers; few of any rank, though, seemed to have footwear that fit. Their dragging feet made a special "sloff-sloff" sound which, walking bow-legged as they did, I tried out for a little while.

From the belt around the commandant's big belly dangled a curved sword and his riding boots gleamed in the sun. He had a tiny moustache like Mr Otten's and stood yelling at us from a three-foot-high wooden platform without steps. He had jumped onto the stand without a run-up, like a cat. I was amazed. Weeks later, at another meeting on the field, we watched him with the same quickness beat up a guard who had broken some rule. In a moment, hands and feet flying, he had the soldier curled up on the ground unconscious, his head a bleeding mess.

The commandant's translator, a young woman who was half-Indonesian, half-Dutch, had told us to bow to him at her order *Keirei!* — and from then on to bow to all Japanese soldiers. She showed us how: stand at attention, then bend your upper body forty-five degrees. You straightened up at the command *Naore!* She said the bowing was really for the Emperor of Japan and warned that an incorrect bow would be seen as an insult to him.

Arms across his chest, legs wide, the commandant shouted at us for a long time. He said we were very fortunate to be under the protection of the Japanese army; we would be told this often. In return we had to keep order, not try to escape, be thrifty with water and electricity, not cause fires, kill flies, keep clean and healthy, always dress decently, not gamble or drink — and practise self-discipline. We would be treated with respect but disobedience would be punished. "You must," he bellowed, "perform useful work in wartime — it's a moral obligation!"

Quietly our mother repeated and explained it all that evening in the "living room." "We will obey them," she said. "They are the strong ones. They have the guns." She pressed her lips together. "We're going to survive. So, don't ever be cheeky — and don't ever look them in the eye!" Then she made us stand up and hissed *Keirei!* Jerry and I bowed and she bowed back. We bowed and we bowed at each other until the three of us flopped down on her mattress laughing.

My mother was made a mover, hauling furniture out of houses and, after sorting — chairs, tables, beds, cupboards, even pianos, also clothes, kitchenware, and paintings — loading it onto huge wooden carts that had been pulled by buffalo before the war. These she and other "furniture ladies" then pushed to already emptied houses for storage for the Japanese: to be used in their quarters or shipped to Japan. She did this all day long in the sun, growing brown and thin. Jerry was put to work in the kitchen where boys his age lifted drums of boiling water or soup or rice from wood fires and toted them around on bamboo poles. I was left alone.

Toy soldiers were new to me. My father had disapproved of our owning any "on principle." He didn't mind Manang's pistols, rifles, knives, swords, spears,

and bows and arrows; but soldiers no. What happened
when I played with Dirk's soldiers was that they
became real men for me, clever or disobedient or
funny, some very brave. Long after the day's battles
were done they went on in my head on my mattress,
for thinking soldiers made unexpected moves. But my
men weren't really mine. Dirk, finally, was general of
both sides.

I needed soldiers of my own — suddenly more than
anything else in the world. There was only my harmonica to trade but Dirk already owned one; he had
a lot of toys. I told my mother that it was important
that I get some soldiers fast, but she was no help. What
then? Could I pray, I asked. We weren't a religious
family; I had even heard my father say that the church
was "nonsense." Still, once in a while on the plantation, when I was sad, maybe after I'd found some dead
animal and buried it, my mother said I could pray if I
wanted to. It wasn't hard: you put your hands
together, closed your eyes, and talked to God inside
your head. He knew who I was, she said. But my
mother wasn't so sure about bothering Him about soldiers. She looked at me. "On the other hand," she said,
"you've already got No — maybe you'll get Yes!"

I prayed for soldiers. I told God I wasn't asking for
many, five, ten at most, and that I needed them to do
battle with as real men who could be smart or stupid
and talk to each other. With ten soldiers I could even
play without Dirk. I thanked Him for listening.

A sort of answer came very quickly. If I wanted soldiers so badly, Dirk said next day, he knew how to get
some. After dark we would climb on the roof of his

father's church where sheets of lead held tiles together. The lead would still be soft from the sun and we could just peel pieces off. He knew somebody who had a mould for soldiers and would melt down the lead and let it cool and harden in the mould. Dirk said he'd filched lead before, even stuff from inside the church, though he didn't say what.

I thought about it. The answer was out of a fairy tale, so simple — but strange: God saying go ahead and steal from a church. It didn't sound like Him, yet it seemed a definite Yes. There was no one to talk it over with. I knew what my mother and brother would say.

That evening I asked if I could play at Dirk's house for a while. I'm not sure my mother liked him: I was always so quiet after our games; but she said yes. It was still behind the locked church and grass and weeds had grown high. Dirk had taken off his socks and shoes. A ladder lay against the wall and he certainly needed my help propping it up; once we were on the roof our bare feet stuck to the tiles and the lead came off like toffee. My unease faded away up there high in the night with bats whooshing by — spirits probably.

A day or so later Dirk told me, sorry, no soldiers; the owner of the mould had botched it. The melted lead had spilled or the mould had broken, whatever. He was impatient. Forget soldiers. He had spotted a papaya tree with several almost ripe fruits in the garden of a house where everybody worked during the day. We'd steal the papayas; maybe we'd get stomach-aches but it was worth it.

Dirk's soldier collection grew larger day by day. I couldn't tell the new ones because he had rubbed them in dirt. It was more fun playing with more soldiers, but they were his and so were the rules. I was angry and then I was sad. I watched Dirk, hair hiding his eyes, digging a trench. He already had lots of soldiers — but he had cheated a friend. What was wrong with him? And what about God's fast answer? It had been a definite No.

Finally I told my mother, not about the lead, just that I thought that Dirk wasn't always a good boy; he was what Indonesians called *pinter busuk*, smart-rotten. I said I felt bad and as a friend, shouldn't I be helping him? She didn't ask me to explain it more. She said the best way to help was just to stay myself. I should also make other friends though.

And just at that time my brother got me interested in something else entirely. Jerry had watched Manang make things, too, and now he said he was going to build me a kite. Somehow he had gathered bamboo sticks, yellow paper, glue, and string. Early on lots of homemade kites flew over the camp, then fewer and fewer, and finally none. Some were run with thread specially coated with glass dust that easily sawed through ordinary string — and then you watched your kite float down, finders keepers for the kite hunter who got to it first. There usually wasn't much point chasing it.

Many of those kiting with glass thread were boys who, like Mr Otten, were half-Dutch, half-Indonesian; just about everybody with European blood, except Germans and, for a while, Italians, was interned. Often from poorer homes, where even the youngest smoked right in front of their mothers, the Indo boys were small for their age, dark-eyed, unsmiling, thin, and quick as crickets. They loved to fight, especially white boys, using their hands and feet; some had even been taught jujitsu by older brothers. If you were bigger, that was more reason to take you on. They roamed the camps in small gangs — and they could smell fear. Often, out of the blue, one would come up, chest out, and push up against you yelling, "I dare you!" and keep at it, his friends goading him on. Talking didn't help: he wanted to fight. You could run but he was probably faster — and you didn't because it wasn't brave and, anyhow, they'd follow and wait in front of the house. The fight ended with the winner sitting on the loser's chest rolling his knees into the muscles of the loser's upper arms until he cried *Ampoen!* meaning "Mercy!" in Indonesian.

The threat of these fights never stopped. If Jerry and I were together we backed each other up, if necessary tackling one of the others in the group; but we were apart a lot. I liked fighting but hated it with those boys. While wrestling they'd rub the clusters of elastic bands they wore around their wrists against your face so it burned. They didn't bathe much and had *daki*, crusts of dried sweat and dirt, on their necks, under their arms, and behind their knees. But mainly I was scared, me, who wasn't afraid of a wild boar! Nearly always smaller, an Indo boy either whipped you — so you lost to a little kid; or, if being bigger you beat him, you were a bully and one of his friends took over — right then, or another day. Loser or bully, you couldn't win.

Yet in time, I have to say, I became friendly with some of them. This was because of my laugh. I had invented a new laugh, a hard, shrill whooping, not for use at home. It sounded wild, even crazy, and at first gave me a little shock: no one laughed like that. I did it out on the street alone for a while, practising. When I thought I had it right, I whooped as I passed people, strangers. I couldn't read their eyes but they noticed: it was a surprise. I tried it on Dirk and he gave me a quick look. Nothing funny needed to happen for me to laugh my laugh; I liked its being unexpected. One day I laughed near a group of Indo boys playing marbles. I was looking down so it didn't seem as if it was aimed at them. I did it again. Was it that the laugh and fear didn't match? I edged up and squatted and watched their game, and they let me, and I whooped again when I wandered away. I kept the laugh and carried it like a weapon through all the camps.

It took Jerry two evenings to put together the kite. I sat with him as if he was Manang. The kite was shaped like a diamond and when we let her up she caught the wind with a rattle and climbed way above the coconut tree in the yard next door. I promised myself that one dark night I would fly her over our house, which is how you chase off bad spirits.

To get the kite in the air alone — Dirk couldn't be bothered to help: it wasn't his kite — Jerry had shown me how to stick the bottom end of the middle spoke just deep enough into the ground so it wouldn't fall over, walk away a few steps letting out string, jerk lightly, and start running. On that cloudless day it took many sweating laps across the damn lawn with the damn thing wobbling behind refusing to catch the damn air. "Damn" was one of my mother's favourite

English swear-words; the others were "hell" and "god-damnit." She muttered them right through her Dutch, which wasn't the best, making people smile. Damn is *verdommen* in Dutch and she used that, too. Anyhow, the damn kite finally took off and in a second scaled our roof. Giving all the line she wanted I sprinted around to the back yard. The space was small but less closed in by trees and wires. She was alive now and with a will of her own, and I was just a little friend on the ground. She looped and climbed as she wished. She raced to the left, streaked to the right. She soared higher and farther, a yellow flash in the blue. She was well beyond the wall of the camp — flying in freedom. If only people could see her!

Then from two streets away there rose a purple kite, slowly first, then climbing quickly — straight and with purpose towards mine. For a moment I didn't understand. Then I furiously started winding her in, but I was too late and too slow: my kite was far and the pull on the string so strong. The killer kite closed in without pity. It never needed to gain great height or make it past the wall. It was low and near to where I was standing when its evil, deadly line crossed mine, just a touch — and at once that yellow angel in the sky began to drift, swoop, and tumble, faster and faster, and then she was gone. But outside the wall.

The worst heat of the afternoon was over and I was walking down our street to meet my mother coming home from work. I had played alone all day, and eaten cold rice with peanut sauce by myself; besides Dirk, there weren't many children nearby. Later I would

become a roamer and wander anywhere in a camp.
Ahead I caught sight of Dirk and some kids I didn't
know in the driveway of a house where no one lived.
He and I had several times circled that house, trying
doors and windows; inside hung paintings and big
mirrors and the furniture was covered with sheets. Dirk
said the owners had run away to Australia before the
Japanese landed. The doors of the garage were wide
open and the group was throwing stones inside.

Dirk was in charge. He said you could only pitch
rocks, one at a time, from behind this line in the gravel
— and drew it again with the heel of his shoe. He had
somehow forced the garage's lock and in the back had
discovered a steamer trunk. He had prodded it open
and found it packed with frilly glassware, vases, bowls,
all sorts of glasses. He showed how a wet finger run
around its rim made a glass sing; the singing came from
around you, not the glass itself. Bigger gravelstones lay
all around the trunk. It seemed a shame to smash that
lovely glass. Dirk said one of these days the movers,
like my mother, would come and carry everything off
for the Japs. Anyway, he said, he was pretty sure I
couldn't hit the mark.

But I did, with my first stone, and heard the rinkling
inside the trunk. The next few missed. You needed
skill, just as with spearing boars and panthers. It wasn't
strength but aiming with narrowed eyes. You lined up
stone with trunk's centre, saw stone flying, saw it
landing in trunk — and then you fired. I wasn't watching how the others made out; I didn't care.

Tired adults were coming down the street, the
workday done; they kept on walking. Some older boys

stopped and joined in, kindly staying behind Dirk's line.

And then, behind me, my mother's voice: "Stop it! All of you — get away! Go home! And Ernest, you come here!"

I was shocked. To yell at children, strangers, and chase them off. To get mad — in public. Other women did that. They screamed at their children, beat them, in front of everybody. Not my mother. If she was angry, she spoke to us, alone, scolded maybe, explained, and sometimes made laws.

She was silent on the fast walk home, and so was I. Once when we were visiting Aunt Ina — she and her children had also been brought to Bloemenkamp — several women talked about how to keep their children from growing wild. One had said she was now both mother and father and hit her children whenever they "asked for it"; kids understood force. Aunt Ina had told the others that Erik was very young, and Ineke and Hanneke were girls and no trouble. Another woman had admitted almost crying that she couldn't beat her daughter and son, couldn't and wouldn't. My mother had said she didn't hit us, didn't believe in it — although her husband did — except if we "insulted" her; but that hadn't happened.

In our room my mother drank a cup of water, and out of her mesh bag fished a *djeruk*, a small green orange, sweet and juicy inside. She first made a cut around the top and bottom, then stripped away the skin in between, and pulled off the round pieces last. It was a little operation I'd seen her do a thousand times. Her hands dealt with many tasks always in the same way; it was restful watching her. She broke the orange in two and handed me the big part. This I expected as well.

"It's never going to happen again," she said, her voice low. "You touched — and broke — what belongs to someone else and that's stealing. You know what stealing is. Well, we are not thieves." Her eyes looked into mine. "And this place is not going to make us thieves. Think about what I'm saying. Understand me. We're not going to discuss it any more."

No scolding, just the law. I felt strange: I couldn't remember ever being angry with her before. But she had yelled in front of other people. She hadn't asked questions, or for my side of the story.

"You yelled," I said, trying to sound like her. "And that stuff is going to the Japs anyway."

She didn't reply. She was thinking. Looking nervous, she leaned forward, hesitated, then smacked my face with her open right hand. I was stunned: it hurt — but most of all because the slap had come from her. My father hit, not my mother.

"The Japanese have nothing to do with this, Ernest," she said quietly. "I told you to think about what I said, to understand me. And you don't talk like that to me: it's insulting." She looked away. She would slap me only once more, towards the end of those months and years — and then she would strike me with all her strength.

I put my mind to what she'd said and mostly understood it. Certainly I felt a little older. I played less and less with Dirk.

3

My Wound

It's hard not to think about food when you're hungry.
All you can do to keep it out of your mind is to play
or sleep.

There was enough to eat the first few weeks in Bloemenkamp. At the communal kitchen you stood in line
with aluminum pans that fitted into each other for
soup, rice, boiled vegetables, bread, chunky brown
sugar, milk for babies, and now and then a piece of
fruit, or an egg. For a short while there was a store in
the camp, which was fine if you had money. But if you
had very little money, like my mother, you bartered
clothes or jewellery or whatever you had for extra food.
You could also trade with Indonesians, at night,
through, over, or underneath the bamboo camp wall.
It was smuggling, *gedekken*, and the Japanese weren't
strict about it — yet. They first just wanted everybody
inside the camp and to have it running right.

But the rations grew smaller over the weeks, the
months, and then the years. It happened so slowly you
didn't notice until you remembered. Also, there suddenly might be a treat, more sugar, more fruit, or a

day, or several days, when the helpings were "larger." Rumours flew then: the Japanese were losing badly, or winning, and having a change of heart — false rumours that never died. And people grew thinner.

Hunger makes you brood about food, dream about it, and, especially, talk about it. At least the women and older girls did, endlessly, about recipes and their preparation, though many, of course, had never cooked before the war; their servants did. I never thought about food on the plantation; it was there. I liked potatoes, when we had them, in thick gravy, green beans and parsley, fried chicken, fried fish, fried eggs, fried rice, fried bananas, tiny fried red onions, condensed milk, boiled tongue, ginger cookies, coconut cookies, buttered corn, shrimp chips, a sweet lemonade in which drifted what looked like frog-spawn — and fruit salad: from mangoes, oranges, papayas, bananas, melons, *rambutans*, *sawos*, and pineapples, sliced above a bowl on the kitchen floor by the cook squatting in her sarong, juice dripping from her fingers. What I didn't like was cheese; all I could think of shouting on the phone to my grandmother in Holland was, "I hate cheese, *Grootmoesje!*" In the camp, food was on my mind a lot and it made me impatient: it shouldn't have been so important.

Adults said we weren't getting enough protein, fats, and vitamins, that our nourishment was out of balance. This made your body weak: if you became ill, your body had little strength to fight — and there was almost no medicine. It was dangerous to get sick. My mother tried to prevent Jerry and me from catching diseases or hurting ourselves; herself, too. She minded herself as much as us. But she didn't go overboard. She used her famous common sense. Many mothers were too fussy and tight with their children, not letting them climb trees, play in the rain, fight, drink unboiled water, explore; their kids turned into soft scaredy-cats. Other mothers seemed tired, confused, frightened, and their children grew wild. They talked back to their mothers, hit them even, never helped, stayed up late. What my mother did was ask us every evening about our day, in detail, and when something came up that was dumb or unsafe we'd discuss it. Climbing trees was fine; going up a dead one, well, its branches snapped off easily and you could fall and break your arm or neck. She almost always talked to us as if we were adults and she was just the oldest and knew most: "Trust me," she said. "I want to trust you." But sometimes she lost her temper and her swear-words would fly. She had laws about bedtime, bathing, not staying in the sun too long, and so on. And she was stubborn about routines: always saying "Good-morning" at the start of the day; drinking tea in the afternoon (or hot water if there was no tea); talking in the evening; and celebrating — our birthdays, those of friends in the camp, my father's, those of family members in Canada and Holland and of the royals of both countries, and all feast days of both. "It's fun," she told us. "This is how we'll survive."

One way she took care of herself was to insist that certain times of every day were hers. There was her reading into the night if she had a book. And when she came home from work, sweaty and tired, she might ask us to get out for a while. "I have to be alone. That's how I restore myself," she would explain. "Take a little walk." It wasn't so bad being kicked out with Jerry. But when he was gone, she kept it up. I'd be waiting for her with stories, and she'd ask me to go away. "I'll listen to you better later," she would say; she would relent if I was sad or not feeling well. [Our mother also never shared with us her regular food ration as some mothers did who couldn't bear seeing their kids hungry. She said it wasn't wise to do so because the women risked illness and death — it happened often enough — and leaving their children orphans.]

The three of us talked while we ate the evening meal, usually thin vegetable soup and boiled rice, and we tried not to complain about the size of the portions. To get more food people grew it: tomatoes, spinach, sweet potatoes, carrots, onions, cabbages, lettuce, beans, hot peppers, herbs. The back yard was divided into five plots, one for each family. We guarded our crops because already people were stealing in the night. One stole in daylight — a guard nicknamed Johnny Tomato.

As Johnny Tomato patrolled the camp on his bicycle, he would keep his eye out for edible tomatoes. If he spotted a red one, he'd jump off his bike, pluck it, and eat it on the spot. It was foolish to let your tomatoes ripen on the plant. One day he snatched a tomato in the front yard of the house across the street. He saw me looking at him eating it, and I quickly straightened my shoulders and bowed from the waist as I was supposed to.

Johnny Tomato grinned at me and swung onto his

bike — he liked kids. Most of the soldiers did, and if a child broke a rule he or she was seldom punished. They would find the mother.

I watched Johnny Tomato slowly ride down our street and then just before he reached the corner there was a woman who hadn't bowed quickly or deeply enough, or maybe he didn't like her face. Anyway, Johnny Tomato got off his bike and wheeled it yelling up to the woman who was still bowed and rammed the front wheel between her legs and hit her with the flat of his other hand, and then with the back of it, many times on the sides of her head, on her ears, until she crumpled onto the road. Then he climbed back on his bike and pedalled around the corner.

I ran over to where the woman lay. Two old women were helping her sit up. Her head was wobbling, blood dripped from the left ear, her eyes stared, not even crying.

I wanted to turn and walk away from the beatings I saw, but I couldn't: my neck was in some grip and my feet seemed nailed down. I sweated and watched. I saw every slap, punch, and kick, heard every yell, shriek, and cry. When Japanese rage erupted, the air quivered; strange anger, dark, their eyes giving no hint of it. Some roared and beat crazily. Some grunted and went at it with all their might. Some silently hit and kicked precisely to hurt, on and on. The women, or teenage girls, were rag dolls with no feelings, with no parts of their bodies special. They could moan and whimper and scream *Ampoen!* but that didn't stop the military men. Mercy was missing. They quit when their minds cleared, or they felt satisfied, or they were tired.

43

For forgetting to bow or bowing wrong I saw so many women and older children slapped and kicked, sometimes until they fell down, that after a while I didn't bother telling my mother about it any more. Because the thrashing by Johnny Tomato had happened on our street, I talked about it at home that evening. By the light from beneath the black cloth we could see each other's eyes shine. My mother listened; she was good at that. She nodded, thinking. From a worker on her team who had visited Japan, she said she had heard how Japanese men treated their own women; they were expected to obey and never to complain. For white women, the woman had said, Japanese men had even more contempt. They also despised prisoners. They themselves would rather die than be captured; honour meant more than life. So white women prisoners were like dirt and guarding them was shameful. Maybe that explained some of the anger and meanness, my mother said.

Then she spoke slowly, saying something she would say again so we would remember it. "They are your enemy," she told us. "They have guns and they are dangerous. They don't like you, even if they smile at you. They don't like any of us. We are their enemy and if we disobey them or get in their way they will kill us. Always be polite, always be serious, always stay calm. Don't laugh, don't smile, don't joke. Don't look them in the eye. You may lie if something in you tells you that you must. I am afraid and I know that you are afraid. But you'll be less afraid if you remember what I'm telling you."

Enemy, enemy — I'd never had an enemy before.

A part of our patch of garden, about as big as a dining-room table, was left empty for me to play in; that's where Dirk had come with his soldiers. The earth was often moist and good for building castles, forts, the decks of ships, and for digging secret tunnels. I had also buried a dead rat there so that, as with the boar's head, the worms could eat it and leave behind a clean, white, little skeleton.

One day, lying on my stomach scooping out a tunnel, I brought out my right hand full of earth and saw a drop of blood on the middle knuckle of my fore-finger. It didn't hurt. Maybe there was a sliver of glass in the ground. I wiped the finger on my pants, but more blood seeped out. So I went to the kitchen and held it under the water tap and when the water washed away the dirt I could see a cut as tiny as an eyelash. I held my finger upright, the bleeding soon stopped, and I went back to digging.

That evening the joint was red and the edges where the skin was slit swollen. My mother cleaned the cut and made a bandage from a strip of bed sheet and wrapped it around the finger. She said it wasn't serious. "You've had lots of cuts." Most aches and pains didn't impress her much, not her own either. She usually laughed them off — except my father's; his were always serious.

Next morning, the whole finger was red and swollen. It hurt, and the pain got worse as the day went by. I didn't feel like playing and lay on my mattress waiting for my mother and Jerry to come home. They brought the evening meal but I had no appetite. In the middle of that night the pain woke me up. I got a cup of water in the dark and dunked the finger in to cool it. My mother turned on the light. The finger was now twice as thick as the others. The cut had turned yellow and was crusted shut; my body felt warm. She made a pan of hot water — the gas still worked in the kitchen — and put salt in it. She set the pan on the suitcase table. Jerry, now awake too, came and sat beside me and put his arm around my shoulder. My mother slowly placed my hand in the pan and told me to let it lie there. She said the hot salt water would soak the yellow dirt out of the cut. It was the dirt that was causing the swelling and the pain.

"It's not a little cut any more," she said. "It's a wound."

She sat at the end of her mattress by the dark lamp and the three of us talked in whispers so we wouldn't wake the others in the house. We each had a spoonful of sugar from our tin can with a lid. The water in the pan cooled and she heated more. The skin of my hand got soft and shrivelly but the wound stayed closed.

Early next morning before she went to work, my mother bandaged the finger and took me to see two nurses who lived in a garage. The nurses had grey hair, thick strong arms, and laughed a lot. One unwound my finger, held it up to the light, felt under my armpit, looked at the other nurse — and they both laughed, maybe to make me feel better. They gave me a piece of cold pancake but said that what I needed was lots of food and vitamins. This was their last pancake, though, and they certainly didn't have vitamins. My mother had to report to work so I trudged home and lay down on her mattress. I listened to insects in the hot air, watched *tjik-tjaks* zip after them on the walls. Lying so very still I had to think of my father's music "lessons." Sure, he had his "discipline," was always so certain he was right, and usually needed all attention for himself, but once, when I had sunstroke, he sat by my bed for hours holding my hand and somehow made himself so small that I wasn't aware of him as a person at all, only of my hand in his; he had been my daddy then. I missed him.

I didn't move on the mattress, but I was soaked in sweat. It was as if a clock was ticking inside my finger. My whole hand was fat and yellow and even my wrist was swollen and red. If I moved my arm even a little, it hurt. When my mother and Jerry came home they leaned over me and saw a thin line running from the finger across my hand and up my arm to the elbow. My mother wiped my forehead with a wet cloth and said, "That's blood poisoning."

She pressed her lips together. "We have to do something. Watch him," she said to Jerry, and went out. Jerry sat and looked at me, frowning, eyes warm, then began to read out loud from a book without pictures that I didn't understand.

My mother's lips were still thin when she returned. It was growing dark. She said she had talked to the nurses again. Drawing on me with her finger, she explained that the red line might run higher and higher up my arm, and then across my chest right to my heart.

That was dangerous. Before that happened, the nurses had said, they would have to put me on a table and cut off my hand or even my arm.

"Well," said my mother, and she took my chin in her hand, "we don't want that. So you're going on a trip — tomorrow."

The houses and trees were still wrapped in mist when she and I walked hand in hand, which I wasn't used to any more, to a house near the camp gate; my wounded hand hung in a sling. A cock crowed, a free, early-morning plantation sound that we'd hear outside the walls of all our camps. My mother knocked on the door and a blonde girl in a thin grey dress that showed her panties opened it; inside the hallway a very old woman sat in a wheelchair with a blue woollen blanket spread over her knees.

"You're going to sit there on that little step," said my mother. "We're going to pull the blanket over you. Then we're going to wheel you down the street and through the gate. Somebody will lift this lady and you into a truck. The truck is going to a hospital where there's food and vitamins." The girl and the old woman were looking at me but didn't say anything.

"Stay under the blanket and be very quiet," my mother said. "If the soldiers at the gate catch you they might not let you or the lady out. Do you understand?" Then she took my face between her hands and kissed me long on one cheek and then on the other. "Remember," she said in my ear, "it's an adventure."

I climbed between the old woman's legs, the blanket came down, and the wheelchair began to move. It bumped out of the door and the bumps shot into my arm. It was hot under the blanket and the old woman smelled sour. We rolled along and no one said a word. We stopped and men's voices started shouting. There was a clank and a squeaking and the chair rolled on again and then it stopped. I felt us swing through the air and thump down, almost falling over — in the back of the truck, I guessed.

We started off. It was an old truck, like the one that brought us down from the mountains; its shaking shoved the chair around and at corners the old lady pressed her hands down on my head below her lap. In the blackness I squeezed my eyes shut against the pain from the jolting and from the heat of her legs. I sucked in my breath and held it longer, I'm sure, than ever in the swimming pool. It had to be so quiet at the pool now, all of us gone. I let myself float in the water, head down, arms dangling, cool, scanning the pale-green bottom: sometimes adults tossed coins in to dive after. When I came up for air I didn't move a muscle — there might be a soldier in the truck. I drifted away again.

We stopped. Outside I could hear only women's voices. "Careful, careful," said the old lady above. The blanket was lifted and my nose was in a long, wide, fresh-smelling white dress. I looked up. It was a tall woman wearing a huge stiff white cap that hid her hair. She bent forward and deep inside the cap, like in a little tunnel, I could see she was smiling and had red cheeks. "You look tired, little man," she said. Holding my good arm she helped me off the truck; a black cross on a silver chain swung from her neck. Other women in white dresses struggled with the wheelchair with the old lady in it. I never saw her again. The woman took my hand and as we walked down a long dark hall her dress whispered. At the end was a large room with many windows, full of beds in rows with children in them, and in the centre a small glass room. The woman pointed to an empty bed and said she would be right back. A bed with legs and sheets. I felt so heavy I could hardly climb onto it. The woman returned and gave me a cup of one of my favourite foods — fruit salad. I should call her "Sister," she said. She studied my yellow hand, not touching it, and said it would heal quickly with lots of food and vitamins. Now I should rest.

At midday a sister brought a tray with soup, rice, meat, gravy, corn, pudding, and more fruit salad and I ate on the bed like at home. With milk I swallowed pills from a tiny paper cup. I asked if I could keep the cup. She said yes, but now it was afternoon-sleep time; I wasn't used to being told what to do during the day.

Most of the children were still sleeping when the first sister came and took me into the glass room. It held a chair and a desk with a bowl of hot water on it. She started to explain, but I said there was salt in the bowl to soak out the dirt. Slowly, without help, I put my hand in it — and wanted to scream. She said I was brave; she would come back when the water was cold. And she whispered away. It hurt so much, I couldn't help it, I had to cry. I sat in the glass room several times a day for many days. Everybody, of course, could see me, so what I did then was sing as loud as I could with my hand in the water so no one would think I was crying. Over and over, I sang:

My bonnie lies over the ocean,
My bonnie lies over the sea,
My bonnie lies over the ocean,
Oh bring back my bonnie to me.

There are many words to this song, but I sang what I knew.

After that first soaking, I was told I was free to roam around, and found I was the healthiest and oldest child on the floor and the only one allowed out of bed. Many kids had tubes sticking out, some twitched, some whimpered, some lay still, staring. I touched a few and their skin burned.

In a little room by himself I discovered a boy about my age named Peter. He had a white face, hair so blond it was almost white, and huge blue eyes. His voice was high and loud. The bed sheet covered him up to his chin; he didn't move except sometimes to lift out his hands and rest them on his chest, thin hands. He told me at once that his left leg had been caught under the wheel of a moving van, the kind my mother pushed around; it happened before the camp, and buffalo had been pulling it. Under the sheet his leg lay inside a wire cage, specially built for it, that he never let me see. He smelled terrible, as bad as the boar's head when I buried it the second time. You couldn't escape his stink; I guessed he didn't notice it any more. I visited him often, stepping in and out of his room. He liked to talk and when I moved outside he just raised that sharp voice.

Peter was a favourite of the sisters. Every day they

ran in to see him and say hello. They were very busy — in the night there would be the same face that I'd seen in the morning reading by a small lamp in the glass room — but there was always time for Peter. When sisters rushed by, I'd ask, "How's Peter?" and I'd get a smile.

You would think Peter liked the attention, but he didn't. He had heard the sisters discuss his leg when they thought he was asleep. He had already had three operations, but was sure his leg would be better soon; or they'd cut it off. One day, he told me, he would be a soldier — like his father who had been killed by the Japanese — and he knew positively you could be a soldier just as well on one leg. He would then talk about weapons, tanks, marching. He knew a lot but he never laughed; didn't smile even for the sisters. With no father and maybe having to live with one leg, he had to be sad inside, and scared. After months in hospital and three operations, the smashed leg still wasn't fixed; maybe it couldn't be; maybe his whole body hidden under that sheet was swollen and yellow and he would die. If my hand smelled bad up close and hurt like crazy, Peter's pain had to be a hundred times worse — too much for a kid. I didn't understand it. Did the sisters understand it? If I had had my harmonica with me, I would have given it to him.

What I didn't like was that Peter did all the talking, and was always so certain about everything. When I showed him my hand on the first day he hardly looked at it. I should see his leg! All I needed was food and vitamins. He overwhelmed me, yet he was really only interested in himself.

That first night, alone after supper, sitting on my bed watching the sun go down through the windows, homesickness hit me. My mother, Jerry, our cozy dark room — it was like a cramp in my stomach. I felt like running away. I could, too. I'd done it before, when I was about six, right there in Bandung, before the war, when my parents were out in the country for a little holiday and Aunt Ina was looking after us; maybe Aunt Ina had been strict with me that day. Jerry and I slept in the same room, and the night before in the dark I had asked him the route out of the city to the house of our parents' friends. He told me, thinking I'd forget about it next day. But I didn't. I sneaked out at dawn and walked and walked along dusty streets crowded with horse-drawn carriages, cars, bicycles, and food stalls on the sidewalks, until I was lost. A policeman was sitting on his motorcycle by the side of the road, so I asked him the way. Did my parents know I was coming? No, it was a surprise. Well, it was far, and he didn't think it a good idea. First he drove me sitting in his sidecar to the police station, phoned Aunt Ina, then we rode home. Hanneke, Ineke, Jerry, Aunt Ina holding Erik, and neighbours were outside waiting. I waved from the sidecar. But, inside, Aunt Ina gave me an angry scolding, and Jerry, too.

I wasn't even homesick then, just missed my parents. I had been really homesick the year before, when I was five — the very first time I was away from home by myself. A couple of hours' drive from our plantation, lived a rich family, also on a plantation, who kept riding horses. Because I'd been good, my parents called and asked if I could come and stay for the weekend; I'd never met them before. There was a father, a mother, and two teenage daughters. I arrived in the morning and the man shook my hand, the woman and the two girls smiled; none of them said much. I was shown my room, the house, the stables. Then came lunch. A room with walls of dark wood, a long table set with shining glasses, napkins in silver holders, and in front of each plate a tiny pewter vase with flowers. The man sat at the head, the mother and I on one side, the daughters across from us. They bowed heads, folded hands, and prayed; I put my head down, too. Indonesians served food and left, and we began to eat. No one spoke. The man leaned his chin on one hand and ate with the other and stared ahead. When his mouth was closed, chewing slowly, it formed a half moon with the points down. He'd take another bite and the mouth would go down again. The woman and girls just smiled, passing things to each other, to him, to me. We were up to dessert and no one had said a word. It was at meals that we talked most at home. Were they waiting for me? Was I being impolite? "This is delicious," I said. The mother smiled and nodded. The girls smiled. The father stared, chewing. I kept quiet.

In the afternoon an Indonesian stable-hand walked me around the grounds on a saddled horse; he knew a lot about the animals, showed where they liked being stroked, told me to always talk softly near them. Dinner around the pretty table was as silent as lunch. At the end of the meal I looked out the window, saw the sun go down, and that strange, sad cramp rose up. Oh to be home! The father at that moment pushed his chair back and crooked his finger at me to follow him. He strode ahead to a room full of leather chairs and a couch; the top of a heavy desk was also leather and books lined the walls even over a fireplace. On the desk was a phone and he dialled a number and handed the phone to me. My mother answered. The man was standing a few feet away. I told her what a great wonderful time I was having, I had ridden a brown horse, brushed it after. The man walked to the end of the room and lifted a book from a shelf. "Mommie," I whispered, "come get me quick!" Well, she would, of course, she said, but it was almost night now and I knew how narrow the roads were. She missed me, too, and so did Daddy and Jerry. Tomorrow, if I wanted to, I could call again. Okay? Sleep well, *jochie*.

The next day the stable-hand helped me ride the same horse and sometimes even let go of it. I sat through the prayers and silent meals, smiled, and thought my own thoughts. After supper the father crooked his finger again. He lit a fire in his room and we sat on the leather couch leafing through books with pictures of horses. In the morning, settled in the front of their car with the chauffeur, I waved goodbye to the family, the mother and daughters smiling, the father not.

It had grown dark in the hospital. A sister sat reading in the glass room. I went to sleep.

It took seventeen days for my wound to heal. In the late afternoon of the last day the sisters hoisted me up into the back of a truck full of mothers and children going to the camp for the first time. When we got to the gate it had grown almost dark. The soldiers yelling at the women and children to get off the truck didn't notice the extra boy. My mother and Jerry had come to the gate every evening, which was when new prisoners arrived, and they were waiting. My mother kissed me long on both cheeks and laughed and said, "Thank God for small mercies," and Jerry smiled his crooked smile. I showed them my finger right away. It was the same as the other fingers, except the skin over the knuckle wasn't rimpled but smooth and showed a tiny pink line no bigger than an eyelash.

4

Christmas 1942

In a hot country people rise early because the first hours are coolest. Mist shreds, cocks cry, and in the camp's crowded houses women and children shuffle out of stuffy rooms to line up for toilets.

If I just had to pee, I went behind two old banana trees in the back yard; nobody noticed. I could have used the toilet that morning without waiting because it was dark out. Nothing stirred. Stars still blinked. I had woken up and couldn't lie on my mattress a second longer. That day we were going to have, as my mother said, "a hell" of a party — the first one in camp. I couldn't believe I was the only one up, but peed in the yard anyway.

For days special food had been sneaked into the house; I'd smelled some of it already being cooked on the gas stove. And I'd heard women and older girls squealing behind closed doors. What was going on there? The evening before, floors had been mopped, windows washed, ledges dusted, and cans, bottles, glasses, even a bucket filled with flowers and weeds and set out where the party would be — in the front hall and in Mrs Witte's room. Scrounged chairs lined the hallway; a scarred Chinese lantern dangled from the ceiling. But giving it all away was what my friend Mrs Plomp had brought in: a Christmas tree made of thick paper. It stood in a place of honour next to the piano. The tree had "snow" painted on its green needles, hanging ribbons, a silver star on top, and small red real candles. They would be lit, she'd promised.

I sat down in the dark in front of our door and exercised my calf muscles. I did this in quiet moments: in bed, on the toilet, listening to my mother or Jerry read. I kept at it; I kneaded the muscles, tensed them and let go, tensed and let go. Strength mattered; calves had become important. I looked out for them; I still walked head down, as in the days when scanning for metal, so I saw feet and calves first. I knew, I suppose, that people's eyes and mouths and voices were more telling, but I liked calves. Thick and round, jumping with power, muscles straining. Some Japanese guards and big boys and surprisingly many women and older girls had them, but few children. From before the war I remembered the sweating *betja* men pedalling their carrier tricycles around Bandung — those were calves! I needed a set. I would work and work on my calf muscles and they would swell up. It was a matter of time. It was also something I couldn't talk about. It wasn't a secret like building the steamship, but it still had to be kept quiet.

It wasn't just that I wanted first-class calves for myself; I enjoyed good calves, enjoyed looking at them, whoever they belonged to. In a few months I would come to live next door to the finest calves in the world. I would watch them in marvellous action; many would — and maybe see more than just calves. But I got to know the calves' owner and I always felt that, privately, she was proud of them. And she had a right to be. Time, though, would go by in the camps, and calves would lose out to breasts.

A day bird tested its voice against the fading night, and others took it up. From behind the camp's wall, a cock shouted he was on duty. Stumblings and mutterings followed from the house, from our room too — and it wasn't even light yet. They hadn't forgotten! Jerry clumped out straight for the toilet, probably thinking he was up first. The day of the party had begun.

Had the camp been given the day off? Was it a Sunday? Anyhow, everybody was home, and busy: cooking, tidying, even raking the gravel path to the front door, scurrying in and out of each other's rooms. Again that hush-hush giggling. It wasn't surprise gifts; I knew that the Dutch didn't give presents on Christmas. Gifts came from St Nicholas on December 5, the old Spanish saint's birthday. I'd been told that every year he sailed from Spain into Amsterdam harbour in the bow of a ship, astride a white horse, dressed in scarlet cape and mitre, clutching a curved staff, white beard blowing, smiling and waving at hordes of singing but nervous children on the docks. Black man-servants surrounded him, shaking white-gloved fingers and birch bundles at the kids in a threatening way. If you'd been good, you got treats, presents, and teasing, funny little gifts. If you'd been bad, well, tough luck.

Christmas was more serious. It was the day God's son, Jesus, was born. He died with nails hammered through his hands and feet on a cross; for us, I had been told. He was a good man who loved children and said everybody should; also your neighbours and your enemies. My mother made me promise to bathe thoroughly, soap the armpits, soap the crotch, put on clean shorts, wear a shirt — and sandals. What! How would I ever get feet like Manang's then? She said it was just for one day, you dressed up for parties, and, besides, Jesus wore sandals. No arguments: she had a lot on her mind.

And she did. Besides cooking and cleaning, readying Jerry, me, and herself, she had taken on a bunch of us kids to perform "Hark the Herald Angels Sing" that afternoon. We couldn't party after dark for fear of alerting the Japanese; visitors also had to slip in just one or two at a time. As it was, the smells of frying onions, chicken, bacon, and bananas, baking cookies, and roasting peanuts wafted out. The women had all dug out money or swapped stuff for the food treats. If soldiers came they'd throw the food out or cart it away. Were parties like ours going on all over the camp? You couldn't tell.

For about a week, when she had time after work, my mother had gathered Ineke, Hanneke, Jerry, me, and four other kids in the back yard and taught us the English hymn, singing softly so it would be a surprise for the others. None of us understood English, except Jerry who knew a little, but my mother had been a teacher in Canada and was a good explainer if not a great singer. We understood the words now and could sing them to her tune very well. Still, she wanted one more rehearsal, so we went through it again in the garden. Her hair was braided around her head and she wore a dress in her favourite colour, green, a thin white belt, white earrings, white sandals, and lipstick. She didn't own lipstick and I was pretty sure the earrings were Mrs Witte's.

The women and girls had all borrowed and switched clothes and jewellery — that was the to-do behind doors. And I had to admit they looked fresh and nice and smelled of soap; Ineke and Hanneke, too, in ironed blouses and skirts, hair damp from bathing. I didn't often look at Ineke and Hanneke closely because, well, they were sisters. We were in all the same camps, but I didn't play with them much because they were older, and working, and girls — and I never noticed them growing into young women. In the Bloemenkamp days, though, when things weren't so bad yet, they always did look neat: Aunt Ina was set on that. She liked order and tidiness and would fret about it. She was often ill and then my mother might go over and do the wash. I was there once when Aunt Ina asked if she would please also iron the sheets and pillow cases, and my mother said, "Certainly not."

Eating started. The hallway and Mrs Witte's room were packed full and half dark with the shutters closed against the sun; but the crowd gave off its own heat and soon the few sweet whiffs of perfume were gone. We ate standing up; there weren't enough plates, so children ate from banana leaves. We ate and ate, and it was quiet. Besides a big bowl of peanuts, there was a lot of avocado salad, fried rice, and fruit salad; adults weren't watching, and I overdid it. But I wasn't the only one.

Dishes were piled up in the kitchen, and we hurried back into the hallway and Mrs Witte's room. Wearing a pale yellow dress and high heels, Mrs Plomp had matches ready and we oohed and aahed as each candle came to life. The tree's flickering brightness bathed the women and children pressed together. Mrs Plomp's smiling, sweating face shone in the light and she looked oh, lovely. Maybe, just then, we all did.

At that moment the damn tree said, "Whooosh!" and was gone in one great lick of flame. There were screams and people jostled to trample on burning bits and candle stubs. But nothing, not the wall, not the piano or the blankets around it to muffle the sound, was even singed, just a small spot on the floor, a little. And then there was laughter. We started to clap our hands and cheer and someone whistled on her fingers. It was a party!

A chair was placed where the tree had been and Mrs Witte sat down with a book. Everybody made themselves comfortable. Mrs Witte wearing a white dress crossed her longer leg over the other, opened the book, and in her soft, polite way began to read the story of the birth of Jesus. It was a children's book and when she came to a picture she would pause to hold it up for us to see, then go on reading. Sitting on the floor Jerry and I leaned against the legs of our mother seated on a chair behind us. I had heard the story before and Mrs Witte was not a good reader; perhaps too polite to speak up. I flexed my calf muscles, let go, flexed, let go. Jesus, when he was older, said we should love everybody. Okay. What about Dirk? And the kite hunters? Well, Dirk, maybe. But what about the Japanese? Love Johnny Tomato, the guards, the commandant? They were the enemy! My mother had said so, again and again. But Jesus had especially mentioned enemies. Had He ever been in a camp though? Had He seen the Japanese beating women and girls? They could be Ineke, Hanneke, Aunt Ina, Mrs Plomp, Mrs Witte — my mother. Men shouldn't hit women. How many times hadn't Jerry and I been told that when Ineke or Hanneke pestered us? Did Jesus maybe have fear spirits in him like Manang's? To hate you needed to be brave, I thought, and I was sure I hated the Japanese: they were the enemy. I'd been told Jesus even loved the men who nailed Him to the cross.

Mrs Witte shut the book then, smiled, and said, "Now we're going to sing." She was a little the boss at the party.

A woman sat down at the piano and we all moved and stood around her. She set several music books on the ledge in front of her, opened one, and began to play. The piano sounded dull. We sang along with her, all Dutch Christmas songs, but kept our voices down. They were familiar songs and we'd sung about six, when Mrs Witte said, "Anna?"

My mother and the eight of us grouped together.

The woman at the piano asked what we were going to sing.

"Hark the Herald Angels Sing."

"Oh, I have that!" said the woman, and she switched her music book for another and flipped the pages.

"Damn!" murmured my mother.

"Sing along with me — *me!*" she whispered to us. "Don't listen to the piano!"

"Ah," said the woman. She spread the book out on the ledge and began to play.

We joined her and for a few lines we were fine, but the piano seemed to go faster or higher, and we stumbled. We tried to catch up, but couldn't, and then, one by one, we children stopped — and my mother was singing alone. We looked at her; everyone did. She wasn't in tune with the music but she kept on singing. The piano stopped, and the woman turned around. In her not perfect voice my mother sang her English song — the only non-Dutch person there. She sang on, unseeing, tears streaming down her face. I'd never seen her cry before and wouldn't again in the camps. When she finished, it was very still, and she ran out of the hallway.

5

Empire of the Sun

The sun was the friend of the Japanese. Even their flag was white with a red sun in the middle. Jerry hated it, didn't want to see it. But it was the only flag and fluttered from poles on the soccer field, in front of the commandant's house, the guards' stations, the administration building, the camp gate; it was in our eyes daily. The Japanese used the sun to hurt us. Day in day out they let it burn down for long hours on workers, weakening and dulling them. A prisoner who broke a rule might be dragged to a shadeless spot to stand at attention, or sit there hunched up in a little bamboo cage, for a day, or two days, eyes burning, lips cracking, with no food or water and kicks and slaps if she blacked out.

Called to the soccer field once again to listen to the commandant, we waited half the afternoon in the sun, people moaning, leaning on each other, no sitting, then jerking straight to bow as, suddenly, he was striding past with his men, sword swinging, boots shining, and making his jump onto the platform. Via the young woman interpreter, he yelled first, as usual, that we were the enemies of Nippon, that only through the goodness of the Emperor were we housed and fed, that we had no home and fatherland any more — "and so you have no religion any more" — and that we must be obedient, polite, humble, and self-disciplined; on and on.

I had begun to find it hard to pay attention at these meetings; afterwards I had to ask what had been said. I watched, instead — the commandant, the officers, the soldiers, the translator, the dusty field of women and children from which the heat trembled upward blurring their faces, the flag above, ants scrambling across my feet. It wasn't just difficult to listen, something in me didn't want to. It wasn't especially because it was a Japanese forcing me — although maybe that's how it started; my mind also wandered when, say, one of the women administrators, just another prisoner, called us together; even when a bunch from our house was chatting on the front steps in the evening, and I kept my eyes glued on the speaker, I would lose track. If I was brought in then with a question, I'd feel dopey; it would get worse, this weird resistance to the grip of another's voice. It didn't happen with those who were close; and I was fine with one or two or three people: a good listener.

Did the commandant have a mother? Was she a yeller? Did he yell back? Did he beat his own wife and children? Or not. Did he miss them terribly? Or not. Was the interpreter his girlfriend? People said so. She watched the commandant bellowing and when he paused and turned to her she'd still be looking up at him, and I saw before she spoke her lips sometimes move a tiny bit, almost in a smile, as if she agreed, as if she thought he was clever; but maybe she was just nervous. She had to be careful, she was a prisoner, too, and thousands of eyes were on her — the commandant was the enemy. "Don't smile at the enemy," my mother had said. Jesus, of course, said, "Love them." What was a "girlfriend"? Probably many of those thousands of eyes, like Jerry's, didn't want to look at the Japanese flag either. None of them, certainly, wanted to look into Japanese eyes. The officers and soldiers stood on either side of the platform, faces closed, but you felt them watching. Once, an officer had suddenly turned to the soldiers behind him pointing to someone standing in the front row. Two soldiers trotted up to a middle-aged woman, grabbed her, and ran her, stumbling and sagging between them, off the field. The other Japanese didn't move. A few days later on the street I spotted the woman rewinding a piece of bed sheet into a turban around her shaven head, her face still blotched and swollen. She had looked into the officer's eyes, I bet. Were the ants at my feet as uninterested in us as the stars at night? A girlfriend might be a girl you could look at naked.

The translator said we must all be at the gate with our belongings early next morning. Then the commandant leapt down and we bowed.

I looked at my mother.

"Moving to Tjihapit!" she whispered. Tjihapit was another section of Bandung also fenced off into a camp, but bigger. The interpreter warned us to bring only what we could carry, not counting mattresses, and not to smuggle anything forbidden — Dutch paper money or coins, any orange ornament (for Holland's House of Orange), pictures of the royal family, cutting tools, foreign flags, radio parts, books, paper, pens and pencils, and so on. There would be searches. And to wear our numbers! At some time in Bloemenkamp we were given numbers. My mother stitched ours on rectangular bits of cloth and sewed them on our pants; mine was 12952.

Why were we moving? Rumours raced. The Japanese were winning, they were losing. Tjihapit was awful, a punishment camp; no, it was better, only three families per house. Nobody knew. There was no explanation.

Well, I didn't care. At least there was action! For me the worst thing about living in Bloemenkamp was not the heat, fear, smells, noise, flies, too many bodies, too little food, scratches that festered, and diarrhea — it was the sameness. The days and weeks and months had dragged by. Women and older children at least swept streets, cooked, cleaned sewers, moved furniture. Mostly on my own, I had sleeps in the middle of the day, wandered around camp, usually unafraid now with my laugh, and sat in shadowy places staring. It was even a relief, it seemed sometimes, that there were always new no-nos: no lights on after eight, no wood-gathering for cooking fires, no meeting in groups, absolutely no *gedekken* through the wall; on and on. But just as the Japanese would get tougher right until the end, some people would disobey right until the end and, for example, smuggle anyway — a few because they were brave and generous, others because they were greedy. And they got us all into trouble.

Packing for us was simple: we had less than what we had carried down from the plantation; it all fitted easily into our three rucksacks and suitcases. The only "thing" I owned was the little harmonica in its hand-kerchief. But there were people living near Bandung who had entered camp with servants pushing piled-high handcarts. One woman, who was a professor, had come with seven cabin trunks full of books. And there were those, like Dirk and his mother, whose home had already been in Bloemenkamp. They had one night to decide what to take; but that's all we'd had, too, wasn't it? Dirk would have to leave behind most of his toys, of course — certainly his lead soldiers. Too heavy. Now he would know what it was like to have no toys, and no soldiers. Maybe, though, his mother should let Dirk keep two or three so he could at least play by himself. They wouldn't take much space. He could carry them in his pocket. Maybe she would.

Early next morning we marked the mattresses with our numbers and piled them up in front of the house for a truck to pick up. Too late I remembered the rat I'd buried in the back yard; maybe someone else would enjoy its little, white skeleton. When we arrived at the gate there was already a long line-up, six or seven women and children across, many wearing several layers of clothing, surrounded by backpacks, suitcases, bags, baskets, sacks made of knotted-up bed sheets, and trunks. Trunks, of course, needed two carriers, but there was no rule about that. Dangling from women's bodies and from their luggage I saw pots, pans, kettles, water canteens, pails, tubs, purses, a chicken-feather duster, a carpet-beater, a hat, a clock, and a doll. Some had brought bird cages with birds in them, rolled-up rugs, fold-up chairs, musical instruments, even a tire from a car. Stuff! How were they going to lug it all? What I didn't know was that Tjihapit's gate was almost across the street from ours.

We nudged luggage forward, a foot maybe, and stopped. Far in front on wobbly bamboo tables outside the gate soldiers rooted through every piece of luggage, taking their time, fingering, shaking out. Once directed, the Japanese slogged away at a job with stiff purpose, rain or shine, entirely absorbed. The sun rose higher; luckily for those overdressed people, there was a breeze. I heard a small scream behind us, then crying: with a rag a mother was wiping off brown trickles running down the legs of her teenage daughter; nothing to cry about really. Murmurs reached us from up front that there was smuggling going on. Several times, way ahead, we heard bursts of yelling and we all tensed up: somebody caught.

When we got closer to the gate I saw two young women standing to the side, straggly hair falling over puffy, bloodied faces, their clothes streaked with red earth — so the soldiers had been mad enough to beat them to the ground. That anger would increase with the day's growing heat. No one, of course, dared approach the women or call to them, and they didn't look up. We said nothing to each other, just shuffled past, but the line-up moved so slowly everyone had a long look at them. I even turned to stare, until my mother twisted my head straight. The whole day the two would shake and sway there trying to stay on their feet; all of Bloemenkamp would file by them. We heard later they had collapsed a few times and been kicked upright again.

Only three rows away from the gate my mother suddenly started groping around in her mesh bag. "Damn it!" she muttered. Then she yanked out something in a pale green handkerchief, held by a knot on top. Looking ahead, as if her hands at her side didn't belong to her, she untied the cloth and slowly, slowly let it slip open.

Not slowly enough! First the woman beside her sneezed, then someone behind her. My mother sneezed, I sneezed, Jerry sneezed — and then everybody around us was sneezing. Taking deep breaths and pinching their noses, wiping their noses on hands and sleeves.

"I'm so sorry, so sorry!" whispered my mother, twirling around so all of us could hear. She wore a faded brown dress that looked too big on her. "It's pepper. I found a whole box. I was going to smuggle it — but I changed my mind. Pepper! Sorry!"

Ten, fifteen, maybe twenty women and children were standing around sneezing, sneezing like mad, eyes watering, coughing, and then one of them started to laugh, and the next second all of us sneezers were laughing. The story of the sneezers raced down the line-up — past the two punished women — and a wave of laughter came back, and then another.

The soldiers looked up from behind their loaded tables into the faces of hundreds of laughing prisoners. Their expressions unreadable, their black eyes flitted to and fro. Did they think the laughter was directed at them? Much less had sparked terrible rage. No. It was just a clutch of women and children sneezing up front. Still, it must have made them angry, but what could they do? Wade in and slap all those laughing mouths? They bent down again to fussing with clothes and hairbrushes and family snapshots.

6

Tjihapit

Our new camp, Tjihapit, held about 15,000 prisoners, three times as many as Bloemenkamp. Bigger in size, it was also a lot more crowded. It swallowed neighbours and friends; many I never saw again: Mrs Witte and Mieke, Dirk, and Mrs Plomp. Since Aunt Ina, Erik, Ineke, and Hanneke were allotted a room some distance from us we seldom visited.

At first, in Tjihapit, time moved fast: everything and everybody was new. Eleven other families lived in our house and it had one toilet. Our room (which in her way our mother at once made a safe space) was about the same size as the one in Bloemenkamp — the mattresses just fit — but it had a window. We looked out on the back yard over a round flower bed, as high and wide as a truck tire, thick with orange and pink hibiscus, and on to a clump of short fruitless palm trees.

Jerry and I went to explore. Besides the palms growing in a tight circle, which formed a decent cave, the garden held two low, climbable trees, and more useless flower beds. Never mind if Johnny Tomato might also move to Tjihapit, the beds would have to be dug up and planted with vegetables. An overgrown lawn ringed the house and in the rear, on our side, it stretched a dozen steps to the edge of a stinking sewer; on the other side of the ditch rose the camp's bamboo fence. Open sewers ran behind all the houses but were usually hidden by man-high whitewashed walls topped with spikes or shards of glass to stop thieves. The foot-wide ditches, with a walkway on either side for cleaners (before the war), made a network of alleys throughout the camp. After a rainstorm, the sewers, not built to service the thousands now crammed into that small section of Bandung, quickly overflowed and the alleys turned into narrow foaming rivers. Some people threw garbage, broken glass, wrecked furniture and appliances, used-up bicycles, anything at all, over those walls. So, when the sun came out and the water level sank, there could be interesting finds amongst the steaming debris; flies, snakes, rats, snails, ravens, and frogs that honked in the night thought so, too. It was stupid to forage there on bare feet and we clappered walking in *klompen*, pieces of wood carved to fit soles and held on by strips of rubber tire across the toes. One girl didn't and stepped on a nail: awful poisons raced through her body and she was soon dead.

Ours was a corner house on a hilly street that climbed towards us and stopped short at the camp's wall. Beyond it was the "outside," from which in the quiet of the evening sometimes drifted sounds, faint and unreal: horseshoes on pavement, a *betja* bell, a vendor's cry nearing and fading. Camp streets were busy with women and teenagers walking to and from work or fetching food, children playing, women pushing the creaking moving vans, and, infrequently, soldiers on bicycles or in a car or truck. Already grass and weeds sprouted from Tjihapit's cracked sidewalks and pitted streets, cut telephone lines drooped from poles, and scum crusted the surface of clogged road-side ditches. Except for vegetable patches, gardens grew wild beneath wash lines strung up helter-skelter. Houses showed broken windows, doors and shutters askew, dangling eavestroughs, peeling paint, sunken roofs, and holes knocked into outside walls as additional entrances; inside, plaster crumbled, roofs leaked, and electrical wiring, plumbing, and gas piping had failed. It would get worse, but we wouldn't notice.

My mother was ordered to chop vegetables in the kitchen. Everybody, of course, wanted to work there — and often those who did looked fitter than the rest. But the preparing and ladling out of food was strictly supervised by certain women who had to report again to the women who ran the camp's administration. Thieves were fired and everyone heard of it. Once, maybe twice, my mother hid a carrot in her clothes and brought it home, but she said it wasn't worth it. She did still manage, though, to get hot water for her important afternoon tea. "It's hard to stay alive," she said, "but even harder to stay alive and decent." I stole anyway, unripe fruit mostly. By now I often stilled her voice in my mind.

Weeks flowed into months and the terrible same-ness of Bloemenkamp took over in Tjihapit too. Heat enervated; only in sleep would food not nag at your mind; the air was thick with smells and flies; and here, too, roamed the gangs of Indo boys. Fear grew: the

Japanese and the *heihos* — uniformed young Indonesians in their service — became angry more quickly and slapped and kicked and punished women for the slightest misconduct. *Gedekken*, smuggling, was now seen as a real crime, though it didn't stop. Once Ineke, at fourteen, actually had the nerve to sneak out of Tjihapit through a sewer alley and carry back fruit. If caught she, and probably Aunt Ina too, would have been beaten and shaved, at the very least. Sometimes a woman, without being allowed to pack or say goodbye to her children, was just hauled out of camp. That usually meant the *Kempetai* — and the end of her. The Germans had the Gestapo, the Japanese the *Kempetai*. They were the military police who beat with whips, tore out fingernails, burned with cigarettes, and killed. When a *Kempetai* officer wandered into camp, it got cold.

Jerry had at once been put to work too, of course. His job was pulling carts with other boys his age, collecting garbage. Quickly rotten in the heat and covered with flies, the piles of rubbish had to be picked up mostly by hand; there were no shovels. But there was a good side: sometimes you found stuff. Jerry would hide his prizes in a bush and retrieve them later.

Extremely important to scrounge at that time were wheels. Bicycle wheels and roller-skate wheels — roller skating had been popular before the war. Jerry was always on the lookout for them on his rounds; me too, on treks through the warren of sewer alleys. If you had wheels, enough of them, you could begin to build one of two types of vehicle that kids had somehow hit upon in Tjihapit: "velos" and "tanks."

There were only three or four velos in the entire camp and they belonged to the oldest boys. Even to be able to say you slightly knew a velo owner was an honour: he had respect. To make a velo you had to have filched all sorts of materials and tools, and you needed know-how. A velo was the size of a small car, made up of four bicycle wheels fixed to the front and back of a frame of two-by-fours. Two bicycle chains running on the back wheels and two sets of pedals (for driver and passenger sitting roughly in the middle) propelled it; and a car's steering wheel and shaft wired to the front wheels gave control. I never rode on a silently whizzing-along velo — it must have been so fine. Older girls liked velos. They smiled at the drivers.

Ankie Crone was an older girl, about fourteen, and I'd seen her smile at Polo who was the owner of a velo. Ankie was one of Mrs Crone's three children; the family lived in the room next to ours. Harry, at fifteen the oldest, tall and bony like his mother but unlike her not a talker, had already decided to become a seaman. His father, a ship's captain who, I noticed in photographs looked a head shorter than his wife, had been away at sea when the Japanese invaded and nobody knew where he was. Greddie, eleven, also tall, I didn't pay much attention to because, well, there wasn't much of my attention left after Ankie.

The Crones were remarkable in that, although thoroughly Dutch from the northern province of Groningen, they all had dark, slanted eyes. Ankie had a way of speaking and smiling at the same time, her pink cheeks narrowing her eyes to slits. When her face closed she looked thoughtful, older. But she smiled

easily, mouth open, showing large white teeth; sometimes a small moan escaped her throat. It was a treat.
In the first days, I watched her face, waiting. But as we
all got to know each other — Mrs Crone and my
mother would become best friends — I began to try
to make her smile, at me. I learned that, while her smile
might come quickly, for serious Ankie there always had
to be a reason: the smile was a sort of reward. So, when
I saw her smile at Polo, I knew it couldn't be just
because of his dumb velo.

Older girls ignored tanks, as did most younger ones.
Tanks were for boys, rough boys, or boys who were
maybe a little crazy. For a tank you needed at least one
and a half roller skates or three pairs of wheels (better
if you had a full set though). From odd pieces of plank
a sturdy floor was hammered together, about as big as
a cabin trunk, under which at the rear end two pairs of
wheels were fastened. The third pair was screwed at the
mid-point of a separate board bolted with some play
beneath the centre of the floor's front end; that board,
with rope running from either end through holes in
the floor, allowed steering. Then, to the height of a
crouched boy, the front, sides, and roof were nailed up
with anything heavy and strong — wood, metal, flat
stones — and wound around and around with wire,
even barbed wire; long nails, slammed in from inside,
stuck out from the sides. Especially reinforced was the
tank's front end. A gash was cut at eye level for the
driver to see through. Entry was from the open back.

One day Jerry found a single set of little wheels on
his garbage route; a week later we dug up a whole roller
skate in a sewer alley. We could start but we needed

patience because Jerry was gone for most of the day. I wandered eyes down along the streets and through the sewer alleys scanning for discarded wood and metal — as in the old days I had collected for the ship of my dreams. I ripped off the doors of a toaster, straightened bent nails with a rock. Because our street was a dead-end, the last few hundred yards, the stretch below our house up to the top of a small hill, had very little traffic. Jerry and I studied that dip in the road. It had possibilities.

About two months went by, and slowly beneath our window, the machine grew. Mostly it was Jerry's work and his planning. Just as when he built the kite, I sat watching him as I used to watch Manang. Like our father, he had clever, sure hands; like Manang he said little. One afternoon he returned with the side of a small icebox: just what we needed. I unearthed a hunk of car tire: perfect. A thin, red-haired boy from our house named Willie, about my age, lent a pair of pliers for twisting wire. A tank was taking shape. It was getting dark, and when he straightened up, Jerry grinned and gave it a couple of good kicks. "Almost," he said, pleased with himself.

My mother watched us through the window. I'm not sure she even knew what we were up to. As on the plantation when we were busy hunting panthers or burying Leo she let us be. She had asked what I wanted for my eighth birthday coming up in a day or so. What a question. What was there to give? I said I would like a fruit salad.

But when I woke up that day, there was a traditional Dutch birthday chair, a chair she'd borrowed (we didn't have one) all decorated with flowers and bits of coloured paper stuck on with the glue-like porridge we were fed. The two of them sang Happy Birthday. On the chair's seat, each with a bit of white ribbon around it, were a pencil and a child's drawing pad. My mother handed me a cup of fruit salad. "There's more tonight," she promised. Who knows how she got the fruit, the presents, and the ribbon.

"Hey — look," said Jerry and pointed out the window. Our monster vehicle had been wheeled to the middle of the lawn; palm leaves lay across the top with a scrap of cardboard tucked upright between them that said: ERNEST'S TANK. That was Jerry for you.

My brother told me he had set up a "race" after work that same day. We'd really have to practise hard when he got home because the other guys were coming around six. That afternoon I climbed inside the tank and Jerry gave it a hard, long push. The weight of the thing made it rumble down our hill terrifically fast, but it listened sharply to my jerking on the ropes — the power of it! Then together we pulled it back up and I went down again and again; Jerry took one ride himself.

The day was cooling and some women and children came out to watch; our mother did, Mrs Crone did, Ankie did — would she think I was pretty brave? And right at six, there appeared a tank and some boys at the top of the opposite hill. Shouting, Jerry made it clear that he would give the starting signal with a towel. He called to a few neighbour boys to help him push.

"Get in, kid," he said.

I wriggled inside and knelt, dripping sweat, forehead

pressed against the piece of car tire, eyes locked on the lookout slit. I felt a jolt and at once the tank was rolling fast, then faster and faster, little wheels roaring, and I heard myself screaming — the wild feel of it rocketing down! And plunging from the other hill, just as fast, the enemy. My tank obeyed my every tug to the last second — and so did his. And when we plowed head-on into each other there was a great crunching, cracking, and clattering. The tanks fell apart around us drivers and running down the hills came our crews, jumping, yelping, and thumping each other.

We'd done it. Never mind the stupid flies, the stink, being hungry or sick all the time, or the *Kempetai*. We'd done it. Maybe we were just numbers who had only to bow. But we had worked a long time to build a fine tank and then in a split second marvellously smashed that tank to pieces — because we damn well felt like it.

7

Willie

In that place where so much was breaking down and wearing out there was a boy who made things whole again.

Willie, his mother, and his older sister who played the accordion were already living in the big house when we came. Outside the door of their windowless room ran an open gully that carried everybody's bath and wash water to the sewage ditch. It was an airless storage room, or *gudang*, like the one we had had in Bloemenkamp. Why they hadn't grabbed our room when it was free, I'll never know. I once overheard a woman in our house, Mrs Slierendrecht, refer to Willie's mother's "humble origin." I didn't understand what she meant, so for a while I thought it was "humbleness" that had stopped Willie's mother from moving into a better room. The sisters in the hospital had talked about being humble; God liked it, they said.

I should have known better, of course, than to think Mrs Slierendrecht would ever say anything about anybody that wasn't meant to be nasty. Her thoughts were ashes. A tall, meaty, red-faced woman, she stomped to and from the toilet, chest out as if she were a queen, in a loose silk housecoat showing hunks of thigh and breast, yellow-grey hair flopping in an untidy braid. No one liked the toilet line-up: because so many had diarrhea there were accidents, but after a while you hardly noticed any more. Mrs Slierendrecht hated the line-ups and always said so. She complained, argued, and mentioned unkind things about people until the door shut behind her. And then she sat there a long time, it seemed to me. When she came out she marched by without a word. From the beginning she and her two grown-up, silent daughters had lived in the best room, in front, with windows. I thought Mrs Slieren-drecht was crazy, but wasn't sure. She had a high-Dutch accent and didn't have to go out to work, perhaps because she was over fifty, but she let on it was because she was a lady. Often I heard yelling behind their door.

Maybe Willie's mother had kept their room because it was separate from the rest of us, private. She was polite but didn't mix; waited to go until there was no line-up. How "humble origin" fitted her, I had no idea. She was a worried-looking woman, though. When she was home she didn't bother Willie — nobody did that — but she kept a sharp eye on him.

Straddling the gully in front of Willie's door were a small kitchen table and a chair protected from sun and rain by a black umbrella with its handle nailed to the table. Soapy water flowing beneath him, this is where Willie spent his days, shoulders rounded, very still, milk-blue eyes fixed on his small fussing fingers. He was shorter than me, skinny, freckled, flop-eared, with thin red hair that grew in tufts; it looked as if he was losing it. His mother made him wear a straw hat, but as soon as she was gone, he'd take it off — no, tear it off. It made him angry.

His mother and sister had jobs, so, like me, he was a lot on his own. I played, visited, fought, stole fruit, roamed the streets, and scavenged in alleys, but Willie had real work. Adults asked for his help and paid him, if they could, with food. Not yet nine, Willie had respect. And this is why: he could repair watches and clocks. He had the little tools, a magnifying glass he could screw in his eye, and a drawer in the table crammed with clock insides, broken watches, and tiny screws and springs and other parts.

Willie's customers came by in late afternoon from all over Tjihapit. He was praised, touched — from which he would bend away — and thanked. He spoke little and curtly, and only about the person's watch or clock; he seldom raised his eyes. Sometimes a piece was beyond repair and Willie would say so with certainty and no concern. Later, he might bring an oil lamp out to the table and keep at it after dark.

This is what Willie did and all he did. When I, at first, sitting by him began stories about the plantation or Bloemenkamp or people I knew, his silence stopped me; he didn't care. If I asked him a question, he'd move his head yes or no or answer in just a few words. I learned little. No, his father wasn't a planter; he worked for the railroad. No, his sister never played her accordion now. Yes, he had always lived in Bandung. And this was his reply to what everybody wanted to know: "I sort of picked it up."

I used to just sit in his doorway for a while and watch him tinkering, eyes inches from the table; he would swing his head in my direction to show he knew I was there. Then I'd wander off: Willie didn't need company. But I'd come back.

One day I went and stood behind him and leaned over. He was snipping off a piece of a very small spiral spring.

"Why?" I asked. That's all. Why?

"Because otherwise it won't fit in here, see?" said Willie promptly and pointed to a little open tunnel in a watch, one of a dozen lying around the table.

"But it's still too big!"

Willie turned and looked up at me.

"No," he said, "look." He picked up the cut spring with tweezers that pressed it down, then tucked the spring in the channel of the watch where it jumped taut.

"There," said Willie.

"And now?"

"We're done," he said, and pressed the back plate of the watch into place with a click, shook it, and put it to his ear. He reached up and held it to my ear. I heard the watch ticking. It was as if Willie had stroked my cheek.

I found a pail and set it upside down beside him. In the next hour or so, as Willie puttered on, everything he did he explained, with words and by showing with his small tools; a really dumb question also got a sort of cackle. Each problem, once he'd solved it, was so simple; but the next one looked horribly complicated. Willie seemed years and years older than I.

I began to spend a lot of time on the pail, peering into watches and clocks, as Willie tightened, filed, cleaned, and murmured whys and hows and wheres. I had a share in the patience he had for his watches. Heads together we'd travel right into a timepiece, Willie leading but not far ahead, stopping to let me catch up, this way, that, and around. And then suddenly it was ticking again — alive. He allowed me to handle his tools; he let me, once, twice, and then more often, do a chore alone. I did well. An alarm clock bell rang again because of me. The hands on a pocket watch now could be relied on. "First class," said Willie. I progressed. This is how far: I once actually set in motion the stuck wheel-works of a watch set in a ring.

But Willie worried me. A few times, in the middle of work, he had suddenly, angrily, got up and saying nothing walked into his room and shut the door. I knocked, he didn't answer, so I left. Later he would only say he had felt tired. It seemed to annoy him I even asked.

And then, sitting close to Willie so often, I noticed he smelled. Not dirty, but sweet, a strange sort of sweet, not nice. Manang had said sometimes bad spirits went to live right inside people. I didn't know why the smell made me remember that. It scared me a little. I asked Willie about the smell in a jokey way, but his whole face tightened up. "Piss off!" he said. He was so furious he trembled. "Just piss off!" he hissed. And after that day Willie found excuses: he was too tired; he was too busy to work with me. He wrapped his silence around him; I had no weapon against it. I wanted my friend back, I liked his world, but it was no use. I had let him down.

About this time it was decided — by my mother, Mrs Crone, and a few other women — that I was big enough to do more around the house. I already swept the hallway and front steps daily; now, my mother said, in rotation with some other children, I was to keep the toilet clean. The toilet was a shame, she said — diarrhea, far too many people using it, some of them unhandy little kids, and maybe some unhandy adults too. Lately, she added, the little room seemed messier than ever; nobody knew why. The walls had pee on them, even smears. I was to inspect regularly, every day, for a week, and use a mop when needed.

I didn't mind. It was a real job, not just a chore such as sweeping. I got there early before the morning rush and straightaway afterwards. Then the windowless little room stank, but not so bad — nothing like Peter under his sheet or the boar's head in the ground. I stopped in at mid-morning, noon, mid-afternoon, after adults returned from work, and before I went to bed. Like a policeman, I stood in line just to check up. Duty undid my own routines, of course, and they were cut short and rescheduled. I missed Willie a little less.

It helped me enormously that first week on the job when Mrs Crone pinned to the wall above the toilet a long poem about shitting. Mrs Crone would say of herself: "I'm not a figure who remains in the shadow." And one way she came out of the shadow was to write stinging or loving or funny lines that rhymed, on any subject. Young and old, small and big, rich and poor, we all have to shit, said the poem, or we die. It went on and on in very correct Dutch except that every line began with the word shit. Finally, it asked the reader, please, to shit properly, to aim true. After two days, when everyone in the house who could read had to have read it, Mrs Crone took the poem down. Months later, though, she could still recite it from memory for my pleasure.

I kept the toilet very clean and adults praised me, which, unlike Willie, I enjoyed. But something was happening there. While mopping, I had the door wide open to let daylight in; usually you sat there with the room lit only by a tiny bulb on the ceiling. Every day, a different spot on one of the toilet's white-painted walls, near the floor, high up, anywhere, was slightly darkened with moisture. Old blots had turned faintly yellow. Worse, here and there, always high up, were small smirches. I couldn't believe it — somebody was dirtying up the toilet on purpose. If I told my mother, what could she do? It could be anybody. There were forty or more people who used the toilet; how would she figure out who it was? Jerry, the same thing; and he might insist we let the adults know. There'd be a terrible ruckus. Mrs Crone might write another poem. Mrs Slierendrecht might have a fit. Ankie? No, I couldn't tell Ankie: her face might close.

I would keep quiet. It was, after all, my toilet that week; and I'd ask, beg even, that they let me take care of it the next week, too. I would wash the walls — not so difficult — and then check for fresh stains; what puzzled me was the spread of the pee marks: how was it done? I would find out. I would hide in a cluster of bushes near the bathroom and the toilet — and watch everybody going in and out. I would join many line-ups. I would look in on the toilet late at night. It could be fun. In time the patient, cunning watcher would run the guilty one to earth. It would be like hunting.

Some people, of course, were definitely innocent. My mother and Jerry, the Crones, Willie and his mother and sister, the Slierendrechts — well, maybe not Mrs Slierendrecht; also, really little kids couldn't have reached the height of the smudges. That still left quite a few suspects though.

And then, when I knew who it was, what would I do? If I told my mother she would perhaps talk quietly with the person; but she also might first want to discuss it with Mrs Crone who didn't like staying in the shadow — and there could be a row. There had to be something wrong with whoever filthied up a toilet on purpose. It was sort of sad. I thought about Dirk long ago cheating over soldiers. Also sad, and bad — and what had my mother answered when I asked how I could help him? Just stay yourself, she'd said.

I knew what to do. I'd write a note. I couldn't write very well, but I'd fox the spelling of the words out of Jerry and then, when I was sure who it was, I would slip the paper to him or her without letting on, of course, that it came from me. The note would say: STOP IT IN THE TOILET.

The toilet was now spotless. I stood in line, made sudden visits, crouched in the bushes watching: some people went often. On the seventh day, about three in the afternoon when it was still and very hot, I saw Willie go in and as he came out again he was stuffing something into his pants pocket. I went into the toilet and there was a wet patch at about the height of my head. I wiped it off.

I went to our room and lay down by the window. It must have been a little can or cup in Willie's pocket. There was one Willie, I thought, a quiet, kind boy who sat hunched over his table hour after hour healing watches. And then there was another who was mad because he had to wear a hat, suddenly needed rest, and lived in a skin that smelled sweet. Was the second Willie so angry, so angry and helpless, that all he could do was, in a half-dark toilet, foul up the walls with his pee and shit? Would I have? I'd never had such an anger. Maybe I would.

I wrote no note. I never told anyone. I just cleaned up after Willie and he must have noticed because before my second week was done he'd stopped. One day, he and his family packed and moved out of our neighbourhood. His mother told someone that a person had died and a nice room had come free.

8

Ankie

Ankie Crone was a mystery. Of course, when I thought about it, everybody was a mystery in a way, even my mother and Jerry. You felt you knew just who a person was, had come to their "end," and then he or she did or said something completely unexpected. But the mystery of Ankie was different again. What it was, I didn't understand. When our lives later moved apart I stopped thinking about the mystery and I stopped thinking about Ankie, although I never forgot her.

On the first day in Tjihapit Ankie had knocked on our door while my mother was still fixing up the new room. She stuck her head in and said she just wanted to say hello and offered tea: neighbourliness was not so common any more. She told us her name and my mother told her ours and said come in. Ankie looked around the room, at every small adornment, the drawings, the flowers, the leaves, and smiled with pleasure. "*Wat gezellig!*" she said. *Gezellig* means cozy, comfortable, homey, friendly, cheerful, snug, festive, hearty, and more; it's an important Dutch word. She confessed her family's room wasn't very *gezellig*. I

93

stared at her. Brown hair fell curling inward to just above slender shoulders. The skin looked baby-soft. The voice was faintly nasal. It was the smile, though, where the mystery began for me: her whole face smiled and she gave that small moan.

Ankie would go back to her family's room and also set out cans and bottles with flowers and leaves; she would find pictures to pin up, cloths to drape. What's more, I thought she came to really appreciate my mother, as did Mrs Crone: value her common sense and lack of self-pity, and enjoy her odd Dutch. I knew this, because Ankie told me so. "Your mother is an example to me," she said once, "and always will be."

It was new to have someone older talk to me seriously, even if only about my mother. In and around the house I grew alert to Ankie's whereabouts and doings. I always first thought what to ask or tell her and then about how she might react. I didn't mind her face closing — all her faces were fine — as long as it wasn't because I had said something childish or ugly or had interrupted her sitting alone on the front steps staring. I didn't come near after overhearing an argument in her family's room, or, of course, if Polo was around. I stayed away when the Japanese said that boys of Harry's and Polo's age had become "a danger to the state" and the next day trucked them out of Tjihapit to nobody knew where. Driving out of the camp gate, many of those big boys waving goodbye were smiling: it was an adventure. I also never forgot that Ankie was older — she had breasts — and that to her I was a little boy. So I was careful approaching her and kept visits short. Mostly we just chatted, her thoughts, I could tell, often straying. The trick for me was to grow beyond cute and sweet to interesting. Now and then it worked and at such moments I briefly felt hot with certainty that her attention was fully on me. Many times, I wouldn't have minded not saying a word. I just wanted to be near her.

Sunlight showed up tiny blonde hairs on her fore-arms. On the front steps she'd sit down, cross her legs, wriggle for comfort, straighten her skirt, and start to swing a foot, and I'd wish she'd get up and do it all again. It was always the same finger that hooked her hair from her eyes. Her mouth looked so soft. The small, quick, busy hands also sometimes lay as if asleep in her lap. Standing up and bending over, her bum stuck out. She hummed a lot. Excitement set off red blotches on her cheeks. When she stretched to hang up washing, her shadow fell slim and curved like young bamboo. Her skin was light pink from the throat down, and on, I supposed. Her voice could soothe like falling water. She wore lipstick on special occasions. If she sat very still I could see her breathing. The eyes, troubled often, were older than she was. When she squatted to pick flowers she tucked her skirt deep between her thighs. She smelled of herself and of laundry soap. Her speaking was sprinkled with "umms" and "ahhs." When she touched me, even by chance, the feel lingered. Sometimes, when happy, she'd run around in long dance jumps. She walked with the sway of a woman. She was a promise.

Across the street, in a house as crowded as ours, there lived a mother and two children, a girl and a boy, about two and five, all with fiery red hair. Sometimes, sitting on our front steps, Ankie and I watched them. Small and muscled, the mother had her hair cut very short and she had a terrible temper. One moment she'd be quietly wandering around their yard, carrying the girl, holding the boy's hand, and in the next the girl had been plunked down crying and the mother was yelling at the boy, shaking a finger in his face. Then the mother would snatch up the girl and, still shouting, grab the boy by the arm and drag him into the house.

It wasn't unusual to see women blow up at their children, or at each other: camp life was dreary but always charged because torment never let up. Just to pester prisoners, a neighbourhood's water or electricity might without warning be cut off for a day or two. A promised truckload of bananas wouldn't arrive. A sugar ration was held back. Soldiers might suddenly burst barking into a house, order everyone out, and ransack it searching for, say, scissors and knives — and so pettily fixed were they then on just those items that they'd miss or ignore any other contraband. And always there were bans: all velos and tanks forbidden; no more religious services; all team sports, such as soccer, prohibited; and, of course, strictly no *gedekken*. *Gedekken* drove them mad; shaving a smuggler's head represented chopping it off with a samurai sword. Over time, though, prisoners' flare-ups slackened: there was no energy.

We got used to the redhead's scenes, but then they began to change. The mother worked and the boy was left in charge of his sister; it couldn't have left him much time to play. She'd come home and later the three of them would go out into the garden. They had a vegetable plot and she and the boy watered and weeded as the girl sat and looked on. The boy seemed to make mistakes or was slow. First she just screamed at him — but then he started to scream back. She would whack him on his behind. He'd run away, she'd catch him, they'd struggle, and the girl sitting in the grass might burst into tears. No one interfered. From that the sessions grew, day by day, to the mother hitting the boy in the face with her open hand while he tried to fight back, to pushing and hitting him until he fell, to finally going at him with her fists and bare feet, just beating and kicking him, screeching that he was a rotten child, a filthy child, a dog.

One day, sitting on our front steps, Ankie said, "That's enough." She got up and crossed the road. I trailed behind. Was she going to fight the mother? Ankie once told me about a boy named Hans who had suddenly given her a kiss, her first, on her cheek, and she had slapped his face. She was soft but there was a limit. The woman now had the boy by the shoulders and was shaking and shaking him so his head flopped around; veins stood out in her neck. Gently, politely, Ankie called the mother's name. Dropping the boy, she swung around; he scurried to where his sister was sitting. The woman stood with her hands in her sides, breathing hard, not saying anything; she wasn't much bigger than Ankie but a lot stronger. Ankie had her hands clasped behind her and she took a few small steps closer. I stayed where I was. In that same voice Ankie said, "I wondered about something — if you have time?" Then she was standing by the mother, finger tips on her arm, murmuring. She pointed to the vegetable bed, moved towards it. The woman stood like a rock at first, then her arms fell, she gave me a look, and she let Ankie steer her away.

I walked backwards to our front steps. First they bent over the vegetable bed, then they knelt by it. The boy had disappeared. Ankie and the woman got up and sat with the girl, played with her. There was a real conversation going.

Maybe half an hour later Ankie came back across. What had she said to the woman, I wanted to know. "I asked about lettuce." But what about the boy, the beatings? She hadn't mentioned him or them. She said she and the woman had talked about his sister and then about themselves as little girls. They had laughed about what an awful lot you can remember from when you were small. Ankie was beginning to stare, her eyes older: I should leave.

The redhead's flare-ups didn't stop altogether — she had a temper — but I didn't see her hit her son again.

The red tile roof of our house hung over so far that in the rain you could sit on the two top front steps and stay dry. Rain came down with the same force as on the plantation, but there you could often see it coming. In Bandung, which lies in a valley, the dark clouds sneaked up from behind the mountains and streaked down to burst apart over the city; in the wet season almost every afternoon, long driving gushes. Streets steamed, sewers gargled, and plants hugged the ground. Those rains could quickly turn gardens into swamps and parts of streets into streams; their drum and clatter, as always, shrank the world.

Ankie, being older, heard more news than I. When I was sitting on the front steps with her once watching the rain, she told me that on the other side of the camp a young Indonesian had tossed a bunch of bananas over the wall to a woman, not to trade, but out of *kasihan*, pity.

She hunched her shoulders as if cold.

The Japanese had spotted the man, she went on, thrashed him, then stood him up in the street where he'd thrown the fruit with a sign around his neck saying, "I gave bananas to the rotten Dutch." He was to stand there for six days without food and water. Late at night women waited for the guard to grow sleepy and then somehow passed food and drink to the young man, and he lived.

The man with the sign must have felt very alone, I said to Ankie, especially in the dark.

Yes, she said, very.

To be alone in the dark was the worst, I said.

She nodded.

There were rumours that soon boys even of Jerry's age were going to be picked up because they were a "danger to the state."

She'd heard that, too.

Jerry would drive out of the camp in a truck like Harry and Polo — and then I wouldn't have a brother any more. My brother would be gone. I wouldn't know where he was or whether he was dead or alive. Sometimes, when I woke in the night, I told her, I climbed over my mother asleep and looked out our window at the stars. Manang, our gardener, had not mentioned spirits living on the stars but I thought they probably did. They had to be lonely so far from the world. On earth, spirits had us at least.

Ankie looked up at the rain. If she went out into it she would look as she did after a bath, her hair clinging flat to her neck, ears, and sides of her face — fresh, like the girl sitting by the holy banyan tree watching the trucks.

And, of course, I said, we had the spirits. If you got really lonely you could think about the spirits all around you, as Manang was positive they were — well, that might make you feel better. But what if Jerry went away? Would thinking about spirits help then? Also, my mother might die. She had a lot of common sense — but it could happen, people died all the time. The women who made coffins had to work hard. If my mother died I'd be completely alone and knowing there were lots of spirits around, well, I didn't think it would cheer me up. No, because I wouldn't have my mother. She would be gone.

I had Ankie's attention.

That was the trouble these days, I told her, you didn't get to keep what you had. Nobody. Nothing. The plantation, my father, Manang, Mr Otten, Uncle Fred, Jerry's bike, my iron collection, Leo, Mr Plomp — gone. The boar's head — gone. Bloemenkamp, Dirk, my yellow kite, Mrs Plomp, Mrs Witte — gone. Peter in the hospital — gone; dead probably. And now perhaps Jerry. If this kept up there'd be nobody and nothing left.

She was still listening.

100

She knew, of course, that Jesus had said "Love your enemy"?

Yes.

Well now, how could anybody — anybody — love the damn Japs? They took away everybody and everything. They were thieves.

It was still pouring. Ankie got up, stretched. I watched her from her toes on up — she looked so smooth all her clothes had to be made of silk. She frowned. She would have to think about that, she said, and went inside.

Another time, maybe also on the front steps in the rain, I brought up Manang again, his squatting all the time, the guns and knives he carved, and the cowardly spirit living inside that made him so afraid of Leo. We talked about fear. That day Ankie was wearing glasses for the first time, rimless: they made her small eyes larger.

There were different kinds of fear, Ankie said. Before we had come to live in Tjihapit, she told me, one night a woman had swapped a pair of pyjama pants at the wall for twelve hard-boiled duck eggs. After she had her eggs she threw up the pants and ran; the pants, though, snagged on top of the wall. The Indonesian outside was trying to free them with a stick when he was caught. The Japanese beat the man until he had to be dragged away. By then it was light and the entire camp was ordered out on a field. An officer yelled for the *gedekker* to come forward. Nobody moved. You will all stand here until she does, he screamed, and marched off. Soldiers with rifles with bayonets kept watch and the camp stood in the sun all morning and all afternoon. People fainted. Children cried.

Ankie shivered. She said the air had been full of fear. People feared for themselves, for their children, for their mothers, for the old, and for the sick. They knew that the officer would let them stand and stand — for days — if the smuggler wasn't found. He would never let them go; whoever had the eggs must be found or he would "lose face." People were going to die on that field. It was towards evening that someone told a soldier who the *gedekker* was. He barked for her to come to him, while another soldier trotted off to fetch the officer. Ankie knew the woman slightly: her name was Loes and she was thirty-seven years old. Ankie was standing nearby when the officer came. He didn't shout at the woman or hit her. He took her by the elbow and leading her away he said quietly in Indonesian, "Too bad, Miss Loes."

What I was afraid of, I told Ankie, was that we would always be prisoners.

No, one day we'll be free, she said.

I didn't think so. The Japanese held us, I said, and they weren't going to let us go. Otherwise, why hadn't they done so already? Why had they even picked up women and children? We weren't men, we couldn't fight them. No, they kept us in camps because they liked it. They hated us. We were the enemy. We were being punished because they thought we were bad, and they were going to keep on punishing us. They would always think we were bad; we would never leave the camp.

Without hope we die, Ankie murmured.

On the plantation I was able to see so far, I told her, and it was green and quiet. Here the wall stopped your eyes, and there were always other people around. I felt cramped.

Ankie nodded. She was leaning forward, hands under her jaw, elbows on her thighs, legs stretched.

I said the Japanese must think we were getting worse because there was less food all the time and more punishment. A woman who hadn't bowed properly was made to kneel on a gravel path for four hours. In Japanese eyes we must be so bad. Maybe we were.

She shook her head no. Raindrops spattered her bare feet.

She turned. I had her attention.

I was an idiot, she said quietly. This was a war — and the Japanese had started it. Now they were fighting us and the Americans and the English, almost everybody, except the Germans and Italians. We were in camp and being starved and hurt because that's how they fought a war. We were victims. None of us were bad. Not me either. I was an idiot, she smiled, to think that maybe I was bad, that maybe I was guilty.

From crashing down, the rain was now just falling steadily.

It was the Japanese who were guilty, she said, her cheeks red. And one day they would pay for it.

What was "guilty," I asked.

If you did something wrong you were guilty, at fault, to blame, for having done it, Ankie said.

I thought that over. And then I said that for a while now I had been feeling guilty about just about everything.

She waited.

I wanted to tell her about Willie and his toilet messes.

Sure they had been his, but just the same I felt guilty about them. I didn't have Willie's anger that made him a little crazy — only he had it. Was that fair? But I kept quiet about Willie. Instead I told her about Peter in the hospital stinking under his sheet. It was long ago, but I could still see the huge eyes in the white face. The pain from his smashed leg had been a hundred times worse than mine from my finger. Was that fair? He shouldn't have suffered so much. And damn, why hadn't I had my harmonica with me to give him?

Ankie had a tiny approving smile for this — as I knew she would. I really had wanted Peter to have the harmonica though.

But I also felt guilty, I said, about the woman Loes and all those people afraid on the field, even whoever had told on Loes, and the woman on the gravel, the Indonesian with the sign around his neck, the coffins being carried out the camp gate, my Aunt Ina in hospital again, Dirk the cheat, my mother's thinness, Jerry maybe leaving, everything. Inside small coffins were dead children. The smallest coffins held babies who must have gone straight from being born to being dead. My father had said religion was nonsense. Well, God was letting it happen, wasn't He? It made me tired.

Ankie was looking down at her wet feet. She sighed, lightly lifting the swellings inside her blouse. She was very serious. She said she thought that perhaps many people felt this guilt. She did sometimes. But she was sure it wasn't right. She touched my forehead. I had to think it away, she said.

I trusted Ankie. I tried.

9

Jerry

We must have looked as if we were celebrating —
sitting cross-legged on the "living-room" mattress,
talking low, laughing, nibbling treats. From somewhere our mother had scrounged a few bananas and
oranges and a bowl of the milk and scraped-out flesh
of a young coconut; earlier Mrs Crone had handed a
saucer of homemade palm-sugar fudge around the
door. The window was shuttered, the one lamp
covered with black cloth. The Japanese hated the dark,
were scared of it some said, and at night kept their own
quarters ablaze while forever badgering us to save electricity. Lights out at eight was the rule — one of the
few my mother ever broke. She read as late as she
pleased, if she had a book and wasn't too tired; it was
at this time that she was copying out *The Hermit*. What
light there was fell at the head end of her mattress
where she was folding clothes and stuffing them into
a rucksack; a little suitcase stood ready by the door.

The awful rumour had come true: boys of Jerry's
age, thirteen-year-olds, were a definite "danger to the
state" to be trucked away to no one knew where. To

stir up panic the Japanese had told the camp only at midday that the boys were to report at the gate next morning at six. They seemed afraid of young boys because some months later there would be a call-up of twelve-year-olds, then eleven-year-olds, which I just missed; ten-year-olds would have been next if the war had gone on. The lower the cut-off age fell, the harder wailed the frantic mothers bunched at camp gates seeing their children hauled away. Once a group of them dared to protest, and were beaten and locked up.

Our mother's lips had grown thin on hearing the news, but then, as expected, she told Jerry it was an adventure, his biggest — and on his own. We stayed up late that night, which didn't matter because my brother had a clock inside that woke him when he told it to. I tried to see his face in the dark. Some people found Jerry dull because he was quiet and seemed shy, but those soft brown eyes could blaze with pain or fun. He read whenever and whatever he could and, like Ankie, would sit still and stare. He wouldn't say what was in his head then; they weren't secret thoughts, he'd explain, just private. I felt they might be a little sad because often that's how his eyes looked. I had overheard our mother say about him that he was "deep." I was the one who made grown-ups laugh. Jerry had no special friends and was alone a lot. When he played it was mostly with me — but no real-fighting games. We never needed to say much; he seemed to feel safe then and even laughed out loud. The age gap still made no difference, except that I got my way a lot. We were as one against outsiders, and never told on each other: that was dishonourable. On his time off we still roamed through the stinking sewer alleys looking for stuff, silent as Indians.

In the dark room I could make out Jerry's shape and the whites of his eyes. He stood up and shuffled this way and that on the mattress, hands in his pockets, saying out loud, it seemed, whatever came into his mind. On the plantation one night he had spied in his pyjamas on the adults playing Monopoly — our parents and Uncle Fred and Aunt Ina. Our parents and Uncle Fred laughed more and more, Jerry said, as a flustered Aunt Ina turned more glum. After a bit he realized the three had ganged up on her and were cheating. He'd started to giggle and had to scramble away.

What an imagination, murmured our mother.

Always calm and gentle and friendly was how Jerry remembered Uncle Fred. He thought Aunt Ina, on the other hand, was usually tense and strict and prickly.

If you can't say something nice about a person, say nothing; our mother slipped an always-useful tea towel into the backpack. But she'd more than once called Uncle Fred "an example of a fine man" and I thought she liked him a lot.

Turning to me, Jerry said that during a New Year's celebration, I'd held a lit firecracker behind my ear to find out just how loud it sounded and after the bang had burst into tears.

Never, I hissed.

Jerry flopped down full length on the mattress. The first book he had ever read was *Robinson Crusoe*. On the plantation he remembered fire-red hibiscus with metal-green leaves and grass so lush it had looked good enough to eat. Why, by the way, he asked our mother, did she never wear trousers?

She felt more womanly in a dress, she said.

Jerry rolled back and forth. He had seen one film in his life, *Snow White and the Seven Dwarfs,* in Bandung; I had been too young to go. Our mother remembered a huge Snow White jigsaw puzzle he had assembled on the dining-room table. In Bloemenkamp, while working in the kitchen, Jerry told us he had seen a soldier beat an older boy with a piece of firewood gripped in both hands. He missed Bloemenkamp: it now seemed almost luxurious — quieter, more to eat, lighter work. Our mother had roasted peanuts there that he sold door to door so we'd have extra money — one egg-cup full for one cent; the Dutch pennies had holes in the centre and he had threaded them on a shoelace with a knot on the end.

Jerry suddenly asked for paper and a pen. Our mother dug a scrap out of her purse and a short pencil. Jerry said a pencil would fade. Sorry, she didn't have a pen. He crawled over to the light and she shifted to make room. Lying on his stomach he held the paper down on *The Hermit* and began to write slowly. My mother and I waited. Then he scrawled his signature, fast like our father did, folded the paper twice, and tucked it and the pencil back into the purse. As if he were an adult, in that tone of voice, he told our mother that we were forbidden to read it until he was gone.

The word "gone" echoed a little, but Jerry wouldn't let it change the mood. After writing his note, he was a little bit in charge. He jumped to the end of the mattress where I was sitting and yanked me up. "Those breasts at the pool on the plantation were pointy, *pointy*," he breathed into my ear (with our mother right there!). "From the cold water," he finished in a normal voice.

What cold water, our mother wanted to know.

But by then Jerry had me in a neck hold and was dragging me across the mattress. He was never the one to start, didn't like it — but I loved wrestling. We fought on, puffing and snorting. Our mother sat by the lamp hugging her knees, rocking herself. We rolled and twisted and leg-pressed the air out of each other. I felt I was beginning to win, but I almost always did with Jerry. He wriggled free and rolled towards our mother. There were three pieces of fudge left on the saucer.

We should eat those, he said, and then we'd better go to bed. Our mother agreed, and lightly held his chin a moment.

But on our side of the room, Jerry wasn't ready for sleep yet. He asked if I remembered Itjeh. I didn't much: she was our cook on the plantation and had a mouth stained red from chewing *sirih*, betel nut. One day, he whispered, Itjeh's husband came to say she couldn't work because she was sick. Jerry decided to visit her; he'd done so before. In front of her one-room bamboo hut on stilts he called "Itjeh!" and she answered from inside to come in. There was a bucket of water by the steps and he first washed his feet. When he opened the door he could just see her half-sitting up in the smoky dimness wrapped in a sarong on a sleeping mat; a child lay asleep nearby. She thanked him for coming, but really she would be fine, she said;

she would cook again tomorrow. He took a step closer to see better. But you're sick, he said. No, not sick, she smiled with red teeth. What is wrong with you then, Itjeh, Jerry said sternly. "Oh, you good boy," Itjeh laughed, "it is only this," and from behind her she lifted a cloth soaked with blood. Jerry shot out of the door and down the steps. He ran home and into our house yelling that Itjeh was bleeding to death, that she was dying, dying.

I'd never heard this story and waited for the end, but that was it. Jerry said no more. Why tell half, I wondered to myself, getting sleepy.

I turned and asked in his ear if he was scared about tomorrow.

No, he said.

On the plantation, he mumbled after a moment, he had liked playing soccer because the Indonesian boys always let him be goalkeeper.

Jerry had set his inside clock early and was already washed and dressed when he woke us. Our mother pushed open the shutters. Grey light showed mist clinging to the ground and a fine drizzle. No cock had cried yet. We heard stumbles next door: the Crones had said they'd come to the gate; Ineke and Hanneke, too. Aunt Ina and Erik were sick. As our mother and I dressed, Jerry swung the backpack on and off his shoulders whistling to himself; the hole his lips formed was never in the centre of his mouth but to the right, giving him a crooked look. We ate small hunks of the glue-like bread and drank water, my brother standing by the door, rucksack on his back.

Once out in the light rain, Jerry began to march, swinging the suitcase, chin up, straight as a soldier. Our mother kept up but I had to trot. I was going to dash forward and imitate him, but it suddenly didn't seem funny. I trudged on behind. From side streets and lanes small solemn groups with a boy at the centre turned onto the main road to the gate. Some women and girls were already crying. I ran to check our mother; but, no, she was calmly stepping at the same pace as Jerry. I slowed down. Puddles were forming, nice to stomp in, but that was too childish this grey-drab morning. That was my brother up ahead, my only brother, going away. In minutes my mother and I would be walking back, without him. He would be on a truck off to no one knew where. He would be gone. Just gone. I tried to imagine it. But he had always been there, always. He was there now, striding along in front of me — brave. He had been brave with Leo, that crazy dog, and now he was brave again, like a man almost. I was nearly crying, but I didn't: Jerry and our mother didn't cry. Damnit, though, he was supposed to stay. He had painted his bike for me, invented invisible girls, shot me in the eye, fought for me, made me a kite, hunted and boxed and swum and smoked with me; together we had mowed down enemy soldiers and pretended to be horses; he had read to me and listened to my Chinese-girl stories. He was the one who had put his arm around me when I had my wound, told me about breasts, and built me a tank. He shouldn't leave me. I was his brother.

At the gate ahead soldiers were herding boys into a line-up behind a truck while others held back family and friends with their rifles. Clothes stuck to bodies and faces shone wetly in the rain. The calling and sobbing by mothers and sisters swelled to loud, raw crying. Two officers holding umbrellas, their flat black gaze missing nothing, flanked a camp-office woman who shouted numbers from a list. As boys responded, soldiers hustled them onto the truck — *Lekas! Lekas!* "Hurry! Hurry!"

The Crones pushed their way through to us and quickly hugged Jerry, and so did Ineke and Hanneke. My mother took his face between her hands and kissed each cheek. They said something to each other that I couldn't hear. Then Jerry gripped my hand, looked me in the eyes, and, like our father had done when he left, said, "Take care of Mom." He freed his hand and knuckle-rapped me on the head. "Don't play *litjik*," he smiled, meaning "false" in Indonesian, and turned and ran for the line-up.

We stayed in place. Mrs Crone put her arm around my mother. The tailboard of the first truck was slammed shut; standing pressed together, the boys waved, some crying, most not. Mothers clawed the air and screamed and surged against the hard rifles. As the truck rumbled out of the gate, a second one hastily backed in, its engine left running. Boys were hoisted into the back with speed. I couldn't spot Jerry at first but then he was clambering up, too, one of the last. He stood on his toes, his eyes searching for us — and he was grinning. Why the hell was he grinning? When he saw us he swung his hands in fists above his head as if he'd won a race; then he just looked. For a second I was inside him, looking over the wet heads of the crowd sealing in the faces of mother and brother, the truck's floor shuddering beneath bare feet. Bolts clanged, gears screaked, and the truck moved off. We waved with two arms, and so did Jerry. He was grinning again. Through the gate, the truck turned sharply right and out of sight behind the bamboo fence. He was gone.

All the way home my mother walked with her hand resting on my shoulder. The Crones and Ineke and Hanneke had stayed to watch the last truck leave. Why, I wanted to know immediately, had he been grinning. Excitement, my mother said, and feeling happy. But wasn't it sad leaving us? Yes, she said, and tonight, wherever he might be, he would be very lonely. But this was also a huge adventure: for the first time Jerry would be his own boss, and that was a great feeling. I didn't bother to imagine her ever not being her own boss. Not only that, she said, but Jerry, who was usually alone when he wasn't with us, was now one of that group of boys; he belonged. She and I would talk about him, she said, just as we talked about my father and his mother and Uncle Fred and her father and mother and grandfather and sister, Ada, and dead sister, Helen, and brother, Alfred, who also had red hair and freckles.

At home our room looked empty. Before she went to work, my mother pulled the folded piece of paper out of her purse. Jerry had written in Dutch: "Herewith I Jerry John Hillen bequeath all my personal belongings to my dear Mother and my little Brother."

Most of that day I stayed in our room lying on my mother's mattress beneath the window. I felt tired. I

113

tried to think about Jerry but it just hurt; it was as if something of myself was gone. Wherever he was, at least there would be spirits around him, even now on the truck, though they would be asleep because it was daytime; but at night they would sit on the roof under which he was sleeping and in the treetops all around. They would keep an eye on him.

"He was my best friend, you know," I said that evening when my mother kissed me good-night. "I'll never have such a friend again."

"You will so," she whispered, "you'll see."

I wanted to believe her, but I didn't really. Jerry was gone.

About half a year later, or maybe it was a year later, we got a postcard from Jerry in Indonesian in block letters, one of three postcards we would receive in total. Besides the required sentences — such as, "We have plenty of food and much recreation" or "The Japanese treat us well so don't worry about me" — the sender had twenty-five "free" words. Into those words Jerry had worked "Baptista," my father's middle name. That told us they were in the same camp. It made my mother very happy. She told everybody: father and son, mother and son — how lucky we were. I was glad, too, of course, that Jerry was safe. But I also knew then that he was certainly not his own boss and that he would be taught a lot of discipline.

10

Corry Vonk

Heroes were always men; all the stories I'd heard said so. The one exception was my own Chinese girl who roamed the countryside without fear in red boots and once fought off a python by pressing her fingers into its nose holes until it fainted. It was men who were brave, clever, wise, proud, and saved everybody. Women were usually helpless and weak, but good at having babies and bandaging wounds. Heroes protected women but didn't take them seriously, unless they were "in love," and then briefly. Women were, or were not, kind, gently strong, and soothing. Women, though, were not heroes. To me this was so. But it has to be said that I was wrong. Tjihapit held no hunters, pilots, cowboys, or Indians, but just the same a couple of real heroes lived there — and they were both women. Maybe my mother was a hero, too, but she was my mother.

Heat, hunger, and the sameness of life in camp, made you slow, even a little stupid, and it took me a while to recognize the first hero. Like a naughty, clownish puppet with huge blue eyes that could suddenly fill with tears, she was not much taller than me and as thin. Her dark-brown hair with three or four silver streaks running through was cut short as a boy's, her large mouth lipsticked deep red, with round touches of it on her cheeks, and her eyelashes thickly blackened. It was a mask. A hundred masks really, because she could, and did, pull her face every which way from grief to delight to shock to innocence. It made people laugh. And they laughed at what she said in her husky strong voice, surprising from someone so small, in exaggerated foreign accents, in high and low Dutch, and in tones from command to snivelling. Sometimes she shocked people a bit, but it was hard not to laugh when you were near her. I was in the same camps with Corry Vonk until the end, and that's what she did: she made us laugh.

Corry Vonk was the wife of Wim Kan and both were cabaret stars. They had gotten stuck on a tour in Indonesia when the Germans invaded Holland. After the Japanese won, Mr Kan was shipped off to a camp in Burma. Mrs Kan-Vonk landed in Tjihapit and at once wangled permission from the Japanese to set up a cabaret by and for prisoners. It was called *Les deux ânes*, "The Two Donkeys," and she ran it with a blonde-haired friend named Puk Meijer. The camp's commandant even gave Corry Vonk a title: *Hanchō main main*, *Hanchō* meaning "boss" in Japanese, and *main main*, "play" in Indonesian.

When we moved into Tjihapit, Corry Vonk and her friend lived next door in a garage. Corry Vonk was slight, noisy, and wore bright cloth twisted into scarfs and belts; Puk Meijer was heavy, quiet, and dressed darkly; both were usually in trousers. Each morning they thrust the garage doors wide apart as if opening a store. In the rear behind a sheet-curtain lay their two mattresses and on nails along the three walls hung unusual clothes and hats, tennis rackets, a broken telephone, an outsize frying pan, beards, all sorts of odd things, and, on a nail by itself, dark-brown and ragged, the camp's only wig. Young women dropped by and sat on the floor sewing costumes, or stood around singing or shouting dialogue at each other. Corry Vonk, in her blunt way, made them repeat the songs and lines over and over and over again. In the afternoon she'd march off to work and the garage would grow quiet.

In an abandoned house, with help from volunteers, the two had knocked down walls so a hundred and fifty women and children could crowd together on the "theatre" floor, and built a stage out of bamboo, chicken wire, old sheets, and coloured rags; from somewhere an old piano had been carted in. The entry fee was one guilder and the proceeds went to poor women or to the camp hospital for medicine and extra food. (At first, people in the camps still had a little money and certain supplies could be bought in the city; later, of course, owning Dutch currency and any dealings with the outside became serious crimes.)

There were always informers in camp — women who for food, cigarettes, light work, and other favours told on the rest of us — so, since Corry Vonk was responsible for every word said on stage, she had to be careful. The Japanese hated criticism, and mockery even more; attention of any sort from them was dangerous, as she very well knew. But with her crazy faces and voices, which were impossible to translate, she was able to make us laugh at the Japanese anyhow, and at ourselves, too.

Still, the authorities didn't make it easy. One day the commandant — who often called for Corry Vonk, perhaps because he too thought she was funny — ordered her to stop charging fees or he'd shut the theatre and punish her. But she seemed to have no fear and she was obstinate. Lookouts were promptly posted so that when spies, most of whom were known to us, showed up at the theatre, cash vanished into deep skirt pockets. Next, the commandant, as a "surprise," had his soldiers build and install a stage backdrop, a huge paper-and-bamboo model of the Japanese holy mountain Fujiyama; he said he was homesick for it. Not to show pleasure would have been insulting, but it looked silly. The commandant invited himself to dress rehearsal and must have been so disappointed at the cast's unreadiness, especially that of three clumsy dancers one of whom misstepped once too often so that her partners tripped, crashed into the mountain, and totally wrecked it.

On another occasion, the commandant told Corry Vonk he'd received a notice from military headquarters in Batavia (Jakarta) banning all religious services, concerts, lectures — and theatrical performances. The story went that she thought hard and fast, pulled her most innocent face, and said that Batavia knew best, of course; it always did. But had Batavia mentioned her acting school and public lessons? The commandant studied the paper on his desk — no, it hadn't.

Hanchō main main's blue eyes opened wide — well? The commandant frowned, then nodded: if Batavia objected to acting schools and public lessons then Batavia would certainly have said so.

When I met Corry Vonk the first time she didn't say hello: she looked at me, and then slowly winked. It was as if she'd known me a long time and we shared some sort of secret. I winked back. And that's how we greeted each other from then on, me letting her wink first to be polite.

Corry Vonk had magic inside her. Up close she sparked. Always the centre, face and voice never still, she jumped from joke to idea to joke. You'd have thought this would tire people, but it didn't. They laughed; she excited them. And when she pulled a sad face — and it could be really sad — she made you want to cry. Around Corry Vonk others also became funny and had ideas, ideas for the cabaret or for cheering up the poor and sick and punished; for cheering up also meant helping out. She never seemed to let up, whether handing out plucks of hair from the camp's only wig to women who'd been shaved bald to sew onto their headcloths, or begging for money or rice or whatever from those she'd heard had more than the rest. I saw her step up to a woman in the street, a stranger, and fall on her knees, hands up as if praying. The woman couldn't say no, of course, and Corry Vonk blew her a smacking kiss. She mostly got her way, and what she scrounged went to those without. The Japanese now and then handed her gifts of food after the show. This was always shared with the cast, but her own portion seldom got as far as the garage. I knew this because, for a while, I was around her a lot. I thought so much giving away was dumb, though; when I, too, got extra bits of food, I sneaked them home through the sewer alleys, or ate them on the way. But then, Corry Vonk was different. I imagined her late at night on her back on her mattress, whispering jokes and ideas in the dark to Puk Meijer, and then suddenly poking her nose into her pillow and falling instantly asleep like a child.

At first, though, I just watched Corry Vonk and Puk Meijer from the branches of one of the climbable trees in our yard. They were a strange pair: one nervous, always talking; the other steady, reserved. People wondered when, actually, they slept. Running the cabaret meant writing sketches and tunes, finding and fitting costumes, scaring up make-up and props, and endlessly rehearsing amateurs. But they, like the others in the cabaret, had camp duties as well. I didn't know what Puk Meijer did, but Corry Vonk held down one of the few volunteer-only jobs: she washed by hand the hospital's linen and bandages, teeming with the bacteria of every imaginable disease; and towards the end, of course, there was no soap. When I met Corry Vonk in Tjihapit she herself was scurrying around with two tropical ulcers on one of her shins. Many people had them, me too; after dysentery, malaria, and, later, hunger edema, sores were the most common ailment. They could start from a scratch like my wound in Bloemenkamp, fester, and turn into aching pus holes that refused to heal for months. Because of Corry Vonk's long pants, no one could tell, except that she limped a little.

Anna Hillen with her sons, Ernest, aged one, and Jerry, aged five, at home in Scheveningen, Holland

John and Anna Hillen reading with their sons at home in Holland, 1936

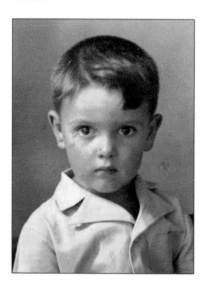

Ernest at about age three

John Hillen, Jerry and Ernest on the tea plantation in the mountains above Bandung, Java

Father and sons watching Indonesians playing soccer on the field below

Anna and John Hillen in the
lush garden of the plantation,
September 1938

Jerry reading out loud to Ernest, 1938. 'Jerry was my best friend'

A visiting *tukang tjukur* at work on Jerry; and the final result of the barber's effort

'What Jerry really liked was to be alone and read'

Anna Hillen and her sons on the front steps of the plantation's main house, 1937

Aerial photograph of the tea plantation, showing the factory, the swimming pool and the Hillen home (top right), 1939

Ernest, Jerry and Ineke and Hanneke Staal. 'They were like our sisters; all four of us had brown eyes'

Jerry, Hanneke, Ernest and Ineke, 1939. 'Every day held the certainty of play in the pool. It was never denied'

Anna shopping in the market, 1939

The last picture the family in
Holland received from Anna,
September 1940

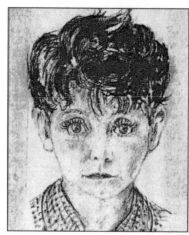

Left: A drawing of Ernest, 1944. 'Events and people that would stir me were like little flames that camp life quickly dimmed or smothered'; *Right*: A drawing of Corry Vonk by a fellow prisoner, 1944. 'She had magic inside her. Up close she sparked'

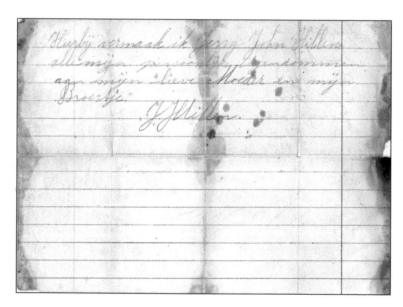

What Jerry wrote when he had to leave his mother and brother in 1943; 'Herewith, I, Jerry John Hillen, bequeath all my personal possessions to my dear mother and my Little Brother. J. J. Hillen' (translated from the Dutch)

Left: Ankie, 1945. 'Ankie had a way of speaking and smiling at the same time'; *Right*: Zuseke Crone, 1945. 'I thought her face should be carved in stone'

A photograph that appeared in the *Toronto Star*, 21 March 1946, upon mother and sons' safe arrival in Canada

Ernest in Canada, aged twelve. 'Memory is, finally, all we own'

Watching from the tree, I was drawn to the two women, the small one especially. I wasn't shy meeting strangers, but all the activity in that garage was a little unnerving. And then one morning I saw the solid Puk Meijer come from behind their "bedroom" curtain in bare feet wearing white, tight, very short pants. She greeted half a dozen young girls who had been waiting and led them onto the red-earth driveway fronting the garage. In shorts she was a whole other lively, lovely person. There was a spring to her step, and no wonder — Puk Meijer's trousers had hidden the most marvellous, most powerful calves I had ever seen in my life. Massive curves of muscle! I dropped out of the tree and moved nearer.

The girls, thin and barefoot, in shorts, with pinned-up hair, formed a circle around Puk Meijer and did as she did. Hands at her waist, she lifted her chin, and for a moment stood straight and still. Then she slowly raised one leg, toes pointed, stretched it inch by inch forward and up, and unhurriedly let it down again — the standing leg's calf nicely twitching with the strain; and the same with the other leg. Her heavy body looked loose and sure and light. She repeated the movement several times; then again with the legs reaching sideways. Usually so quiet, she kept up a steady patter, coaxing the girls, cheering them on. She joined their circle and showed them how to take long steps like a stork, feet pointed, arms out like wings, hands like butterflies. Round and round they paced under a whitening sun, the skinny girls and the big woman, faster and faster, steps turning into leaps and then into running and flying, like Ankie when she was

121

happy. Hands stuffed in my pockets, I stared from only yards away.

Puk Meijer clapped once and the girls froze. She turned to me and asked smiling if I would like to learn to dance. I said no thank you politely; if only there had been even one boy in the group. The exercises went on. The girls never looked my way again nor did Puk Meijer. After about an hour she clapped twice and the students stood still, flushed and panting, heels touching, feet out in V's. Puk Meijer would now dance alone, a treat for her pupils, I learned, and the way every lesson wound up. For a few minutes, to music only she could hear, spinning and leaping and swaying, her shining-wet body told a little story that ended with her sinking, one leg behind, one in front, right down flat to her crotch, body bent forward as if crushed, wild hair brushing her knee. Then she raised her head and, calves bunched to bursting, slowly drew herself up. The girls applauded and she curtsied to them.

For a while, Puk Meijer, who also performed in the cabaret, held three or four ballet classes a week and I tried to catch them all. By hanging around, I got to know her and Corry Vonk. The two women never really said much to me, but they let me sit on the ramp, or right inside the garage when it rained, and listen and watch and knead my calves. The others who came and went got used to me. The songs and skits they rehearsed I heard so often I learned some by heart. At night I acted them out for my mother, and for Jerry in the beginning when he hadn't left yet — and just like Corry Vonk, I could make them laugh. That was a good feeling, and I would do it again and again, until I was told to shut up.

I asked Corry Vonk if I could come to the theatre with her. She said yes. The most fun was not where the audience sat — I never once saw a performance from there — but in the cramped backstage where in a great muddle women stripped to near nakedness and wrestled their sweating bodies into costumes, and, at two small tables with mirrors, took turns painting their faces, fingers trembling. They were nervous, and giggled and snapped, and ran to the toilet a lot. Mumbling lines, some puffed hard at cigarettes made of straw. Before my eyes, tired, thin women became actresses and dancers, turned beautiful or witchy, or even male. Corry Vonk, the director, had lead roles in nearly every sketch, but it was she who darted around readying and calming the others, often saying, "Don't worry. I'm a professional. You're wonderful."

Through a hole in the curtain I'd watch the room filling up, and heating up: later, every face would gleam. Women and children brought old cushions or stools, or sat on the floor. In the front row were a half-dozen kitchen chairs, always there in case Japanese officers decided to show up. They did, too, though they couldn't have understood much and their faces stayed mostly like stone; but sometimes they laughed when the audience did, and also when it didn't.

The first time backstage I wasn't of any use, unless someone asked for water, so I pressed myself away in corners. The disorder and hurry didn't stop once the show started because between numbers, when the lights were briefly turned off, props had to be switched and people who had several roles, most of all Corry Vonk, needed to change costumes fast. That commotion almost scared me: the actresses weren't jittery any more, but suddenly serious and so alive. By the second performance I knew what to expect, even helped set up props in the dark — and Corry Vonk began giving me a share of her food gifts: at different times I carried home two eggs, some sugar wrapped in banana leaf, and four small green oranges.

I watched from the wings and, especially when Corry Vonk was on, heard the laughter swelling and breaking, swelling and breaking. I now knew that feeling, and wanted it again. One character I especially would like to have played was the one Corry Vonk was famous for herself — a mischievous Amsterdam ragamuffin with a too large, peaked cap over one ear who sometimes sang sorrowful songs. Adults in the audience knew some of the tunes so well they hummed along. I mentioned to Corry Vonk that I had a harmonica. I still knew only a few bars of "Silent Night, Holy Night" but even so hoped I'd be asked to play it in the cabaret. It was all I could think of but she showed no interest.

So I fetched water, lugged props, and waited. I waited through rehearsals and performances of a cabaret version of *Pinocchio*. I waited through the writing of a whole new set of skits. I waited — and then one day Corry Vonk told me I was going to be a boy who had swallowed a *rijksdaalder*, a large silver two-and-a-half-guilder piece. She would play my mother, another woman would be my father, and a third a maid. I was very happy. Sitting at table with my parents I had to pretend to accidentally gulp down the coin hidden in a slice of "cake," then look concerned while the others made a great to-do — and never smile. I had nothing to say. We rehearsed and rehearsed, in the garage, then the theatre. On opening night I was ready early, in shorts, shirt, knee socks, shoes, and red lips. My heart was thumping, but I wasn't scared — until I heard the buzz from the audience coming in. Corry Vonk as usual was everywhere at once. She stopped and looked at me. "You're green," she said in that voice all could hear. "If you need to puke, puke. I'm a professional. You're wonderful." I did and felt better. On stage I swallowed, looked concerned, and never smiled. I was wonderful.

The best role, though, came in the next, and last, full-scale cabaret. Over the months the Japanese had been steadily sending off groups of Tjihapit prisoners, from hundreds to a few thousand, "on transport" to nobody knew where. Rumours had them ending up in filthy camps in Batavia or on old ships to be torpedoed out at sea. The unexplained relocations scared people: the whispers never stopped that the Japanese really just wanted to kill us all off. By now the upper half of the camp was almost empty. It was said a fence was going to go up through the middle and we in Lower Tjihapit would be herded into Upper Tjihapit. If this were true, *Les deux ânes* would lose its theatre. So Corry Vonk worked us hard.

By opening night we knew the move to Upper Tjihapit could come any day. The mood in camp was nervous. Change, adults said, was now never for the better. I was already sure that just as my brother had

125

left my life, so would the Crone family, Corry Vonk and Puk Meijer, our room with the window, being an actor, everybody, everything. That's how it went.

Corry Vonk wasn't down, though. The theatre was packed as usual. She looked through the hole in the curtain, then held up a hand with fingers spread, and told us loudly, "Five Japs out front!" She seemed to like danger. The word "Jap" was strictly forbidden because the Japanese had learned it was meant as a slur; if children said it, their mothers were punished; everybody used it anyway, but quietly.

The curtain rose and there in the kitchen chairs, in starched uniforms and gleaming riding boots, swords dangling, sat the commandant and four unknown officers. Corry Vonk was on first and, in her street-boy clothes, gave a short speech she'd memorized in Japanese. The audience was silent, but the military men clapped hard. The commandant had asked her for it especially, to impress his visitors.

Once the show was on the way it moved fast, everyone trying to keep pace with the star who switched from urchin to parlour maid to poet to radish vendor to rabbit to professor. My number was towards the end but I'd wriggled into my tight, hot costume long before curtain time. The skit was about water, which in the sapping heat was always on people's minds. The Japanese pestered and punished us by cutting water off unexpectedly. That was the point of our routine, that never ever could you take water for granted. Two women dressed as pine trees, straight and unmoving, would first hold a long, comical conversation, then drift into a song that ended in a six-line chorus. I would come on during the chorus. Timing was everything. I wasn't nervous, just very ready: the cast had applauded me during dress rehearsal.

When we got to the sketch there was the quick black-out in which the pine trees rushed to centre stage. The lights went on and from the wings I watched the pines talking. There were a few smiles, but no laughs from the audience: to the barefoot women and ragged children, jokes about water or food weren't really funny. The trees went into their song and I bent down, fingertips to the floor. Then the trees sang the first line of the chorus.

"It's grand to be a pine tree,"

And I trotted out on all fours and moved between the trees, tongue out, rear end wagging.

"One of the upper ranks,"

I looked down into the blank faces of the five officers. I sniffed one tree, then the other. There was a chuckle starting, some children pointed.

"Who need but wait and get for free"

The chuckle rose into laughter — as I lifted my leg high to the first tree.

"The special water they deserve, you see!"

Laughter.

"Who need but wait and get for free"

Laughter and applause — as I raised my other leg and "peed" on the second tree.

"The special water they deserve, you see!"

The Japanese below were laughing and clapping, one hitting his thigh.

At the end of the show the cast jogged one by one on stage to applause, and there was, truly, a quick surge for me. But it was nothing compared to the roar that greeted the small woman who, after a moment's pause, and then at a run, came out last. That's who they had been waiting for, those tired, skinny women and children scrambling upright now. For a short while she had held off hunger, fear, and pain, squelched misery, and scattered amongst them like fireflies sparks of her courage and joy. For a long moment then, the audience ignored the five sitting military men, and stomped bare feet, held up children, shouted "Bravo!" and whooped and clapped and whistled. "You're wonderful," she mouthed, eyes wet, "you are wonderful."

11

Zuseke Crone

If the first hero looked like a toy, the second, Mrs Crone, was like a tree. She wrote the poem on shitting and was the mother of Ankie, Greddie, and now long-gone Harry. Tall and lean, she had a bony face with the family's slanted eyes, and thick black hair; all her parts were big. Soon after we moved into Tjihapit, she and my mother became good friends. My mother had few friends, although she liked everybody — no, that's wrong: what she did, as she often enough said I should do, was "take people as they are, enjoy the good and forget the bad" and "mind your own business." This was smart because, through all the camps, she never once had a fight, not even a real argument. Anyway, she was friends with Mrs Crone so I trusted Mrs Crone.

Even long after Mrs Crone wasn't in our lives any more, my mother would say that she was the most "forthright" person she'd ever met; and I overheard Mrs Crone call my mother "exceptional." But Mrs Crone wasn't "a figure who remains in the shadow" and she did not "forget the bad." She was a fighter, and I never saw her back off or lose. In our house and at her job, she went after bullies, liars, thieves, cheats, slackers, loudmouths, and dirt-makers. She fought with words. She had her sharp poems, and she had at her command a million sayings. Her tongue was as fast as Corry Vonk's, though not as funny, and because she had a saying for everything she usually also had the last word — which, of course, could be irritating. Yet, adults in our house repeated her sayings; it seemed to cheer them up. They said she was "full of truth," but also nicknamed her "Boss Crone." The sayings were old ones from Holland that she called "the daughters of daily experience." Many, to be honest, I didn't understand. I told her this once and she said I shouldn't worry because "In the concert of life no one gets a program."

Mrs Crone was paid attention wherever she happened to be, but she had no "centre" to her life the way Corry Vonk had her cabaret. No one did. Women worked all day in the sun and then trudged home to take care of children or the sick or old, wash and repair clothes, and sleep. They seldom visited. Early on in Bloemenkamp, yes — we'd even had our party — but in Tjihapit they were too tired and, later, too weak. So my mother and Mrs Crone were good friends in passing; they had no real conversations, not like Ankie and I. They chatted in line-ups in the back of the house where the toilet and bathhouse were and by a short, uncovered length of gas pipe. (It was forbidden to cook at home and stoves had been confiscated, but for a while the gas wasn't cut off. Someone, perhaps Willie — he was smart enough — had fixed a piece of hose to the pipe so it fed a secret little burner. Women met there when they had an extra bit of food to fry or boil; if soldiers suddenly appeared, the all-purpose alarm cry sounded, "Coffee is ready!") Otherwise, they stayed mostly in their own rooms. At one point my mother was taken out of the camp kitchen and made a furniture lady again, on the same team as Mrs Crone. But they wouldn't have talked much hauling the big carts around.

"A friend at your back is like a firm bridge," was a Mrs Crone saying. When Harry was taken away, my mother stood next to her waving goodbye. And later, when Jerry was trucked out of camp, Mrs Crone put her arm around my mother. One day my mother turned yellow, copper yellow, even the whites of her eyes; her forehead burned, and she was suddenly so weak she could hardly speak. She had yellow fever, jaundice. Except to bathe her with wet cloths, Jerry and I hadn't known what to do. I'd never seen her ill and I wouldn't again in the camps; she wouldn't "allow" it. I once watched her late at night in her white cotton nightgown, hair falling over her face, drag herself out of our room on hands and knees, down the hall, and outside to the toilet. I didn't help her because I was sure she'd waited until she thought we were asleep to be private.

The only foods she apparently should and could take in were yoghurt and buttermilk. Mrs Crone found some. I wanted to hear how, but you never asked: it was better not to know. And it was Mrs Crone who every morning would half-carry my mother to wherever their team gathered because the movers' payment of an extra chunk of bread was only handed out to the worker herself. Mrs Crone would hide my mother in an already emptied house nearby, where she lay on the floor until the bread was delivered. Then Mrs Crone would fetch her, prop her up in the breadline, and later sneak away to help her home again. The reason for all this effort was that I didn't get extra bread like Jerry, who also earned it at his job, because I was too young to work. My mother had always split this ration with me and she wasn't going to let me go without. Mrs Crone dragged my mother around the whole two weeks she was sick.

I thought Mrs Crone's face should be carved in stone. With her hollow, lined cheeks, high forehead, and sharp nose, she looked like a hawk. Or maybe a painting would be better. Because how, in stone, could you cut a twinkle or a glare? You could read the eyes of the animals Hanneke Staal drew. And it was the expression in Mrs Crone's eyes that told me how she meant a saying, as a joke or a swipe, even if its sense went over my head. She was a hero I didn't understand very well but that was all right. Her phrases rolled and echoed around in my mind:

> That helps as much as a mosquito peeing in the Rhine.
> She's like a winter's day: quick and dirty.
> Old love doesn't rust.
> Whores and crooks are always talking about honour.
> Revenge is honey in the mouth but poison in the heart.
> What gain is there if a lazy wench for once rises early?

I know my way around there like a herring in a
    hayloft.

Quick is dead but Slow is still alive.

Grief is a long death; death is a short grief.

A cow quickly forgets she was a calf.

Don't hoist old horses out of the canal.

Hunger eats through stone walls.

When children are small they step on your toes,
    but when they grow up they step on your
    heart.

Young and old, in the end all turn cold.

A warm bed and lazy ass are like lovers: they don't
    part easily.

Better to have ridden a good horse for half a year,
    than a donkey your whole life.

Avarice is never satiated until the mouth is full of
    earth.

Good is good, but better is better.

All things are possible except biting off your own
    nose.

She's as comfortable as a salmon on a pyramid.

Mrs Crone had two favourites: "Be trustworthy, but
trust no one" and "That (some annoyance) is unim-
portant in the drama of the here and now."

I couldn't, as with Ankie, have serious talks with Mrs
Crone: she had no patience discussing death, fear,
guilt, and certainly not Manang's spirits; for that sort
of thing she had all the answers. But she liked reports.
She listened to the killing of Leo the dog, burying the
boar's head, food line-up gossip, cabaret adventures,
and anything on the horrid Mrs Slierendrecht. They

were enemies: "Mrs Slierendrecht," said Mrs Crone, "crept out of hell while the devil was sleeping."

If I had news, I felt free to knock on her door. The room was neat as I imagined Mr Crone's cabin was on his ship, but, as Ankie had said, not *gezellig* like ours. Sitting on their one chair, Mrs Crone might suddenly pull me onto her huge lap, her arms sticky from the heat. "A good listener needs only half a word," she'd told me once, so I'd keep the report short, jump down, and leave.

Then came the morning they took Jerry away, and for a few days I kept to myself. At night my mother and I talked about him, his smell and shadow not gone yet. I was surprised, after my father, Manang, Mrs Plomp, and all the others, how much missing a person could still hurt. Closing my eyes so only a glimmer of light slipped in I thought I could see his face. But I knew that, really, like everybody else, Jerry was fading into mist.

During one of those days, returning from the toilet, I passed Mrs Crone's door and she called me to come in. She was alone, sitting on her chair. In her quick way she yanked me onto her lap. She had been thinking, she said, and she needed to tell me something privately.

"You and I are friends, aren't we?" she asked, her glinting, slanted eyes looking into mine.

I nodded.

"True true friends?"

I nodded again.

"Ernest, a true friend doesn't call me Mrs Crone. He doesn't call me aunt. He calls me — from now on — Zuseke. All right?"

And then the toughest woman in the house, maybe in the whole camp, gave me sweaty hug.

I was flabbergasted. It was unheard of. Even Dutch adults usually used first names only with family or good friends; in camp many women still said Mrs to each other. For a child to speak like that — like a grown-up — to a woman with children, to a woman who always won, to a woman who should be carved in stone, well, it was hard to believe. It was like a present, maybe as big as Jerry's bike. I was very pleased.

Mrs Crone set me down. Then she shook my hand.

"Sleep well, Ernest," she said.

"Sleep well . . . Zuseke," I said.

For the first few days after that I tore around looking for her so I could call out, "Hello, Zuseke!" even if I'd just seen her. Others in the house looked up surprised — most of them couldn't be that familiar with her. Was I being cocky? But who got cocky with Mrs Crone? Ankie and Greddie had to get used to it. I never completely got used to it myself.

Time drifted on. But it often felt as if it wasn't real time, as if we were all standing still. The events and people that would stir me were like little flames that camp life quickly dimmed, or smothered. One morning, coming out of a sewer alley, I saw a boy run by chewing a piece of sugar cane. I chased him, but he disappeared. I could *taste* the sugar cane. I crisscrossed the camp looking for him: maybe he had more, to swap, or he'd at least tell me where he got it. As the sun climbed, its heat softened the surface of streets so that bubbles formed; some would burst, leaking drops

135

of shiny black asphalt that stuck to my feet. Hours later I sat down, feeling dizzy. I'd also forgotten what I was doing on the other side of the camp.

It was the same, in a way, when for a few days men prisoners came in to put up the bamboo fence cutting Tjihapit in two. It was exciting at first to see white men after seeing none for two years or more, and guards were posted to keep us apart. The Japanese soldiers, though, faced the women because it was women who risked and got beatings, pressing close and shouting the names of husbands and sons; the men hardly responded and, backs turned, obediently stuck to the job. Their clothes were shabbier than ours — maybe they didn't know how to patch and wash them, or maybe they didn't care. Most of them shuffled about, round-shoul-dered, heads down — even though women and chil-dren were watching. Zuseke mockingly called them "the bruised ones" or "bruisies." I thought they just looked sorry for themselves, not the way men should, and after the second day didn't bother going to the work site any more.

The rumours of moving to Upper Tjihapit turned ur-gent. Three performances of the last cabaret had been held when, with less than a day's warning, we were or-dered to show up by number at the gate in the new fence. As usual we could bring what we could carry; once again sidewalks were piled with tagged mattresses to be carted away. Relocation would take two days. Our house emptied on the first morning, except for my mother and me because we had higher numbers.

Lifting one of their suitcases on my head, I said I'd see the Crones through inspection. That earned an

Ankie smile, as I knew it would, and pleased Zuseke, who said, "The bad get worse here, the good better." There was a line-up at the gate, of course, and each foot forward seemed to take an hour. Finicky guards dug through every piece of baggage while the owners stood bowed; there were no tables, and bags, trunks, and baskets were spread out on the street. To possess anything forbidden had become almost as bad a crime as *gedekken*. In the murmuring crowd behind us a retarded boy stared at a hard turd in his fist. Why did his mother let him? His mother had grey straggly hair; two little girls clutched her legs and she looked ahead shielding her eyes with her hands. She went on standing like that.

Finally, in early afternoon, when the sun was pure white, Zuseke, Ankie, Greddie, and I reached the soldiers. We quickly opened the suitcases, took a step back, and bowed, feet together. A soldier named Tesuka bent and rummaged through the cases, spilling contents on the asphalt. At the bottom of the last and biggest one he flicked open a little cloth-covered jewel box. It held a tangle of girl things of Ankie's and Greddie's: ribbons, hairpins, bits of cloth, a lipstick, a necklace, dried flowers, spools of thread. Tesuka bent deeper, plucked inside it. Then, with a grunt, he fished out a small photograph of Mr Crone in his captain's uniform — I heard Ankie sucking in her breath — and after more fingering, a silver Dutch ten-cent piece as big as a shirt button.

Tesuka grunted again, his face showing nothing. He kicked the suitcase shut, stepped over it, and yelled something in Japanese at Zuseke, thrusting with his

137

right hand the picture and coin under her bowed face. She shook her head no. It was suddenly silent around us. He yelled something else, and I thought one of the words was *andjing*, Indonesian for "dog." Again Zuseke shook no. Then Tesuka slapped her face, snorting with the effort, and the things in his hand fell to the street. He slapped her again, so hard that big as she was she staggered. But just the once: she parted her feet for a better grip. He beat her several times with his left hand. Each time flesh struck flesh he snorted. But he favoured his right, hitting then swinging back with the nail-side. That hand just streaked back and forth, landing all over Zuseke's face. With each blow sweat sprayed, her hair jumped, blood drops flew from her nose, but her body and her head hardly moved. Tesuka was sweating, too. And then, just as the beating had begun to take on a rhythm, Zuseke slowly came out of her bow and straightened to her full height. Head up, chest out, she towered over him. Tesuka kept on hitting, but he was off balance reaching up. Snarling, he grabbed her arm jerking her forward, stood on the big suitcase, and started again. But something was wrong. The slaps had less force. Hundreds of eyes had seen the big woman rise up and a soldier of the Japanese Imperial Army have to climb on luggage to reach her. Or maybe Tesuka was tired and knew he still had work ahead in the sun. He stopped hitting, stepped off the suitcase, and mopping his face clumped over to another family of prisoners.

Zuseke sagged through her knees and toppled over. Ankie and Greddie, both crying, stretched her out with rolled-up dresses under her head. Two women

138

wetted cloths from water bottles and wiped her bloody face, dribbled water on the swelling welts and bruises, on her chest, on her arms. More women leaned over her with water. That's what she needed, to be cooled off. She lay unmoving, eyes closed, breathing deeply. On my hands and knees beside her, I blew into her hair. The pounding hadn't shaken me up: I'd seen worse. I felt no pity, just pride.

"You're wonderful, Zuseke," I whispered.

She didn't respond. Near her head still lying on the street was the crumpled picture of Mr Crone. I picked it up and slipped it into her still hand. Her lifelessness made me nervous.

"Zuseke," I whispered again, "what would Mr Crone say if he ever met Tesuka?"

Her eyes flew open. She lifted her head. Her daughters and the women hovering around at once began telling her to lie back. Instead, she half sat up.

"Say?" she croaked through thick, cut lips. "What would my husband *say*? 'Here's my hand,' he'd tell that Jap. 'You did what I haven't managed to do in twenty years.'"

Ankie and Greddie and the women around us giggled and laughed. I was shocked. A few minutes later, the Crones gathered their luggage, Zuseke still unsteady, and walked through the gate and out of sight.

The next morning my mother and I moved into Upper Tjihapit, our third camp.

12

Upper Tjihapit

In Upper Tjihapit we were allocated a windowless kitchen that was as dark as but even smaller than the storeroom we had had in Bloemenkamp. It was at the back of the house, next to the toilet; the line-up formed outside our door. The room had a built-in counter entirely covered with blue-and-white tiles that showed windmills, sailing boats, and skaters wearing muffs; the walls were speckled with black-green moisture patches. Two mattresses lying flat couldn't fit on the floor, so mine curled up against the tiles. The house was smaller than the one in Lower Tjihapit and more crowded. We had thought the Japanese couldn't shrink space and privacy more, but, as we'd discover soon again, they certainly could. We knew no one in the house.

Earlier that day we had come through the new gate without trouble, except that the guard who searched our two small suitcases and rucksacks tossed away the exercise book in which my mother had copied *The Hermit*. She knew, of course, that anything to do with reading or writing was forbidden, but she'd brought it anyway hoping the Japanese might be less strict on the second moving day. She was wrong: our soldier was as fussy as Tesuka had been with the Crones. The soldier didn't hit her because she'd placed the book at the top of her backpack, unhidden. She didn't read again in camp.

That first evening in Upper Tjihapit as we sat on our mattresses talking the day through, my mother told me what had happened the night before and how frightened she had been. Just the two of us had been left in the house in Lower Tjihapit, it was late, and I had fallen asleep after describing in detail Zuseke's beating and braveness. My mother was reading *The Hermit* for the sixth time, knowing she might lose it the next day, when she heard soldiers suddenly slamming into the house. She quickly shut off her light under the black cloth. They flung open doors to empty rooms, thumped their rifle butts, barked at each other. They rattled our door, but it was locked. My mother lay stiff, not breathing; if they kept at it she'd have to open. She wasn't afraid of the Japanese — our high camp numbers would explain why we were still there — but of how I might react to being jerked awake by shining flashlights and yelling. She was, she said, very scared that, groggy and with Zuseke fresh in mind, I might do "something crazy." I was only about nine but big for my age, and in the dark and confusion the soldiers could hurt me badly before realizing I was a child. What she hadn't thought through was that the moment they did realize it, of course, they would pitch me aside, and go after her. The soldiers joggled the doorknob once more, then stamped away; I slept on.

142

I was pleased that my own mother could think I had the nerve to attack two of the enemy no less. What struck me more, though, was that she'd actually been frightened. I'd never known her to be afraid. She was, I thought, like a jujitsu fighter. From watching the Indo boys, and from having been their mark, I knew the trick with jujitsu was to flow with the other's swing, or kick or chop, help it along even, so a lot of power just walloped air, and again and again the attacker lost his balance. My mother seemed to live like that, yielding but springy, like rubber. She didn't get hit. She was cautious and patient, broke few rules, accepted people and situations as they were — but not from fear. It was always "using my common sense," which, in turn, was somehow linked to her other rule, the big one, endlessly repeated to me, "try to be true to yourself" — which, really, meant your "best" self: a long list of dos and don'ts that came down to being just plain good. If you were that, she said, well, then, you'd be all right. It seemed to work for her. I asked often enough, "Did that scare you?" "Were you afraid then?" The answer was always no, and she didn't lie.

My mother was made a furniture lady yet again, and I was on my own. Sameness was at its worst in Upper Tjihapit; later, in the fourth and last camp, monotony eased up because heat and hunger and dying got so bad. The Crones lived in Upper Tjihapit, so did Puk Meijer and Corry Vonk, and Ineke, Hanneke, Erik, and Aunt Ina. I rarely visited though: everyone's daily-life circle grew tighter and tighter — food, work, rest. So, like Jerry and all the others, they began fading away; sometimes, I felt I was passing into mist too —

away even from myself. I made no new friends. Sameness flowed on. It was as if I was half-asleep. My eyes felt like glass: I saw only what was close, anything far-off was blurred. I walked with my head down, but not, as before, looking for things to play with, only for what might be edible: snails, unripe fruit, spoiled greens in the camp kitchen's garbage ditch. I would sit in shade in small spaces where people couldn't surprise me and stare down at the red earth between my legs; if an ant came along, I'd watch the ant, let it run up a finger and around my hand. I lay on my mattress in our shadowy room, listened to rain, studied the tiles; outside our half-open door, I could hear the toilet line-up shuffling, murmuring. Willie must have lain like that listening to the wash water gurgling in the ditch outside his door.

In the evenings my mother and I talked. She remembered a sweet moment as a girl when she and her mother had been walking arm-in-arm, shopping in Toronto, Canada, and her mother, who never used endearing names such as "Honey" or "Darling," had suddenly called her "Sister" instead of "Anna." To her first high-school dance she had worn her older sister Ada's new yellow dress with puffed sleeves and not one but two boys, "Red" and Cyril, had walked her home. She believed her father didn't think she was very smart, but one day he'd said, "Anna, at least you know what you want — you want to teach. That's something." The brown eyes were far away for a moment. But her days in the sun were long, she was tired, and she'd start yawning. She would loosen her long red hair, turn on her side and, hands folded between her thighs, fall asleep.

One morning my mother said she wasn't going to work — so no extra bread — because all night an infected wisdom tooth had hurt her. Her cheek bulged. There was a nurse who had the tools to pull teeth. I wanted to come along and watch, but no. When she returned, her face was white and she was spitting blood. She mumbled that the nurse, of course, had had to rip the tooth out without a local anaesthetic. We owned five aspirins — but those were for an "emergency." "I'm not sick," she said tightly. "It'll go away." She sat on her mattress, eyes closed, arms around her shins, rocking and rocking, going inside herself. In a singsongy voice like Manang's, I told her a few Chinese-girl stories from the old days. In one, the girl pretended she was a horse and foolishly galloped through a field of *alang-alang*, tall sharp-edged grass. She came out looking a bloody mess, with bleeding gashes on her legs and arms and face, blood dribbling into her clothes and red boots. She stuck small leaves on some cuts, but that didn't help; she sucked them, but they bled on. Luckily, there was a river nearby. She took off her clothes, scooped out river clay, smeared it all over, and sat down cross-legged in the sun. All day she sat covered in caked bloody clay. She looked scary, and panthers and boars kept their distance. In the evening she washed herself in the river, with spirits in the trees and water spiders watching, and saw that all the cuts had closed. She never ran through *alang-alang* again. Still clasping her legs, my mother had rolled on her side like a ball and was asleep.

Another day, trucks loaded with Red Cross packages drove into camp. This was some time in late 1944, when cats and dogs had been eaten long ago and it was no use hunting rats any more — with so little to feed off, they had disappeared. The Japanese ordered the bulk of the cargo carted out of sight; what was left was to be distributed among the several thousand prisoners. That called for a special announcement. Out on a field in the sun an officer shouted at the interpreter that while we were *busuk*, "rotten" in Indonesian, *busuk* to the ground — even so, the hearts of the good Japanese had only compassion for us. He told us to keep the camp cleaner, dress neater, wear shoes, and not lick our fingers after eating to avoid dysentery. My mother and I shared a can of Spam with three other people, and we were all counted out ten raisins, four dried figs, one Lucky Strike cigarette, and a postage-stamp-size piece of dark chocolate; my mother at once swapped our cigarettes for twenty raisins. There was another Red Cross shipment in 1945.

Then — suddenly as always — we were told that for the second time the Emperor was permitting us to write a postcard; he was to do so only once more. All cards, though, had to be in by six that evening, and there was to be no time off from work. Also, we couldn't mention the date, the name of the camp, sicknesses, weight loss, or anything else "negative"; we could only report, in Indonesian, "good" news. There was excitement, anxiety, panic. How, first, to draft the so-important twenty-five "free" words allowed per card? Then, how to say it in Indonesian? And, finally, how to copy that version onto the card in print the authorities could read? Possession of all writing materials, after all, was strictly forbidden, not many people knew Indonesian very well, and there was little time. All day women and children raced around the camp bartering, begging, and lining up for pens, pencils, and scraps of paper from those few who'd dared smuggle them in. Next they ran about for help with translation; it always took more words to say something in Indonesian than in Dutch, and women cried cutting short their messages. We sent ours to my father and could really just let him know we were all right and I was growing. Then came the mad sprint to deliver the cards in time to the administration office. The Japanese were good at fine as well as coarse torment.

One afternoon my mother brought home from a house she'd emptied a framed picture of sunflowers in a vase by a painter named Vincent van Gogh. The print flamed with yellows. "Our own sun," she said, and set it on the blue-and-white-tiled counter against the wall. Another day, she and a woman from her moving team carried in a dainty, carved desk of dark, shiny wood. In the cramped half-dark it stood glowing in a corner, unused, tiny drawers empty. "It's beautiful," my mother explained. Now when I lay down during the day, I had, not only the tiles, but the painting and the desk to stare at. We knew, of course, we couldn't keep these things; we could just live with them for a short time.

Reports of transports had started up again. And soon they were true. Groups of some hundreds of prisoners, according to number, got a day's or a night's warning to pack and report at the camp gate at a certain hour. Again no one knew where they were going. It was whispered that this time the Japanese definitely planned to kill us all — perhaps with machine guns, or by setting fire to churches and schools with us locked inside. And I also heard about the "Borneo Plan" — rumours of which floated until the end: the Japanese would ship the women to the island of Borneo to work in mines for about an ounce of rice a day so they'd quickly starve to death, and scatter the children around Java for Indonesians to raise.

The Crones were among the first to be called up. We went over to say goodbye. We hugged, and Ankie cried, but I didn't see them off to the gate. A few days later it was our turn.

Early in the morning the few hundred of us waiting at the camp gate were counted — twice. The Japanese were poor counters, the officers as well as the soldiers. Maybe arithmetic was taught badly in Japan, for whenever they counted us, they almost always made mistakes, and had to begin over again. Flustered, they could quickly get angry then and start yelling and slapping. We were counted often in the camps to make sure no one had escaped — though where could you hide amongst all the brown-skinned people outside?

Again we were weighted down with worn suitcases, sheets knotted into carry-alls, and rucksacks, with pots, pans, and pails dangling from belts. It was a bright day, not hot yet. I wore khaki shorts and my one shirt with, in the buttoned pocket, my harmonica wrapped in its handkerchief. Walking to the gate my mother told me again and again that, no matter what, we had to stick together, hold hands if necessary, even if it meant dropping baggage.

Once through the gate we were jammed into old buses with the windows painted black. *Lekas! Lekas!* "Hurry! Hurry!" The buses started off, and in minutes stopped again. We were rushed out onto the platform of a deserted little railway station with holes in its roof. There was no train and we slumped against our luggage for two hours. But what I was breathing was free air. There was a world outside the camp. In a circle around us, soldiers leaned on rifles; two officers smoked in the shade of the station house. The tracks glittered until they disappeared under a distant bridge. No Indonesians showed themselves. My mother and I had a small mouthful from the bottle of water she carried in a string bag.

Finally, a short train puffed in and came to a stop hissing. I got excited then. This would be fun. I'd almost forgotten my other train ride when I was four from a mountain depot down to Bandung. Because I'd been good, my father, who had a boil in his nose, had let me come along on the trip to the hospital. But the hospital wanted him to stay a few days, so he phoned home, and I travelled back into the mountains alone that night, up front in the locomotive's dark cabin asking the Indonesian engineer a hundred questions. He had let me pull and push oily levers — so I was really driving the train — and, many times, tug at the knotted cord that set off the steam whistle.

The soldiers shouted and pushed us into a line-up — to be counted again. How could our number have changed? There were mistakes; it took a while. Then, with a lot of *Lekas! Lekas!* we were run aboard the wooden fourth-class coaches with benches along the sides. Planks and bamboo matting covered the few windows. My mother and I were lucky and got seats about midway, but more and more prisoners were pressed into our carriage until the floor space between the benches, too, was packed with luggage and children and women, some standing. Then the doors slammed shut. The temperature inside soared and sweat started running out of my hair. I fumbled for the water bottle, but my mother said softly, "Wait." I could hardly make out her face.

"I'm thirsty," I said.

"I know. Me too."

Except for some small children crying and mothers shushing, it was quiet at first. We were waiting for the train to start — but it didn't. It stood there for another hour, or maybe longer, the midday sun beating down on the roof; a few shafts of light shot into the coach when women parted strands of the bamboo window screening. Then with a wrench the train moved off, squealing and clanging, rocked along for ten minutes, and jarred to a stop again. Word went around we were at Bandung's main station. My mother and I ate a little of the boiled rice she'd brought with a swallow of water. The train didn't move again until mid-afternoon.

Inside the coach, one moment in the thick heat and stink became the next moment and then the next and then the next until they melded into just one unending moment. I couldn't think. Thinking was impossible, so all the people and events that might have helped, didn't. They refused to come into my mind: Manang's spirits, the yellow kite, Ankie's smile. I

knew the moment had to end, but then I began to
believe that it wouldn't. I would always be in the dark
with hot wet bodies pushing into me. I felt I would
start screaming and keep on screaming and begin
hitting around me and keep on hitting. Was I
"crazy"? The feeling was like vomit rising and I had
to swallow and swallow to keep it down. Some in the
coach didn't swallow and there were outbursts of
shrieking and flailing around; there was groaning and
sobbing, and mothers whacking children. An argument started and turned into a fight. Fights were
usually interesting, but not now. Women yelling with
voices that broke; slaps; women shouting to stop it,
to shut up, to stay calm. There were more arguments,
more fights. My mother sat very still, probably with
her eyes closed, touching me only now and then
because it was so hot. Near us in the dark a woman
fell over, crashing into her neighbours; more women
and children fainted. Someone began to sing, about
a Dutch admiral who'd sunk the Spanish fleet. Others
joined her, but it was hard just to breathe, and the
song died. Many times people took up a tune, and
stopped again. The stink in the coach was of sweat
and fear, and of pee and shit. Just about everybody
had stomach trouble. There may have been a toilet
hole at the front or back of the carriage, but only for
those nearby; the rest of us couldn't move. We did it
in our pants. It was a long journey, so everyone
must have.

When the train lurched out of the big station, the
moaning about thirst had already begun. It would not
stop. By then the small supply of water people could

carry was gone. My mother had said "Wait" many times, but finally our bottle was empty, too.

In a half-hour the train screeched to a stop again. Those who could spy out said it was a little station on the way to Batavia. They said there was no one about. So it went the rest of the afternoon, the evening, and all that night, halting at tiny, empty depots, hunched together swaying and bumping. No food, no water. After dark the heat lessened slightly for some hours and with it angry voices and crying; not the whimpering about thirst, though. At one of the stations Indonesians had lined up pails and basins of water along the platform; our guards kicked them over. Thirst is much worse than hunger. Like a terrible pain in one place, it shuts out all other feeling.

"I'm thirsty," I whispered.

"I know," my mother whispered back.

"Really thirsty."

"Me too."

"I'm thirsty."

"Yes."

"Very thirsty."

"I know," she sort of hummed.

"But I am thirsty."

"I know you are."

"I've never been this thirsty," I hummed, too.

"No, you haven't."

"I want water."

"Our bottle's empty."

"I want water."

"We don't have any more."

"I'm thirsty."

"I know. We'll have to wait."

"I can't."

"We'll have to."

"I want water."

"We'll get water."

"When?"

"When we arrive."

"Where?"

"We'll see."

"There'll be water?"

"Yes."

"Promise?"

"Yes."

"You promise?"

"I promise."

"There'll be enough?"

"Yes."

"You're sure?"

"Positive."

"Lots?"

"Yes, lots."

As the train clattered through the night down towards the sea, heat returned and with it high humidity. In the moist air you could almost taste our stink. I'd heard adults say that compared to Batavia's wet heat, Bandung was dry and cool. When dawn broke, the lookouts said we were nearing Batavia. The usual three-hour Bandung-Batavia run had taken us about twenty.

The train slowed down, halted with a jerk; after the night of stops and starts, most of us stayed stiff and in place. Another small station. But this time, the watchers reported, guards were running up and down the platform. We could hear them yelling. Fear rose again. Were we there? What now? Mothers shook children awake, yanked at luggage; some people stood up. My mother said, "Let's not rush." Then the doors screaked open and soldiers' heads stuck through grey light and bawled at us to come out. *Lekas! Lekas!* People staggered and slithered across the coach's filthy floor, banging into each other, falling, children howling. *Lekas! Lekas!* Out on the platform we huddled in a warm drizzle, a tired, frightened, smelly group, licking rain from our hands and arms. Soldiers carted several old women and a limp child out of the train and laid them down one next to the other. "Dead," I said. My mother nodded. Some women leaned on others, children held tight to legs and handbags. The guards prodded us into a line-up and started to count — until an officer screamed impatiently and we were rushed off the platform, stumbling, clutching each other, and into canvas-covered military trucks. The still figures and a broken suitcase were left on the platform.

The truck's rear flap was struck down tightly, and we were once again all riding, standing up, through an unknown outside, unseeing in the dark. Our truck drove fast, tires sizzling, honking a lot, so it was probably in the lead. The trip lasted about half an hour. The truck stopped, turned sharply, throwing many off their feet, and backed up a bit. I heard the other trucks roaring up, stopping, turning, and reversing. Our flap was slung open and we could see a few yards away a wide gate made of bamboo poles strung with barbed wire: you could look right through it. On either side, though, rounding away from view, ran the familiar high dense *bilik* wall. Where were we? In the air hung a smell like that in the railroad car. Soldiers yelled at us to come down — *Lekas! Lekas!* Off to the side, a small thin officer, legs in shiny boots wide apart, stood watching us from under his umbrella. Behind him I could see a corner of the wide veranda of a grey stone house and some purple bougainvillaea. Clambering off the truck I kept my eyes on the man because, in a very un-Japanese way, his face showed expression: the small mouth looked as if it was smiling.

Lined up facing the gate, we were counted thoroughly this time. Three tired-looking women in patched-up clothes like ours approached the gate from the inside. They bowed to the soldier who opened it for them, bowed towards the officer.

In a loud, not unkind voice, one of the women, wearing a frayed straw hat with a string under her chin, told us we had arrived at camp Kampung Makasar. She didn't smile; nor did the other two. "Kampung Makasar," she said again, as if the name should have meaning for us. The three of them, she said, were the *kaichōs*, "camp leaders" in Japanese. We were tired and sleeping space had been arranged. We would be shown where. We must want to wash and eat and that was arranged also. My mother stood in front of me, her khaki shirt dark from sweat, her skirt stained. Today, said the woman, was *yasumi*, "rest time." Tomorrow, the adults and older children would be told what their jobs were. This was a work camp. She repeated that, too — "This is a work camp." Now we should keep to our line-up and follow.

The three turned and bowed to the officer. The soldier at the gate kicked it open so the taut barbed wire trembled. We shuffled inside.

13

Kampung Makasar

It was night, and we lay waiting for the sound of the *tokkeh* up in the bamboo rafters. A *tokkeh* is a lizard, with large bulging eyes and four toes on each foot, that eats flies. When it grew dark and there was one in the barrack you waited for it to clear its throat, just like a human being, and go "*tokkeh, tokkeh.*" If it *tokkehed* seven times it meant good luck. Kampung Makasar's barracks were risky for flies because, besides *tokkehs* and *tjik-tjaks,* a lot of spiders lived there. By order of the Japanese, a team of women in each barrack spent half a day every month swiping at cobwebs with home-made besoms. But webs were quickly spun again — as dense and bulky as those around the pavilion on the plantation, that dream place. And flies had another worry. Every barrack had to deliver a certain number of dead flies to the administration office — at one point, ten per adult per day; I usually caught my mother's quota. The Japanese also endlessly insisted that our barracks be kept clean and swept, mattresses be aired regularly, and clothes be washed with soap. But the insects that infested mattresses didn't seem to mind the sun and there was of course no soap; people rinsed their few clothes and slapped them a little on the stone floors of the bathing huts. Flies loved the blood in the barracks, the smears of squashed-bug blood that streaked bodies, clothing, mattresses, sheets, mosquito nets, luggage, the *bilik* walls, and the bamboo poles supporting the palm-frond roofs. The crushed bugs smelled like lanced boils.

At eight exactly, every night, the barrack's three light bulbs went out and it was instantly very dark; any show of light afterwards was severely punished. Usually, talk went down to whispers then, and stopped. Adults said sleep was needed for strength — for the next day's work in the kitchen, hospital, latrines, or shadeless vegetable gardens with water only at noon. That didn't mean, though, that it grew really quiet. Each of the camp's fourteen barracks built amidst coconut trees — it was a plantation once — held from 200 to 300 women and children, by the end some 3,800 people in a space put up for 800. Sleeping platforms of bamboo slats about six feet deep ran the length of a barrack on either side of a red-earth path; high over the path zigzagged rainy-season wash lines although when it rained, the palm-leaf roofs leaked like sieves. Our mattresses had had to be made smaller because an adult's bed space was just under twenty-four inches, a child's under twenty. So on about forty-four inches my mother and I slept, ate, and kept our clothes, spoons, mugs, and bowls. She and I also had a fork, and our small, lidded tin with four tablespoons of brown sugar we'd saved up; we would have had more but she had bartered three

spoons and half a spool of thread for a brassiere sewn
from a tea towel. With sheets, old curtains, or clothes
hung from string, families walled themselves off
from neighbours — but we could still hear each other.
In the night there was a steady, inescapable rumble
of sighing, moaning, snoring, coughing, hawking,
burping, farting, retching, teeth grinding, sudden
cries, sleep-talking, children whining or sobbing,
mothers snapping or shushing, feet shuffling to and
from the latrines, and, up above, the creak and swish
of low-hanging palm leaves grazing the roof.

It was only just past eight. This evening was different because people talked right on in the dark, even
laughed. It was a feast day of some sort, Easter perhaps.
My mother was lying next to me under half a bed sheet;
I had the other half. It was so hot you didn't really
need covering but it kept off the mosquitoes, and
tucked between sweaty legs prevented them from
sticking together. Even this small space my mother had
made *gezellig* with a silk scarf, some of Hanneke's
animal drawings pinned to our "walls," and a can with
leafy papaya branches. She lay on her back with hands
under her head, the half-sheet just reaching her knees.
Mine covered me; I could even get my head under it.

In the beginning my mother's job had been to clean
latrines, narrow ditches behind the bathing huts into
which used bath water drained and trickled to
cesspools. She poked clog-ups loose — though during
rains flooding was unstoppable; the whole camp
turned into a steaming red-mud bog then, dangerous
for small children — and she scraped clean the soiled
edges of the ditches over which people squatted.

Nothing the "latrine ladies" did, though, could lighten the stench in the moist air over Makasar. I had no real job, except some sweeping in and around our half of the barrack, and trotting about yelling that bread or soup or rice were ready at the camp kitchen. Now and then I was sent there to fetch pails of steaming tea, a chore I didn't like because, especially after rain, I could slip and fall. It wasn't the scalding but spilling the tea I feared: not the sort of accident easily forgiven. Later, my mother worked in the vegetable gardens and I, too, put in a few hours with other children my age weeding, watering, hacking at the ground; by then I was the biggest boy in camp.

This morning our holiday had begun, as every day, with the six o'clock *tenko*, "roll-call" in Japanese, when we lined up five deep in front of our barrack; there was another one at six in the afternoon. Ours was one of the first barracks, 4A, near the gate, near the officers' stone house. Usually a low-ranking officer and an interpreter did the rounds, but sometimes it was the commandant himself, Lieutenant Tanaka, the officer with the smile-shaped lips I'd seen on our first day.

Kiotsuke! was shouted and we came to attention, then *Keirei!* and we bowed. Heads down, the women in front counted loud and very fast in Japanese: *Ichi-ni-san-shi-go-roku-shichi* . . . up to ten; then again up to ten, and on. The barrack *hanchō* reported those too sick to show up, and those who had died. When the totals matched, not often on first count, it was *Norei!* and we could stand upright, then troop off. My mother was the first in our line, me behind her, and seven, *shichi*, was her number. You said it like a sneeze, *Shichiiii!*

One afternoon some weeks before the holiday, with Tanaka taking *tenko*, when it came to *Shichi*, my mother said nothing. Bowed, I could see Tanaka's high boots stop in front of her. Someone coughed in the silence, but she didn't react. Tanaka enjoyed hurting women; I'd seen him; I'd heard the screams in the night from his house. Seconds went by. Maybe ten or twenty. Then she said, "*Shichi!*" and the counting raced on. The boots, though, didn't move: for an awful moment Tanaka's eyes were regarding my mother's bowed head, then he slouched on. Afterwards women crowded around. What had gotten into Anna? Her excuse made no sense. "His boots were so shiny," she said. "I forgot where I was." What had Tanaka been thinking looking down on my mother's head? My mind shut off. I stayed near her, but asked nothing. I'd never before been so scared.

Late that night I slipped out to the bath hut and filled a bottle with water to clean myself, then settled outside over the latrine ditch. I was alone there. The sky was full of stars, though it wasn't good to look at them for too long; they were free. People in *Kempeitai* cells never saw stars. Above me rustled the crowns of palm trees, or it could have been spirits whispering. A few times I had climbed such trees in the deep of the night and twisted loose a young coconut spotted during the day. Dangerous, because patrols were out; if they caught me, they'd find my mother. Barrack roofs shimmered in the arc light of the sentry box on stilts close by the stone house.

Tanaka was greatly feared. I had been looking for a smile on the lips of the most brutal camp officer we'd ever had. It was rumoured that once he had even been reprimanded for his cruelty by his superiors in Batavia. A few months before we came, sixteen women led by a doctor had gone to Tanaka to complain about small bread rations. Tanaka was said to have yelled, "You can all die here. There's room enough in the cemetery." He had ordered the kitchen fires doused, the day's cooking fed to the pigs, food withheld from the whole camp for forty-eight hours, and the sixteen protesters beaten, shaved, and locked up in a bamboo cage for five days. When Tanaka punished in person, women couldn't work for days, so no wages of extra bread or soup, and often they had to be hospitalized. That could have happened that afternoon to my mother — and my mind shut off again. I couldn't finish the thought. The other one, that she might die, I never allowed in at all.

Yet, squatting there over the stinking latrine, I realized that soon after coming to Makasar, I could think about other people dying, anybody really — and that I could finish those thoughts. I could think it about Corry Vonk and Puk Meijer and the Staals, who had landed in camp after us, and about people living beside and across from us in the barrack. I could *see* them dead, and it didn't make me sad: dead was dead. The administration office kept the numbers of deaths secret: they didn't want to scare us. People got sick, went to hospital, then disappeared out the gates on stretchers. It was hard to tell how many died because, with new arrivals from other camps, the barracks stayed packed.

I also discovered, after a while in Makasar, that I could walk down our barrack, gloomy even in daylight, past women and children with broken teeth and bleeding gums, hair growing in tufts like Willie's, faces and stomachs and legs bloated from hunger edema and beriberi, boils as big as ping-pong balls, and oozing tropical ulcers for which they had no bandages, nor clothes nor towels to rip into bandages — and not let myself really *see* them: pain was pain. Just as I could play with other kids, run around, do mischief — but make no friends, on purpose: friends went away. Just as, by then, I could admit to myself that I wasn't especially brave — all I had was my crazy laugh; that I'd never hunted wild boars on the plantation, only pretended to. Just as I could still my mother's voice in my head because I'd learned that her common-sense, be-true-to-yourself dos and don'ts always had their opposites and that the choice was mine — and if I did wrong it wasn't so hard to forgive myself. In Upper Tjihapit I had been half-asleep, not in Kampung Makasar. Hunger shrunk bodies here, and fear minds, but they also kept you awake, and you had to be awake to stay alive.

It was quiet at the latrine. Night creatures whirred about, some of them biters. I tried again to imagine what might have happened that afternoon, and again failed. But then — it had to be a spirit's trick — just for a second, there appeared Tanaka's smiling face, down below me in the black filthy ditch where it belonged.

When I crept in next to my mother I was still a bit angry about her behaviour at *tenko*. She didn't wake up. But later she must have, as all of us did nearby, when, suddenly cutting into the barrack's usual night noises and silencing them, a solitary old woman who lived on the berth across from us began in a clear, ringing voice to sing "Ave Maria." She sang the whole hymn. When she was done the only sound for long moments was soft crying here and there.

This Easter holiday was to be made special really only by what the camp office had promised for the evening meal: double rice rations, soup with meat — *babad*, the guts of one of the small, fierce pigs prisoners raised for the Japanese — and half a hard-boiled egg per person. We hadn't had egg for a long time. Sometimes I told my mother that the first thing I wanted when we were free was eggs and cold fruit salad. We discussed the different kinds of fruit we would cut up above a bowl to catch the juice. Eggs we would eat in just a few bites because there would be lots of them. Now when we got an egg she'd take our fork and mash it and we'd eat it slowly. That way, she explained, you got all the goodness.

All day, in the gardens, workers looked forward to the feast meal. The gardens were outside the camp. Under guard, prisoners were marched through the gate, past the grey stone house, and across an asphalt highway that led from Batavia to a town called Buitenzorg (Bogor). The vegetables and fruit fed the women's camps in Batavia as well as ours. In the middle of the garden stood a shed where in hot, still air the pigs were fattening for the Japanese. The sky turned white in the heat of the sun, but water for the women and older girls who worked from early morning until mid-afternoon didn't come until noon, in gasoline cans strung by wire to bamboo poles that women carried on their shoulders.

We boys and young girls wore only shorts, so that even if we had a chance to steal vegetables or a small green papaya, we had no place to hide them; and neither, really, did the women who wore blouses, or brassieres, or tea towels tied across their breasts. I never saw it, but I'd heard that one or two guards sometimes turned their eyes away to let a prisoner gobble up a carrot or a handful of beans. On the return to camp, soldiers watched workers closely for suspicious lumps which, if spotted, nearly always earned a beating. Not all Japanese guards and *heihos* aped their commandant when it came to punishing, but many did. And, although in our earlier camps there had always been a few women who betrayed others to the Japanese for favours, tough Kampung Makasar was full of them. It was a dangerous place to break rules.

After roll-call, we stood in line for bread, soup, and the egg. We ate on our bed, saving the egg for last. My mother's long hair in two braids was wrapped around at the back of her head. When we were done with the bread and had drunk the thin soup out of our half-coconut bowls, she looked at me and said:

"Erik was put in hospital this morning."

The Staals lived a couple of barracks away. Erik was about four then, a quiet, nice boy. I liked him. Sometimes we played, me lying down on my stomach while he sat on my bum "drawing" with a wood chip on my back.

"Dysentery," my mother said.

I was sorry about that. I really was. Little kids who went into camp hospital usually didn't come out again. If Erik died, it would make Aunt Ina and his sisters extremely sad. And me too. Just as I thought of Ineke and Hanneke as sisters, I saw him as a sort of little brother. Right now, though, I wanted my mother to start peeling the egg and mashing it.

"I think," she said, "we should give half our egg to Aunt Ina for Erik. We can do that because we are still strong, and we'll have the other half between us."

I didn't know what to say. My mother never said silly things but this seemed silly. You kept what you had and got what you could. People were eating *larongs*, flying ants, if they could catch them, not to mention fried rat and boiled snake. Give half our egg away? Just like that? It didn't make sense, and she'd said it as if it were a natural thing to do, and as if I were a small child who'd just go along with it. Well, I wasn't talked to like that any more. When had anyone last asked me what I wanted to be when I grew up? I wasn't a kid: I didn't pee, I pissed. You didn't give things away — not food; you traded.

"Erik may die, you know."

I understood that. But Aunt Ina, as far as I knew, never mashed eggs for her children; they just ate theirs in a few bites. Besides, how could half an egg possibly make Erik better? He wasn't a strong boy, and he never got brown in the sun, just red.

"It may not help Erik get better, but we should try. . . ."

She paused.

"I think your brother would say yes."

166

I slid the palm of my hand up and down the bamboo pole by our bed, one of the poles that held up the roof. It felt, cool, smooth, a little oily from being grabbed there so often by us climbing in and out. Fastened higher up was one end of a string that held our rolled-up mosquito net, bloodied and full of holes — my mother was a poor seamstress. There was still light, and down the barrack I could see children curled up already asleep, adults lying down or sitting in their "rooms," as every evening, playing cards, sewing, combing each other's hair, staring, but also chatting which wasn't done much any more. I clamped my teeth tight. I did not want to give in to giving. But it was true, Jerry probably would have said yes.

So, in the end, we put away the half-egg for Aunt Ina . . . who probably let Erik just gulp it down.

Our own half she mashed with the fork in one of the licked-clean coconut bowls, then divided it into two neat piles which we ate slowly. Next she gave herself a spoonful of sugar from the tin can and me a spoon and a half because, she said, I was a child and on a feast day children should always be given a bit extra. We ate the sugar slowly too.

In a little while it was eight o'clock and the light bulbs went out. She lay next to me under our mosquito net, and I knew that her hair was not in braids any more but lying loose about her head. Long ago, when I was about Erik's age, she had let me brush it.

People went on talking softly and sometimes laughing, even though they should save their strength. But it didn't go on for very long. I was sure that they, like me, were waiting for the *tokkeh* to clear its throat.

14

Hubie and I

Hubie van Boxel became my best friend, but I did have to get used to him. He and his mother and two grown-up sisters moved into our barrack a couple of months after my mother and I had settled in. I watched Hubie and the three women put away clothes, bedding, tin mugs, eating pans; his mother strung a pair of riding boots from a rafter above their sleeping space. The women's eyes seemed always to be on Hubie. I would learn later that anything he asked for they gave him, if they had it, or brought to him, like a drink of water. He looked about my age, going on eleven, and my size, which made him the other biggest boy in the camp.

It wasn't just Hubie's family who treated him as if he were special — everybody did. He smiled a lot, which wasn't usual, and he was respectful, which many children weren't any more. I was polite when my mother was around and when it was useful. I roamed Kampung Makasar always with an eye out for "helping" people: fetch, carry, lift, watch a child so its mother could sleep or visit the hospital; if it paid off in a little fee of food, fine, I'd be back. I also drifted around the kitchen and the food sheds, to help, friendly and polite.

I thought, though, that the real reason for the interest in Hubie was probably his hair, which grew in tiny curls tight against his head and was golden. That's the word people used, golden. And because his mother and sisters looked after him so well, so that in the muggy heat he always looked fresh and clean, there was a shine to it, like light. Anyhow, people seemed to enjoy seeing Hubie; the guards, too. I heard some women and girls and even my mother say about him, "He looks like an angel."

On Hubie's first day I hung around his part of the barrack until he had to come over and talk to me. He was wearing only shorts but, whatever camp he'd come from, his mother must have made him wear a shirt because he wasn't very tanned. I was as dark as an Indo boy. His mother's eyes were on us as we wandered away. We sat down on the barrack's shaded side; there wasn't much room because that's where pails, basins, and boxes were stored, washing hung, and a few vegetables and even flowers grown. Maybe Hubie had had to wear a shirt, but I noticed the bottoms of his feet were as hard and full of criss-cross cuts as mine and Manang's. I had no wish to become friends — friends went away — but I knew that we would otherwise have to fight until it became clear which one of us won most often. I was to discover, though, that Hubie, like Jerry, didn't like fighting, not even for fun, so I needn't have made friends at all. But by then it was too late. By then, although it wasn't easy, I had even learned not to mind that people's eyes were always on him.

The smile, politeness, and hair had nothing to do with why we immediately got along. Hubie wanted to know all about Kampung Makasar — food, rules, work, the commandant — and I was the perfect person to tell him. Inmates always snubbed new arrivals at first because they used up space and food supplies, and I knew what it was like to have to poke around on your own. It was a fine, new feeling to be a guide and teacher. Before and after my afternoon shift in the gardens, which Hubie would also take on, I showed him around the camp and explained its workings. Soon he knew the place as well as I did, but I found out he could never know enough. He'd watch women repair a shed roof, dig out wood-eating white-ant colonies, water the hospital's herb garden — and, smiling and polite, pepper them with whys and hows. My trips to the kitchen were strictly to finagle a bite of food, but Hubie would fix his blue eyes on cursing cooks trying to fire wet kindling, then sound them out on baking bread or spicing the vegetable-water soup; often, he'd also walk away with an extra nibble. Everything seemed to interest Hubie, as it had me — once. Then I began to ape him a little and, when we weren't tired, we rambled around camp, both of us asking questions. We were a team. Because we were big, people noticed us and, for the same reason, Indo boys rarely took us on. I had no need for my crazy laugh any more.

It was the "now" that concerned Hubie, this hour, this day. I was the same. We told each other little about people, events, or places from before — they were gone. And the future, well, it was clear to us. Rumours never stopped in camp, switching from bad to good to bad news; lately they were of the good sort. Just as the Japanese had often sunk Allied fleets, so now the Allies repeatedly sank the Japanese fleet. France was free, Hitler was dead, only the Japanese were fighting on. Definitely, they said, the war would end soon. But Hubie and I knew better: the war wouldn't end at all. All of us, we agreed, would always live in camp and die there, one a little faster than the other, but everybody would get their turn. How could we believe anything else? We were forgotten. Hubie and I didn't tell anyone this, especially our mothers: they would have fretted.

On the side of a barrack was scrawled in charcoal, DON'T SPEAK ABOUT FOOD! But everyone did, all the time, as they always had, going on about pre-war meals, recipes, postwar feasts, and, endlessly, about the shrinking fare of the day. It was hunger that did it, clamping the insides of the body, nesting in the mind, and wearing out both. Daily rations by then were, for breakfast, a slice of bread either so hard it had to be softened with water or so doughy it could barely be swallowed, or a cup of thin sago gruel, weak tea or warm water, and a spoonful of sugar when it wasn't held back; in late afternoon a cup of the lowest-grade rice with sometimes a few peanuts or tiny salted fish, and a cup of vegetable-scrap soup; once a week we got a spoon of salt, and occasionally a teaspoon of hot-pepper paste, a banana, a cup of coffee-water. The two meals stilled hunger for about an hour. Hubie and I agreed we wouldn't talk about food, or try not to.

Everybody else seemed outraged when a baby was born in the camp hospital — the father, of course, had to be an enemy soldier; the mother, therefore, a traitor — but Hubie and I agreed this very rare event in camp was marvellous, and climbed on each other's shoulders to peek through a hospital air vent at that new life in Makasar.

We agreed about a lot; many of our thoughts were the same, although mine might have been a little darker than Hubie's. He trusted more, while I remembered Zuseke's "trust no one." Sometimes he'd still give or share; I didn't. He could feel pity; I could, too, but I'd also learned not to *see* the pain and fear and death around all day. And I'm not sure Hubie understood yet about all dos and don'ts having their opposites; though he did know about a few, such as lying, stealing, and at sunset watching freshly bathed women and girls comb their hair.

Like everyone, we tired quickly, had dizzy spells, or suddenly felt shivery; this was from hunger, we knew. Still, Hubie liked playing — more than I did — and I'd go along. The game of *katrik* needed only two sticks, one about two feet long, the other one foot, and two players or more. The person at bat, at a spot marked with a stone, dangled the small stick from an outstretched hand and with the big stick hit it as far as he could. The fielder had to throw the little stick back as near to the rock as possible; the distance between where it landed and the rock was measured with the short stick and the number scratched in the ground; then the batter switched with a fielder. After the players had had, say, eight turns each, the numbers were added and whoever had the lowest total won. *Katrik* involved no running so it didn't wear you out in the sun. Kids might also gather and set up a *tenko* with bowing, counting, and "punishment" that could get a bit rough. Or we'd pretend to line up for food and in cupped hands receive measured portions of sand and bits of leaf. "Hospital" had snippy nurses, groaning, dying patients, and guards coming to haul off "fakers."

I preferred stalking chores-for-food around camp, but Hubie fussed that my "helping" was too much like begging, so we merely roamed, slowly, alert to any-thing edible. Just as Makasar held many who told on others, so it also teemed with thieves. The Japanese never intervened; they didn't care if we died, never mind being robbed. We simply weren't worth much attention and, aside from punishment and pestering, it was really their indifference that was to blame for many camp conditions. Hubie and I, for part of the day, had the camp to ourselves, except for the old, the young, and the sick. We could have stolen a lot — stuff to swap for food — but we never did: that was a real "don't." From the Japanese, of course, we swiped at every chance, which wasn't often.

When Hubie visited, my mother was nice to him, and so were Ineke and Hanneke, who had come to live next to us in the barrack; this was after Aunt Ina had some-how arranged permission to take sick Erik to a hospital in Batavia. When I showed up at Hubie's bed space, though, his mother and sisters were cool. His mother had at once found work in the camp office, mine sweated in the gardens. His father was a high-up army officer, mine just an employee on a plantation. Mrs van Boxel held her head high and seldom spoke to anyone, unusual after years of no one caring who you'd been.

Around that time my mother said that I was becoming a big boy and that after work I should bathe separately. A day or so later, Hubie reported he'd been told the same thing. Our mothers, we were sure, had not discussed this. On most days after work, prisoners were permitted to use the bath huts — dark slippery places that held oil drums brimming with water. Dust from the outside garden's red earth mixed with sweat dried into crusts. You dipped a can in and splashed yourself, rubbed at the dirt with a rag, and rinsed again. People laughed in there and yelped. The water falling from arms stretched high made women's bodies glisten. Hubie and I obeyed our mothers and waited until the women and girls were done. While waiting, we'd sometimes go to a hole in the back of the bath hut and stare.

I might have been looking for a Hubie all those years in camp, someone I could feel safe and restful with as I had with Manang. Hubie and I meandered around or lay about in the shade, and half the time we didn't even need to talk. And this was a boy my own age, an equal. Well, not entirely equal: he did have something that, the moment he showed it to me, I envied and immediately and badly wanted for myself. It was a helmetted plaster soldier, probably Belgian — Hubie wasn't sure — in a greatcoat, seated on a horse with a broken tail. It was his one possession, carried from camp to camp. It lit a fierce old longing in me. I dug up my one and only object of value, my harmonica, and pressed Hubie to trade. But no, he liked his soldier. I tried several more times, and he refused; it wasn't as if he ever played with it either.

If after we had bathed and eaten it was still light, Hubie and I might once more circle a few barracks, the office, the hospital, the kitchen, always on the lookout for food, and check the high fence for hidden holes. Sometimes we'd find one, which meant that even though most people had little left to barter and our commandant was so harsh, a few women were still smuggling. When a *gedekker* was caught, always at night, the guard would run her over to the officers' stone house, up the steps onto the veranda. There the usual happened: her hair was cut off with barber's clippers and Tanaka yelled at her and hit and kicked her until he grew tired. Our barrack would grow still then and we could hear every blow. Afterwards she'd be locked in a cage for some days, dependent on brave friends to sneak food and water to her. Some women took these risks to feed themselves and family, some to help the sick, and some to trade the eggs and fruit and sugar for huge profit or services from fellow prisoners.

Hubie and I didn't prowl only in daylight. Sometimes we'd sneak away long after lights-out when it was forbidden to leave the barrack except to use the nearest latrine. We did this knowing that if we were caught we might get a slap, but that our mothers would be severely punished. We'd meet at the latrine, then flit from shadow to shadow through the empty camp to the kitchen. There might be some burnt rice at the bottom of a cooking drum, or a swallow of soup. A food shed might have been left unlocked. One of those sheds was stocked with pig food, hard, brick-sized, soya-bean cakes called *bungkil*. It was mixed with water into swill for the pigs; people could eat it like that, or roasted. A blue line ran through some cakes and this was said to be poisonous to humans. Once or twice we'd found a hunk of *bungkil*; it tasted like sand.

On what was to be our last night run, Hubie and I had found nothing in the drums, and the storage huts were locked — but then we spotted a hole near the ground in the wall of the *bungkil* shed. Hubie reached in and brought out almost half a cake. We broke it into pieces and roasted them in the still-hot ashes of a kitchen fire hole, then climbed onto the slithery palm-leaf roof of the kitchen and sat very still, close together, gnawing at the *bungkil*. We felt it filling us. We felt strong and wanted to laugh and punch each other. We ate it all — there was no thought of sharing with anyone else. In a little while we slid down the roof, sprinted back to the barrack, and lay down beside our sleeping mothers.

Two or three hours later that same night beating sounds and screams welled up from the stone house. They didn't stop until just before the six o'clock roll-call for which the commandant himself came by. Beside him walked the interpreter and behind him, wearing only panties and brassieres, stumbled two trembling young women, each held up by a soldier; their bodies were blotched with welts and black bruises, and smeared with blood, even their bald heads. Tanaka shouted, appearing as always to smile, and the transla-tor told us that he had decided that no prisoner must ever again try to smuggle in food of which he gave us plenty. He had punished the women, as we could see, and now he would punish the whole camp because "your spirit is not good." We must remain inside our barrack for the next two days and we would not be fed. Then the little group moved on.

No one now felt sorry for the two young women, especially after we heard they were *gragas*, "greedy," smugglers. It was rumoured that the Indonesian they had bartered with was beaten to death. It had been a dangerous night for Hubie and me to have taken our run.

People hurriedly carried water in mugs and eating pans into the barracks, lay down on their beds, talked softly, dozed. My mother said we should stay this quiet to save our strength; like most, we had no reserves of food. Hubie and I remained in our own spaces. The two hunger days made many people very ill; some died, older women, patients in hospital, and the woman across from us who'd sung "Ave Maria."

At the *tenko* that ended the punishment, the interpreter read out a harangue by Tanaka. The last words caused great excitement: "You are not stateless, you have a fatherland. Look to the future, conduct yourselves as true patriots, and cast no shame on your country." It could mean only one thing: Holland was free. But why had he told us? Why now? Were the Allies winning against the Japanese? Were they close by? Where?

On the third day, Hubie didn't show up in the gardens. One of the other working children said that during the hunger days she'd seen him being carried to the hospital. I ran there when I got back to camp, but the nurse wouldn't let me in because I wasn't family. Mrs van Boxel and her daughters in the meantime had hung up more sheets around their bed space, curtaining it tightly shut. The next day we heard something that was hard to believe: the Japanese were taking Hubie to their own military hospital in Batavia.

Along with his crying mother and sisters, at least a dozen people were waiting at the camp gate early next morning when Hubie was carried through on a stretcher and lifted into the back of a small truck. He lay curled up, not seeing us, looking about half my size.

The van Boxels stayed behind their sheets. I went to work, and lay on my mattress. Don't die, Hubie. Don't die. Don't let him die, Jesus. Some days passed and then my mother took me for a little walk. She said she had heard that the military doctors had done their very best for Hubie. They had all liked him, she said; anything he wanted they had given him. Apparently he had asked for sliced bananas with milk and brown sugar.

I stood outside the van Boxels' sleeping space that evening and listened to the sobbing. I stayed awake and much later crept near again. It was quiet. Then someone slipped from behind the sheets and moved outside, and I followed. It was Mrs van Boxel wrapped in a big towel with a smaller one over her head. At the latrine I squatted a distance behind her; there must have been stars because I could see the white skin of her shoulders. As soft as a spirit I whispered that I was sorry that Hubie was dead. The head under the towel turned a little and nodded. I asked if she knew we had eaten from the same piece of *bungkil*. She nodded again. Then I heard her whisper that she didn't want to face her husband because, oh, he would be so sad about losing his son.

Time in Makasar speeded up. So many good rumours were flying that people hardly even talked about food.

The war was ending, the war was ending — really, this time, really. I learned there was actually a radio hidden in camp, smuggled in by brave women each carrying a tiny part. One evening, it must have been in the second half of August, 1945, the administration office asked us to assemble on a field on the other side of Makasar. I'd once or twice seen Puk Meijer and some girls dance in a corner of the field. It was dark when we got there; even those who could hardly walk had come. I saw no guards. You could have heard a butterfly when one of the camp *kaichōs* began to speak. She said she had news but, please, we must not shout or sing. Outside, Indonesians were in rebellion — they wanted Indonesia back. They already knew our news and if they suddenly heard loud cheering they might become angry and there weren't enough soldiers to defend us. When she was done there would be two minutes of silence. Then she said, "The war is over." American pilots had bombed Japan and the Japanese had capitulated. Allied soldiers would land on Java any day now. Until then, camp life should go on as normal, though no working in the gardens, and no more bowing either. Rations would be increased, but food would still have to be cooked and latrines cleaned. Everyone was to stay calm. Three thousand or more women and children were on that field, but the two minutes were very still. A few people cried, but most, like my mother, just stood there, like stones. Hubie had died two weeks before, believing he and I were right, that the war would never end.

A few days later, I was sitting with other kids on the high bamboo fence, barbed wire jabbing our bony bums, screaming and waving at an airplane dropping parachutes on Makasar from which swung big wooden boxes. The plane turned and roared back low, tossing out more boxes. Chocolate, canned food, milk powder, medicine, cigarettes. That on top of the oil, fruit, sugar, soap, toothpaste, and extra rice and bread already distributed in camp.

There was no lights-out any more and that night I watched young women wind up a gramophone — from who knows where — in a dimly lit, stone-floored shed, open on three sides, where Corry Vonk had performed a few times. They put on jazz records, and talked and smoked. Word spread and women of all ages began drifting in; many had pinned on their clothes a bit of orange ribbon or cloth for Holland's royal House of Orange. Some wore their "for-when-we're-free" dresses, hoarded for years, but most had on the usual flimsy odds and ends. All, though, looked fresh and clean and combed; there were red lips in the hut and even traces of perfume. One woman shyly put her arms around another and slowly, awkwardly, they started to dance. Other women made room, and a second couple stepped out, and then another, and in moments the stone floor was full of thin and clumsy dancing women. Laughing and tripping, shrieking and pushing, they soon drowned out the music. A few cried and partners hugged them; others smiled like children; some had cigarettes dangling from their mouths; and in the close hot air all sweated, blouses and shirts clinging to their wonderful swellings, breasts small and medium, none big.

Shirtless, and also sweating, I leaned against a bamboo support pole on the edge of the dance floor hedged now by clapping, swaying women. All around me they were smoking; one woman pinched a cigarette in two, offered half, and lit it for me. I felt their eyes, and inhaled, and then exhaled through my nose. "A man," the woman sighed to her friends. I couldn't help myself: slowly I heaved my chest up and gripped the pole so arm muscles would show. "Thank you very much," I said to her, and she grinned and looked into my eyes. I breathed deeply — mystery, mystery — and strolled on to the next pole. "How are you?" and "Are you happy?" I asked, smiling at complete strangers. At the second pole, a whole cigarette was placed between my lips and lit for me. Then a hand reached out from the dancers, yanked me on the floor, and I was hopping to keep up with a tall twirling woman as old as my mother. Sweat ran down her cheeks and her hands kept slipping off my shoulders. Face turned aside, she just swung around and around, until I was suddenly loose and staggering backwards, cigarette in my mouth, right into a younger, smaller woman. She grabbed me and began to dance quite differently, slowly, holding me against her. It started to rain and those outside jostled to get under the hut's roof. There wasn't room to dance then and women stood pressed together smoking, talking, humming to the music. I moved amongst their moist, warm bodies, smelling them, feeling so fine that my legs were trembling.

My mother was awake when I slid in next to her. It was very late, she murmured, I should have let her know where I was. But she didn't really seem to mind, and said nothing about my smokey breath. After I'd described the night, she whispered only, "Are you a good dancer?"

Next morning I was squatting with my back against the barrack wall by the front door when two young women in shorts approached carrying pails with washing. My eyes moved slowly up their ankles, calves, thighs, and lingered on their breasts as they walked by. And then, out of nowhere, my mother was leaning down in front of me, lips very thin. She hit me open-handed across the face with such force I fell over. "Don't you dare look at girls or women like that," she said, as angry as I'd ever seen her. She glowered down at me a moment longer. We'd had lots more to eat in the last ten days, but it didn't show yet. Her eyes dark and hollow, the sallow skin of her face was stretched so tight it made the bones stick out. She turned and took long steps back into the barrack. I wasn't entirely sure why I'd been slapped, and didn't really want to ask. I would be careful, though, when my mother was around, how I watched girls and women.

For some time even before the end of the war, the Japanese had stopped coming into camp, except for *tenko*. It was thought then that, clean, healthy men themselves, they had begun to dread our filth and disease. Now they hardly appeared at all and, when they did, avoided looking at us — yet at the sight of a Japanese soldier, everything in you still shouted to bow. Tanaka no one saw again. And then one day there were English soldiers in the stone house who turned a radio on full blast. Soon after, a truck drove off carrying our guards, prisoners now, helpless — but in their uniforms, to me, still frightening; it was a fear that would linger in the months to come even when I would see them in gangs under armed guard repairing roads and bridges.

Things were happening so fast. The camp gate was swung wide open, and left so, with a white soldier on duty who whistled to himself. When a group of English officers first marched into Makasar, some women bowed to them, until they were told to stop. The military men criss-crossed the camp, grim and quiet, walking through barracks, with kids following. What did they think of the fleshless women and children with open sores and swollen legs and faces, the rags on wash lines, the spattered bug blood, the smell? The Englishmen tried not to look at the women they stopped to speak to, I noticed, especially not into their faces. Some women sat crying when we came by and didn't lift their heads: already news of dead men-prisoners had begun filtering in. Well, that was to be expected. Adults told each other with great certainty we'd all have died had the camps lasted another six months.

My father walked through the camp gate one afternoon. We'd been told he was coming, and were waiting. I hadn't seen him for three and a half years. He was not a big man. For this day my mother had saved the green dress she'd worn at the Christmas party in Bloemenkamp; I had on my shirt. My father and mother embraced long with closed eyes, patting each other's shoulders. Then he hugged me and said, "I'm your father." I answered, "Yes, sir." We climbed on our bed and he held my mother's hand. She sat looking at his face. Jerry was fine, my father said, waiting in the camp where they'd lived together in Tjimahi, a town near Bandung. Early the next day we were going there by train, he told us. So soon? What about Ineke and Hanneke, I interrupted. It was all right, my mother assured me, they would join Aunt Ina and Erik in Batavia. Except for clothes, we should leave all our stuff behind, my father directed; everything would be provided in Tjimahi. What about our mattresses, sheets, Hanneke's drawings, I asked; I didn't want anyone else to have them. My father gave me a look, but the blue-grey eyes no longer went inside my head. "*Jongetje*, let your mother and me talk," he said in the low tone I also remembered very well. But no one called me *jongetje*, "little boy," any more; old little boy, maybe. I said nothing and went out. My mother remained silent.

Before we left next morning, one of Hubie's sisters came over to our bed space. She said her mother wanted me to have some of his things. She handed me a soft wool cap like Frenchmen wear, the riding boots that had hung from the rafter, and the soldier on horseback. The boots, she told me, her mother had carried all those years so Hubie could wear them to run to his father when he saw him again; they fitted me perfectly. The soldier I wrapped in the yellowed handkerchief I'd had around my harmonica.

It was hard not to cry when I saw Jerry again; for him, too, I thought, when he saw my mother. He wasn't much taller but even more quiet. He had changed and not changed. For about a year and a half he had carried on his own the brunt of our father's "discipline," yet the two of them seemed to get along fine. Jerry was as gentle and generous as I remembered, but I noticed one thing — he'd made a teasing habit of our father's a bit his own. It came down to interrupting another's comment or story, even in mid-sentence, and slightly, cleverly, twisting the words, so that what had been said took on a different meaning and sounded silly; it was done in fun but could stop conversation cold. I didn't like it, nor, I think, did my mother. I wrestled with thoughts about Jerry. Had our father emptied Jerry of himself a little? Still, the four-year age gap between us seemed to have shrunk and he and I played as I hadn't played since he left.

We lived in a house again inside Kamp Tjimahi, in a camp still because it was easier to protect against the Indonesians fighting the Dutch over who owned Indonesia. Jerry and I liked to climb to the ridge of the roof and straddle it. One afternoon we were, as in long-ago days, fighter pilots, arms stretched sideways, weaving and diving, strafing enemy soldiers running below. We had turned and were swooping back — when I put my arms down and started to cry. Jerry flew on a moment, looked back, then carefully clambered around me and off the roof. It was real crying, sobbing and coughing — Hubie was so alive in my mind I kept saying his name. Why was he dead? And why, if he was, wasn't I? Jesus, how could Jesus have let him die? After a while Hubie began to fade and I went on with the day.

It happened again, during a meal, and I left the table and sat down on the floor in another room facing the wall. My family let me be. I thought of Hubie certainly as I cried, and of all the others who one way or another had gone into mist.

And one last time — at the start of an evening in that camp that wasn't one but was, when a violinist from Hungary stood on a chair in a field near our house and played for hundreds of men and women and children sitting around him on the ground. It was music that danced on the air, thrilling, free. I put my head down when the thought of Hubie came along, but then I looked up and saw that playing the violin was such hard work that the man's face was actually shining with sweat.

There was long applause when the Hungarian finished and, as he bowed, and people got up still clapping, some with tears in their eyes, and moved towards him, I felt an urge I hadn't had in a long time. It was a strange feeling. I whispered to my mother and she frowned at first, then nodded yes.

I ran home, dug around in my rucksack brought from Makasar, and ran back. The crowd was tight around the violinist, and I had to struggle through it. When I stood in front of him, a short man with curly black hair, I put out my hand with my harmonica in it. He looked at the harmonica and at me for a moment. Then he smiled, took it, dropped it in his shirt pocket, and turned to an adult admirer. I swallowed. It was gone.

Safe in my backpack was Hubie's soldier on horseback, a thing not for giving.

Notes

Most of the people named in *The Way of a Boy* survived the war except for Uncle Fred Staal who died of dysentery working as a prisoner of war on the Burma-Siam railway; I don't know what happened to Manang, Mr Otten, Peter, Dirk, Johnny Tomato, Willie, Tesuka, or Lieutenant Tanaka.

A few months after the war had ended in 1945, my mother took my brother and me to Canada, her homeland, to recuperate — we were the first civilian survivors from the camps to arrive there — while my father remained in Jakarta and worked for the then still-in-power Dutch government. In 1947, we rejoined my father in Jakarta where the revolution for independence, as throughout Indonesia, had been raging since the Japanese capitulated.

In 1968 I lost Hubie van Boxel's soldier on horseback (shown on the cover), but it was found and kindly returned to me twenty-three years later.

Epilogue: Back on Java

I sat near the edge of the pond and watched for fish jumping; I never saw any, only the widening rings they left behind. The ample pond was stocked with carp and gourami. Monsoon rains had raised the brown water almost level with the lush lawn and shrubs. My wrought-iron chair stood beside the front door of a two-room guest-house overgrown by an orange bougainvillaea. It was light but the sun didn't show yet; ordinary birds had taken over from the noisy creatures of the night. This was the best hour. Once the sun appeared the heat would soon follow — heat that you breathed and tasted and could see dancing in the hazy air.

There was time; by now a routine had evolved. Renni wouldn't come over from the main house with the tray of tea and sliced papaya for another half hour. I had been awake for hours already: tropical nightlife was still disconcerting. In the dark, inside my little house and around it, there was much rustling, whirring, and the odd squeal, and around 4:30 the muezzins' voices calling the faithful to prayer would swell to a great wail.

During the writing of this book, magazine assignments had brought me back to Java after more than forty years. Throughout most of my short stay, I had been moving along in a kind of dream state — every sight and sound and smell set off waves of memories.

Somewhere in the rear of the garden a woman began to sing tonelessly on and on. I watched big red ants marching along a branch of the bougainvillaea up to the roof, one behind the other. This morning I would be leaving Bogor, a town between Jakarta and Bandung (where three of our camps had been located). I was going on a small journey that would take me about ninety miles south into the mountains in search of the tea plantation, difficult of access, which was our home before the war. I had lived on Java from three to the age of fourteen. For me, remembered consciousness began there. I had come home.

I had landed in Jakarta, as most visitors do, and escaped that city's furor quickly. On the way out, I asked my elderly, English-speaking driver to help me inquire whether anything was left of Kampung Makasar, our last camp. We discovered that the village, which had been near the camp and after which the camp had been named, was now an entire city district. Clerks at the municipal office had never heard of a camp, but then none of them looked more than forty. They wanted to help, though, and guided us to the house of Hajji Mohamad Nur, a retired fruit farmer, who had been a village official in the 1940s.

Tall, straight, seventy-five years old, and a chain smoker of Indonesia's clove-spiced cigarettes, Nur waved his big hands around and was inclined to shout though he wasn't deaf. It was a pleasure, though unexpected, he said, to have us in his home. He was called Hajji, I should understand, because he had made the pilgrimage to Mecca. The camp, he said, had been "a bad and secret place" — bamboo barracks surrounded by a high fence in the middle of vegetable gardens. White women and children worked there. Nur thought that his wife, his blind, ninety-year-old mother-in-law, and he himself were probably the only ones left who remembered it. About three quarters of the people in the area had died in those years, first when the Japanese army took away the food the farmers grew and afterwards during the revolution. He pointed at my driver, at me, at himself, clapped his hands, and laughed loudly: "We have survived!"

I didn't know what to say.

And neither did he then, so he showed us around his small stone house. Oil-lamp smoke had blackened the ceilings. We were allowed a glimpse of a room where a window let in the afternoon's hard light on the child-size, nearly bald figure of his mother-in-law sitting on a brass bed facing a wall.

I asked if anyone had ever felt *kasihan*, pity, for those whites.

"Of course!" Nur said. Young men from the village would make their way to the camp after midnight with fruit and other food, to exchange for clothes or jewellery. But sometimes they'd feel such *kasihan* they'd just throw the food over the fence and run home. He shrugged. After the women and children had been evacuated from Makasar, he said, the Allies had filled the barracks for a while with Japanese prisoners. How those fastidious men must have hated it, I thought, living amidst our filth and bugs and deadly germs.

Nur told us the location of Makasar and we drove by. Today it is an army garrison built of stone, but there's still, as then, a lot of barbed wire about. The road running by is wider and busier, but the main gate, through which I'd peered at freedom, is just where it used to be. Nur had said that neighbourhood people are superstitious about that gate: since 1945, a lot of accidents in which someone invariably is killed have happened right in front of it. It's a puzzle because there's no cross-road. "Many people died inside that place," was Nur's explanation, "and their spirits are still there."

It's easy, in Indonesia, to accept the spirit world's mysteries. Certainly it seemed to be the kindly connivance of "silent forces" that was charting my unplanned rambling.

In Canada I had been asked to deliver a package to Renni Samsoedin in Bogor. I found her to be an immensely cheerful woman in her early thirties with degrees in botany and chemistry. She spoke fluent English and promptly asked why I was in her country. I said I was seeing some places where I'd lived as a boy; now I hoped to seek out the tea plantation. Renni nodded and smiled and nodded. When you talk to Indonesians, it seems sometimes as if part of their consciousness is elsewhere, as if they are dreaming and yet awake.

"Ah well," Renni interrupted, "we must make a plan. You must come and stay where I live — there's lots of room. You will meet my father. He will help with the plan."

Renni was intrigued by the idea of someone returning to where he'd been small — and in *her* Indonesia. It would not do to muddle on alone, though, and try to find the plantation. Just rent a car and go? It wasn't that simple. Or maybe it was, but it was no fun. Or at least it was more fun if Indonesians came along to explain things. Her whole family would help make a plan. There were three girls and seven boys, all adults; Cucu, the youngest, was twenty-two.

Would I return to her office in late afternoon when Cucu picked her up in the family Land Rover — and would I like *saté ayam* (chicken roasted on bamboo skewers in spicy peanut sauce) with *nasi goreng* (fried rice) for dinner?

The rest of the day I explored Kebon Raya, the city's world-famous botanical garden, with its rolling lawns, holy banyan trees, cactus gardens, lily ponds, and forest groves. It was green and still. Left unharmed by the war, it had probably been as green and still while we were in camp. Upside down from the branches of a dead-looking tree hung bats with bodies the size of rats. Now and then one would wake up with a sad cry, spread its cloaklike wings, float to another branch, and fold up again. The huge, many-trunked holy trees possessed massive self-assurance: roots grew down from their branches into the earth, enlarging and renewing the trees forever.

Later at Renni's house the rest of the family wasn't home yet. She first showed me a room where, spread out on the floor, polished and ready, there lay enough flutes, bamboo xylophones, gongs, and other percussion instruments for an entire gamelan ensemble. On Sundays the Samsoedins got together and performed Indonesia's rhythmically complex, liquid, thousand-year-old music for hours on end; but I missed that. Renni walked me around the family's terraced fairy-tale garden, full of still places, to the little guest-house by the fish pond where I would sleep. I bathed, splashing water over myself in the way I had done so many years ago.

Most of the family came around that evening. Word got out about Renni's foreigner, though none of them had a phone. All knew some English. Pak Samsoedin, the father, also remembered a few words of Dutch. Soft-spoken and much less direct than his daughter, he did eventually ask why I was in Indonesia. Halfway through my reply his attention shifted in that curious Indonesian way.

"So," he said abruptly in English-Dutch, dropping in a word of French as well, "you are going on a journey of *nostalgie*?" He stared ahead. The room was quiet. "I too would like to go on a journey of *nostalgie*. And in the same area. It is beautiful. High in the mountains with the tea. . . . I was stationed there, you know — in 1947, with the army.

That would have been the revolutionary army fighting us, the Dutch.

"I remember we were put up in a nice house," he went on. "In the morning I would go out and do my exercises on the big downhill lawn. . . ."

He paused, remembering.

I thought I felt some neck hairs rise. I reached for

my camera bag and groped inside for a half-dozen tiny black-and-white pictures taken before the war.

"And then I would walk to the edge of the lawn to a bridge over a little stream. . . ."

I held out a photo.

"This house?"

He looked.

"That house, yes."

It was a picture of *our* house on *our* plantation. We'd been trucked away in *1942*. The population of Java is more than a *hundred million* . . . and *forty-seven years later* . . . ! The family was amused but not awestruck: these things happen. Manang would have understood. Renni laughed and said, "Magic!" Her father took it entirely in stride and continued to reminisce about his army days. But yes, the journey of *nostalgie*. . . .

Cucu would drive me, Cucu was on a break from law school and had time. In a corner on the floor with his seven-year-old niece Dini in his lap, Cucu nodded sleepily. Short and slight, he rarely spoke and always looked sleepy. Renni said that if I could wait a day, she'd take time off and come as interpreter. Absolutely. The map was spread out on the floor, a jug of chilled coconut juice did the rounds, a route was plotted. The "silent forces" were at it all right. There was a great honking of frogs in the fish pond.

And so, after tea and papaya, we were driving out of Bogor, Cucu at the wheel, Renni in the back. The road at once started to ascend and the air grew drier and clearer. Every day there had been the season's sudden rain squalls, but this day it stayed dry and mostly sunny, allowing the views along the twisting, climbing roads to come spectacularly into their own. Early on, patches of mist had raced over the valleys, over the tender green, terraced rice fields. Where the hillsides carried cuts or stood too steep to cultivate there was unruly jungle growth from which poked the familiar heads of coconut trees. Later, high up where the tea plantings began, the terrain acquired the long sweep of mid-ocean waves: the flat-topped, black-green bushes fell and rose in patterned clusters against red earth from the shadows of one mountain into those of the next. Renni called the weather "magic," as she labelled almost everything slightly fortuitous. But she was right. At a certain point the narrow asphalt roads turned into roads of rock and earth — we'd gone wrong. Had it rained, even the Land Rover might have bogged down.

We were quite alone by then, except for the occasional clutch of women tea pickers in their conical hats, chest-deep among the bushes, hands quick as sparrows pinching off the pale green youngest leaves. The car jolted along in first gear for what seemed hours, but the windows were open and the sun was gentle. A stop for pictures let the uplands' immense stillness settle for a moment.

We were getting closer to Pasirnanka, the plantation, and my mind was moving awfully fast. We turned a corner and were suddenly amidst houses and people — some of them in dark-blue uniforms, gesticulating at us with night sticks! Security guards yelling, What were we doing here? Who were we? They were clearly astonished to see us: we had come in the back way.

How had we known the bridge on the main road had collapsed yesterday. Renni murmured, "Magic" — and cheerfully set about explaining. Cucu, unperturbed, passed around cigarettes.

Was this the plantation? Nothing looked familiar, not a house, not the shape of a hill. I wandered away from the car. My mind was slowing down again. By the guard house a road turned left and down towards a large grey metal shed. I could hear a humming that grew louder as I came closer . . . the factory! If that was the factory, then up that hill had to be the swimming pool. And to the right, beyond those new houses, the home of the lovely Mrs Plomp. And from way up their hill, Mr and Mrs Plomp had looked down — on us!

I started to run, and the group by the car followed. A few steps only and there was the Plomp house, a dilapidated bungalow on a little rise, not a hill. And there — our house . . . the garden still the same shape; buried deep in the rear a wild boar's skull. On those fieldstone steps my father made Jerry and me promise to look after our mother; the last time we came down them, my mother, Jerry, and I were loaded into the back of the truck with the other white mothers and children. But such a little house! The shape unchanged but walls cut into picture windows, the "pavilion" gone.

The others had caught up. The guards were laughing and calling to someone inside the house. A woman in a pink dress came out; a little boy and girl followed and clung to her legs. The woman looked a bit apprehensive and didn't speak. One of the guards urged her to invite me inside, which she did with her hand. But I said thank you, no, because I knew right then that I had no need to enter, and no curiosity. I took some pictures, thanked her, and started down the steps, the group following. There were quite a few new homes, but those the whites had lived in were still in use too. The biggest had been the chief administrator's, Mr Witte's; his home was in even worse shape than the Plomp place.

Friends and guards in tow, I now marched towards the pool on the hill. At the bottom of the slope there was a tall vine-covered wire fence, broken and flattened in places, the gate hanging open. I knew for certain that there had been no fence there in our time. Inside, high wild grass ran up the hill. I reached the edge of the pool. One rusted handrail still stood upright by the steps leading down; weeds sprouted from the cracked concrete. The guards looked around with interest. The hilltop was quiet, shadowy, neglected — where once it had resounded with life. It was like an old cemetery.

A half-hour out of the plantation, on the way back, Cucu drove off the narrow road to let a small bus pass. He cut the motor and lit a cigarette. As the noise of the bus receded, stillness set in again. Cucu had hardly spoken on the whole trip. He listened to what others said and responded with his eyes or his smile. But then he turned to me sitting next to him and unexpectedly asked, "Are you happy now?"

I thought of the place we had just left and that I'd travelled so far to visit, and I said: "I am, yes" — and realized I was already seeing it again, in my mind's eye, as I'd always seen it, and probably always would. Memory is, finally, all we own.

A REDBIRD CHRISTMAS

Fannie Flagg, film, TV and stage actress, writer, producer and performer, is the bestselling author of *Fried Green Tomatoes at the Whistle Stop Café* (filmed with her own award-winning screenplay), *Daisy Fay and the Miracle Man, Welcome to the World, Baby Girl!* and *Standing in the Rainbow*.

Fannie Flagg

A REDBIRD CHRISTMAS

A Novel

VINTAGE BOOKS
London

Published by Vintage 2005

14

Copyright © Willina Lane Productions, Inc. 2004

Fannie Flagg has asserted her right under the Copyright,
Designs and Patents Act, 1988 to be identified as the author
of this work

This book is sold subject to the condition that it shall not by
way of trade or otherwise, be lent, resold, hired out, or
otherwise circulated without the publisher's prior consent in
any form of binding or cover other than that in which it is
published and without a similar condition including this
condition being imposed on the subsequent purchaser

First published in Great Britain in 2004 by
Chatto & Windus

Vintage
Random House, 20 Vauxhall Bridge Road,
London SW1V 2SA

www.vintage-books.co.uk

Addresses for companies within The Random House Group
Limited can be found at: www.randomhouse.co.uk/offices.htm

The Random House Group Limited Reg. No. 954009

A CIP catalogue record for this book
is available from the British Library

ISBN 9780099490487

Penguin Random House is committed to a sustainable future for
our business, our readers and our planet. This book is made from
Forest Stewardship Council® certified paper.

Printed and bound in Great Britain by Clays Ltd, St Ives plc

FOR JONI, KATE, AND RITA

❧ A ❧
REDBIRD
CHRISTMAS

The Windy City

※

I T WAS ONLY November sixth but Chicago had just been hit with its second big blizzard of the season, and Mr. Oswald T. Campbell guessed he had stepped in every ice-cold ankle-deep puddle of dirty white slush it was possible to step in, trying to get to his appointment. When he finally arrived, he had used up every cussword in his rather large vocabulary of cusswords, owed in part to his short stint in the army. He was greeted by the receptionist and handed a clipboard.

"We received all your medical records and insurance forms, Mr. Campbell, but Dr. Obecheck likes to have a short personal history of his new patients, so could you please fill this out for us?"

Oh, God, he thought, why do they always make you fill something out? But he nodded cordially and sat down and started.

Name: *Oswald T. Campbell*
Address: *Hotel De Soto, 1428 Lennon Avenue, Chicago, IL*
Sex: *Male*
Age: *52*
Hair: *Some . . . Red*
Eyes: *Blue*
Height: *Five feet eight*
Weight: *161 pounds*
Marital status: *Divorced*
Children: *No, thank God.*
Closest living relative: *Ex-wife, Mrs. Helen Gwinn, 1457
    Hope Street, Lake Forest, IL*
Please list your complaints below:
The Cubs need a new second baseman.

There were many more questions to fill out, but he just left them blank, signed his name, and handed it back to the girl.

Later, after his examination was over, as he sat shivering in a freezing room wearing nothing but a backless thin gray cotton gown, a nurse told him to get dressed; the doctor would meet him back in his office. Not only was he chilled to the bone and sore from just having been probed and prodded in many rude places, but now, to make matters worse, when he tried to put his shoes and socks back on they were still ice cold and sopping wet. He tried to wring the excess water out of his socks and managed to drip dye all over the floor. It was then he noticed that the dye from his socks had stained his feet a nice dark blue. "Oh, great!" he muttered to himself. He threw the socks in the trash basket and squished down the hall in cold wet leather shoes.

As he sat in the office waiting, he was bored and uncomfortable. There was nothing to read and he couldn't smoke because he had lied to the doctor and told him he had given it up. He wiggled his toes, trying to get them warm, and glanced around the room. Everywhere he looked was gray. It was gray outside the office window and gray inside the office. Would it kill them to paint the walls a different color? The last time he had been at the VA hospital, a woman had come in and given a talk on how colors affect the mood. What idiot would pick gray? He hated going to doctors anyway, but his insurance company required him to have a physical once a year so some new bozo could tell him what he already knew. The doctor he had just seen was at least friendly and had laughed at a few of his jokes, but now he just wished the guy would hurry up. Most of the doctors they sent him to were old and ready to retire or just starting out and in need of guinea pigs to practice on. This one was old. Seventy or more, he guessed. Maybe that's why he was taking so long. Gray walls, gray rug, gray gown, gray doctor.

Finally, the door opened and the doctor came in with his test results. Oswald said, "So, Doc, will I be able to run in the Boston Marathon again this year?"

This time the doctor ignored Oswald's attempt to be humorous and sat down at his desk, looking rather somber.

"Mr. Campbell," he said, "I'm not too happy about what

I have to tell you. I usually like to have a family member present at a time like this. I see you have listed your ex-wife as immediate family. Would you like to call and see if she can come in?"

Oswald suddenly stopped wiggling his toes and paid attention. "No, that's all right. Is there a problem?"

"I'm afraid so," he said, as he opened his folder. "I've checked and rechecked your charts and records. I even called in another associate from down the hall, a pulmonary specialist, to consult, but unfortunately he agreed with my diagnosis. Mr. Campbell, I'm going to tell it to you straight. In your present condition you won't live through another Chicago winter. You need to get out of here to a milder climate as soon as possible, because if you don't—well, frankly, I'm not sure I would give you till Christmas."

"Huh?" Oswald said, as if he were thinking it over. "Is that right?"

"Yes, it is. I'm sorry to report that since your last checkup the emphysema has progressed to the critical stage. Your lungs were already badly damaged and scarred from the childhood tuberculosis. Add all the years of heavy smoking and chronic bronchitis, and I'm afraid all it would take is one bad cold going into another bout of pneumonia."

"Is that right? Huh," Oswald said again. "That doesn't sound too good."

The doctor closed his folder and leaned forward on his desk, looked him right in the eye, and said, "No, it doesn't. In all honesty, Mr. Campbell, considering the alarming rapidity with which this condition has advanced, even with you going to a better climate, the most optimistic prognosis I can give you is a year . . . maybe two."

"You're kidding," said Oswald.

He shook his head. "No, I'm afraid not. At this stage, the emphysema is a strain on your heart and all your other organs. It's not just the lungs that are affected. Now, I'm not telling you this to scare you, Mr. Campbell; I only tell you so you have time to make the appropriate plans. Get your estate in order."

As stunned as he was at the news, Oswald almost laughed out loud at the word *estate*. He had never had more than two hundred and fifty dollars in the bank in his entire life.

The doctor continued. "Believe me, I wish the diagnosis had been better." And the doctor meant it. He hated having to hand out bad news. He had just met Mr. Campbell, but he had liked the personable little guy at once. "Are you sure you don't need me to call anyone for you?"

"No, that's all right."

"How will this news affect your future plans, Mr. Campbell?"

Oswald looked up at him. "Pretty damn adversely, I would say, wouldn't you?"

The doctor was sympathetic. "Well, yes, of course. I just wondered what your future plans may have been."

"I didn't have anything in particular in mind . . . but I sure as hell hadn't planned on this."

"No, of course not."

"I knew I wasn't the picture of health, but I didn't think I was headed for the last roundup."

"Well, as I said, you need to get out of Chicago as soon as you can, somewhere with as little pollution as possible."

Oswald looked puzzled. "But Chicago is my home. I wouldn't know where else to go."

"Do you have any friends living somewhere else— Florida? Arizona?"

"No, everybody I know is here."

"Ah . . . and I assume you are on a limited budget."

"Yeah, that's right. I just have my disability pension."

"Uh-huh. I suppose Florida might be too expensive this time of year."

Never having been there, Oswald said, "I would imagine."

The doctor sighed and leaned back in his chair, trying to think of some way to be of help. "Well, let's see. . . . Wait a minute, there was a place my father used to send all his lung patients, and as I remember the rates were pretty reasonable." He looked at Oswald as if he knew. "What *was* the name of that place? It was close to Florida. . . ." The doctor suddenly remembered something and stood up. "You know what? I've still got all his old files in the other room. Let me go and see if by any chance I can find that information for you."

Oswald stared at the gray wall. Leave Chicago? He might as well leave the planet.

It was already dark and still freezing cold when Oswald left the office. As he rounded the corner at the Wrigley Building, the wind from the river hit him right in the face and blew his hat off. He turned and watched it flip over and over until it landed upside down in the gutter and began to float like a boat on down the block. Oh, the hell with it, he thought, until the frigid air blew through what little hair he did have left and his ears started to ache, so he decided to run after it. When he finally caught the hat and put it back on his head he realized he was now wearing wet shoes with no socks, a wet hat, and he had just missed his bus. By the time another bus finally came, he was completely numb from the cold plus the shock of the news he had just received. As he sat down, his eye caught the advertisement above his seat for Marshall Field's department store: MAKE THIS THE BEST CHRISTMAS EVER. START YOUR CHRISTMAS SHOPPING EARLY THIS YEAR. It suddenly dawned on him that, in his case, he had *better* start early and it might already be too late. According to the doctor, if he did live to see it, this Christmas could be his last.

Not that Christmas had ever meant much to him, but still it was a strange thought. As he sat there trying to comprehend the world without him, the bus jerked and lurched in short spurts all the way down State Street, now packed with bumper-to-bumper rush-hour traffic and loud with the angry sounds of the blaring horns of frustrated people. As more passengers began to crowd onto the bus, they weren't in such a good mood either. One woman glared at Oswald and said to her friend, "Gentlemen used to get up and give a lady a seat." He thought to himself, *Lady, if I could get up, I would,* but he still couldn't feel his legs.

After about five minutes, when he could begin to move

his fingers, he reached in his pocket and pulled out the brochure the doctor had given him. On the front page was a photograph of what looked to be a large hotel, but it was hard to make out. The brochure was faded and looked as if it had water damage, but the print underneath was still legible:

THE WOODBOUND HOTEL
IN
THE SUNNY SOUTH
UNDER NEW MANAGEMENT

Horace P. Dunlap
Formerly of Gibson House, Cincinnati, Ohio

Deep in the southernmost part of Alabama, along the banks of a lazy winding river, lies the sleepy little community known as Lost River, a place that time itself seems to have forgotten.

LOCATION

This pleasant health resort sits nestled between Perdido and Mobile bays, in the subtropical district, especially adapting it for a winter home. To the south lies the Gulf of Mexico, the soft breezes from which seem at all times to temper the climate. The near presence of a large body of salt water furnishes an atmosphere charged with ozone, chlorine, and other life-giving constituents. Instead of the barren bleakness of the northern winter, there is the luxurious warmth and color of the Southern Clime, where a gloomy day is the exception and where the azure sky and a wealth of sunshine rule. This section of the country, when in the possession of the Spaniards, was called "The Charmed Belt."

HEALTH-GIVING CONDITIONS

Many a consumptive, rheumatic, nervous, worn-out, and overworked person has found health and a new lease on life by spending a few months in this region; the influence of the saline breezes from the Gulf will bring you a good sharp appetite even if you have not enjoyed a meal for years. *It is the ideal spot for complete recreation and rest from the hustle-bustle whirl of society and the noise of the city. It will quiet your nervous system no matter how badly it may be wrecked. As a winter resort, the climate is all that could be desired and the crystal springwater found everywhere cannot be beat.* "I would call the entire region one of the garden spots of America," says Dr. Mark Obecheck of Chicago.

Oswald guessed that must have been his doctor's father. He turned the page and as the bus jerked along he read further.

COMMENTS FROM WINTER VISITORS

Dear Mr. Dunlap,
 We so enjoyed the fishing and boating and the pleasant walks

in the dense pine woods. The sweet songs of the mockingbird at early morn, the fragrance and balmy air as it drifted into our rooms.

Mr. S. Simms, Chicago, Illinois

Another faded photo captioned: RIVER VIEW FROM THE LARGE VERANDA. He turned the page.

"I fled from the North, from blizzard, frost and snow
To see the Sunny South where sweet and balmy breezes blow."
(A poem by Mrs. Deanne Barkley of Chicago, inspired by a recent winter visit)

Another faded photo: MR. L. J. GRODZIKI AND HIS CATCH OF FINE FISH.

A FISHERMAN'S PARADISE!

Game fish are plentiful here in our southern waters. The following is a partial list of the varieties: redfish, silver and speckled trout, pike, flounder, croakers, mullet, brim, perch, catfish, gar, and tarpon (sometimes called the silver king). Oysters, shrimp, and clams abound.

Another faded photo was captioned A GROUP OF CHICAGO GENTLEMEN ENJOYING A GOOD SMOKE AFTER AN OYSTER BAKE.

Oswald turned the page and there was a photo he could not make out: A ROSEBUSH UNDER WHICH THIRTY PEOPLE CAN STAND COMFORTABLY!

As he approached his bus stop he put the booklet back in his pocket and wondered who in the hell would *want* to stand under a rosebush with thirty other people, comfortably or not?

When he reached the De Soto Apartment Hotel for Men, where he had lived for the past eight years, a few of the guys were down in the lobby looking at the TV. They waved at him. "How did it go?"

"Terrible," he said, blowing his nose. "I may be dead before Christmas."

They all laughed, thinking he was joking, and went back to watching the news.

"No, I'm serious," he said. "The doctor said I'm in terrible shape."

He stood there waiting for some reaction, but they weren't paying any attention and he was too tired to argue the point. He went upstairs to his room, took a bath, put on his pajamas, and sat down in his chair. He lit a cigarette and looked out at the blue neon Pabst Blue Ribbon beer sign in the window of his favorite neighborhood bar across the street. Damn, he thought. At a time like this, a man ought to be able to have a drink. But a year ago another doctor had informed him that his liver was shot and if he took one more drink it would kill him. But so what? Now that he was going to die anyway, drinking himself to death might not be such a bad idea after all. It would be fast anyway, and at least he could have a few laughs before he checked out.

He toyed with the idea of getting dressed and heading across the street, but he didn't. He had promised his ex-wife, Helen, he'd stay sober and he would hate to disappoint her again, so he just sat there and tried his best to feel sorry for himself. He had had bad luck from the get-go. He had contracted his first bout of tuberculosis when he was eight, along with 75 percent of the other boys at St. Joseph's Home for Boys, and had been in and out of hospitals fighting chronic bronchitis and pneumonia all his life. Being an orphan, he had never known who he was or where he had come from. Whoever left him on the church steps that night left no clues, nothing except the basket he came in and a can of Campbell's soup. He had no idea what his real name was. Oswald was the next name on St. Joseph's first-name list and, because of the soup, they gave him Campbell as a last name and the initial T. for Tomato, the kind he was found with. Nor did he know his nationality. But one day, when he was about twelve, a priest took a good look at his rather large nose, red hair, and small squinty blue eyes and remarked, "Campbell, if that's not an Irish mug, I'll eat my hat." So Oswald guessed he was Irish. Just another piece of bad luck as far as having a problem with booze was concerned.

But it had not been just the drinking. Nothing had come easy to him. School, sports, or girls. He had never been able to keep a job for long, and even the army had released him early with a medical discharge. It seemed to Oswald that everyone else had come into this world with a set of instructions but him. From the beginning he had always felt like a pair of white socks and brown shoes in a roomful of tuxedos. He had never really gotten a break in life, and now it was all over.

After about an hour of trying to work up as much sympathy for himself as he possibly could, he suddenly realized that despite all of his efforts, he wasn't all that upset! At least not as upset as a man *should* be who had just been handed his walking papers. The real truth was, the only two things he would really miss when he checked out were the Cub games and Helen, unfortunately in that order, one of the reasons for their divorce in the first place.

In all honesty, Helen was probably the only one who would really miss him. Although she was remarried with two kids, she was still the person closest to him. He used to go over to her house for dinner quite a bit, but not so much anymore. The new husband was somewhat of a jerk and her two kids had grown from obnoxious young boys into whiny and obnoxious teenagers, who did nothing but give her grief. He couldn't go there anymore without wanting to strangle one or both, so he just didn't go. You can't tell other people how to raise their kids, especially since the other reason for the divorce was because she wanted kids and he didn't. Having spent the first seventeen years of his life in a room with five hundred other screaming and yelling kids, he had had enough of children to last him a lifetime. Still, despite the apparent apathy he felt about his own imminent demise and not knowing the correct protocol for this sort of thing, he supposed he should tell *someone* about his prognosis. He guessed he should tell Helen at least. But after thinking about it a little longer, he wondered why tell her? Given the kind of woman she was, an ex-nurse and a nice person, if she knew how sick he was she would probably insist on his coming to live with them so she could take care of him. Why put her through that? Why worry her? She didn't deserve it. He had caused her enough trouble already. She had enough problems of her own, and besides there *were* those teenagers.

No, he concluded, the best thing he could do for her was just go away and let her get on with her life. Then if he *wanted* to take a drink nobody would be the wiser or care. He just had to find a place he could afford on his small $600-a-month government pension.

He went over and sat down, took the Woodbound Hotel brochure out of his coat pocket, and turned to the next page, where Horace P. Dunlap asked the reader:

WHY GO TO FLORIDA?

Why go to Florida with its low lands and deficiency of good water? Why go to New Mexico and be exposed to alkali dust? Why go to California, with its cold uncomfortable houses two to three thousand miles away, when Baldwin County can be reached from Chicago in twenty-six hours? On both sides of the river you will find a magnificent growth of fine timber. Among the many varieties are the magnolia, sweet bay, sweet gum, Cuban pine, ash, maple, evergreen, and white cedar, with a great variety of shrubs and Spanish moss hanging from the live oaks. Satsuma trees, pecan, kumquat, pear, fig, and apple are plentiful.

The winters here are like the northern spring or early autumn. In fact, you can enjoy nature walks in comfort nearly every day of the year. . . . Along the river, ducks, geese, wild turkey, dove, quail, raccoon, and squirrel abound. Here is an abundance of sparkling-clear springs, and good water is found at 20 to 30 feet. All the various fruits and vegetables by reason of the mild climate are about two weeks in advance of other sections of the country. What does this mean for the health seeker? It means relief and cure to those who suffer from bronchitis, catarrh, and rheumatism and absolute safety from pneumonia; it means an easy recovery for those few who get grippe in this county. It means a carefree romping out-of-doors for the pale or delicate boy or girl, the joy of picking beautiful flowers at Christmastime.

RENT A LOVELY ROOM OR A DANDY LITTLE BUNGALOW!

We extend a hearty welcome for you to visit our fair county. We are just as large as Chicago, only we haven't quite so many houses. Don't say we are giving you only exaggerations. Come visit and see for yourself the sunshine, flowers, and orange blossoms in December.

On the back page was a song complete with words and music.

"Dreamy Alabama"

Words and music by Horace P. Dunlap

Evening shadows falling
where the southland lies,
whip-poor-will is calling
'neath the starlit skies I love

Dreamy Alabama where sweet folks are waiting,
there my heart is ever turning, all day long.
Dreamy Alabama, where songbirds are singing,
waiting to greet me with their song.

Winding river flowing
through the whispering pines
like a stream of silver
when the moonlight shines above.

Oswald put the brochure down. This had to be one of the dullest places in America, but he had to hand it to Horace P. Dunlap. He sure as hell was trying hard to get your business. He had thrown in everything but the kitchen sink. Tomorrow he would give old Horace a call and see how much it would cost to rent a lovely room or a dandy little bungalow, and find out where the nearest bar was.

Hello, Operator

THE NEXT MORNING after his usual thirty to forty-five minutes of coughing, Oswald lit his first cigarette, picked up the phone, and called the number on the brochure.

"I'm sorry, sir, but that number is invalid. Are you sure you have the right number?"

"I know it's the right number. I'm looking at it right now."

"What area code are you trying to call?"

"Well, I don't know. It's the Woodbound Hotel in Lost River in Baldwin County, Alabama."

"Let me connect you with information for that area." In a moment another operator answered. "May I help you?"

"I hope so. I'm trying to reach the Woodbound Hotel."

"Just a moment, sir, I'll check that for you right away." This operator had such a thick southern accent he thought she must be joking with him. "I'm sorry, sir, but I don't have a listing for a Woodbound Hotel anywhere in Baldwin County."

"Oh. Well, where are you?"

"I'm in Mobile."

"Is that in Alabama?"

"Yes, sir."

"Have you ever heard of a place called Lost River?"

"No, sir, I haven't."

"Is there a listing for *anything* down there?"

"Just a moment. Let me check that for you. . . . Sir, I have a listing for the Lost River community hall and one for the post office. Would you like me to connect you to either one of those numbers?"

"Yes, let me try the first one. They might be able to help me."

Not five minutes earlier, Mrs. Frances Cleverdon, an attractive, slightly plump woman with white hair as soft as spun cotton candy, and her younger sister, Mildred, had just entered the back of the community hall through the kitchen. It was 72 degrees outside and the hall was hot and stuffy, so they opened all the windows and turned on the overhead fans. It was the first Saturday of the month. Tonight was the monthly meeting and potluck dinner of the Lost River Community Association. They were there early to deliver what they had made for the potluck dinner and to get the place ready for the evening. Frances had brought two covered dishes, one a green-bean casserole, the other a macaroni and cheese, and several desserts.

Mildred, who had prepared fried chicken and a pork roast, heard the phone ringing first but ignored it. When Frances came back in from the car, Mildred said, "Don't answer that. It's probably Miss Alma, and we'll never get her off the phone."

After another trip to the car for two cakes and three pecan pies, the phone was still ringing.

Frances said, "You know she's not going to give up," and picked up the receiver one second before Oswald was going to hang up.

"Hello?"

"Hello!" he said.

"Hello?" she said again.

"Who is this?"

"This is Frances. Who's this?" she asked, in the same southern accent as the operator.

"This is Oswald Campbell, and I'm trying to find the phone number for a hotel."

"Well, Mr. Campbell, this is the community hall you've reached."

"I know. The operator gave me this number."

"The operator? Where are you calling from?"

"Chicago."

"Oh, my!"

"Do you happen to have the number of the Woodbound Hotel? It's a health resort that supposed to be down there."

"The Woodbound Hotel?"

"Have you ever heard of it?"

"Yes, I've heard of it . . . but it's not here anymore."

"Did it close?"

"Well, no. It burned down."

"When?"

"Just a minute, let me see if my sister knows." Frances called out, "Mildred, when did the old hotel burn down?"

Mildred looked at her funny. "About 1911, why?"

"Mr. Campbell, it was in 1911."

"In 1911? You're kidding!"

"No, they say it burned right to the ground in less than an hour."

"Oh . . . well . . . could you give me the name of another hotel I could call?"

"Down here?"

"Yes."

"There isn't any."

"Oh."

"There used to be a few, but not anymore. If you don't mind me asking, how on earth did you hear about the old Woodbound all the way up there in Chicago?"

"My doctor gave me a brochure, but obviously it was a little out-of-date. Thanks anyway."

"Hold on a second, Mr. Campbell," she said, and called out, "Mildred, close that screen door, you're letting the flies in. I'm sorry, Mr. Campbell. What kind of place were you looking for?"

"Just somewhere to spend a couple of months this winter, get out of the cold weather for a while. I have a little lung problem."

"Oh, dear. That's not good."

"No. My doctor said I needed to get out of Chicago as soon as possible."

"I can understand that. I'll bet it's cold up there."

"Yes," he said, trying not to be rude but also wanting to hang up. This call was probably expensive. But Mrs. Cleverdon continued talking. "Well, it's hot down here. We just had to open the windows and turn all the fans on. Oh. Hold on. Mr. Campbell, I've got to go close that door. . . ."

While he was waiting, he could actually hear the sounds of birds chirping in the background over long distance. It must be some of those damn whip-poor-wills, he thought, and they were costing him money.

Frances picked up the phone again. "Here I am, Mr. Campbell. Now, would this be a place for you and your wife or just you?"

"Just me."

"Have you tried anywhere else?"

"No. I wanted to try there first, it sounded like a nice place. Oh well, thanks anyway."

"Mr. Campbell. Wait a minute. Give me your number. Let me see if I can come up with something for you."

He gave her his number just to get her to hang up. What a crazy place. Evidently they would just talk the head off of any stranger that happened to call.

Mildred came back in the kitchen after putting flowers on the two long tables in the other room. "Who were you on the phone with so long?"

"Some poor man from Chicago with bad lungs who needs a place for the winter. His doctor had given him a brochure for that old hotel, and he thought he might want to come here." She walked over and pulled out the huge coffeepot. "Why *did* it burn down, I wonder?"

"They say it was rats and matches."

"Oh, lord," said Frances, opening a large dark-brown can of A&P Eight O'Clock coffee. "They'll just chew on anything, won't they?"

Around three o'clock the next afternoon, Oswald was about to pick up the phone and make another call to Florida when it rang. "Hello?"

"Mr. Campbell, this is Frances Cleverdon, the lady you spoke to in Alabama yesterday. Do you remember me?"

"Yes, of course."

"Listen, have you found a place yet?"

"No, not yet, not one I can afford, anyway."

"Yes. Well, if you still have a mind to come down here, I think I found a place for you. We have a very nice lady next door to me, and she said she would be happy to rent you a room for however long you want it."

"Huh," said Oswald. "How much do you think she would charge?"

"She told me that fifty dollars a week would suit her just

fine, if that was all right with you. Of course, that would include all your meals. Is that too much?"

Oswald added up his $600-a-month pension, plus the small military medical-discharge check from the government, and figured he could handle it. The places in Florida he called had been double and triple that amount.

"No, that rate sounds fine to me. When would it be available?"

"Betty said for you to just come on anytime, the sooner the better; the river is so pretty this time of year. But now, Mr. Campbell, before you decide on anything, I need to warn you. We are just a small place down here, all we have is one grocery store and a post office, but if it's warm weather and peace and quiet you want, I can guarantee you'll get plenty of that."

"Sounds good to me," he lied. He couldn't think of anything worse, but the price was right. He figured he should probably grab it before they changed their minds.

"Well, all right then," she said. "Just call me back and let me know when you're coming, and we'll have somebody pick you up."

"OK."

"But one more thing, Mr. Campbell, just so you know. We are very friendly and sociable down here and good neighbors when you need us, but nobody is going to bother you unless you want them to. By and large we mind our own business."

. . .

What Frances had told Mr. Campbell was true. The people in Lost River did mind their own business. However, after having said that, Frances, a romantic at heart, could not help being a little optimistic. With four widows and three single women living in the community, having a new man around would certainly be interesting. One of the three single women was her sister Mildred. Frances was one of the widows, but she did not put herself in the running. She had been very happily married for twenty-seven years and was perfectly content to live on memories, but as for the rest of the ladies she was willing to let fate take a hand. After all, she was a Presbyterian and believed strongly in predestination. Besides, the day Mr. Campbell called happened to be the first Saturday of the month, usually the only day someone was at the hall, and that could not have been just a coincidence. Wouldn't it be wonderful if he turned out to be someone's knight in shining armor? The only other eligible man in Lost River was Roy Grimmitt, who ran the grocery store. But he was only thirty-eight, too young for most of the women. Besides, after what had happened to him, it looked as if Roy was a confirmed bachelor for life. Too bad, she thought, because he was a handsome man and a nice one, but she more than the others understood it. Once you've experienced true love, you don't want anybody else.

The Store

✦

ROY GRIMMITT, WHO ran the grocery store in Lost River, was a big friendly guy and everybody liked him. He was also one of the few people who had actually been born and raised in the area, except for the Creoles across the river, whose families had been there since the 1700s. Roy had inherited the store from his uncle, who had run it for fifty years. The tin Coca-Cola sign across the front of the brick building advertised it simply as GRIMMITT'S GROCERY, but it was much more than that. It was a landmark. If the store had not been on the corner, most people would have driven right by, never knowing there was a river or an entire community of people living there. For the sixty or seventy residents, it was the place where they did their shopping and kept up on all the news, good and bad. It was an especially favorite stopping-off spot for the many fishermen in the area, the place where they bought their tackle and live bait and swapped lies about how many fish they had caught—all except Claude Underwood, the best fisherman there, who never said how many he had caught or where he had caught them. There were two gas pumps outside the store; inside was rather plain, with wooden floors and a meat counter in the back. The only concession to decoration was the large array of mounted fish, game birds, and deer heads that lined the walls and a stuffed red fox on top of the shelf in the back. One of the Creoles, Julian LaPonde, the only taxidermist in the area, had once been a good friend and poker pal of Roy's uncle. Most of the produce was local. Roy bought his meat from area hunters and always had plenty of fresh shrimp, crab, and oysters from the Gulf and fish from the river. He got his milk, poultry, eggs, fruits, and vegetables from nearby farms. Because his was the only store around, he stocked much more than just food and gas; he sold everything from work gloves, rakes, shovels, and pickaxes to rubber boots. Kids loved the store because of its great selection of candy, potato chips, and ice cream, and the deep box of ice-cold drinks he kept by the front door filled with every kind you could want: Orange Crush, root beer, Grapettes, Dr Pepper, and RC Cola. Name it, he had it. But Roy also had something that no other store in the world could offer.

It had been just a few weeks after Christmas about five years ago, when Roy heard the popping of guns out in back of the store. A pair of kids that lived back up in the woods had gotten high-powered pump-action BB guns that year and were busy shooting everything in sight. Roy was a hunter and a fisherman, but those damn mean little redneck boys would shoot anything and leave it to die. He hated that, and he walked out the back door and yelled at them, "Hey, you boys, knock it off!" They immediately scattered back into the woods, but they had just shot something, and whatever it was it was still alive and on the ground flopping around. Roy walked over and picked it up. It was a baby bird.

"Damn those little bastards." It was a scruffy tiny gray-and-brown thing, so young he could not tell what it was. Probably a sparrow or a mockingbird or a wren of some kind. He had picked up many dead or hurt birds that these boys had shot but this was the youngest by far. It probably had not even learned to fly. He knew he couldn't save it, but he took the little bird back inside the store anyway, wrapped it up in an old sock, and put it in a box in a warm dark place in his office so some hawk or owl or other predator could not get it. At least he could save the baby bird from that and let the thing die in peace. Other than that, there was nothing more he could do for it.

Most of the kids that lived around there were pretty nice and Roy had a good relationship with all of them, but these two new boys were surly. Nobody knew who they were or where they had come from. Somebody said their family lived in an old run-down trailer way back up in the woods. He had never seen the parents, but he had seen the boys throwing rocks at a dog and he had no use for them after that, even less now. Anybody that would deliberately shoot a baby bird ought to have their heads knocked together. If he could get his hands on them, he would do it himself.

The next morning when he opened the store he had almost forgotten about the baby bird when he heard something chirping away in the sock. He walked over and touched it and up it popped with his mouth wide open, still very much alive and hungry for breakfast.

Surprised, Roy said, "Well, I'll be damned, you little son of a gun."

Now he didn't know what to do. This was the first hurt bird he had ever picked up that had survived the night, but this little thing was definitely alive and carrying on like something crazy. He went to the phone and called his veterinarian friend who lived in Lillian, a small town ten miles away.

"Hey, Bob, I've got this baby bird over here, I think it's been shot."

His friend was not surprised. "Those kids with the BB guns again?"

"Yeah."

"What kind of bird?"

"I don't know." Roy looked over at the bird. "He's kind of ugly . . . looks like some kind of mud hen. He's gray and brown, I think. Could be some kind of sparrow or mockingbird or—oh, I don't know what the thing is, but it looks like it's hungry. Should I feed it?"

"Sure, if you want to."

"What should I give it?"

"Give it the same thing its mother would, worms, bugs, a

little raw meat." He laughed. "After all, Roy, you're its mother now."

"Oh, great, that's just what I need."

"And Roy . . ."

"What?"

"Seriously, it probably won't live, but you might want to check and see if you can get those BBs out. If you don't, it will die for sure."

Roy went over, picked up the bird, and examined it and was surprised at how strong it was as it squawked and struggled to get free. He held out the wings and could see four BBs lodged right under its right wing close to the breast. He got a pair of tweezers. After having to dig around for a moment, he carefully lifted the BBs out one by one as the bird squawked and squirmed in discomfort. "Sorry, fella, I know that hurts, but I've got to do it, pal." He cleaned the spot with alcohol and put him back in the sock. Then he went over to the live bait section of the store and pulled out a large English red worm and a few grubs and took a razor blade and chopped up a nice breakfast for the bird, who proceeded to gobble the entire thing down and scream for more.

Roy continued to keep the bird in his office. He did not want anyone to know that he was hand feeding a baby bird three times a day and twice at night. He did not want to take the ribbing he would get from his friends. After all, he was a strapping six-foot-two man, and taking care of a baby bird might have seemed sissylike to them. As the days went by Roy tried not to become too attached. He knew how fragile they were and how hard it was to keep them alive. Every morning he half expected to find it dead, but each morning when he opened the door and heard the bird chirping away, he was secretly as pleased as punch and proud of the little bird for hanging on. He never saw anything want to live so bad in all his life, but he still didn't tell anyone. He planned to keep feeding it, and if it survived he would release it when it got old enough to fly.

Several weeks went by. The bird grew stronger and stronger and pretty soon was hopping all around the room, trying to flap his wings, but he could not seem to get off the ground. Roy noticed that each time he tried he kept falling over to the right. As this continued to happen, Roy began to worry about him. One day he put him in a shoe box and drove him over to his friend Bob's office.

The vet looked the bird over and said, "That wing is just too badly damaged, Roy. He's never going to be able to fly like he should, and he'll certainly never survive in the wild. We probably should just go ahead and put him to sleep."

Roy felt as if someone had kicked him in the stomach.

"Do you think so?" he asked, trying to hide his disappointment.

"Yes, I do. You shouldn't keep a wild bird like this inside. It would be cruel, really."

"Yeah, I guess you're right. I was just hoping he would make it."

"I can do it for you right now if you want me to."

"No, it's my bird. I'll do it."

"All right, that's up to you. I'll give you a bottle of chloroform. Just put it on some cotton and hold it over the beak; he won't feel anything. He'll just go to sleep."

Roy put the bird back in the shoe box and drove home, and every time he heard the bird jumping around in the box, trying to get out, he knew his friend was right. It would be cruel to keep a thing meant to be free closed up inside. That night he gave the bird as much food as he would eat, and around nine o'clock he sat down and took out the chloroform and a ball of cotton. He sat there, staring at the bird hopping around the room, jumping on everything in sight and pecking at the papers on his desk. He picked him up and examined him more closely under the light. It was then he noticed that some of his feathers were just beginning to turn from brown to red. Upon closer inspection he began to see the beginnings of a small crest forming on the back of his head and a black mask starting to form around his eyes. Then it hit him. This was a redbird! What a shame, this little guy was not going to get the chance to grow up and become the beautiful bird he was meant to be. Damn! All of a sudden Roy felt like going back in the woods and finding those two boys and cracking their heads together right then and there. Finally, after sitting and staring at the bird for a few more hours, Roy stood up and threw the bottle in the trash can. "Oh, the hell with it, buddy. See you in the morning." He turned the lights out and went home to bed. He could no more have put that bird to sleep than fly to the moon.

After that night Roy started keeping the bird in the front of the store with him. Eventually word got out that a baby redbird was living at the grocery store, and everybody who came in got a big kick out of it. At first the bird sat on the counter beside Roy and hopped all over the cash register, but as the weeks went by he was able to fly in short spurts, many times missing his mark, but he was getting stronger and more active every day, so much so that just in case Roy put a sign on the front door:

DON'T LET THE BIRD OUT!

At night when Roy locked up and went home he left the bird in the store so he could have the whole place to himself to roam as freely as he pleased, and roam he did. One morning Roy came in and found he had pecked his way through the top of a Cracker Jack box and was hopping around with a large Cracker Jack stuck on his beak. Roy removed it and laughed. The crazy bird must like Cracker Jacks! From then on he called the bird Jack. But as Roy found out later, Jack also liked Ritz crackers, potato chips, peanut butter, and vanilla wafers, and he especially liked chocolate-covered Buddy Bars. The little bird's appetite for sweets was relentless and not exclusive. He once pecked his way inside a large bag of marshmallows, and by the time Roy found him the next morning he was completely covered with powdered sugar. Eventually, everybody got used to buying things that had been pecked at by Jack first.

Everyone who went in the store got a big kick out of Jack except one person. Frances's younger sister, Mildred, made it clear that she did not like the bird and constantly complained to Frances. "I just know he walks all over everything," she said. "There's little peck holes in everything I pick up. He's just a pest. The last time I was up there he landed in my hair and messed up my hairdo and I had to go home and redo the whole thing."

Frances, who liked the bird, said, "Oh, Mildred, he never does that to me. I think he does it just to aggravate you because he knows you don't like him."

"Well, I don't care what you say, I don't think a place where you sell food is a sanitary place to have a bird, and I told Roy; I said, "It's a good thing we don't have health inspectors around here, or that bird would be against the law."

"Then why do you keep going up there if all you are going to do is fuss about that bird night and day?"

"Where else am I going to shop? It's not like we are living in the middle of twenty-five supermarkets. I don't have a choice; I'm stuck. I'm telling you that bird is a nuisance. You can't go up there without having it jump on you. He's a menace to society and that's all there is to it, and I don't want to talk about it anymore."

Frances said, "Well, I don't either. Just make out a list of what you want and I'll go and get your groceries for you so I don't have to listen to you complain."

Mildred looked at her, highly incensed. "And just how am I supposed to know what I want until I get there? That's why it's called shopping, Frances!" And with that she marched out the door.

Although Jack was a real handful and, without a doubt, could be a pest at times, he had grown from the tiny ugly mud hen he started out as in life into a beautiful scarlet-red and black-masked bird. With his lipstick-colored beak and shiny little reddish-brown eyes, he looked exactly like a red-bird should, but for some reason when Jack looked right at you, he seemed to have a silly smile on his face. One day Roy told Claude Underwood, "I swear that crazy bird has a sense of humor. Every morning I come in and he's done something else just to make me laugh. I came in yesterday, and the fool was hanging upside down swinging back and forth in the fishnet."

As time went on, Roy saw how smart the bird was and began to teach him tricks. Pretty soon he had Jack riding around on his finger and eating sunflower seeds out of his hand. His favorite game was when Roy would hide a sunflower seed in someone's pocket and Jack would go inside the pocket of the surprised person and come back out with it and fly over and hand it to Roy. Then Roy would give him ten more.

Jack clearly loved all the attention he was getting. When he saw himself in the mirror for the first time, he hunched down and bobbed his head at his reflection and tried to attack it, so Roy had to get rid of all the mirrors. Jack had made it known that as far as he was concerned the store was his territory, and he did not want another bird around. When the bird in the mirror had disappeared so quickly, Jack was convinced that he and he alone had run the intruder off, so he puffed up and strutted around and became bolder and bolder. Most of the time he rode on Roy's shoulder or on his hat, but he pretty much went where he pleased. Eventually that turned out to be dangerous.

One day, the postmistress Dottie Nivens's big fat orange cat named Henry sat outside the store all day, looking in the window at Jack fluttering around the cash register, just waiting with his tail swishing back and forth, his eyes never losing sight of the bird. He was determined to catch it one way or another. Around three-thirty, when the kids from Lost River got off the school bus from Lillian and started coming in for candy and cold drinks, the cat saw his chance. He lunged through the open screen door, and before anyone saw him he had leaped up on the counter and made a grab for Jack. Jack shot straight up in the air, just barely managing to escape Henry's claws, and landed on top of a shelf. Not to be deterred, Henry went tearing through the store right behind him, knocking racks of potato chips, cigarette cartons, cans and bottles on the floor as he chased Jack all around the room. And then everybody was running through the store chasing the cat and yelling. What a racket! It sounded like an earthquake. Poor Jack with his feathers flying and his crest standing straight up on his head, was hopping and leaping as fast and high as he could, with the cat continuing to miss him by mere inches. Jack somehow flapped and hopped his way all the way to the back of the store and landed on top of the meat counter, and the cat immediately sprang up after him and slid on all four feet all the way down the other end, knocking off bottles of ketchup, barbecue sauce, and horseradish in his wake. In the meantime, Jack, in one herculean effort, took a tremendous leap from the counter and flapped his wings long enough to land on the deer head, just out of the cat's reach. Roy was finally able to shoo the frustrated

Henry out the back door with a broom while Jack, with his feathers still all fluffed up, sat on his safe perch and fussed at the cat as he slunk out of the store.

Jack did not come down for the rest of the day and continued to fuss at Roy for letting the cat inside in the first place. The next day a new sign was added to the screen door:

DON'T LET THE BIRD OUT!
DON'T LET THE CAT IN!

River Route

❋

Back in Chicago, Oswald Campbell met with his insurance agent and signed over his death benefits and anything that might be left from his pension after he died to Helen, stipulating that she spend it on herself and not let those kids get ahold of it. He knew they would anyway, and it galled him, but there was nothing he could do about it. He closed out his bank account and had only a little money left. The train was the cheapest way to go, so he made his reservations. The next morning he phoned Mrs. Cleverdon to tell her when he would arrive and find out the new address to have his pension forwarded.

Frances said, "Send it in care of Miss Betty Kitchen, River Route Forty-eight."

"River Route? Is that the name of the street?"

"No, that's the river," she said.

"Oh. Well, I need a street address."

"That *is* the address, Mr. Campbell. We get our mail by boat."

Oswald was confused. "By boat? I don't have a boat."

She laughed. "You don't need a boat, the mailman brings it by boat."

"Where does he bring it?"

"Right to your dock."

He was still confused. "Don't I need a zip code or anything?"

"No, you don't need to fool with that, Mr. Campbell. Our mailman knows where everybody lives."

"I see . . . so it's just River Route Forty-eight?"

"That's right, I'm River Route Forty-six. My sister Mildred is Fifty-four." She wanted to mention Mildred to him as much as possible.

Oswald hung up and wondered what kind of place he was headed to. She had not mentioned they got their mail by boat, for God's sake. He was starting to have second thoughts but he had already given up his room and said goodbye to Helen on the phone, so he guessed he'd just go on as planned. After all, he had not told Mrs. Cleverdon he was a walking time bomb and would probably die on them. Besides, it was too late now. He couldn't afford to go anywhere else at this point. He only hoped the grocery store down there sold beer at least. There was no reason to stay sober too long. Not when you had nothing to look forward to anyway.

The moment Frances had hung up, she realized that she had forgotten to at least *warn* him about Betty Kitchen's mother, Miss Alma. She thought about calling him back but changed her mind. Maybe it was for the best; after all, she didn't want to scare him off before he even arrived. Besides, she had to run over to Mildred's house and help get ready for the meeting of the Mystic Order of the Royal Polka Dots Secret Society. Christmas was just around the corner and they had to make arrangements for the Mystery Tree. Every year in the dead of night, all the club members would get together and decorate the large cedar tree standing in front of the community hall. The Polka Dots did a lot of good works and they did all their good works in secret. The club motto was "To Toot One's Own Horn Is Unattractive." The only honorary male member of the Polka Dots was Butch Mannich, whom everybody called Stick, because he was six-four and weighed 128 pounds. He was Sybil Underwood's twenty-six-year-old nephew and a good soul who did anything the ladies needed. He supplied the ladder and was the only one tall enough to hang the lights on the top of the tree each year.

When Frances walked in the house for the meeting, Mildred was lounging on the couch in the living room wearing a bright floral Hawaiian muumuu and reading the new book she had just borrowed from the bookmobile entitled *Romance on the Bayou: A Steamy Story of Forbidden Love Deep in the Bayou Country of Louisiana*. When Frances saw what her sister was reading, she said, "Oh, for God's sake, Mildred, when are you going to stop reading all that trash?" Mildred closed the book, laid it on the coffee table, and answered, "When are you going to stop eating all that candy?"

Frances never could get the best of Mildred. As girls they had both attended one of the finest finishing schools in Chattanooga, but even then Mildred had always been somewhat of a maverick. She had been the first girl in town to ever wear a pants suit inside the Chattanooga Country Club: too independent, long before it was fashionable. Frances thought it was probably the reason that the boy Mildred had been engaged to ran off and married someone else. It could also account for the fact that you never knew what color Mildred's hair was going to be the next time you saw her. She dyed her hair on a whim and according to how she felt from day to day. Today it was some sort of plaid. Frances hoped that by the time Mr. Campbell arrived it would be at least close to the color of something natural. But she did not say anything. If Mildred knew she was trying to fix her up with a man she would do something crazy for sure. Frances worried about her sister. Mildred had retired after twenty-five years of work, had good insurance, owned her own home, and had plenty of friends, but she did not seem happy. Frances worried that Mildred was getting bitter as she aged and turning into an old curmudgeon right before her eyes. It was one of the many reasons that Frances was holding such high hopes for Mr. Campbell. Mildred needed to get over that boy who had left her, and move on with her life before it was too late.

Dreamy Alabama

As the doctor had suggested, Oswald tied up all loose ends and settled his estate, a task that took him no more than five minutes. It consisted of throwing away three pairs of old shoes and giving away one of his two overcoats. He packed the one baseball he had caught at a game and all his other belongings into a single suitcase. That night a few of his friends from AA took him out for a farewell cup of coffee. He told them he would most probably be back in the spring. No point in getting anyone upset.

The next morning he took a cab to the L&N railroad station at LaSalle Street. He found his seat, and the train pulled out of the station at 12:45 P.M. As the familiar buildings passed by his window, he knew he was seeing Chicago for the last time and he thought about going to the club car for a drink right then and there, but the "One Day at a Time" chip his friends had given him last night was still in his pocket. He felt he should probably wait until they got farther away from Chicago and his AA group, so he just sat and looked out the window and soon became preoccupied with the scenery passing by. As they traveled south, through Cincinnati and Louisville to Nashville, the landscape slowly began to change. The deeper south they went, the more the brown land started to turn a different color, and by the time he woke up the next morning the barren black trees that lined the tracks the day before had been replaced with thick evergreens and tall pines. He had gone to sleep in one world and awakened in another. Overnight, the gray gloomy winter sky had turned a bright blue with huge white cumulus clouds so big that Oswald's first thought was, You've got to be kidding!

When they reached Mobile late that afternoon, the moment he stepped off the train, a tall thin man with a small head, who looked to Oswald exactly like a praying mantis wearing a baseball cap, stepped up. "Are you Mr. Campbell?" He said he was, and the man took his bag and said, "Welcome to Alabama! I'm Butch Mannich, but you can call me Stick; everybody else does." As they walked along he added, "Yeah, I'm so skinny that when I was a child my parents wouldn't let me have a dog because it would keep burying me in the yard." Then he laughed uproariously at his own joke.

When they came out of the station, the warm air of Mobile was moist and fragrant and a surprise to Oswald. To see it from the train was one thing; to feel it and smell it was another. Their mode of transportation was a truck that Butch apologized for. "It ain't pretty, but it'll get us there." Butch was a cheery soul and talked the entire hour and a half it took them to drive down to Lost River. He handed Mr. Campbell his business card, which had a drawing of a big eye in the middle. Underneath was printed:

BUTCH (STICK) MANNICH
PRIVATE INVESTIGATOR
AND PROCESS SERVER

Oswald was surprised. "Is there a lot of call for private detective work here?"

"No, not yet," said Butch, a little disappointed. "But I'm available, ready, willing, and able, just in case." It was just getting dark as they went over the long Mobile Bay causeway, and they were able to see the last of the sunset. There was nothing but miles of water on both sides and the sun that was now dipping into the bay was so large and orange it almost scared Oswald.

"Is that normal?" he asked Butch.

Butch glanced out the window. "Yeah, we get a nice sunset most of the time."

By the time they turned off the highway to Lost River it was pitch-black outside. "There's the store," said Butch, as they whizzed by. Oswald looked out but saw nothing. They drove about a block and stopped in front of a large house. "Here we are, safe and sound."

Oswald took out his wallet. "What do I owe you?"

Butch's reaction was one of genuine surprise. "Why, you don't owe me a thing, Mr. Campbell."

Just as Oswald reached out to knock on the door, it was flung open by a huge woman, standing at least six feet tall. "Come on in!" she said, in a booming voice, and snatched his suitcase away from him before he could stop her. "I'm Betty Kitchen, glad to have you." She grabbed his hand, shook it, and almost broke it. "Breakfast is at seven, lunch at twelve, and dinner at six. And if you see a little funny-looking woman spooking around don't let it bother you; it's only Mother. She doesn't know where she is half the time, so if she wanders in your room just chase her out. Let me show you around."

The house had a long hallway down the middle, and he trailed behind her. She walked to the back of the house, pointing as she went: "Living room, dining room, and this is the kitchen." She switched the lights on and then off. She turned around, headed back to the front, and pointed to a small door under the stairs. "And this is where I sleep," she said. She opened the door, and inside was a closet just big enough for a single bed. "I like to be close to the kitchen where I can keep an eye on Mother. It's small but I like it; it reminds me of being on a train. I always slept well on a train, and I was on a lot of them in my day. Come on upstairs. I'll show you your room."

As he followed her up the stairs, Oswald felt that there

was something familiar about her manner and her way of speaking. It was almost as if he had met her before, but he was sure he had not; she was a person you would not forget.

"Mother used to be a baker in Milwaukee, specialized in petits fours and fancy cakes, but that was before she slipped on a cigar wrapper." She turned around and looked at him. "You don't smoke cigars, do you?"

Oswald quickly said no. Even if he had, from the tone of her voice he would have quit on the spot. "No, I have emphysema; that's why I'm here. For my health."

She sighed. "Yes, we get a lot of that. Most of the people that come down here have something or another the matter with them . . . but not me. I'm as healthy as a horse." That was evident as they walked into his room and she heaved his suitcase onto the bed with one arm. "Well, here it is, the sunniest room in the house. It used to be mine before I moved downstairs. I hope you like it."

He looked around and saw it was a spacious open room with yellow floral wallpaper and a small yellow sofa in the corner. The brown spindle bed was made up with a crisp white chenille spread, and above it hung a framed embroidered plaque that read HOME SWEET HOME.

She pointed at two doors. "Closet to the left, bathroom on the right, and if you need anything just holler. If not, see you at oh-seven-hundred."

He went in the bathroom and was surprised to see it was almost as big as the bedroom, with a green sink and tub. Another surprise: It had a window. He had never seen a bathroom with a window. He was so tired he just wanted to go lie down, but he felt grimy from the train ride so he took a bath and put his pajamas on and got into the soft bed with its clean sweet-smelling sheets. He lay there and looked around his new room once more before he turned off his lamp and fell into a deep peaceful sleep.

After Oswald had gone upstairs to bed, the phone rang. It was Frances calling Betty to inquire if Mr. Campbell had arrived safe and sound. After she was told yes, Frances's next question was, "Well?"

Betty laughed. "Well . . . he's a cute little man, with crinkly blue eyes and red hair. He sort of looks like an elf."

Frances said, "An elf?"

"Yes, but a nice elf."

Somewhat disappointed that Mr. Campbell was not as handsome as she had hoped for—Mildred was so picky where men were concerned—nonetheless Frances looked on the bright side. An elf, she thought. Oh, well, it *is* close to Christmas. Maybe it was some kind of sign. After all, hope springs eternal.

Oswald opened his eyes at six-thirty the next morning to a room filled with sunlight and with the sound of those same birds chirping he had heard over the phone, only twice as loud. To a man used to waking up for the past eight years in a dark hotel room around nine-thirty or ten to the sounds of traffic, this was unsettling. He tried to go back to sleep but the birds were relentless and he started coughing, so he got up. As he was dressing, he noticed an advertisement on the wall that Betty Kitchen had obviously cut out of a magazine. It was a picture of a ladies' dressing table and alongside a compact, lipstick, comb, and a pack of Lucky Strike Green cigarettes was a WAC dress uniform hat. The caption underneath said SHE MAY BE A WAC—BUT SHE'S A WOMAN TOO!

Then it dawned on him. That's what had seemed so familiar. The old gal must have been in the service, probably as an army nurse. God knows he had been around enough army nurses, in and out of so many VA hospitals. He had even married one, for God's sake. Downstairs in the kitchen, while eating a breakfast of eggs, biscuits, grits, and ham, he found out he was right. Not only had she been an army nurse, she was a retired lieutenant colonel, supervisor of nurses, and had run several big hospitals in the Philippines.

He informed her that he had been in the army as well.

She looked up. "Somehow, Mr. Campbell, I wouldn't have pegged you for a military man."

He laughed. "Neither did they. I never got out of Illinois."

"Ah, that's too bad."

"Yeah, I guess, but I don't have any complaints. I got a nice medical discharge and went to school, thanks to the old U S of A Army."

About that time, the mother, who was half as tall as her daughter and looked like a dried-up little apple doll, appeared in the doorway. She ignored Oswald and seemed highly agitated. "Betty, the elephants are out in the yard again. Go see what they want."

"Yes, Mother," said Betty. "I'll go find out in just a minute. Go on back upstairs now."

"Well, hurry up. They're stepping all over my camellia bushes."

After she left, Betty turned to him. "See what I mean? She thinks she sees all kinds of things out in the yard. Last week it was flying turtles." She walked over and picked up his dishes. "I'm not sure if it was that fall she took a while ago or just her age; she's older than God." She sighed. "But that's the Kitchen curse, longevity—on both sides. How about yourself, Mr. Campbell? Do you have longevity in your family?"

Not having any information about his real family, but considering his own current condition, he said, "I sincerely doubt it."

After breakfast, Oswald went back to his room and finished unpacking, and a few minutes later he heard Betty call up the stairs, "Yoo-hoo! Mr. Campbell! You have a visitor!"

When he came out, a pretty woman in a white blouse and a blue skirt looked up and said, "Good morning!" He recognized the voice at once and went downstairs to meet Frances Cleverdon. Although her hair was white, he was surprised to see that up close she had a youthful-looking face, with blue eyes and a lovely smile. She handed him a large welcome basket filled with pecans, a cranberry cream-cheese coffee cake, little satsuma oranges, and several jars of something. "I hope you like jelly," she said. "I made you some green pepper and scuppernong jelly."

"I do," he said, wondering what in hell a scuppernong was.

"Well, I won't stay, I know you must be busy. I just wanted to run in for a second and say hello, but as soon as you get settled in and feel like it, I want you to come over for dinner."

"Well, thank you, Mrs. Cleverdon, I will," he said.

As she got to the door, she turned and asked if he had been down to the store and met Roy yet. "Not yet," he said.

"No?" She smiled as if she knew a secret. "You need to go and see what's down there. I think you're in for a treat."

After she left, Oswald guessed he should take a walk and at least see the place, and he asked Betty how to find the store. She instructed him to go out the front door, take a left, and it was four houses past the post office at the end of the street.

When he opened the door and walked out onto the porch, the temperature was the same outside as it was inside. He still could not believe how warm it was. Just two days ago he was in an overcoat and icy rain, and today the sun was shining and he was in a short-sleeve shirt. He went out, took a left, and saw what he had not been able to see last night.

The street was lined on both sides by fat oak trees, with long gray Spanish moss hanging from each one. The limbs of the oaks were so large that they met in the middle and formed a canopy of shade in each direction for as far as he could see. The houses he passed on both sides of the street were neat little well-kept bungalows, and in every yard the bushes were full of large red flowers that looked like roses. As he walked along toward the store, the fattest squirrels he had ever seen ran up and down the trees. He could hear birds chirping and rustling around in the bushes, but the undergrowth of shrubs and palms was so thick he couldn't see them. He soon passed a white house with two front doors and an orange cat sitting on the steps. One side of the house had POST OFFICE written above the door.

As he went by, the door opened and a thin willowy woman with stick-straight bangs came out and waved at him. "Hello, Mr. Campbell. Glad you're here!"

He waved back, although he had no idea who she was or how she knew his name. When he got to the end of the street he saw a redbrick grocery store building with two gas pumps in front and went in. A clean-cut man with brown hair, wearing khaki pants and a plaid shirt, was at the cash register.

"Are you Roy?" Oswald asked.

"Yes, sir," the man said, "and you must be Mr. Campbell. How do you do." He reached over and shook his hand.

"How did you know who I was?"

Roy chuckled. "From the ladies, Mr. Campbell. They've all been waiting on you. You don't know how happy I am you are here."

"Really?"

"Oh, yeah, now they have another single man to pester to get married besides me."

Oswald put his hands up. "Oh, Lord, they don't want me."

"Don't kid yourself, Mr. Campbell. If you're still breathing they want you."

"Well"—Oswald laughed—"I'm still breathing, at least for the moment."

"Now that you're here we have to stick together and not let any of those gals catch us off guard. Unless, of course, you're in the market for a wife."

"Noooo, not me," said Oswald. "I've already made one poor woman miserable. That's enough."

Roy liked this little guy right away. "Come on back to the office and let me get you a cup of coffee, and I'll introduce you to my partner."

As they walked back, Roy whistled and called out, "Hey, Jack!"

Jack, who had been busy all morning running up and down the round plastic bird wheel with bells that Roy had ordered through the mail, heard the whistle, flew out of the office, and landed on Roy's finger.

Oswald stopped dead in his tracks. "Whoa. What's that?"

"This is Jack, my partner," Roy said, looking at the bird. "He really owns the place. I just run it for him."

"My God," said Oswald, still amazed at what he saw. "That's a cardinal, isn't it?"

Roy held Jack away from him so he could not hear and confided, "Yes, officially he's a cardinal, but we don't tell him that; we just tell him he's just a plain old redbird. He's too big for his britches as it is." Then he spoke to the bird. "Hey, Jack, tell the man where you live."

The bird cocked his head and Oswald swore the bird chirped with the same southern accent Roy had. It sounded exactly like he was saying, "Rite cheer! . . . Rite cheer! . . . Rite cheer!"

When Roy was busy waiting on some customers, Oswald wandered around the store, examining the mounted fish and stuffed animals that covered the walls. They looked almost alive. The red fox seemed so real Oswald jumped when he first saw him up on the counter. He later remarked to Roy, "That's really nice stuff you have here. For a second I thought that damn fox was alive. And those fish up there are really great."

Roy glanced up at them. "Yeah, I guess so. My uncle put them up there. He won most of them in a poker game."

"Who did them, somebody local?"

"Yeah, Julian LaPonde, an old Creole, lives across the river."

"A Creole? What's that? Are they Indians?"

Roy shook his head. "Who knows what they are—they claim to be French, Spanish, Indian, you name it." He indicated the mounted animals. "And in that guy's case, I'm sure there's a little weasel thrown in." He changed the subject. "All those fish you see up there were caught by our mailman, Claude Underwood. That speckled trout is a record holder. Do you fish? 'Cause if you do, he's the man to see."

"No," Oswald admitted, "I'm not much of a fisherman, or a hunter either, I'm afraid." He wouldn't have known a speckled trout from a mullet.

Oswald had spent about an hour roaming around the store and watching that crazy redbird of Roy's run around on his wheel when the phone rang. Roy put the phone down and called out, "Hey, Mr. Campbell, that was Betty. She said your lunch is ready."

Oswald looked at his watch. It was exactly twelve o'clock, on the dot. "Well, I guess I'd better go."

"Yep, you don't want to get her riled. Hey, by the way, have you met the mother?"

"Oh, yes," Oswald said, rolling his eyes.

"They say she's harmless, but I'd lock my door at night if I were you."

"Really? Do you think she's dangerous?"

"Well," said Roy, looking up at the ceiling, "far be it from me to spread rumors, but we don't know what happened to the daddy, now, do we?" By the look on Oswald's face, Roy could tell he was going to have a lot of fun kidding around with him. He would believe anything he told him.

As he left the store and headed back, Oswald realized he had been so busy looking at Jack and talking he forgot to notice if the store sold beer.

Oh, well, there was always tomorrow.

When he got home he asked Betty about the woman with the bangs at the post office who had waved at him, twice now. "Oh, that's Dottie Nivens, our postmistress. We got her from an ad we put in *The New York Times*. We were afraid when she got here that she'd see how small we were and leave, but she stayed and we sure are glad. She gives one wingding of a party and makes a mean highball; not only that, she can jitterbug like nobody's business." Oswald wondered if the postmistress might be a little off her rocker as well, to leave New York City for this place.

Around twelve-thirty, while Oswald was having his lunch, Mildred, who had been in Mobile all morning buying Christmas decorations for the Mystery Tree with money from the Polka Dots' jingle-bell fund, called Frances the minute she got home and said, "Well?"

Frances, trying to be tactful, said, "Well . . . he's a cute little man, with cute little teeth, and of course he has that funny accent and . . ."

"And what?"

Frances laughed in spite of herself. "He looks like an elf."

"Good Lord."

"But a nice elf," she quickly added. Mildred was always one to make snap judgments, and Frances did not want her to make up her mind about Oswald before she even met him. She could be so cantankerous.

As a rule, Oswald rarely ate three whole meals in one day, but on his first day, in Lost River, after a huge breakfast, for lunch he ate baked chicken, a bowl of big fat lima beans, mashed potatoes, three pieces of corn bread and honey with real butter (not the whipped margarine spread he usually bought), and two pieces of homemade red velvet cake. He had not had real home cooking since he had been married to Helen and since the divorce he had been eating out at greasy spoons or off a hot plate in his room. That night at dinner he finished everything on his plate, plus two servings of banana pudding, which pleased Betty no end. She liked a man with a big appetite.

He was still somewhat tired and weak from the trip and went up to bed right after dinner. As he reached the top of the stairs, the mother, who had no teeth, poked her head out of her room and yelled, "Have the troops been fed yet?"

He did not know what to say so he said, "I think so."

"Fine," she said, and slammed her door.

Oh dear, thought Oswald. And even though he suspected that Roy had been kidding around with him earlier, he did lock his door that night, just in case.

The next morning the birds woke him up once more, but he felt rested and hungry again. While eating another big breakfast, he asked what had brought Betty and her mother all the way from Milwaukee to Lost River, Alabama.

Betty threw four more pieces of bacon into the pan. "Well, my friend Elizabeth Shivers, who at the time worked for the Red Cross, was sent here to help out after the big hurricane, and when she got here she just fell in love with the area and moved down, and when I came to visit her, I liked it too so I moved here myself." She flipped the bacon over and mused. "You know, it's a funny thing, Mr. Campbell, once people find this place, they don't seem to ever want to leave."

"Really? How long have you lived here?"

Betty said, "About fourteen years now. We moved down right after Daddy died."

At the mention of the father, Oswald tried to sound as casual as possible. "Ah . . . I see. And what did your father die of, if I may ask?"

"Will you eat some more eggs if I fix them?" she asked.

"Sure," he said.

She went over to the icebox and removed two more eggs, cracked them and put them in the frying pan, and then said, "Well, to answer your question, we're really not sure what Daddy died of. He was twenty-two years older than Mother at the time, which would have put him right at a hundred and three. I suppose it could have been old age, but with the Kitchens you never know. All I know is that it was a shock to us all when it happened."

Oswald felt better. Obviously the old man's exit from the world had not been by violent means as Roy had suggested, but at age 103, just how much of a shock could it have been?

The following morning when he went downstairs, Betty Kitchen looked at him and said, "That's quite a cough you have there, Mr. Campbell. Are you sure you're all right?"

Oswald quickly downplayed it. "Oh, yeah. . . . I think I may have caught a little cold coming down, but I feel fine." He realized he would have to cough quieter and try not to let her hear him from now on.

After breakfast he thought he would take another walk and asked Betty where the river was. "Right out the kitchen door," she said.

Oswald walked out the back of the house into a long yard filled with the tallest pine, evergreen, and cedar trees he had ever seen. He figured some must have been at least six or eight stories high. As he walked toward the river, the fresh early morning air reminded him of the smell of the places around Chicago where they sold Christmas trees each year.

He followed a small path that had been cut through the thick underbrush, filled with pine needles and pinecones the size of pineapples, until he came to a wooden dock and the river. He was amazed at what he saw. The bottom of the river was sandy and the water was as clear as gin—and he should know. He walked out onto the dock, looked down, and could see small silver fish and a few larger ones swimming around in the river. Unlike Lake Michigan, this water was as calm as glass.

As he stood there looking, huge pelicans flapped down the river not more than four feet away from him, flying not more than two inches off the water. What a sight! He had seen pictures of them in magazines and had always thought they were all gray. He was surprised to see that in person they were many colors, pink and blue and orange, with yellow eyes and fuzzy white feathers on their heads. A few minutes later they flew off and then came back and crashed with a loud splash and floated around with their long beaks in the water. He had to laugh. If they had been wearing glasses they would have looked just like people. The only other birds he had ever seen this close up were a few pigeons that had landed on his windowsill at the hotel.

The river was not very wide, and he could see the wooden docks of the houses on the other side. Each one had a mailbox, including the one he was on; he looked down and saw the number 48 on it, as Frances had said. So far, everything he had been told or had read about Lost River in that old hotel brochure was true. Old Horace P. Dunlap had not been lying after all. Who would have guessed Oswald would now be living in one of those dandy little bungalows that old Horace had talked about. From that day just a month ago, when he was headed for the doctor's office, to today, his life had taken a 180-degree turn. Everything was upside down. Even the seasons were flipped. In his wildest dreams, Oswald could never have imagined a month ago that he would wind up in this strange place, with all these strange people. As far as he was concerned, he might just as well have been shot out of a cannon and landed on another planet.

The next day he did not know what to do with himself, so after breakfast he asked Betty what time the mail came. She said anywhere between ten and eleven, so he went down to the dock and waited. At about ten-forty-five a small boat with a motor came around the bend. As Oswald watched, the man in the boat went from mailbox to mailbox, opening the lid and skillfully throwing the mail in while the boat slid by. He was a stocky man in a jacket and a cap who looked to be about sixty-five or seventy years of age. When he saw Oswald, he pulled up and turned off his motor.

"Hello, there. You must be Mr. Campbell. I'm Claude Underwood. How are you?"

"I'm fine, happy to meet you," said Oswald.

Claude handed him a bundle of mail wrapped in a rubber band. "How long have you been here?"

"Just a few days."

"Well, I'm sure the ladies are glad you're here."

"Yeah, it seems they are," Oswald said. "Uh, say, Mr. Underwood, I'm curious about this river. How big is it?"

"About five or six miles long. This is the narrow part you're on now. The wide part is back that way."

"How do you get to it?"

"Do you want to take a ride with me sometime? I'd be happy to show it to you."

"Really? I sure would. When?"

"We can go tomorrow, if you like. Just meet me at the post office around nine-thirty and bring a jacket. It gets cold out there."

Walking back home, Oswald thought it was pretty funny that Mr. Underwood would worry about him getting cold anywhere down here. It might say December on the calendar, but the weather felt just like a Chicago spring and the beginning of baseball season to him.

The next morning, as Oswald walked up to the porch of the post office, a striking-looking woman wearing a lime-green pants suit came out of the other side of the house. The minute she saw Oswald she almost laughed out loud. Frances had described him perfectly. She walked over and said, "I know who you are. I'm Mildred, Frances's sister, so be prepared. She's already planning a dinner party, so you might as well give up and come on and get it over with." Mildred chuckled to herself all the way down the stairs. Oswald thought she was certainly an attractive, saucy woman, very different from her sister. She had a pretty face like Frances, but he had never seen hair that color in his life.

He went inside the post office and met Dottie Nivens, the woman who had waved to him the first morning. She shook his hand and did an odd little half curtsy and said in a deep voice, "Welcome, stranger, to our fair community." She could not have been friendlier. Oswald noted that if she had not had a large space between her two front teeth and such straight hair she could be a dead ringer for one of Helen's sisters.

He walked through the door and found Claude in the back of the post office, sorting the last of the mail and putting it in bundles. As soon as Claude finished he put it on a small cart with wheels and they walked to his truck and drove a few blocks down a dirt road to an old wooden boathouse. "This is where I keep my boat," he said. "I used to keep it behind the store, but those redneck boys that

moved here shot it up so bad I had to bring it up here."
When they got in the boat Oswald looked around for a life
jacket but did not see one. When he asked Claude where it
was, Claude looked at him like he thought he was kidding. "A
life jacket?"

"Yes. I hate to admit it, but I can't swim."

Claude dismissed his concern. "You don't need a life
jacket. Hell, if you do fall in, the alligators will eat you before
you drown." With that, he started the motor and they were
off, headed up the river. Oswald hoped he was kidding but
was careful not to put his hands in the water just in case he
wasn't. As they rounded the bend and went under the bridge
and on out the length and breadth of the river was amazing.
It was extremely wide in the middle, with houses up and
down on both sides. As they went farther north, delivering
the mail at every dock, Claude maneuvered the boat inside
tiny inlets where the water in some spots could not have
been more than six or seven inches deep, opening mailboxes
of all sizes, tall and low, and while the boat was moving past
them, he never missed a beat or a mailbox.

Oswald was impressed. "Have you ever missed?"

"Not yet," Claude said, as he threw another bundle of
mail in a mailbox. "But I'm sure the day will come."

On some of the docks people were waiting and said hello,
and on some dogs ran out barking and Claude reached in his
pocket and threw them a Milk-Bone.

"Have you ever been bitten?"

"Not yet."

About an hour later, they turned around and headed back

the way they came. Oswald noticed that Claude did not deliver mail on the other side of the river. When he asked him about it, Claude said, "No, I don't go over to that side anymore. I used to but that's where the Creoles live. They have their own mailman now."

Oswald looked across and asked, "Is that where that Julian LaPonde lives?"

"How do you know about Julian LaPonde?" Claude said.

"Roy told me he mounted all those fish and animals at the store."

"Huh," said Claude, lighting his pipe. "I'm surprised he even mentioned him." But he did not say why he was surprised.

"Well, he sure is a good taxidermist, but I got the impression that Roy doesn't think much of him as a person."

"No, he doesn't," said Claude, and left it at that.

They had been out on the river about two and a half hours when they returned to the boathouse. Oswald was exhausted and as he got out of the boat his legs were shaky. He needed a nap. All that fresh air was too much for one day. He asked Claude what he did after he got off from work every day.

Claude's eyes lit up. "Ah. Then I go fishing."

Dinner at Eight

OSWALD HAD BEEN unable to avoid running into Frances Cleverdon, since she lived right next door, and finally agreed to have dinner at her house the next week. After all, he could not hurt her feelings; she had been responsible for his coming to Lost River in the first place.

Frances's house was a neat blue bungalow. It was very nice inside as well, with a completely pink kitchen—pink stove, icebox, and sink—right down to the pink-and-white tiles on the floor. Frances showed him her prize gravy boat collection, and Mildred, whose hair to Frances's dismay was now the color of root beer, remarked, "I'll never understand why anybody in their right mind would collect gravy boats." Although Oswald had not wanted to go that night, the food was delicious, especially the macaroni and cheese, and after dinner they played a good game of gin rummy.

However, much to her sister's disappointment, Mildred

did *nothing* to help things along in the romance department. All she did all night was crab and complain about everything under the sun, including how much she hated that bird Roy had up at the store, and in between her complaints about Jack she managed to tell several blue jokes that Oswald laughed at. Frances smiled, but was secretly horrified and wanted to strangle her sister. How was she ever going to get a man? A perfectly good dinner wasted, as far as she was concerned.

The next day, true to form, Mildred was back down at the store fussing at Jack, who fluttered around her head. She said, "You've heard about the four-and-twenty blackbirds baked in a pie? Well, mister, I'm going to bake one big redbird pie if you don't quit pestering me!"

Roy laughed. "You better watch out, boy, or she'll have you for dinner one day."

Despite all her complaints Roy liked Mildred a lot. He got a kick out of her and how she was always dyeing her hair different colors. Besides, as Oswald had just found out, she sure could tell a joke.

After just a few weeks, Oswald found that he was beginning to get into a routine. Every morning after breakfast he would go to the store, hang around awhile, and then go down to the dock to smoke cigarettes and wait for Claude Underwood to come by with the mail. He didn't dare smoke in Betty's house. As he sat waiting, sometimes for an hour or two, he saw that the river was full of things he had never seen before. All kinds of large birds, loons and egrets, geese and ducks of different kinds, swam up and down the river. A few swam in pairs but most were in flocks that took off together and landed in the water together.

One day while he was waiting, Oswald noticed a black duck out in the river all by himself and he wondered about it. Why did this one lone duck not swim with a mate or with the flock? Did the duck even know he was supposed to be with the others? What had caused that duck to separate from the rest? The more he watched it out there, swimming around, the sadder it made him. He realized he was just like that duck. All his life he had been out in the world alone while the rest of the world swam by, happy in their own flock, knowing who they were and where they belonged.

Oswald was feeling a little sad these days anyway. Christmas was just around the corner, and Betty was already playing Christmas carols on the radio. He supposed it put some people in a good mood, but all those "I'll be home for Christmas" and "There's no place like home for the holidays" songs just made him feel lousy. For him, Christmas had always been a season with everything set up just to break your heart. As a kid, all he had ever gotten were cheap toys handed out by a bunch of once-a-year do-gooders, toys that by the next day were either broken or stolen. Even as an adult, when he had spent the holidays with Helen's family, it just made him feel more of an outsider than ever. Each year was the same; all her brothers and sisters would sit around, looking at home movies and reminiscing about their wonderful childhood Christmases. No, Christmas for him had always been like someone shining a great big spotlight down in that dark empty space inside him, and the only way he had been able to handle it in the past was to get drunk. A hangover was nothing compared to feeling all alone in a roomful of people. This year he would be spending what could turn out to be his very last Christmas on the river with the birds and ducks. That, he guessed, was better than nothing.

The next time Oswald went in the store he found himself eyeing the cartons of beer stacked over in the corner and was almost headed over there but when Betty Kitchen came in, he decided to stick to his original plan and asked Roy if there was some kind of book he could get so he could try and figure out what kinds of birds and ducks he was looking at. Roy said, "Come on back in the office with me, I think I have something for you." The office was a mess, with stacks of papers and old ledgers and Jack's toys everywhere, but Roy rummaged through a pile on the floor and handed Oswald an old ripped paperback copy of *Birds of Alabama: A Birdwatcher's Guide*.

"May I borrow this?" asked Oswald.

"Oh hell, you can have it. I don't need it."

Oswald took the book up to his room. While he was thumbing through it, he found an old postcard from 1932 that described Lost River as

A magical spot, invisible from the highway by reason of its location in masses of shade trees, along the winding banks of the river, where it lies in a setting of flowers and foliage and songbirds, like a dream of beauty ready for the brush and canvas of the landscape painter.

That's the damn truth, he thought. It *would* be a great place for a painter or a birdwatcher. Then it dawned on him that he, Oswald T. Campbell, was actually studying to become a birdwatcher. Birdwatching was certainly not one of the things he would ever have put on his THINGS TO DO list. As a matter of fact, he had never even had a THINGS TO DO list, and now it was almost too late to do anything. Oh, well, he thought, live and learn. Better late than never. And then he wondered why in the hell he was thinking in clichés.

From that day on, after he had gone down and had a cup of coffee with Roy and shot the breeze with him for a while, he would take his birdwatcher's guide and go down to the river and try to match the birds he was seeing with the pictures in the book. So far he had identified a great blue heron that cracked him up by the way it walked. It picked its feet up and down as if it were stepping in molasses. He had seen cranes, a snowy egret, mallards, wood ducks, and a belted kingfisher, and by December 19 he had already identified his first pileated woodpecker. He was hoping to see an osprey one of these days.

On the morning of December 22, when Oswald walked over to the store for coffee with Roy, he saw that the huge cedar tree outside the community hall had been decorated with hundreds of Christmas ornaments and silver and gold tinsel. When he went in the store, he asked Roy who had done it. Roy shook his head.

"We don't know. Every Christmas it happens overnight and nobody knows who did it, but I have my theories. I think it's that bunch of crazy women that do it."

"Who?"

"Oh, Frances, Mildred, and Dottie; probably Betty Kitchen is in on it, too. I can't prove it but I'll tell you this: Anytime you see all of them wearing polka dots on the same day, watch out."

Just then the door opened and Frances Cleverdon walked in, looking sunny and cheerful. "Well, good morning, Mr. Campbell," she said with a smile. "How are you getting along?"

"Oh, fine," he said.

"I hope you're coming to the annual Christmas Eve Dinner at the community hall. Roy's coming, aren't you? We're going to have a lot of good food."

Roy said, "I'll be there. Hey, Frances, have you seen the tree yet?" He winked at Oswald as she turned around and looked across the street.

"Well, for heaven's sake!" she said, feigning surprise. "When did that happen?"

"Last night."

Frances turned to Oswald. "Last year the same exact thing happened on the twenty-third. I just wish I knew who was doing it."

"Yeah, me too," said Roy. "I was just telling Mr. Campbell, it's a mystery, all right."

Walking back home Frances was so pleased. The Polka Dots had done it again! Frances and Betty Kitchen had started the club twelve years ago and the founding members, after herself and Betty, were Sybil Underwood and, later, Dottie Nivens and Mildred. They had named themselves after a Mardi Gras group over in Mobile because they wanted to have fun as well as do good works. And thanks to Dottie Nivens and her amazing ability to make delicious highballs, which they drank out of polka-dotted martini glasses after every meeting, they did have fun. When their friend Elizabeth Shivers over in Lillian heard about it she started another secret society, the Mystic Order of the Royal Dotted Swiss. They also did a lot of good work, but Frances was convinced that they could never top the Mystery Tree caper.

The Christmas Dinner

OSWALD HAD ALWAYS been shy and was no good at social events. Although it was the last thing on earth he wanted to do, it seemed that on Christmas Eve he had no choice but to put on his one blue suit and tie and go with Betty and her mother to the Dinner and Tree Lighting Ceremony at the community hall. It was made clear to him over and over that everyone was expecting him. So at five-thirty he and Betty Kitchen and her mother, Miss Alma, wearing three giant red camellias in her hair, strolled down the street. It was still about 69 degrees outside and hard for Oswald to believe it was really December twenty-fourth. When they arrived, the hall was already packed with people, and the minute they saw Oswald everyone made a point to come up and shake his hand and welcome him to the area. After about thirty minutes of being pulled around the room like a wooden toy, Oswald was thrilled to see Roy Grimmitt come in, looking as uncomfortable in his blue suit and tie as Oswald felt in his. At around six-thirty, after a prayer was said, it was time to eat and someone called out, "Let Mr. Campbell start the line."

Oswald was handed a plate and pushed to the long table, full of more food than he had ever seen: fried chicken, ham, turkey, roast beef, pork chops, chicken and dumplings, and every kind of vegetables, pies, and cakes you can imagine. At the end sat two huge round cut-glass punch bowls of thick, delicious-smelling eggnog. One was labeled LEADED, the other bowl said UNLEADED. Oswald hesitated for a moment and seriously thought about it, but at the last second went for the unleaded. He did not want to get drunk and make a fool out of himself and embarrass Frances. After all, everyone knew she was responsible for getting him there. The long tables with the white tablecloths had centerpieces decorated with sprigs of fresh holly and pinecones that had been dipped in either shellac or gold or silver paint and sprinkled with glitter. On the pine walls, huge red paper bells hung from twisted red and green crepe paper that wrapped around the room, interspersed with pictures of the nativity. Oswald sat next to Betty's mother and Betty sat on the other side and about halfway through dinner the old lady punched him in the ribs and said, "Ask me what time it is."

"OK," he said. "What time is it?"

"Half past kissing time; time to kiss again!" she said, then screamed with laughter and continued to repeat it over and over until Betty had to get up and take her home. It seems Miss Alma had gotten into the leaded eggnog.

Oswald had just dropped whipped cream from the sweet potato pie all down the front of his tie when Dottie Nivens, the president of the association, made an announcement. "Before we start the program this evening, we have a first-time visitor with us tonight and I would like for him to stand up and tell us a little bit about himself." Everyone clapped and they all turned around and smiled at him and sat waiting for him to speak.

Oswald's ears turned as red as the bells on the wall. Frances, seeing how uncomfortable he was, quickly stood up and said, "Keep your seat, Mr. Campbell. Mr. Campbell is my guest tonight, and I can tell you he came all the way down here from Chicago to get away from bad old cold weather and to spend the winter with us and maybe longer, if we don't run him off with all our crazy doings." They all laughed. "So welcome to the community, Mr. Campbell." They all clapped again and he made an attempt at a nod.

The program for the evening was a reading of " 'Twas the Night Before Christmas" by Dottie Nivens, an unfortunate selection for a woman with a lisp, followed by a solo rendition of "Rudolph the Red-Nosed Reindeer" played on the musical saw, and ending with a visit from Santa Claus, who came in the room with a large sack thrown over his shoulder.

Santa sat in the front and called out the names of the children in the room, and one by one each went up for their present. Oswald noticed that when they got back to the table and opened their packages, they all seemed to like what they got. After everyone had received gifts, Santa Claus stood up and said, "Well, that's all, boys and girls." But then, as he lifted his sack, he pretended to find just one more present. "Oh, wait a minute," he said. "Here's another one." He read the card, looked out, and asked, "Is there a little boy here named Oswald T. Campbell?" Everybody laughed and pointed. "Come on up, Oswald," said Santa. When he got there Oswald saw it was Claude Underwood under the beard, who asked, "Have you been a good boy?" Oswald laughed and said he had, received his present, and went back to his seat.

The evening ended with the lighting of the tree. As soon as everyone was outside they all mashed together in a large clump, and Oswald found himself in the middle. He could not help but think about the photo in the old hotel brochure of those thirty people standing under a rosebush. People in Alabama must love to stand around in clumps. Butch Mannich was stationed in the doorway. When the children, standing over to the side mashed together in their own smaller clump, started singing "O Christmas Tree," he switched on the lights and they all applauded.

After it was over, Oswald walked home with Frances and Mildred. He told them the most amazing thing about the evening to him, besides all the food, was that all the kids seemed to love their presents. He said he almost never liked what he had gotten for Christmas. They smiled and explained that the reason they were all so pleased was because each year Dottie Nivens, the postmistress, opened the letters they had written to Santa Claus and told their parents exactly what they wanted. As they walked farther up the street, Oswald noticed that one side of the sky seemed to be glowing red off in the distance. Frances told him it was caused by the fires the Creoles lit along the riverbanks every Christmas Eve to light up the night for "Poppa Christmas" and help him find his way to the homes of the Creole children. "We used to go and watch him come up the river, but we don't go over there anymore," she said.

Although it was around ten o'clock, the night was still mild and it was very pleasant with the moonlight shining through the trees, walking past all the houses with their Christmas lights twinkling in the windows. As they strolled along in silence listening to the night birds singing, Oswald suddenly began to experience an unfamiliar feeling he could not quite identify. He was actually glad he had gone to the dinner; it had not been that bad after all.

When he got home, Betty, who was downstairs in her nightgown with cold cream on her face, said, "You don't have to worry about waking Mother up tonight, she's as drunk as a skunk and out like a light, so maybe I'll finally get some rest."

When he got upstairs to his room, he unwrapped his present and saw that it was a brand-new hardcover copy of *Birds of Alabama*. It was signed *Merry Christmas, from the Lost River Community Association*. It was just what he wanted. And he had not even written Santa a letter.

The gift was really from Claude and Roy. A few days before Christmas, Claude had told Roy he felt sorry for Mr. Campbell.

"Why?"

"Aw, the poor guy, he comes down to that dock waiting for the mail, and all he ever gets is some pension check from the government. The whole time he's been here, he hasn't received one personal letter, not even one lousy Christmas card."

What they did not know was that Oswald did not expect to receive any mail. He was down at the dock every day only because he did not have anywhere else to go, except to the store and back to his room again. All he was doing was just sitting around killing time, looking at the birds and waiting to die.

Being aware that his days were numbered was not easy. Oswald found the hardest part was to wake up each morning with nothing to look forward to but getting worse. From what the doctor had told him, Oswald had assumed that as time passed he would start to feel weaker and weaker. However, on December 31 he woke up and noticed he was not coughing as much as he used to. He was really starting to feel pretty good, and somehow for the first time in his life, certainly for the first time since he was fifteen, he had actually managed to get through Christmas sober. In the past he had never been able to get more than one year in AA because he could never make it through the holidays without falling off the wagon, usually on Christmas Day. And also for the first time, he was experiencing another unfamiliar feeling. He was proud of himself and wished he had someone to tell. Not only had he made it through Christmas, he had also put on about five extra pounds since he had been there and he noticed in the mirror that he had a lot more color in his cheeks. This place was obviously agreeing with him. Damn, he thought. If he hadn't known better he could have sworn he *was* better.

On New Year's Day, Frances and Betty and everybody up and down the street made him come in, and they all insisted that he eat a big bowl of black-eyed peas. They said it was good luck to eat them on New Year's Day, and by that night he was up to his ears in black-eyed peas. Maybe they were right. Maybe he would get lucky and last a little longer than he had expected.

A few mornings later when Oswald sat down for breakfast, Betty announced, "Well, Mr. Campbell, you're famous. You've made the papers," and she handed him a copy of the local newsletter that came out once a month.

ALONG THE RIVER

The Lost River
Community Association Newsletter

Oh, my, what a busy and happy Christmas season we had on the river! Everyone agreed that the "Mystery Tree" was prettier than ever this year. Kudos to those secret elves, who must have come down from the North Pole to surprise us yet again! If we only knew who they were we would thank them in person.

Christmas Eve Dinner was especially delicious. We are mightily blessed with an abundance of good cooks down here and mucho thanks to the good ladies and gents who made the hall so festive and so full of Christmas cheer. A special nod goes to Sybil Underwood, who supplied the centerpieces; we are all amazed at what she can do with only simple pinecones and a few sprigs of holly. Thanks also to husband Claude for the fried mullet. Yum, yum. We had the largest crowd ever and it was good to see Betty Kitchen's mother, Miss Alma, out and about again. As usual, the highlight of the evening for the children was a visit by good old Santa Claus himself. All the boys and girls loved their presents, including our newest member, Mr. Oswald T. Campbell. Welcome!

The evening ended as usual with the annual tree-lighting ceremony, and amid the oohs and ahhs of the crowd I heard someone say that those folks up at Rockefeller Center in New York have nothing on us. I could not agree more.

And so ends another Christmas season, with all of us worn down to a frazzle and exhausted from all the busy activity but already looking forward to next year's happy Noel. In the meantime, all you lovebirds out there, married or single, don't forget to grab your sweetheart for the annual Valentine's Dinner on February 14. Yours truly and Frances Cleverdon will be the hostesses again this year, and we promise that love will definitely be in the air!

—*Dottie Nivens*

After he finished reading, Betty said, "You know, Mr. Campbell, Dottie's no stranger to the written word. When she was younger she had herself quite a little literary fling up there in Manhattan."

"Is that so?" he said, although he was not surprised. She certainly did look the artistic type, since she usually wore a long black scarf and a black velvet beret on her head.

"Oh, yes," said Betty. "She lived in Greenwich Village and was a genuine bohemian, from what I understand. Dottie told me she thought she was going to be the next Edna Ferber or Pearl Buck, but it didn't work out so she had to get a job."

"That's too bad," he said.

"Yes, but she's a good sport about it. When Dottie became our official postmistress she said she'd always hoped she'd wind up a woman of letters, but this was not quite what she had in mind."

Oswald understood how she felt. He had always dreamed of becoming an architect someday but instead wound up working as a draftsman all his life. His ambitions had never quite panned out either. He might have a lot more in common with her than he had thought, which would please Frances. Although Oswald did not know it, in her secret scheme to get him married, Dottie Nivens was second in line to get him if he and Mildred did not work out. And at the moment that did not seem to be going anywhere, at least as far as she could glean from Mildred. After that first dinner with Oswald at her house she had tried her best to get at least a clue as to how she felt. After he had left that night she had asked Mildred, "Well, what do you think?" Mildred had looked at her as if she had no idea what she meant. "About what?" She knew full well what Frances had meant and was just being cantankerous to irritate her. But far be it from Mildred to tell you what she was really thinking!

Sunday mornings in Lost River were quiet. Almost everyone, including Betty Kitchen and her mother, went over to the little town of Lillian for church. Frances and Mildred had asked Oswald to go with them, but he was not a churchgoing man. Another person who did not go was Claude Underwood, who went fishing. When asked why, he told everyone that he attended the Church of the Speckled Trout and would much rather be on the river than be in a suit and tie cooped up in some hot stuffy building.

One Sunday in early January, Claude rode by the dock, noticed Oswald sitting there in his chair with his book, and pulled over to him.

"I see the girls haven't drug you off to Lillian with them," Claude said, smiling.

"No, they tried, but I escaped."

"What are you doing?"

"Oh, nothing, just looking."

"Then why don't you come fishing with me?"

"I don't know how to fish. Could I just tag along for the ride?"

"Sure, get in."

It was a clear bright blue morning and the sun sparkled on the water as Claude rode all the way up to the wide part of the river. Flocks of pelicans flew beside the boat, almost close enough to reach out and touch. While they were sitting in the middle, the river was so still and peaceful; the only sound was the faint whirring of Claude's fishing reel and the soft *plop* as the lure hit the water. Oswald was amazed at the ease and grace with which Claude cast his line out and drew it back, with almost no effort.

While they were sitting there in the quiet, Oswald heard church bells ringing way off in the distance. He asked Claude where they were coming from.

"That's the Creole church across the river. You can hear it sometimes if the wind is right." He laughed. "Sometimes on Saturday night you can hear them playing their music, whooping and hollering and carrying on. They like to have a good time, I'll say that for them."

"Do any of the Creoles ever come over to our side of the river?"

Claude sighed. "They used to, but not anymore."

"What are they like?"

"Most of them are as nice as you could want, would give you the shirt off their backs. I had a lot of good Creole friends at one time, but after that thing with Roy and Julian we just don't mix. After that happened everybody was more or less forced to take sides. Since the Creoles are all pretty much related to one another they had to side with Julian whether they agreed with him or not, and all of us over here had to do the same. It's sort of a Hatfield and McCoy kind of a thing, I guess. We don't go over there; they don't come over here."

Oswald, curious, asked, "What happened?"

"Didn't the women tell you about it?"

"No."

Claude threw his line out in the water and began to reel it back in. "Well, back about seventeen or maybe eighteen years by now we had ourselves a real-life Romeo and Juliet situation, and it's a dang miracle somebody wasn't murdered over it. It was touch and go there for a long time, with threats going back and forth across the river. Roy swore he was going to kill Julian and Julian swore he was going to kill Roy, and to this day there's still a lot of bad blood between them. I think if either one of them got caught on the wrong side of the river, look out."

Roy seemed like such an even-tempered man to Oswald. "Do you really think Roy would kill him?"

"You better believe it. Julian would do the same if he got the chance, and it's a damn shame, too. Roy was practically raised by Julian and thought the world of him until that mess over Julian's daughter. I don't know the exact details of what happened, but the women do. I'm sure there is right and wrong on both sides, but I do think Julian's pride caused most of the trouble."

"Really?"

"Oh, yeah, back in the seventeen hundreds the LaPonde family used to own all of Baldwin County all the way up to Mobile. Julian's great-grandfather got the original land grant from the king of Spain, but over the years the family sold most of it off bit by bit, got cheated out of some of it, lost a lot of it in poker games, and eventually wound up with just the land on the other side of the river."

A small boat came around the corner and two men waved at Claude. "Having any luck?"

Claude waved back. "Not much," he said as they went by. "Anyhow, about sixty years ago some of the farmers that came down to Baldwin County and bought land thought the Creoles were just a little too dark for their tastes and also they were Catholic and did their share of drinking and that didn't set too well with the farmers, so there was some talk about maybe they shouldn't be going to the same schools as their children and evidently there was going to be some sort of vote, but Julian's father got wind of it and he pulled all the Creoles out of the county school and started one of their own. Julian was just a kid then, and he swore that when he grew up he was going to get his family's original Spanish land grant back and kick the farmers off their land or some such crazy idea. He wanted his daughter, Marie, to marry the Voltaire boy so he could get some of the LaPonde land back in the family, but Marie wanted to marry Roy. As I say, I don't know what all took place, but after it was over the girl wound up marrying the Voltaire boy and Roy ran off and joined the marines."

Oswald had not been aware that Claude had hooked something while he was talking, but at that moment Claude casually reached over and pulled a mean-looking fish with a long skinny snout full of teeth out of the water and into the boat.

"What is *that*?" asked Oswald, moving aside.

"This old boy is a gar, puts up a nice little fight but not

good to eat," he said, unhooking the fish. Putting him back in the water he said, "Sorry, fella."

The next week, when Oswald went over to have dinner with Frances and Mildred again, he asked Frances about the feud between Roy and Julian LaPonde.

Frances looked at him. "Oh, Mr. Campbell, you don't even want to know about that; it was just terrible. I just don't want to tell you how awful it was." She then sat down on the couch and proceeded to tell him the entire story. "When that mess was going on, Ralph, my poor husband, had to get up and go down there in the middle of the night and help try and stop Roy from going across the river and killing Julian. And evidently, from what I heard, his relatives had to hold Julian back from coming over here and killing Roy. Julian accused Roy of ruining his girl's reputation or some such nonsense and said he was going to shoot him if he got the chance. Ralph said poor Roy was down at the store having a fit, he was so in love with Marie LaPonde, and you can't blame him; she was a beautiful girl. But then, as mean as he was, Julian was always a good-looking man, you have to say that for him don't you, Mildred?"

Mildred, who tonight had black hair with a white streak down the middle, said, "I don't know. I never saw the man."

"Oh, that's right," said Frances. "You weren't here yet, but he was as good-looking as a movie star with those blue-green eyes; all the women were crazy about him. Anyhow,

Roy and Marie had practically grown up together and had been in love with each other since they were children. So when he was eighteen, Roy told Julian that he and Marie wanted to get married, and Julian had a fit and said no, absolutely not, that the only way Roy could marry Marie was over his dead body. Marie's mother, who loved Roy like a son, begged Julian to change his mind, and so did Roy's uncle, who was his good friend, but he would not budge. He claimed he was against it because Roy was not Catholic, but the truth was Julian wanted that Voltaire land back and the only way he could get his hands on it was to have Marie marry into the family. So when all else failed Roy somehow got a note to Marie and rowed over there late one night to get her so they could run off and get married, but Julian caught them just as they were leaving the dock and drug Marie out of the boat and shot at Roy. Oh, it was terrible. People said they heard poor Marie screaming and crying and pleading with her father all the way across the river. The very next day Julian took Marie off and stuck her in a convent somewhere where Roy couldn't find her."

Mildred said, "Why didn't she just leave? That's what I would have done."

"I don't think it was that easy, Mildred. I think she was afraid her father would hurt Roy, or maybe being a good Catholic girl she felt obligated to do what he said, but anyway about a year later she managed to get a letter to Roy and told him she had decided to go ahead and marry the Voltaire boy. And do you know what the worst part of this story is?"

Mildred, who had already knocked back two vodka martinis, said, "That the dinner is getting cold."

Frances ignored her sister and continued. "The worst part is after all that, the Voltaire boy lost all his family's land gambling, and he and Marie had to move to Louisiana. So Julian broke two hearts and destroyed two lives, all for naught. It's a real-life tragedy so we just don't talk about it. Especially to Roy. I know he's still in love with her."

Mildred turned to Oswald. "It sounds like the plot of a really bad novel, doesn't it?"

You should know, thought Frances, as she stood up to go to the kitchen, but she did not say it. She did not want Mr. Campbell to know what kind of junk her sister read and wished Mildred could be more like Dottie Nivens, who at least aspired to better herself. She read great literature, Chaucer, Proust, and Jane Austen, not those cheap romance novels Mildred always picked. As she pulled the roast out of her pink stove she also wondered why Mildred had worn that low-cut blouse that showed the top of her more than generous where-withals. Was she interested in Mr. Campbell? Or was she just not paying attention to what she put on? With Mildred you never knew.

A Small Visitor

ONE AFTERNOON OSWALD was standing around the cash register talking with Roy, when Roy suddenly picked up a pencil, pretended to be writing something, and said, "Don't look now, but that little girl I was telling you about is back."

The first time Roy had seen the little girl was a few weeks before, and then it was only the top of a small blonde head slowly rising up and appearing in the side window, then two big wide blue eyes staring in at Jack running on his plastic wheel and ringing his bells. But the minute she saw Roy she quickly disappeared from sight. Roy walked back and went outside, but by the time he got around the side of the building she was nowhere to be seen. He had noticed her only a few times, but it was always the same; as soon as she saw him looking at her, she disappeared into thin air.

The next time she came he was able to catch sight of her

before she saw him. He quickly turned his back and pretended not to notice her. From what he had seen of her, she was a pretty little thing, and was clearly shy and afraid of people, but obviously fascinated with the bird. She came every day after that, and Roy got a big kick out of it.

"Who is she?" asked Oswald, not turning around.

"I don't know. I've asked Frances and Dottie, but nobody knows who she is or where she came from. I just wish I could get her to come in."

As the days went by the girl became bolder and bolder, until one afternoon when Roy opened the back door she did not run away. "Don't you want to come inside?" he said. "He can't come out, but if you come in you can pet him if you want. He doesn't mind."

Roy, seeing how small she was, guessed the girl could not have been more than five or six. She was barefoot and wearing a dirty ripped cotton dress, and she stood there, clearly torn between being terrified of Roy and wanting to see Jack up close.

"Come on in," he said. "Nobody's going to hurt you." The girl started to turn around and leave but Roy said, "Wait a minute, don't go," and went back in and picked Jack up and held his feet between his forefinger and thumb and walked to the door so she could see him. "Look. You can hold him if you want. He's tame, he won't hurt you."

Jack looked at her through the screen and sang out, "Chip, chip, chip, birdie, birdie, birdie."

After a moment the girl could not resist and slowly began to move toward the door. It was then Roy noticed that there was something wrong with her. As she came closer and closer he could see that her body was slightly twisted and she was dragging her right leg behind her. "What's your name?" he asked as she came in, with her eyes never leaving Jack.

She answered "Patsy" so softly he could barely hear her.

"Well, Patsy. This is Jack."

It had been Roy's experience that at first most children this young were afraid to touch the bird, but not her. She may have been frightened of people but not of Jack. She said, "Can I hold him?"

"Sure."

She lifted her finger and held it up, and Jack walked from Roy's finger over to hers and sat there cocking his head and blinking his eyes. Usually in the past when he had put Jack on someone else's finger, he had always hopped right back to him. Not this time.

"He likes you," said Roy.

Her eyes were wide with wonder. "He does?" she said.

"Oh, yes." At that point Jack bobbed up and down on her finger and walked all the way up her arm, sat on her shoulder, and nuzzled against the side of her cheek. "Well, I'll be darned," said Roy.

This was the beginning of the love affair between Jack and Patsy.

When Patsy left the store that first day, Roy walked out and watched where she was headed. He finally figured out where she lived and why nobody in town knew who she was. She had headed in the same direction where those people who lived way back up in the woods were located. She probably belonged to the same family as the two mean boys who had shot Jack in the first place, and most likely had heard about the bird from them. He remembered the first day she had appeared was the same day he had seen those boys walk by the store and look in at Jack. What a shame, thought Roy; he could just imagine what kind of life she had. But all he could do was to be as nice as possible to her while she was here. The kind of people who lived back there in the woods never stayed anywhere long. They were mostly itinerant farm workers passing through the area to pick strawberries or work the pecan crop and then move on to the next place.

After that first time, the girl came back to the store every day and played with Jack for hours. She was still terrified of people and shy with Roy, although he found she was no trouble to have around. She was as quiet as a mouse. The only time he ever heard her at all was when she was alone in the office with Jack. If he happened to pass by, he could hear her in there, just chattering away to the bird—and darned if the bird wasn't chattering back at her. He would have loved to hear what she was saying, but he couldn't make it out. As the weeks went by she got to the point where she would come out of the office and talk to people. When Roy first introduced her to Oswald, who was not very comfortable around children, he awkwardly reached down and shook her hand and said, "Hello little girl, how do you do," and was amazed at her tiny hand. As she walked away and he saw how badly crippled she was, he turned to Roy and said softly, "That's a damn shame. She's such a pretty little kid, too."

Roy glanced back as she went into the office. "Yeah, it makes you want to kick the living tar out of somebody, don't it?"

The next time Oswald came up to the store, he saw Patsy in the back and she shyly motioned for him to come over. "Do you want to know a secret?" she asked.

"Why, yes, I do."

She then motioned for him to lean down and whispered in his ear. "Jack is my best friend."

"Really?" he said, pretending to be astonished. "How do you know?" he whispered back.

"He told me."

"He did? And what did you say?"

"I told him first and then he told me."

"I see."

"But he said I could tell you."

"Well, tell him I said thank you."

"OK," she said.

When he walked over to the cash register he was laughing to himself. "Hey, Roy, did you know she's back there, talking to that bird?"

"Oh, yes, I hear her all day, just chattering away, lost in her own world. But you know what, considering what she must go home to every night, the kid probably needs some magic in her life. She can stay back there forever, as far as I'm concerned."

Of course, when Frances and the other women saw the girl they were appalled, not only at her condition but also at how thin and dirty she was. Butch Mannich got mad and fumed over it. He had no patience with that kind of child neglect. Being a process server he had dealt firsthand with the type of people that lived back in the woods and knew what they were like. He said, "They treat their kids worse than you and I would treat a dog."

From then on, every time Frances went in the store the sight of the girl broke her heart. She told Roy, "I'm just worried to death about her, and you just wonder what her mother must be like, to let a crippled child roam around like some wild animal. Somebody ought to do something."

"I know, Frances," said Roy, shaking his head. "I've tried to feed her but she won't take a thing from me but a few pieces of candy. All she wants is to play with Jack all day. I feel bad for her, but she doesn't belong to us and there's nothing we can do about it."

Something New

✺

AS THE DAYS went by, Patsy charmed everyone who met her. Even Oswald found that now when he went to the store he was looking forward to visiting with Pasty as much as anything else. As a matter of fact, after a while he realized much to his amazement that he was crazy about the little girl. She was the first and only child he had ever liked. He had mostly always been around boys, so he figured it must be because she *was* a girl, so tiny and frail. Or maybe it was that he felt a kinship with Pasty—and Jack, too, for that matter. They were all three handicapped in one way or another. He went up to the store one morning as usual and when he got there she was in the back office playing with Jack.

"How are you today, Patsy?"

"Fine."

"What are you up to?"

"Nothing. Jack and I are just playing."

She was busy pretending to serve tea to Jack and offered Oswald a cup of imaginary tea.

"Hey, Patsy, how old are you?" he asked.

"I don't know."

"Well, when is your next birthday?"

She thought about it. "I don't know. I don't think I have one."

"You don't have a birthday?"

"No."

He took another cup of imaginary tea from her and pretended to drink it. "You know what? You're not going to believe this, but I don't have a birthday either. I have an idea. Let's you and I make one up. Then every year you and I will have the same birthday, OK? And we won't tell anybody; it will be our secret."

"OK," she said.

He looked at the calendar on the wall. "How about Wednesday, three days from now?"

"Can it be Jack's birthday, too?"

"I don't see why not."

"OK," she said, and they shook hands.

The next day, Oswald asked Butch if he could get a ride over to Lillian. Never having bought a present for a child before, he was at a loss. He wandered around the general merchandise store in the small town, looking for something she might like. He didn't know how to pick out a doll, or what kind of toys girls played with, but then he spotted a black beanie decorated with Dr Pepper bottle caps.

Wednesday came, and they had their secret birthday back in the office. He gave her the hat and she gave him two pieces of candy she had saved and wrapped up in brown paper and string. She was as thrilled with her hat as he hoped she would be. Oswald sat there eating the candy and drinking more imaginary tea and watching Jack peck away at his present of sunflower seeds. Then he remarked, "You know, Patsy, this is the best birthday I ever had."

She sat across from him wearing her new Dr Pepper hat and declared, "Me too!"

After a while Oswald had another idea and went out to the cash register.

"Hey, Roy, do you have a camera?"

"Yeah."

"Can I borrow it? I want to take a picture of Patsy."

"Sure, let me put some film in and we'll do it."

After some time deciding where the best light was, they stood Patsy outside the front door of the store and took her picture, holding Jack and wearing her new beanie. A week later, Oswald brought the finished black-and-white photo and showed it to her. He had had three copies made, one for Roy and one for Patsy and one to keep for himself. Roy taped his photo to the side of the cash register so everyone who came in could see it. Across the bottom was written *Pasty and Jack on their birthday.*

A Dilemma

ONE FEBRUARY MORNING Roy came in the store and whistled for Jack, but the bird did not answer. He whistled again. No answer. He looked around the store and wondered what the crazy thing was into today when he suddenly saw a large man's work glove walking across the top of the lettuce and across the lemons. During the night Jack had somehow gotten himself tangled up inside the glove and could not get out. Roy went over and pulled it off. Jack was all ruffled up and mad; he must have been in there for hours. He shook his feathers and stomped all over the lemons and slipped in between two of them and got even madder. Roy laughed at him. "You nutty bird, you." Always getting himself in trouble. Last week he had caught him pecking holes in all the tomatoes and later that day when Mildred had come in she had screamed bloody murder. "There's not one good tomato here!" she said. "How can a person be expected to make a decent salad as long as that horrible little bird is around?"

Jack responded by running around on his wheel and ringing his bells, almost as if he were laughing at Mildred. Roy thought it was hilarious but Mildred was not amused.

Oswald had recently started getting up at daybreak and was usually down at the store by seven to have a cup of coffee with Roy before going out on the river. But the next morning Oswald seemed flushed and was already banging at the window at six-thirty. Roy walked over and opened the door. "Oh, hell, let me in," Oswald said, and ran into the store.

"What's the matter?"

"Man, I'm in trouble," he said, holding up an envelope. "Betty, Mildred, Frances, and now Dottie Nivens have all asked me to this Valentine thing over at the hall, and I don't know what to do. Oh, man," he said, wringing his hands. "These women are going to drive me to drink."

"Well, which lucky lady are you going to go with?"

"It doesn't matter. Whoever I pick, the other three are going to be mad at me."

Roy thought about it. "If I were you I would explain it to Frances and let them fight it out among themselves."

After he left, Roy had to smile. Oswald was certainly the most unlikely Lothario he had ever seen.

Oswald could not have agreed with him more. He had never been asked out on a date in his life, much less by four women on the same night. Reluctantly he explained the situation to Frances.

As it turned out, all four had invited him because they wanted to make sure he would not feel left out and did not know the others had done the same. And so it was decided that all four women were to be his date.

On Valentine's night poor Oswald, wearing a red bow tie and even though he was a terrible dancer, had to dance every dance. He waltzed with Frances to a sappy version of "Dreamy Alabama," jitterbugged with Dottie Nivens, did some odd tango thing with Mildred, and ended the evening being dragged around the floor by his six-foot landlady to the tune of "Good Night Sweetheart."

ALONG THE RIVER

The Lost River
Community Association Newsletter

Oh, what a delightful evening was had by all who attended the annual Sweethearts dance! The melodious tunes that had all of our toes literally dancing inside our shoes was supplied by the ever-popular Auburn Knights Swing Band, and we were all mighty impressed by their musicality and wide range of repertoire, from the fox-trot to the jazzy idioms and interpolations of the bossa nova. But the highlight of the evening was the nimble Terpsichore of our own Fred Astaire in the person of Os-

> *wald T. Campbell, who if I may borrow a phrase was*
> *truly the belle of the ball!*

After Oswald read that first paragraph and later when Roy and Claude started calling him Belle, he decided that all of this female attention was making him a nervous wreck. He had so many dinner invitations he had to write them down.

He needed to get to an AA meeting fast.

Butch Mannich knew a lot of people in the nearby towns, so the next time Oswald saw him walking up the street he stopped him and asked if he by any chance knew anyone in AA.

Butch brightened up. "Yes, by gosh, I sure do. I know a man over in Elberta who belongs. I didn't know you were in that, Mr. Campbell."

"Yes," said Oswald, "but it's not something I'm particularly proud of, and I would appreciate it if you could sort of keep it under your hat. I don't want anybody to know, especially Frances."

Butch nodded and conspired in a whisper. "I understand completely, Mr. Campbell, and I don't blame you, but don't you worry. Your secret is safe with me. I won't say a word to anybody." Butch glanced around to see if anyone was looking and quickly wrote a name and number down on a piece of paper. He looked around again to make sure no one saw him and then slipped him the piece of paper on the sly.

Oswald called the number that afternoon, and a man answered.

"Is this Mr. Krause?"

"That's me."

"Mr. Krause, I was given your number by Butch Mannich over in Lost River."

"You mean Stick?"

"Yes, sir."

"Well, any friend of Stick's is a friend of mine. What can I do for you?"

"Uh . . . I understand you are in AA, and I wanted to ask you when the next meeting was." Mr. Krause told him there was a weekly meeting at eight o'clock on Friday nights at the Knights of Columbus hall in downtown Elberta and to please come. "We will be glad to have you. We are always happy to have new members. Where are you from?"

"Chicago."

Mr. Krause was impressed. "Ah, Chicago. I bet there are a lot of great meetings up there. We are just a small group over here. Are you a beginner, Mr. Campbell, or have you been at it for a while?"

"No, I'm not a beginner, I have a few years, but I haven't been to a meeting in quite a while and you know once you stop going it's hard to start all over in a new town."

"You got that right, Mr. Campbell. You have to keep coming or you get out of practice. But don't you worry, we'll get you right back in the swing in no time."

"By the way, is this a men's meeting?" Oswald asked.

"We have one or two women but mostly men."

Good, thought Oswald. It would be a nice break for him.

. . .

Friday night Butch said he would be glad to drive Oswald over to the meeting. He had some people he needed to see anyway, so they drove over before dark. Elberta was a small German farming community about ten miles to the east, and the houses had an almost Bavarian look to them. Butch took him to the Elks Club where he was a member and introduced him around to a few friends. Around seven-thirty after they had eaten hamburgers at the lodge, Butch drove him downtown, parked on a side street, and furtively glanced around in all directions to make sure the coast was clear before he let him out. "I'll be back to get you in an hour," he said.

Oswald asked if he could give him an hour and a half. "Since this is my first meeting here, I'd like to try and get to know some of the fellows."

"No problem," said Butch. "And don't you worry, Mr. Campbell, mum's the word." And with that he sped off into the night.

Oswald went inside the large Knights of Columbus hall and found a sign that said ALABAMA AA with the arrow pointing upstairs. A heavyset man in suspenders greeted him with a big beefy handshake and a pat on the back that nearly knocked him down.

"Mr. Campbell? Ed Krause. Welcome to our little group."

Oswald looked around the room. There were already six or seven other friendly-looking men sitting in wooden chairs, smiling and nodding at him.

Mr. Krause led him to a chair. "Where's your instrument, Mr. Campbell?"

Oswald was not sure what he had heard. "I beg your pardon?"

It was only when he looked around the room again that he noticed that all the men were pulling accordions out of the cases beside each chair.

When another man walked by with a big black case and carrying an armload of sheet music, Oswald suddenly realized that he had walked into an Alabama Accordion Association meeting!

He turned to the man and said, "Ah . . . I tell you what, Mr. Krause, I believe I'll just listen tonight. My instrument is sort of on the blink."

"That's too bad," said a disappointed Ed Krause. "We were looking forward to a little new blood."

Oswald went over in the corner and sat and listened. He sat through quite a few polkas and one pretty lively version of "The Poor People of Paris" before it was time for Butch to come and pick him up. Outside, Butch asked how the meeting went and he answered, "Just fine."

On the way back home, Oswald thought about it and wondered which was worse, being an accordion player or being an alcoholic. He figured it was a toss-up.

He was sorry there were no AA meetings around, but Oswald figured he was doing pretty well just hanging out on the dock and meeting with the birds every day. It seemed to keep him calm, and it was certainly interesting. He was not bored. There were plenty of them to see. One day when Oswald was sitting there on the dock busy watching the birds, a great blue heron stared right back at him, and it suddenly occurred to him that they might be busy watching him as well. He wondered what they thought he was, and how would they identify him.

His *Birds of Alabama* book had given him guidelines as to how to identify birds by size and color and by location, so he decided to look in the book and figure out what the birds would write down for him. He searched for himself up under LOCATION:

PERMANENT RESIDENTS: Live in the same geographic region all year long.

SUMMER RESIDENTS: Breed and raise their young in one geographic region, then leave to winter in warmer regions.

WINTER VISITORS: Come to a geographic region only during winter months after their breeding season.

TRANSIENTS: Pass through a geographic region only once or twice a year during their spring or fall migrations.

ACCIDENTALS: Birds not expected in a particular region and, therefore, are surprise visitors.

As he read on, he decided that according to the book, he was definitely a medium-sized, redheaded, nonbreeding accidental. At last he knew what he was, and it amused him to no end. He was a rare bird, after all.

Winter

❄

ON THE MORNING of February 21, everybody up and down the street declared, "Well, winter is here," and noted with horror that last night the temperature had dipped all the way down into the 50s. That afternoon, Oswald looked across the river and for the first time saw blue smoke curling out of the chimneys of the houses on the other side. The air was suddenly fragrant with the smell of wood smoke from the burning of local pine, hickory, and cedar logs.

Oswald welcomed the cooler weather because in the following days he discovered it brought winter sunsets, and the river sunsets were different from anything else he had ever seen. They mesmerized him. He loved sitting there on the dock in the cool crisp air, the river so quiet you could hear a dog bark a mile away. Every afternoon he watched the sky turn from burnt orange to salmon, pink and lime green to purple. Navy blue and pink clouds were reflected in the water, and as the sun slowly disappeared he watched the river change from teal blue to an iridescent green and gold that reminded him of the color of the tinfoil that came wrapped around expensive candy and then from rich tan to a deep chocolate brown. As the evening became darker, the birds and ducks that flew by became black silhouettes against the sky. He sat each night watching the evening change colors and the currents of the water make circles, until the moon came up behind him and rose over the river.

With the last of the sun fading, he could see the reflection of the green lights on the docks across the way and the stars twinkling in the river like small diamonds. What a show. This was better than any movie he had ever seen, and it was different every night. It was so wonderful at times he felt he wanted to do something about it, to try and stop time, make it last longer, but he didn't know what to do. How can anyone stop time? He knew with each passing day his own time was running out, and there was nothing anybody could do to stop it. If he could, he would have stopped it right then and there on the river, while he was still well enough to enjoy it.

A few weeks later, Oswald was still feeling well, and Jack was still making everyone laugh except Mildred, and everything was going along as usual until Saturday morning, when Patsy showed up at the store to see Jack. One side of her face was red, and it was obvious that someone had hit her. Roy asked her how it had happened, but she said nothing. Butch, who had been in the store first thing that morning, was in a rage over it. Afterward all six-feet-four-inches and 128 pounds of him stormed down the street to Frances's house in a fit and threw open the door.

"That just aggravates the fire out of me!"

"What?" asked Frances.

"Somebody hit Patsy!"

"Who?"

"I don't know!"

"Are you sure?"

"Sure, I'm sure. There's a big old handprint on the side of her face."

That afternoon an emergency meeting of the Mystic Order of the Royal Polka Dots secret society was called to discuss what could be done. After much talk back and forth, Betty Kitchen allowed that Roy might be right. She said, "There may be nothing we can do without getting those people back there all riled up. You all know what they are like."

Mildred said, "Trailer trash."

Frances said, "Oh, now, Mildred, that's not a very Christian thing to say."

"No," said Mildred, "but it's the truth."

Butch admired her ability to hit the nail on the head. Frances got back to the point. "Now, I think we all agree that this is definitely a Polka Dot matter, and I think the least we can do is offer to buy her some decent clothes. Here it is, the dead of winter, and the little thing is still running around with no coat or shoes."

"How much money do we have in our Sunshine fund?" asked Betty.

Frances went over to her gravy boat display, and lifted the top off the third one from the left, and pulled out $82. They took a vote to spend it all on Patsy, and the motion passed unanimously.

Betty said, "The next question is who and how are we going to ask the family if we can do it."

Mildred said, "Why don't we just take her to Mobile and do it ourselves? Why ask?"

Frances looked at her. "We can't just take her, Mildred. They might have us all arrested for kidnapping. That's all we need is to go to jail."

"Yes, but if you go back there where they live they're liable to turn the dogs on you," warned Dottie. "Or shoot you."

"Well, two can play that game," said Butch, patting the sidearm he wore under his shirt. "They're not the only ones around here with guns, you know."

"Oh, Lord," said Frances. "That's all we need is gunplay."

"Why don't we go as a group?" asked Mildred.

Frances shook her head. "No, that might be too threatening. I think one of us should just casually pay a visit like a friendly neighbor. Who wants to go?"

Butch raised his hand.

"No, not you, Butch, it has to be a woman," said Mildred.

Betty Kitchen said, "Well, I'll go. I'm not afraid of any

man. They fool with me and I'll sling them into tomorrow and back."

Dottie, who knew that Betty was not exactly capable of being subtle, said quickly, "I think you should go, Frances. You're the nicest and least likely to get thrown out."

The following Sunday, Frances parked her car at the store and walked down the white sandy path in her high heels, carrying a purse on one arm and a large welcome basket on the other, hoping she would live through the day. Throughout the years a variety of people had moved back up in the woods, and her husband had told her it was best to let them alone. Some were hiding from the law and were not very friendly to strangers. They usually stayed awhile, threw trash everywhere, and then moved on. A few years ago, the sheriff's department had arrested some of them, so there was no telling what she was walking into today. A few moments later she suddenly heard a loud crack, which almost scared her to death. She thought she had been shot. She turned to see Butch, who had been darting back and forth in the woods trailing behind her and had stepped on a branch. "Oh, my God, Butch, what are you doing? You nearly gave me a heart attack!"

Still darting, he jumped behind a tree and said in a whisper, "Don't worry about me, you just go on. I'm here just in case you need me."

Oh, Lord, she thought. Butch had clearly seen too many movies. She continued on until she reached a clearing and saw a broken-down trailer sitting up on concrete blocks. An old rusted ice box lay on its side in the yard, along with an assortment of worn tires and motorcycle and car parts. As she got closer, some kind of pit-bull-mix dog came rushing toward her, barking furiously, baring his teeth, and straining at his chain. Frances stopped dead in her tracks. In a moment a five-foot-tall fat woman in a tank top and short shorts opened the door, yelled at the dog to shut up, and then saw Frances standing there.

"Hello," said Frances, trying to sound casual, "I hope I'm not bothering you. I'm Mrs. Frances Cleverdon, and I was wondering if I might speak to you for a moment."

The woman stared at her. "If you're a bill collector, it won't do you no good. My husband ain't here."

Frances, trying to reassure her, said, "Oh, no, I'm just a neighbor lady come to chat and bring you a little gift."

The woman shifted her small pig eyes to the basket. "You wanna come in?"

"Yes, thank you." Frances climbed the concrete steps while the dog leaped up and down and literally foamed at the mouth. The place was a mess. She took note of the empty beer cans on the counter and a box of stale doughnuts. The woman sat down and crossed her enormous white leg with the tattoo of a snake around her equally enormous ankle. After Frances had moved a few things and made a place to sit, she said, "I'm sorry, I don't know your name."

"Tammie Suggs."

"Well, Mrs. Suggs, I really came here today to discuss your little girl."

The woman's eyes narrowed. "What about her, what did she do? Patsy!" she yelled. "Get out here!"

"No, that's all right, she didn't do anything—"

"If she stole something, I ain't paying for it."

Patsy appeared from the back of the trailer, looking frightened.

"No. It's nothing like that, Mrs. Suggs. Hello, Patsy," she said, and smiled.

Frances leaned forward. "I was hoping we could speak in private."

The woman turned and said to Patsy, "Get out of here."

Frances waited until she was gone. "Mrs. Suggs, it's just that I . . . well, a group of us, actually—have grown very fond of Patsy and wondered if you had had a doctor look at her lately?"

"What for?"

"Well, her condition—her leg?"

"Oh, yeah, she drags that thing bad, don't she. But she was already like that when her daddy left her here. She ain't even my kid. She was just dumped on me. I don't have no money for doctors for my own kids, much less her. Then after her daddy took off, I got stuck with her and the next thing I know my old man up and runs off, and me and them kids is about to starve to death."

Tammie Suggs looked far from starving, but Frances refrained from comment and continued. "Do you know what causes her to walk like that? Was it an accident of some kind?"

Tammie Suggs shook her head. "Naw, he told me it happened when she was born. Her mother was real delicate-like and was having a hard time delivering, so the doctor jerked her out with forceps, and it left her all twisted like that."

"Oh, no!"

"Yeah. And the mother died anyway."

"I see. Did he say if anything could be done about it, maybe special shoes of some kind?" Frances said, as a subtle hint.

Tammie shook her head and scratched her large arm. "Naw, her daddy said she's always gonna be like that. That there weren't no use to put shoes on her, she just ruins every pair, dragging that foot like she does."

"And where is the father now?" asked Frances, trying her best to remain pleasant.

"I don't know, but he better get his butt back here soon. I'm tired of putting up with her." Frances could not help herself and winced slightly at the last statement. Tammie saw it and snapped at her. "Look, lady, I'm doing the best I can. You try raising three kids with no man."

"Oh, I'm sure it's very difficult, but maybe we could help you buy Patsy a few things, maybe some toys or clothes?"

Tammie thought it over for a moment. "Well, me and the boys needs things, too."

After she could see that there was really no use to try and reason with her, Frances put the envelope with the money on the table and left. When she got outside she was so disgusted with the woman she didn't know what to do. She walked by the dog, who was having another jumping-up-and-down fit, straining to break free from its chain and eat her alive. Frances, a lady to the core, uncharacteristically turned on him and said, "Oh, shut up, you!" Butch caught up with her halfway to the car and Frances, who had never been able to have children of her own, said, "What kind of a man would leave his child with that horrible woman? You just wonder what the Good Lord is thinking about when he gives people like that children."

For the next week, everybody watched Patsy to see if she showed up in shoes or anything other than that old dress, but she never did.

Although Patsy had no new clothes, Frances was determined to make sure the little girl had at least one good meal a day. At twelve o'clock each day, she walked down to the store with a hot lunch and sat with her in the office while she ate it. At first, Patsy was shy and afraid to eat, but Frances, who had once been a schoolteacher, was finally able to convince her that it was all right, and pretty soon she had her talking a lot more. As she left one day, Frances told Roy, "You know, that is the sweetest little girl. It's all I can do not to just pick her up and squeeze her to death. Can you imagine a father leaving a child like that?"

Roy shook his head. "No, I can't." Then he said sadly, "You know, Frances, there are a lot of people that should be shot."

Roy would have shot Julian LaPonde a long time ago, if he had not been Marie's father and if her mother had not begged him not to. He was not over Marie yet and still remembered how she looked that night, the last time he ever saw her.

He still wondered how she was doing. He could have found out from her mother, who liked him, or gone through the Catholic priest on the sly, but it would have been painful to know she had forgotten him and equally painful to know she had not. In her last letter to him, she had said that if he loved her he would forget her and find someone else and have a happy life. He loved her, all right, but have a happy life without her? That was something he had not been able to do.

Roy and Mildred had a lot in common. Mildred, although not as young as she used to be, still had a good figure, small hips, and large full breasts and years ago could have had any boy in Chattanooga but instead she had thrown her life away over Billy Jenkins. Why she had picked him over all the other boys that were lining up at her door was beyond Frances. He was certainly not up to her. A no-good lazy bum from the wrong side of the tracks, as their father had put it, but nothing would do at the time than for Mildred to settle on the one boy nobody in the family liked. Frances suspected that if they had liked him, Mildred would not have wanted to marry him. It was as if Mildred went out of her way to find the one unsuitable boy in town and go after him. It had been a small scandal and had cost their father a small fortune. The bridesmaids' dresses had been bought and fitted, the country club rented, food ordered, and invitations sent, and one week before the wedding the groom skipped town on a motorcycle, leaving a note saying *Sorry, I guess I wasn't ready. Love, Billy.* Mildred had been inconsolable and heartbroken for years. But Frances wondered if it was not so much over love as it was that Mildred always wanted what she couldn't have. Mildred had had a few men friends after that, but she never really loved any of them. None could ever compete with the one that got away.

An Awakening

SPRING CAME TO Lost River around the middle of March. The nights were slowly becoming warmer, and each evening as the sun went down, the mullet started jumping and splashing around in the river, almost as if they too were happy spring was here. Soon all the flowers Oswald had not seen when he arrived began to bloom. Almost overnight, the entire area was heady with the smell of gardenias, azaleas, wisteria, night-blooming jasmine, and honeysuckle. Oswald thought, if this were to be his last spring on earth, it was certainly the most spectacular one he had ever witnessed.

A few weeks later, on one balmy night as Oswald walked down the street, he saw fireflies flitting in and out of the bushes, and the wind blowing the Spanish moss through the trees forming shadows on the road. As he reached the river, Oswald suddenly felt as if he were walking around in a painting. Then it dawned on him. Everywhere he looked was a painting! Everything was alive with color: the water, the sky, the boathouses that lined the river, with red tin roofs, silver tin roofs, and rusted orange tin roofs. Red boat in a yellow boathouse. Green, pink, blue, tan, yellow, and white boathouses. The wooden pilings sticking out of the water were a thousand different shades of gray, and each individual piling was encrusted with hundreds of chalk-white barnacles and black woodpecker holes. Even the grain of the wood and the knots on each post differed from inch to inch and pole to pole. Vibrant color everywhere he looked and it all changed from season to season, from minute to minute. At that moment he thought, God, if he could only paint all the beautiful things he saw! He could live a thousand years and never run out of things to paint. Birds, trees, ducks, flowers. After Oswald had gotten out of the army, he had signed up for a course in architecture, but he never finished it. He had certainly never painted anything in his life, but when he had been younger, before he made a career out of drinking, he had always been tempted by those DRAW ME advertisements in magazines. One time he had gone so far as to actually send one in and they had written back and told him in glowing terms that he had talent and invited him to send off for a series of art courses, taught by famous artists, but Helen had discouraged him. She said it was just a scam and that they told everybody they had talent just to get you to buy lessons—so he had not followed up. But now he wondered if maybe they had been right. Maybe he might have talent.

He could try a few things on his own; after all, he didn't have a thing to lose.

The next day he started by just doing the black silhouettes of the birds and trees in pen and ink on the backs of old paper sacks, and after a week or two he had about ten drawings he thought were not half bad. He even gave one a name, "The Lone Duck," and signed it *O. T. Campbell.* A few weeks later he strolled around the store to the area where Roy kept the school supplies, picked up a long black tin box of watercolors, and asked Roy how much it was. "A buck," Roy said. "OK," he said, pulled out a dollar, and left. Roy thought he had bought the watercolors for Patsy, but he was wrong. Oswald felt a little foolish dipping his brush into paint shaped like stars and half moons, but he had to start somewhere and he needed to get as much practice as he could.

ALONG THE RIVER

The Lost River
Community Association Newsletter

Well, it's official. Spring has sprung, and as that gentle-man bard Browning once said, "Oh, to be in England now that April's there." But with all our flowers burst-ing with color and splash, I say I would much rather be in Lost River. Have you ever seen a prettier spring? And of course it's getting to be that time of year when Mr. Peter Cottontail is about ready to come hopping down that bunny trail. All you boys and girls out there be sure to come for the big Easter egg hunt that will be held at the community hall, and a big thanks to Mr. Oswald T. Campbell for volunteering to help dye Easter eggs this year.

—Dottie Nivens

A Visit

MISS ALMA WAS having her nap and Oswald was out on the river, so Betty Kitchen had a moment to walk next door and have a cup of coffee with Frances. After they had finished discussing Polka Dot business, she said, "You know, Frances, we are all going to have to be extra special nice to Mr. Campbell."

"Why?"

"Last night I asked him if he had any family and he told me no, he was an orphan named after a can of soup. He said he did not have a living relative that he knew of."

Frances was appalled. "Oh, poor Mr. Campbell, and he never mentioned a word to me about it. Betty, can you think of anything worse than being an orphan?"

Betty thought it over for a moment. "Well," she said, "I wouldn't mind giving it a try, for a day or so at least. Mother is about to drive me batty. I came in this morning and she had poured four boxes of oatmeal and two bottles of Log Cabin syrup all over my kitchen floor. You try cleaning that up."

"What possessed her to do that?"

Betty shrugged. "Who knows what possesses her to do anything? Yesterday she was hiding from Eskimos she saw flying around in the yard and locked herself in the attic. Poor Butch had to come over in the middle of the night and break the lock to get her out. She's worse than trying to keep track of a litter of kittens."

After Betty left, Frances thought about poor Mr. Campbell. Even though she did have her sister Mildred and plenty of relatives, she knew what it felt like to be lonely. Mr. Campbell deserved to find someone, even if it was late in his life. There was always hope, and now that he had put on a little weight he was almost nice-looking. Why Mildred would waste so much time over that Billy Jenkins who had left her practically at the altar was beyond her. She knew Mr. Campbell liked Mildred. Why else would he laugh at her terrible jokes?

Just as she was finishing the dishes, she heard someone knocking at her door and wondered who it was. She dried her hands and walked to the door, and there stood Tammie Suggs and she did not look happy. Oh dear, thought Frances, I could be in trouble. She had bought Patsy a pair of gloves on the sly. But she put on her best smile and said, "Well, hello, Mrs. Suggs, how nice to see you. Won't you come in?"

As Frances opened the door she looked out and saw a banged-up maroon truck parked in front of her house with a long-haired man sitting in the driver's seat. Tammie marched into the living room, flopped down in her best chair, and said, "The reason I've come here is because my husband showed back up yesterday, and we're fixing to leave for Arkansas in the morning."

Frances's heart sank. She had known this day was coming, but she had hoped to have a little more time with Patsy.

"I'm sorry to hear that, Mrs. Suggs. I'm sure we will all miss Patsy."

"Here's the thing," Tammie said. "I know you took sort of an interest in her and all, and my husband said he don't want to fool with her no more, so I was wondering if you knew anybody that might be willing to have her for a while."

Frances was totally unprepared for the question but, not missing a beat, she looked Tammie right in the eye. "I do know somebody, Mrs. Suggs," she said. "Me. I would just love to have that little girl."

Tammie said, "Well, all right, then, you can have her this afternoon if you want." And she gave the child away with no more concern than if she had just given away an old sweater.

After Tammie and the husband drove off, Frances was beside herself with joy. She had prayed for a child for years and every Christmas Eve had secretly longed to have a little girl of her own to send up and get a present from Santa Claus. When her husband died she had given up hope. But now her prayers had been answered. She was so grateful, she thanked the Good Lord that Tammie had come to her first and wondered why she had ever doubted Him. She ran upstairs to get the room ready for Patsy and to think about all the things she was going to buy her. She would buy her a hundred pairs of shoes, and Patsy could ruin all of them, as far as she was concerned.

Frances called everyone she knew and told them the good news. They were all delighted and relieved that Patsy was finally going to have a good home. Later that day, after Frances had the room ready, she went down to the store and explained to Patsy that she was coming home to live with her now. Patsy, who had been left in so many different places in her short life and always went where she was told to go, said OK. She told Jack goodbye and that she would see him in the morning. That first afternoon as Frances walked down the street with Patsy, holding her hand all the way back up to her house, people up and down all came out on their porches and waved at them as they passed. Dottie called out with a flourish, "Helloo, Miss Patsy, we're all so glad you're going to stay with us!"

It soon became a familiar sight, Frances walking the little girl in the Dr Pepper hat to the store every morning and back home every afternoon.

In all the excitement of getting Patsy, it was not until a few days later that Frances realized Tammie Suggs had left without giving her a forwarding address. Not only that, she also realized she had no idea what Patsy's last name was. But it didn't really make any difference. Frances had her now, and that was all that mattered. She and Mildred took Patsy to

Mobile and bought her shoes and socks, underwear, dresses, coats, and sweaters. They tried to buy her a few cute hats but Patsy did not want any hat other than the Dr Pepper beanie Mr. Campbell had given her. She wore it with everything. Even when Frances washed her hair and combed it out so nice and shiny, she put the hat right back on. On the first Sunday, when Frances dressed her up in a frilly white dress, she put the beanie on again and Frances didn't have the heart to make her take it off, so she wore it to church. She would have slept in it if Frances had let her.

As the days went by, Frances worried that Patsy might be upset at coming to live with a complete stranger, but if she missed Tammie Suggs or her father, she never said so. She never complained about anything, really. She was basically a very shy and quiet child and seemed perfectly happy to do what she was told. Although Frances did not know how old Patsy was, she guessed she must be at least six and planned on sending her to first grade in the fall. But before she went, Frances wanted to teach her a few basic things so she would have a head start. Even though December was still eight months away, she wanted to make sure that Patsy would be able to write a letter to Santa Claus next Christmas and go up and get her present from Santa with all the other children.

Every afternoon after the store closed, Patsy would come home and have her lessons. Mildred came by and asked how Patsy was doing, and Frances beamed with pride. "Oh, Mildred, she's as bright as a penny, she can already write her name and she's reading like a house afire." She turned and exclaimed, "Why, she may be a genius for all we know!"

Mildred was genuinely happy for her sister, but she was also worried. "Now, Frances, don't let yourself get too attached to this child, you're just setting yourself up to have your heart broken when that father comes back for her. It's not like you can keep her forever."

"I know that," said Frances. "I know I only have her for a little while."

"Well, just as long as you understand," Mildred said. "I don't want you to get too attached and forget that she belongs to someone else." But her sister's warning was too late. Frances had already become attached. Secretly she hoped that the little girl would never have to leave.

When Oswald wasn't at the store visiting with Patsy or at the river, he worked on his sketches on the back porch of the Kitchen house. One rainy afternoon when he was on the porch, Betty walked out to get something from the extra ice box she kept out there, glanced at his latest picture, and exclaimed, "That looks just like a blue jay!" And then she added, "I hate blue jays," and went back in the kitchen.

But Oswald was very encouraged. Not that Betty hated blue jays but that she had recognized what he had drawn. When he had first started, all his birds looked alike. He must be getting better.

Oswald was now spending most of his cigarette money on painting supplies, but that was all right with him. He was smoking less anyway.

A few days later, Oswald asked Claude Underwood, who

went fishing every morning at 6 A.M., if he would take him back up in the marshes. He wanted to see the large ospreys and their nests that he had been told were there. There was a picture of them in his Alabama birds book, but so far he had not spotted any.

"Sure," said Claude, happy to oblige. "I can get you right up to them and leave you there for a couple of hours, if you like." Claude had seen some of his drawings and was pleased that Oswald had found something he seemed to enjoy. He noticed that Oswald was getting a lot of mail now from the Alabama Ornithological and Audubon Society.

The next morning at five-thirty Oswald walked over to Claude's house. He saw a light on in the kitchen and knocked gently. Claude's wife, Sybil, opened the door and greeted him with a big smile. "Come on in, Mr. Campbell, and have a cup of coffee. Claude's getting the boat ready." He stepped into a big room, with pine walls and a brick fireplace that had a large circular brown-and-cream rug in front of it. The sofa and the easy chair and the curtains in the windows all had the same brown-checked material, and hanging over the fireplace was a picture of the Last Supper. A round honey-colored maple dining table, with a lazy Susan and chairs, was across the room. The place was neat and clean and looked as if it had not changed one bit since it was first decorated, which by the look of the pinecone wallpaper in the kitchen, Oswald guessed was probably sometime in the forties. "A place where time itself stood still," came to his mind as he sat down and was handed a cup of coffee and a homemade cinnamon bun by Sybil, who also looked like she was from the forties. She had on a white frilly apron over her housedress and still wore her hair in tight curls that only old-fashioned bobby pins could create. "Claude tells me you are going across the river to look at some birds for your art."

He laughed. "Mrs. Underwood, I don't know if you can call it art, but yes, I'm going to try and do a few sketches."

Sybil poured him another cup of coffee. "I think it's very exciting," she said. "Claude tells me you are a wonderful artist. Who knows, Mr. Campbell, one day you may be hanging in a museum and make us all famous."

Claude came through the front door. "Good morning," he said. "We can take off anytime you're ready."

"I'm ready," said Oswald, picking up his sketch pad. Sybil handed each of them a small paper bag.

Mr. Campbell looked at his sack. "What's this?"

"Your lunch," she said. "You don't think I'd send you boys off with nothing to eat, do you?"

It had been years since anyone had called Oswald a boy, and he liked it. As they walked to the river, he said, "Your wife is really nice. How long have you been married?"

"Forty-one years this July."

Then Claude, who was usually a man of few words, said something surprising. "And I don't mind telling you that there has not been a day in all those years that I haven't thanked the Good Lord for her."

The river was still covered with early morning mist as they headed out. After about an hour, the mist lifted and the sun came up over the salty marshes that now lay before them. Claude pointed to some tall gray trees that had great nests on the tops of them. "There they are." As they approached the bank of the river, a big hawklike bird rose up and gently flapped to another tree, and perched there, looking at them. "If you're lucky you'll see all kinds of owls and hawks and cranes, they live up in these marshes." Claude pulled up alongside a dock with a wooden bench and let him out. "I'll be back to get you in a few hours."

As Claude pulled away and disappeared around the bend and the sound of his motor faded away Oswald realized that he was truly out in the middle of nowhere. After a while back up in the marshes with only the sound of occasional wings flapping and a hoot owl way off in the distance to break the silence, Oswald began to lose all sense of time and place. All the years of catechism, and years of drinking, had not done it, but now, sitting in the silence, away from "the whirl of society and the noise of city life," he felt himself becoming one with nature. For the first time in his life he was at peace. He had finally caught a glimpse of what they had been talking about.

Around ten o'clock he started to get hungry, so he opened the sack and looked in. Sybil had packed him a typical fisherman's lunch: a box of saltine crackers and small tins of potted meat, tiny Vienna sausages, and sardines. She had included a white plastic knife and several packets of mustard and he ate the whole thing and it was delicious. An hour later, Claude came to pick him up, and when he got in the boat Claude said, "Any luck?"

"Oh, yes, I must have seen a hundred birds," he said. "What about you?"

"A little," Claude said, as they headed home. Oswald found out later that for Claude a little luck meant he had caught more fish and bigger fish than anyone on the river, not just that day but also that week. There was no question that he had a talent for fishing. He knew the currents and how to read them, how the wind affected the fish, how deep they were at what time of the year. Some who had been with him said he could hear them. But he was modest, and when he was asked how he did it he just said, "I do a lot of it and stick with it longer, I guess." The only time he did not fish was on Saturday afternoon when everybody in Lost River had the Saturday opera on the radio and you could hear it up and down the river. Claude said there was no point to try because all those Italians screaming like that scared the fish so bad they wouldn't bite anyway.

When Oswald had first been told that Claude Underwood went fishing every day of his life he could not comprehend how anybody could be so obsessed with one thing. But since he had started painting he understood completely. Still, he had a different reason to paint every day for as long as he possibly could. He wanted to be good enough to paint that one picture he had in mind and he hoped to finish it by Christmas. So while Claude fished, Oswald painted, and the river just kept quiet and let them do it.

. . .

At the next Mystic Order of the Royal Polka Dots Secret Society meeting, the annual election of officers was held. As usual, Frances was voted back in as president, Sybil Underwood as vice president, Mildred as treasurer, and Dottie Nivens as secretary. Betty Kitchen never stood for election. Because of her height and her military background, she had been named sergeant at arms, in perpetuity.

When the election was over, Mildred complained. "I don't know why we even bother to have the dumb thing anyway; we always elect the same old people." And after another show of hands, a vote was taken to change the election to every other year. At the same meeting, before they concluded their business, they also voted to reciprocate and invite the members of the Mystic Order of the Royal Dotted Swiss secret society over for a luncheon. Although they were a sister organization and often did projects together, there was also a small friendly rivalry between the two, and so elaborate plans were made. When they had been the Dotted Swiss's luncheon guests over at Lillian, they were served Pineapple Chicken Salad with date-nut bread and cream cheese. The Polka Dots decided that they would serve tomato aspic, three different breads, and a floating island for dessert. Nobody could top Sybil's floating island. Plus they would make table favors of polka-dotted pot holders to be at each plate. "That ought to impress them," declared Betty Kitchen.

A Sighting

A FEW WEEKS later, after Claude had dropped him off way up in the marshes again, Oswald had quite a start. He had been lost in his work and had not heard it coming, but when he looked up there was a boat sitting not more than five feet in front of him. The dark-skinned man in the boat was staring at him with a look that made his blood run cold. After a long moment he slowly began to paddle away, never saying a word. When Claude came back, Oswald described the man with blue-green eyes and silver hair to him and asked if he knew who he was.

Claude asked if he had a net in the back of his boat.

Oswald said he did.

Claude nodded. "I have a pretty good idea who it was, all right."

"Who?"

"I can't say for sure, but I think you might have just had yourself an up-close look at Julian LaPonde."

"The Creole?"

"Sounds like him."

"He didn't look too friendly, I can tell you that."

"No, he wouldn't."

"I didn't say anything."

"It's best that you didn't. You never know which way he's liable to jump."

"What should I do if he comes back?"

"He won't . . . believe me. He doesn't want a thing to do with any of us. If he could pick up his side of the river and move it to Louisiana, he would."

Claude was right. Oswald did not see him again.

As the days got warmer, Patsy would sometimes go out with Claude and Oswald to the marshes and sit with Oswald for hours while he painted. One day he looked over and said, "Hey, Patsy, what are you going to be when you grow up, do you know yet?"

She thought about it. "Hmmm . . . maybe a . . . I don't know."

"Well, is there anything you like to do?"

"I like to play with Jack. I like birds."

"Ah," he said. "Maybe you can be a veterinarian one day. Do you know what a veterinarian is?"

"No, sir."

"It's a doctor who takes care of animals and birds. Would you like that?"

"Yes, I would. Could I be a real doctor?"

"Sure. If you want to bad enough you can."

"Really? Could Jack come and see me?"

"Absolutely."

Her eyes suddenly lit up. "If I was a doctor, maybe I could fix his wing so he could fly so good that the hawks and owls couldn't catch him and eat him."

"Maybe you could." Then Oswald handed Patsy a small picture he had drawn for her of a large white crane, wearing glasses, tap shoes, and a top hat and carrying a walking stick under his wing. Underneath was written: *For Patsy, Mr. Ichabod Crane, Putting on the Ritz.*

That night when she came back home, Frances was at the sewing machine busy making borders for the pot holders and Patsy said, "Mrs. Cleverdon, guess what I'm going to be when I grow up?"

"Oh, I just wouldn't have any idea."

"Guess."

"Let's see. A teacher?" said Frances.

"No."

"A cowboy?"

"No." She laughed. "Do you want me to tell you?"

"Yes."

The girl's eyes lit up. "A bird doctor!"

"A bird doctor? Oh, my, where did you come up with that?"

"Mr. Campbell. He said if I wanted to bad enough I could. He said all you have to do is want something really, really bad, and if it's supposed to it will happen."

"He did?"

"Yes, he said he always wanted to paint and he wished and wished really really hard, and now he's doing it!"

Patsy showed her the picture Oswald had done for her that day. "Oh, this is very good," Frances said. "He's just getting better and better, isn't he? Your aunt Mildred should see this." She gave her back the picture. "You like Mr. Campbell, don't you?"

"Yes, ma'am, he's funny."

After Patsy went to bed, Frances thought about what Mr. Campbell had told Patsy and realized he might be right. She must have wanted a child *really* badly because she got one. Now she found herself actually praying that Patsy's father would never come back and take her away. She knew it was wrong to pray for something like that, but she couldn't help it.

The Stranger

I T WAS A warm humid afternoon in late May when a black car drove up in front of the store and parked. Roy was behind the counter by the cash register, laughing and telling Oswald that when he had come in that morning Jack had had his foot stuck in a flyswatter. Betty Kitchen was over in the produce department, examining the potatoes. When the man in the white shirt and dark shiny pants walked in and stood looking around the store, Roy looked up. "Can I help you find something?"

The man wiped his brow and the back of his neck with a handkerchief and said, "Yeah, I'll take something cold to drink if you have it. It's a hot one out there."

Roy pointed to the drink box. "Help yourself."

"Thanks," the man said.

Roy didn't know why, but he had a strange feeling about the guy, so he looked out the window and saw that his car was from Montgomery, the state capital, and it had an official state seal on the door. This guy was not lost or just stopping in for a drink. He was here on some sort of official business. While the man was looking in the box with his back turned, Roy slowly walked around and stood in front of the photograph taped against the side of the cash register.

The man came over with his drink. "I wonder if you could help me out. I'm trying to locate a Mrs. Tammie Suggs. I understand that she and her family used to live around here." When Betty Kitchen heard the name Suggs, she started throwing potatoes in her bag a mile a minute.

Roy leaned back up against the cash register, crossed his arms, and thought out loud. "Hmm, Suggs . . . Suggs. . . . Nope, doesn't ring a bell."

In the meantime, Oswald had slowly floated away from the cash register back into the store and was pretending to be looking for something on the shelf.

Roy took a toothpick out of his pocket, looked at it, then put it in the corner of his mouth and calmly asked, "Why are you trying to locate this Suggs woman. Any special reason?"

The man said, "I'm really looking for the little girl we were told she has in her possession." All of a sudden Jack started running around his plastic wheel and ringing his bells like crazy, as if he too understood the danger of the moment. The man continued, "I'm looking on behalf of the father"— he took a piece of paper out of his pocket and read, "A James Douglas Casey who left her in custody of the Suggs family. We have this area on file as their last known location."

"Huh," said Roy and turned around. "Miss Kitchen, does the name Suggs ring a bell with you?"

"Never heard of them," Betty said, as she moved on to the squash.

Roy called out to the back of the store. "Hey, Mr. Campbell, do you know of any Suggs family that used to live around here? Had a little girl with them?"

Oswald, who had been standing frozen in one spot, staring at a can of pork and beans said, "Suggs? No, the only family that might have been them moved to Mexico. I think they said they were going to Juárez or was it Cuernavaca? One of those places down there."

"Mexico?" the man asked. "Are you sure they said Mexico?"

"Yeah," said Oswald, picking up a can of butter beans and pretending to read the label. "They told me they weren't coming back, either, some trouble with the law or something."

"Huh," said the man.

About that time Claude came in the door carrying a bucket of fish and Roy immediately said, "Oh, hello, Mr. Underwood, how are you today?" and cleared his throat. "Maybe you can help us out. This gentleman here is looking for a girl that lived back up in the woods with a family named Suggs. Mr. Campbell remembers there was a family back there with a little girl that took off and went to Mexico, Juárez or Cuernavaca. Isn't that right, Mr. Campbell?"

"That's right," said Oswald, who was now in the breakfast cereal section.

Claude had figured out something was wrong the minute

Roy called him Mr. Underwood. He put the bucket of fish up on the counter and said, "I hate to disagree with you, Oswald, but I heard those folks you are talking about say they were headed out to Canada."

The man looked at him. "Canada?"

Claude took his cap off and scratched his head. "Yeah, as I recall it they said they were going up to Quebec."

"Maybe you're right," said Oswald, picking up a box of Blue Diamond stove matches. "I knew it was somewhere that began with a Q."

Claude said, "No, wait a minute. . . . Now that I think about it, it *could* have been Mexico. I know it was one of those places but if I were you I'd try looking in Mexico first."

"Oh, brother." The man sighed. "By the time I go through all the red tape down there, the kid will be grown."

"So," said Roy, as casually as he could, even managing a yawn, "the father wants the girl back?"

The man took a swig of his Coke and shook his head. "No, not really. The father's dead. Fell off the back of a truck a couple of months ago. The grandmother claims she's too old to take care of the little girl so she signed her over to us, and now all I have to do is find her."

"Who is us?" asked Roy.

"The State of Alabama. She's an official ward of the state now."

At that moment, Betty Kitchen glanced out the window and saw Patsy coming down the street, headed straight for the front door. Betty immediately grabbed her sack of groceries and swept her way past the men at the cash register.

"I'll pay you tomorrow," she said, and was out the door. With her sack in one arm, she snatched Patsy up off the ground with the other and had her headed back home to Frances in less than five seconds. Betty had not been an emergency room nurse for nothing. She could move fast when she had to. The man in the store, who had missed the entire episode, continued to complain about his job. "I waste half my life running up and down the roads trying to track these people down and—" He stopped in mid-sentence. "What are those bells I'm hearing?"

Roy said, "It's just a bird I've got back there."

"Oh," he said.

"Say," said Roy. "Just out of curiosity. What will happen to her when you do find her?"

"Well," he said, looking around at all the mounted fish and animals on the wall, "being she has no other living relatives, she'll most likely be sent to a state home until she's eighteen."

Oswald flinched when he heard that. Just the thought of Patsy being raised in a state home almost made him sick to his stomach. The man walked over, looked into the bucket, and said, "Nice fish." Then he put his empty bottle on the counter and sighed again. "Well, thanks for your help, but from what you fellows tell me it doesn't look likely that I will find that little girl anytime soon. *You* try tracking somebody down in Mexico or in Canada." He then asked Roy what he owed for the Coke.

"Nothing," said Roy. "I'm always happy to accommodate a government man."

"Much obliged," he said, and handed Roy his card. "My name is Brent Boone: that's my numbers on the bottom. Call me if you hear anything."

Roy said, "Yeah, we sure will, Mr. Boone."

Boone went to the door muttering to himself. "Mexico, of all the damn places." Then he turned around at the door and said, "Well, wish me luck, fellows. God knows I'll need it."

"Yeah," said Roy. "Good luck." And they all watched him drive away. Roy picked up the phone to call Frances. As far as they were concerned, from that day on Patsy was officially theirs, and Oswald walked home that night grinning from ear to ear. Patsy Casey was her name. She was Irish, just like him!

The Assistant

As THE SUMMER progressed, it seemed everything was looking up. Oswald continued to feel well, and the Dotted Swiss luncheon was a huge success. The Dotted Swiss ladies, who tended to lord it over the Polka Dots as far as their needlework was concerned, had been very impressed with the pot holders, and Frances could tell they were green with envy over the tomato aspic. Not only had the luncheon been a hit, Patsy was very happy. She had a brand-new job.

In the past, when asked, Roy had taken Jack out and done a few little shows with him for local schools or church bazaars to raise money. But the next time he and Jack were asked to do a show, Roy asked Frances if Patsy could come along. She said yes, she thought it was a fine idea. After that, whenever he and Jack did a show, he started taking Patsy along as his assistant. Frances even bought her a special red-striped dress to wear to match Roy's red-and-white-striped jacket and straw hat. Oswald went with them and helped set up chairs for the performance. Roy would start the show with Patsy standing beside him and Jack perched on his finger.

"Come one, come all, come and see the Amazing Redbird of Baldwin County. He walks, he talks, he crawls on his belly like a snake. The only redbird in captivity that actually knows his own name! And now, my lovely assistant Miss Patsy and I will demonstrate. Is your name Jack?" The bird would bob up and down as if he were agreeing. "*Yes!* he says. Absolutely amazing. But wait. Now you might think a poor dumb bird would not know his right from his left. But observe the Amazing Redbird of Baldwin County." At this point Patsy would hold out her right finger and Jack would land on it. "That is correct, sir! And now the left." Jack would fly over to her left hand. "Absolutely amazing! The only redbird in America, ladies and gentlemen, boys and girls of all ages, that can tell me exactly what I have hidden here in my hand." Then the bird would walk up her arm to her shoulder and nudge her ear. "And what did he say the object was, Miss Patsy?" He would lean down while Patsy whispered something to him. "The bird has said, *Sunflower seeds.*"

Roy then opened his hand to reveal about ten shiny black sunflower seeds. "He is absolutely correct yet again! Ladies and gentlemen! I can hardly believe it myself." Then Patsy would pretend the bird said something else in her ear and tug on Roy's jacket and Roy would hold up his hand and say, "Wait a moment, ladies and gentlemen, the bird has spoken again." Then Patsy would whisper again to Roy. "Ah-ha!" said Roy. "The Amazing Redbird of Baldwin County says he would like to demonstrate his powers of detection. Very well. At this time I will hide certain objects and test his abilities. Please turn your back, Miss Patsy, while I hide the objects." Patsy would turn away with Jack, as Roy would make a big show out of hiding seeds in all his pockets; later of course Jack, who was a glutton for sunflower seeds, amazed the audience as he crawled in and out of all Roy's pockets and found every one.

After the shows children would come up and try to talk to Patsy, but Roy noticed that she seemed shy and afraid of other children.

Frances saw it too, and it worried her. She tried to invite a few children over to the house to play with Patsy, but it was no good. All Patsy wanted to do was play with Jack. Frances wondered if, in the past, children had been mean to her because of her leg. The first time she had bathed her she had been surprised to see how badly twisted her little body was. She just hoped, when Patsy went to school in the fall, that the other children would not make fun of her.

Two Men in a Boat

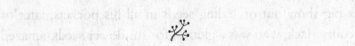

CLAUDE HEARD THE redfish were biting and had gone all the way up the river over to Perdido Bay. As he was coming home up the backside of the river late that afternoon, he heard somebody yelling, "Help! Help! Help!"

He saw two men standing up in a shiny brand-new blue-and-white twenty-two-foot boat in the middle of the river, frantically waving.

He throttled down his motor and pulled up alongside them. "Hey, fellows, what's up?"

"Thank God you came along! We've been stranded out here all day," one man said.

The other man said, "We must have hit something, because the motor just died and wouldn't start again and we've been drifting around for hours. We must have drifted five miles."

Claude asked, "Why didn't you use your paddles?"

"They didn't give us any," the man said.

Claude calmly pointed over at the right side of the boat. "Look in that compartment down there. There should be a couple."

The larger man opened the long side panel and saw two paddles. "Oh."

"Where did you fellows come from?"

"We started out at the Grand Hotel at Point Clear. Where are we now?"

"You're all the way to Lost River, about fifteen miles south."

"How are we going to get all the way back?"

"Well, let me take a look at this thing." Claude maneuvered around the back of the boat and quickly assessed the situation. "You got your motor all twisted up with silt and mud."

"Can it be fixed?"

"Oh, sure, but we've got to pull it out of the water to do it." He threw them a rope and towed them back to his house. When they pulled up to the dock, Claude looked at the setting sun and said, "It'll be too dark to get you to the hotel by boat tonight, but I'll get Butch to drive you back and the hotel can send somebody to get your boat tomorrow."

As the two men gathered up their expensive fishing gear and heavy rods and reels, Claude chuckled. "What were you boys aiming to catch out there today?"

Embarrassed that they had to be towed in, they tried to sound like they knew what they were doing. "Oh, speckled trout, redfish. I hear they're running pretty good this time of year."

"Uh-huh," said Claude. "About the only thing you're liable to catch with that stuff you got there is a shark—or a whale, maybe."

He opened a box and pulled out a string of the biggest bass, redfish, and speckled trout they had ever seen.

"Come on up to the house and I'll call Butch."

"Thanks, that's mighty nice of you."

"By the way," said the larger one, "my name is Tom and this is Richard."

"I'm Claude Underwood. Nice to meet you."

As the three of them headed up the yard, Claude said, "You boys down here on a vacation?"

"No," said Tom, "we're attending a medical convention at the hotel, but we thought we might try to get a little fishing in while we're here."

When they got to the house Sybil fixed them some coffee and a few minutes later Butch came in the door whistling. He was used to being called to take amateur fishermen back home. It gave him a chance to have some fun. "Hey, guys, I hear you got lost. That's why we call it Lost River, 'cause if you're up this far, you must be lost." And as always he laughed at his own joke, thinking it was the funniest thing he had ever heard.

When they were leaving, Claude said, "How long are you here for?"

Tom said, "Just three more days. Unfortunately this one was shot to hell." He looked over at Sybil. "Excuse me, ma'am."

Sybil laughed. "Don't worry, I'm married to a fisherman so I've heard that kind of language before."

Claude, who felt sorry for them, said, "If you want to do some more fishing, come back tomorrow and I'll take you out and show you a few good spots."

Later, when Butch was driving them back to the hotel, he said, "You might not know it, but you just met the best fisherman in the state. If he's offered to take you out, you need to take him up on it."

"Thanks! We will," they said.

The next afternoon Butch picked them up and drove them back down to the river to where Claude was waiting for them at the dock.

"Hey, boys, get in," he said. They climbed into his old green fourteen-foot flat-bottom boat powered by a small five-horse Johnson motor and headed out. Claude handed them both a simple rod and reel and explained his method. "I only use this little guy here." He held up a red and white Heddon vamp spook. "Now I modify it a bit, I take the front lip off and it runs deeper for you. Or else I just use a little lead head jig, but that's all you really need."

Before the day was over, the two men were so excited they could hardly believe it. They had caught more fish and learned more about fishing in one day than they had all their lives. They thought Claude must have some sort of secret knowledge about fish. Claude, always philosophical, said, "Naw, there's no secret to it. Either they're biting or they ain't."

* * *

The men came down the next two afternoons and had a wonderful time going up and down the river with Claude, and he got a kick out of the two who were obviously city boys, full of enthusiasm and excitement every time they caught something. On the last day they were to be there, they tried to pay him for being their guide, but Claude said, "No. You don't owe me a thing."

Tom said, "We'd love to pay you for your time."

"Thank you, but no, it was my pleasure."

"Are you sure?"

"Yes, I'm sure. You fellows don't owe me a dime. But I am going to ask you to do me a favor."

"If we can, sure, what is it?"

"I know you fellows are both doctors, and I wondered if you would take a look at a little girl for me and tell me what you think."

In the past few days Claude had found out that the two men were at the hotel for the southeastern convention of elbow and shoulder surgeons. He did not know if they could help Patsy but he thought it might be worth a try, so he told Frances to have Patsy up at his house that afternoon just in case they agreed to see her.

Frances dressed Patsy in her best dress and brought her over, and they sat in the living room with Sybil and Butch and waited for them. When the two men walked in with Claude, he introduced them to Frances and then to Patsy. Tom leaned down and shook her hand. "Hi, Patsy, how are you?" Then he said, "Honey, could you do me a big favor? Would you walk across the room for me?" Patsy looked at Frances, who smiled and motioned for her to do it. Patsy walked across the room and stopped. Tom whispered something to his friend and said, "Now come on back for me." She did. "That's fine, thank you, honey," he said. After a few more minutes of small talk, they said their goodbyes and walked out the door.

Claude and Butch followed them out, and they stood in the yard and talked. Tom said, "Mr. Underwood, unfortunately that sort of birth injury is not our specialty. We deal mostly with sports injuries. I wish we could help, but that girl needs a specialist."

"What kind of specialist?"

"She needs a pediatric orthopedic surgeon," said Richard. "Kids' bones are tricky, and you need someone with a lot of skill and expertise in that area."

Tom looked at his friend and said a name: "Sam Glickman."

Richard nodded. "Yeah."

Later that night the phone rang. "Mr. Underwood, this is Tom. Listen. If you can get that little girl up here to the hotel before eight o'clock in the morning, Sam says he will take a quick look at her before he has to catch his plane back to Atlanta."

Claude called Frances and told her to have Patsy ready and that Butch would pick them up at six-thirty and drive them over to the hotel. When Frances told Patsy that they were going for a ride in the morning, she asked if Mr. Campbell could go with them.

"Well, if you want him to, I'll call and see."

When she phoned and asked, Oswald said, "If Patsy wants me to come, I'll be there."

When he hung up he was so pleased that Patsy had wanted him to go along, he felt like a million bucks. Would he go? Why, he would have gone to the moon and back if she had asked.

The next morning Butch drove the three of them all the way over to Point Clear, to the Grand Hotel on the Mobile Bay. At seven-thirty, wearing only her underwear and her Dr Pepper hat, Patsy was lying on a banquet table in the main dining room being examined by Dr. Samuel Glickman. Frances and Oswald both cringed as they watched the doctor push and pull her leg back and forth, up and down. Then he turned her over and felt all the way up her spine, talking to her the whole time he was examining her. "You know, Patsy," he said, "I have a little granddaughter about your age named Colbi, and do you know what she told me? Does that hurt?" Patsy made a face like it did but said, "No, sir." Then he turned her back over. "She said, 'Granddaddy, I already have two boyfriends.' Can you imagine that?" As he sat her up and had her bend over to the left as far as she could and then to the right, he asked, "Do you have a boyfriend?"

"No, sir," she said.

"Yes, you do, Patsy," Frances said. "You told me the other day that Jack was your boyfriend. Tell the doctor about Jack, honey."

After it was all over, the doctor looked at his watch, picked up his suitcase, and said to Frances, "Come walk to the car with me, Mrs. Cleverdon." Then he turned and smiled and waved. "Goodbye, Patsy."

He talked as they walked through the lobby.

"Mrs. Cleverdon, I would need to do X-rays, of course, but from what I felt I would say that her pelvis and right hip were broken in four, maybe five places, and whoever did it never bothered to set the bones straight. Does she complain much about pain?"

Frances, running to keep up with him, said, "No, Doctor, she's never said a word about pain."

"Well, I don't know why she hasn't, because I know it has to hurt. Those bones are pressing on the nerves in her hip and spine, and the more she grows the worse it will get."

As he got in the waiting car, Frances blurted out the one question they all wanted answered. "Can anything be done?"

Dr. Glickman looked up. "Mrs. Cleverdon, it's not a question of can anything be done. Something has to be done." He handed her a card. "Call my office and set up an appointment," he said, and the car drove away.

Frances went back inside and found them all waiting in the lobby for her. "He wants to see her in his office," she said.

Two weeks later they were swerving in and out of Atlanta traffic while Frances and Oswald reached back and forth over Patsy trying to read the map. Finally, they found the medical building and made it on time.

Frances said, "How anybody can find their way in or out of this town is a mystery to me."

After a series of X-rays were looked at and all the tests were done, Dr. Glickman called Frances and Oswald into his office while a nurse took Patsy down to the cafeteria for something to eat.

"With a malformation as severe as this," he said, "if we let it go uncorrected any longer, what will happen is that she will begin to lose mobility and eventually she won't be able to walk at all."

Frances grabbed Oswald's hand for support. "Oh, dear."

"And as she continues to grow it will begin to affect her central nervous system as well. The sooner we can reset those bones and relieve her skeletal and muscular area from all the stress and strain the better. But we are talking about two—maybe three—separate surgeries. With a child that young and frail it's a pretty serious undertaking, and it's going to require a lot of strength and stamina on her part to get through it."

Frances was alarmed. "You don't mean she could die, do you?"

"With any major surgery there's always that possibility, of course, but from what I have seen she seems like a pretty happy little girl with a lot to live for. But let me be clear. She will need a lot of emotional support from all of us for the long haul, and even after going through it all there are still no guarantees she will heal properly."

"Oh, dear," said Frances again.

"Having said all that, in my opinion it has to be done. I just want you to know up front that it is going to be a long hard process, no matter what the results."

Oswald asked, "Will it be expensive?"

"I wish I could say no, Mr. Campbell, but yes. It will be terribly expensive." He glanced down at the picture of his granddaughter on his desk. And then he flipped through his calendar and looked over his glasses. "I'll tell you what I'll do. I'll waive my surgical fees. That ought to help some. If you promise to have her here with a few more pounds on her by the end of July, we can do her first operation the morning of August second."

Frances told the doctor that they would be there and that Patsy would have more pounds on her if she had to feed her twenty times a day. How they would get the rest of the money was another question, but she did not tell him that.

For the next month everybody up and down the street plied Patsy with cookies and candies and as much ice cream as she could eat. They were determined to get those extra pounds on her by the end of July. But the main problem was going to be the money. Even without the doctor's fees it was estimated that the long hospital stay plus the following months of therapy would run over a hundred thousand dollars. Frances and Mildred had a little saved, but it was not nearly enough. The Lost River Community Association had several fund-raisers, and a large jar that said THE PATSY FUND sat by the cash register in the grocery store. Pretty soon, as more people found out about it, other organizations began to help them as well. When Elizabeth, their friend over in Lillian who was president of their sister group, the Mystic Order of the Royal Dotted Swiss, heard about it, her group held a bake and rummage sale. Lost River had a huge fish fry at the community hall every Saturday, thanks to Claude Underwood, and people came from all over the county for that. As word spread, and courtesy of Butch's friends, the Elks Club over in Elberta decided to have a fund-raiser. They planned a barbecue, and everybody in Lost River attended, along with hundreds of other people from all over the county. When Oswald got there he was in for a surprise. The members of the Alabama Accordion Association had donated their services and were giving a free concert in the park to raise money. They were up on the bandstand, dressed in lederhosen. Mr. Krause spotted Oswald and waved while playing "The Beer Barrel Polka." Frances and Mildred and Patsy joined him, and they sat in the wooden chairs and listened along with the rest of the people. Patsy was on her second cotton candy when suddenly Oswald saw something that made his blood run cold. He had just spotted Brent Boone, the government man, sitting in the front row across from them, and he was looking right at Patsy.

Oswald felt his ears turn red. After a few minutes Boone stood up and walked over to the large wooden barrel that had THE PATSY FUND written across it, threw in ten dollars, and headed up the aisle right toward him. As he walked past Oswald, who had stopped breathing, he looked down at him and said out of the side of his mouth, "Mexico, my ass," and kept going.

As August approached, Oswald wanted to do something for Patsy, but of course he had no money. But there was one thing he could try. Even if he only got a few dollars it might help.

Butch drove him over to the big Grand Hotel on the Bay in Point Clear. The last time they had been there with Patsy, he had noticed an art gallery in the lobby. Today he mustered up all his courage, walked in, and a nice lady looked at his watercolors, one at a time, but did not offer an opinion.

When she finished, she asked, "How much are you asking for these, Mr. Campbell?" He was thrown completely; he had never sold anything in his life, much less his own work, so he said, "Why don't you name a price?"

She looked at them again and counted. "You have eighteen paintings here, is that right?"

"Yes."

She looked again and then said, "I can offer you two hundred and fifty dollars."

"You're kidding," he said, thrilled beyond belief that she was willing to buy them for so much money.

"I wish I could offer you more, Mr. Campbell, these are just excellent, but we're just a small shop."

"No, that's fine. I'll take it."

When she handed him the check, she said, "I'd be interested in seeing anything else you have, Mr. Campbell."

When he got outside and looked at the check, he almost fainted.

She had meant $250.00 dollars apiece!

By the end of July, almost all the money they needed had been raised and everyone was pretty optimistic that the rest would be there on time. The morning before Patsy was to go to Atlanta for her operation, Oswald and Roy had planned to have a little going-away party for her up at the store. Roy came in around 6:45 A.M. to get ready to open and whistled for Jack. "Hey, buddy, your girlfriend is coming to see you." No answer. "What have you gotten yourself into today, you nutty bird? You better not be in the marshmallows again; I don't have time to give you another bath." He wandered around whistling and looking for the bird, and when he walked toward the front of the store he saw Jack over in the corner on the floor by the produce, his favorite place to scavenge. "What do you have down there? You better not be pecking the tomatoes again. Mildred will be after you for sure." He went over and looked; Jack was lying on his side. "What are you doing, you silly thing?" When he picked him up, Jack's body felt stiff, and his usually bright eyes were strangely dull and glassed over. He looked at the bird again. Then it suddenly hit Roy like a ton of bricks. Jack was dead.

Roy stood there in shock. He could not believe that this cold lifeless thing he held in his hand was really Jack. At that moment it seemed the whole world went silent and all Roy could hear was the sound of his own heart beating. He continued to stand there stunned and not moving until after a while he finally heard Oswald knocking loudly on the front window. He looked up and Oswald waved at him. Roy went over and opened the door. Oswald could see that Roy was white as a sheet. Something was wrong.

Roy said, "Come back to the office."

Oswald followed him back. "What's the matter, Roy?"

Roy closed the door and held him out. "Jack's dead."

"Oh, my God," said Oswald. "What happened?"

Roy sat down at his desk and shook his head. "I don't know. I just found him this very minute." Roy picked up the phone and called his veterinarian friend, who told him to look and see if Jack seemed hurt in any way. Roy looked him over. "No, he looks fine, there's no blood or anything unusual anywhere."

"Well, I don't know what to tell you, Roy, he could have eaten something, or caught some virus; it could have been one of a hundred things. But these things can happen very fast with birds. One day they're OK and the next day they're gone. I sure am sorry."

Roy hung up and looked at Oswald. "He doesn't know."

The two men just sat there, not knowing what to say, when Oswald suddenly thought of something.

"Hey Roy," he said. "What about Patsy? What are we going to tell Patsy?"

Roy looked up. "Oh, God, I didn't think about that. Get Frances on the phone and tell her not to let Patsy come up here until we figure out what to do. I'm going to put the CLOSED sign on the door."

Oswald dialed Frances while Roy closed the blinds and turned out the lights. Frances picked up the phone.

"Hello?"

Oswald said, "Frances, it's Oswald. I'm at the store. Where's Patsy?"

"She's right here, Mr. Campbell, just finishing her breakfast, why?"

"Thank goodness she's still there. Whatever you do, don't let her come up to the store today."

"Oh?" she said, looking over at Patsy and not quite understanding. "Well, that's going to be mighty hard."

"I know it is but you have to do it. I'll explain later. You just keep her there."

Frances could tell by the tone in Mr. Campbell's voice that whatever was going on must be pretty serious. Patsy was just standing up to leave, and Frances blurted out, "Oh, honey, I can't let you go up to the store today."

Patsy's eyes got big. "Why?"

"Oh, the most awful thing has happened."

"What?"

She looked at the little girl who stood waiting for an answer. "Poor Roy has the measles!" she said, thankful that something came to her at the very last second.

Patsy suddenly looked frightened. "Oh, no! Does Jack have the measles too?"

"No, darling, birds don't get measles, only people."

Frances could not imagine what had really happened. Both of them knew Patsy was leaving for the hospital tomorrow and not seeing Jack before she left would upset her terribly. The only thing she could imagine serious enough was that maybe that crazy Julian LaPonde had finally come across the river and gone on a shooting spree and shot Roy.

In a few minutes Oswald came into the backyard and caught Frances's eye from the kitchen window. He motioned for her to come over to his house.

Frances dried her hands. "Honey, I have to run over to Betty's but I'll be right back. Now promise me you will not move from this house, OK?" She handed Patsy a coloring book and went next door. Betty and Oswald were in the living room, huddled together in hushed conversation. "What in the world is going on?" she asked.

Betty said, "Sit down, Frances, we have terrible news."

Frances put her hand over her mouth, "Oh, no, it's Roy, isn't it? He's been shot, hasn't he? Is he dead?"

Betty said, "No, it's not Roy, it's Jack. Roy came in this morning and found him."

"Oh, my God, what happened?"

"We don't know, but that's why we didn't want Patsy coming down to the store," Oswald said.

Frances sat down, "Oh, dear God in heaven, what in the world are we going to tell her? You know how she feels about that bird."

Oswald said, "Yes, I do. How did you keep her home today?"

"I told her Roy had the measles, I didn't know what to say; I wasn't thinking straight. I also promised her she could go up to the store and say goodbye to Jack tomorrow. I didn't know he was *dead*."

Just then Mildred came barging in the front door. "What's going on? I went down to the store and it was closed."

Betty shut the door behind her. "Jack is dead."

Mildred gasped and looked at her sister.

Frances said, "It's true. Roy came in this morning and found him on the floor."

"Oh, no," cried Mildred, and then proceeded to collapse on the couch in a heap, wailing "Oh, no! Oh, poor little Jack. . . . Oh, that poor little bird. Oh, I just feel so terrible! Oh, the poor little thing."

Frances looked at her like she had lost her mind. "Mildred, what is the matter with you? Why are you suddenly carrying on like that? You did nothing but complain about him when he was alive."

"I know I did," Mildred wailed, "but I always liked him. It never occurred to me he would die! Oh, poor little Jack." She then grabbed a lace doily from the back of Betty's couch and used it as a handkerchief, which Betty did not appreciate.

"Mildred," said Frances, "you are, without a doubt, the strangest woman I ever knew. All you ever did was to threaten to cook him."

"Oh, I know I did!" Mildred wailed even louder, and threw herself back down on the couch again.

Frances said, "Oh, for God's sake, Mildred, pull yourself together," and turned to Betty and Oswald in amazement. "The very time I need her is the very time she decides to fall apart."

* * *

Later that afternoon, while Patsy was having her nap, Butch, Betty, Dottie, Frances, and Oswald gathered in Roy's office, trying to figure out what to do. Frances explained the problem. "The doctor told us that the operations are going to be very difficult and dangerous and right now, that bird is the one thing in this world she cares the most about. Jack is her best friend. How do you tell a child who's getting ready to go through major surgery that her best friend is dead?"

Oswald agreed with Frances. "I don't see how we *can* tell her. I think we have to figure out what is more important here, telling the truth or taking a chance on her not making it through the operation."

Dottie said, "But we can't lie to her, can we? That would be wrong, wouldn't it?" She looked around the room. "We can't lie to a child, can we?"

Betty said, "Why not, Dottie? You do it every year at Christmas. What's the difference? Speaking as an ex-nurse with some psychological training, I say just go on to Atlanta as if nothing happened. Then later after her operations and her therapy is over, when she's healthy and out of the woods, then we tell her."

"Yeah, Frances," said Butch. "Just don't tell her now."

Frances shook her head. "That sounds easy and I agree with you, but the problem is that I know she will not want to leave here in the morning until she tells Jack goodbye. It was all I could do to keep her at home today."

Dottie thought for a moment. "Could we get another redbird by morning? They all look pretty much alike, don't they? I couldn't tell one from another myself."

Betty looked at Dottie as if she were insane and asked, "How are we going to catch another redbird by morning? Besides, she'll know that's not the same bird. Do you think a strange bird is going to sit on her finger and do tricks?"

"Well, you think of something then," said Dottie.

After everybody left, Roy sat holding Jack in his hand. He had been the one to realize that the only person who could help them was the one man in this world he hated. The one man he had vowed never to forgive. But there was no other way. After trying their best to think of something else, they all came to agree that this was the only solution. Poor skinny, brave Butch offered to go, and so did Betty Kitchen, but since neither of them were familiar with the other side of the river, it was decided that Roy had to go, and he had to go alone. It was the hardest thing he would ever have to do in his life: swallow every ounce of pride he had. But he made the decision to do it anyway. He had to forget about the past just this once. This was for Patsy.

He wrapped Jack in a handkerchief and placed him in his jacket pocket. Just as the sun was starting to get low in the sky, he rowed across the river to a place where he had spent most of his childhood playing on the river with the Creole families and children he had grown up with, eating gumbo and jambalaya at their mothers' tables. The happy, sunlit place he had once loved was now nothing but a shadowy murky swamp full of painful memories.

Around dusk, he pulled his boat up to the dock, walked to

the long gray wooden Creole cottage where Julian LaPonde lived, and knocked on the door. No answer.

After a while he called out, "Julian, it's Roy. I need to talk to you." Still no answer, but someone was moving around inside. A few seconds later, when he heard the unmistakable sound of a gun click, he knew it was Julian on the other side of the screen door.

Roy was suddenly overwhelmed with old feelings of rage and humiliation. Rage at the fact that this man had ruined his life, humiliated that he had to ask for a favor instead of doing what he wanted to do—reach through the door, pull Julian out into the yard, and stomp him to death. As he continued knocking, he was even further humiliated because, for some inexplicable reason beyond his control he began to cry. He stood there with tears running down his face, as he tried to talk and hold back the sobs at the same time.

"Julian, I know you hate my guts and I hate you . . . but I want you to look at a picture of this little girl." He took out the photograph of Patsy and Jack and held it up against the screen so he could see. "She's a little crippled girl, Julian, and she's going off to have a really bad operation tomorrow, and the bird who was her friend died last night. If she finds out, I don't think she can make it. So I need your help." Then he broke down completely and stood sobbing on the porch like a ten-year-old.

Julian, who had the gun aimed right at his chest and was fully prepared to shoot, hesitated for a moment. He must have seen the boy in Roy he had once known so well. After another moment he slowly put the gun down at his side and walked up closer to the door, looked at the picture, and then said to Roy in his thick Creole accent, "I tell you . . . I kill you dead if you ever was to come over here."

"I know." Roy sighed. "You can kill me later if you want to, I don't care anymore, but tonight you have to help me. I'll pay you whatever you want."

Julian stood staring at him but made no move. He could see that in the years that had passed Roy had grown into quite a man. The only thing Roy noticed in the dim light was that Julian's thick black curly hair had turned silver. As they stood there, with Roy still pressing the picture of Patsy and Jack against the screen, Roy heard a woman's voice from inside the cottage say "Let him in."

After another moment, Julian growled. "Well . . . I do it for the little gull, not you, you understand?" Roy nodded. "Come on then," Julian said roughly.

As Roy stepped in the room, someone said, "Hello, Roy," and as his eyes adjusted to the light he saw the woman, looking more beautiful than she had the last time he had seen her years ago. It was Marie.

Time had not changed the way he felt about her, and from the look in Marie's eyes, it seemed she felt the same.

As the sun was coming up Julian came in the kitchen and handed Jack's body back to Roy. He had worked all night and done a skillful job. All of Jack's feathers had been carefully cleaned and fluffed up, and his eyes were bright and shiny. Somehow Julian had managed to take the poor dead bird he had been handed the night before and make it look alive again. Even the way the head was cocked to one side and the expression was Jack's. Roy looked at Julian and shook his head. "It's better than I could have hoped for. I don't know what to say, Julian, except thank you." Roy stood up and reached for his wallet in his back pocket. "How much do I owe you?"

Julian's eyes flashed with anger. "I tell you, I do it for the little gull. Now go." Roy looked at Marie and nodded good-bye and then rowed back across the river with his friend.

What Roy didn't know was that the Creoles already knew about the little crippled girl named Patsy and the redbird who lived on the other side of the river. Their parish priest had been in the audience at one of the shows with Jack that he and Patsy had done for the Catholic Church over in Lillian. When he had talked about it in his sermon the following Sunday, all the Creole children who were not allowed to go across the river longed to see the redbird and the girl. And later, when the priest heard about the Patsy Fund, he had taken up a collection for her in church and sent it over as an anonymous gift. Julian, who had grown even more cold-hearted over the years and hated everybody on the other side, had not donated a dime to the fund and resented those who did. Why should they care about those people? He wouldn't lift a finger to help any of them. But last night, seeing Patsy's face in the photograph smiling at him through the screen door, something happened that made him change his mind. He really had done it for the little girl.

Leaving Home

✣

THE NEXT MORNING, from the moment Patsy awakened all she did was ask when she could see Jack. Frances didn't know what to tell her until she heard from Roy. Roy had gotten back to the store at around eight and Oswald was there waiting for him with his painting kit. It was around eight-thirty when Oswald finished painting red spots all over Roy's face to back up the measles story. Roy finally called a nervous Frances. When the phone rang she picked it up on the first ring.

"Hello?"

"It's me," said Roy. Frances, pretending the call was from a boyfriend she had dated thirty-seven years ago who had been dead for six years, said, "Oh, hello, Herbert, what a surprise to hear from you after all these years!" She was not sure if Patsy could hear her conversation but she did not want to take any chances. "Well. So everything is OK with you?"

Roy had no idea who Herbert was and said, "Yes, we're ready to go here. Come on anytime. Drive her up to the window, keep the motor running, slow down and stop for just a few seconds, then take off."

"Oh, dear," said Frances, in a high-pitched voice. "That will be mighty hard to do."

"I know, but I think a few seconds is all we can chance it. Jack looks good, but if she gets too long a look she's liable to figure it out."

"I understand completely. I'll try my very best," she said, to the imaginary man. "And Herbert, I'm so glad you are feeling better. Well, goodbye, and thanks for calling."

The second she put the phone down, it rang again and she almost jumped out of her skin.

"Hello!" It was Mildred. "Did you get the message? Roy said to drive by but don't stop for long."

"Yes, I got the message," she said. "Don't be calling me now, Mildred. I've got to go!"

Frances was so nervous about the upcoming surgery, and now the bird situation, that she went to the bathroom and nearly plucked every one of her eyebrows out. She had to quickly pencil them back in with a black eyebrow pencil, but when she did they were shaped like upside down half moons. When she saw what she had done, she muttered to herself, "Dear God, I look like a cartoon, but that just can't be helped. I'm late as it is." She powdered her nose and fluffed her hair a few times and called out, "Patsy, honey, it's time to go." She put Patsy in the backseat of the car with a pillow so she could lie down along the way. Patsy looked worried and asked again, "Can we go by and see Jack now?" Frances pretended not to hear her and reached in and honked her horn for Oswald. He walked over and put his suitcase in the trunk and got in the car. "Good morning, Patsy," he said, trying to sound casual, but Frances could tell he was as anxious as she was. When Frances came around the other side of the car and got in, she said, "I hope I have everything, I can't trust myself to remember anything. If I've left something, so be it. We have to leave right now or we will never get there on time." She looked down and checked the gas. "Good, we have a full tank." Butch had filled it for her last night and thank goodness, because with everything that was going on she would have forgotten to do it. "Well," she said, "for better or worse, here we go."

As she pulled out of the driveway a worried Patsy said, "Can't I go and say goodbye to Jack?"

Frances looked at her in the rearview mirror and said, "Oh, for heaven's sake. In all this rush I almost forgot you wanted to go by and see Jack, didn't you?"

"Yes, ma'am."

"Well, all right, I'll whip you by there, but for just a second."

Oswald sat completely still, afraid to move a muscle, but he could not help but be impressed by the way Frances managed the sharp turn perfectly and pulled up on the other side of the gas tanks not more than fifteen feet from the front window, and stopped the car on a dime. Roy stood waiting with Jack perched upon his finger, looking as bright and alive as he ever had.

"Can't I go in?" asked Patsy.

"Oh, no, honey. Roy still has the measles. Look at him! You can't get near him. Not with you just about to be operated on. Just wave, honey," she said as she stepped on the gas and took off. Patsy turned around and waved at Jack bobbing up and down on Roy's finger until the store and the little redbird were out of sight. As they turned onto the highway, safely headed to Atlanta, Frances was happy she had worn her dress shields. At one point after they drove off she half expected Patsy to say something, but at the moment she seemed content to at least have seen Jack, even if it had only been for a moment.

After they had been on the road awhile, Patsy took out her birthday picture with Jack and whispered to it, "I'll be back . . . you be good now."

The Big City

✢

WHEN THEY ARRIVED in Atlanta and checked Patsy into the hospital, Oswald went to a pay phone. He called Roy and told him that Patsy had been fooled completely and had talked to the picture of Jack all the way. "Honest to God, Roy," he said, "I know Jack is dead and it even fooled me, when you were standing there. I half expected him to fly!"

It was true. Julian had done an incredible job that night and Jack had never looked better. Roy picked him up and said, "You pulled off your best trick ever this morning, buddy, and you didn't even know it."

After the phone call, he carefully wrapped Jack in a soft white cloth and placed him inside something he knew Jack would appreciate being buried in. It was to be their last little joke together. Then Roy walked him way back up in the woods and dug a grave and placed the bird in the ground and covered him up. As he stood at the spot, looking down where his friend now slept in a Cracker Jack box, an old song his father used to sing ran through his head.

> *Nights are long, since you went away,*
> *I think about you all through the day,*
> *My buddy, my buddy, your buddy misses you.*

Roy wondered why a six-foot-two man would cry over something no bigger than a pinecone. Damn you, Jack, he thought to himself as he walked back through the woods, if you were here I'd ring your scrawny little neck.

Roy was not a religious man, but that day he hoped if there was such a thing as a spirit, a small part of Jack's had somehow managed to escape and maybe he was up there right now, flying around looking down and laughing at all the poor earthbound creatures below. That would be just like him, Roy thought, and looked up half expecting to see him.

Frances and Oswald met at the hospital at six the next morning and sat with Patsy as nurses came in and out of the room preparing for the first operation. Oswald was busy drawing pictures for her, trying to distract her and make her laugh, while Frances tried to explain what was going to happen next. Patsy sat up in bed, wearing a hospital gown and her beanie, and seemed to be a little frightened by all the activity, but soon another nurse came in and gave her a shot to relax her and she started to get sleepy. Dr. Glickman opened the door. "Well, good morning, young lady," he said, as he walked over to the bed. "How are you?"

"Fine," she said, slightly groggy.

"The nurses tell me you gained four pounds since the last time I saw you. That's just terrific," he said, and smiled at Frances and Oswald. Then he turned back to Patsy. "In just a little while we're going to take you down the hall to another room and work on your leg a bit, but you won't feel a thing and when you wake up everybody will be right here waiting for you."

He picked up the photograph of Patsy and Jack from her bedside table. "Is this the bird you were telling me about?"

"Yes, sir," she said, smiling sleepily.

"Well, he's a fine-looking fellow," he said, patting her arm. "And we are going to get you fixed up as good as new and back home again as fast as we can, OK?"

"OK."

When Frances went out with Dr. Glickman to ask a few last-minute questions a woman came in with papers to sign and asked Oswald if he were the father. "No," he said.

"Grandfather?"

"No, just a friend. The lady you need to see is right down the hall."

When Frances came back they went over the papers together and she signed on the line where it said LEGAL GUARDIAN, even though she was not legal. She had just perjured herself on an official document, but as she told Oswald, "If I go to jail, I go to jail. At least Patsy's leg will be fixed."

Oswald's admiration for Frances grew even more during the long hours they waited. He was as jumpy as a cat and could not sit still for a minute, so he walked up and down the hall. He wanted a drink so badly he was about to jump out of his skin. But he could not leave Frances. He wondered why the nurses don't give a shot to the people who are waiting for the operation to be over to calm them down?

While he paced, Frances sat quietly and prayed and waited.

Everybody in Lost River was waiting to hear as well.

That afternoon, around one-thirty, when Frances called from the hospital to report that the first operation was over, everybody was relieved to hear that Patsy, according to the doctor, came through it "just fine."

That night as they were on the elevator leaving the hospital, tired but happy, Frances said to Oswald, "Thank heavens you were here with me. I don't think I could have gone through this alone."

Oswald had been lucky enough to find a room at a YMCA just two blocks from the hospital, and Frances was able to stay with a cousin who lived in Atlanta. They wanted to make sure that someone was with Patsy every day, at least through the next two operations.

* * *

Back in Lost River, everyone was coming to realize just how much a part of their lives Jack had become. They had all gotten used to seeing him flying around, hearing him sing, and ring the bells on his plastic wheel. Everybody missed the bird more than they could have guessed. But the one most struck by just how much she missed him was Mildred. Mildred found out that she had loved Jack as much as anyone, but she had not known how much until he died. She had loved him all along but did not know how to express herself in any way other than complaining.

A week after he died she went in the store with her head hanging and said, "Roy, I'm here to apologize and ask you to forgive me. I'm so ashamed of myself I just don't know what to do."

"What for?" asked Roy.

"For being so mean to that poor little crippled bird, always fussing at him, telling him I was going to cook him." She looked at Roy with tears running down her face. "I don't know why I did it. I really liked him."

Roy said, "Oh, I know you did, Mildred, and so did he. He knew you didn't mean all those things."

"Really?"

"Sure he did. That's why he was always pestering you."

Mildred looked up. "Do you think so?" she asked hopefully.

"Oh, I know so. No question about it. You see, Mildred," said Roy, handing her his handkerchief, "old Jack was a master at judging people, much better than me. One time these two girls I had never seen before came in, and I tried to get

Jack to do a few tricks for them, but as hard as I tried he wouldn't do anything. He just flew around, acting all agitated. And it really made me mad that he acted like that until later, when I found out that while I was busy talking to one girl, the other was back in the office robbing me blind."

"Oh, no," said Mildred.

"Yeah, they sure did, and Jack tried his best to warn me. He knew they were up to no good. You can fool me, but you couldn't fool him. I tell you, Mildred, it sure seems empty in here without him. I guess I got so used to having him around I never figured he'd go and die on me, but that's what life's about, isn't it; you get attached to something and then you lose it. Thank God Patsy is making it through those operations, or I don't know what we would do around here."

Mildred went home feeling at least a bit better, but somehow the loss of Jack made her realize that she never wanted to lose another living thing without them knowing how she really felt. From then on, after every phone conversation with Frances she would add, "Love you," before she hung up.

At the Hospital

IT HAD BEEN an anxious few weeks, but everyone was relieved when Oswald and Frances came home with the good news that the last of the operations had gone well. Next would come the long and boring weeks that Patsy would have to spend in the hospital lying flat on her back in a body cast. From then on, every other weekend the Polka Dots would ride up to Atlanta and visit as a group.

Although he was anxious to get back and visit Patsy, Oswald rode up with them only once. Once was enough. Seated in a car full of women, squashed between his six-foot landlady and Sybil Underwood, having to listen to them talk nonstop all the way to Atlanta and back, was too much for him to bear. After that fateful trip he only went with Frances alone or hitched a ride with Butch. He also rode with Roy, who sometimes went on Sunday and came back Sunday night.

Everybody brought her games or picture books to try and keep Patsy occupied. Oswald always brought her little drawings that made her laugh, especially the one of him in the car with all the women. One day when the Polka Dots came to visit they were surprised to learn that a delegation from the Dotted Swiss had just been there and presented Patsy with a beautiful hand-sewn quilt for her bed, with GET WELL SOON appliquéd in the middle. Although they were pleased that the Dotted Swiss had come, Betty Kitchen examined the quilt and remarked, "It just galls me to say it, girls, but look at those little stitches. They have us beat in needlework, hands down." Dottie put on her glasses and looked more closely and had to agree. Mildred said, "Maybe so, but you have to admit nobody can beat Frances's macaroni and cheese; we always have that, not to mention our floating island. "And," added Sybil, "I know we are not to blow our own horn, but don't forget the tomato aspic." "Ah," they all said, nodding, and felt better about the whole thing. Patsy suddenly giggled in the bed. Frances walked over and squeezed her big toe with affection. "What's so funny, young lady?"

"Tomato aspic," she said, and giggled again.

Finally, the day came when the cast was removed. Now, according to the doctor, came the hardest part, the long months of therapy. The goal was to improve Patsy's range of motion more each day and eventually get her back up on her feet and walking. But walking again was not going to be easy. They had to change her gait completely from what it had been before and retrain all the muscles.

Her physical therapy nurse was a pretty, dark-eyed woman

named Amelia Martinez, who was impressed with the way Patsy tried so hard and never complained through the long grueling hours of painful exercise. One day, when Patsy was in water therapy, Amelia pulled Frances aside. "You know, Mrs. Cleverdon, she's the bravest little girl I have ever worked with. With all the pain we have had to put her through . . . well, let's put it this way. I've seen grown men cry over less. Dr. Glickman told me he'd never seen anybody improve so fast in all his life." Then she smiled and waved at Patsy. "That little girl wants to get better and go home."

During Patsy's therapy everyone came to visit as often as they could, and when they were not able to be there in person, they all sent her cards and letters that Amelia would read to her. Amelia soon got to know everybody in Lost River by their letters. Each time Frances and Oswald came to visit they were pleased Patsy was doing so well, but still her first question was always, "How is Jack?" and of course they always said, "Just fine," and felt terrible about it. But what else could they do? All that mattered now was that she was improving. Even though all the strengthening exercises she was put through each day were painful and exhausting, they were starting to work. She was now able to walk a few feet without support. As far as Patsy was concerned, each new step was just one step closer to getting home to see Jack.

ALONG THE RIVER

The Lost River
Community Association Newsletter

Fall is here, and it's hard to believe that old Father Time is in such a hurry. Seems like it was only yesterday when summer arrived, but "tempus fugit," as they say, and Thanksgiving is around the corner. And we have a lot to be thankful for in our community this year, as the news from Atlanta is still very positive and Patsy's therapy continues to go well. All good things come to those who wait, and we can hardly wait until our own Miss Patsy is back home again. Don't forget to start planning for potluck and get those pumpkin pies and turkeys ready to go!

—Dottie Nivens

The days passed and Patsy's future was looking brighter. Amelia continued to report that she was making great progress. Even Mildred seemed to be getting happier but as fate will sometimes do, it threw Mildred a curve in the form of a letter from her old lost love, Billy Jenkins, who wrote telling her that he was now a widower and would love to see her again. And, surprise of all surprises, Mildred told Frances she was going to drive up to Chattanooga and visit him. It was the last thing in the world Frances figured she would ever do, but as she so often said, with Mildred you never knew which way she was going to jump from one minute to the next.

She had left on Friday and it was already Tuesday, and Frances had not heard one word from her the entire time and didn't know what to think. Then, around four that afternoon, Mildred pulled into the driveway. She could hardly wait to see her sister. She threw open the front door and yelled, "Frances, I'm back!"

The minute Frances saw her she knew something big had happened. There was a glow about Mildred as she stood there wearing a new lavender pants suit, and she looked younger and prettier than she had in years. With her face flushed with excitement, she exclaimed, "I've got news!"

Frances felt her heart start to pound. "Oh, dear, do I need to sit down?" she asked, then sat down anyway.

After she was seated, Mildred announced, "Well, I saw him."

"And . . ."

"And Frances, I am the luckiest woman alive!"

Frances put her hand up to her mouth. "Oh, my God. I don't believe it, after all these years."

"I don't believe it either. I have dodged a bullet. Thank the Good Lord that the idiot got cold feet and I didn't get stuck with him. The man is a perfect fool. What I ever saw in him is beyond me."

"What?"

"You know what he wanted, don't you? He wanted a nurse and a cook and even had the nerve to ask me how big my house was and how much money I was getting a month from Social Security. Then he showed me a picture of his six daughters, and Frances, that was the ugliest bunch of women I have ever seen. They all looked like him in bad dresses. When I saw that I thought to myself, I could have been looking at my own children. Then he wanted to know if I had enough room for his granddaughter, who is just out of drug rehab, and her four kids to come and live with us. They need a mother, he said."

Frances was flabbergasted. "Oh, my word. What did you say?"

"I said, 'Billy, you broke my heart and ruined my life, and you want me to take you back now that you are old and all worn out, move into my house, and have me cook and clean for six people?' I said, 'Well, you are going to have to look around some more to find that fool, because it's not going to be me.' And then I left."

Frances said, "Mildred, I hope you are not too upset. Maybe it was for the best that you saw him."

"I'm not upset at all, I feel great."

After Mildred left, Frances thought about how strange life had turned out for Mildred. At age fifty-one she was finally over Billy Jenkins once and for all. Now maybe, just maybe, she would be able to see how nice Oswald really was. Not only was he nice, he had talent. Maybe there was hope for the two of them after all. Frances had grown very fond of Oswald in the past weeks and could not think of anybody she would rather have as a brother-in-law. She immediately put on her thinking cap about how to help things along. It wasn't meddling. Everybody needs a little help, she thought.

* * *

Frances was planning another dinner party for Oswald and Mildred as soon as she and Oswald got back from their next trip to Atlanta, but something much more important came up. When they went to visit, Amelia told Frances once more that she was very pleased with Patsy's progress; she was getting better every day. Then she said, "But I know from experience when a child has something to look forward to it makes all the difference in the world, and all she talks about is going home to see her friend Jack." Frances's heart sank when she heard that, and Oswald felt sick. Frances did not tell Amelia that the bird was dead, but it was just a matter of time before Patsy would be coming home and going into the store expecting to find Jack. When he had died so suddenly they had all been worried about how it would affect her before she had her operations. Now they had another dilemma on their hands.

When the two of them arrived home, a special meeting of the Polka Dots was called and Oswald was invited to attend, the second male ever to be invited. Frances felt he had earned the right if Patsy was going to be discussed.

Dottie spoke first. "We can't let her come all the way home and then when she gets here tell her he's dead, we have to at least warn her or something."

"Maybe we should just bite the bullet and go ahead and tell her the truth," said Mildred.

"What truth?" asked Frances. "That all the hard work she's been doing, thinking she was going to get to come home and see Jack, was for nothing?"

Betty said, "Listen, she still has six more weeks of therapy left. Maybe if we tell her just a little something now to soften the blow, it won't be so hard on her."

Mildred asked, "How can you soften the blow, tell her he's sick?"

Oswald spoke up. "No, we can't do that. I know Patsy and that would only worry her."

"He's right," said Frances.

After much discussion, they finally decided what they would do. A letter would be written as soon as possible and because of her literary background, Dottie would be the one to write it. And her nurse Amelia, the one Patsy liked so much, would be the one to read it out loud to her.

After it was finished, Butch got in his truck and drove it to Atlanta, hand-delivered it to Amelia Martinez, and then turned around and ran like a bandit. That afternoon after therapy, Amelia sat by Patsy's bed and read the letter out to her.

Dear Patsy,

I am writing to you on behalf of all your friends here in Lost River to tell you the most wonderful news! Not more than a week after you left a man came into the store and took a look at Jack. As it turned out, the man was a top veterinarian who specialized in treating injured birds. After examining Jack, he told Roy he could fix that wing and he took Jack to his clinic and did just that, like your doctor did for you. When he came back you can imagine how happy we all were to see Jack flying around the store as good as new. We all wanted to wait until you came home so you could be there with us when we set him free, but the doctor said it was best to let him go now. After we knew he was nice and strong and had fully recovered, we all gathered at the store, and when Roy opened the door he flew straight to the very top of the big cedar tree across the street. And oh, Patsy, how we all wished you could have been there with us to see it! Jack looked so happy to be free and flying around way up in the sky, and to be back in nature again, among his friends. Just as happy as all of us here will be to have you back, among all your friends who love you. I know we will all miss not seeing Jack at the store anymore, but the other day Mrs. Underwood said she saw him looking fat and healthy sitting on a branch with a lady friend, so perhaps we may see a bunch of little Jacks flying around here in the near future. We all hope you will be home very soon and, just like Jack, be healthy, happy, and as good as new!

Best wishes from Dottie and
all your friends at Lost River

Neither Sybil Underwood nor anyone else had spotted a redbird since Jack died, but Dottie said, "I'll just have to believe the Good Lord will forgive me for lying just this once. And if He doesn't, then He's not half the man I thought He was."

After Amelia read the letter to Patsy, she said, "Well, that's good news, isn't it? Your little bird friend is all cured and well, just like you are going to be. Aren't you happy?" But Patsy did not look happy. She looked worried and upset. She remembered exactly what Roy had said about why Jack should not be outside and it scared her.

"Oh, Amelia, you don't think a hawk or an owl will get him, do you?" And then, for the first time since she had come to the hospital, she started to cry.

Amelia was alarmed. "What's the matter?" she asked.

"I want to go home. I want to see Jack."

A couple of weeks later Frances was in the kitchen when the phone rang.

"Mrs. Cleverdon, this is Dr. Glickman."

"Yes, Doctor?"

"I'm afraid we've had a little setback here. I think you need to get to Atlanta as soon as possible."

Frances and Oswald left Lost River at 5 A.M. the next morning and were sitting in Dr. Glickman's office by 11:30.

"What happened?" asked Frances.

"Well, the main problem is, she's not progressing. If anything she seems to be getting worse. We've done everything we can, but it's almost as if she's lost her will to get better, and without that, all the medicine and therapy in the world is not going to help."

"Oh, no, what can we do?"

"At this point, for you people to spend what you are spending to keep her here is a waste, so I'm recommending that you take her home for a while, give her a rest."

Oswald said, surprised, "Is she ready to leave?"

"No, physically she is not ready; she needs much more therapy if she is going to improve beyond the point where she is today. I don't like to release a patient who is not fully healed, but in this case it seems Patsy no longer cares about improving . . . and she was doing so well. Do you have any idea what might have caused this?"

Frances looked at Oswald and then at the doctor. "I think she's just heartbroken over that bird."

"Are you talking about the bird in the picture she has?" asked the doctor.

Oswald said, "Yes, it was a little crippled redbird."

He brightened a little. "Well, maybe a visit with him could cheer her up. We can try, at least. Is there any way we could get the bird here?"

"No," said Oswald. "That's the problem. The bird died."

"Oh, I see," said Dr. Glickman. "And you told her?"

Frances said, "No, we were afraid to tell her the truth so we lied and told her a veterinarian fixed him and he flew away. I wish we hadn't but we did."

Oswald said, "We didn't know what else to do."

Dr. Glickman looked at the two distraught people across the desk. "Don't be too hard on yourselves. At least for the time being she can still think he's alive somewhere. That's something for her to hang on to. Then maybe after some time passes she'll get over it and we can get her back up here and finish what we started."

"How much time?" asked Frances.

Dr. Glickman shook his head. "Not much, I'm afraid. My

concern is that without continuing therapy the muscles will weaken, the leg will start to move back into the old position, and all our work will have been for nothing. Let's hope we can get her back right after Christmas."

Patsy, looking thinner than the last time they saw her, was so excited when they told her she was going home she could hardly wait to leave. Amelia was sorry to see her go but helped get her packed up. As they wheeled her out to the car, Amelia waved goodbye and hoped Patsy would be back, but she wondered if she would ever see her again.

Patsy chattered happily to her picture of Jack all the way to Lost River, and Oswald and Frances both felt terrible.

When she got home she was still weak and could not walk very far. She had to stay inside most of the time. Everybody did everything they could to cheer her up, but all she wanted to do was look for Jack. Frances tried to reason with her. "Darling, Jack is probably way off somewhere, busy with his own family, and he might not ever come back."

But Patsy would not be convinced. "Mr. Campbell says if you want something really really bad it will happen, and I want to see Jack really really bad."

Patsy woke up each day thinking she would see him and was disappointed when she didn't, but she did not say so. On the days it rained, she sat in her room looking out the window hoping to get a glimpse of him. Frances could not tell her the truth. Dr. Glickman said it was good to have hope, even if it was only false hope. Christmas was coming and

Frances was hoping for something as well: She was hoping that Christmas would be a distraction for Patsy and help get the bird off her mind once and for all. She told Mildred, "This will be Patsy's first Christmas with us, and I don't care what anybody says, I'm going to spoil her to death." Day after day Claude came up the river and delivered Christmas packages for Patsy sent from every store that had a catalog. Stuffed animals, books, games, and clothes arrived every day, and Mildred, who did some sewing occasionally, was busy making a dozen monkey-sock dolls for her bed.

Three days before Christmas, after the Mystery Tree had been decorated, Dottie called and said, "Frances, I need to see you right away." Frances walked into the post office and Dottie, looking grim, handed her a letter she had just pulled out of the letters-to-Santa-Claus box. Frances recognized the childish scrawl immediately.

> *Deer Santa Klause,*
> *Please let me see Jack. I am sacred he is hurt. I do not want any presents. I have been a good girle I poromise. I am living at Mrs. Cleveaton's now. It is the blue hose by the post offiec.*
>
> *Love your firend Patsy*

The first Christmas Eve dinner at the community hall with her own child was not as happy as Frances had imagined. There was a pall on the entire evening. When Santa called her child up to receive her present it would not be the *one* thing she wanted most in the world. What was so heart-breaking for Frances and Oswald as well was that she wanted something that neither of them could give her.

Even the tree lighting that year was a bust. When Butch flipped the switch, there was a brief flare, a pop, and then nothing. When they left, Butch was still trying to fix it. But despite the tree fiasco, Patsy was cheerful on the way home. She didn't tell anyone, but she believed with all her heart that she was going to see Jack tomorrow and she could hardly wait. She fell asleep with his picture in her hand.

Another Christmas

CHRISTMAS MORNING, PATSY woke up early and came in the kitchen already dressed for the day, so excited that she told Frances, "I'm going to see Jack today, I know I will!"

Frances winced. "Now, honey, don't get your heart too set on it, you don't know that he's not off somewhere with his own family. Don't you want to open your presents? It's Christmas morning!"

"Can I do it later? After I've seen Jack?"

"But, sweetheart, you're supposed to open them on Christmas morning. If I had that many presents I just couldn't wait another minute. Mildred is coming up here to see you later. Besides, I don't think you're strong enough yet to be out all by yourself." But Patsy was not listening, and as soon as she ate her breakfast she was out the door with her presents left unopened.

When Mildred arrived, Frances was alone in the living room looking upset and worried.

"Where's Patsy?"

"She's gone off looking for Jack. She left here an hour ago saying she was sure she was going to see him today."

"Oh, no. Somebody's got to tell her the truth; you can't let that little girl wander around all day thinking she's going to see that bird."

"Well, if you want to break her heart on Christmas, go ahead. I can't. We should have done it sooner. But I just thought she'd get over it. Forget about him."

Mildred went to the window and looked out. "Ohh . . . there she is, over in Betty's backyard. I'll tell you, Frances, this is the worst Christmas I can ever remember. This is what we get for lying. I'll never do it again." She turned around and looked at Frances with some alarm. "If she ever finds out what we did she's going to grow up and hate us. She'll be scarred for life! Maybe she'll turn out to be a criminal. She could flip out and come back someday and murder us all in our beds for this, and it will be all our fault."

"Oh, for God's sake, Mildred, you've got to stop reading those trashy novels. Things are bad enough as it is without you making them worse."

But even the day seemed sad. The sky was gloomy and overcast. The usual Christmas blue skies and sunshine had deserted them.

Next door, Oswald sat in his room thinking about what an odd concept time was and how it never seemed to be just right. There was either too much of it or never enough. Before his doctor's prognosis, time had been just a round circle ticking on his wrist to check now and then, to see if he was late or early. Looking back on his life now, it seemed most of his time had been spent waiting for something to happen. As a kid, waiting to be adopted. Waiting to grow up. Waiting to get over some cold or for some broken bone to heal. Waiting to meet the right girl, find the right profession, find a little happiness, some reason to live, until his time was up. Now the waiting was over and he had never found one thing he had been looking for until he found painting, and it had come too late. Somebody had sure handed him the short stick in life. And this year, probably his last, Patsy, just as he had, was also waiting for something that was never going to happen. He had watched her from his window walking around in the yard, looking for a dead bird she was never going to see, and it made him mad. This kid was going to have her heart broken. He was one thing, he was tough, but she didn't deserve it. He sat looking at the painting he had worked on all year, of Patsy and Jack on their birthday. He had wanted to give it to her for Christmas, but again it was too late. She didn't want a picture, she wanted to see the real Jack, and he wanted to get drunk. He knew all the dangers of picking up that first drink but he didn't care. He couldn't bear the pain of having to watch Patsy grow up and realize that nothing is real. There is no God. No Santa Claus. No happy endings. Things die. Nothing lasts.

And there was not a damn thing he could do to spare her from any of it. Even if there had been a God, that morning he wanted to punch Him in His great big liar's nose.

That afternoon Oswald hitchhiked over to Lillian, walked into the VFW bar, and took a stool next to a man in a John Deere cap drinking a Budweiser. Sitting in the dark room full of cigarette smoke and the smell of stale beer and the sound of the jukebox playing bad music, he began to feel that old familiar feeling. He was back where he should be. He was finally home.

He motioned to the bartender. "I'll have a Bud, and give my friend here one on me."

The guy said, "Well thanks, buddy. Merry Christmas."

Oswald Campbell said, "Merry Christmas to you too, buddy."

Frances had waited all day for Patsy to come home. By four-thirty that afternoon, when it was just starting to get dark, she gave up waiting, went out to look for her, and finally found her in the woods behind the store. The store was closed on Christmas Day but with great effort, Patsy had somehow managed to make it all the way up there, thinking that this is where Jack might be.

"Honey, you need to come on home now. You're not strong enough yet to be out this long. It's turned chilly, and you don't even have a sweater on. You know the doctor doesn't want you to catch cold."

But Patsy would not give up. She wanted to keep looking as long as there was even a little daylight left. "Can't I stay out just a little bit longer? Please?"

Frances could not bear to make her come in. "All right, just a little while. But put this on for me." Frances took off her pink sweater, put it on Patsy, and buttoned it up. "I want you home by dark. Do you hear me?"

"Yes, ma'am."

"You still have your presents to open. Have you forgotten that?"

"No, ma'am."

She looked so small and frail, standing there in the pink sweater down to her knees, that Frances almost burst into tears on the way home.

Mildred was right. This was the worst Christmas she had ever been through in her life.

About an hour later, Frances heard Patsy coming up the steps and greeted her at the door. She had turned on all the Christmas lights and had hot chocolate and cookies ready for her. "Well, *here* you are. Santa Claus has left you a whole bunch of things, you better come in and see what they are. Won't that be fun?" Frances had hoped that the presents would cheer her up, and Patsy tried her best to act surprised and happy at each gift she opened. But Frances could see that nothing, not the dolls, the stuffed animals, the games, or the new clothes, could mask her disappointment. For Patsy, the thing that really mattered was that Christmas had come and was almost gone, and she had not seen Jack.

That evening, after Patsy was in bed, the phone rang. It was Betty Kitchen.

"How's Patsy doing?"

"Terrible I'm afraid."

"Well, I figured as much. Is Mr. Campbell there?"

"No. I haven't seen him all day. Why?"

"He didn't come in for his Christmas dinner so I wondered if he was over there with you. You know it's not like him to miss a meal."

A little after midnight, Oswald had finally passed out and fallen off the bar stool. It was 12:45 A.M. when Betty woke up to the sound of loud knocking. She came out of her closet, put on a robe, and went to the door. The good Samaritan in the John Deere cap had Oswald slung over his shoulder. He tipped his cap and said, "Sorry to disturb you, ma'am, but I'm afraid he's had a little too much Christmas cheer. Where do you want him?"

Betty had never seen Oswald take a drink before, but having dealt with many a drunk in her day she said, "Bring him on in, no need to drag him upstairs tonight. Put him in my bed and I'll deal with him tomorrow."

The man, who had obviously had a snootful of booze himself, walked into the closet and deposited Oswald on her bed. "Merry Christmas, and to all a good night," he said as he left. Betty took Oswald's shoes off, covered him up, and shut the door. She tiptoed upstairs, went into the spare bedroom down the hall, and got in bed, thinking to herself that this had been the worst Christmas she ever remembered. Patsy had had her heart broken, her mother had eaten almost all the wax fruit out of the bowl on the dining room table, and now her boarder had come home dead drunk.

Good God, what next? she wondered.

Betty did not have much time before she found out. At around 5:45 A.M. the next morning the screaming started. Betty's mother, Miss Alma, was standing in the hall in her nightgown screaming for her daughter at the top of her lungs. "Betty! Betty! Get up! Get up! My camellias are flying off the bushes. Help! Betty!"

Betty woke up and heard her mother carrying on out in the hall, but she was so tired—she had not slept well—so she lay there hoping her mother would give up and wander back to bed. But no luck. The old lady continued to run back and forth in and out of her room, yelling about her camellias. Finally poor Betty got up, went down the hall, and tried to calm her mother down. "OK, Mother, it's all right. Go back to bed. There's nothing wrong, you just had a bad dream."

But the old lady would not be calmed. She grabbed Betty by the wrist and pulled her to her room and pointed out the window and screamed, "Look! Look, there they go! Go get them!"

Betty sighed. "Come on, Mother, calm down, you are going to wake Mr. Campbell. Let's just get back in bed."

Miss Alma continued to point out the window. "Look, look, look!" she said, jumping up and down.

"OK, Mother," Betty said, and, just to appease her, walked over and looked out and could hardly believe what she saw. At almost exactly the same time in the house next door, Patsy sat up in bed and screamed for Frances. "Mrs. Cleverdon! Mrs. Cleverdon!"

Her screaming startled Frances and she came running to the room. When she opened the door she saw Patsy, her eyes wide with excitement, jumping up and down at the open window. "I saw him, I just saw Jack! He was here! I knew he would come!"

"Where did you see him?"

"Here. He landed right here on my windowsill and blinked at me. I know it was him. He came back!"

Frances went over and looked out the window and she too could not believe what she saw. It almost took her breath away. Although it was just beginning to get light outside, she could see that the entire yard and all the trees *were completely covered with snow!*

Everywhere she looked, for as far as she could see, was absolutely white, until all of a sudden she saw a flash of a powerful, incredible red streak by the window, then two, then four. When she leaned out and looked down, she saw that the ground was filled with big red camellias that must have fallen off the bushes. It was not until she saw one fly away that she realized that the whole yard was alive with redbirds!

By this time Betty Kitchen was running down the stairs, her large arms flailing in the air, yelling, "Oh my God, oh my God, oh my God, get up, Mr. Campbell!"

Oswald opened his eyes and sat up in the small dark closet, and immediately hit his head on a shelf. He didn't know where he was or how he got there and with all the yelling and screaming he was not sure if he had died and gone to hell or what. Just then Betty jerked the closet door open and yelled, "It's *snowing*!"

Pretty soon, people up and down the street were out in their yards, in various stages of undress, screaming and hollering, jumping up and down, and pointing at all the redbirds that continued to swarm up and down the street. There were hundreds of redbirds, in flocks of twenty or thirty, sitting in trees and flying around the bushes. With his head ringing with pain from a hangover and having just hit his head, Oswald struggled to get his shoes back on. When he finally walked out he was further startled. He had walked out of a pitch-black closet into a blindingly white world just in time to see a flock of redbirds fly by.

What a sight. It was still snowing big soft white flakes, and as he stood in the street it was as if he were standing inside one of those paperweights that had just been turned upside down. He didn't know if he was still drunk or not but he suddenly felt like he was inside a picture of some fairyland that could have been an illustration for a children's book. The Spanish moss, now covered with snow, looked like long white beards hanging down from the trees. As soon as she saw Oswald, Patsy went up to him and took his hand and—

with her face flushed and her eyes shining—said, "I *saw* him, Mr. Campbell. He came back just like you said he would if I wished hard enough. He came right to my window and blinked at me. Look," she said, and pointed to the birds. "There are all his friends. I just knew he'd come back!"

He looked up as a flock landed in the tree above and shook snow down on the two of them.

At that moment Oswald was not sure if he had died and gone to heaven, but if by any chance he was still alive he swore to God he would never take another drink as long as he lived.

Oh, what a morning!

Betty ran in, called her friend Elizabeth Shivers over in Lillian, and said excitedly, "Can you believe it? Have you ever seen anything like it in your life?"

"What?" she said.

"The snow, look out the window! And we're full of redbirds. Are you?"

Elizabeth, who had been asleep, looked out the window and said, "Betty, there's no snow over here. What redbirds?"

In the meantime, the Creoles had heard the screaming all the way across the river and wondered what was happening. When they came out and looked, they saw that it was snowing on the other side. As they all stood on the docks, the Creole children who had never seen snow were having a fit to go see it up close. And finally even the adults could not resist, and they did something they had not done in nineteen years. The snow was still falling as one by one, they all got in their boats and started rowing across the river to join the people on the other side. Pretty soon the entire street was filled with Creole men, women, and children who had joined their neighbors laughing and dancing in the snow. In less than an hour, word had spread by phone and the entire place was packed with people who had come from all around to see the snow and the redbirds. For most of the children who came, this was the first snow they had ever seen, and for the adults, it was certainly the first time they had ever seen snow in Lost River. But nobody there that morning, child or adult, had ever seen that many redbirds.

Frances and Sybil and Dottie went down and opened up the community hall and made coffee and hot chocolate for everyone, and when they switched on the interior lights the Christmas tree outside suddenly lit up. It was almost like Christmas Day all over again. Even though it was Sunday, Roy opened the store in honor of the snow and gave away candy to the kids and free beer to the adults. He was busy opening a can for Mildred, who had joined the party, when he looked up and saw Julian LaPonde standing outside looking in. As soon as the others saw him, a hush came over the store. They all held their breaths, wondering what was going to happen next. The two men looked at each other, neither moving. Then Roy walked over and held the door open and said, "Come on in, Julian, let me buy you a beer." He knew how proud a man Julian was and how hard it must have been for him to come that far. To the astonishment of everyone, Julian walked in and took the beer.

Later, Oswald walked down to the river and watched the pelicans and the ducks and the egrets try and figure out what all the white stuff on the river was. Three pelicans skidded off the top of a piling and fell into the water and were mad about it and Oswald had a good laugh.

As the morning went on and the sun came out, the snow began to melt, but not before three people who had no idea how to drive in it slid into one another. A lot of strange and unusual things happened that day. Oswald in his excitement had forgotten about his condition and against the doctor's orders was out in the snow all morning. But he did not catch pneumonia and die; he didn't even catch a cold. But the best thing by far was that Patsy got her wish. She had seen her friend Jack again.

Naturally, after that day there were many questions. Why had it snowed in just that area? Why had so many redbirds come? Why had that one bird blinked at Patsy? Of course no one person could be 100 percent sure what had really happened that morning, but Mildred had a theory. She went over to her sister's house, stood in the middle of the living room with her hand on her hip, and declared with defiance, "Frances, I believe her. I believe she *did* see Jack."

"But Mildred, how could she? We both know he's been dead for months."

"I don't care," Mildred said, "I think she saw him, I don't

know how or why, but she did." Then Mildred looked her sister right in the eye as serious as a heart attack and said, "Frances, I think it was a miracle of some kind."

Frances thought about it. "Well, I don't know what it was, if she really saw Jack or if she just thinks she did. But I'm not going to question it. She's eating again, and that's all I care about."

Of course, if the exact same event had taken place on Christmas morning instead of the day after, many more people might have believed a miracle had occurred. Still, everyone had his or her own personal explanation as to why it had happened. As far as Patsy was concerned, it was Santa Claus who caused it; he had just been a day late. And according to all the meteorologists, there was a perfectly good scientific reason for the sudden snow. A cold snap from the East swept down from Canada and dipped all the way down to northern Florida, causing the temperature to drop to 38 degrees, and the moisture of the river may have caused snow to fall only in and around the river area. The bird experts who appeared explained it away saying that the Northern Cardinal has been known to flock together in large numbers in cold weather; and not being a migratory bird, they most probably had been in the area all along, hidden among the thick foliage. However, Roy and Butch believed it was the fifty pounds of sunflower seeds they had spread all around in the dead of night on Christmas Eve trying to attract a red-bird for Patsy that caused them to come. Roy had said if there was a redbird out there within a hundred miles that liked sunflower seeds as much as Jack, they might have a chance. But as to *why* that particular redbird had landed on Patsy's windowsill and blinked at her was a question for which nobody really had an answer.

As time passed, even more strange and unusual things started to happen. The night after Roy had rowed across the river to Julian LaPonde's house with Jack, he had found out that Marie was divorced from her husband. And after being apart for so long, Marie and Roy were finally able to get back together again. With her two children, the confirmed bachelor of Lost River was soon going to become a family man.

But romance did not stop there. A few months after the redbird event, Frances Cleverdon made a surprise decision. One morning she marched over to Betty's house and said to Oswald, "Listen. I never thought I'd want a new husband, but I'll have you, if you'll have me. Patsy needs a daddy. She likes you, and so do I."

Oswald was stunned. But after she left he thought about it and realized that he absolutely adored everything about the woman, from her gravy boat collection right down to her pink kitchen. He had just been too dumb to see it before. The truth was, he would love to be married to her and be Patsy's daddy. But before he gave Frances his answer, Oswald decided he'd better go back to Chicago and see his doctor. It was only fair that she know what she was getting for a husband and for how long.

When he arrived in Chicago and called, he found out his doctor had died. However his son, Dr. Mark Obecheck III, had all Oswald's charts and agreed to see him the next day. After he examined him and came back in with the results, he looked at Oswald. "Well, Mr. Campbell, I've got good news and bad news. What do you want to hear first?"

Oswald's heart sank. He had hoped against hope that it would all be good news. "Let me have the bad news first, I guess," he said.

"The bad news is you are no long eligible to receive your disability check."

"What?"

"The good news is that those lungs of yours have cleared up quite a bit since your last checkup. You are doing great, Mr. Campbell. Keep up the good work."

"Really? How long do I have?"

"How long do you want?" asked the doctor with a smile.

"Forever."

"Well, Mr. Campbell, I can't promise that, but you can try."

"Thanks, Doc. I'll do my best."

Before he left, he called his ex-wife, Helen, and told her all the great news, and she was very happy for him.

On his way home to Frances and Patsy, Oswald felt like he was the luckiest man alive. And he owed it all to old Horace P. Dunlap and that faded old brochure. He was no longer an "accidental visitor" in Lost River. He was now a permanent resident. And if that wasn't enough wonderful news, one day right after Oswald came back from Chicago, Miss Alma, Betty's mother, came downstairs and out of a clear blue sky announced, "I think I'll do some baking today," and started up again. Everyone was so thrilled with her fancy cakes and petits fours that eventually Betty Kitchen started her own bed and breakfast and bakery.

Patsy, content that Jack was alive and well, returned to the hospital and finished her therapy. Within a year she was walking without even a hint of a limp. However, Butch Mannich continued to drive to Atlanta every weekend, even after Patsy finished her therapy, and within six months two new dishes of tamales and enchiladas were permanently added to the community potluck dinner by his new bride, Amelia Martinez.

The most unexpected development involved Mildred. On that morning after Christmas when Julian LaPonde had walked in the store, she thought he was the best-looking man she had ever seen. And when Julian, a widower, had spotted Mildred he had asked Roy, "Who is that?"

After a whirlwind courtship, Mildred, now a platinum blonde, had run off with Julian, and they were now living in New Orleans, having a wonderful time.

Dottie Nivens remarked, "That's what comes from reading all those racy books," and sat down and started writing one of her own, which won a first novel award from the Romance Writers of America. At last she was a real Woman of Letters both professionally and at the post office.

Five years later, right before another Christmas, Oswald T. Campbell came in from a meeting at the county courthouse and informed Frances with a chuckle, "Well, honey, it looks like we are not lost anymore. We've been found!"

On Christmas Eve a new sign was to be unveiled in front of the community hall that said:

WELCOME TO REDBIRD, ALABAMA
A Bird Sanctuary
Population 108

That night, when Butch switched on the Christmas tree lights and the new sign lit up, Oswald squeezed Frances's hand, and they both smiled and waved at Patsy, who was standing over with all the other children.

Then Oswald leaned over and whispered to Frances, "Isn't it amazing how one little bird changed so many lives?" And it was.

Epilogue

❊

ALTHOUGH OSWALD LOST his medical pension, thanks to the wealthy clientele that patronized the art shop at the Grand Hotel his work was soon discovered and much to his surprise he became quite a well-known artist. But as successful as he became, everyone agrees that his best work hangs in the Redbird community hall, and people come from miles around just to see the portrait of Jack and Patsy on their birthday.

And as for Patsy, she is a now a veterinarian who specializes in the treatment of birds and has grown into a lovely young woman with children of her own. Sometimes when she walks down the street, especially around Christmastime, a redbird will fly by . . . and it always makes her smile.

Fannie Flagg

DAISY FAY
AND THE
MIRACLE MAN

"Sheer unbeatable entertainment'
Cosmopolitan

Fannie Flagg takes us on a journey to a South that only
Southerners know, to a time when 'Blue Velvet' was played
at the Senior Prom, and into the life of Daisy Fay Harper, a
sassy, truth-telling heroine who just can't stay out of trouble. What's more she tells us everything – from what (or
who) made her Daddy and Momma split up to what is really
stashed in the freezer of the family's malt shop.

Daisy Fay is coming of age in the Gulf Coast's Shell Beach,
which is The End of the Road of the South, but a dandy place
to meet the locals like hard-drinking Jimmy Snow, former
debutante Mrs Dot and Daisy's own Daddy. They're all part
of the fun that takes us down home, back to the '50s, and
into the best story ever written east of Texas...

'A born storyteller'
New York Times

VINTAGE BOOKS
London

Fannie Flagg

WELCOME TO THE WORLD, BABY GIRL!

'Utterly irresistible'
Time

'Suspenseful, in an edge-of-your-seat, Hitchcock sort of way...It has the feel-good quality of an Anne Tyler...Totally enjoyable, intricately plotted, touching, hugely comic'
Mail on Sunday

Sweeping from the gentler confines of late 1940s small-town America to the tough side of the New York media circus in the '70s, it mines golden seams of goodness and gritty deter-mination, prejudice and despair, love and survival, in the story of a young TV interviewer, Dena Nordstrom, whose future looks full of promise, whose present is an emotional mess, and whose past is marked by mystery.

With a cast of unforgettable characters, from the comic masterpiece that is Neighbor Dorothy (broadcasting home tips and good news to the midwest from her own front room) to the monstrosity that is Ira Wallace, TV network head – *Welcome to the World, Baby Girl!* is a funny, constantly surprising novel that keeps you guessing and turning the page right up to the last.

VINTAGE BOOKS
London

Sicily

Aeolian Islands
p131

Western
Sicily
p84

Palermo
p48

Tyrrhenian Coast
p112

Central Sicily
p216

Ionian
Coast
p158

Mediterranean
Coast
p233

Syracuse &
the Southeast
p188

Contents

PALERMO P51

RESERVA NATURALE DELLO
ZINGARO P89

Contents

SPECIAL FEATURES

Welcome to Sicily

Eternal meeting point between East and West, Africa and Europe, the gorgeous island of Sicily is a linchpin of Mediterranean culture and one of Europe's most alluring destinations.

Classical Crossroads

Seductively beautiful and perfectly placed in the heart of the Mediterranean, Sicily has been luring passersby since the time of legends. The land of Scylla, Charybdis and the Cyclops has been praised by poets from Homer to Virgil and prized by the many ancient cultures – Phoenicians, Carthaginians, Romans and Greeks – whose bones lie buried here. Whether in the classical perfection of Agrigento's Concordia temple, the monumental rubble of Selinunte's columns or the rare grace of a dancing satyr statue rescued from Mazara del Vallo's watery depths, reminders of bygone civilisations are everywhere.

Sparkling Sea, Restless Mountains

Sicily's varied landscape makes a dramatic first impression. Fly into Catania and the smoking hulk of Etna greets you; arrive in Palermo and it'll be the sparkling mountain fringed Golfo di Castellammare. This juxtaposition of sea, volcano and mountain scenery makes a stunning backdrop for outdoors activities. Sicily and its dozen-plus offshore islands offer enough swimming, diving, hiking and climbing to build an entire vacation around.

Mediterranean Flavours

A crazy layer-cake of culinary influences, Sicily's ancient cuisine continues to rely on a few key island-grown ingredients: shellfish and citrus, tuna and swordfish, pistachios, hazelnuts and almonds, ricotta and wild herbs. Traditional ties to the land run deep here. Talk to the septuagenarian chef at a Catania restaurant and she'll not only confide that she still uses her grandmother's recipe for *pasta alla Norma*, but will also share the poetic imagery that links it to Mt Etna: the tomatoes are lava, the aubergines cinders, the basil leafy greenery, the ricotta snow. Modern chefs may play with the details, but Sicily's timeless recipes – from the simplest *cannolo* to the most exquisitely spiced fish couscous – live on.

Byzantine to Baroque

As if its classical heritage weren't formidable enough, Sicily is bursting at the seams with later artistic and architectural gems. In a short walk around Palermo you'll see Arab domes and arches, Byzantine mosaics, baroque stuccowork and Norman palace walls. This embarrassment of artistic riches remains one of the island's most distinctive attractions.

Why I Love Sicily

By Gregor Clark, Author

Decades after my first visit, I still find Sicily one of the world's most mesmerisingly beautiful places. Among the island's innumerable charms, here are a few personal favourites: the ever-present scent of lemon trees, the purity of dawn light on terracotta walls, the colourful decrepitude of Palermo's markets, the drama of Stromboli erupting against a darkening sky, the sense that history lurks always just around the next corner, the reflective marble glow of late-night Ortygia and Marsala streets, the lonely majesty of Segesta, the exotic flavours of Sicilian food and the kindness of its people.

For more about our authors, see p336

Above: Ragusa Ibla (p213)

Sicily

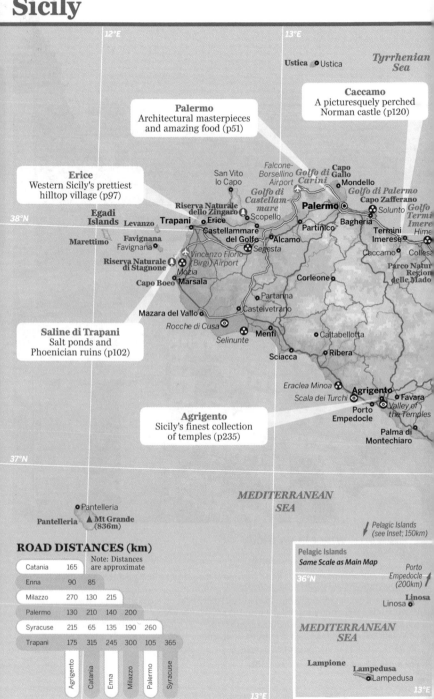

Ustica • Ustica

Tyrrhenian Sea

Palermo
Architectural masterpieces
and amazing food (p51)

Caccamo
A picturesquely perched
Norman castle (p120)

Erice
Western Sicily's prettiest
hilltop village (p97)

San Vito
lo Capo
*Falcone-
Borsellino
Airport*
*Golfo di
Carini*
**Capo
Gallo**
Mondello
Golfo di Palermo
Capo Zafferano
Solunto
*Golfo
Termi
Imere*
Hime

**Egadi
Islands** Levanzo
**Riserva Naturale
dello Zingaro**
*Golfo di
Castellam-
mare*
Palermo
Bagheria
Scopello
Partinico
**Termini
Imerese**
Trapani • Erice
Castellammare
del Golfo
Alcamo
Segesta
Caccamo
Collesa

Marettimo
Favignana
Favignana
**Riserva Naturale
di Stagnone**
*Vincenzo Florio
(Birgi) Airport*
Mozia
Capo Boeo **Marsala**
Corleone
*Parco Natur
Region
delle Mado*

Partanna

Saline di Trapani
Salt ponds and
Phoenician ruins (p102)

Mazara del Vallo
Rocche di Cusa
Castelvetrano
Menfi
Caltabellotta
Selinunte
Sciacca
Ribera

Eraclea Minoa
Scala dei Turchi
Agrigento
Favara

Agrigento
Sicily's finest collection
of temples (p235)
Porto
Empedocle
*Valley of
the Temples*
Palma di
Montechiaro

*MEDITERRANEAN
SEA*

• Pantelleria
▲ Mt Grande
(836m)
Pantelleria

*Pelagic Islands
(see Inset; 150km)*

ROAD DISTANCES (km)

	Agrigento	Catania	Enna	Milazzo	Palermo	Syracuse
Catania	165					
Enna	90	85				
Milazzo	270	130	215			
Palermo	130	210	140	200		
Syracuse	215	65	135	190	260	
Trapani	175	315	245	300	105	365

Note: Distances
are approximate

Pelagic Islands
Same Scale as Main Map

Porto
Empedocle
(200km)

Linosa
Linosa •

*MEDITERRANEAN
SEA*

Lampione
Lampedusa
• Lampedusa

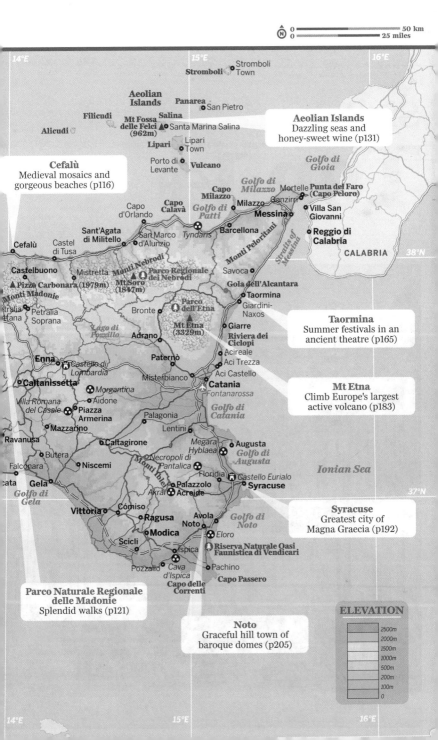

N 0 ——————— 50 km
0 ——————— 25 miles

14°E · 15°E · 16°E

Stromboli ○ Stromboli Town

Aeolian Islands **Panarea**
○ San Pietro
Filicudi **Salina**
Mt Fossa delle Felci (962m) ▲○ Santa Marina Salina

Aeolian Islands
Dazzling seas and
honey-sweet wine (p131)

Alicudi ○
Lipari Lipari Town
Porto di ○ **Vulcano**
Levante

Golfo di Gioia

Cefalù
Medieval mosaics and
gorgeous beaches (p116)

Capo Milazzo
Golfo di Milazzo Mortelle **Punta del Faro (Capo Peloro)**
Capo d'Orlando **Capo Calavà** *Golfo di Patti* Milazzo ○ Ganzirri
Sant'Agata ○ ○ **Messina** ○ ○ **Villa San Giovanni**
di Militello San Marco ○ *Tyndaris* **Barcellona**
○ d'Alunzio
Cefalù Castel di Tusa

○ **Reggio di Calabria**
CALABRIA 38°N

Straits of Messina

Castelbuono Mistretta **Monti Nebrodi** **Parco Regionale dei Nebrodi**
▲ **Pizzo Carbonara (1979m)** ▲ **Mt Soro (1847m)** Savoca ○
Monti Madonie
Petralia ○ **Gola dell'Alcantara**
○ ○ Petralia **Parco dell'Etna** ○ **Taormina**
Soprana Bronte ○ Giardini-
Naxos
Lago di Pozzillo **Mt Etna (3329m)** ○ **Giarre**
Riviera dei Ciclopi
Adrano ○ Acireale
Aci Trezza
Enna ○ **Castello di Lombardia** Paternò ○
Caltanissetta ○ **Morgantina** Misterbianco ○ Aci Castello
○ **Aidone** **Catania**
Villa Romana del Casale ○ **Piazza Armerina** *Fontanarossa*
Mazzarino Palagonia *Golfo di Catania*
Ravanusa Lentini
Caltagirone Megara ○ **Augusta**
Butera Hyblaea *Golfo di Augusta*
Falconara **Niscemi** *Monti Iblei* ○ **Necropoli di Pantalica**
cata **Gela** Floridia ○ Castello Euriale
Golfo di Gela **Palazzolo** ○ **Syracuse**
Akrai **Acreide**
Taormina
Summer festivals in an
ancient theatre (p165)

Mt Etna
Climb Europe's largest
active volcano (p183)

Ionian Sea

37°N

Vittoria ○ Cómiso **Ragusa** Avola
Noto ○
Modica ○ Eloro
Scicli ○ **Riserva Naturale Oasi Faunistica di Vendicari**
Ispica ○
Pozzallo ○ *Cava d'Ispica* ○ Pachino
Capo delle Correnti **Capo Passero**

Syracuse
Greatest city of
Magna Graecia (p192)

Parco Naturale Regionale delle Madonie
Splendid walks (p121)

Noto
Graceful hill town of
baroque domes (p205)

ELEVATION

2500m
2000m
1500m
1000m
500m
200m
100m
0

14°E · 15°E · 16°E

Sicily's
Top 14

Syracuse

1 Syracuse's charms will sneak up on you. Alight from the train or bus station into the city's sterile modern centre, and you just might wonder what the fuss is all about. But turn a corner or two and its layers of history will soon have you swooning. Suddenly you're standing in a vast field of Greek ruins (p193), gazing down over delicate papyrus plants in an ancient pool (p193) or wandering through a glimmering marble-paved square (p192) where ancient temple columns peek out from under a cathedral's baroque facade. Below left: Piazza del Duomo (p192), Ortygia

Sicilian Cuisine

2 Where to start? Simply put, Sicilian cuisine will radically alter your concept of Italian food and bring you back, begging for more. Aubergines, ricotta, citrus, wild fennel and mint, cherry tomatoes, capers and olives, tuna and sardines, swordfish and shrimp: these are just a few of the ingredients that find their way repeatedly into the island's delectable dishes. But wait – there's more! Spectacular street food, couscous with saffron and cinnamon, and desserts that just won't quit. Bring a healthy appetite and prepare to gain a little weight! Below right: Taormina (p165)

Aeolian Islands

3 Extraordinarily beautiful and surprisingly diverse, the seven islands of the Aeolian archipelago are packed with standout attractions – Stromboli's lava-spewing crater (p151), Salina's verdant vineyards (p146) and Panarea's whitewashed luxury hotels (p260) – yet their greatest appeal may lie in their slower rhythm. With very few cars and zero stress, this place feels like a world apart from the Sicilian mainland; indeed, when leaving the islands, locals speak of 'going to Sicily'. You might just want to adopt the same mindset, lingering here your whole vacation and saving 'Sicily' for later. Above: Lipari (p133)

Erice

4 With every hairpin curve on the long climb to Erice, it seems that the views can't possibly get any better. But they do. Save your camera battery for the top of the hill, where the Norman Castello di Venere (p98) and its public park afford 360-degree views clear out to San Vito Lo Capo and the Egadi Islands. It's small wonder that earlier cultures considered this a sacred site, building a temple to Venus that even earned a mention in Virgil's *Aeneid*.

Open-Air Performances

5 Aeschylus himself would be pleased to see Greek drama still flourishing in Syracuse's great amphitheatre (p193), two-and-a-half millennia later. Every spring, the Cycle of Classical Plays (p198) brings a solid month's worth of live performances to the very venue where the venerable playwright once sat. From June through August, the action moves up the coast to Taormina's Teatro Greco (pictured right; p167), where you can watch everything from international film premieres to famous rockers, dancers and divas performing under the balmy night air, all with Mt Etna as the scenic backdrop.

JEAN DU BOISBERRANGER GETTY IMAGES ©

Volcanoes

6 Never content to sit still, Sicily's great volcanoes keep belching sulphurous steam and sending fireworks into the night sky. Three-and-a-half centuries after burying Catania in volcanic ash, Mt Etna (p183) still broods over the city, keeping locals on their toes, while Stromboli (pictured above; p151) continues lighting the way for passing ships as it did in ancient times. Climbing either or both of these fiery beauties is easily done in a day, or you can just admire them from afar. Either way, they're an unforgettable part of the Sicilian experience.

Cefalù

7 With its long sandy beach hugging the sparkling Tyrrhenian Sea, and its twin cathedral towers juxtaposed against the rugged heights of La Rocca, Cefalù (p116) provokes many a 'love at first sight' reaction. The dazzling Byzantine mosaics of the cathedral's apse and the carved columns of its cloister will keep you busy on a rainy day, but once summer rolls around it's hard to resist the waterfront's allure. You won't find a better blend of beach resort and medieval town centre anywhere in Italy.

Hill Towns

8 Sicily's interior is a rugged place, full of rocky outcroppings, precipitous hillsides and fields parched by the summer sun. It can sometimes look downright uninhabitable, but scan the horizon and you'll quickly find evidence of the island's long centuries of human settlement. Gorgeous hill towns such as Enna, Petralia Soprana, Ragusa (pictured above), Noto and San Marco d'Alunzio are sprinkled throughout the island, most of them clinging to impossible heights and crowned by crumbling Norman castles or traces of other long-past civilisations.

Agrigento

9 The temples of Agrigento's Valley of the Temples (p235) make an impression like no other ruins in Sicily. Strung out along the long rocky promontory where the ancient Greeks erected them 2500 years ago, their magical aura is enhanced at night, when they're brilliantly floodlit. On summer evenings, don't miss the chance to walk among the temples of the Eastern Zone after dark, an experience not to be had at any other Sicilian ancient site. A short way up the hill, Agrigento's Museo Archeologico (p239) is also one of the island's finest.

Saline di Trapani

10 After so many dramatic mountainous landscapes in the rest of Sicily, the Saline di Trapani come as a revelation. These vast flats between Trapani and Marsala, dotted with windmills and shimmering pools, have been prized since ancient times as a source of salt. Zigzag through the watery landscape under big skies, then take the ferry across to ancient Mozia (p103), an island whose Phoenician relics are some of Europe's most significant, displayed in situ and in the adjoining Whitaker Museum (p103). Bottom: Mozia

Parco Naturale Regionale delle Madonie

11 Deluged with so many seaside attractions, many visitors never get around to exploring Sicily's interior. Big mistake! All it takes is a half-hour drive into the lofty reaches of the Madonie regional park (p121) and the world completely changes. Coastal heat gives way to mountain breezes, overcrowded beach resorts yield to tranquil hill towns, and high-country trails offer endless outdoor recreation. Add to this one of Sicily's most unique regional cuisines and you just might be tempted to alter your beach vacation plans.

Markets

12 A feast for the senses, Palermo's Mercato di Ballarò (p56) is as much akin to a north African bazaar as to a mainland Italian market: fruit vendors raucously hawking their wares in Sicilian dialect, the irresistible perfume of lemons and oranges, and the crackle of chickpea fritters emerging from the deep-fryer. Across the island, Catania's La Pescheria (p174) offers an evocative slice of Sicilian life, with gesticulating fish vendors presiding over a crush of market stalls where swordfish heads cast sidelong glances across heaps of sardines on ice. Below: Antico Mercato (p201), Syracuse

SABINE LUBENOW/GETTY IMAGES ©

Palermo

13 Unapologetically gritty and fascinating, Palermo (p48) is an urban adventure. You may find yourself cursing the traffic, but you'll also find moments of absolute grace – gazing up at the carved ceilings and mosaic-covered arches of the Cappella Palatina, listening to the singing fruit vendors at Mercato del Capo or the perfection of the opera at Teatro Massimo, poring through well-catalogued treasures at the Museo Archeologico Regionale or stumbling across baroque facades on a backstreet.

Caccamo

14 Formidable Norman strongholds straddle the hilltops throughout the Sicilian countryside, but perhaps nowhere as dramatically as at Caccamo (p120). The castle's spiky crenellations and the underlying crag appear fused into a single impregnable mass, towering above the valley floor. Climb up top and survey the vast domains below, then stop in for lunch downstairs under the atmospheric brick-and-stone arches of the castle's former grain stores. You'll feel transported back to the Middle Ages, yet modern downtown Palermo is only an hour's bus ride away.

Need to Know

For more information, see Survival Guide (p304)

Currency
euro (€)

Language
Italian

Visas
Generally not required for stays of up to six months.

Money
ATMs widely available. Credit cards accepted in most hotels and restaurants.

Mobile Phones
Local SIM cards can be used in European and Australian phones – use a local SIM card for cheaper rates on local calls. Other phones must be set to roaming.

Time
Central European Time (GMT/UTC plus one hour)

When to Go

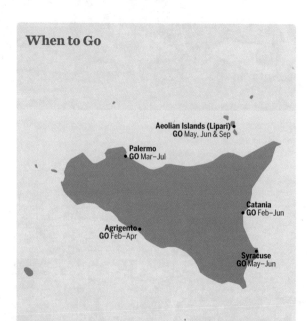

Aeolian Islands (Lipari)
GO May, Jun & Sep

Palermo
GO Mar–Jul

Catania
GO Feb–Jun

Agrigento
GO Feb–Apr

Syracuse
GO May–Jun

High Season
(Jul–Aug)

➡ Prices skyrocket, especially surrounding Ferragosto (15 August), and roads and beaches are jam-packed

➡ Festival season in Taormina, Palermo, Piazza Armerina and elsewhere

➡ Good time to hike in the mountains

Shoulder
(Apr–Jun & Sep–Oct)

➡ Best period for good weather coupled with reasonable prices

➡ Spring is ideal for coastal hiking, wildflowers and local produce

➡ June and September are best for diving

➡ Easter is marked by colourful religious festivities; book ahead

Low Season
(Nov–Mar)

➡ Accommodation prices drop by 30% or more

➡ Offshore islands and coastal resorts largely shut down

➡ Experience local culture without the crowds

Useful Websites

Sicily for Tourists (www
.regione.sicilia.it/turismo)
Sicily's official online tourism
portal.

Best of Sicily (www.bestofsicily
.com) Comprehensive coverage
of the island.

Sicily Web (www.sicilyweb.it)
History and culture.

Lonely Planet (www.lonely-
planet.com/italy/sicily)

Important Numbers

To dial listings in this book from
outside Italy, dial your international access code, followed by
Italy's country code, the relevant
city code (including the initial
'0') and the number.

Italy's country code	☎39
Ambulance	☎118
Fire	☎115
Police	☎113

Exchange Rates

Australia	A$1	€0.69
Brazil	R$1	€0.34
Canada	C$1	€0.74
Japan	¥100	€0.77
New Zealand	NZ$1	€0.60
Switzerland	Sfr1	€0.81
UK	UK£1	€1.16
US	US$1	€0.77

**For current exchange rates
see www.xe.com**

Daily Costs

Budget:
up to €100

➡ Double room in a B&B or
budget hotel: €60–80

➡ Pizza or pasta: €7–12

➡ Bus or train tickets: €5–10

Midrange:
€100–200

➡ Double room in a hotel:
€80–150

➡ Lunch and dinner in local
restaurants: €30–60

Top end:
over €200

➡ Double room in a four- or
five-star hotel: from €150

➡ Lunch and dinner in top
restaurants €60–120

Opening Hours

Banks 8.30am–1.30pm and
2.45–3.45pm Monday to Friday

Restaurants noon–3pm and
7.30–11pm; many close one day
per week

Cafes 7am to 8pm (or later if
offering bar service at night)

Shops 9.30am–1.30pm and
4–7.30pm Monday to Saturday

Museums Hours vary, but most
close on Monday

Arriving in Sicily

Falcone-Borsellino Airport
(p311; Palermo). Trains (€5.80)
and buses (€6.10) run to the
city centre every 30 to 60 minutes from 5am to 11pm. Taxis
cost €45. The journey takes
from 30 minutes to an hour.

Fontanarossa airport (p311;
Catania). AMT's Alibus (€1, 30
minutes) runs from the airport
to the train station every 20
minutes. Taxis cost €28.

Vincenzo Florio airport (p311;
Trapani). Buses (€4.70, 20
minutes) run hourly to Trapani's
bus station and port between
8.30am and 12.30am. Taxis
cost €35.

Getting Around

Train Trenitalia service is fast
and frequent along the coast
from Palermo to Messina and
Syracuse to Messina. Less
frequent and slower trains run
from Palermo to Agrigento,
Trapani and Marsala.

Ferry/hydrofoil Efficient ferries
and hydrofoils serve Sicily's
outer islands. Milazzo is the
main port for services to the
Aeolian Islands, Trapani for the
Egadi Islands, Palermo for the
island of Ustica.

Car This is the most convenient option if you're travelling
away from the coast or visiting
smaller towns and remote
archaeological sites (Segesta,
Selinunte, Piazza Armerina etc).
Car hire is readily available at all
airports and many towns.

Bus Slow, infrequent service.
Useful for more remote villages
not served by train.

For much more on
getting around,
see p313

First Time Sicily

For more information, see Survival Guide (p304)

Checklist

➡ Verify validity of your passport

➡ Organise travel insurance

➡ Pre-book popular festivals, opera and theatre performances, rental cars and accommodation

➡ Inform your credit card company of your travel plans

➡ Check if you can use your mobile (cell) phone

What to Pack

➡ Sturdy shoes for walking or hiking and sandals for the beach

➡ Round two-pin electrical adapter (to fit Italian sockets)

➡ Picnic-friendly pocket knife with corkscrew

➡ Sunglasses, sunscreen and a hat

➡ Driver's licence and map if hiring a car

➡ Mobile (cell) phone charger

Top Tips for Your Trip

➡ Late spring and early autumn are ideal times to visit Sicily; temperatures are more moderate, prices are lower and crowds are much smaller than during July and August

➡ Most hotels and other accommodation in Sicily include a simple breakfast in the price

➡ Sicilians dine late, especially in bigger cities, where restaurants don't typically start filling until after 9pm

➡ *Cannoli* are meant to be eaten with your fingers, not a fork and knife!

What to Wear

Appearances matter in Italy. The concept of *la bella figura* (literally 'making a good impression') encapsulates the Italian obsession with beauty, gallantry and looking good. In cities, suitable wear for men is generally trousers and shirts or polo shirts, and for women skirts, trousers or dresses. Shorts, T-shirts and sandals are fine for summer and at the beach. For evening wear, smart casual is the norm. A light sweater or waterproof jacket is useful in spring and autumn, and sturdy shoes are advisable at archaeological sites.

Sleeping

Advance booking is recommended during Easter Week and in the busy summer months, especially along the coast.

➡ **Agriturismi** Working farms or country houses that offer rooms and often delicious home-cooked meals. In the best cases, they offer guests a first-hand perspective on local rural culture.

➡ **B&Bs** The fastest growing category of accommodation in Sicily. They range from the basic to the luxurious. Most have five rooms or fewer, sometimes with a shared bathroom outside the room.

➡ **Pensioni** Family-run guesthouses – facilities tend to be more basic (and prices lower) than at hotels.

➡ **Alberghi (hotels)** Ranked on a star system (one to five) based on amenities.

Money

Credit and debit cards can be used almost everywhere. Exceptions include some rural areas, as well as smaller family-run businesses such as B&Bs that are only set up to take cash. Visa and MasterCard are widely recognised. American Express is only accepted by some major chains and big hotels, and few places take Diner's Club. Ask if bars and restaurants take cards before you order. Chip-and-pin is the norm for card transactions. ATMs are everywhere, but be aware of transaction fees.

For more information, see p306.

Bargaining

Gentle haggling is common in markets; in all other instances you're expected to pay the stated price.

Tipping

➡ **Restaurants** Most have a cover charge (*coperto*, around €2), and some also levy a service charge (*servizio*, 10–15%). If there is no service charge, consider rounding the bill up, though it is by no means obligatory.

➡ **Bars** In cafes people often place a €0.10 or €0.20 coin on the bar when ordering coffee. There is no need to tip for drinks at a bar, although some people may leave small change.

➡ **Taxis** Optional, but most people round up to the nearest euro.

Language

English is not as widely spoken in Sicily as in northern Europe. In the main tourist centres you can get by, but in the countryside it will be helpful to master a few basic phrases. This will improve your experience no end, especially when ordering in restaurants, some of which have no written menu.

1 **What's the local speciality?**
Qual'è la specialità di questa regione?
kwa·le la spe·cha·lee·ta dee kwes·ta re·jo·ne

A bit like the rivalry between medieval Italian city-states, these days the country's regions compete in speciality foods and wines.

2 **Which combined tickets do you have?**
Quali biglietti cumulativi avete?
kwa·lee bee·lye·tee koo·moo·la·tee·vee a·ve·te

Make the most of your euro by getting combined tickets to various sights; they are available in all major Italian cities.

3 **Where can I buy discount designer items?**
C'è un outlet in zona? che oon owt·let in zo·na

Discount fashion outlets are big business in major cities – get bargain-priced seconds, samples and cast-offs for *la bella figura*.

4 **I'm here with my husband/boyfriend.**
Sono qui con il mio marito/ragazzo.
so·no kwee kon eel mee·o ma·ree·to/ra·ga·tso

Solo women travellers may receive unwanted attention in some parts of Italy; if ignoring fails have a polite rejection ready.

5 **Let's meet at 6pm for pre-dinner drinks.**
Ci vediamo alle sei per un aperitivo.
chee ve·dya·mo a·le say per oon a·pe·ree·tee·vo

At dusk, watch the main piazza get crowded with people sipping colourful cocktails and snacking the evening away: join your new friends for this authentic Italian ritual!

Etiquette

➡ **Greetings** Shake hands and say '*buongiorno*' (good day) or '*buona sera*' (good evening) to strangers; kiss both cheeks and say '*come stai?*' (how are you?) to friends. Use '*lei*' (formal 'you') in polite company; use '*tu*' (informal 'you') with friends and children. Only use first names if invited.

➡ **Asking for help** Say '*mi scusi*' (excuse me) to get someone's attention; say '*permesso*' (permission) when you want to pass someone in a crowded space.

➡ **Religious etiquette** Dress modestly (cover shoulders, torsos and thighs) and be quiet when visiting religious sites.

➡ **Eating and drinking** At restaurants, summon the waiter by saying '*per favore*' (please). When dining in an Italian home, bring a small gift of sweets (*dolci*) or wine and dress well. Let your host lead when sitting and starting the meal.

➡ **Avoid** Discussing the Mafia can be a touchy subject.

If You Like...

Ancient Sites

Teatro Greco, Taormina Divine architecture and a dreamy setting come together at this splendid Greek theatre with a front-row view of Mt Etna. (p167)

Segesta Sitting in moody isolation on a windswept hillside, the Elymians' perfect Doric temple is one of Sicily's most magical spots. (p88)

Villa Romana del Casale This Roman villa's ancient floor mosaics are among the most extensive and best-preserved anywhere. (p226)

Valle dei Templi Splendidly arrayed on Agrigento's craggy heights, five temples and a superb archaeological museum make this the granddaddy of Sicilian ancient sites. (p235)

Parco Archeologico della Neapolis Syracuse's vast complex of amphitheatres and altars is backed by citrus groves and limestone caves. (p193)

Selinunte One of western Sicily's top draws, Selinunte blends an idyllic coastal setting and a magnificent diversity of ruins.

Necropoli di Pantalica This honeycomb of Iron- and Bronze-Age tombs may have once been the capital of the ancient Sicilian culture. (p203)

Coastal Walks

Stromboli Crater Nothing in Sicily compares to climbing Europe's most active volcano and watching sunset over the Tyrrhenian Sea. (p151)

Riserva Naturale Oasi Faunistica di Vendicari Flamingos migrate through this peaceful southeastern coastal reserve, a prime birdwatching spot. (p209)

Riserva Naturale dello Zingaro In Sicily's oldest nature reserve, a spectacular coastal trail zigzags past secluded coves and museums of local culture. (p89)

Pianoconte to Quattropani Tracing the bluffs of Lipari's western shore, this walk affords stunning views of the other Aeolian Islands. (p138)

Punta Troia From Marettimo's whitewashed main village to a crumbling Norman castle, this walk is one of the Egadi Islands' prettiest.

Sentiero del Mezzogiorno Leading to a lighthouse at Ustica's western edge, this scenic hike can be extended into a full-island loop.

Zucco Grande An easy day hike leads to this abandoned village on Filicudi's wildflower-strewn coastal bluffs. (p156)

Italian Food

Pasta alla Norma, **Trattoria di De Fiore** Catania's signature pasta dish, made with aubergines, ricotta, basil and tomatoes. (p176)

Bucatini con le sarde, **Piccolo Napoli** A Palermitan classic: tube-shaped pasta with sardines, wild fennel, pine nuts, raisins and toasted breadcrumbs. (p67)

Couscous alla trapanese, **Osteria La Bettolaccia** Trapani's North African–inspired fish couscous, seasoned with saffron, cinnamon, garlic, tomatoes and nutmeg. (p95)

Caponata, **A Cannata** Sicily's classic appetiser of eggplant, tomatoes, olives and capers, at its best in the Aeolian Islands. (p147)

Pane e panelle, **Francu U Vastiddaru** Chickpea fritters, fried eggplant and potato

IF YOU LIKE...AVANT-GARDE ART

Castel di Tusa's eclectic outdoor sculpture garden, Fiumara d'Arte, extends from the Tyrrhenian Sea to a hilltop pyramid where white-clad revellers celebrate the summer solstice.

croquettes with a touch of mint, served on a sesame roll. (p66)

Pesce alla messinese, **Al Duomo** Fish fillets, Messina-style, with tomatoes, capers and olives. (p169)

Antipasto montagnolo, **Nangalarruni** Cheeses, sausages and wild mushrooms of the Madonie mountains. (p123)

Frittura mista, **Trattoria Il Veliero** Heavenly fried shrimp and calamari. (p102)

Beaches

Cefalù The Tyrrhenian's prettiest beach town boasts a long stretch of sand backed by medieval streets and a palm-fringed cathedral. (p118)

Scala dei Turchi Just west of Agrigento, this chalky white staircase of natural stone makes a dazzling sunset-watching spot.

Spiaggia dei Faraglioni Scopello's rough-pebbled beach has shimmering turquoise waters backed by towering rock formations.

Area Marina Protetta Isola di Ustica This fabulous marine reserve off Ustica's western shore is one of the Mediterranean's top dive sites.

Lido Mazzarò Sparkling far below Taormina, this idyllic cove's crystal-clear waters cradle the islet of Isola Bella. (p168)

Piscina di Venere On Capo Milazzo, an idyllic natural pool at the Mediterranean's edge. (p129)

Spiaggia Valle i Muria Fabulously far from civilisation, save for its cavelike beachside bar, this cliff-backed beach is one of the Aeolians' finest. (p137)

(Top) Stromboli (p150)
(Bottom) Cefalù (p116)

IF YOU LIKE...ROCK-CLIMBING

Check out the recently launched Climbing Festival in San Vito Lo Capo, an up-and-coming adventure sports hotspot at the foot of a rugged coastal promontory. (p91)

Performing Arts

Cycle of Classical Drama Watch classic Greek dramas in the same Syracusan theatre where Aeschylus once sat.

Teatro Massimo Palermo's great opera house makes for an elegant night out. (p63)

Teatro Massimo Bellini Classical concerts in classy surrounds are the hallmark of this opera house named for Catania's native son. (p179)

Taormina Arte This popular summer festival brings Taormina's ancient theatre back to life with music, dance, theatre and film. (p168)

Cuticchio Mimmo Sword-wielding knights and damsels in distress delight multi-aged crowds at Palermo's outstanding traditional puppet theatre. (p68)

Dessert

Delizia di pistacchio, **Pasticceria Cappello** Possibly the world's tastiest pistachio dessert, with an exquisite mix of creaminess and granular crunch. (p67)

Cannoli, **Ti Vitti** Perfect pastry tubes hand-filled on the spot with homemade ricotta from the nearby Madonie mountains. (p118)

Granita alla mandorla, **Da Alfredo** This refreshing blend of crushed ice, local almonds and sugar is the perfect summertime treat. (p147)

Gelato, **Caffè Sicilia** A perennial favourite stop for ice cream in the baroque town of Noto. (p208)

Xocoatl chocolate, **Dolceria Bonajuto** At Modica's famous chocolate factory, hot peppers add an Aztec-inspired kick. (p210)

Frutta martorana **Maria Grammatico** Marzipan fruit from Erice's famous confectioner. (p98)

Panoramic Vistas

Castello di Venere Fairy-tale coastal views extend from Erice's castle to the distant point of San Vito Lo Capo. (p98)

Quattrocchi Arched sea-rocks, precipitous cliffs and a smoking volcano on the horizon make this one of the Aeolians' unmissable viewpoints. (p138)

La Rocca A long-abandoned hilltop castle provides the moody backdrop for perfect views of Cefalù and the Tyrrhenian Sea beyond. (p116)

Piazza IX Aprile On a clear day, Taormina's main square offers mesmerising perspectives of Mt Etna and the Ionian Sea. (p167)

Chiesa di Santa Maria delle Scale Stunning views of Ragusa's lower town from this church astride a panoramic staircase. (p214)

Capo Grillo Spy all six of the other Aeolian Islands from this prime perch on Vulcano's east coast. (p143)

Getting off the Beaten Track

CIDMA Learn about Sicilian resistance to the Mafia in Corleone. (p82)

Rocche Di Cusa This olive-shaded ancient quarry near Selinunte makes a prime picnic spot.

Filo dell'Arpa Climb to the top of Alicudi, the Aeolians' least visited island.

Riserva Naturale Torre Salsa Wild beaches line the coast between Agrigento and Selinunte. (p243)

Mistretta A lost-in-time hill town at the edge of Sicily's largest nature preserve.

Markets

La Pescheria Catania's morning market is alive with noisy banter and swordfish heads casting sidelong glances across silvery heaps of sardines. (p174)

Mercato di Ballarò Vendors croon the merits of artfully stacked artichokes, wild strawberries and lemons at Palermo's liveliest market. (p56)

Antico Mercato Syracuse's top spot for fresh seasonal produce. (p201)

Mercato del Capo Plump olives, pungent cheese and voluptuous vegetables fill this popular Palermo market. (p56)

Month by Month

January

Hot on the heels of the New Year comes Epiphany (6 January). On Etna and Monte Mufara in the Madonie it's ski season, while many coastal resort towns are firmly shut.

February

Temperatures aren't exactly balmy, but citrus orchards are heavy with fruit, and almond blossoms begin to appear in Agrigento. Carnevale also heats up in places like Acireale and Sciacca.

✺ Festa di Sant'Agata

One million Catanians follow a silver reliquary of St Agata through the city streets. This festival takes place from 3 to 5 February and is accompanied by spectacular fireworks.

✺ Sagra del Mandorlo in Fiore

Performances of drama and music among the almond blossoms in the Valley of the Temples on the first Sunday in February (www.sagradelmandorlo.net).

✺ Carnevale

During the week before Ash Wednesday, many towns stage carnivals. The most flamboyant are in Sciacca (www.ilcarnevaledisciacca.com) and Acireale (www.carnevaleacireale.com).

March

Weather in March is capricious, alternating between sun, wind and rain. Easter Week brings marzipan lambs to bakery windows and marks the opening date for many seasonal businesses.

✺ Pasqua (Easter)

Holy Week is marked by solemn processions and passion plays. The most famous are in Trapani, Enna, Lipari and Erice.

April

Markets overflow with wild strawberries, artichokes and fava beans. Weather is moody; it can be chilly or blissfully springlike.

✺ La Processione dei Misteri

For four days, Trapani's 20 traditional *maestranze* (guilds) parade life-sized wooden statues of the Virgin Mary and other Biblical figures through the streets, accompanied by a band that plays dirges to the slow, steady beat of a drum.

May

Many places on outer islands are just opening for the season. With wildflowers blooming, this is a glorious season for walking on the Aeolians or in the Vendicari and Zingaro reserves.

☆ Ciclo di Rappresentazioni Classiche

Combining classical intrigue with an evocative setting, the Cycle of Classical Plays, held from mid-May to mid-June, brings Syracuse's 5th-century BC amphitheatre to life with performances from Italy's acting greats (www.inda-fondazione.org).

Infiorata

At Noto's big annual jamboree, held around the third Sunday in May, the highlight is the decoration of Via Corrada Nicolaci with works of art made entirely from flower petals (www.infioratadinoto.it).

June

Great month for walking in the mountains. Beaches are crowded on weekends but still not at peak capacity. Summer ferry schedules start at month's end, bringing an influx of visitors to the islands.

Taormina Film Fest

Hollywood big shots arrive in Taormina in mid-June for six days of film screenings and press conferences at the Teatro Greco (www.taorminafilmfest.it).

July

School is out and Sicilians everywhere are headed away from cities and to mountains or beaches for summer holidays. Prices and temperatures rise.

Festino Di Santa Rosalia

Palermo's biggest annual festival celebrates Santa Rosalia, the patron saint of the city. The saint's relics are paraded through the city amid three days of fireworks and partying.

☆ Taormina Arte

Opera, dance, theatre and live music performances are staged at the Teatro Greco during July and August, with big-name performers from all over the world (www.taormina-arte.com).

August

Hot, expensive and crowded. Everyone is on holiday and many businesses and restaurants close for part of the month.

Ferragosto

After Christmas and Easter, Ferragosto, on 15 August, is Italy's biggest holiday. It marks the Feast of the Assumption, but even before Christianity the Romans honoured their gods on Feriae Augusti. Beaches are jam-packed and city attractions open for limited hours only.

Palio dei Normanni

Piazza Armerina's medieval pageant (between 13 and 14 August) commemorates Count Roger's taking of the town from the Moors in 1087 (www.paliodeinormanni.it).

September

Warm weather and sea but without the summer crowds. Hotel prices drop from their midsummer peak. Prime time for diving on Ustica.

Festival Internazionale del Cuscus

San Vito Lo Capo's famous fish couscous is celebrated annually at this six-day September event. The multicultural festivities involve musicians and chefs from around the world (www.couscousfest.it).

October

Businesses in the outer islands begin to curtail services, even as the chestnut harvest and wild mushroom seasons begin in earnest on Mt Etna and in the Madonie and Nebrodi mountains.

November

Chilly, rainy weather creeps in, and many accommodations in beach and island communities close for winter. Opera season in Palermo and Catania is in full swing.

Ognissanti

Celebrated all over Italy as a holiday, All Saints' Day on 1 November commemorates the Saint Martyrs, while All Souls' Day on 2 November honours the deceased.

December

Natale

During the weeks preceding Christmas, many churches set up cribs or nativity scenes known as presepi; these are particularly notable in Caltagirone and Erice.

Itineraries

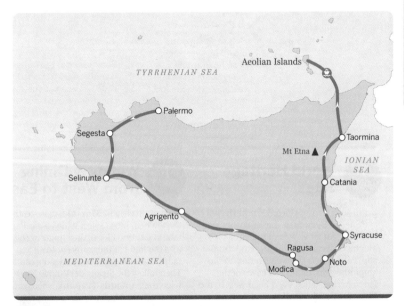

2 WEEKS: Only the Best

Fly into Palermo, Trapani or Catania and pick up a hire car to begin your circumnavigation of the island. Your destinations should be the same regardless of where you start: Agrigento, Selinunte, Segesta, the Val di Noto, Syracuse, Catania, Mt Etna, Taormina, the Aeolian Islands and Palermo. From **Palermo**, for instance, after exploring the capital's magnificent architectural monuments, you could head southwest to the temples at **Segesta**, **Selinunte** and **Agrigento**, then cut east across the island to the Unesco-listed Val di Noto, where the baroque beauties of **Ragusa**, **Modica** and **Noto** are all obligatory stops. Next it's on to **Syracuse**, a highlight of any trip to Sicily: split your time here between the pedestrian-friendly ancient island city of Ortygia and the vast classical ruins of the Parco Archeologico. Continue up the coast to bustling **Catania** and circle **Mt Etna** to reach **Taormina**, a town whose abundant attractions include its ancient Greek theatre and the gorgeous beaches just below. Finally, hop a ferry to the **Aeolian Islands** for some sun, swimming and beautiful coastal scenery.

7 DAYS World Heritage Sites

Begin your tour of Unesco World Heritage Sites in **Syracuse**, one of the ancient world's great cities, where traces of Magna Graecia are omnipresent – from papyrus-fringed Fontana Aretusa to the amphitheatres, altars and caves of the Parco Archeologico. Next head west to the **Necropoli di Pantalica** – an eerie array of several thousand Bronze Age tombs built into limestone cliffs – before continuing to the captivating Val di Noto. The devastating earthquake of 1693 may have wrought havoc on this corner of the island, but it also led to the creation of some of Sicily's greatest treasures. The late-baroque towns of **Noto**, **Modica** and **Ragusa** are the stars, but it's also worth seeking out the small villages of **Scicli** and **Palazzolo Acreide** and the famed ceramics centre of **Caltagirone**, with its grand staircase of 142 distinctively tiled steps. Continue west to dazzling **Villa Romana del Casale**, whose newly restored Roman mosaic floors depict bikini-clad gymnasts and African beasts prancing side by side. The trail ends at the most magnificent archaeological site in Sicily: **Agrigento**'s Valley of the Temples, with its five Doric structures perched on a ridge near the coast.

7 DAYS Wining & Dining from West to East

Start off in elegant **Marsala**, taste-testing the town's famous sweet wine on a cellar tour at Cantine Florio, then lingering late into the night at the many *enoteche* and restaurants in the pedestrian-friendly centre. Then follow the Strada del Vino Erice DOC wine route towards **Trapani**, where you can lunch on fabulous fish couscous, followed by dessert with a breathtaking view in **Erice**, renowned for its marzipan fruit, nougat and other nut-based sweets. Next, park your car for a day or two in **Palermo**, whose supremely colourful markets, delicious street food, irresistible bakeries and countless fine eateries are highlights of any Sicilian food trip. Take a cooking course, either at Palermo's Butera 28 or down the road at the 400-hectare **Regaleali estate** near Vallelunga, one of Sicily's leading wine producers. Meander east along the southern edge of the Madonie and Nebrodi mountains, refuelling frequently with local black pork, ricotta, pecorino, mushrooms and hazelnuts in pretty hill towns like **Petralia Sottana** and **Nicosia**. Last, circumnavigate spectacular **Mt Etna**, stopping for tastings of local honey, pistachios and Etna DOC wine before enjoying a final evening in cosmopolitan **Catania**.

4 DAYS — Mountain Retreats

Relax into your journey in postcard-perfect **Cefalù**, where you can lounge on the beach, visit the splendid medieval cathedral and enjoy panoramic coastal views from the ruins of the hilltop Norman citadel. Follow the coast to **Castel di Tusa**, breaking for lunch on the waterfront before exploring the town's unique open-air sculpture garden. Next climb through the lost-in-time mountain town of **Mistretta** into the Nebrodi mountains, where grand views of Mt Etna begin to unfold. After brief detours to explore the medieval village of **Nicosia**, continue south to **Enna**, a handsome hill town that marks the geographic centre of Sicily – a fact best appreciated from atop the heavily fortified walls of the Castello di Lombardia. Snake back north through Gangi into the heart of the **Parco Naturale Regionale delle Madonie**, a magnificent natural landscape dotted with hazelnut orchards, ash forests and photogenic hilltop towns. Linger a couple of days along the mountains' western edge in beautiful **Petralia Soprana, Petralia Sottana**, **Collesano** and **Castelbuono**, each of which boasts fine regional restaurants and makes a good base for hikes into the mountains. From Castelbuono an easy downhill jaunt takes you back to Cefalù.

7 DAYS — Smoke & Fire: Volcanic Sicily

Start in **Catania**, a city built of lava from the devastating volcanic eruption of 1669. Your first logical step is to climb the volcano that did all the damage, **Mt Etna**, nowadays one of Sicily's leading tourist attractions. As legend would have it, it was from Etna's lofty heights that the Cyclops hurled his stones at the fleeing Odysseus – you can still see their jagged forms along the dramatic **Riviera dei Ciclopi** coastline, where traditional fishing villages have been reinvented as summer resorts. Next follow our **driving tour** of Etna's western flank and continue north to **Milazzo**, where you can catch a ferry to **Lipari**, the largest of the Aeolian Islands. Read up on the archipelago's fiery past at Lipari's Museo Archeologico, then go tour a few volcanoes for yourself. Nature lovers can explore the verdant island of **Salina**, whose twin extinct cones are one of Sicily's most harmonious sights. Those looking for something a little more 'active' can climb smoking **Fossa di Vulcano**, with its sulphur-belching crater and gloopy mudbaths, or scale the 'lighthouse of the Mediterranean', **Stromboli**, an eternal lava-lamp whose eruptions continually light up the night sky.

Beach Hopping
7 DAYS

Unpack your beach towel for the first time at **Mondello**, Palermo's summer playground. Then head west to the stunning Golfo di Castellammare, where the popular beaches of **Castellammare del Golfo** and **San Vito lo Capo** offer an urban counterpoint to the pristine **Riserva Naturale dello Zingaro**, home to a series of sparkling coves spread out along a 7km walking trail. Next stop is Sicily's west coast. Beach aficionados will love the untrammelled **Riserva Naturale Torre Salsa**, the town of **Eraclea Minoa**, whose fabulous beach is complemented by an archaeological site, and the blindingly chalk-white **Scala dei Turchi**. Continue your beach-hop along Sicily's Ionian Coast, with visits to the isolated shores of the **Riserva Naturale Oasi Faunistica di Vendicari** and the blue waters at **Aci Castello**, where a Norman castle broods over the beach scene. Wrap it all up with stops at bustling **Lido Mazzarò** just below Taormina, **Piscina di Venere** at the tip of Capo Milazzo, and the long sandy beach in **Cefalù**. From here it's a quick trip back to Palermo.

Offshore Islands
10 DAYS

Your island-hopping adventure begins with a half-hour hydrofoil trip from Marsala or Trapani to **Favignana**, gateway to the Egadi Islands. Tour the old Florio tuna factory and cycle through Favignana's landscape of abandoned tufa quarries and beaches, then ferry across to see prehistoric cave art at **Levanzo** and hike the trails of **Marettimo**. Next stop is the offshore diving paradise of **Ustica**, whose pristine waters and easygoing pace will make you forget you're only 90 minutes from downtown Palermo. When you're ready for a culture shock, boomerang back to the Sicilian 'mainland' for the train from Palermo to Milazzo, then hydrofoil out to the **Aeolian Islands**, seven volcanic beauties with seven personalities. Start on the biggest, **Lipari**, where you can tour the superb archaeological museum, linger over drinks in the pleasant town centre or explore the island's outlying beaches and walking trails. From Lipari, frequent hydrofoils allow easy day trips to all the remaining islands: smoky **Vulcano**, chic **Panarea**, lush green **Salina**, remote **Alicudi**, off-the-beaten-track **Filicudi** and the most spectacular of all, actively erupting **Stromboli**.

Plan Your Trip

Eat & Drink Like a Local

If food isn't already one of your prime motivations for visiting Sicily, it should be! Over the centuries, Sicilian chefs have combined culinary influences from mainland Italy, north Africa and countless other places, with tasty and unexpected indigenous twists to create a unique cuisine, one of the world's most magnificent.

Food Experiences

Meals of a Lifetime

➡ **Trattoria Ai Cascinari**, Palermo (p67)
A traditional neighbourhood trattoria serving some of Palermo's best meals

➡ **Osteria La Bettolaccia**, Trapani (p95)
The perfect place to sample Trapani's famous fish couscous and other refined seafood dishes

➡ **Ristorante La Madia**, Licata (p248)
Exciting modern Sicilian cuisine that showcases the best regional produce.

➡ **Ristorante Duomo,** Ragusa (p215)
Faultlessly cooked and presented classics.

Cooking Classes

Serious epicureans can learn their way around the Sicilian kitchen at one of the island's cooking schools.

➡ **Cooking with the Duchess** (www. cookingwiththeduchess.com) Gregarious, multilingual duchess Nicoletta Polo Lanza opens the tiled kitchen of her 18th-century seaside *palazzo* for half-day Sicilian cooking courses. After taking students to shop in Palermo's markets and pick herbs in her backyard garden, she shares secrets of the island's multifaceted cuisine, from street food to classic main courses to gorgeous desserts.

The Year in Food

While *sagre* go into overdrive in autumn, there's never a bad time to raise your fork in Sicily.

Spring (Mar–May)

Asparagus, artichokes and little wild strawberries flood the local market stalls, and Easter specialities fill bakery windows. Tuna and swordfish both come into season.

Summer (Jun–Aug)

Time for eggplants, peppers, berries and seafood by the sea. Beat the heat Sicilian style with gelato on a brioche, or fresh mulberry *granite*.

Autumn (Sep–Nov)

Food festivals galore, wine harvest season and a perfect time to visit the mountains for gems like chestnuts, hazelnuts, mushrooms and wild game.

Winter (Dec–Feb)

Time for Christmas and Carnevale treats.

⇒ **Anna Tasca Lanza Cooking School**
(p231) Affiliated with one of Sicily's leading wine producers, this fabulous school in the middle of the Sicilian countryside has been around since 1989. Classes are taught at a century-old agricultural estate, with all ingredients sourced from the family garden or surrounding farms. Courses run from one to five days, with the option of overnight stays and additional food-related excursions to vineyards, permaculture gardens or the famous sweet shop of Maria Grammatico in Erice.

⇒ **La Corte del Sole Cooking School**
(p209) These half-day lessons are offered by the chef at the pretty Corte del Sole *agriturismo*, tucked between the baroque town of Noto and the beautiful coastline of the Riserva Naturale Oasi Faunistica di Vendicari.

Cheap Treats

⇒ *Arancini* – rice balls stuffed with meat or cheese, coated with breadcrumbs and fried

⇒ *Crocchè* – fried potato dumplings made with cheese, parsley and eggs

⇒ *Panelle* – fried chickpea-flour fritters, often served in a sesame roll

⇒ *Sfincione* – a Palermitan pizza made with tomatoes, onions and (sometimes) anchovies

⇒ *Quaglie* – aubergines (eggplant) cut lengthwise and fanned out to look like the feathers of a bird (the Italian name means 'quails'), then deep fried

THE ARK OF TASTE

The Ark of Taste is an international catalogue of endangered food products drawn up by the Slow Food Foundation for Biodiversity. It aims to protect indigenous edibles threatened with extinction by industrialisation, globalisation, hygiene laws and environmental dangers, and actively encourages their cultivation for consumption. Foods included in the list must be culturally or historically linked to a specific region, locality, ethnicity or traditional production practice, and must also be rare. There are 47 Sicilian foods on the list, ranging from the Ustica lentil to Trapani artisan sea salt and the Monreale white plum. For a full list, go to www.slowfoodfoundation.com/ark.

Dare to Try

⇒ *Pani ca muesa* – a roll filled with calf's spleen, *caciocavallo* cheese, a drizzle of hot lard and a squeeze of lemon juice

⇒ *Stigghiola* – seasoned and barbecued lamb or kid intestines served on a skewer

Sagre

The sharing of food is a central feature of Sicily's most important social occasions, and the Sicilian calendar is dotted with *sagre* (festivals dedicated to a culinary item or theme). The classic way is to precede it with a day of eating *magro* (lean), because the feast day is usually one of overindulgence. Here's a list of some of the best-known food festivals:

Sagra del Mandorlo in Fiore (Almond Blossom Festival; www.sagradelmandorlo.net) Agrigento, first Sunday in February

Sagra della Ricotta (Ricotta Festival; www.sagradellaricotta.it) Vizzini, near Caltagirone, late April

Sagra del Carciofo (Artichoke Festival; www.sagradelcarciofocerda.it) Cerda, near Palermo, 25 April

Sagra del Cappero (Caper Festival) Salina, in the Aeolian Islands, first Sunday in June

Festival Internazionale del Couscous (International Couscous Festival; www.couscousfest.it) San Vito Lo Capo, late September

Sagra del Miele (Honey Festival; www.sagradelmiele.it) Sortino, between Catania and Syracuse, late September or early October

Sagra del Pistacchio (Pistachio Festival; www.sagradelpistacchio.it) Bronte, late September or early October

Festa dei Sapori Madoniti d'Autunno (Festival of the Madonie Mountains' Autumn Flavours) Petralia Sottana, mid-October

Don't Miss

⇒ Dessert wines – skip straight to the dessert course so that you can order a glass of Marsala, Moscato or Malvasia

⇒ Honey tasting on Etna – sample mountain honey made from orange blossoms, chestnuts and lemons

⇒ *Brioche e gelato* – where else is it acceptable to eat an ice-cream sandwich for breakfast?

➡ *Granita con panna* – crushed ice mixed with coffee, almonds, pistachios, strawberries or mulberries, crowned with a dollop of fresh whipped cream

➡ Porcini mushrooms – head to the Madonie mountains to feast on freshly gathered fruits of the forest

➡ *Couscous alla trapanese* – Trapani's North African–influenced fish dish is so good it has its own festival

LOOK OUT FOR

➡ Interdonato lemons – natural hybrid of lemon and citron with a slightly bitter taste

➡ Almonds from Noto – intense and aromatic nuts from ancient trees

➡ Pistachios from Bronte – emerald-green nuts with an unctuous texture and intense flavour

➡ Black pork from the Nebrodi Mountains – can be enjoyed in succulent ham, sausages and bacon

➡ Capers from Salina – known for their firmness, perfume and uniform size

Local Specialities

Palermo

Snack in street markets on the local classic *pane e panelle* (a chickpea fritter sandwich with optional potato croquettes, fried eggplant and lemon), or sit down to a restaurant meal of *pasta con le sarde* (pasta with sardines, pine nuts, raisins and wild fennel) followed by *involtini di pesce spada* (thinly sliced swordfish fillets rolled up and filled with breadcrumbs, capers, tomatoes and olives).

Western Sicily

Savour this region's marked North African influence with a plate of *couscous di pesce alla trapanese* (fish couscous in a broth spiced with cinnamon, saffron, parsley and garlic) or a *bric* (savoury Tunisian pastry filled with tuna or shrimp). Top your pasta with *pesto alla trapanese* (made with fresh tomatoes, basil, garlic and almonds), and be sure to tour Marsala's world-renowned wine cellars.

Tyrrhenian Coast

Seafood is king along the coast, but some of the region's most interesting cuisine lies inland. The Madonie and Nebrodi mountains are recognised throughout Sicily for their delicious hazelnuts, chestnuts, wild mushrooms, fresh sheep's milk ricotta, provola cheese and *suino nero* (pork from local black pigs).

Aeolian Islands

With seven islands to choose from, you'll never run out of seafood. You'll also want to try *pasta all'eoliana*, with a sauce that incorporates the islands' renowned capers and olives, and sip the smooth and sweet Malvasia dessert wine grown on verdant Salina island. Other local treats include *pane cunzato* (sandwiches piled high with tuna, ricotta, eggplant, capers and olives) and the delicious *granite* (crushed ice flavoured with fresh fruit or nuts) at Da Alfredo (p147) in Lingua.

Ionian Coast

Hit Catania for one of Sicily's most beloved first courses, *pasta alla Norma* (pasta topped with eggplant, basil, fresh ricotta and tomatoes), and if you're passing through Messina, don't miss *agghiotta di pesce spada* (swordfish with pine nuts, sultanas, capers, olives and tomatoes). Several other regional specialities are grown on Mt Etna's volcanic slopes, including Bronte pistachios, Zafferana Etnea honey and Etna DOC wine.

Syracuse & the Southeast

Celebrate the earthy flavours of the southeast with *macco di fave* (fava-bean puree with wild fennel) or *lolli con le fave* (hand-rolled pasta with fava beans), and don't miss *ravioli di ricotta al sugo di maiale* (ricotta ravioli with a pork-meat *ragù*). The Syracuse region is famous for its lemons, blood oranges and tomatoes, and Ragusa is home to the excellent Ragusano DOP cheese. Local desserts include Modica's spiced chocolate creations and Noto's fine gelati (ice cream).

FABIO BIANCHINI/GETTY IMAGES ©

Above: *Linguine con cernia* (linguine with grouper)

Left: Sicilian *cannoli*

Central Sicily

The only place in Sicily without a coastline, the interior hill towns around Enna build their menus around meat, sausages and wild game, accompanied by mushrooms and fresh vegetables such as fava beans and wild asparagus. If you're here in September or October, don't miss the region's delicious yellow-and-red-streaked Leonforte peaches.

Mediterranean Coast

Seafood takes centre stage along Sicily's southwestern shoreline, most notably in the busy fishing port of Sciacca. Inland, the region's sun-baked fields and orchards produce excellent almonds, Canicatta grapes, Ribera oranges and Nocellara del Belice olives.

How to Eat & Drink

When to Eat

Sicilians love to eat at virtually any time of day. The three set meals are interspersed with breaks for coffee, street snacks and early evening *aperitivi*.

➡ *Colazione* (breakfast) – Many Sicilians eat the standard Italian breakfast of coffee with *cornetti* (croissants filled with cream or marmalade), *brioche* or *fette bicottate* (packaged dry toast), but they also enjoy a couple of sweet alternatives in summertime: *brioche e gelato* (a sweet roll filled with ice cream) and *granita con panna* (flavoured crushed ice, often topped with whipped cream).

➡ *Pranzo* (lunch) – Traditionally the biggest meal of the day, especially on Sundays. A full *pranzo* typically lasts at least two hours, with antipasti, a first course, second course, side dishes, fruit, wine, water and dessert. Standard restaurant hours are from noon to 2.30pm, though most Sicilians eat after 1pm.

➡ *Aperitivo* – Sicilians enjoy post-work drinks between 5pm and 8pm, often at outdoor tables when weather permits. At many places, the price of your drink includes an offering of snacks.

➡ *Cena* (dinner) – The courses available at dinnertime are the same as at lunch, though you'll be hard pressed to finish two meals of this size in a single day. In restaurants it's always perfectly permissible to order just a *primo* or *secondo*. Another less substantial alternative

---

SICILIAN SWEET TREATS

Most traditional Sicilian dishes fall into the category of *cucina povera* (cooking of the poor), featuring cheap and plentiful ingredients such as pulses, vegetables and bread. Supplemented by fish (locally caught and still relatively inexpensive), this diet is still widely embraced today, but differs in one major respect to that of previous generations – the inclusion of decadent desserts.

The two most beloved are *cassata siciliana* (a mix of ricotta, sugar, candied fruit and chocolate that is flavoured with vanilla and maraschino liqueur, encased by sponge cake and topped with green icing) and *cannoli* (crisp tubes of fried pastry dough filled with creamy ricotta and sometimes decorated with a maraschino cherry, candied fruit, grated chocolate or ground nuts). You'll find both on restaurant menus throughout the island.

---

is pizza, which is widely served in the evenings throughout Sicily. Standard restaurant hours are from 7.30pm to 11pm, though locals don't arrive in earnest until 9pm or later.

Where to Eat

Sicilian eateries range from the humblest of street-side stalls to top-of-the-line gourmet restaurants, with plenty of options in between. Here's a breakdown of the most common places to eat. Menus for most places are posted by the door.

➡ Trattoria – Often family-run, this is a less formal restaurant serving regional specialities, with a focus on traditional pasta, fish and meat dishes. Many of Sicily's best eateries fall into this category.

➡ *Ristorante* (restaurant) – Can be anything from a conservative hotel-based establishment with crisp white linen and formal service to a trendy up-and-coming eatery. Restaurants tend to serve a wider selection of dishes and charge higher prices than trattorias.

➡ *Osteria* – Historically a tavern focused on wine, the modern version is usually an intimate, relaxed trattoria or wine bar offering a handful of dishes from a verbal menu.

COFFEE, SICILIAN STYLE

Sicilians take their coffee seriously, and order it in the following ways.

Espresso A tiny cup of very strong black coffee; usually called a *caffè* or *caffè normale*

Caffè macchiato An espresso with a dash of milk

Cappuccino Espresso topped with hot foaming milk; only drunk at breakfast or in the mid-morning

Caffè latte Coffee with milk that is steamed but not frothed; an extremely milky version is called a *latte macchiato* (stained milk); again, only drunk in the morning

Caffè freddo The local version of an iced coffee

➡ Pizzeria – A top place for a cheap feed, cold beer and a buzzing, convivial vibe. Many open only at night.

➡ *Enoteca* (wine bar) – Wines are the clear focus, but most places also serve a limited menu of deli-style snacks or simple meals.

➡ *Agriturismo* – In rural areas, this is an eatery on a country estate or working farm where much of the produce is cultivated on-site.

➡ *Friggitoria* – These street food venues range from portable carts pushed through local markets to hole-in-the-wall eateries with small kitchens and limited, informal seating. The common denominator is the emphasis on simple fried snacks and the ultra-low prices, usually no more than a euro or two.

➡ *Tavola calda* – A simple canteen-style eatery serving pre-prepared pasta, meat and vegetable dishes, along with snacks and *panini* (bread rolls with simple fillings).

➡ Bar-*caffè* – Typically varying its functions depending on the time of day, a bar-*caffè* will serve coffee and *cornetti* (Italian croissants) in the morning, drinks in the afternoon and evening, and sweet and savoury snacks all day long. Many also serve ice cream.

➡ *Pasticceria* (pastry shop) – Typically serves a wide selection of pastries and cakes, including classic Sicilian treats like *cannoli* and *cassata*. Some have a *caffè* attached, others do not.

➡ Gelateria (ice cream shop) – One of the best reasons to come to Sicily, generally with a vast rainbow of flavours. Don't miss *gelato e brioche* (ice cream served on a roll), a common Sicilian treat.

Menu Decoder

While tourist-oriented restaurants sometimes provide bilingual menus, you'll be better off learning some Italian food terminology. Below are a few key terms that will help you decipher Sicilian menus.

➡ *Menu a la carte* – choose whatever you like from the menu

➡ *Menu di degustazione* – tasting menu, usually consisting of six to eight 'tasting size' courses

➡ *Menu turistico* – the dreaded 'tourist menu', a fixed-price, multi-course affair that often signals mediocre fare aimed at gullible tourists

➡ *Piatto del giorno* – dish of the day

➡ *Nostra produzione* or *fatta in casa* – made in house, used to describe anything from pasta to olive oil to *liquori* (liqueurs)

➡ *Surgelato* – frozen, usually used to denote fish or seafood that has not been freshly caught

➡ Antipasti – hot or cold appetisers; for a tasting plate of mixed appetisers, request an *antipasto misto*

➡ *Primi* – first courses of pasta, rice, couscous or soup

➡ *Secondi* – second courses of *pesce* (fish) or *carne* (meat)

➡ *Contorni* – side dishes of *verdura* (vegetables) or *insalata* (salad) intended to accompany your main course

➡ *Dolci* – sweets (many Sicilian menus also use the English word dessert)

➡ *Frutta* – fresh fruit, served in more traditional eateries as the epilogue to your meal

Plan Your Trip

Outdoor Activities

Sicily's outdoor appeal is all-encompassing – the favourable climate and variety of landscapes mean you can pretty much do any outdoor activity that's imaginable in the Mediterranean. There is a wealth of coast and islands to dive and snorkel from, if mere swimming doesn't suffice; a number of volcanoes (Mt Etna and Stromboli being the main ones) to climb; and a range of regional parks to trek and explore both on foot and bike. There's also birdwatching, skiing, and World Heritage sites to hop around. You name it, you can do it.

Volcanoes

Mount Etna

There are a number of tours and treks you can do around Etna. Two treks leave from Piano Provenzano (p185), on the mountain's northern slopes: to Pizzi Deneri and the Volcanic Observatory at 2800m (a two-hour trip), or up to the main crater at 3200m (three hours). Both offer spectacular views of the Peloritani, Nebrodi and Madonie mountain ranges and the Valle del Bove. Further down, there's lovely walking in the pine, birch and larch trees of the Pineta Ragabo, a vast wood accessible from the Mareneve road between Linguaglossa and Milo.

The ascent of the southern slopes begins at Rifugio Sapienza (p185; 1923m), from where you can take the Funivia dell'Etna (p185) and walk the 2km up to the four craters: Bocca di Nord-Est (northeast crater), Voragine, Bocca Nuova and Cratere Sud-Est (southeast crater).

You can ski (p186) on Etna (both downhill and cross-country) between December and March. The Mufara (northern slopes) skiing complex goes to heights of 1840m

Don't Miss Experiences

Diving & Snorkelling
Explore the underwater worlds of Lipari, Ustica or Isola Bella.

Volcano Viewing
Watch Stromboli's nocturnal fireworks from the summit or a boat, or teeter on the edges of Etna.

Cycling
Use pedal power to explore the Mt Etna area.

Sailing Trips
Explore the coastlines and hidden coves of Lipari, Alicudi and Filicudi.

Guided Nature Walks
Join local naturalists on a walk around the Syracusan countryside or on the slopes of Etna.

Mud Baths
Wallow in the mud at Vulcano or Eraclea Minoa.

and serves 3.5km of runs, while the Mufaretta (southwest slopes) reaches 1680m, with a run of about 500m. Always check the latest volcanic activity and the state of the slopes and how many lifts are working at www.etnasci.it.

Tough bikers can also cycle around the mountain – check out Etna Touring (p165) for details.

Stromboli

With Stromboli's constant spray of liquid magma, trekking up to its crater is always a magical experience – especially since the walk takes place at dusk. The demanding trek (up to three hours up, and one-and-a-half hours back) takes you up in time for sunset, and you get to observe the crater's fireworks for about 45 minutes against the night sky. Crater explosions take place around every 20 minutes or so and are great fun to watch.

Those less keen on the climb can observe the crater from L'Osservatorio (p154), a viewpoint that has a restaurant on the side, for dinner with a view – with a difference.

Aeolian Islands

Vulcano is more of an olfactory than visual experience – the stench of sulphur is omnipresent on the island. You can walk up the 391m Fossa di Vulcano (p142) without a guide, and see the steaming crater while enjoying the beautiful views of the rest of the Aeolian Islands to the north.

URBAN ESCAPES
• •

Orto Botanico, Palermo (p63) A tranquil botanic garden in the midst of the city's chaos.

Villa Comunale, Taormina (p168) Superb views, shady paths and botanical species galore.

Villa Bellini, Catania (p175) This charming retreat in the centre of the city is named after the great composer.

Latomia del Paradiso, Syracuse (p195) An ancient limestone quarry pitted with caves and full of orange and olive trees.

Don't miss taking a mud bath at the Laghetto di Fanghi (p143), a smelly but exhilarating and healing experience – there's even a natural Jacuzzi attached!

Salina has the Aeolians' highest point, Monte Fossa delle Felci (p145; 962m), and after the two-hour climb, which can be quite tough at times, you'll emerge to the most magnificent views of the Lingua salt lagoon and all the way to Lipari and Vulcano.

Regional Parks

There are no national parks in Sicily, but there are many protected natural landscapes, including 79 regional nature reserves, six marine protected areas and one protected wetland. For information about visiting them, go to www.parks.it.

The following are the largest and most significant. These parks are large, and each deserve a few days of exploration; fortunately, all offer plenty of places to sleep and eat. Each park offers the visitor a very different experience.

➡ **Parco dell'Etna** (p186) Taste home-grown wine and honey on the volcano's slopes, and trek to the crater

➡ **Parco Fluviale dell'Alcantara** (p170) Swim, picnic, ride quad bikes, hike or canyon

➡ **Parco Regionale dei Nebrodi** (p126) A wealth of beech, oak, elm, ash, cork, maple and yew trees that shelter the remnants of Sicily's wildlife: porcupines, San Fratello horses and wildcats, as well as a healthy population of birds of prey such as golden eagles, lanner and peregrine falcons and griffon vultures

➡ **Parco Naturale Regionale delle Madonie** Excellent walking and picnicking opportunities

Top Treks

➡ Piano Battaglia – walk among the wildflowers in the Parco Naturale Regionale delle Madonie

➡ Mt Etna – hike the picturesque northern slopes of the famous volcano

➡ Vulcano – climb the short but steep path to the steaming rim of an active volcano's crater

Above: Mt Etna (p183)
Right: Scuba diving, Ustica (p82)

JEFF ROTMAN/ALAMY ©

BATHE YOURSELF IN MUD

People spend many euros on beauty treatments, but Sicilians only have to hop over to the island of Vulcano or the beach of Eraclea Minoa to dip into a healing, beautifying and overall health-enforcing mud bath.

Vulcano's Laghetto di Fanghi (p143) is a large are of gloopy sulphurous mud that has long been considered excellent treatment for skin disorders and arthritis. Get your oldest bikini on (the smell of sulphur will *never* leave the fabric, so act wisely and don't go in your new shiny swimsuit) and relax for a while – apply a mud face mask while you're at it. Finish off with a natural Jacuzzi (hot bubbling springs in a small natural seawater pool) on the side.

You'll see green people emerging from the western end of the beach of Eraclea Minoa, west of Agrigento. This is because sunbathers flock to the beach's natural mud rock: they scrape the mud and spread it all over their bodies and faces – a wonderful natural skin treatment. Let it dry on your skin and wash it off with a refreshing swim in the sea. What could be better?

➡ Riserva Naturale dello Zingaro (p89) – hike the coastal path between Scopello and San Vito Lo Capo

➡ Stromboli (p151) – complete the demanding six-hour guided walk to the summit

➡ Valle dell'Anapo – take a gentle walk through an unspoiled valley

➡ Riserva Naturale Torre Salsa (p243) – admire sweeping panoramic views of the surrounding mountains and coast

Climbing Festival

San Vito Lo Capo has blossomed as a climbing destination in recent years, with a variety of challenging crags just outside town. The San Vito Climbing Festival (www.sanvitoclimbingfestival.it/eng) is a four-day, mid-October festival that, apart from climbing, features kayaking, mountain biking, trail running in the nearby Riserva Naturale dello Zingaro, and an outdoor adventure film festival.

Birdwatching

➡ Riserva Naturale dello Zingaro (p89) – this nature reserve has more than 40 species, including the rare Bonelli eagle, hawks, buzzards, kestrels, swifts and Imperial crows, as well as the 'Greek Partridge of Sicily' – an endemic species nearly extinguished in the province of Trapani, but which has started to repopulate the area from the reserve.

➡ Parco Regionale dei Nebrodi (p126) – the park has some 150 species of birds, among them endemic species like the Sicilian marshtit and the Sicilian long-tailed tit. Birds of prey populate the edges of the park, and you can spot buzzards, kestrels and the peregrine falcon, as well as the golden eagle. Species like the little grebe, the coot, the dipper and the kingfisher live in the wetlands.

➡ Mozia (p103) – this tiny island is a haven for many species, including flamingos, herons, storks and cranes, as well as grey herons.

➡ Riserva Naturale Oasi Faunistica di Vendicari (p209) – the wetlands are home to flamingos, herons, spoonbills, cranes, ducks, cormorants and collared pratincoles.

➡ Lingua (p146) – Salina's lagoon attracts huge numbers of migrating birds in April; scores of Eleonora's falcons (Falco eleonorae) return to nest here.

Driving Tours

Tour striking landscapes, sampling great regional food and wine as you go.

Monti Madonie Admire hilltop medieval villages and majestic mountain scenery, dining in acclaimed restaurants along the way.

Etna's western flank Pass Norman castles, baroque towns and pistachio groves, and feed yourself mountain fare in *agriturismi*.

Baroque towns Discover Unesco-listed hilltop towns such as Noto, Modic and Ragusa, and get in a spot of birdwatching, swimming and sunbathing at the Riserva Naturale Oasi Faunistica di Vendicari.

Enna to Etna Traverse an undulating landscape of sun-baked hills, historic towns and mountain honey.

Way out West The tour around Western Sicily showcases the best of the region, with natural reserves, medieval towns and the best wine on the island. It can be done in one day or over a leisurely couple of days.

Mediterranean The Med Coast tour encompasses an excellent and eclectic mix: wild beaches and fresh fish along the coast, spectacular Greek temples at Agrigento and contemporary art in Favara.

Diving & Snorkelling

Ustica

Divers from all over the world come to Ustica between May and October to explore its magnificent underwater sites.

Highlights include the underwater archaeological trail off Punta Cavazzi, where artefacts including anchors and Roman amphorae can be admired. Other popular dive sites are the Scoglio del Medico, an outcrop of basalt riddled with caves and gorges that plunge to great depths; and Secca di Colombara, a magnificent rainbow-coloured display of sponges and gorgonias.

Ustica's western shores are home to a protected marine reserve, the Riserva Naturale Marina, which is divided into three zones. Zone A extends along the west flank of the island from Cala Sidoti to Caletta and as far as 350m offshore (marked with special yellow buoys): you can swim within its boundaries at designated spots, but fishing and boating are prohibited. Two of the island's most beautiful natural grottoes – the Grotta Segreta (Secret Grotto) and the Grotta Rosata (Pink Grotto) – are located here.

Zone B extends beyond Zone A from Punta Cavazzi to Punta Omo Morto; swimming and underwater photography are permitted within its boundaries, as is hook-and-line fishing. Zone C applies to the rest of the coast; swimming and boating are allowed and national fishing regulations apply. Always check your itinerary

with a dive centre or the Marine National Park headquarters before you dive.

There are plenty of dive centres that offer dive itineraries and hire equipment. Among them, Diving Center Ustica (p83) stands out: it's the only operator managed and staffed entirely by local residents.

Aeolian Islands

There are good dives off most of the Aeolian Islands, but the best are in Lipari. Our favourites are: Punta Castagna, a spectacular dive with a 10m white pumice platform interrupted by multicoloured channels; Secca del Bagno, a breathtaking collection of colourful walls that are swathed with schools of technicolour fish; Pietra Menalda, with octopuses, eel, groupers and other sea critters; Pietra del Bagno, circumnavigating the Bagno rock, while witnessing colourful surfaces and sea life; and La Parete dei Gabbiani, a black-and-white dive with black lava rock streaked with white pumice stone, hiding cracks that are home to lobsters.

Other Spots

The Riserva Naturale dello Zingaro is great for diving too. Cetaria Diving Centre (p91) in Scopello organises guided dives in the waters off the nature reserve between April and October, visiting underwater caves and two shipwrecks; it also offers boat excursions with snorkelling.

Taormina's Isola Bella (p168) has some good diving for children and adults.

TOP BEACHES

➡ **Forgia Vecchia, Stromboli** (p154) Relax on this black volcanic beach

➡ **San Vito Lo Capo** Join the sun worshippers on this crescent-shaped sandy beach

➡ **Spiaggia dei Conigli, Lampedusa** Visit one of the Mediterranean's finest beaches

➡ **Scala dei Turchi** A bright white rock that's shaped like a staircase, perfect for off-beat picnicking and swimming

WORLD HERITAGE LANDSCAPE

The Aeolian Islands (*Isole Eolie*) are one of only two Italian natural landscapes included on the World Heritage list (the other is the Dolomites). Unesco's citation describes the Aeolians as providing an outstanding record of volcanic island building and destruction, and ongoing volcanic phenomena. It also notes that the islands have played a vitally important role in the education of vulcanologists for over 200 years.

Of course it's not only vulcanologists who are fascinated by these islands. Tourists from around the world flock here in summer to take advantage of the great hiking, swimming, snorkelling, diving and boating on offer.

Boating & Kayaking

Those who are keen to observe the underwater world in Ustica but don't wish to dive or snorkel can hop aboard a glass-bottomed Acquario Motorship; ask at the **Marine National Park** (☑091 844 94 56; www.parks.it/riserva.marina.isola.ustica; Piazza Umberto 1) office for details.

You can go boating around the Aeolian Islands, both with a tour or by renting out your own boat or dinghy. In Lipari try **Gruppo di Navigazione** (Map p136; ☑090 982 22 37; navigazioneregina.com; Via Garibaldi), and in Vulcano, Centro Nautica Baia di Levante (p144).

Sicily in Kayak (p144) offers kayaking tours around Vulcano and the other Aeolians, ranging from half a day to an entire week.

Marine Reserves

Sicily has six *area marina protetta* (protected marine reserves).

Isole Pelagie (www.isole-pelagie.it) Includes the three islands of the Pelagic archipelago: Lampedusa, Lampione and Linosa.

Isole Ciclopi (www.isoleciclopi.it) On the Riviera dei Ciclopi outside Catania.

Capo Gallo (www.ampcapogallo-isola.org) In the Tyrrhenian Sea.

Isola di Ustica (www.ampustica.it) Around the island of Ustica.

Plemmirio (www.plemmirio.it) The waters off Syracuse.

Isole Egadi (www.ampisoleegadi.net) Includes the islands of the Egadi archipelago: Favignana, Levanzo, Marittimo and Formica.

Plan Your Trip

Travel with Children

There can be few places as friendly to children as Sicily. Families are welcomed with open arms at restaurants, cafes and hotels, and staff usually go out of their way to accommodate your needs. Your brood will have an easy time enjoying museums, galleries and archaeological parks.

Best Regions for Kids

Palermo

Excellent for teenagers, who should enjoy the buzz and weird variety of offerings at the food markets and on Palermo's labyrinthine streets.

Western Sicily

The wonderful beaches and natural reserves will appeal to all generations, while taking the funicular (p99) up to the magical hilltop town of Erice should entertain older kids.

Tyrrhenian Coast

Great beaches at Cefalù and along this part of the coast make for good family times.

Aeolian Islands

Teenagers should love island hopping and climbing the steaming cone of Stromboli (p151), while smaller kids, toddlers and babies will love the beaches and clear waters that encircle all the islands.

Ionian Coast

Climb Etna (p185) with your teenagers or swim off the many volcanic beaches.

Practical Tips

When to Go

Spring, early summer and autumn are generally best for families with small children, because high summer temperatures can make life miserable for the very little ones although good beaches and all that coast should make this more bearable.

Before You Go

Car seats for infants and children are available from most car-rental firms, but you should always book them in advance.

Stock up on sun cream even in spring and autumn, when it can still be quite warm in Sicily.

Insect repellent (especially for mosquitoes) is highly advised.

For more information see Lonely Planet's *Travel with Children* book or look up the websites www.travelwithyourkids.com and www.familytravelnetwork.com.

Catania's Pescheria (p174) fish market should entertain kids and adults alike, while the resorts of Giardini-Naxos and small towns on the Riviera dei Ciclopi are great for family days on the beach.

Syracuse Southeast

Toddlers and little children will revel in the open running space on Syracuse's Piazza Duomo (p192), while the whole family will enjoy exploring the beaches at Oasi Faunistica di Vendicari (p209) nature reserve. The pedestrianised centre of Noto is a wonderful running ground for toddlers and small children.

Central Sicily

Visit at springtime for endless fields of wild flowers that smaller children will adore to run around in, or escape the heat in the summer months.

Mediterranean Coast

Agrigento's Valley of the Temples (p235) should prove a wonderful day for the whole family in the spring and autumn months, while the many beaches along the coast will be loved by all generations. Farm Cultural Park (p249) in Favara is just perfect for teenage art lovers.

Sicily for Kids

It's a safe bet that in Sicily you and your kids will be met with a friendly, accommodating and relaxed attitude. Eating out should be a breeze, even for the fussiest of kids – you can choose from the basics like pizza and pasta with a tomato sauce – while the more adventurous eaters will be able to 'expand' their palate with varied seafood, fish, meat and a variety of vegetables and fruit. *Gelati* (ice cream), *granite* (crushed ice with various flavours), and the many fantastic Sicilian *dolci* (desserts) will be fought over by the entire family.

The entire island, and the smaller islands off Sicily, have something engaging for the family, be it the mix of history and nature at the Valley of the Temples (p235) in Agrigento, the beaches at the many natural reserves, vibrant street markets at Palermo and Catania, or a simple *passegiata* (evening stroll) with the locals, ice cream in hand. Teenagers will be able to break up lazy days with the parents with some swimming off organised boat trips, while families who are activity seekers have two volcanoes to climb, many mountain-biking trips to take and lots of snorkelling and diving options. Norman castles are scattered around the island and are ripe for exploration.

Away from the beaches, smaller kids can be kept entertained at the local main square – the piazzas are usually equipped with fun rides and, well, other kids! Traditional puppet shows are a great way to introduce your children to local culture – it helps if they're into battles!

Babies will be cooed over, and breast feeding is common and attitudes are relaxed.

While it's generally safe for kids to run around small town squares, keep an eye on the scooters that sometimes zip in and out – pedestrian areas are something of a relative concept in Sicily.

Children's Highlights

Food & Drink

Gelato Kids love the local ice cream, especially for breakfast, when ice cream is served in a sweet bun!

Granita There's nothing more refreshing (and yummy) than this crushed-ice drink on a hot day.

In & On the Water

Visiting a sea cave Visit Filicudi's spectacular Grotta del Bue Marino by boat.

Snorkelling and diving Water-loving families and older kids and teenagers can snorkel and dive to their heart's desire at Ustica.

The Outdoors

Volcano climbing #1 A glance at the glowing insides of Stromboli (p151) volcano on a night climb should put a smile on any teenager's face.

Volcano climbing #2 Follow the pongy path to the steaming crater of Fossa di Vulcano (p142).

Castles Storm the ramparts of Norman castles across the island

Cable Car to Erice Take the kids on a steep ride to the hilltop town of Erice (p99).

The Arts

Farm Cultural Park Teenagers will love the edgy art kasbah (p249) in Favara, and little ones can run around the many installations.

Puppet theatre Watch brave knights defeat evil monsters in a traditional puppet play in Palermo, Acireale (p181) or Syracuse's Teatro dei Pupi (p201).

Sicilian Culture

Farm stays Enjoy animals, swimming pools and lots of space while staying in an agriturismo.

Passeggiata Search out carousels, cafes and convivial company of every age during the evening stroll.

What to Expect

➡ Admission to many cultural sites is free for under-10s or under-18s (particularly EU citizens).

➡ In restaurants, high chairs are usually available and it's perfectly acceptable to order a *mezza porzione* (half portion) off the normal menu for little ones.

➡ On trains, the *offerte familia* allows a discount of 50% for children under 12 and 20% for other family members if you are travelling in a group of three to five people (see www.trenitalia.com for conditions).

➡ You can stock up on nappies, baby formula and sterilising solutions at pharmacies and supermarkets.

➡ Fresh cow's milk is sold in bars that have a 'Latteria' sign and in supermarkets.

Regions at a Glance

Palermo

Art & Architecture
Food
Nightlife

Cultural Treasure Chest

Palermo has everything from Byzantine mosaics to Arab-Norman palaces to exuberant rococo chapels. This city is full of surprises: verses from the Koran scrawled on church columns, Arabic marble inlay beside glimmering images of an all-powerful Christ, and baroque domes atop medieval foundations.

Culinary Capital

From appetisers such as *sarde in beccaficco* (pine-nut-and-raisin-stuffed sardines rolled in breadcrumbs) to the world's most scrumptious *cannoli,* every menu page is worth lingering over. Don't limit yourself to restaurants – stroll through the city's bustling markets and discover its superb street food.

Puppets & Prima Donnas

Nights out in Palermo can mean many things: live music at one of Italy's great opera houses, medieval tales performed by exquisite handcrafted puppets, an evening soak in a Moorish steam bath, or bar-hopping the buzzing late-night streets.

p48

Western Sicily

History
Outdoors
Food & Wine

Ancient Eyries

For idyllic natural setting, few ruins can match Segesta and Selinunte; where hilltop temples sit in splendid, moody isolation, peeking through fields of tall grass and wildflowers. Erice's Norman castle comes close, though, perched on a spectacular hilltop that's been coveted by everyone from the Phoenicians to the ancient Greeks.

Fun in the Sun

Whether you're climbing San Vito's crags, hiking the Zingaro's trails, or sunbathing on an Egadi Island beach, western Sicily offers endless supplies of outdoorsy fun.

Saracen Seasonings

North African influences have always been close at hand in western Sicily, as reflected in the seductively spiced fish couscous that appears on every menu. Some of Sicily's finest wines are also produced here, most notably around Marsala and Erice.

p84

Tyrrhenian Coast

Beaches
Hill Towns
Food

Sea & Sand

Dotted with pretty resort towns such as Cefalù and Castel di Tusa, the Tyrrhenian Coast becomes a jam-packed beach playground every summer.

Mountain Retreats

Pretty villages such as Castelbuono, Mistretta and Petralia Sottana hunker down against the Nebrodi and Madonie mountains' high slopes, offering a welcome home base to outdoors enthusiasts who are increasingly discovering the region's charms.

Fabulous Fungi

Kiss seafood goodbye and prepare to be impressed by the entirely different cuisine of the Nebrodi and Madonie mountains. Wild mushrooms and roast meats, notably from the indigenous *suino nero* (black pig), are mainstays of the menu, as are local hazelnuts, chestnuts, ricotta and *provola* cheese.

p112

Aeolian Islands

Outdoors
Food & Wine
Volcanoes

Natural Paradise

If stunning coastal beauty is your idea of paradise, you've come to the right place. Each of the seven Aeolians has its own natural charms, with enough diving, swimming, kayaking, walking and climbing to satisfy outdoors enthusiasts of all stripes.

Island Flavours

Fresh seafood figures prominently in the Aeolians' divine cuisine, along with local capers and olives. The island of Salina is famous for its honey-sweet Malvasia wine, available at shops and restaurants throughout the archipelago.

Smoke & Fire

Yes, most of the Aeolians' volcanoes are now extinct. But Vulcano and Stromboli just keep on smoking, the former luring visitors with its therapeutic mud baths, the latter with its awe-inspiring fiery eruptions.

p131

Ionian Coast

Volcanoes
Festivals
Food & Wine

Volcano Views

Mt Etna's spellbinding form dominates this stretch of coast from every imaginable angle, looming on the horizon at the end of Catania's busy boulevards, peeking through the stage at Taormina's Greek theatre, providing four-season outdoor recreation and feeding local agriculture with its fertile volcanic soil.

Fabulous Festivals

This place really knows how to throw a party. Taormina buzzes all summer long with world-class festivals of film, theatre, music and dance, while winter revellers are lured into the streets by Acireale's Carnevale and Catania's massive Festa di Sant'Agata.

Markets & Vineyards

Foodies will find plenty to love in this corner of Sicily, from the acclaimed Etna DOC wine to Catania's colourful fish and produce markets.

p158

Syracuse & the Southeast

Architecture
History
Food

Baroque Beauty

Devastated by a 1693 earthquake, southeastern Sicily's hill towns rose like a phoenix from the ashes, adopting the appealing baroque aesthetic you see today in the Unesco-listed towns of Noto, Modica, Ragusa and their smaller sisters throughout the southeast.

Ancient Greek Echoes

Modern-day Syracuse still glows with the glory of its Greek past, in the repurposed temple columns of Ortygia's cathedral, the papyrus-fringed pool at the heart of town and the cycle of Greek dramas that still draws crowds to the city's ancient amphitheatre each summer.

Sweet Temptations

From Modica's chocolates to Noto's *granite* to the wine-flavoured ice creams of Ragusa, this is a region that any sweet tooth will love.

p188

Central Sicily

Hill Towns
History
Shopping

Norman Strongholds

Bearing traces of their Norman past, Central Sicily's hill towns float like islands in the sky above the surrounding landscape. The regional capital of Enna lords over them all from its prime position at Sicily's geographic centre.

Roman Splendour

The world's most extensive and best-preserved late-Roman mosaic floors are shining brighter than ever thanks to recent renovations. Look for them in the ancient Villa Romana del Casale outside Piazza Armerina.

Ceramics Central

Ceramics lovers beware! Caltagirone's dozens of artisans' shops, ceramics museum, and whimsical 142-step staircase covered top to bottom in hand-painted tiles may seduce you into an acquisitive frenzy.

p216

Mediterranean Coast

History
Beaches
Food

Transcendent Temples

Agrigento's unparalleled array of ancient temples, coupled with the superb collection of artefacts at the nearby archaeological museum, constitutes Sicily's greatest classical legacy.

White Cliffs, Wild Sands

Stellar beachgoing spots dot the coast west of Agrigento, including the long, unspoiled shoreline of Riserva Naturale Torre Salsa, the golden sands of Eraclea Minoa and the stunning white rock formation called Scala dei Turchi, at its best when illuminated by the setting sun.

Superb Seafood

You can eat well all along this coast, but at no place better than Sciacca, where seafood is delivered straight from the boat into the kitchens of the many port-side restaurants.

p233

On the Road

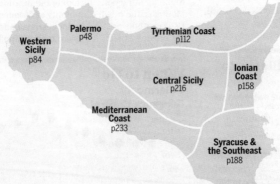

Palermo

Includes ➡

Best Places to Eat

➡ Trattoria Il Maestro del Brodo (p66)

➡ Trattoria Ai Cascinari (p67)

➡ Piccolo Napoli (p67)

➡ Ferro di Cavallo (p64)

➡ Antica Focacceria San Francesco (p65)

Best Places to Stay

➡ Palazzo Pantaleo (p252)

➡ BB22 (p252)

➡ B&B Amelie (p252)

➡ Butera 28 (p252)

➡ Grand Hotel Piazza Borsa (p253)

Why Go?

Flamboyant, feisty and full of life, Palermo evokes a strong response from visitors and residents alike. Its car-choked streets, rubbish-strewn pavements and decrepit infrastructure cause everyone to pull out their hair at one stage or another, but it's easy to overlook the city's problems when you enter a church full of luminously beautiful Byzantine mosaics, wander along a street of stately baroque *palazzi* or witness the genial banter between canny stall owners and bargain-hunting housewives at a street market. Exploring can be exhausting, but it's well and truly worth it.

Palermo is also an ideal base for excursions to surrounding attractions, including the magnificent mosaics at Monreale, the beach community of Mondello, the island of Ustica with its pristine marine reserve, and the inland town of Corleone, famous for its groundbreaking Mafia museum.

When to Go
Palermo

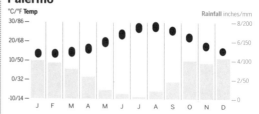

April–May Lower prices and nice weather make spring perfect for visiting, with displays of fruit and veg jazzing up the markets.

July Join the party in celebration of Santa Rosalia, the city's patron saint, whose image is paraded on a decorated carriage.

September–October Enjoy optimal late-season diving conditions without the crowds in the crystal-clear waters off Ustica.

Getting Around

Walking is the best way to experience central Palermo's markets and architecture. Traffic and limited parking make driving challenging, and there's excellent public transport into town from the airport. Palermo's port is a 10-minute walk from Piazza Politeama, heart of the new city. From here, local buses whiz down Via Roma and Via Maqueda to Palermo Centrale, where trains serve destinations near and far.

THREE PERFECT DAYS

Medieval Masterpieces

Palermo's wealth of Arab, Norman and Byzantine masterpieces is enough to fill an entire day. Begin with the city's crown jewel, Palazzo dei Normanni (p55), where the sparkling mosaics of King Roger's royal bedroom are only a prelude to his magnificent Cappella Palatina (p55). In the afternoon, visit the dazzling Cattedrale di Monreale (p80) or the architectural smorgasbords at Palermo's Cattedrale (p56) and San Giovanni degli Eremiti (p56). End your day at Piazza Bellini (p53), home to the exquisite domed churches of La Martorana (p53) and San Cataldo (p53).

Baroque Beauties

Admire the quartet of baroque facades at Quattro Canti (Map p58) and the exuberant cascade of naked nymphs at Fontana Pretoria (Map p58). Lunch nearby at Ferro di Cavallo (p64) or Maestro del Brodo (p66), then tour the city's fabulous oratories (Santa Cita (p60), San Domenico (p61), San Lorenzo (p61)), where Giacomo Serpotta's masterful stucco relief steals the show. After dinner, catch an opera at the equally ornate Teatro Massimo (p68).

Under the Palermitan Sun

Wander through the bustling markets of Capo (p56) and Ballarò (p56) in the morning. Lunch on street snacks from a sidewalk vendor amid the greenery of Orto Botanico (p63) or Giardino Garibaldi (Map p58; Piazza Marina; ☺24hr), then spend the afternoon on the beach in nearby Mondello. In the evening, head to the Teatro di Verdura (p68), Palermo's open-air summer theatre, and dine under the stars at the onsite cafe.

Getting Away From It All

⇒ **Ustica** Catch a ferry to one of the Med's top dive spots.

⇒ **Villa Malfitana** Wander through the serene salons and gardens of this belle époque mansion.

⇒ **Hammam** Sip mint tea on cushions after an evening relaxing in Palermo's Arabic-style steam baths.

DON'T MISS

Taking time to stumble upon unexpected surprises. Join the *passeggiata* (evening stroll), plunge into the maelstrom of a street market, go bar-hopping on Via Chiavettieri or Via Spinuzza, or seek out rare architectural treasures like the Capo building facade that's half baroque church, half industrial rolling doors (yes, it really exists!).

Best Nights Out

⇒ Teatro Massimo (p68)
⇒ Kursaal Kalhesa (p67)
⇒ Cuticchio Mimmo (p68)
⇒ Hammam (p62)
⇒ Teatro di Verdura (p68)

Best Street Food

⇒ Francu U Vastiddaru (p66)
⇒ I Cuochini (p66)
⇒ Antica Focacceria San Francesco (p65)
⇒ Friggitoria Chiluzzo (p66)

Resources

⇒ **www.seepalermo.com** English-language info.

⇒ **www.unospiteapalermo.it** Info about hotels, restaurants, museums, churches, monuments and transport.

⇒ **www.balarm.it** For cultural events.

⇒ **www.lonelyplanet.com/italy/sicily/palermo** Planning advice, author recommendations, traveller reviews and insider tips.

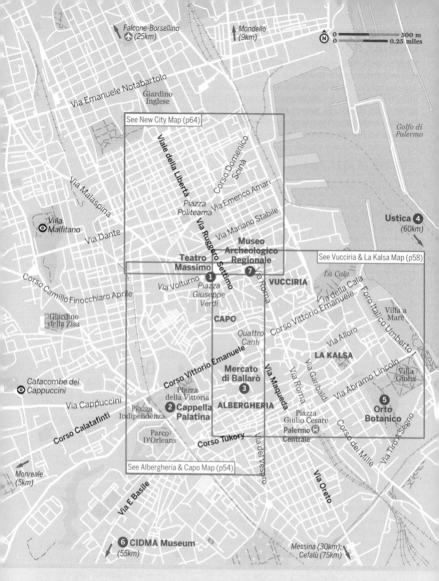

Palermo Highlights

1 Joining the ranks of impeccably dressed opera-goers at elegant **Teatro Massimo** (p68).

2 Basking in medieval Palermo's multicultural brilliance amid the Byzantine mosaics and Arabic marble-work of the **Cappella Palatina** (p55).

3 Admiring perfect piles of produce and the symphony of early morning vendors' voices at **Mercato di Ballarò** (p56).

4 Diving into the blue-green waters in the marine reserve at **Ustica**, Palermo's offshore island paradise.

5 Finding refuge from the traffic, crowds and street noise

among the trees and gardens of the **Orto Botanico** (p63).

6 Learning all about the Mafia – and Sicilian resistance to it – at the **CIDMA museum** (p82) in Corleone.

7 Admiring archaeological treasures from all over Sicily at the **Museo Archeologico Regionale** (p60).

PALERMO

POP 656,829

Sicily's main city is draped in a mantle of unpredictability and adventure: its streets are chaotic, its buildings are magnificently dishevelled and its residents – many of whom have a penchant for rule bending and a healthy suspicion of outsiders – can be an inscrutable lot. To gain an initial understanding of the city's unique culture, start by wandering the streets of the old city. The mix of architectural styles points to the wave upon wave of invaders who have claimed the city as their own, as does the look of the locals. Put simply, there's no one style or people in this urban melting pot, and there never has been.

History

The city looks old for a reason – it is. Nearly 3000 years old, at that. It started life as a huddle of Phoenician stores on a peaceful bay surrounded by the fertile Conca d'Oro, a prime piece of real estate that long made it a target for Sicily's colonisers. As the Carthaginians and Greeks began to flex their territorial muscles, the little depot grew in strategic and economic importance, eventually becoming known as Panormus (the Greek word for 'port').

Conquered by the Arabs in AD 831, the port flourished and became a very fine city. So much so that when the Normans invaded in 1072, Roger I (1031–1101) made it the seat of his kingdom, encouraging the resident Arabs, Byzantines, Greeks and Italians to remain. In Sicily, the Normans found their longed-for 'kingdom of the sun' and under their enlightened rule Palermo became the most cultured city of 12th-century Europe.

The end of Roger's line (with the death of William II in 1189) was to signal a very long and terminal decline of the city. A series of extraordinary and often bloody political struggles saw the island pass from German (Hohenstaufens) to French (Angevins) to Spanish (Aragonese) and English rule. None of these powers – who were nearly always uninterested and removed from Palermo – could regain the splendour of the Norman era. The only physical change to the city occurred under the Spaniards, with the imposition of a rational city plan that disguised the original Moorish layout. If you see the city from an altitude, you'll notice the baroque domes rising like islands above a sea of alleyways.

Industrial entrepreneurs such as the Florios and the Whitakers gave the city a brief flash of brilliance in the pre-WWI period by dressing it in the glamorous and decadent Liberty (Italian art nouveau) style, resulting in Palermo's final belle époque. But two world wars and massive material damage sank the city into despair and disrepair. At the end of 1945, the city was flooded by impoverished rural labourers and gripped by Mafia violence.

The middle classes moved out into newly built housing estates, escaping the new wave of violence (and the bad plumbing). By the 1980s the city was virtually a European pariah, notching up weekly murders. After the Mafia super-trials of the 1990s, Palermo slowly began to emerge from its troubled past and city authorities embarked upon an ambitious program of revitalisation. Walk through the ancient quarters of La Kalsa, Vucciria and Albergheria today and you will notice restoration projects galore, signalling the fact that this great city is working towards reclaiming its proud past and forging a prosperous future.

◉ Sights & Activities

Though there are a couple of world-class museums, a sprinkling of historic palaces as well as a bevy of notable baroque churches to visit, your most uplifting and engaging experiences will come courtesy of a walk through the city's streets.

Most museums offer a discounted entry price for EU citizens under the age of 18 and over the age of 65.

◉ Around the Quattro Canti

The busy intersection of Corso Vittorio Emanuele and Via Maqueda marks the Quattro Canti (Four Corners), the centre of Palermo. This intersection is surrounded by a perfect circle of curvi-linear facades that disappear up to the blue vault of the sky in a clever display of perspective. It is known locally as Il Teatro del Sole (Theatre of the Sun) as each facade is lit up in turn throughout the course of the day.

★ Piazza Pretoria   SQUARE

(Map p58) Fringed by imposing churches and buildings, this piazza is visually dominated by the over-the-top Fontana Pretoria, one of Palermo's major landmarks. The fountain's

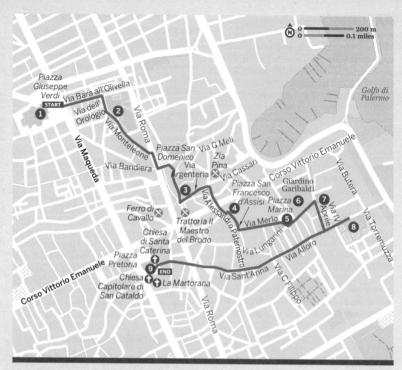

City Walk
Historic Palermo

START TEATRO MASSIMO
END PIAZZA BELLINI
LENGTH 2.5KM; SIX HOURS

Dense but compact, central Palermo is best explored on foot. This tour covers the eastern half of the city and the labyrinthine alleys of La Kalsa.

Start at Piazza Giuseppe Verdi, dominated by the neoclassical **1 Teatro Massimo** (p63). Cross Via Maqueda and follow narrow Via Bara all'Olivella to the newly renovated **2 Museo Archeologico Regionale** (p60), which houses one of southern Italy's finest classical art collections.

After a short hop south along Via Roma, descend the steps alongside Chiesa di Sant'Antonio into **3 Mercato della Vucciria** (p56). You'll find several good lunch spots near the market, including Trattoria Il Maestro del Brodo, Ferro di Cavallo and Zia Pina. Leaving the market, follow Via Alessandro Paternostro to pretty Piazza San Francesco d'Assisi and look into the 16th-century

4 Oratorio di San Lorenzo, adorned with the remarkable rococo stuccowork of Giacomo Serpotta. From here, Via Merlo leads east to the fine 18th-century **5 Palazzo Mirto** (p63), replete with silken wallpaper, embroidered wall hangings, frescoes, chandeliers and colourful tile and marble floors.

Take a break in **6 Giardino Garibaldi**, a fenced formal garden that is home to Palermo's oldest tree, a 150-year-old *ficus benjamina* (weeping fig). Overlooking the square is the imposing 14th-century Palazzo Chiaromonte Steri, former headquarters of the Inquisition, where you can tour the prisoners' cells and see their graffiti at **7 Museo dell'Inquisizione** (p62).

Next, head south to Via Alloro, where a left turn leads to the splendid **8 Galleria Regionale della Sicilia** (p61). Exiting the gallery, head west along Via Alloro, and end your tour at magnificent **9 Piazza Bellini** (p53), home to three of the city's most distinctive churches: Santa Caterina, La Martorana and San Cataldo.

tiered basins ripple out in concentric circles, crowded with nude nymphs, tritons and leaping river gods. Such flagrant nudity proved a bit much for Sicilian churchgoers, who prudishly dubbed it the Fontana della Vergogna (Fountain of Shame).

Designed by the Florentine sculptor Francesco Camilliani between 1554 and 1555 for the Tuscan villa of Don Pedro di Toledo, the fountain was bought by Palermo in 1573 and proudly positioned in front of the Palazzo Pretorio (Municipal Hall) in a bid to outshine the newly crafted Fontana di Orione installed in Messina.

Piazza Bellini   SQUARE

(Map p58) The disparate architectural styles and eras of the buildings adorning this magnificent piazza should by rights be visually discordant, but in fact contribute to a wonderfully harmonious public space. The piazza's eastern edge is adorned by the delightful Teatro Bellini (Map p58) (Bellini Theatre), built in the late 19th century and named after the great Sicilian-born opera composer, Vincenzo Bellini.

★ La Martorana   CHURCH

(Chiesa di Santa Maria dell'Ammiraglio; Map p58; Piazza Bellini 3; donation requested; ⊘ 8.30am-1pm & 3.30-5.30pm Mon-Sat, 8.30am-1pm Sun) On the southern side of Piazza Bellini, this luminously beautiful, recently restored 12th-century church was endowed by King Roger's Syrian emir, George of Antioch, and was originally planned as a mosque. Delicate Fatimid pillars support a domed cupola depicting Christ enthroned amid his archangels. The interior is best appreciated in the morning, when sunlight illuminates magnificent Byzantine mosaics.

In 1433 the church was given over to an aesthetically challenged order of Benedictine nuns – founded by Eloisa Martorana, hence its nickname – who tore down the Norman apse, reworked the exterior in a fussy baroque fashion and demolished most of the stunning mosaics executed by Greek craftsmen, replacing them with the gaudy baroque ornamentation of their own frescoed chapel. The few remaining original mosaics include two magnificent portraits, one representing George of Antioch, crouched behind a shield at the feet of the Virgin Mary, and one of Roger II receiving his crown from Christ (the only portrait of him to survive in Sicily). Mussolini returned the church to the Greek Orthodox community in 1935, and the Greek Mass is still celebrated here.

Chiesa Capitolare di San Cataldo   CHURCH

(Map p58; Piazza Bellini 3; admission €2.50; ⊘ 9.30am-12.30pm & 3-6pm) This 12th-century church in Arab-Norman style is one of Palermo's most striking buildings. With its dusky-pink bijou domes, solid square shape, blind arcading and delicate tracery, it illustrates perfectly the synthesis of Arab and Norman architectural styles. The interior, while more austere, is still beautiful, with its inlaid floor and lovely stone-and-brickwork in the arches and domes.

The building was founded in the 1150s by Maio of Bari (William I's emir of emirs, or chancellor) but Maio's murder in 1160 meant it was never finished – hence the lack of additional adornment within.

Chiesa di Santa Caterina   CHURCH

(Map p58; ⌨ 338 7228775; Piazza Bellini; admission €2; ⊘ 9.30am-6.30pm Mon-Sat, 9.30am-2pm Sun Apr-Oct, 9.30am-1.30pm daily Nov-Mar) On Piazza Bellini's northern edge, this ornate baroque church was built between 1566 and 1596, though many of its smooth white statues and whirling frescoes and much of its gilded stucco were added in the 18th century. Noteworthy features include the carved marble presbytery, the altar's silver angels and the statue of St Catherine in the right transept, carved by Antonello Gagini in 1534.

Chiesa di San Giuseppe
dei Teatini   CHURCH

(Map p58; Corso Vittorio Emanuele; ⊘ 8.30-11am & 6-8pm) In the southwestern corner of the Quattro Canti is the Chiesa di San Giuseppe dei Teatini, topped by a soaring cupola. The monumental interior is baroque at its brashest, and has been lovingly restored after it suffered substantial damage during WWII.

Chiesa del Gesù   CHURCH

(Map p54; Via del Ponticello; ⊘ 7-11.30am & 5-6.30pm Mon-Sat, 7am-12.30pm Sun, closed afternoons Aug) Also known as Casa Professa, Palermo's recently restored Jesuit church was built in the 16th century and its interior was decorated over the next 200 years with no cost (or inclination towards ostentation) spared. It's a veritable blizzard of baroque, with inlaid marble and sculptures galore.

◉ Albergheria

Once inhabited by Norman court officials, Albergheria has been a poor and ramshackle quarter since the end of WWII – indeed, you

Albergheria & Capo

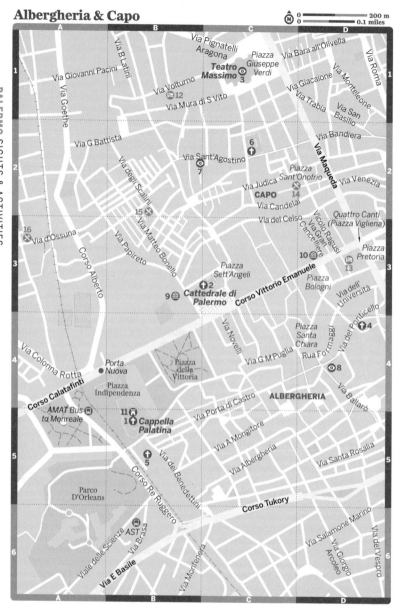

N 0 ——————— 200 m
0 ——————— 0.1 miles

Via Pignatelli Aragona

Via Bara all'Olivella

Via Roma

Via Giovanni Pacini

Via B Latini

Via Goethe

Piazza Giuseppe Verdi

Teatro Massimo 3

Via Monteleone

Via Volturno 12

Via Mura di S Vito

Via Giacalone

Via Trabia

Via San Basilio

Via G Battista

Via degli Scalini

Via Sant'Agostino

6

7

Via Bandiera

Via Maqueda

Piazza Sant'Onofrio

Via Judica 14

CAPO

Via Venezia

15

Via Matteo Bonello

Via Candelai

Via del Celso

Via Ragusi

Quattro Canti (Piazza Vigliena)

16

Via d'Ossuna

Corso Alberto

Via Papireto

Via Gran Cancelliere

Vicolo Ragusi

Piazza Pretoria

10 13

Piazza Sett'Angeli

9 **Cattedrale di Palermo** 2

Corso Vittorio Emanuele

Piazza Bologni

Via dell' Università

Via Novelli

Piazza Santa Chiara

Rua Formaggi

Via del Ponticello

4

Via Colonna Rotta

Porta Nuova

Piazza della Vittoria

Via G M Puglia

8

Corso Calatafinti

Piazza Indipendenza

ALBERGHERIA

Via Ballarò

AMAT Bus to Monreale

11

1 **Cappella Palatina**

Via Porta di Castro

Via A Mongitore

Via Santa Rosalia

Via dei Benedettini

5

Via Alberghería

Parco D'Orleans

Corso Re Ruggero

Corso Tukory

AST

Via Brasa

Viale delle Scienze

Via Montenera

Via Salamone Marino

Via Giorgio Arcoleo

Via del Vespro

Via E Basile

can still see wartime bomb damage scarring some buildings. The area is now home to a growing immigrant population that has revitalised the streets with its aspirations. It is also the location of Palermo's busiest street

market, the Mercato di Ballarò. Far and away the top tourist draws here are the Palazzo dei Normanni and its exquisite chapel, Cappella Palatina, both at the far western edge of the neighbourhood.

Albergheria & Capo

PALERMO SIGHTS & ACTIVITIES

★**Cappella Palatina**   CHAPEL
(Palatine Chapel; Map p54; adult €8.50; EU citizen 18-25yr €6.50; EU citizen 65+ €5; EU citizen under 18yr free; ◎8.15am-5pm Mon-Sat, 8.15-9.45am & 11.15am-12.15pm Sun) On the middle level of the Palazzo dei Normanni's three-tiered loggia, this mosaic-clad jewel of a chapel, designed by Roger II in 1130, is Palermo's premier tourist attraction. Gleaming from a painstaking five-year restoration, its aesthetic harmony is further enhanced by the inlaid marble floors and wooden *muqarnas* ceiling, a masterpiece of Arabic-style honeycomb carving that reflects Norman Sicily's cultural complexity.

The chapel's well-lit interior is simply extraordinary. Every inch is inlaid with precious stones, giving the space a lustrous quality. Swarming with figures in glittering, dreamy gold, the exquisite, highly sophisticated mosaics were mainly the work of Byzantine Greek artisans brought to Palermo by Roger II in 1140 especially for this project. They capture expressions, detail and movement with extraordinary grace and delicacy, and sometimes with enormous power – most notably in the depiction of Christ the Pantocrator and Angels on the dome. The bulk of the mosaics recount the tales of the Old Testament, though other scenes recall Palermo's pivotal role in the Crusades. Some of the mosaics are later and less-assured additions (eg the Virgin and Saints in the main apse under Christ the Pantocrator) but fortunately these don't detract too much from the overall achievement.

It's not only the mosaics you should be gazing at – don't miss the painted wooden ceiling featuring *muqarnas*, a decorative device resembling stalactites that is unique in a Christian church (and, many speculate, a sign of Roger II's secret identity as a Muslim). The walls are decorated with handsome marble inlay that displays a clear Islamic aesthetic, and the carved marble in the floor is breathtaking: marble was as precious as gems during the 12th century, so the floor's value at the time of its construction is almost immeasurable by today's standards.

Be prepared to queue to enter and once inside don't let the attendants hurry you through. Note that you will be refused entry if you are wearing shorts, a short skirt or a low-cut top – uncovered navels are also forbidden. If you visit the chapel on a day when the rest of the *palazzo* is closed (Tuesday through Thursday most weeks), the adult and youth entry prices are reduced to €7 and €5, respectively (price for EU senior citizens remains €5).

Palazzo dei Normanni   PALACE
(Palazzo Reale; Map p54; Piazza Indipendenza 1; incl Cappella Palatina adult €8.50, youth 18-25yr €6.50, senior 65+ €5, child under 18yr free; ◎8.15am-5pm Fri, Sat & Mon, to 12.15pm Sun) On weekends, when Palermo's venerable Norman Palace isn't being used by Sicily's parliament, visitors can take a self-guided tour of several upstairs rooms, including the gorgeous blue Sala Pompeiana, with its Venus & Eros frescoes; the Sala dei Venti, adorned with mosaics of geese, papyrus, lions, leopards and palms; and the Sala di Ruggero II, King Roger's mosaic-decorated bedroom.

DON'T MISS

STREET MARKETS

Palermo's historical ties with the Arab world and its proximity to North Africa are reflected in the noisy street life of the city's ancient centre, and nowhere is this more evident than in its markets.

Each of the four historic quarters of Palermo has its own market, but the Vucciria, Ballarò and Capo are the 'Big Three' in terms of popularity and history.

The Mercato della Vucciria (Map p58; Piazza Caracciolo) is the most dishevelled of the three, with rough-edged customers, carts selling street snacks, a small number of produce stalls and often-grumpy stallholders. The Mercato di Ballarò (Map p54) is filled with stalls displaying household goods, clothes and foodstuffs of every possible description – this is where many Palermitans do their daily shop. The Mercato del Capo (Map p54), which extends through the tangle of lanes and alleyways of the Albergheria and Capo quarters respectively, is the most atmospheric of all. Here, meat carcasses sway from huge metal hooks, glistening tuna and swordfish are expertly dismembered, and anchovies are filleted. Long and orderly lines of stalls display pungent cheeses, tubs of plump olives and a huge array of luscious fruits and voluptuous vegetables.

The markets open from 7am to 8pm Monday to Saturday (until 1pm on Wednesday), although they are busier in the morning. Remember: keep an eye on your belongings while exploring.

Chiesa di San Giovanni
degli Eremiti   CHURCH
(Map p54; ☏ 091 651 50 19; Via dei Benedettini 16; adult/reduced €6/3; ☉ 9am-6.30pm Tue-Sat, 9am-1pm Sun & Mon) This remarkable, five-domed remnant of Arab-Norman architecture occupies a magical little hillside in the middle of an otherwise rather squalid neighbourhood. Surrounded by a garden of citrus trees, palms, cacti and ruined walls, it's built atop a mosque that itself was superimposed on an earlier chapel. The peaceful Norman cloisters outside offer lovely views of the Palazzo dei Normanni.

◉ Capo

Bordering the Albergheria quarter, Il Capo is another web of interconnected streets and blind alleys. As impoverished as its neighbour, it too has a popular street market, the Mercato del Capo, which runs the length of Via Sant'Agostino and terminates at Porta Carini, one of Palermo's oldest town gates. The centrepiece of the quarter is the imposing monastery of Chiesa di Sant'Agostino (Church of Saint Augustine; Map p54; Via Sant'Agostino; ☉ 8am-noon & 4-6pm Mon-Sat, 8am-noon Sun), which ran the region in medieval times.

★ Cattedrale di Palermo   CATHEDRAL
(Map p54; www.cattedrale.palermo.it; Corso Vittorio Emanuele; Norman tombs & treasury adult/reduced €3/1.50; ☉ 8am-7pm) A feast of geometric patterns, ziggurat crenulations, majolica cupolas and blind arches, Palermo's cathedral has suffered aesthetically from multiple reworkings over the centuries but remains a prime example of the extraordinary Arab-Norman style unique to Sicily. The interior, while impressive in scale, is essentially a marble shell whose most interesting features are its treasury and royal Norman tombs.

Construction began in 1184 at the behest of Palermo's archbishop, Walter of the Mill (Gualtiero Offamiglio), an Englishman who was tutor to William II. Walter held great power and had unlimited funds at his disposal, but with the building of the magnificent cathedral at Monreale he felt his power diminishing. His solution was to order construction of an equally magnificent cathedral in Palermo. This was erected on the location of a 9th-century mosque (itself built on a former chapel); a detail from the mosque's original decor is visible at the southern porch, where a column is inscribed with a passage from the Koran. The cathedral's proportions and the grandeur of its exterior became a statement of the power struggle between Church and throne occurring at the time, a potentially dangerous situation that was tempered by Walter's death (in 1191), which prevented him from seeing (and boasting about) the finished building.

Since then the cathedral has been much altered, sometimes with great success (as in Antonio Gambara's 15th-century three-arched portico that took 200 years to complete and became a masterpiece of Catalan Gothic architecture), and sometimes with less fortunate results (as in Ferdinando Fuga's clumsy dome, added between 1781 and 1801). Thankfully Fuga's handiwork did not extend to the eastern exterior, which is still adorned with the exotic interlacing designs of Walter's original cathedral. The southwestern facade was laid in the 13th and 14th centuries, and is a beautiful example of local craftsmanship in the Gothic style. The cathedral's entrance – through Gambara's three magnificent arches – is fronted by gardens and a statue of Santa Rosalia, one of Palermo's patron saints. A beautiful painted intarsia decoration above the arches depicts the tree of life in a complex Islamic-style geometric composition of 12 roundels that show fruit, humans and all kinds of animals. It's thought to date back to 1296.

To the left as you enter the cathedral are several royal Norman tombs, which contain the remains of two of Sicily's greatest rulers, Roger II (rear left) and Frederick II of Hohenstaufen (front left) as well as Henry VI and William II. A joint ticket grants access to the tombs along with the cathedral's other most interesting feature, the treasury (p57) and crypt.

Tesoro della Cattedrale   MUSEUM
(Cathedral Treasury; Map p54; Corso Vittorio Emanuele; adult/reduced €3/1.50; ☺9am-5pm Mon-Sat Apr-Oct, 9.30am-1.30pm Mon-Sat Nov-Mar) This small collection of Norman-era jewels and religious relics is accessed via the cathedral's right aisle. Most extraordinary is the fabulous 13th-century crown of Constance of Aragon (wife of Frederick II), made by local craftsmen in fine gold filigree and encrusted with gems. More bizarre treasures include the tooth and ashes of Santa Rosalia, kept here in silver reliquaries.

The treasury entrance ticket also grants access to the cathedral's crypt and to the Norman tombs at the cathedral's southwestern corner.

Museo Diocesano   MUSEUM
(Map p54; ☏091 60 77 215; www.museodiocesanopa.it; Via Matteo Bonello 2; adult €4.50, 6-17yr & 65+ €3, under 6yr free; ☺9.30am-1.30pm Sun & Tue-Fri, 10am-6pm Sat) Opposite Palermo's cathedral, this museum houses an important collection of artworks from local churches

destroyed during WWII. The ground floor holds 15th-century frescoes, along with Byzantine paintings, icons and mosaics. Especially beautiful are the 1171 *Madonna della Perla*, the haunting 13th-century *Madonna della Spersa* and the 12th-century *Madonna Orante*, whose face is rendered in remarkably minuscule stones.

Seek out the room dedicated to the 17th-century Sicilian painter Pietro Novelli (1603–47), who was one of the region's finest and served as a court painter to Spain's ruler, Philip IV. Much influenced by Anthony Van Dyck and Raphael, Novelli often portrayed himself in his chiaroscuro works. The museum's basement level is a mixture of sculpture, finds from destroyed churches, and paintings of Palermo.

Museo Regionale d'Arte
Moderna e Contemporanea
della Sicilia (Riso)   MUSEUM
(Map p54; ☏091 32 05 32; www.palazzoriso.it; Palazzo Riso, Corso Vittorio Emanuele 365; adult €6, youth 18-25yr €3, under 18yr & 60+ free; ☺10am-7.30pm Sat, Sun, Tue & Wed, 10am-9.30pm Thu & Fri) The newest addition to Palermo's art scene is this multi-level museum housed in a restored 18th-century neoclassical *palazzo*. Its curators work with other city and regional institutions to provide alternative interpretations of Sicily's artistic heritage and to stage challenging international survey shows. It also has a good bookshop and a stylish ground-floor cafe (the latter closed indefinitely at research time).

◉ Vucciria

The shabby Vucciria neighbourhood is known throughout Sicily for its Mercato della Vucciria, the inspiration for Sicilian painter Renato Guttuso's most important work, *La Vucciria* (1974), described by writer Leonardo Sciascia as 'a hungry man's dream'.

Once the heart of poverty-stricken Palermo and a den of crime and filth, the Vucciria illustrated the almost medieval chasm that existed between rich and poor in Sicily up until the 1950s. Though it's still quite shabby, the quarter is one of Palermo's most fascinating areas to explore, with most of its interesting buildings in the vicinity of the imposing 17th-century Chiesa di San Domenico (Church of Saint Domenic; Map p58;

Vucciria & La Kalsa

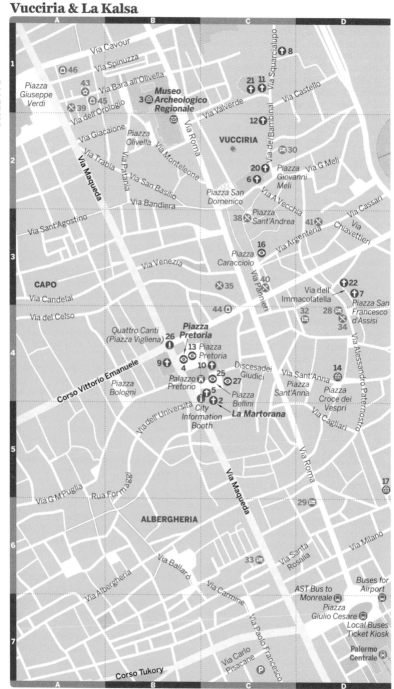

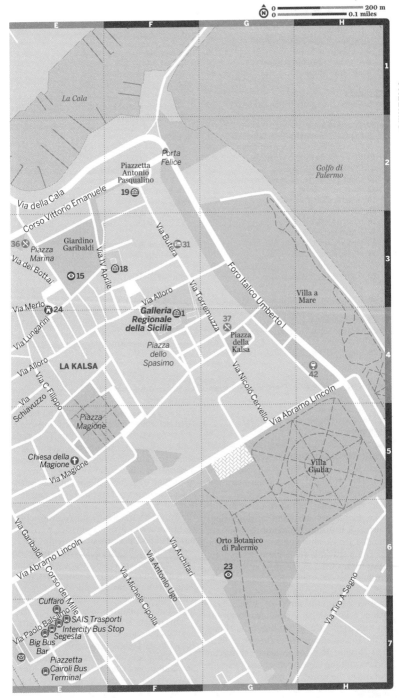

Vucciria & La Kalsa

091 58 91 72; Piazza San Domenico; ⊙9.30am-noon Tue-Sat).

★**Museo Archeologico
Regionale**   MUSEUM
(Map p58; ✆091 611 68 05; www.regione.sicilia.it/beniculturali/salinas; Piazza Olivella 24; ⊙8.30am-1.30pm & 3-6.30pm Tue-Fri, 8.30am-1.30pm Sat & Sun) This splendid, wheelchair-accessible museum is scheduled to reopen in late 2013 after renovations. Situated in a Renaissance monastery surrounding a gracious courtyard, it displays some of Sicily's most valuable Greek and Roman artefacts. The museum's crown jewel is the series of decorative friezes from the temples at Selinunte, but there are countless other treasures from archaeological sites throughout the island.

Other important finds on display here include a Phoenician sarcophagus from the 5th century BC, Greek carvings from Himera, the Hellenistic *Ariete di Bronzo di Siracusa* (Bronze Ram of Syracuse), Etruscan mirrors and the largest collection of ancient anchors in the world.

**Oratorio del Rosario in
Santa Cita**   CHAPEL
(Map p58; Via Valverde; admission €2.50, for joint ticket incl Oratorio del Rosario in San Domenico €4; ⊙9am-6pm Mon-Fri, 9am-3pm Sat) This 17th-century chapel showcases the breathtaking stuccowork of Giacomo Serpotta, who made a name for himself by introducing rococo to Sicilian churches. Of special note is the elaborate *Battle of Lepanto* on the entrance wall. Depicting the Christian victory over the Turks, it's framed by stucco drapes held by hundreds of naughty cherubs who were modelled on Palermo's street urchins.

The side walls are awash with further examples of Serpotta's virtuosity, with sculpted white stucco figures holding gilded objects, including swords, shields and a lute, and a golden snake (Serpotta's symbol) curling around a picture frame on the left wall.

This chapel is associated with four other nearby churches, collectively known as the Tesori della Loggia (Treasures of the Loggia). Three of the churches (Santa Cita, San Giorgio dei Genovesi and Santa Maria di Valverde) are free; a combined ticket (available here) offers a small discount on admission to the remaining chapel, the Oratorio del Rosario in San Domenico.

Oratorio del Rosario in
San Domenico
CHAPEL

(Map p58; Via dei Bambinai 2; admission €2.50, for joint ticket incl Oratorio del Rosario in Santa Cita €4; ⊙9am-6pm Mon-Fri, 9am-3pm Sat) This small chapel was commissioned by the Society of the Rosary of San Domenico and is dominated by Anthony Van Dyck's fantastic blue-and-red altarpiece, *The Virgin of the Rosary with St Dominic and the Patronesses of Palermo*. Van Dyck left Palermo in fear of the plague, and painted the work in Genoa in 1628.

Also gracing the chapel are Giacomo Serpotta's amazingly elaborate stuccos (1710–17), vivacious and whirling with figures. Serpotta's name meant 'lizard' or 'small snake', and he often included one of the reptiles in his work as a sort of signature – see if you can find one here!

Chiesa di Santa Cita
CHURCH

(Map p58; Via Valverde; ⊙9am-7pm Mon-Fri) This 14th-century church is named after the patron saint of domestic servants. The Dominican priests who acquired the church in the 16th century cleverly allowed rich families to bury their dead here, thus both collecting income for the priests' monastery and endowing the church with particularly lavish funerary chapels. There are also some sculptures by Antonio Gagini.

Chiesa di San Giorgio dei
Genovesi
CHURCH

(Map p58; Via Squarcialupo; ⊙9am-1.30pm Mon-Fri) Boasting an elegant Renaissance-style facade, this church was built between 1575 and 1591 to a design by Piedmontese architect Giorgio di Faccio. Its interior is as pleasing as its exterior, featuring Corinthian tetrastyle columns and a gravestone-laden marble floor. During the WWII Allied bombing of Palermo, the entire area around the church was flattened but it was miraculously spared.

Chiesa di Santa Maria di Valverde CHURCH

(Map p58; Largo Cavalieri di Malta; ⊙9am-1.30pm Mon-Fri) In 1633 this 14th-century Carmelite church underwent a lavish transformation courtesy of wealthy Genovese Camillo Pallavicino, whose only daughter had entered the convent of Valverde. It is graced by *The Madonna of Mount Carmel with Saints*, painted by Pietro Novelli in 1640.

◉ La Kalsa

Plagued by poverty, La Kalsa has long been one of the city's most notorious neighbourhoods. However, a recent program of urban regeneration has resulted in many of its long-derelict *palazzos* being restored and these are rapidly being turned into museums, boutique hotels and upmarket residential accommodation.

★ Galleria Regionale
della Sicilia
MUSEUM

(Palazzo Abatellis; Map p58; ☑091 623 00 11; www.regione.sicilia.it/beniculturali/palazzoabatellis; Via Alloro 4; adult/EU 18-25/EU under 18 & over 65 €8/4/free; ⊙9am-6pm Tue-Fri, to 1pm Sat & Sun) Housed in the stately 15th-century Palazzo Abatellis, this fine museum features works by Sicilian artists from the Middle Ages to the 18th century. Its greatest treasure is *Triunfo della Morte* (Triumph of Death), a magnificent fresco in which Death is represented as a demonic skeleton mounted on a wasted horse, brandishing a rather wicked-looking scythe while leaping over his hapless victims.

Represented at the heart of the painting, under Death's horse, are the vain and pampered aristocrats of Palermo, while the poor and hungry look on from the side. The huge image, carefully restored, has been given its own space on the ground level to maximise its visual impact.

Widely regarded as Palermo's best art museum, the gallery is full of countless other treasures, which collectively offer great insight into the evolution of Sicilian art. The exhibition space itself was designed to fill this gorgeous Catalan Gothic *palazzo* in 1957 by Carlo Scarpa, one of Italy's leading architects.

Galleria d'Arte Moderna
MUSEUM

(Map p58; ☑091 843 16 05; www.galleriadarte-modernapalermo.it; Via Sant'Anna 21; adult €7, 19-25yr & 60+ €5, under 19 free; ⊙9.30am-6.30pm Tue-Sun) This lovely, wheelchair-accessible museum is housed in a sleekly renovated 15th-century *palazzo*, which metamorphosed into a convent in the 17th century. Divided over three floors, the wide-ranging collection of 19th- and 20th-century Sicilian art is beautifully displayed. There's a regular program of modern-art exhibitions here, as well as an excellent bookshop and gift shop. English-language audioguides cost €4.

PALERMO SIGHTS & ACTIVITIES

DON'T MISS

STRESS RELIEF, SICILIAN STYLE

For a sybaritic experience, head to **Hammam** (Map p64; ☑ 091 32 07 83; www.hammam.pa.it; Via Torrearsa 17d; admission €40; ☺ women only 2-9pm Mon & Wed, 11am-9pm Fri, couples only 2-8pm Thu, men only 2-8pm Tue, 10am-8pm Sat), a luxurious marble-lined Moorish bathhouse, where you can indulge in a vigorous scrub-down, a steamy sauna and many different types of massages and therapies. There's a one-off charge (€10) for slippers and a hand glove.

The collection includes everything from 19th-century monumental historical genre paintings to futuristic romps from the early 20th century. Works are dedicated largely to Sicily and Palermo in their subject matter, with themes and landscapes that will be familiar to anyone who's already toured the island and will serve as inspiration for newcomers just embarking on their Sicilian adventure. Examples include Michele Catti's *Ultime foglie* (Last Leaves; 1906), a beautiful image of a wet Viale della Libertá on a late autumn day; Antonio Leto's *Saline di Trapani*, depicting the reflective salt pools of western Sicily; Ettore de Maria Bergler's *Taormina;* and Gennaro Pardo's paintings of the temples at Selinunte.

Museo dell'Inquisizione   MUSEUM
(Map p58; Piazza Marina 61; adult/reduced €5/3; ☺ 10am-6pm) Housed in the lower floors and basements of the 14th-century Palazzo Chiaromonte Steri, this recently opened museum offers a chilling but fascinating look at the legacy of the Inquisition in Palermo. The honeycomb of former cells has been painstakingly restored to reveal multiple layers of prisoners' graffiti and artwork (religious and otherwise). Excellent guided visits are available in English or Spanish with advance notice.

Guides help point out small details that would otherwise be easily missed. Depicted are religious themes such as Christ tortured by Spanish soldiers and images of local protector saints San Rocco and Santa Rosalia. Also depicted are profane themes, including hearts pierced with arrows or instruments of torture, elaborate maps of Sicily where other prisoners were invited to add missing details,

an inquisitor holding the scales of justice, or a caricature of another inquisitor astride a defecating horse adjacent to the latrine.

Look also for two works by noted Sicilian modern artist Renato Guttuso: first, a graphic depiction of the strangulation murder of inquisitor De Cisneros by the handcuffed 22-year-old prisoner Diego La Mattina; and Guttuso's masterful 1974 painting of the Vucciria market, whose vibrant colors jump out at you after so many rooms full of prison art executed in simple reds and blacks (the red from crumbled bricks, black from burnt wood and candles).

Museo Internazionale delle Marionette   MUSEUM
(Map p58; ☑ 091 32 80 60; www.museomarionettepalermo.it; Piazzetta Antonio Pasqualino 5; adult/reduced €5/3; ☺ 9am-1pm & 2.30-6.30pm Mon-Sat year-round, plus 10am-1pm Sun Sep-May) This whimsical museum houses over 3500 marionettes, puppets, glove puppets and shadow figures from Palermo, Catania and Naples, as well as from further-flung places such as Japan, Southeast Asia, Africa, China and India. From October through May, weekly puppet shows (adult/child €6/4) are staged on the museum's top floor in a beautifully decorated traditional theatre complete with hand-cranked music machine.

Established by the Association for the Conservation of Folk Traditions of Palermo, the museum takes puppeteering seriously, researching the art form, providing informative labelling alongside museum exhibits and hosting the annual **Festa di Morgana** (www.festivaldimorgana.com), when puppeteers from all over the world converge on the museum for lectures and performances.

Museo delle Maioliche   MUSEUM
(Stanze al Genio; Map p58; ☑ 340 0971561; www.stanzealgenio.it; Via Garibaldi 11; adult/reduced €7/5; ☺ by appointment) Lovers of handpainted Italian maiolica should make a beeline for this unique museum, which contains a private collection of over 2300 tiles, most from Sicily and Naples, amassed over three decades by founder Pio Mellina. The tiles fill the walls and floors of the lovingly restored 16th-century Palazzo Torre-Piraino, itself a work of art with vaulted and frescoed ceilings.

Operated as a nonprofit association, the museum plans to add four to five new rooms by 2015 and expand its collection to include over 4500 tiles.

Palazzo Mirto
PALACE

(Map p58; ☑ 091 616 75 41; www.regione.sicilia.it/ beniculturali/palazzomirto; Via Merlo 2; adult €4, EU citizen 18-25yr €2, under 18yr or 65+ free; ☺ 9am-6pm Tue-Sat, 9am-1pm Sun) Just off Piazza Marina, this *palazzo* is one of the few in Palermo open to the public. The walls of its 21 rooms are covered in acres of silk and velvet wallpaper, with vast embroidered wall hangings, frescoed ceilings, gaudy chandeliers and floors paved in coloured marbles, maiolica tiles and mosaics. English-language cards in each room provide information for visitors.

Memorable rooms include the tiny but extravagant Salottino Cinese (Chinese Salon) full of black lacquer, silken wallpaper and a rather conceited ceiling painting of European aristos viewing the room from above. It also features a leather-walled Fumoir (Smoking Salon), with walls of colourfully dyed Cordovan leather, and the Salottino di Diana (Lounge of Diana), with a swivelling statue of Apollo that leads to a secret passageway.

Parco Culturale del Gattopardo Giuseppe Tomasi di Lampedusa
WALKING TOUR

(☑ 091 625 40 11, 327 6844052; www.parcotomasi.it; c/o Kursaal Kalhesa, Foro Italico Umberto I; ☺ by arrangement) This organisation runs two-hour literary walks in English, French, German or Italian focusing on the life and masterwork of Sicily's most famous novelist, Giuseppe Tomasi di Lampedusa. As you stroll through the Kalsa district, you'll learn the history of Palermo's ties with Lampedusa's great novel *Il Gattopardo* (The Leopard).

Orto Botanico
GARDEN

(Map p58; ☑ 091 2389 1236; www.ortobotanico. unipa.it; Via Abramo Lincoln 2; adult €5, child 10-16yr €3, under 10 or 65+ €2; ☺ 9am-8pm May-Aug, to 7pm Apr & Sep, to 6pm Mar & Oct, to 5pm Nov-Feb) Laid out by Léon Dufourny and Venanzio Marvuglia, this subtropical paradise shelters massive fig trees, tall palms and dazzling hibiscus bushes, an avenue of bizarre-looking bottle, soap and cinnamon trees, as well as coffee trees, papaya plants and sycamores. It's a real haven of silence and fascinating botany, with a large herb garden that focuses on Mediterranean plants.

☉ The New City

North of Piazza Giuseppe Verdi, Palermo's streets widen, the buildings lengthen, and the shops, restaurants and cafes become more elegant (and more expensive). Glorious neoclassical and Liberty examples from the last golden age in Sicilian architecture give the city an exuberant and grandiose feel that contrasts with the narrow, introspective feel of the historic quarter.

★ Teatro Massimo
OPERA HOUSE

(Map p54; ☑ tour reservations 091 605 32 67; www. teatromassimo.it/servizi/visite.php; Piazza Giuseppe Verdi; guided tours adult/reduced €8/5; ☺ 9.30am-4.30pm Tue-Sun) Palermo's grand neoclassical opera house took over 20 years to complete and has become one of the city's iconic landmarks. The closing scene of *The Godfather: Part III*, with its visually stunning juxtaposition of high culture, crime, drama and death, was filmed here. Guided 25-minute tours are offered in English, Spanish, French and Italian daily except Monday.

☉ Outside the City Centre

Villa Malfitano
VILLA

(☑ 091 682 05 22; www.fondazionewhitaker.it/ villa.html; Via Dante 167; adult/student & child €6/3; ☺ 9am-1pm Mon-Sat) A showcase of Liberty architecture, set in a 9-hectare (22-acre) formal garden planted with rare and exotic species, this villa is most notable for its whimsical interior decoration, which includes a 'Summer Room' with walls painted to resemble a conservatory, and a music room draped with 15th-century tapestries illustrating the *Aeneid*. It's a 20-minute walk west from Piazza Castelnuovo.

The villa was built in 1886 by Joseph Whitaker, a member of the entrepreneurial English business dynasty that made a fortune in the Marsala trade in Sicily in the 19th century. Joseph and his wife Tina were leading figures in Palermo's high society and entertained their belle époque buddies here in lavish style, even hosting King Edward VII in 1907 and George V in 1925.

Catacombe dei Cappuccini
CATACOMB

(☑ 091 652 41 56; Piazza Cappuccini; adult €3, child under 8 free; ☺ 9am-1pm & 3-6pm) These catacombs house the mummified bodies and skeletons of some 8000 Palermitans who died between the 17th and 19th centuries. Earthly power, gender, religion and professional status are still rigidly distinguished, with men and women occupying separate corridors, and a first-class section set aside for virgins. From Piazza Independenza, it's a 15-minute walk.

New City

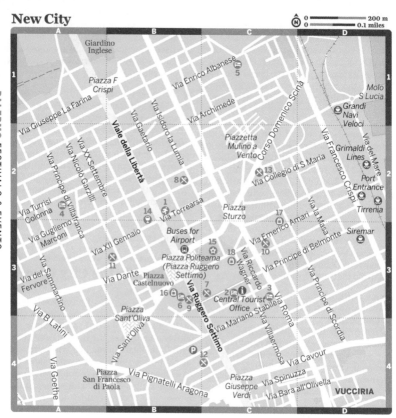

★ Festivals & Events

Festino di Santa Rosalia
RELIGIOUS

(www.festinosantarosalia.it; ⊙ 13-15 Jul) Palermo's biggest annual festival celebrates Santa Rosalia, the patron saint of the city. The saint's relics are paraded through the city amid three days of fireworks and partying.

Provincia in Festa
CULTURE

(www.provinciainfesta.it) Four months of art, music and sport events; from September through December.

✗ Eating

Palermitans generally dine late, and although kitchens open around 7.30pm, you'll eat alone if you get to a restaurant before 9pm, particularly in summer.

Local specialities include *bucatini con le sarde* (pasta mixed with sardines, wild fennel, raisins, pine nuts and breadcrumbs) and *frutta martorana* (colourfully decorated marzipan modelled into fanciful shapes and named after the convent of La Martorana).

Two other quintessentially Palermitan eating experiences are the city's bustling markets (p56) and street food stalls (p66). Don't miss either one!

★ Ferro di Cavallo
TRATTORIA €

(Map p58; ☑ 091 33 18 35; Via Venezia 20; meals €13-17; ⊙ lunch daily, dinner Wed-Sat) Tables line the sidewalk, while inside religious portraits beam down from bright-red walls upon the bustling mixed crowd of tourists and locals at this cheerful little trattoria near the Quattro Canti. Nothing costs more than €7 on the straightforward à la carte menu of Sicilian classics. Sweet tooths should save room for one of Palermo's very best cannoli (only €1.50).

Zia Pina
TRATTORIA €

(Map p58; Via Argenteria 67; meals €15-25) Tucked under a red-and-white-striped awning on a

New City

PALERMO EATING

Vuccria backstreet, this highly informal eatery is run by elderly Aunt Pina and a bevy of her brothers. There's no fixed menu, but everything's dependably tasty. Grab a plate full of antipasti, choose your fish from the display up front, and pull up a plastic chair to one of the sidewalk tables.

Other items usually on offer include Sicilian classics like *spaghetti alle vongole veraci* (spaghetti with clams, garlic, olive oil and parsley), *frittura mista* (mixed fried seafood) and antipasti such as grilled peppers, artichokes, zucchini and aubergines in tomato sauce.

Osteria Lo Bianco   SICILIAN €
(Map p64; ☎ 091 251 49 06; Via Enrico Amari 104; meals €18-19; ☺12.30-3.30pm & 7.30-10.30pm Mon-Sat) As traditional a place as you'll find in the new town, this bustling, down-to-earth *osteria* between Piazza Politeama and the port is atmospherically decked out with red-checked tablecloths, black-and-white photos of old Palermo and colourful ceramic plates. Potbellied guys in T-shirts crank out a host of Palermitan classics, including plenty of seafood and a delicious homemade *cassata*, all at very reasonable prices.

Pizzeria Frida   PIZZERIA €
(Map p54; www.fridapizzeria.it; Piazza Sant'Onofrio 37-38; pizzas €4.50-11; ☺7pm-midnight, closed Tue) With sidewalk tables under umbrella awnings on a low-key Capo piazza, this local favourite makes pizzas in a variety of shapes, including *quadri* (square, picture-frame-shaped pizzas) and *vulcanotti* (named after famous volcanoes and looking the part). Toppings include Sicilian specialities like tuna, capers, pistachios, mint, aubergines and fresh ricotta. Desserts (strawberry tiramisu, almond parfait) are tasty.

Ristorantino Spanó   SICILIAN €
(Map p54; www.ristorantinospano.it; Via degli Scalini 6; meals from €20; ☺1-3pm & 7.30-10pm) Conveniently located near the Capo market, this family-run neighbourhood trattoria offers sidewalk seating on warmer days. The two small interior dining rooms have brown-and-white-checked tablecloths and a large window looking into the kitchen, where you can glimpse classic Sicilian ingredients being put to use in dishes such as *casarecce al lido* (pasta with swordfish, mint, tomatoes and eggplant).

Trattoria Basile   TRATTORIA €
(Map p58; ☎ 091 33 56 28; Via Bara all'Olivella 76; meals €9-14; ☺noon-3.30pm Mon-Sat) At this unpretentious, cafeteria-style eatery, pay first, take a number at the window for your pasta (€2.50 to €4) or main course (€3.50 to €7), then sidle over and choose three antipasti for €2 or six for €4. While enjoying your appetisers, listen for your number – they'll bellow it out (in Italian) when your order is ready.

Avoid the busy period between 1pm and 2pm when every workman in town is elbowing in for his plate of pasta.

★ Antica Focacceria
San Francesco   STREET FOOD €
(Map p58; ☎ 091 32 02 64; www.afsf.it; Via Alessandro Paternostro 58; snacks €2-7; ☺10am-11pm) This historic *focacceria* opposite Chiesa di San Francesco d'Assisi first opened its doors in 1834 and is known for its *panino con la milza* (veal spleen boiled in lard, served on a roll with optional lemon and ricotta). Display

PALERMO'S STREET FOOD

If you were taught that it was bad manners to eat in the street, you can break the rule in good company here. The mystery is simply how Palermo is not the obesity capital of Europe given just how much eating goes on! Palermitans are at it all the time: when they're shopping, commuting, discussing business, romancing...basically at any time of the day. What they're enjoying is the *buffitieri* – little hot snacks prepared at stalls and meant to be eaten on the spot.

Kick off the morning with a *pane e panelle*, Palermo's famous chickpea fritters – great for vegetarians and a welcome change from a sweet custard-filled croissant. You might also want to go for some *crocchè* (potato croquettes, sometimes flavoured with fresh mint), *quaglie* (literally translated as quails, they're actually aubergines/eggplants cut lengthwise and fanned out to resemble a bird's feathers, then fried), *sfincione* (a spongy, oily pizza topped with onions and *caciocavallo* cheese) or *scaccie* (discs of bread dough spread with a filling and rolled up into a pancake). In summer, locals also enjoy a freshly baked brioche filled with ice cream or *granite* (crushed ice mixed with fresh fruit, almonds, pistachios or coffee).

From 4pm onwards the snacks become decidedly more carnivorous and you may just wish you hadn't read the following translations: how about some barbecued *stigghiola* (goat intestines filled with onions, cheese and parsley), for example? Or a couple of *pani ca meusa* (bread roll stuffed with sautéed beef spleen). You'll be asked if you want it 'schietta' (single) or 'maritata' (married). If you choose *schietta*, the roll will only have ricotta in it before being dipped into boiling lard; choose *maritata* and you'll get the beef spleen as well.

You'll find stalls selling street food all over town, especially in Palermo's street markets.

cases brim with other Palermitan snacks, including *sfinciuni* (Palermo-style pizza), focaccia sandwiches and *cassatelle* (fried dough pouches filled with sweet ricotta).

In bygone days, the *focacceria* hosted the first Sicilian parliament and was a favourite haunt of notorious Mafia boss 'Lucky' Luciano. Under new management as of 2013, it now also operates an upstairs restaurant serving a more substantial menu year-round, with tables set out on the cobblestones in the pretty piazza out front in warm weather.

Francu U Vastiddaru
STREET FOOD **€**

(Map p58; Corso Vittorio Emanuele 102; sandwiches €1.50-3.50; ⊙8am-late) Palermitan street food doesn't get any better or cheaper than the delicious panini hawked from this hole-in-the-wall sandwich stand just off Piazza Marina. Options range from the classic *panino triplo*, with *panelle* (chickpea fritters), *crocchè* (potato croquettes) and eggplant to the owner's trademark *panino vastiddaru* (with roast pork, salami, emmental cheese and spicy mushrooms).

I Cuochini
STREET FOOD **€**

(Map p64; Via Ruggero Settimo 68; snacks from €0.70; ⊙8.30am-2.30pm Mon-Sat, plus 4.30-7.30pm Sat) Hidden inside a little courtyard off Via Ruggero Settimo, this long-standing Palermitan favourite specialises in low-cost snacks, including delicious *arancinette* (rice balls filled with meat sauce) and divine *panzerotti* (stuffed fried dough pockets). The latter come in countless delectable varieties: ricotta and mint, squash blossoms and cheese, mozzarella, cherry tomatoes and anchovies, just to name a few.

Friggitoria Chiluzzo
STREET FOOD **€**

(Map p58; Piazza della Kalsa; sandwiches €1.50-2; ⊙8.30am-3pm Mon-Sat) This beloved street vendor makes some of Palermo's best *best pane e panelle* (sesame bread with chickpea fritters). Add some *crocchè* (potato croquettes), fried eggplant and a squeeze of lemon and call it lunch!

★ Trattoria Il Maestro del Brodo
TRATTORIA **€€**

(Map p58; Via Pannieri 7; meals €19-30; ⊙12.30-3.30pm Tue-Sun, 8-11pm Fri & Sat) This no-frills, Slow Food–recommended eatery in the Vucciria offers delicious soups, an array of ultra-fresh seafood, and a sensational antipasti buffet (€8) featuring a dozen-plus homemade delicacies: *sarde a beccafico*, eggplant involtini, smoked fish, parslied artichokes, sun-dried tomatoes, olives and more.

★ Trattoria Ai Cascinari SICILIAN €€
(Map p54; ☑ 091 651 98 04; Via d'Ossuna 43/45;
meals €20-28; ☺ lunch Tue-Sun, dinner Wed-Sat)
Friendly service, simple straw chairs and
blue-and-white-checked tablecloths set the
relaxed tone at this neighbourhood trattoria, 1km north of the Cappella Palatina.
Locals pack the labyrinth of back rooms,
while waiters perambulate nonstop with
plates of scrumptious seasonal antipasti and
divine main dishes. Save room for homemade ice cream and outstanding desserts
from Palermo's beloved Pasticceria Cappello.

★ Piccolo Napoli SEAFOOD €€
(Map p64; ☑ 091 32 04 31; Piazzetta Mulino a Vento
4; meals €25-34; ☺ lunch Mon-Sat, dinner Tue-Sat)
Known throughout Palermo for its fresh seafood, this bustling eatery is another hot spot
for serious foodies. Nibble on toothsome
sesame bread and plump olives while perusing the menu for a pasta dish that takes
your fancy, then head to the seafood display
(often still wriggling) to choose a second
course. The genial owner greets his many
regular customers by name.

Sant'Andrea MODERN SICILIAN €€
(Map p58; ☑ 091 33 49 99; www.ristorantesantan-
drea.eu; Piazza Sant'Andrea 4; meals €31-36;
☺ dinner Mon-Sat) Tucked into the corner
of a ruined church in a shabby piazza,
Sant'Andrea's location doesn't inspire much

confidence, but its creative Sicilian dishes
and congenial high-ceilinged dining room
keep well-heeled customers picking their
way across the broken flagstones nightly.

Cucina Papoff SICILIAN €€
(Map p64; ☑ 091 58 64 60; www.cucinapapoff.
com; Via Isidoro la Lumia 32; meals €27-37; ☺ lunch
Mon-Fri, dinner Mon-Sat) Specialising in Sicilian
classics like *trancio di pesce in umido con
capperi e olive* (slow-simmered fish stew
with capers and olives), Papoff creates an
elegant ambience with stone walls, grand
arched doorways, carved wooden ceilings,
exposed brickwork and torch-style lighting.

Drinking & Nightlife

Lively clusters of bars can be found along
Via Chiavettieri in the Vucciria neighbourhood (just northwest of Piazza Marina) and
also in the Champagneria district due east of
Teatro Massimo, centred on Piazza Olivella,
Via Spinuzza and Via Patania. Higher-end
drinking spots are concentrated in Palermo's
new city. In summer many Palermitans decamp to Mondello by the sea.

★ Kursaal Kalhesa BAR
(Map p58; ☑ 091 616 21 11; www.kursaalkalhesa.
it; Foro Italico Umberto I 21; ☺ noon-3pm & 6pm-
1.30am Tue-Sat, noon-1.30am Sun) This bar of
choice for the city's avant-garde occupies
the remnants of a handsome early-19th-

DON'T MISS

CAFES

Palermo is justly famous for its cafe society. To indulge in an excellent espresso accompanied by a creamy *cannolo* or decadently sweet *cassata*, head to the following:

Pasticceria Cappello (Map p64; www.pasticceriacappello.it; Via Nicoló Garzilli 10;
☺ 7am-9.30pm Thu-Tue) Famous for the *setteveli* (seven-layer chocolate cake) that was
invented here – and has long since been copied all over Palermo – this bakery-cafe with
its boudoir-style back room creates splendid pastries and desserts of all kinds. Not to
be missed is the dreamy *delizia di pistacchio*, a granular pistachio cake topped with
creamy icing and a chocolate medallion.

Antico Caffè Spinnato (Map p64; ☑ 091 32 92 20; www.spinnato.it; Via Principe di
Belmonte 107-15; ☺ 7am-1am Sun-Fri, to 2am Sat) At this sophisticated cafe dating back to
1860, Palermitans throng the sidewalk tables daily to enjoy afternoon piano music, coffee, cocktails, ice cream, sumptuous cakes and snacks.

Pasticceria Mazzara (Map p64; Via Magliocco 19; ☺ 7.30am-9.30pm) Tucked into the
upscale locale between Teatro Massimo and Teatro Politeama, this venerable and bustling corner bakery has been satisfying Palermitan sweet tooths since 1909.

Pasticceria Alba (☑ 091 30 90 16; www.pasticceriaalba.it; Piazza Don Bosco 7; ☺ 7am-
10pm Tue-Sun) Aficionados insist that the city's best coffee is served here, and they're
equally evangelical about Alba's delectable *arancine* (rice balls). It's about 3km north of
the city centre; take Viale della Liberta' north to Via Antonino di Giorgio, turn right and
look for the *pasticceria* on your right in Piazza Don Bosco.

DON'T MISS

PALERMO'S OPERA DEI PUPI

Sicily's most popular form of traditional entertainment is the *opera dei pupi* (rod-marionette theatre), and the best place to attend a performance is in Palermo.

Marionettes were first introduced to the island by the Spanish in the 18th century and the art form was swiftly embraced by locals, who were enthralled with the re-enacted tales of Charlemagne and his heroic knights Orlando and Rinaldo. Effectively the soap operas of their day, these puppet shows expounded the deepest sentiments of life – unrequited love, treachery, thirst for justice and the anger and frustration of the oppressed. Back then, a puppet could speak volumes where a man could not.

There are traditionally two types of *opera dei pupi* in Sicily: Palermitan (practised in Palermo, Agrigento and Trapani) and Catanese (in Catania, Messina and Syracuse). Carved from beech, olive or lemon-tree wood, the marionettes stand some 1.5m high, have wire joints and wear richly coloured costumes. The knights are clad in metal suits of armour that make the figures shine and resonate when they engage in swordfights with bloodthirsty Saracen warriors or mythical monsters.

Good puppeteers are judged on the dramatic effect they can create – lots of stamping feet, thundering and a gripping running commentary – and on their speed and skill in directing the battle scenes. Nowadays the *opera dei pupi* has been relegated to folklore status, maintained by a few companies largely for the benefit of tourists and children. The best places to attend a performance are at the Museo Internazionale delle Marionette Antonio Pasqualino (p62) or at the **Teatro dei Pupi Cuticchio** (Map p58; ☑ 091 32 34 00; www.figlidartecuticchio.com; Via Bara all'Olivella 95; ☉ 6.30pm Sat & Sun Sep-Jul), a company run by the Associazione Figli d'Arte Cuticchio (check website for performance times).

century palace, built into the city walls next to the monumental 16th-century town gate Porta dei Greci. Recline on silk-covered divans beneath soaring vaulted ceilings and choose from an extensive list of cocktails and snacks while listening to live music or selections from the in-house DJ.

There's a roaring fire in winter, plus art exhibits, a good program of music and literary events and a bookstore with foreign newspapers. Meals (from €30) are served upstairs on the leafy patio flanked by 15th-century walls.

Pizzo & Pizzo   WINE BAR
(Map p64; ☑ 091 601 45 44; www.pizzoepizzo.com; Via XII Gennaio 1; ☉ dinner Mon-Sat) Sure, this sophisticated wine bar is a great place for aperitifs, but the buzzing atmosphere and the tempting array of cheeses, cured meats and smoked fish might just convince you to stick around for dinner.

☆ Entertainment

Teatro Massimo   OPERA
(Map p54; ☑ 091 605 35 80; www.teatromassimo.it; Piazza Giuseppe Verdi) Ernesto Basile's six-tiered art nouveau masterpiece is Europe's third-largest opera house and one of Italy's most prestigious, right up there with La Scala in Milan, San Carlo in Naples and La Fenice in Venice. With lions flanking its grandiose columned entrance and an interior gleaming in red and gold, it stages opera, ballet and music concerts from September to June.

Teatro Politeama Garibaldi   PERFORMING ARTS
(Map p64; Piazza Ruggero Settimo) This grandiose theatre is a popular venue for opera, ballet and classical music, staging afternoon and evening concerts from October through June. It's home to Palermo's symphony orchestra, the **Orchestra Sinfonica Siciliana** (☑ 091 607 25 32; www.orchestrasinfonicasiciliana.it).

Teatro di Verdura   PERFORMING ARTS
(☑ 091 765 19 63; Viale del Fante 70; ☉ mid-Jun–Sep) A summer-only program of ballet and music in the lovely gardens of the Villa Castelnuovo, about 6km north of the city centre. Take Viale della Liberta' to Viale Diana to Viale del Fante. There's a delightful open-air bar that opens during shows.

Cantieri Culturali alla Zisa   PERFORMING ARTS
(☑ 091 652 49 42; Via Paolo Gili 4) West of the centre, this newly renovated industrial space has recently emerged as Palermo's

Continued on page 77

DIANA MAYFIELD/GETTY IMAGES ©

Sicilian Architecture

Architecture lovers will find themselves in heaven in Sicily. There is hardly a town that isn't graced with at least a mini-masterpiece of architecture – the particular style of Sicilian baroque is a feast for the senses. There are many Classical structures, fantastic, shimmering and ancient mosaics, Byzantine churches and Norman forts to explore.

Contents

Above Doric temple, Segesta (p88)

Baroque Cathedrals

The sight of Sicily's baroque cathedrals is one of the foremost reasons for visiting the island. They range from reformed ancient temples, to mixtures of baroque and neoclassical, and whirling and overstated places of worship. Each gives its city centre a unique lushness and grandeur.

Duomo

Syracuse's flamboyant cathedral (p192) lords it over the city's beautiful showpiece square. Its sumptuous facade is typically baroque, but the columns that run down the sides tell of a former life as a temple to the Greek goddess Athena.

Cattedrale di San Nicolò

In Noto, a town noted for its sublime baroque buildings, the spectacular Cattedrale di San Nicolò (p205) trumps the lot. Standing in monumental pomp at the top of a grandiose staircase, it stylishly fuses the best of baroque and neoclassical architecture.

Cattedrale di San Giorgio

Fans of the TV series *Inspector Montalbano* might recognise Ragusa's towering baroque cathedral (p212), often used as a backdrop. The work of Sicily's grand baroque maestro Rosario Gagliardi, it's a masterclass in overstated style and unrestrained passion.

1. Duomo (p192), Syracuse **2.** Cattedrale di San Giorgio (p212), Ragusa **3.** Cattedrale di San Nicolò (p205), Noto

Chiesa di San Giorgio

A commanding presence, Modica's great church (p209) looms over the town's serpentine streets and bustling medieval centre. Its stentorian facade is a stunning example of baroque on a grand scale while the echoing interior drips with silver and gold.

Cattedrale di Sant'Agata

The highlight of Catania's centre is its wedding-cake cathedral (p172). Dedicated to the city's patron saint, Agata, it's unique among Sicily's baroque churches for its black and white tones, a reflection of the volcanic stone used in its construction.

SICILIAN BAROQUE

After being devastated by an earthquake in 1693, Sicily was presented with an opportunity to redesign many of its cities and experiment with a new architectural style that was taking Europe by storm: baroque. A backlash against the pared-down classical aesthetic of the Renaissance, this new style was dramatic, curvaceous and downright sexy – a perfect match for Sicily's unorthodox and exuberant character. Aristocrats in towns such as Noto, Modica, Ragusa, Catania and Syracuse rushed to build baroque *palazzi* (palaces), many decorated with the grotesque masks and *putti* (cherubs) that had long been a hallmark of the island's architecture. Even the church got into it, commissioning ostentatious churches and oratories aplenty.

72

JOHN HESELTINE/GETTY IMAGES ©

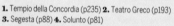

1. Tempio della Concordia (p235) **2.** Teatro Greco (p193)
3. Segesta (p88) **4.** Solunto (p81)

Classical Masterpieces

Sicily is renowned for its classical masterpieces, the best of which is to be found in Agrigento. Ancient-history lovers can choose from wonderfully preserved Greek amphitheatres and temples, and rich Roman ruins.

Valley of the Temples

The model for Unesco's logo and one of the world's best-preserved Greek temples, the Tempio della Concordia is the star turn of stunning Agrigento. The ruins (p235) are what's left of Akragas, once the fourth-largest city in the ancient world.

Parco Archeologico della Neapolis

A major power in ancient times, Syracuse boasts one of Sicily's great classical monuments – the Teatro Greco (p193), a supremely well-preserved Greek amphitheatre. In the theatre's shadow, you can explore caves where slaves once laboured.

Selinunte

You don't have to be an archaeologist to be bowled over by the Greek temples at Selinunte (p256). They are beautifully set against a sunny seaside backdrop that looks particularly fabulous in spring, when wildflowers set the scene ablaze with colour.

Segesta

Standing in proud isolation amid rugged, green hills, the ruins of ancient Segesta (p88) are an unforgettable sight. Pride of place goes to the stately 5th-century-BC temple but don't miss the amphitheatre, dramatically gouged out of the hillside.

Solunto

Originally founded by Phoenicians in the 8th century BC, ancient Solunto underwent several incarnations, including a period as the Roman city of Soluntum. Its remaining ruins (p81), sprawled attractively over a steep seafront hillside, mostly date to the Roman era.

Inspiring Mosaics

The island's many invaders left behind great architectural riches, one of which was a variety of exquisite mosaics. Dedicated to celebrating the Divinity, they range from Roman, Byzantine and Arab-Norman periods.

Cappella Palatina

Sicily's greatest work of Arab-Norman art is this sparkling mosaic-encrusted chapel (p55) in the Palazzo dei Normanni in Palermo. Every inch of the arched interior is emblazoned with golden mosaics and biblical figures. Precious inlaid marble and an Arabic-style carved wooden ceiling complete the picture.

Villa Romana del Casale

This villa (p226) in Piazza Armerina is home to some of the world's finest Roman mosaics. Buried for centuries under a layer of mud, they stand out for their scale, use of colour, and scenes of mythological monsters and bikini-clad girls working out with weights.

1. La Martorana (p53) **2.** Villa Romana del Casale (p226) **3.** Duomo di Cefalù (p116)

Duomo di Cefalù

The robust, fortress-like exterior of Cefalù's hulking Norman cathedral (p116) guards one of Sicily's most celebrated mosaics: the depiction of Christ Pantocrator in the apse. Dating to the mid-12th century, it's a remarkably lifelike depiction of a severe man with drawn cheeks and a dark beard.

La Martorana

A favourite venue for local weddings, Palermo's most popular medieval church (p53) is a treasure trove of Byzantine mosaics.

Cattedrale di Monreale

An outstanding example of Norman architecture, Monreale's famous cathedral (p80) harbours a dazzling interior of Byzantine-influenced mosaics depicting stories from the Old Testament.

Castello di Caccamo (p120)

Captivating Castles

Sicily's castles have played a vital role in the island's history, serving as forts during the Norman rule, when most of them were built. They continue to tower over landscapes and cities, and are some of the island's most impressive sights. Some are even said to be still holding ancient ghosts captive!

Palazzo dei Normanni

This palace (p55) in Palermo has long been the nerve centre of island power. It once housed one of Europe's most glittering courts and it is now the seat of Sicily's regional government. Politics becomes religion which becomes art in the Cappella Palatina.

Castello di Lombardia

As impressive as this formidable 14th-century castle (p220) in Enna is, the real highlight is the sweeping panorama that unfolds from the top of Torre Pisana, the tallest of the castle's six remaining towers. As far as the eye can see, great swaths of rolling green countryside stretch off in all directions.

Castello di Caccamo

One of Italy's largest castles, Caccamo's impregnable fort (p120) served as a Norman stronghold and then a base for the powerful 14th-century Chiaramonte family. It's protected by a series of forbidding walls and ingenious fortifications, and commands magnificent views.

Castello dei Ventimiglia

An evocative sight, the enormous castle (p121) that gives Castelbuono its name is said to be haunted. Every month the ghost of a long-dead queen runs the lengths of its corridors, which now host a small museum and art gallery.

Continued from page 68

trendiest contemporary and experimental arts venue, with frequent live performances and a brand-new modern art gallery, ZAC (Zona Arti Contemporanee), which opened in December 2012.

🛍 Shopping

⭐ **Gusti di Sicilia**   FOOD & DRINK
(Map p64; Via Emerico Amari 79; ⊗ 8.30am-11pm Mon-Sat, 8.30am-2pm & 6-11pm Sun) This recently expanded gourmet grocery is a stellar spot to stock up on edible Sicilian souvenirs, from tins of tuna to jars of caponata, capers and marmalade to bottles of wine and olive oil to unexpected treasures like *'pasta con le sarde'* sauce. Everything's packaged beautifully, making this a perfect source for gifts as well as personal souvenirs.

Siculamente   CLOTHING
(Map p64; www.siculamente.it; Via Emerico Amari 136; ⊗ 9.30am-1.30pm & 4-8pm) Wear a little Sicilian slang with one of the T-shirts and hats sold at this trendy little shop. All bear captions in local dialect, from pithy Sicilian proverbs to cheeky, humorous or political statements. The store's catalog provides translations into English and Italian to help your friends decipher what the heck kind of statement you're trying to make.

Le Ceramiche di Caltagirone   CERAMICS
(Map p58; www.leceramichedicaltagirone.it; Via Cavour 114; ⊗ 9am-1pm & 4-8pm Mon-Sat, 9am-1pm Sun) This little shop near Teatro Massimo specialises in tiles and pottery from Caltagirone, the ceramics capital of southeastern Sicily. Various artists are represented and the selection is good, even if the prices are a bit higher than you'd pay at the source.

Casa Merlo   CERAMICS
(Map p58; www.casamerlo.it; Corso Vittorio Emanuele 231; ⊗ 9am-1pm & 4-7.30pm Mon-Sat) For exquisite and innovative Sicilian ceramics and pottery, stop by this shop, which ships abroad. Near the Quattro Canti.

Il Laboratorio Teatrale   ARTISANAL
(Map p58; Via Bara all'Olivella 48-50; ⊗ 10am-1pm & 4-7pm Tue-Sat) A true artists' workshop, this enchanting space is where the Cuticchio family constructs puppets for their famous theatre across the street. High-quality puppets dating from the late 1800s to the present are displayed here, and are available for purchase by serious enthusiasts.

Bottega dei Sapori e dei Saperi della Legalità   FOOD & DRINK
(Map p64; www.liberapalermo.org; Piazza Castelnuovo 13; ⊗ 4-8pm Mon, 9.30am-1.30pm & 4-8pm Tue-Sat) For edible souvenirs with a dollop of social consciousness, consider buying some wine, olive oil, pasta, couscous or marmalade – all grown on lands confiscated from the Mafia – at this unique store. It's run by the Libera Terra organisation, famous for its outspoken resistance to the Mafia's influence in Sicilian society.

ℹ Orientation

Palermo is large but easily walkable – if you can brave crossing the street, that is. Via Maqueda is its central street, extending from the train station in the south and then changing name to Via Ruggero Settimo at Piazza Giuseppe Verdi, the gateway to the new city. At Piazza Castelnuovo (also commonly known as Piazza Politeama), it continues into Viale della Libertà, a grand boulevard lined with 19th-century apartment blocks.

Via Maqueda is bisected by Corso Vittorio Emanuele, running east to west from the port of La Cala to the cathedral and Palazzo dei Normanni. The intersection of Via Maqueda and Corso Vittorio Emanuele, known famously as the Quattro Canti (Four Corners), divides historic Palermo into four traditional quarters: La Kalsa (southeast), Vucciria (northeast), Il Capo (northwest) and Albergheria (southwest). These quarters contain the majority of Palermo's sights.

Parallel to Via Maqueda is another major street, Via Roma. A one-way system moves traffic north up Via Roma from the train station and south down Via Maqueda.

ℹ Information

EMERGENCY
Ambulance (☑ 091 666 55 28, 118)
Ospedale Civico (☑ 091 666 11 11; www.ospedalecivicopa.org; Via Carmelo Lazzaro) Emergency facilities.
Questura (☑ 091 21 01 11, 113; Piazza della Vittoria 8)

TOURIST INFORMATION
Central Tourist Office (Map p64; ☑ 091 58 51 72; informazionituristiche@provincia.palermo.it; Via Principe di Belmonte 42; ⊗ 8.30am-2pm & 2.30-6pm Mon-Fri) Palermo's provincial tourist office offers maps and brochures as well as the helpful booklet *Un Ospite a Palermo* (www.unospiteapalermo.it), published bimonthly and containing listings for museums, cultural centres, tour guides and transport companies.
City Information Booth (Map p58; Piazza Bellini; ☑ 8.30am-1pm & 3-7pm Mon-Sat)

MOVING ON?

For further information, head to shop.
lonelyplanet.com to purchase a downloadable PDF of the Naples & Campania, Florence & Tuscany and Turin, Piedmont & the Italian Riviera chapters from Lonely Planet's *Italy* guide.

The most dependable of Palermo's city-run information booths, next to the churches of San Cataldo and La Martorana. Other booths around the city – at the port, the train station, Piazza Castelnuovo and Piazza Marina – are only intermittently staffed and have unpredictable hours.

Falcone-Borsellino Airport Information Office (☑ 091 59 16 98; in downstairs hall; ☺ 8.30am-7.30pm Mon-Fri, 8.30am-2.30pm Sat)

❶ Getting There & Away

AIR

Falcone-Borsellino Airport (PMO; Punta Raisi Airport; www.gesap.it) is at Punta Raisi, 30km west of Palermo on the A29 motorway. There are regular flights between Palermo and most mainland Italian cities.

BOAT

From Palermo's port, just east of the corner of Via Francesco Crispi and Via Emerico Amari, **Grandi Navi Veloci** (Map p64; ☑ 010 209 45 91, 091 58 74 04; www.gnv.it; Calata Marinai d'Italia) runs ferries to Civitavecchia (from €73), Genoa (from €90), Naples (from €44) and Tunis (from €72); **Tirrenia** (Map p64; ☑ 091 976 07 73; www.tirrenia.it; Calata Marinai d'Italia) goes to Cagliari (from €51, Saturday only) and Naples (from €47); **Grimaldi Lines** (Map p64; ☑ 081 49 64 44, 091 611 36 91; www.grimaldi-lines.com; Via del Mare) goes to Salerno (from €65, nine to 11½ hours); and **Siremar** (www.siremar.it) goes to Ustica (€18.35, 2¼ hours).

Siremar and **Ustica Lines** (☑ 092 387 38 13; www.usticalines.it) both operate hydrofoils year-round to Ustica (€22.95, 1½ hours). In summertime, Ustica Lines also runs one afternoon hydrofoil to the Aeolian Islands – with stops in Alicudi (€27, two hours), Filicudi (€32.50, 2½ hours), Rinella (€34.70, 3¼ hours), Santa Marina Salina (€38.30, 3½ hours), Lipari (€38.70, four hours), Vulcano (€38.70, 4½ hours), Panarea (€47.40, 4¾ hours) and Stromboli (€54.10, 5¼ hours).

BUS

Offices for all bus companies are located within a block or two of Palermo Centrale train station. The two main departure points are the brand-new **Piazzetta Cairoli bus terminal** (Map p58; Piazzetta Cairoli), just south of the train station's eastern entrance, and the **intercity bus stop** (Map p58) on Via Paolo Balsamo, two blocks due east of the train station. Check locally with the bus company you'll be travelling with to make certain that you'll be boarding at the appropriate stop.

Salemi tickets are sold at **Crystal Viaggi** (☑ 091 617 54 11) in Palermo Centrale train station, and buses leave from Piazzetta Cairoli just outside. Segesta is the agent for the Interbus service to Syracuse, and AST tickets can be purchased from the **Big Bus Bar** (Map p58; ☑ 091 617 30 24; Via Paolo Balsamo 32). **Societá Autolinee Licata** (SAL; ☑ 0922 40 13 60; www.autolineesal.it) runs a service between Palermo's Punta Raisi airport and Agrigento (€12.10, 2¼ hours, three daily).

CAR & MOTORCYCLE

Palermo is accessible on the A20-E90 toll road from Messina, and from Catania (A19-E932) via Enna. Trapani and Marsala are also easily accessible from Palermo by motorway (A29), while Agrigento and Palermo are linked by the SS121/189, a good state road through the interior of the island.

TRAIN

Regular services leave from **Palermo Centrale train station** (Piazza Giulio Cesare; ☺ 6am-9pm) to Messina (from €11.80; 2¾ to 3½ hours, hourly), Catania (from €12.50, three to 5¾ hours, six to 10 daily, including one direct train on weekdays) and Agrigento (€8.30, two hours, eight to 10 daily), as well as to nearby towns such as Cefalù (from €5.15, 45 minutes to one hour, hourly). There are also Intercity trains to Reggio di Calabria, Naples and Rome. Inside the station, there are ATMs, toilets and left-luggage facilities (first five hours €5 flat fee, next seven hours €0.70 per hour, all subsequent hours €0.30 per hour; office staffed 8am-8pm).

❶ Getting Around

TO/FROM THE AIRPORT

Prestia e Comandè (☑ 091 58 63 51; www.prestiaecomande.it) runs an efficient half-hourly bus service between 5am and 11pm that transfers passengers from the airport to the centre of Palermo, dropping people off outside the Teatro Politeama Garibaldi and Palermo Centrale train station. To find the bus, follow the signs past the downstairs taxi rank and around the corner to the right. Tickets for the journey, which takes anywhere from 35 to 50 minutes depending on traffic, cost €6.10 one-way or €11 return and are purchased on the bus. Return journeys to the airport run with the same frequency and pick up at the same points. This is definitely the best way to travel to Palermo from the airport.

The Trinacria Express (091 704 40 07) runs between the airport and the train station (€5.80, 45 minutes to 1¼ hours). Trains depart from Palermo Centrale station every 30 to 60 minutes between 4.55am and 8.09pm, returning from the airport between 5.54am and 10.05pm.

There is a taxi rank outside the arrivals hall and the set fare to/from central Palermo is €45, and all the major car-hire companies are represented at the airport.

CAR & MOTORCYCLE

When making a booking, ask your hotel about parking; many hotels have a *garage convenzionato*, a local garage that offers special rates to their guests (typically between €10 and €20 per day). Alternatively, you'll need to find a legal space on the city's streets or piazzas. For spaces marked by blue lines, you must get a ticket from a machine (usually every day except Sunday; see the hours of operation posted at the machine nearest your vehicle). For spaces with signs stating a maximum parking time but with no ticket machine in evidence, you'll need to purchase a green form called a *scheda* –

BUSES FROM PALERMO

COMPANY	DESTINATION	PRICE (€)	DURATION (HR)	FREQUENCY
AST (Azienda Siciliana Trasporti; Map p54; 091 680 00 32; www. aziendasicilianatrasporti.it; Via Rosario Gregorio 46)	Ragusa	13.40	4	4 daily Mon-Sat, 2 Sun
AST	Modica	13.40	4½	4 daily Mon-Sat, 2 Sun
Cuffaro (Map p58; 091 616 15 10; www.cuffaro.info; Via Paolo Balsamo 13)	Agrigento	8.70	2	8 Mon-Fri, 6 Sat, 3 Sun
Interbus	Syracuse	12	3¼	3 daily
SAIS Trasporti (Map p58; 091 617 11 41; www.saistrasporti.it; Via Paolo Balsamo 20)	Petralia Soprana	9.90	2	3 Mon-Sat, 2 Sun
SAIS Trasporti	Petralia Sottana	9.90	1¾	3 Mon-Sat, 2 Sun
SAIS Trasporti	Polizzi Generosa	8.90	1¼	3 Mon-Sat, 2 Sun
SAIS Trasporti	Cefalù	5.70	1	4-6 Mon-Sat
SAIS Trasporti	Rome	48	12	1 daily (overnight service)
SAIS Autolinee (091 616 60 28; www.saisautolinee.it; Piazza Cairoli)	Enna	9.90	1¾	1-2 daily Mon-Sat
SAIS Autolinee	Messina	15.80	2¾	5 daily Mon-Fri, 3 Sat & Sun
SAIS Autolinee	Catania	14.90	2½	14 daily Mon-Sat, 10 Sun
Salemi (0923 98 11 20; www. autoservizisalemi.it)	Mazara del Vallo	8.70	2	10 Mon-Sat, 4 Sun
Salemi	Marsala	9.20	2½	20 Mon-Sat, 11 Sun
Salemi	Trapani's Birgi airport	10.60	1¾-2	8 Mon-Fri, 6 Sat & Sun
Segesta (Map p58; 091 616 79 19; www.segesta.it; Piazza Cairoli)	Trapani	9	2	hourly 6am-8pm

available from AMAT (Palermo's transit authority) or tobacconists – and place it on your dashboard, first making sure to scratch off the circles corresponding to the time and date you parked there. If you neglect to do this, or if you park longer than the time allowed, you may be fined.

PUBLIC TRANSPORT

Palermo's orange **AMAT buses** (☎848 80 08 17; www.amat.pa.it) are overcrowded and often slow due to the city's appalling traffic. Ask at the tourist booths for a leaflet detailing the different lines; most stop at the train station. Tickets should be purchased before you get on the bus and are available from tobacconists or AMAT booths at major transit hubs around town, including Piazza Independenza, Piazza Politeama, Piazza Sturzo and **Piazza Giulio Cesare** (Map p58) (in front of the train station). They cost €1.30 (€1.70 if purchased from the bus driver) and are valid for 90 minutes. Once you get on the bus you need to validate the ticket in the orange machine, which prints a 'start' time on it.

TAXI

Taxis are expensive in Palermo, and heavy traffic can make matters worse. Official taxis should have a *tassametro* (meter), which records the fare; check for this before embarking. Hailing a passing taxi on the street is not customary; rather, you'll need to phone ahead for a taxi or wait at one of the taxi ranks at major travel hubs such as the train station, Piazza Politeama, Teatro Massimo and Piazza Independenza.

AROUND PALERMO

Palermo is in turn both exhilarating and exhausting, and after a few days visitors often find that they need a respite from its noisy, dirty and crowded streets. Fortunately, there are plenty of options for an easy urban escape.

Mondello

In the summer months, it sometimes seems as if the entire city population has packed a beach towel, an iPod and a pair of D&G shades and decamped to this popular beach resort only a 20-minute drive north from the centre of town.

Originally a muddy, malaria-ridden port, Mondello only really became fashionable in the 19th century, when the city's elite flocked here in their carriages, thus warranting the huge Liberty-style pier that dominates the seafront and kicking off a craze for building opulent summer villas. Most of the beaches are private (two loungers and an umbrella cost around €10 per day), but there is also a wide swath of public beach crammed with swimmers, pedalos and noisy jet skis.

Seafood restaurants and snack stalls have colonised the lido (Viale Regina Elena) and the main piazza hosts numerous cafes with outdoor seating. One of Sicily's trendiest restaurants, **Bye Bye Blues** (☎091 684 14 15; www.byebyeblues.it; Via del Garofalo 23; meals €50; ⊗closed Mon), is located a few streets back from the beach.

Catch AMAT bus 806 (€1.30, 20 minutes, every 20 to 30 minutes between 4am and 11.30pm, fewer services on Sunday) from Piazza Politeama.

Monreale

Inspired by a heavenly vision of the Virgin and driven by earthly ambition, William II set about building the sumptuous **Cattedrale di Monreale** (☎091 640 44 03; Piazza del Duomo; admission to cathedral free, north transept €2, terrace €2; ⊗8.30am-12.45pm & 2.30-5pm Mon-Sat, 8-10am & 2.30-5pm Sun), 8km southwest of Palermo. Living in the shadow of his grandfather, Roger II – who was responsible for the cathedral in Cefalù and the Cappella Palatina – and vying with Walter of the Mill, who was overseeing construction of a grand Duomo in Palermo, William was determined that his cathedral should be the biggest and best of all. The result was Monreale, considered to be the finest example of Norman architecture in Sicily. The mosaicists were from Sicily and Venice, but the stylised influence of the Byzantines pervades their work. Completed in 1184 after only 10 years' work, the mosaics are an articulate and fitting tribute to William's ambition and to the grandeur of Sicilian culture at that time.

The interior is among the most impressive creations of the Italian Middle Ages. A catalogue of shimmering mosaics depicts Old Testament stories, from the creation of man to the Assumption, in 42 different episodes. The beauty of the mosaics cannot be described – you have to see for yourself Noah's ark perching atop the waves or Christ

Around Palermo

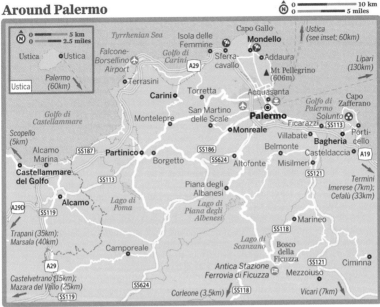

healing a leper infected with large leopard-sized spots. The story of Adam and Eve is wonderfully portrayed, with a grumpy-looking, post-Eden-eviction Eve sitting on a rock while Adam labours in the background. The large mosaic of Christ, dominating the central apse, is stunning. Binoculars make viewing the mosaics easier, although they are still impressive to the naked eye. Take €1 coins to illuminate the ill-lit mosaics in the apses. For a guide to the various scenes, print out the handy key and map at www.seepalermo.com/monrealekeyprint.htm.

Outside the cathedral is the entrance to the **cloister** (adult €6, EU citizen 18-25yr €3, under 18 & 65+ free; ⏱ 9am-6.30pm Tue-Sat, 9am-1pm Sun & Mon), which illustrates William's love of Arab artistry. This tranquil courtyard is an ode to Orientalism, with elegant Romanesque arches supported by an array of slender columns alternately decorated with shimmering mosaic patterns. Each capital is different, and taken together they represent a unique sculptural record of medieval Sicily. The capital of the 19th column on the west aisle depicts William II offering the cathedral to the Madonna.

To reach Monreale, take AMAT bus 389 (€1.30, 30 to 40 minutes, every 25 to 60 minutes) from Piazza Indipendenza in Palermo. The bus will drop you off outside the cathedral in Piazza Duomo. Alternatively, you can catch an AST bus for Monreale from in front of the Palermo Centrale train station (one way/return €1.80/2.80, 40 minutes, roughly hourly from 6.25am to 7.45pm). Note that at the time of research service on AMAT's bus 389 was temporarily disrupted – enquire locally to see if normal service has resumed.

Solunto

About 20km east of Palermo are the remains of the Hellenistic Roman town of **Solunto** (☏ 091 90 45 57; adult €2, EU citizen 18-25yr €1, EU citizen under 18 or 65+ free; ⏱ 9am-5.30pm Tue-Sat, 9am-1pm Sun), founded in the 4th century BC on the site of an earlier Phoenician settlement. Although the ancient city is only partially excavated and the ruins less impressive than others you'll see around Sicily, the setting on the slopes of Monte Catalfano is beautiful, with spectacular sea views. Wander along the Roman *decumanus* (main street), and take detours up the steep, paved side streets to explore the ruined houses, some of which still sport remnants of original mosaic floors.

CORLEONE: AN OFFER YOU CAN'T REFUSE

Having suffered centuries of poverty and possessing a well-documented history as a Mafia stronghold, the town of Corleone – 60km from Palermo and best known through Francis Ford Coppola's classic *Godfather* trilogy – has been trying to reinvent itself over the last decade. It is now home to **CIDMA** (Centro Internazionale di Documentazione sulla Mafia e Movimento Antimafia; ✆340 4025601, 091 845 242 95; cidmacorleone@gmail.com; Via Giovanni Valenti 7, Corleone; admission €5; ⊙ by arrangement), an absorbing and extremely moving anti-Mafia museum located in a small cobbled street off Piazza Garibaldi. The centre aims to promote speaking out against organised crime rather than succumbing to the Mafia-promoted culture of *omertà* (silence).

English-, Spanish- and Italian-speaking tour guides recount the terrifying history of the local Mafia but focus on the brave efforts of anti-Mafia campaigners and judges. A huge 'No Mafia' sign greets visitors at the entrance, as does a quote from murdered anti-Mafia judge Giovanni Falcone: 'It's necessary to keep up your duty to the end at all costs, however hard may be the sacrifice to bear, because this is the essence of human dignity'. Three rooms are visited: the first holds the documents from the maxi trials of 1986–87; the second exhibits photos by photojournalist Letizia Battaglia, who documented Mafia crimes in the 1970s and 1980s; and the third displays photos of Mafia bosses, the men of justice who fought them and people who have lost loved ones.

The museum can be visited by guided tour only. Call or email ahead to reserve a space, as tour frequency and the availability of multilingual guides vary.

AST buses travel between Palermo and Corleone (€4.80, 1½ hours, nine daily). In Corleone, passengers are dropped off at Piazza Falcone e Borsellino, a five-minute walk from the museum. If you'd like to eat here or stay the night, **Al Capriccio** (✆091 846 79 38; http://trattoria-alcapriccio.it; Via Sant'Agostino 39, Corleone; s/d €30/60) offers low-cost, very basic B&B accommodation a stone's throw from the museum, with an attached pizzeria-trattoria. A better lodging and dining option for those traveling by car is the converted train station Antica Stazione Ferrovia di Ficuzza (p254), a 20-minute drive northeast of Corleone on the road to Palermo.

To get there, take the train from Palermo to the Santa Flavia-Solunto-Porticello stop (€2.25, 20 minutes, hourly). Turn right as you leave the train station, then right again to cross the tracks, following the main road (Corso Filangeri) towards the sea. After about 200m, you'll see a signposted turn-off to your left. From there, the ancient city is a 30-minute steep uphill walk.

Ustica

POP 1291

This tiny island floats alone almost 60km north of Palermo in the Tyrrhenian Sea. Part of the Aeolian volcanic chain, the land mass is actually the tip of a submerged volcano. Its black volcanic-rock landscape is sprinkled with blazing pink-and-red hibiscus flowers and prickly green cacti, the shoreline is littered with dramatic grottoes and the surrounding waters – protected within Area Marina Protetta Isola di Ustica (Island of Ustica Protected Marine Area) – are kept sparklingly clean by an Atlantic current and are thus replete with fish and coral.

Palermitans flock here in July and August for their summer holidays – consider visiting in June and September to appreciate the dramatic coastline and grottoes without the crowds. Note that between October and Easter most of the island's restaurants and accommodation options close down during the week and ferry services from the mainland can be cancelled in bad weather.

◎ Sights & Activities

Scuba Diving & Snorkelling

Divers from all over the world come to Ustica between May and October to explore its magnificent underwater sites. Highlights include the **underwater archaeological trail** off Punta Cavazzi, where artefacts such as anchors and Roman amphorae can be admired. Other popular dive sites are the **Scoglio del Medico**, an outcrop of basalt riddled with caves and gorges that plunge to great depths; and **Secca di Colombara**, a magnificent rainbow-coloured display of sponges and gorgonias.

There are plenty of dive centres that offer dive itineraries and hire equipment. Among them, Diving Center Ustica (☑ 380 4745118; www.usticadiving.it; Contrada Piano Cardoni) – affiliated with Hotel Diana – stands out as the lone operator managed by local residents born and raised on Ustica.

Area Marina Protetta Isola di Ustica (Island of Ustica Protected Marine Area) is divided into three zones. Zone A extends along the west flank of the island from Cala Sidoti to Caletta and as far as 350m offshore (marked with special yellow buoys). You can swim within its boundaries at designated spots, but fishing and boating are prohibited. Two of the island's most beautiful natural grottoes – the Grotta Segreta (Secret Grotto) and the Grotta Rosata (Pink Grotto) – are located here.

Zone B extends beyond Zone A from Punta Cavazzi to Punta Omo Morto; swimming and underwater photography are permitted within its boundaries, as is hook-and-line fishing. Zone C applies to the rest of the coast; swimming and boating are allowed and national fishing regulations apply. Always check your itinerary with a dive centre or the marine national park headquarters before you dive.

Hiking

Ustica is only 8.7 sq km in area, so it's easy to explore on foot. There are a number of walking trails.

For a grand tour of the coastline, start by following the signposted Sentiero del Mezzogiorno south from town. The trail soon curves west, skirting high bluffs and traversing occasional patches of pine forest before eventually rejoining the coast at Ustica's western lighthouse (simply called Faro on local maps). From the lighthouse, continue north on foot or by local bus to Cappella della Madonna della Croce, an 18th-century white adobe church high on the hillside. Here another footpath splits off, following the northern coastal bluffs to the Villaggio Preistorico, a rather poorly maintained remnant of a Bronze Age village. Finish the loop by following the main road back into town. The whole circuit takes between three and four hours.

Another scenic trail passes through pine woods to the summit of Guardia di Mezzo (248m), before descending to the best part of the coast at Spalmatore, where it's possible to swim in natural rock pools.

Closer to town, shorter walking paths lead to the Rocca della Falconiera, a defensive tower above the church; to the lookout point above the lighthouse at Punta Omo Morto; and to the Torre Santa Maria, a Bourbon-era tower just south of the town centre. Ask at the tourist office for directions.

✖ Eating

La Luna sul Porto SICILIAN €€
(☑ 091 844 97 99; Corso Vittorio Emanuele; meals €25; ⊙ lunch & dinner year-round) Since 2000, friendly proprietress Annamaria Baldini has been producing delicious home cooking at this sweet eatery along the steps between the port and main square – one of Ustica's few year-round dining options. In the off-season there's no menu: Annamaria simply swings by your table and announces what she can make with whatever's in the kitchen.

Ristorante Giulia SEAFOOD €€
(☑ 091 844 90 07; Via San Francesco 16; meals €25-35; ⊙ dinner late May–mid-Sep) Just north of Ustica's central square, this family-run eatery is renowned for its seafood and considered by many to serve the island's best meals. If you're lucky enough to be around when it's open, make a beeline for it!

ℹ Information

VisitUstica (☑ 091 748 24 30; www.visitustica.it; Piazza Umberto I; ⊙ 10am-1pm & 5-9pm Jun-Sep) On Ustica's main square; offers info on the island and the marine reserve.

ℹ Getting There & Away

Siremar (Map p64; ☑ 091 749 31 11; www.siremar.it; Via Francesco Crispi 118) operates a year-round car-ferry service between Ustica and Palermo (€18.35 one way, 2¼ hours, one daily), with additional hydrofoils twice daily in the tourist season (€23.55 one way, 1¼ hours). **Ustica Lines** (☑ 0923 87 38 13; www.usticalines.it) runs hydrofoils year-round from Palermo to Ustica (€22.95, 1½ hours, two daily in summer, one in winter) and also operates a Naples–Ustica hydrofoil service on Saturdays from June to the end of September (€80 one way, four hours).

Climbing the hill through Ustica's church square, look for both companies' ticket offices on your left.

ℹ Getting Around

A local bus (€1.20) makes regular circuits of the island, leaving every hour or so. In summertime Bicincittà (☑ 800 75 55 15; www.bicincitta.com) also provides rental bikes that can be picked up and dropped off at four sites around the island using an automated credit-card-based system.

PALERMO USTICA

Western Sicily

Includes ➡

Best Places to Eat

Best Places to Stay

Why Go?

Sicily's windswept western coast has beckoned invaders for millennia. Its richly stocked fishing grounds, hilltop vineyards and coastal saltpans were coveted by the Phoenicians, Greeks, Romans and Normans, all of whom influenced the province's landscape and culture. Even the English left their mark, with 18th-century entrepreneurs lured here and made rich by one of the world's most famous sweet wines, Marsala. Today, this part of the island is a largely unexploited tourism treasure, perfect for those who savour slow travel. There's an amazingly diverse range of experiences to be had here. Standout attractions include the ancient ruins of Segesta and Selinunte, the hilltop village of Erice and the Golfo di Castellammare, with its stunning juxtaposition of sea and mountain scenery. Adding to Western Sicily's appeal are its unique local cuisine and the region's proximity to both the Palermo and Trapani international airports.

Road Distances (KM)

	Marsala	Scopello	Segesta	Selinunte
Scopello	75			
Segesta	50	30		
Selinunte	45	70	60	
Trapani	30	35	30	95

Getting Around

Efficient train service links the coastal cities of Mazara del Vallo, Marsala and Trapani. Elsewhere you'll benefit from having your own vehicle. Bus schedules are limited and become virtually non-existent on Sundays.The north-south A29 autostrada and its east-west counterpart A29D (A29dir on road signs) make driving a breeze between Palermo, Selinunte, Segesta and Trapani. Smaller roads to San Vito Lo Capo, Scopello and Saline di Trapani – all linked by the Strada del Vino Erice wine route – are scenic if slow.

THREE PERFECT DAYS

Hike the Zingaro
This 7km ramble dips in and out of several wild and gorgeous coves as it follows the rugged coastline north through Sicily's oldest nature reserve (p89). Museums, beaches and picnic tables along the way offer ample opportunities to catch your breath, catch some rays, or take a swim.

Commune with the Ancients
Start your day at ancient Segesta (p88), strolling down from the majestic hilltop amphitheatre to the site's star attraction, a perfectly preserved Doric temple on the edge of a precipitous gorge. In the afternoon, picnic under the trees at the Rocche di Cusa quarry, surrounded by half-finished columns abandoned by the Greeks over two millennia ago, then move on to Selinunte, where the remains of eight great temples sit in splendid isolation by the sea. After a last look at the ruins from the beach below, it's time for seafood and sunset at Da Vittorio (p110) just down the road.

Wine & Dine
Tour the famous cellars (p105) of Marsala in the morning, then head to Trapani for fish couscous or *pesto alla trapanese* (pasta with fresh tomatoes, basil, garlic and almonds). After lunch, climb through vineyards to the hilltop castle (p98) at Erice, snack on some of Sicily's most famous sweets at Maria Grammatico (p98) and admire the setting sun over the stunning promontory at San Vito Lo Capo.

Getting Away from It All

→ **Explore Mozia** Once a thriving Phoenician settlement, this off-the-beaten-track island (p103) is now home to abundant bird life and an excellent archaeological museum.

→ **Get marooned on Marettimo** The outermost of the Egadi Islands, Marettimo is as attractive for its lone whitewashed village as for its fabulous network of pine-shaded walking trails.

DON'T MISS

The cinnamon- and saffron-infused fish couscous brought to this stretch of coast by the Saracens centuries ago. Prime venues for a taste-test include La Bettolaccia (p95) in Trapani, Eyem Zemen (p107) in Mazara del Vallo and the annual couscous festival (p91) in San Vito Lo Capo.

Best Historical Sites

→ Segesta (p88)

→ Selinunte ruins (p109)

→ Museo del Satiro (p107)

→ Museo Archeologico Baglio Anselmi (p104)

→ Whitaker Museum (p103)

Best Beaches

→ Spiaggia dei Faraglioni (p89)

→ Cala Minnola (p101)

→ Lido Burrone (p100)

→ Castellammare del Golfo (p251)

→ San Vito Lo Capo (p91)

Resources

→ **Trapani Welcome** (www. trapaniwelcome.it) Detailed information about Trapani province.

→ **EgadiWeb** (www. egadiweb.it) Guide to the Egadi Islands.

→ **Selinunte On Line** (www. selinunte.net) Information about Selinunte's archaeological park.

Cagliari (140km)

Ustica (90km)

Tyrrhenian Sea

Mt Eryx (750m)

Valderic

Erice ②

Trapani

Capo Grosso

Grotta del Genovese ◎ Levanzo

Levanzo ③

Nubia◦ ◦**Paceco**

Saline di Trapani SS187

SS115

Marettimo◦

Egadi Islands

Vincenzo Florio (Birgi) Airport

Marettimo

Favignana

Favignana

Stagnone Islands

Riserva Naturale di Stagnone

◦Mozia San Pantaleo

⑤**Marsala**

Capo Boeo

SS188

Tunis, Tunisia (150km)

MEDITERRANEAN SEA

SS115

Mazara del Vallo ④

Pantelleria (85km)

Pantelleria (90km)

Western Sicily Highlights

① Contemplate one of the world's most perfect classical temples on the idyllic slopes of **Segesta** (p88).

② Plan your next move while surveying western Sicily's stunning landscape from Erice's Norman castle, **Castello di Venere** (p98).

③ Explore ancient cave art at **Grotta del Genovese** (p101) on the island of Levanzo.

④ Admire hand-painted wall tiles and stop in for fish couscous in the narrow lanes of **La Casbah** (p107), the old Saracen quarter of Mazara del Vallo.

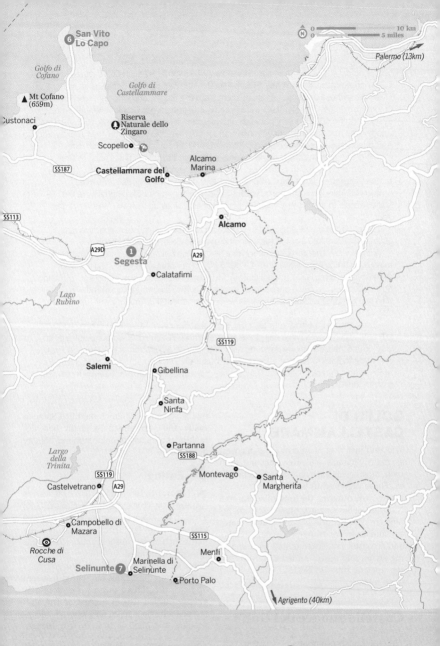

San Vito
Lo Capo

Golfo di
Cofano

Golfo di
Castellammare

Palermo (13km)

▲ Mt Cofano
(659m)

Custonaci

Riserva
Naturale dello
Zingaro

Scopello

Alcamo
Marina

Castellammare del
Golfo

SS187

Alcamo

SS113

A29D

A29

Segesta

Calatafimi

Lago
Rubino

SS119

Salemi

Gibellina

Santa
Ninfa

Largo
della
Trinita

Partanna

SS188

Montevago

Santa
Margherita

SS119

Castelvetrano

A29

Campobello di
Mazara

SS115

Rocche di
Cusa

Menfi

Selinunte

Marinella di
Selinunte

Porto Palo

Agrigento (40km)

5 Join the evening
passeggiata through the
marble-paved streets of
Marsala (p103), then people-
watch over aperitifs at a
streetside *enoteca*.

6 Splash in the vibrant
turquoise waters of **San Vito
Lo Capo** (p91), backed by
the imposing rock-climber's
favourite, Monte Monaco.

7 Gain a sense of historical
perspective as you roam
through gargantuan piles
of crumbled columns on the
seaside bluffs at **Selinunte**
(p108).

SEGESTA

The principal city of the Elymians, Segesta (☎092 495 23 56; adult €6, EU citizen 18-25yr €3, EU citizen under 18 or 65+ free; ☉9am-4pm Oct-Mar, 9am-6pm Apr-Sep) was an ancient civilisation whose peoples claimed descent from the Trojans and who settled in Sicily in the Bronze Age. The Elymians were in constant conflict with Greek Selinunte, whose destruction (in 409 BC) they pursued with bloodthirsty determination. Such mutual antipathy was to have fatal consequences, and more than 100 years later the Greek tyrant Agathocles slaughtered over 10,000 Elymians and repopulated Segesta with Greeks.

Today, the remains of the city form one of the world's most magical ancient sites, which comprises a theatre high up on the mountain and a never-completed Doric temple. The latter dates from around 430 BC and is remarkably well preserved.

Every 30 minutes a shuttle bus (€1.50, five minutes) runs 1.5km uphill from the site entrance to the theatre. If you've got the energy, walk up instead – the views are spectacular.

The site is set on the edge of a deep canyon amid wild, desolate mountains and is accessed off the A29D autostrada running between Palermo and Trapani.

Autoservizi Tarantola (p96) operates a bus service between Segesta and Trapani's main bus station (one way/return €3.80/6.20, 35 minutes each way). The most convenient departures leave Trapani at 8am and 10am, returning from Segesta at 1pm and 4pm. Alternatively, catch a train from Trapani (€3.45, 30 minutes, two Monday to Saturday, one Sunday) to Segesta Tempio; the ruins are about a 20-minute walk uphill from the station.

Coming from Palermo, your best bet is the Autoservizi Tarantola (☎0924 3 10 20) bus, which leaves twice daily (one way/return €6.70/10.70, 70 to 80 minutes each way). Buses leave from Via Balsamo near Palermo's train station at 8.30am and 2pm, returning to Palermo at noon and 4pm; all buses also pick up and drop off passengers at Palermo's Piazza Politeama. Train service from Palermo is impractical, as it requires a time-consuming connection in Alcamo.

GOLFO DI CASTELLAMMARE

This gulf just west of Palermo is as far west as many Sicilians will ever get, and even then, most locals have only visited its beaches. Those prepared to be a bit more adventurous will discover the unspoiled Riserva Naturale dello Zingaro, quaint settlements built around historic *baglios* (manor houses) and *tonnare* (tuna-processing plants), and a coastal landscape dotted with tempting swimming coves. Added to all this are the ancient ruins of Segesta, only a short drive inland.

Castellammare del Golfo

POP 14,606

The stunning promontory between Castellammare del Golfo and Monte Cofano (659m) is perhaps the most beautiful in all of Sicily. At its foot lies the fishing village of Castellammare del Golfo, founded by the Elymians as the port for the city of Segesta. It has a pleasant harbour that is overlooked by the remains of a much-modified Saracen castle and surrounded by sandy beaches, making it a hugely popular summer holiday destination.

✖ Eating

★**Ristorante Del Golfo**   SEAFOOD €€
(☎0924 3 02 57; Via Segesta 153; meals €30-40; ☉closed Tue, except in summer) This perennial Castellammare favourite serves seafood delights such as *scampi marinati all'arancia* (prawns marinated in orange juice), *linguine gamberi pistacchio e bottarga* (pasta with shrimp, pistachios and cured fish roe) or *pesce del giorno in crosta di sale alla griglia* (grilled fish in a crust of Trapani's famous salt). Save room for *cassatelle* (deep-fried pastries filled with ricotta) for dessert.

Il Ristorantino Del Monsù   SEAFOOD €€
(☎0924 53 10 31; Piazza Petrolo 2; meals €25-30; ☉closed Mon & 2 weeks in both Feb & Nov) Seafood rules the menu at this restaurant in Castellammare's upper town, just opposite a panoramic terrace overlooking the harbour. Dishes include *tagliolini con cernia,*

pomodorini e mandorle (fresh pasta with grouper, cherry tomatoes and almonds), *cous cous del Monsù* (couscous with black squid ink) and *involtini di pesce spada* (swordfish rolls stuffed with breadcrumbs, currents and pine nuts).

ⓘ Getting There & Around

BUS

Buses depart from Via della Repubblica. **Autoservizi Russo** (☑ 0924 3 13 64; www.russoautoservizi.it) runs services to Piazza Politeama and the central train station in Palermo (€5.70, 1¼ hours, six daily Monday to Saturday, one Sunday), as well as services to Scopello (€2.50, 30 minutes, four daily) and San Vito Lo Capo (€5.70, 1½ hours, two Monday to Saturday, one Sunday). Extra buses operate in July and August. **Azienda Siciliana Trasporti** (AST; ☑ 840 110323; www.aziendasicilianatrasporti.it) runs buses to Trapani (€4.10, one to 1¼ hours, four daily Monday to Saturday).

CAR

Castellammare del Golfo is only 44km from Palermo's Falcone-Borsellino (Punta Raisi) airport via the A29 autostrada.

TRAIN

The train station is an inconvenient 3km out of town, although there is a shuttle bus (€1.50). There are frequent trains from Palermo (€5.75, 1½ to 1¾ hours, eight daily) and Trapani (€4.65, one hour, four daily).

Scopello

The hamlet of Scopello couldn't be any more charming if it tried. Built around an 18th-century *baglio* fortified with a high wall and huge gates, its white houses and smooth-stone streets look like they belong in a 1950s Italian movie. In fact, the historic *tonnara* (tuna-processing plant) on the shore below is a popular film location – the 2004 Hollywood blockbuster *Ocean's Twelve* was filmed here, as was an episode of the *Inspector Montalbano* TV series.

Favourite pastimes in Scopello include sipping a coffee on the main piazza, hiking in the nearby Riserva Naturale dello Zingaro and swimming in one of Sicily's most idyllic coves, which is next to the *tonnara*. Flanked by two tall rocks, one of which is crowned by a medieval tower, the cove has incredibly blue waters and a rough-pebbled beach, Spiaggia dei Faraglioni.

The beach is private property, so you'll have to pay €3 admission, plus a parking fee, and abide by other restrictions – no beach umbrellas or photos of the *tonnara*, which is for the private use of the owners and their guests.

Try to avoid Scopello in August, when it becomes unpleasantly crowded.

✖ Eating

If you're staying at Pensione Tranchina (p254), make sure to take advantage of its fabulous home-cooked meals. Unfortunately, the *pensione* doesn't cater for outsiders unless one of its own guests opts to skip dinner; interested nonguests are welcome to check around 5pm to see if a table has opened up.

Bar Pasticceria Scopello   BAKERY, CAFE €
(☑ 388 101 07 72; Via Diaz 13; pastries from €1) This tempting *pasticceria* sells a huge range of Sicilian sweet treats and is the town's social epicentre. Claim one of its outdoor tables and settle back for a session of people-watching fuelled by coffee and cake or a refreshing fruit-based *gelato* or *granita* (crushed-ice drink).

ⓘ Getting There & Around

BUS

Autoservizi Russo buses run between Castellammare del Golfo and Scopello (€2.50, 30 minutes, four daily).

Around Scopello

Riserva Naturale dello Zingaro

Saved from development by local protests, the tranquil Riserva Naturale dello Zingaro (☑ 092 43 51 08; www.riservazingaro.it; adult €3, child 8-14 €2, under 8 or 65+ free; ⊙ 7am-7.30pm Apr-Sep, 8am-4pm Oct-Mar) was established in 1981 as Sicily's first nature preserve. It has become the star attraction on the gulf, drawing an ever-growing number of nature-lovers and outdoors enthusiasts, both Italian and foreign.

Zingaro's wild coastline is a haven for the rare Bonelli eagle, along with 40 other bird species and 700 plant varieties, some unique to this stretch of coast. Mediterranean flora dusts the hillsides with wild carob and bright yellow euphorbia, and hidden coves provide excellent swimming spots.

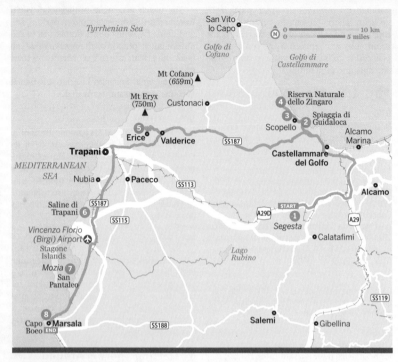

Driving Tour
Best of the West

START SEGESTA
END MARSALA
LENGTH 109KM; ONE TO THREE DAYS

This tour weaves together two ancient archaeological sites, a coastal nature reserve, a medieval hilltop town, and one of Sicily's prime wine-growing regions. While the route can be driven as a one-day rental-car loop (the start point is only 30 minutes from either Palermo or Trapani airport), it's more rewarding to spread the journey over two or three days.

Start at ❶ **Segesta** (p88), just off the A29D autostrada. One of Sicily's most evocative ancient sites, Segesta consists of a perfectly preserved, hauntingly beautiful Doric temple at the edge of a precipitous gorge, and a hilltop amphitheatre with views clear out to the Mediterranean.

From here, meander north to the dazzling blue-green waters of ❷ **Spiaggia di Guidaloca**. Stop for a dip here, or continue north to ❸ **Scopello**, where you can swim in the shadow of some supremely photogenic

faraglioni (rock spires). Alternatively, take a day hike into the ❹ **Riserva Naturale dello Zingaro** (p89), Sicily's oldest nature reserve, just 2km further north.

Double back to the SS187, which winds lazily through vineyards before climbing a dizzying set of switchbacks to ❺ **Erice**. Perched high above a fairy-tale coastal landscape, this hilltop has been prized by every civilisation that's passed through, from the Elymians to the Normans to the day-trippers who come now to sample its fabulous views and addictive sweets.

Descend next to the ❻ **Saline di Trapani**, a mirror-like landscape of salt pools and windmills that has been a centre for salt production since ancient times. From here take a short boat ride to the island of ❼ **Mozia** (p103), home to one of Europe's finest Phoenician archaeological sites.

Back on the 'mainland', it's a short jaunt down to ❽ **Marsala**, capital of one of Sicily's great wine-producing regions. Tour the marsala cellars at Florio, then settle in for aperitifs and dinner among the glimmering marble-paved streets of the historic centre.

Cetaria Diving Centre (☏092 454 11 77; www.cetaria.com; Via Marco Polo 3) in Scopello organises guided dives in the waters off the nature reserve between April and October, visiting underwater caves and two shipwrecks; it also offers boat excursions with snorkelling.

The main entrance to the park is 2km from Scopello. The 7km walk up the coast between the Scopello and San Vito Lo Capo entrances will take about two hours each way, not counting stops. The route follows a clearly marked track, passing several fine beaches along the way. Note that the San Vito entrance is 10km from the town of San Vito Lo Capo and there is no public transport, so backtracking to Scopello is the most practical option for hikers. There are also several trails inland, which are detailed on the free maps available at the information offices at the park's two entrances. You can also download these from the park website.

Spread out along the coastal trail are four museums and a visitor centre administered by park staff (all with the same hours as the park itself). Starting from the north, these include the Museo delle Attività Marinare, housed in a former tuna-processing plant, with exhibits ranging from photos of local fishermen to treatises on the importance of tuna to the ancient Greeks; Museo della Cultura Contadina, documenting the farming traditions of the Zingaro region; Museo della Manna, explaining how sap from local ash trees is processed into the ancient delicacy known as manna; Centro di Visitanti, the park's main visitor centre; and Museo Naturalistico, featuring displays on the Zingaro's flora and fauna.

Various organisations around the park organise guided walks – see the park's visitor centre for a list.

San Vito Lo Capo

POP 4407

Occupying the tip of Capo San Vito is the seaside town of San Vito Lo Capo, full of beachcombers and sun worshippers in summer but akin to a graveyard in winter.

◉ Sights & Activities

San Vito is renowned for its crescent-shaped sandy beach, where limpid turquoise and ultramarine waters are juxtaposed against the dramatic mountain backdrop of Monte Monaco.

The town's other noteworthy sight is the fortress-like 13th-century Chiesa di San Vito, about halfway down Via Savoia.

Excellent local hiking opportunities include the 3km ascent of Monte Monaco (about 2½ hours round trip; look for the trailhead just southeast of San Vito) and the splendid coastal trails of Riserva Naturale dello Zingaro, whose northern entrance lies about 10km southeast of San Vito. San Vito has also blossomed as a climbing destination in recent years, with a variety of challenging crags just outside town and an autumn climbing festival drawing enthusiasts from throughout the Mediterranean.

✦ Festivals & Events

Cous Cous Fest   FOOD
(www.couscousfest.it) San Vito is famous for its fish couscous, which is celebrated annually at this six-day September event. The multicultural festivities involve musicians and chefs from around the world, with a couscous cook-off (Italy against teams from other countries), free World Music concerts, and couscous workshops given by chefs from San Vito, Trapani and North Africa.

San Vito Climbing Festival   OUTDOORS
(www.sanvitoclimbingfestival.it/eng) Launched in 2009, this four-day, mid-October festival bills itself as the Mediterranean's biggest and most exciting multisports event. Its traditional focus on climbing has recently expanded to include kayaking, mountain biking, trail running in the nearby Riserva dello Zingaro, and an outdoor adventure-film festival.

✗ Eating

★Syráh   MODERN SICILIAN €€
(☏0923 97 20 28; Via Savoia 5; meals €25-40; ⊙Tue-Sun, closed Nov) Offering prime people-watching a few steps from the beach in San Vito's pedestrianised restaurant row, this relative newcomer shows off chef Vito Cipponeri's creative twists on classic Sicilian ingredients. Audacious appetisers (mixed raw fish with Modica chocolate and lemon marmalade) share the menu with couscous and other delicious mains such as seafood ravioli with shrimp, artichokes and tuna roe.

Al Ritrovo   SICILIAN €€
(☏0923 97 56 56; www.alritrovo.it; Viale Cristoforo Colombo 314; meals €25-32; ⊙closed 2 weeks in both Nov & Jan) Acclaimed by the international Slow Food organisation, this roadside

eatery 8km south of San Vito features cous-cous prominently on the menu. However, there are also plenty of seafood and meat alternatives, including the house speciality *gran frittura con pescato del golfo* (mixed fried seafood), all complemented by an excellent wine list. There are also 13 rooms with modern decor (€50 to €97 per person with half-board).

Pocho   SEAFOOD €€
(☑ 0923 97 25 25; www.pocho.it; fixed-price meals €38; ☺ lunch Sun & dinner Wed-Mon, closed Oct-Mar) Dinner is as much a feast for the eyes as for the palate at this hotel restaurant overlooking dramatic Isulidda beach, 2km south of San Vito. In warm weather, guests are seated on a terrace with panoramic views of the Golfo di Cofano. The menu, which changes daily, leans heavily towards seafood-based local specialities such as fish couscous.

The adjacent hotel (per person with breakfast €55 to €75, with half board €75 to €95) has 12 comfortable rooms and an impressive pool terrace.

Tha'am   TUNISIAN, SICILIAN €€
(☑ 0923 97 28 36; www.sanvitoweb.com/thaam; Via Duca degli Abruzzi 32; meals €30-40; ☺ Easter-Oct) A North African theme is evident in both menu and decor at this popular restaurant, which dishes up fish and chicken cous-cous beneath tented canopies in the heart of San Vito town. It also offers attractively decorated rooms (doubles €55 to €120).

❶ Getting There & Away

BUS

Buses arrive at/depart from Via Piersanti Mattarella, just near the beach and parallel to Via Savoia – look for street signs marking the stops. AST services travel between San Vito Lo Capo and Trapani (€4.40, 1½ hours, seven daily Monday to Saturday) and Autoservizi Russo travels to/from Palermo's train station and Piazza Politeama (€8.90, 2½ to three hours, two Monday to Saturday, one Sunday, more in summer).

TRAPANI

POP 69,183

Hugging the harbour where Peter of Aragon landed in 1282 to begin the Spanish occupation of Sicily, the sickle-shaped spit of land occupied by Trapani's Old Town once sat at the heart of a powerful trading network that stretched from Carthage to Venice. Traditionally the town thrived on coral and tuna fishing, with some salt and wine production. Over the past century, there has been much construction here – most of it unattractive – and it is often alleged that this is the result of healthy injections of Mafia-laundered money into the local economy. The busy port is the main embarkation point for the Egadi archipelago and the remote Moorish island of Pantelleria; ferries to Tunisia also leave from here.

❂ Sights & Activities

Although the narrow network of streets in Trapani's historic centre is Moorish, the city takes most of its character from the fabulous 18th-century baroque of the Spanish period. A catalogue of examples can be found down pedestrianised Via Garibaldi, most notably the **Palazzo Riccio di Morana** and **Palazzo Fardelle Fontana**. The best time to walk down here is in the early evening, when the *passeggiata* (evening stroll) is in full swing.

Another busy place during *passeggiata* is Corso Vittorio Emanuele, which is punctuated by the huge **Cattedrale di San Lorenzo** (☺8am-4pm), with its baroque facade. At the east end of the *corso* is another baroque concoction, the **Palazzo Senatorio** (cnr Corso Vittorio Emanuele & Via Torrearsa).

Chiesa del Purgatorio   CHURCH
(☑ 0923 56 28 82; Via San Francesco d'Assisi; voluntary donation requested; ☺ 7.30am-noon & 4-7pm Mon-Sat, 10am-noon & 4-7pm Sun) Just off the *corso* in the heart of the city, this church

Trapani

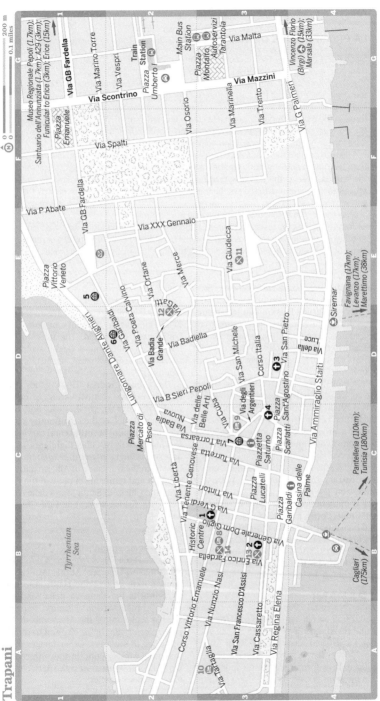

Tyrrhenian Sea

Museo Regionale Pepoli (1.7km);
Santuario dell'Annunziata (1.7km); A29 (3km);
Funicular to Erice (3km); Erice (15km)

Vincenzo Florio (Birgi) (15km);
Marsala (33km)

Favignana (17km);
Levanzo (17km);
Marettimo (38km)

Pantelleria (110km);
Tunisia (180km)

Cagliari
(175km)

Via GB Fardella
Via Marino Torre
Via Vespri
Via Scontrino
Piazza
Emanuele
Via Spalti
Via P Abate
Via GB Fardella
Via XXX Gennaio
Piazza
Vittorio
Veneto
Via Ortane
Via Merce
Via Badiella
Via Giudecca
Via Badia Grande
Via Poeta Calvino
Lungomare Dante Alighieri
Piazza
Garibaldi
Piazza
Mercato di
Pesce
Via Libertà
Via Tenente Genovese
Via G Verdi
Via Turretta
Via Tintori
Via B Sieri Pepoli
Via delle Belle Arti
Via Badia Nuova
Via Cuba
Via degli Argentieri
Via San Michele
Via Torrearsa
Piazzetta Saturno
Piazza Lucatelli
Piazza Scarlatti
Piazza Sant'Agostino
Corso Italia
Via San Pietro
Via della Luce
Via Ammiraglio Staiti
Piazza Garibaldi
Casina delle Palme
Corso Vittorio Emanuele
Via Nunzio Nasi
Via San Francesco D'Assisi
Via Cassaretto
Via Regina Elena
Via Tartaglia
Via Enrico Fardella
Via Generale Dom Giglio
Historic Centre
Train Station
Main Bus Station
Piazza Umberto I
Piazza Montalto
Autoservizi Tarantola
Via Malta
Via Mazzini
Via Osorio
Via Marinella
Via Trento
Via G Palmeri
Siremar

200 m
0.1 miles

LA PROCESSIONE DEI MISTERI

Since the 18th century, the citizens of Trapani – represented by 20 traditional *maestranze*, or guilds – have begun a four-day celebration of the Passion of Christ on the Tuesday before Easter Sunday by parading a remarkable, life-sized wooden statue of the Virgin Mary through the town's streets. Over the course of the next three days, nightly processions of the remaining *Misteri* (life-sized wooden statues) make their way through the old quarter and port to a specially erected chapel in Piazza Lucatelli, where the icons are stored overnight. Each procession is accompanied by crowds of locals and a Trapanese band, which plays dirges to the slow, steady beat of a drum.

The high point of the celebration is on Friday afternoon, when the 20 guilds emerge from the Chiesa del Purgatorio and descend the steps of the church, carrying each of the statues, to begin the 1km-long procession up to Via Giovanni Battista Fardella; the procession then returns to the church the following morning. The massive crowds that gather to witness the slow march often reach a peak of delirious fervour that is matched only by that of the Semana Santa parades in Seville, Spain.

To witness the procession, you'll need to book your accommodation well in advance. At other times, the figures are on display in the Chiesa del Purgatorio (p92). For more information, check out www.processionemisteritp.it (in Italian, Spanish and French only).

houses the impressive 18th-century *Misteri*, 20 life-sized wooden effigies depicting the story of Christ's Passion that take centre stage during the city's dramatic Easter Week processions every year. Explanatory panels in English, Italian, French and German help visitors to understand the story behind each figure.

Some of the statues are originals; others are copies of statues that were destroyed by WWII Allied bombings or irreparably damaged after being dropped by their bearers during a procession (the statues are heavy and unwieldy, and mishaps sometimes occur).

Each statue was commissioned and is now carried by members of a particular profession. For example, *Jesus Before Herod* was commissioned by the Millers and Bakers Guild; *Jesus Entombed*, by the Pasta-Makers Guild; and *The Whipping,* by the Bricklayers and Stonemasons Guild. One of the figures, *The Ascent of Calvary,* isn't claimed by a particular guild but is instead accompanied by the Trapanese people at large.

Museo Nazionale Pepoli　　　MUSEUM
(☑0923 55 32 69; Via Conte Pepoli 200; adult €6, EU citizen under 18 or 65+ free, EU citizen 18-25yr €3; ☉9am-1.30pm & 2.30-7.30pm Tue-Sat, 9am-12.30pm Sun; tours hourly 9am-noon & 2.30-6.30pm) In a former Carmelite monastery, this museum houses the collection of Conte Pepoli, who devoted his life to salvaging Trapani's local arts and crafts, most notably the garish coral carvings – once all the rage in Europe before Trapani's offshore coral banks were decimated. The museum also has a good collection of Gagini sculptures, silverwork, archaeological artefacts and religious art.

Don't miss Andrea Tipa's gaudy 18th-century *presepe* (Nativity scene or crèche) made of alabaster, coral, shells and other marine material, or the significantly less ornate but far more beautiful coral carvings by Fra' Matteo Bavera. Other highlights include an extraordinary *cassetta reliquaria* (relic box) from the workshop of Alberto and Andrea Tipa and remnants of painted tile floors from the Chiesa di Santa Maria delle Grazie (featuring fishing scenes) and the Chiesa di Santa Lucia (with scenes of Trapani's city centre).

Santuario dell'Annunziata　　　CHURCH
(Via Conte Pepoli 179; ☉7am-noon & 4-7pm Mon-Sat, 7am-1pm & 4-7pm Sun) At this 14th-century church, 4km east of the centre, the main attraction is the Cappella della Madonna, which contains Nino Pisano's venerated marble sculpture of the *Madonna di Trapani,* patron saint of the city and traditional protector of seafarers. Other images of the Madonna can be found in the 16th-century Cappella dei Marinai and the 15th-century Cappella dei Pescatori.

Chiesa di Santa Maria del Gesù
CHURCH

(Via San Pietro; ☉ 8am-1pm) This Catalan-Gothic church in the historic centre houses the exquisite *Madonna degli Angeli* (Madonna of the Angels), a glazed terracotta statue by Andrea della Robbia.

Chiesa di Sant'Agostino
CHURCH

(Piazza Sant'Agostino; ☉ 8am-1pm) The austerity of this 14th-century church near the port is relieved by its fine Gothic rose window and portal.

✕ Eating

Trapani's unique position on the sea route to Tunisia has made couscous (or *cuscus*, as it is sometimes spelled here) something of a speciality, particularly when served *alla trapanese* (in a soup of fish, garlic, chilli, tomatoes, saffron, cinnamon and nutmeg). Another irresistible staple is *pesto alla trapanese* (pesto made from fresh tomatoes, basil, garlic and almonds), eaten with *busiate,* a small hand-twirled pasta.

La Rinascente
PASTRIES & CAKES €

(☑ 0923 2 37 67; Via Gatti 3; cannoli €1.80; ☉ 9am-1pm & 3-7pm, closed Sun afternoon & Wed) When you enter this bakery through the side door, you'll feel like you've barged into someone's kitchen – and you have! Thankfully, owner Giovanni Costadura's broad smile will quickly put you at ease, coupled with some of the best *cannoli* on the planet, which you can watch being created on the spot.

★ Al Solito Posto
SICILIAN €€

(☑ 0923 2 45 45; www.trattoria-alsolitoposto.com; Via Orlandini 30; meals €20-35; ☉ closed Sun & 15-31 Aug) A 15-minute walk east of the centre, this wildly popular trattoria is a well-deserved wearer of the Slow Food badge. From superb *primi* (try the trademark *busiate con pesto alla trapanese*) to super-fresh seafood *secondi* (don't miss the local tuna in May and June) to the creamy-crunchy homemade *cannoli*, everything is top-notch. It's wise to book in advance.

★ Osteria La Bettolaccia
SICILIAN €€

(☑ 0923 2 16 95; www.labettolaccia.it; Via Enrico Fardella 25; meals €30-45; ☉ closed Sat & Sun lunch all year, plus Sun dinner Nov-Easter) An unwaveringly authentic, Slow Food favourite, this centrally located eatery just two blocks from the ferry terminal is the perfect place to try *cous cous con zuppa di mare* (couscous with mixed seafood in a spicy fish sauce, with tomatoes, garlic and parsley). In response to its great popularity, the dining room was expanded in 2013, but it's still wise to book ahead.

Tavernetta Ai Lumi
SICILIAN €€

(☑ 0923 87 24 18; www.ailumi.it; Corso Vittorio Emanuele 73-77; meals €30-40; ☉ closed Tue Oct-May) Converted from an 18th-century stable block, this tavern is rustic to the core. Exposed brickwork, heavy wooden furniture and huge arches lend the dining room great character, while the outside terrace, in the heart of historic Trapani, is delightful on summer evenings. The menu features plenty of fresh seafood along with superbly prepared Trapanese classics.

Cantina Siciliana
SICILIAN €€

(☑ 0923 2 86 73; www.cantinasiciliana.it; Via Giudecca 36; meals €20-30; ☉ lunch & dinner) The reasonably priced regional specialities here are enticing, as are the pretty blue-tiled front rooms. Service can range from lacklustre to borderline rude, as owner Pino sometimes regales his Italian friends to the exclusion of other guests. Still, it's one of Trapani's better-regarded eateries and worth a visit if you're willing to focus on the food.

ℹ Information

EMERGENCIES

Hospital (Ospedale Sant'Antonio Abate; ☑ 0923 80 94 50; Via Cosenza; ☉ 24hr)

Police Station (☑ 0923 59 81 11; Piazza Vittoria Veneto)

TOURIST INFORMATION

Tourist Office (☑ 0923 54 45 33; point@stradadelvinoericedoc.it; Piazzetta Saturno; ☉ 9am-1pm & 4-7pm Mon-Sat) Trapani's tourist office offers city maps, bike sightseeing tours, bike rental (€8 per day), tour guides and information about wineries along the Strada del Vino Erice DOC. The subsidiary **Casina delle Palme** (☉ 9am-1pm & 4-7pm Mon-Sat) branch is in Piazza Garibaldi, opposite the ferry terminal.

ℹ Getting There & Around

TO/FROM THE AIRPORT

Airport

Sicily's third-busiest airport, **Vincenzo Florio airport** (TPS; Birgi Airport; www.airgest.it), is 15km south of Trapani at Birgi and is commonly known as Birgi. **Ryanair** (www.ryanair.com) serves three dozen destinations throughout Italy and Europe, including Brussels, London, Manchester, Rome and Stockholm. Other airlines

STRADA DEL VINO E DEI SAPORI ERICE DOC

Representing more than a dozen local wine producers, the **Associazione Strada del Vino e dei Sapori Erice DOC** (☎ 0923 81 17 00; www.stradadelvinoericedoc.it) celebrates the Erice DOC (Denominazione di Origine Controllata; Controlled Origin Denomination) wine that is produced in the province of Trapani.

The Erice DOC appellation recognises several indigenous grape varieties from the Zregion, including Catarratto, Nero d'Avola, Grillo, Insolia, Frappato, Perricone and Zibibbo. These grapes owe their distinctive flavour to the fact that they're grown in vineyards that lie between 250m and 500m in altitude, but are also located close to the sea.

The Strada del Vino association offers customisable four-day wine tours, as well as free downloadable itineraries that feature local wineries alongside the area's other cultural attractions. As you drive around western Sicily, you'll see plenty of Erice DOC wine route signs, but bear in mind that it's not always the easiest route to follow. Signposts are intermittent and the number of wineries regularly open to the public is limited – **Fazio** (www.faziowines.it) and **Caruso & Minini** (www.carusoeminini.it) are among those that dependably offer guided tours and tasting.

serving domestic Italian destinations from Birgi include **Alitalia** (www.alitalia.com), **Air One** (flyairone.com) and **Darwin** (www.darwinairline.com), which fly to Rome, Milan and Pantelleria respectively.

Bus

From a curbside bus stop just outside the arrivals hall, **AST** (Azienda Siciliana Trasporti; www.aziendasicilianatrasporti.it) runs buses (€4.70, 20 minutes) to Trapani's port and main bus station on Piazza Montalto approximately every hour from 8.30am to 12.30am, and also offers regular service to Mazara del Vallo (€3.80, three daily). There are also direct buses from Birgi airport to Marsala (45 minutes) operated by AST (€2.50, four daily) and Salemi (€4.70, six to eight daily). **Salemi** (☎ 0923 98 11 20; www.autoservizisalemi.it) teams up with **Terravision** (☎ 0923 48 23 71; www.terravision.eu) to provide direct bus service to Palermo's Piazza Politeama and train station (€10.60, 1¾ to two hours, six to eight daily); buy tickets online or from Terravision's office directly adjacent to the rental-car counters in Birgi's arrivals hall.

Taxi

A taxi between Birgi and Trapani costs €30 to €35.

BOAT

Trapani's **ferry terminal** (☎ 0923 54 54 11) is opposite Piazza Garibaldi. Both **Siremar** (☎ 0923 54 54 55; www.siremar.it; Via Ammiraglio Staiti) and **Traghetti delle Isole** (www.traghettidelleisole.it) operate car ferries to the Egadi Islands of Favignana (€8.20, one to 1½ hours, five to six daily), Levanzo (€8.20, one to 1½ hours, five to six daily) and Marettimo (€13.10, three hours, one to two daily), as well as to Pantelleria (€34, 5¾ to six hours, two daily June to September, one to two daily the rest of the year). **Grimaldi Lines** (www.grimaldi-ferries.

com) runs a Thursday morning service to Tunis in Tunisia (deck/cabin from €60/85, 8½ hours). **Tirrenia** (☎ 0923 03 19 11; www.tirrenia.it) runs a Sunday evening service to Cagliari on Sardinia (deck/cabin from €40/160, 12 hours).

For hydrofoils you will need to head east a few blocks down Via Ammiraglio Staiti. Both Siremar and **Ustica Lines** (☎ 0923 87 38 13; www.ustica-lines.it; Via Ammiraglio Staiti) run regular hydrofoils to Favignana (€9.80, 15 to 40 minutes, nine daily each company), Levanzo (€9.80, 15 to 40 minutes, eight to nine daily each company) and Marettimo (€17.30, one to 1½ hours, one to three daily each company). Ustica Lines also operates summer-only, Saturday-morning hydrofoils to Ustica (€28, 2½ hours) and Naples (€94, seven hours). Get tickets at the **hydrofoil terminal**. A surcharge of €1.50 to €5 is levied on all Ustica and Siremar tickets booked in advance via the website or an agent.

BUS

All intercity buses arrive and depart from the **main bus station** (☎ 0923 2 00 66; Piazza Montalto). Tickets can be bought from the bar in the station building. AST (p96) serves Erice (€2.80, 40 minutes to one hour, five daily Monday to Saturday, three Sunday), San Vito Lo Capo (€4.40, 1½ hours, eight daily Monday to Saturday), Marsala (€3.40, one to 1¼ hours, four Monday to Saturday) and Mazara del Vallo (€5:10, 1¾ hours, three Monday to Saturday). **Autoservizi Tarantola** (☎ 0924 3 10 20) operates a service to Segesta (€6.20 round trip, 35 minutes each way, four to five daily) and **Lumia** (☎ 0923 2 17 54; www.autolineelumia.it) operates services to Agrigento (€11.80, 2¾ to 3½ hours, three daily Monday to Saturday, one on Sunday). **Segesta** (☎ 0923 2 84 04; www.segesta.it) runs express buses connecting Trapani with Palermo (€9, two to 2¼ hours, at least every hour between 5.30am and 8pm). Note that all services decrease dramatically on Sundays, as well as on public holidays and from October to May.

PARKING

There are plenty of parking spaces at the port and near the train station. Purchase tickets from the machines on the street (prices range from €0.50 to €0.80 per hour, with rates increasing as you get closer to the city centre).

PUBLIC TRANSPORT

Tickets for local ATM buses – valid for 90 minutes – cost €1 at *tabacchi* (tobacco shops) or €1.20 if purchased on board the bus. The Trapani Welcome Card (€12), available at the tourist information office and some hotels, covers one return trip on the Erice funicular and one three-day local bus pass.

TRAIN

From Trapani's train station, 1km east of the centre on Piazza Umberto, trains run to Palermo (€8, 2½ hours, five daily), Marsala (€3.45, 30 minutes, 10 daily) and Mazara del Vallo (€4.65, 50 minutes, 14 daily).

AROUND TRAPANI

There's not a lot in Trapani itself to keep tourists occupied, but the city has a good range of hotels and restaurants, making it a convenient base for those keen to explore the surrounding region. A trip to the medieval eyrie of Erice will often end up being a holiday highlight, as will an itinerary built around

sampling Trapanese food and wine, which is among the most impressive on the island.

Erice

POP 27,970 / ELEV 751M

Erice watches over the port of Trapani from the legendary mountain of Eryx, situated a giddy 750m above sea level. It's a mesmerising walled medieval town with stern-looking forts and churches, and its mountain charm is enhanced by the unpredictable weather that can take you from sunny afternoon to foggy evening in the space of a few minutes.

Erice

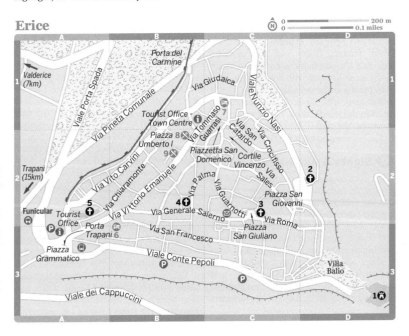

MARIA GRAMMATICO

This **pasticceria** (☑ 0923 86 93 90; www.mariagrammatico.it; Via Vittorio Emanuele 14; ☺ 9am-10pm May, Jun & Sep, to 1am Jul & Aug, to 7pm Oct-Apr) is owned and run by the delightful Maria Grammatico, Sicily's most famous pastry chef and the subject of Mary Taylor Simeti's book *Bitter Almonds*.

In the early 1950s, Maria's father died suddenly of a heart attack. Her impoverished mother, pregnant with a sixth child, decided to send Maria, aged 11, and her younger sister to the cloistered San Carlo orphanage in Erice to learn the art of pastry-making from the nuns. There, the children toiled in brutally hard conditions – beating sugar mixtures for six hours at a time, rising before dawn to prime the ovens, shelling kilos of almonds and surviving on an unrelenting diet of meatless pasta and vegetable gruel. At 22, Maria left the orphanage after having a nervous breakdown and started making sweets and pastries to survive. The rest, as they say, is history.

The world-famous *pasticceria*, with its shady courtyard out back, and the associated **Caffè Maria** (www.caffe-maria-erice.it; Via Vittorio Emanuele 4; ☺ 8.30am-9pm Oct-May, till midnight Jun-Sep), with its panoramic upstairs terrace, are good places to take a break as you wander around Erice. At either place you can sample Sicilian treats such as *cannoli* filled with fresh ricotta; green *cassata* cakes made of almonds, sugar, vanilla, buttermilk curd and candied fruit; perfectly formed marzipan fruits; lemon-flavoured *cuscinetti* (small fried pastries); and *buccellati* (hard, baked cookies) twisted around fig, cinnamon and clove comfit. At Easter, the shop is filled with super-cute almond-citron baby lambs that are made to celebrate Erice's *I Misteri* celebration. Be warned that the produce here uses more sugar than is usual – your dentist would certainly not approve!

The town has sweeping views of the valley beneath it and the sea, and is home to Sicily's most famous cake shop, Maria Grammatico.

Erice has a notorious history as a centre for the cult of Venus (Astarte to the Phoenicians and Aphrodite to the Greeks). The mysterious Elymians claimed descent from Venus' famous Trojan son, Aeneas, who mentions the sanctuary as a holy landmark in the *Aeneid*. Inside the holy temple, acolytes practised the peculiar ritual of sacred prostitution, with the prostitutes accommodated in the temple itself. Despite countless invasions, the sacred site long remained inviolate – there's no need to guess why!

◉ Sights & Activities

Virgil once compared Eryx to Mt Athos for its altitude and spiritual pre-eminence. Not that the town resembles a sanctuary today – temples and convents have given way to carpet shops selling the town's famous *frazzate* (bright rugs made from colourful rags) and innumerable souvenir stalls. Still, Erice is about wall-hugging alleys, votive niches and secret courtyards, all of which are best appreciated in the evenings and early mornings after the battalions of day-trippers leave.

Erice Monuments Circuit CHURCH
(admission €5; ☺ 10am-6pm Apr-Jun & Oct, 10am-8pm Jul & Aug, 10am-7pm Sep, 10am-12.30pm Nov-Feb, 10am-4pm Mar) A single ticket grants admission to the town's five major ecclesiastical attractions: the **Campanile** and **Treasury** at the Duomo, the wood sculptures at **San Martino**, the Gruppa Misteri (Good Friday group sculptures) at **San Giuliano** and the marble sculptures at **San Giovanni**. Buy your ticket at any of the churches.

Of Erice's 60-odd churches, the **Duomo** is the most interesting. It was built in 1312 by order of a grateful Frederick III, who had sheltered in Erice during the Sicilian Vespers uprising (1282–1314). The church's interior was remodelled in the neo-Gothic style in 1865, but the 15th-century side chapels were conserved. Views from the top of the 28m-high Campanile, with its mullioned windows, are impressive.

Castello di Venere CASTLE
(www.comune.erice.tp.it/minisitocastello; Via Castello di Venere; adult €3, 8-14yr or 65+ €1.50, child under 8 free; ☺ 10am-6pm daily Apr-Oct, 10am-4pm Sat & holidays Nov-Mar) The Norman Castello di Venere was built in the 12th and 13th centuries over the Temple of Venus, which had long been a site of worship for the ancient Elymians. The views from up top, extending

to San Vito Lo Capo on one side and the Saline di Trapani on the other, are spectacular.

Eating

Caffè Maria offers a well-priced simple tourist menu comprising an antipasto, *primo* (first course), sweet, coffee and water for €13, which is worth considering as most of the town's restaurants serve mediocre food solely geared towards a tourist clientele.

ⓘ Orientation

All vehicles arrive in Piazza Grammatico, from where you enter the town through the Porta Trapani. The funicular station and the bus stop are also here. From the piazza, Corso Vittorio Emanuele, the town's steep main road, heads up to Piazza Umberto I, the central piazza. The other main road, which branches off Vittorio Emanuele, is Via Generale Salerno. This eventually brings you out at the castle.

ⓘ Information

EMERGENCIES

Police (Questura; ☑ 0923 55 50 00; Piazza Grammatico; ⊗ 24hr)

TOURIST INFORMATION

Tourist Office (☑ 0923 50 23 22; strerice@ regione.sicilia.it; Porta Trapani; ⊗ 10.30am-1.30pm & 3.30-5.30pm Tue-Sat, 10.30am-1.30pm Sun, 2.30-5.30pm Mon) Main booth adjacent to the Porta Trapani parking lot; subsidiary office in the town centre (☑ 0923 86 93 88; Via Tommaso Guarrasi 1; ⊗ 10.30am-1.30pm Tue-Sun).

ⓘ Getting There & Away

BUS

There is a regular AST bus service to/from Trapani (€2.80, 40 minutes to one hour, five daily Monday to Saturday, three Sunday). All buses arrive and depart from Porta Trapani.

FUNICULAR

The best way to travel between Erice and Trapani is on the **funicular** (Funivia; ☑ 0923 56 93 06; www.funiviaerice.it; one way/return €5.50/9; ⊗ 1-8pm Mon, 8.10am-8pm Tue-Fri, 10am-10pm Sat, 10am-8pm Sun). The funicular station in Erice is just below, and across the street from, Porta Trapani. To reach the funicular from Trapani, catch bus 21 or 23 from Via GB Fardella down to the end of Via Alessandro Manzoni, which is the point where Trapani ends and Erice begins. You can walk from downtown Trapani to the funicular station, but it takes around 45 minutes.

PARKING

Parking is available next to Porta Trapani and along Viale Conte Pepoli. There's a ticket machine adjacent to the main Porta Trapani lot.

EGADI ISLANDS

POP 4163

The Egadi Islands (Isole Egadi) are popular destinations for swimming, diving, eating and general relaxation. Their proximity to the mainland (only 20 minutes to an hour from Trapani or Marsala by hydrofoil) make them an appealing, hassle-free island getaway, either for a day trip or for a longer stay.

For centuries, the Egadi Islanders have lived from the sea, as the prehistoric cave paintings on Levanzo illustrate. Later, when the islands were a key Carthaginian stronghold, one of the most critical battles of the Punic Wars was fought in 241 BC at Cala Rossa (Red Cove), which earned its name from the amount of Carthaginian blood spilt. When the Arabs decided to take Sicily, they used the islands as a stepping-stone en route to their invasions, fortifying them heavily to prevent anyone else getting the same idea.

In the 17th century the islands were sold to Genovese bankers, who in turn sold them to the Florio family in 1874. The Florios established a branch of their lucrative tuna industry here, bringing great prosperity to the locals. Unfortunately, the waters around the islands have been terribly overfished, causing a dent in the local economy. The islands only became part of the Italian state in 1937.

ⓘ Getting There & Away

Both Siremar and Ustica Lines run hydrofoils from Trapani to Favignana (€10.30, 20 to 40 minutes), Levanzo (€10.30, 20 to 40 minutes) and Marettimo (€17.80, one to 1½ hours). Ustica Lines also offers year-round services from Marsala to Favignana (€10.30, 30 minutes), and summer-only service from Marsala to Marettimo (€17.80, 1¼ hours).

Both companies offer year-round inter-island services: from Favignana to Levanzo (€5.80, 10 minutes), Favignana to Marettimo (€10.40, 30 minutes) and Levanzo to Marettimo (€10.40, 50 minutes). In summertime, Ustica Lines also offers Saturday-only service from Favignana to Ustica (€28, two hours) and Naples (€90, 6½ hours).

LA MATTANZA

One of the Egadi Islands' most ancient traditions, the *mattanza* (ritual tuna slaughter) has come to a halt in recent years due to the the ever-decreasing number of tuna swimming into the local waters.

For centuries schools of bluefin tuna have used the waters around western Sicily as a mating ground. Locals can recall the golden days of the island's fishing industry, when it was not uncommon to catch giant breeding tuna of between 200kg and 300kg. Fish that size are rare these days and the annual catch is increasingly smaller due to the worldwide commercial overfishing of tuna. Climate change also appears to have disrupted the tuna's normal breeding and migration cycle in recent years.

Traditionally, the *mattanza* occurred in late May or early June. Fishermen would organise their boats and nets in a complex formation designed to channel the tuna into a series of enclosures, which culminated in the *camera della morte* (chamber of death). Once enough tuna were imprisoned, the fishermen closed in and the *mattanza* began. It was a bloody affair – with up to eight or more fishermen at a time sinking huge hooks into a tuna and dragging it aboard. Anyone who has seen Rossellini's classic film *Stromboli* will no doubt recall the *mattanza* scene, one of the most famous accounts of this ancient tradition.

The number of tuna caught by this method was relatively small and sustainable – the fact that the *mattanza* took place for around 900 years without overfishing is testament to this. Problems arose with the increase in commercial fishing in the 1960s: tuna were caught year-round, and deep waters were exploited using long-line fishing and indiscriminate means such as drift and gill nets. Anything that passed by was caught, and thus the oceans' fish resources were depleted.

According to some scientists, additional problems such as high legal fishing quotas and illegal fishing are causing 'irreversible' damage to bluefin tuna stock. Fishermen have largely lost their livelihoods; for several years, La Mattanza was reinvented as a tourist attraction, but even that was finally discontinued in 2007.

Favignana

The largest of the islands is butterfly-shaped Favignana, which is dominated by Monte Santa Caterina (287m) to the west. You can easily explore it on a bicycle, as the eastern half of the island is almost completely flat. Around the coast, deep gouges in the cliffs are reminders of tufa quarrying that occurred in the past; many of these have now been reclaimed by the crystal-clear waters and are atmospheric swimming spots.

◉ Sights & Activities

The first thing you'll see as you step off the boat is the Ex-Stabilimento Florio della Tonnara, the town's historic tuna factory. Vincenzo Florio Sr (1799–1886), a brilliant Palermitan businessman who had built an empire in the sulphur, shipping and Marsala industries, also invented a way of steam-cooking and preserving canned tuna that revolutionised the fish-packing industry and cemented the success of his family's business empire. This *tonnara* was one of many the Florios ran around Sicily and it operated until 1977.

Since 2010, the tuna factory has housed a museum (☎ 335 7957210; www.facebook.com/ex.favignana; Via Amendola) focused on the Egadi Islands' fishing industry, displaying tuna boats, nets and videos that feature local fishermen and women talking about their work in the seas around Favignana and in the cannery itself. Unfortunately at the time of research the museum had been closed indefinitely due to lack of funds from the Sicilian government.

Favignana town's other significant building, Palazzo Florio, was built in 1876 for Vincenzo's son Ignazio, who purchased the Egadis in 1874. It now houses the tourist office, among other things.

The best beaches are on the southern side of the island at Miramare or Lido Burrone, a long, graceful stretch of sand lapped by clear aquamarine waters and backed by nice views of Monte Santa Caterina. On the north side, the bays at Cala Rossa and Scalo Cavallo are also lovely swimming spots.

Eating

Not surprisingly, tuna is the thing to eat on the islands, served in a multitude of ways. There's a clutch of popular eateries at the port. The food at Albergo Egadi (p255) is also highly regarded.

La Bettola SEAFOOD €€
(☑ 0923 92 19 88; Via Nicotera 47; meals €24-30; ⊙ closed Wed Oct-May) Family-run and Slow Food–recognised, La Bettola serves well-prepared seafood dishes such as *zuppa di cozze* (mussel soup), *linguine con sarde* (linguine with sardines) and *tonno in agrodolce* (tuna in a sweet-and-sour sauce). You can also order Trapanese specialities including couscous and *busiate*. There's a limited list of local and regional wines to accompany your meal.

Camarillo Brillo MODERN SICILIAN €€
(☑ 329 7726127; www.camarillobrillo.it; Via Vittorio Emanuele 18; meals €30-35) With a youthful, energetic atmosphere that sets it apart from Favignana's more traditional restaurants, this classy, high-ceilinged *osteria* specialises in putting traditional Sicilian ingredients to new and sometimes surprising uses – for example, red shrimp with melon and local Trapani salt, or grilled octopus with sauteed potatoes and minted zucchini. Upon request they'll also prepare vegan-friendly fare.

ⓘ Information

EMERGENCIES
Ambulance (☑ 0923 92 12 83)
Police (Carabinieri; ☑ 0923 91 12 02; Via Simone Corleo)

TOURIST INFORMATION
Tourist Office (☑ 0923 92 54 43; www.welcometoegadi.it; ⊙ 8.30am-2pm & 3-7pm Mon-Sat, 8.30am-2pm Sun Apr-Oct) Helpful office on the ground floor of the elegant Palazzo Florio, one block from the hydrofoil dock. Supplies information on diving and boating operators, accommodation and excursions.

ⓘ Getting There & Around

BICYCLE & SCOOTER
This is the best way to get around Favignana, giving you access to all the little coves and beaches dotting the island. The port area is swarming with places offering bikes, scooters and motorbikes for hire. Bicycle hire in the high season costs approximately €10 per day; scooter hire €35 to €45. Prices are cut nearly in half during low season.

BUS
Tarantola runs orange buses (€1) to various points around the island. There are three different routes, all of which originate at Piazza Marina near the main port in Favignana town. Schedules are posted at Piazza Marina and at Favignana's tourist office.

Levanzo

There are two main reasons to visit Levanzo: to examine the prehistoric cave paintings at the Grotta del Genovese, and to spend some time swimming off the island's pebbly beaches.

◉ Sights & Activities

Grotta del Genovese CAVE
(☑ 339 7418800, 0923 92 40 32; www.grottadelgenovese.it; guided cave tour €10, incl transport 1-way/round trip €16/22.50; ⊙ tours 10.30am daily, extra tour 2.30pm or 3pm Jul & Aug) Between 6000 and 10,000 years old, the Upper Palaeolithic wall paintings and Neolithic incised drawings at the Genovese Cave were discovered in 1949 by Francesca Minellono, a painter from Florence who was holidaying on Levanzo. Mostly featuring animals, the later ones also include men and tuna. Visits to the grotto are by guided tour only, and reservations are required.

The all-inclusive tour takes two hours; transport is by boat if weather conditions are favourable – otherwise, it's by 4WD. You can also reach the grotto by foot from the port (1½ hours each way), or walk one way and take a jeep or boat the other way. Advance booking of the cave visit is imperative, regardless of how you get there.

Swimming SWIMMING
Three spots on the island offer great swimming. To get to **Faraglione**, walk 1km along the road west of town until you see a couple of rocks sticking out of the water just offshore. For something a little quieter, continue to **Capo Grosso**, on the northern side of the island, where there is also a lighthouse.

Alternatively, take a right out of town and walk along the dirt road. The road forks 300m past the first bend; take the rocky path down towards the sea and keep going until you get to **Cala Minnola**, a small landing bay with crystal-clear water where, outside the month of August, you can swim in peace and tranquillity.

MARETTIMO

The wildest, most westward and least developed of the Egadi Islands, Marettimo is a collection of green mountain peaks and whitewashed houses dipping into a little harbour packed with bobbing fishing boats. With the overfishing of tuna affecting fishermen's incomes, the villagers are increasingly focusing on the economic potential of tourism, and more accommodation options have cropped up in the last few years; however, this doesn't mean that you'll find Marettimo packed at any time of the year – indeed, the island still virtually shuts down in winter, and remains sleepier than its neighbours even in peak summer season.

There's only one road on the island, and the main mode of motorised transport is electric carts, making this a prime destination for walkers. Fanning out in all directions from the town centre, a well-marked network of trails leads quickly into unspoilt nature, climbing through fragrant pine forests to dramatic coastal lookouts, then descending again to remote beaches. At various points along the way, well-placed picnic benches invite hikers to take a shady break.

Three of the most popular trails are the hike north from town to the crumbling Norman castle perched on the lonely promontory of **Punta Troia**, the short climb west to **Case Romane**, where the remains of Roman houses share the stage with a spare, whitewashed Byzantine church, and the longer hike following the island's southwestern shores to the secluded beach at **Cala Nera**.

Marettimo is also a perfect place for relaxation and swimming – other good beaches include **Cala Sarda** and stunning **Cala Bianco**.

Ustica Lines (p96) and Siremar (p96) hydrofoils serve the island from Trapani, Levanzo and Favignana; Ustica Lines also has service from Marsala. See their websites for schedules and fares.

Just north of Marettimo's hydrofoil dock you'll find one of western Sicily's best family-run restaurants, **Il Veliero** (0923 92 32 74; Via Umberto 22; meals €30). Chef-owner Peppe Bevilacqua goes to the market daily, picking out the freshest catches. The resulting menu is a seafood-lover's fantasy, featuring superbly prepared Sicilian classics like *pasta con le sarde* and *frittura mista* (fried shrimp and calamari) alongside perfectly grilled seasonal fish.

✖ Eating

Ristorante Paradiso   SEAFOOD €€
(0923 92 40 80; www.albergoparadiso.eu; Via Lungomare 8; meals €30-45; ☺Apr-Oct) A family-run Slow Food favourite, Paradiso offers a charming terrace overlooking the port and a menu filled with seafood delicacies such as *spaghetti con i ricci* (spaghetti with sea urchins), *lasagne di mare* (seafood lasagne) and *calamari fritti* (fried calamari). The attached hotel also rents out simple rooms.

THE SOUTHWEST

This flat and often windswept corner of Sicily is now solidly on the tourist map, in part thanks to a surge in low-cost flights to nearby Birgi airport. The elegant town of Marsala, home to the island's famous fortified wine, is an ideal base for exploring the region. From here, destinations such as Saline di Trapani, the world-famous archaeological site at Selinunte and the multicultural fishing port of Mazara del Vallo are only a short trip away.

Saline di Trapani

Follow the SP21 coastal highway (the Via del Sale or Salt Road) between Trapani and Marsala and you'll soon find yourself in a flat and featureless landscape of *saline* (shallow pools), softly shimmering heaps of salt and small decommissioned *mulini* (windmills). The salt from these marshes is considered the best in Italy and has been big business since the 12th century; now, however, salt production has fallen massively and only a cottage industry remains, providing for Italy's more discerning dinner tables. The best time to travel here is in summer, when the sun turns the saltpans rosy pink and makes the salt heaps glint. In winter, the heaps are covered with tiles and plastic tarpaulins to keep out the rain and are nowhere near as picturesque.

Sights & Activities

The most attractive stretch of coast, where the saltpans glitter undisturbed by modern construction, is protected within the Riserva Naturale di Stagnone and the Riserva Naturale Saline di Trapani e Paceco (www.salineditrapani.it). These wetland preserves encompass the Stagnone Islands (Isole delle Stagnone) – one of which is home to the noted archaeological site of Mozia – as well as the long arm of Isola Lunga, which protects the shallow waters of the lagoon.

Mozia   ARCHAEOLOGICAL SITE
Located on the tiny island of San Pantaleo, ancient Mozia (also known as Motya or Mothia) was one of the Mediterranean's most important Phoenician settlements. Established in the 8th century BC and coveted for its strategic position, Mozia is today the world's best-preserved Phoenician site.

The entire island was bought by the ornithologist and amateur archaeologist Joseph Whitaker (1850–1936) in the early 20th century and bequeathed to the Joseph Whitaker Foundation by his daughter Delia on her death in 1971. Joseph, who was a member of an English family that gained great wealth from the Marsala trade, built a villa here and spent decades excavating the island and assembling a unique collection of Phoenician artefacts, many of which are now on display in the museum that bears his name.

The fields around the museum are strewn with ruins from the ancient Phoenician settlement. Visitors can wander at will around the island to explore these, following a network of trails punctuated with helpful maps and informational displays. Excavations include the ancient port and dry dock, where you can see the start of a Phoenician road – now approximately 1m underwater – that once linked San Pantaleo with the mainland. There's also a bar/cafe serving drinks and snacks.

Whitaker Museum   MUSEUM
(☑0923 71 25 98; adult/child €9/5; ☺9.30am-1.30pm & 2.30-6.30pm Mar-Sep) Housed in Joseph Whitaker's former villa on San Pantaleo island, this museum displays the amateur archaeologist's unique collection of Phoenician artefacts, assembled over decades. The museum's greatest treasure (on loan to the Getty Museum in Los Angeles at the time of research) is *Il Giovinetto di Mozia*, a marble statue of a young man in a pleated robe suggesting Carthaginian influences.

Museo Saline Ettore e Infersa   MUSEUM
(☑0923 73 30 03; www.salineettoreinfersa.com; Contrada Ettore Infersa 55; adult/student €6/2; ☺9.30am-sunset Apr-Oct, by appointment Nov-Mar) Housed in a beautifully restored old windmill opposite the Mozia boat dock (on the 'mainland' side of the channel), this small salt museum has displays about the history of salt production in the area, including a film in multiple languages. From 4pm to 6pm on Wednesday and Saturday afternoons in summer, you can see the windmill in action.

Ask at the reception about renting bikes (€10 per half-day) and canoes (€6 per hour, summer only).

Getting There & Away

To access Mozia, you'll need to take one of the boats operated by Mozia Line (☑0923 98 92 49; www.mozialine.com) from the landing point opposite the island. Boats make the short crossing every 20 minutes from 9.15am to 6.30pm, and the round trip costs €5 (€2.50 for children under 14).

Marsala

POP 80,145

Many know about its sweet dessert wines, but few people realise what a charmer the town of Marsala is. Though its streets are paved in gleaming marble, lined with stately baroque buildings and peppered with graceful piazzas, pleasures here are simple – a friendly *passeggiata* (evening stroll) most nights, plenty of aperitif options and family-friendly restaurants aplenty.

Marsala was founded by the Phoenicians who escaped from Mozia after it was defeated in 397 BC by an army led by Dionysius I of Syracuse. They settled here on Capo Lilibeo, calling their city Lilybaeum and fortifying it with 7m-thick walls that ensured it was the last Punic settlement to fall to the Romans. In AD 830 it was conquered by the Arabs, who gave it its current name Marsa Allah (Port of God).

Marsala

N 0 ____ 200 m
0 ____ 0.1 miles

Marsala

◉ Sights
1 Chiesa Madre C3
2 Complesso Monumentale San
   Pietro C3
3 Insula Romana B1
4 Museo Archeologico Baglio
   Anselmi A2
5 Museo degli Arazzi Fiammingi C3
6 Palazzo VII Aprile C3
7 Piazza Della Repubblica C3

⊟ Sleeping
8 Hotel Carmine B3
9 Il Profumo del Sale C3

⊗ Eating
10 Divino...Rosso B2
11 Il Gallo e l'Innamorata D4
12 San Lorenzo Osteria B3

⊖ Drinking & Nightlife
13 Enoteca Comunale B2

◉ Sights & Activities

**Museo Archeologico
Baglio Anselmi**   MUSEUM
(☑ 0923 95 25 35; Lungomare Boeo; adult €4, EU
citizen 18-25yr or 65+ €2; ⊙ 9am-8pm Tue-Sun,
9am-1.30pm Mon) Marsala's finest treasure
is the partially reconstructed remains of a
Carthaginian *liburna* (warship) sunk off
the Egadi Islands during the First Punic
War. Displayed alongside objects from its
cargo, the ship's bare bones provide the only
remaining physical evidence of the Phoenicians' seafaring superiority in the 3rd century BC, offering a glimpse of a civilisation
extinguished by the Romans.

Among the objects found on board the
ship and displayed here are ropes, cooking
pots, corks from amphorae, a brush, olive
stones, a sailor's wooden button and even a
stash of cannabis. In an adjacent room are
other regional archaeological artefacts including a marble statue known as *La venere*

di lilybaeum (The Venus of Lilybaeum) and some mosaics from the 3rd and 5th centuries AD.

In early 2013 the museum was expanded to include the adjacent Insula Romana, an archaeological site that encompasses the remains of a 3rd-century Roman villa and a splendidly preserved *Decumanus Maximus* (Roman ceremonial road) paved with giant stones.

Cantine Florio   WINERY
(☑0923 78 11 11; www.duca.it/cantineflorio; Via Vincenzo Florio 1; tours €10; ☺wine shop 9am-1pm & 3.30-6pm Mon-Fri, 9.30am-1pm Sat, English-language tours 3.30pm Mon-Fri & 10.30am Sat year-round, plus 11am Mon-Fri Apr-Oct) These venerable wine cellars just east of town open their doors to visitors to explain the Marsala-making process and the fascinating history of local viticulture. Afterwards visitors can sample the goods in Florio's spiffy new tasting room (tastes of two Marsalas and a moscato, accompanied by hors d'oeuvres, are included in the tour price). Take bus 16 from Piazza del Popolo.

Other producers in the same area include Pellegrino, Donnafugata, Rallo, Mavis and Intorcia.

Complesso Monumentale
San Pietro   MUSEUM
(☑0923 71 87 41; Via Ludovico Anselmi Correale; ☺9am-1pm & 4-8pm Tue-Sun) FREE Housed in a beautifully restored 15th-century convent, this arts centre is home to an intriguing complex of small museums. Most noteworthy is the upstairs space devoted to Giuseppe Garibaldi, who landed in Marsala on 11 May 1860 with his army of 1000 red-shirts in the first stage of their successful campaign to conquer the kingdom of the Two Sicilies.

The Garibaldi collection includes weapons, documents, uniforms and portraits but unfortunately lacks interpretive labels in English. Other museums include a small collection of local archaeological finds and a space devoted to Marsala's unique Easter Thursday procession. On the upper floor, close to the courtyard entrance, you'll find the newest addition to the complex, the Museo dei Pupi, which displays Marsala-designed puppets and their theatrical backdrops.

Piazza Della Repubblica   PIAZZA
Marsala's most elegant piazza is dominated by the imposing Chiesa Madre. Just across the way, on the eastern side of the square, is the arcaded Palazzo VII Aprile, formerly known as the Palazzo Senatorio (Senatorial Palace) and now the town hall.

Chiesa Madre   CHURCH
(www.chiesamadremarsala.it; Piazza della Repubblica; ☺7.30am-9pm) Divided into three aisles highlighted by tall columns, the cavernous interior of Marsala's 'mother church' contains a number of sculptures by the Gagini brothers. Although construction commenced in 1628, the church's facade wasn't completed until 1956 (courtesy of a cash donation by a returning emigrant).

THE SWEET SMELL OF SUCCESS

Fresh out of sherry country in southern Spain, John Woodhouse's 'sweet nose' knew a business opportunity when he smelled it. The English soap merchant swiftly based himself in Marsala aiming to market its wine to the seemingly insatiable sweet palate of 18th-century England, but had to grapple with one problem: how was he to get the wine to England without it going bad? He added a dash of pure alcohol and, *voilà*, Marsala's fortified wine was born.

The real success of the wine came when the British Navy used it as an alternative to port in order to supply the sailors' ration of one glass of wine per day. Lord Nelson placed a huge order in 1800, and soon other entrepreneurs wanted to get in on the action. Benjamin Ingham and his nephew, Joseph Whitaker, set up the first rival winery, exporting to the USA and Australia in 1806. The third big producer was canny Vincenzo Florio, who already owned the Egadi Islands and their lucrative tuna plants. All of the wineries were eventually bought by Cinzano in the 1920s, which merged them under the Florio label. In 1988, Cinzano sold the company to Illva Saronno, which now operates three labels: Florio, Duca di Salaparuta and Corvo.

For more information on Marsala and the companies that produce it today, see www.stradavinomarsala.it.

Museo degli Arazzi Fiammingi   MUSEUM
(☑ 0923 71 29 03; Via Giuseppe Garraffa 57; adult €4, EU citizen 18-25yr or 65+ €2; ⊗ 9.30am-1pm & 4-6pm Tue-Sat, 9.30am-12.30pm Sun) Tapestry fans should check out this tiny museum just behind Marsala's Chiesa Madre. The eight 16th-century Flemish tapestries on display were woven in Brussels for Spanish king Philip II.

🍴 Eating & Drinking

Divino...Rosso   PIZZERIA, SICILIAN €
(☑ 0923 71 17 70; www.divinorosso.it; Via XI Maggio; pizzas €6-8, meals €25-30; ⊗ 6pm-1am Tue-Sun) With outdoor tables on Marsala's main pedestrian thoroughfare, this lively restaurant and wine bar serves pizzas, more than 150 different wines and an extensive menu of local dishes.

⭐ San Lorenzo Osteria   SICILIAN €€
(SLO; ☑ 0923 71 25 93; Via Garraffa 60; meals €25-35; ⊗ closed Tue; 🐾) With roots as a wedding-catering business, this stylish eatery opened to universal acclaim in 2012. It's a class act all around – from the ever-changing menu of market-fresh seafood scrawled daily on the blackboard to the interior's sleek modern lines to the gorgeous presentation of the food. The stellar wine list features some local choices you won't find elsewhere.

Il Gallo e l'Innamorata   SICILIAN €€
(☑ 0923 195 44 46; www.osteriailgalloelinnamorata. com; Via Bilardello 18; meals €25-30; ⊗ closed Tue) Warm orange walls and arched stone doorways lend an artsy, convivial atmosphere to this Slow Food–acclaimed eatery. The à la carte menu is short and sweet, featuring a few well-chosen dishes each day, including the classic *scaloppine al Marsala* (veal cooked with Marsala wine and lemon).

Enoteca Comunale   WINE BAR
(Via XI Maggio 32; ⊗ 11am-1pm Tue-Sat, 6-11.45pm Tue-Sun) Sponsored by the local association of Marsala wine merchants, this atmospheric wine bar in the heart of the pedestrian zone has tables invitingly spread under the arcades of its interior courtyard. It's a good place to sample a variety of local vintages, starting at €3 per glass.

ℹ Information

EMERGENCIES

Ambulance (☑ 0923 95 14 10)
Police (Questura; ☑ 0923 92 43 71; Corso Antonio Gramsci; ⊗ 24hr)

TOURIST INFORMATION

Tourist Office (☑ 0923 99 33 38, 0923 71 40 97; ufficioturistico.proloco@comune.marsala. tp.it; Via XI Maggio 100; ⊗ 8.30am-1.30pm & 3-8pm Mon-Sat) Spacious office with comfy couches right off the main square; provides a wide range of maps and brochures.

ℹ Getting There & Away

BOAT

Ustica Lines (www.usticalines.it) operates services between Marsala and Favignana (€10.30, 30 minutes, five daily in summer, three daily in winter), with connections to the other Egadi Islands.

BUS

From Marsala's **bus terminal** at Piazza del Popolo (off Via Mazzini in the centre of town), **AST** (Azienda Siciliana Trasporti; www.aziendasicilianatrasporti.it) travels to/from Trapani (€3.40, one hour, four daily except Sunday) and Mazara del Vallo (€3.25, 25 to 45 minutes, three daily except Sunday). **Salemi** (☑ 0923 98 11 20; www. autoservizisalemi.it) also runs regular daily services to/from Palermo (€9.20, 2½ hours).

TRAIN

The best way to travel along this stretch of coast is by train. Regular services go to/from Trapani (€3.45, 30 minutes, 10 daily), Mazara del Vallo (€2.85, 15 to 30 minutes, 10 daily) and Palermo (€9.10, 3¼ to 3½ hours, five daily). You'll usually have to change at Alcamo, Trapani or Piraine for Palermo. To access the centre of town from the train station, walk straight down Via Roma, which meets Via XI Maggio at Piazza Matteotti.

Mazara Del Vallo

POP 50,017

Vaguely redolent of a North African kasbah (and still bearing the Casbah name), Mazara's historic quarter is a labyrinth of narrow streets, sprinkled with magnificent baroque and Norman-period buildings. It's small enough that you won't ever really get lost, and the dilapidated old buildings give it a rugged charm.

Mazara was one of the key cities of Saracen Sicily and the North African influence is still strongly felt here – the town is said to have one of the highest percentages of immigrants in Italy, with hundreds of people from Tunisia and Maghreb arriving annually to work on Mazara's fishing fleet.

In summer, Mazara is inundated with holidaymakers who head straight to Tonnarella beach, on the western side of the city.

THE SATYR THAT ROSE FROM THE SEA

The **Museo del Satiro** (☑ 0923 93 39 17; Piazza Plebiscito; adult €6, EU citizen 18-25yr €3, EU citizen under 18 or 65+ free; ☺9am-7pm) is the jewel in Mazara's crown. This memorable museum revolves around its central exhibit, a bronze statue known as the *Satiro danzante* (Dancing Satyr), hauled from the watery depths by local fishermen in the late 1990s. The sculpture depicts a bacchanalian satyr dancing wildly like a whirling dervish, arms outstretched, head flung back, the centrifugal force evident in his flowing hair.

The museum is located in the deconsecrated shell of the Chiesa di Sant'Egidio. On entering, make sure you watch the 25-minute video before looking at anything else. In Italian, with English subtitles, the film tells the story of a group of fishermen who were working their nets 40km off the shores of Tunisia in 1997 when they pulled up the bronze leg of a statue. Time elapsed and they continued to fish in the same area, wondering if they would ever find the rest of the statue. Extraordinarily, they did so the next year – a rare original casting from the Hellenistic era. Overcome by romanticism, the boat's captain tells the camera: 'Lying on the deck with its face turned to the sky, it looked like someone who'd clung on, waiting to be rescued'. What followed was a 4½-year period of painstaking restoration, during which time Mazara strenuously tussled with the powers in Rome to ensure the return of the satyr, which only came home in 2003.

And what a beauty. Originally, it would have been used in Dionysian processions – today it commands its own form of no-less-passionate worship here.

◉ Sights & Activities

Mazara's streets and alleys are decorated with colourful hand-painted tiles, a subtle touch that adds to the pleasure of randomly strolling through town.

Piazza della Repubblica   PIAZZA

Mazara's central piazza is an attractive space edged by elegant buildings, including the town's 11th-century **Cattedrale del San Salvatore** (admission free; ☺irregular), the elegant, two-storey **Seminario dei Chierici** (dating from 1710) and, on the opposite side of the square, the 18th-century **Seminario Vescovile**, with an impressive 11-arched portico.

The cathedral was completely rebuilt in the 17th century in the baroque style. Over the portal is a relief from the 16th century of Count Roger trampling a Saracen. Unfortunately, the 1970s office tower on the west side of the square is a visual affront of the highest order – how it managed to get a construction permit beggars belief.

La Casbah   HISTORIC QUARTER

At the northwest corner of the historic centre, this multicultural maze of narrow streets was once the heart of the Saracen city. The main thoroughfare was Via Bagno, which still has its *hammam* (public baths). Today, the area is run-down but interesting, in large part because it retains a strong Arab connection through the Tunisians who now live here.

Castle   RUIN

(Piazza Mokarta) Just in from the waterfront, the ragged remains of Count Roger's Norman Castle have definitely seen better days, but their forlorn ruination is wonderfully atmospheric at night (when they are floodlit).

Chiesa di Sant'Ignazio   CHURCH

Across from the Museo del Satiro, this early 18th-century church collapsed in the 1930s, but its roofless remains make a photogenic detour, with their circular colonnade of twin columns backed by a vine-draped stone wall.

✖ Eating

★ Eyem Zemen   TUNISIAN €

(☑ 347 3869921; Via Porta Palermo 36; meals €15; ☺closed Tue) For a little taste of Tunisia, try this delightful hole-in-the-wall in the heart of La Casbah, marked by a bilingual Italian-Arabic sign. Tunisian owner Fatima serves specialities from her homeland, including excellent cous cous and classic savoury pastries known as *bric*, filled with either tuna or shrimp. In warm weather, sit at tables on the little piazza outside.

La Bettola   SICILIAN €€

(☑ 0923 94 64 22; www.ristorantelabettola.it; Via Maccagnone 32; meals €30-44; ☺closed Wed) Mazara is Sicily's largest fishing centre, so it's not surprising that most restaurants here specialise in seafood. La Bettola is one of the very best. Over the past four decades, owner Pietro Sardo has established a reputation as one of Sicily's top chefs, creating sensational dishes in his immaculate kitchen. It's right around the corner from Mazara's train station.

ℹ Information

EMERGENCIES

Hospital (Ospedale Civico A Ajello; ☑ 0923 90 12 33; Via Salemi 175)

Police (☑ 0923 93 27 66; Via Carlo Alberto della Chiesa 10)

TOURIST INFORMATION

Tourist Information Point (☑ 0923 94 27 76; www.comune.mazaradelvallo.tp.it; Piazza Mokarta; ⊙ 10am-12.30pm Tue & Thu, 10am-12.30pm & 4-6pm Wed, Fri & Sat) Municipal government info centre, just off the *lungomare* (seafront promenade), next to the castle.

ℹ Getting There & Away

BUS

Mazara's bus station is next to the train station. **AST** (www.aziendasicilianatrasporti.it) travels to/from Marsala (€3, 25 to 45 minutes, three daily except Sunday) and Trapani (€5, 1¾ to 2¼ hours, three daily except Sunday). **Lumia** (www.autolineelumia.it) runs services between Mazara and Agrigento (€8.90, two to 2¼ hours, three daily Monday to Saturday, one on Sunday) and **Salemi** (www.autoservizisalemi.it) runs regular services to/from Palermo (€8.70, two hours).

TRAIN

Regular services go to/from Trapani (€4.65, 50 minutes, 10 daily), Marsala (€2.85, 15 to 30 minutes, 10 daily) and Palermo (€8.50, three to 3¼ hours, five daily). You'll need to change at Piraineto or Alcamo for most Palermo services.

Rocche di Cusa

Most of the buttery yellow stone used to construct the great temples of Selinunte was hewn at these ancient Greek quarries. The setting is charming – overgrown and wild, it's dotted with olive trees and wildflowers. Huge column drums forever awaiting transport to Selinunte are scattered around, and if you look carefully you will come across two carved columns ready for extraction. When removed, the columns would have

been transported to Selinunte across wooden logs by oxen or slaves.

At the time of research, the site had just started levying a €2 admission fee, though free admission was still being granted to visitors holding a ticket for the Selinunte ruins issued within the preceding three days.

To get here from Mazara del Vallo, take the SS115 to Campobello di Mazara, then follow the signs to the Rocche di Cusa (Cave di Tufo).

Selinunte

The ruins of Selinunte are some of the most impressive of the ancient Greek world, and the site is one of the most captivating in Sicily.

Selinos (as it was known to the Greeks) was once one of the richest and most powerful cities in the world, with over 100,000 inhabitants and an unrivalled temple-building program. The most westerly of the Greek colonies, it was established by a group of settlers from nearby Megara Hyblaea in 628 BC who had been attracted by its wonderful location atop a promontory between two major rivers (now silted up), the Modione and Cottone, the latter forming a secure natural harbour. The plains surrounding the site were overgrown with celery (*selinon* in Greek), which served as inspiration for the new colony's name.

Originally allied with Carthage, Selinunte switched allegiance after the Carthaginian defeat by Gelon of Syracuse at Himera in 480 BC. Under Syracusan protection it grew in power and prestige. The city's growth resulted in a litany of territorial disputes with its northern neighbour, Segesta, which ended abruptly in 409 BC when the latter called for Carthaginian help. Selinunte's former ally happily obliged and arrived to take revenge.

Troops commanded by Hannibal utterly destroyed the city after a nine-day siege, leaving only those who had taken shelter in the temples as survivors; they were spared not out of a sense of humanity but because of the fear that they might set fire to the temples and prevent their looting. In a famous retort to the Agrigentan ambassadors who sought to negotiate for the survivors' lives, Hannibal replied that as they hadn't been able to defend their freedom, they deserved to be slaves. One year later, Hermocrates of

Selunte

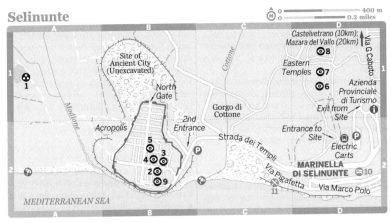

Syracuse took over the city and initiated its recovery. In 250 BC, with the Romans about to conquer the city, its citizens were relocated to Lilybaeum (Marsala), the Carthaginian capital in Sicily, but not before they destroyed as much as they could. What they left standing, mainly temples, was finished off by an earthquake in the Middle Ages.

The city was forgotten until the middle of the 16th century, when a Dominican monk identified its location. Excavations began in 1823, courtesy of two English archaeologists, William Harris and Samuel Angell, who uncovered the first metopes.

Sights & Activities

Selinunte's **ruins** (☑092 44 62 51; www. selinunte.net; adult €6, EU citizen 18-25yr €3, under 18 or 65+ free; ☉9am-6pm summer, 9am-4pm winter) are divided into the acropolis, the ancient city, the eastern temples and the Sanctuary of Malophoros. The archaeological site is spread out over a vast area dominated by the hill of Manuzza – the location of the ancient city proper – and deserves a visit of at least three hours to do it justice.

The ticket office and main parking lot are near the eastern temples, on the western edge of Marinella di Selinunte. There are **electric carts** (€3-12 depending on number of sites visited) that can help mobility-impaired visitors get around the site.

★**Acropolis** ARCHAEOLOGICAL SITE
(Strada dei Templi) The Acropolis, the heart of Selinunte's political and social life, occupies a slanted plateau overlooking the now-

Selinunte

silted-up Gorgo di Cottone. Huddled in the southeastern part are five temples (A, B, C, D and O). Virtually the symbol of Selinunte, **Temple C** is the oldest temple on the site, built in the middle of the 6th century BC.

The stunning metopes found by Harris and Angell were once a part of this formidable structure, as was the enormous Gorgon's mask that once adorned the pediment; both of these can be viewed in the Museo Archeologico Regionale in Palermo. Experts believe that the temple was dedicated to Apollo.

Northernmost of the remaining temples is **Temple D**, built towards the end of the 6th century BC and dedicated to either Neptune or Venus.

The smaller **Temple B** dates from the Hellenistic period and could have been dedicated to the Agrigentan physiologist and philosopher Empedocles, whose water-drainage scheme saved the city from the scourge of malaria (a bitter irony for William Harris, who contracted the disease during the initial excavations and died soon after).

The two other temples, Temple A and Temple O, closest to the sea, are the most recent, built between 490 and 480 BC. They are virtually identical in both style and size, and it's been suggested that they might have been dedicated to the twins Castor and Pollux.

★ Eastern Temples ARCHAEOLOGICAL SITE

The Eastern Temples are the most stunning of all Selinunte's ruins, crowned by the majestic Temple E. Built in the 5th century BC and reconstructed in 1958, it stands out due to its completeness. It is the first of the three temples close to the ticket office.

Temple G, the northernmost temple, was built in the 6th century BC and, although never completed, was one of the largest temples in the Greek world. Today it is a massive pile of impressive rubble – as is its counterpart directly to the south, Temple F.

Sanctuary of Malophoros ARCHAEOLOGICAL SITE

Walk west about 20 minutes from the acropolis across the now-dry river Modione (formerly the Selinon), then up a dirt path, and you'll reach the ravaged ruins of the temple dedicated to Demeter, the goddess of fertility. Amid the debris, two altars can be made out; the larger of the two was used for sacrifices.

Although they're not much to look at, these are some of the most important finds of the site as they provide an insight into the social history of Selinunte. Thousands of votive offerings to Demeter have been found in the area (nearly 12,000), including stelae crowned with real human heads.

Ancient City ARCHAEOLOGICAL SITE

Occupying the hill of Manuzza, to the north of the acropolis, the Ancient City, where most of Selinunte's inhabitants lived, is the least excavated of all the sites. Exploration of the area has only begun in recent years, and evidence suggests that survivors of the destruction of 409 BC may have used the city as a necropolis.

Lido di Zabbara BEACH

No visit to Selinunte is complete without a walk along this attractive stretch of beach below the archaeological site, which affords marvellous views back up to the cliff-top temples. A path once led here from the acropolis parking area, but it has now been fenced off, so the only access is via the beachfront town of Marinella di Selinunte.

✖ Eating

Unfortunately, the modern village of Marinella di Selinunte hasn't retained any of its ancient predecessor's grandeur and beauty. Amid the profusion of shoddily constructed holiday accommodation, you'll find a largely uninspiring clutch of restaurants by the waterfront, along with a few tourist cafes around the archaeological site's car park. Below are a couple of better options, one in town, the other further afield.

Lido Zabbara BUFFET €

(☑ 0924 4 61 94; Via Pigafetta; buffet per person €12) For tasty, reasonably priced food near the temples, head straight for this low-key eatery on the beachfront. The outdoor terrace here makes a delightful spot to enjoy grilled fish and the varied buffet of two dozen items, including many salads and vegetables.

★ Da Vittorio SEAFOOD €€

(☑ 0925 7 83 81; www.ristorantevittorio.it; meals €28-45) Travellers with their own vehicles should consider driving 15km east of Selinunte to this venerable eatery on the Porto Palo beachfront. In business for more than 45 years, Da Vittorio has earned a reputation as one of western Sicily's best spots for fresh seafood. The front-row view of crashing breakers is wonderful any time of day, but especially at sunset.

Rooms are available upstairs for anyone too stuffed to drive home (single €50 to €60, double €80 to €90).

❶ Information

Azienda Provinciale di Turismo (☑ 0924 4 62 51; ⊙ 8am-1pm & 2-6pm Mon-Sat) On the roundabout just outside Selinunte's main car park, this office supplies a photocopied map of the ruins with multilingual text, plus bus timetables to Castelvetrano and points beyond, including Agrigento.

ⓘ Getting There & Around

BUS

Autoservizi Salemi (☎ 0924 8 18 26; www.
autoservizisalemi.it) runs regular buses between Marinella di Selinunte and Castelvetrano's
train station (€2, 25 to 35 minutes, seven
Monday to Saturday, five Sunday), where you
can make onward rail connections to Mazara,
Marsala, and Trapani. For eastbound travellers,
Lumia (www.autolineelumia.it) runs buses from
Castelvetrano to Agrigento (€8.30, 1¾ to two
hours, three Monday to Saturday, one Sunday).

CAR

Coming from Palermo and other points north,
take the Castelvetrano exit off the A29 and follow the brown signposts for about 6km. If you're
driving from Agrigento, take the SS115 and follow the signposts.

TRAIN

There are services from Castelvetrano to Mazara
del Vallo (€2.85, 20 minutes, 10 daily), Marsala
(€3.95, 35 to 55 minutes, 10 daily) and Palermo
(€7.65, 2½ hours, three to six daily). Note that
unless you take the direct evening train to Palermo (Monday to Saturday only), you'll have to
change at Cinisi, Alcamo or Piraineto.

Tyrrhenian Coast

Includes ➡

Why Go?

The coastal stretch between Palermo and Milazzo is packed with dramatic beach and mountain scenery, and appealing coastal towns like Cefalù and Castel di Tusa – but once summer rolls around, it's holiday central, characterised by crowded roads and beaches. Somehow neither this nor the ever-growing proliferation of ugly concrete buildings marring the coastline can dissuade locals from coming here for their annual vacation and having a whale of a time.

Few sun-worshippers head inland from these sybaritic summer playgrounds to visit the nearby Madonie and Nebrodi mountains, but those who do are swiftly seduced. These superb natural landscapes enfold hilltop villages where the lifestyle is traditional, the sense of history palpable and the mountain cuisine exceptional, featuring wild forest mushrooms, *suino nero* pork, and ricotta straight from the sheep.

Best Places to Eat

➡ Ti Vitti (p118)

➡ Casale Drinzi (p125)

➡ Da Salvatore (p124)

➡ Nangalarruni (p123)

➡ A Castellana (p120)

Best Places to Stay

➡ Atelier sul Mare (p257)

➡ Green Manors Country Hotel (p258)

➡ B&B L'Alberghetto (p258)

➡ Albergo Il Castello (p257)

➡ Agriturismo Pardo (p257)

Road Distances (KM)

	Caccamo	Castelbuono	Cefalù	Milazzo
Castelbuono	75			
Cefalù	50	20		
Milazzo	185	135	130	
Petralia Sottana	90	35	60	175

Getting Around

Trains are frequent and dependable along the coast, but once you head inland, your own wheels are nearly indispensable, especially for exploring the scenic backroads of the Madonie and Nebrodi mountains. Buses from coastal hubs like Palermo and Cefalù service interior towns such as Castelbuono, Collesano, Petralia and Caccamo, but they have limited schedules, and there's no public transport linking these interior towns to one another once you get there.

THREE PERFECT DAYS

Explore Beaches

Take the squiggly SS113 along the coast, or zip down the A20 autostrada, admiring the engineering wizardry of its bridges and tunnels. Either way, a few stops are mandatory. Prowl the pretty sands at Capo d'Orlando, brake for avant-garde art (and lunch by the waterfront) at Castel di Tusa and pull into Cefalù by mid-afternoon, in time to savour the region's prettiest town-plus-beach combo before sundown.

Travel Back in Time

Start in Cefalù with a visit to the Byzantine mosaics of its cathedral and a wander through its enchanting tangle of back streets. Next head inland to Castelbuono, where you can tour the 14th-century castle and enjoy superb mountain cuisine in a pair of atmospherically rustic eateries. End the afternoon at Caccamo, touring its imposing cliff-top Norman castle and then enjoying a meal fit for a foreign invader at A Castellana (p120) next door.

Meander Through Forgotten Mountains

Link the Madonie and Nebrodi mountains with a scenic inland jaunt through a series of little-visited hill towns. From Cefalù climb south to the mountain town of Castelbuono, then circle the dramatic Madonie mountains to Petralia Sottana. Next, head east through the gorgeous villages of Gangi, Sperlinga and Nicosia, all perched high on rocky ledges and surrounded by rolling, wildflower-draped hills. From here, it's an easy trip north to Mistretta in the Parco Regionale dei Nebrodi.

Getting Away from It All

➡ **Explore Mistretta** A tranquil time capsule perched on the Parco Regionale dei Nebrodi's western border.

➡ **Savour the silence in Petralia Soprana** The cobbled streets of this ancient mountain village are often deserted.

➡ **Hike the high country** Walk across carpets of spring wildflowers in Piano Battaglia after the ski bunnies have decamped for the beach.

DON'T MISS

Climbing to the top of La Rocca (p116) in Cefalù. This ancient eyrie with its ruined temple and castle commands spectacular views of the medieval town centre, the Tyrrhenian Sea, and the surrounding beaches.

Best Hill Towns

➡ Petralia Sottana (p124)

➡ San Marco d'Alunzio (p126)

➡ Mistretta (p127)

➡ Castelbuono (p121)

Best Panoramic Viewpoints

➡ Castello di Caccamo (p120)

➡ La Rocca (p116)

➡ Ancient ruins, Tyndaris (p128)

➡ Belvedere, Petralia Soprana (p124)

➡ Belvedere, Santuario di Gibilmanna (p122)

Resources

➡ **Parks.it** (www.parks.it) English-language info on the Madonie and Nebrodi parks.

➡ **Parco dei Nebrodi** (www.parcodeinebrodi.it) Official site.

➡ **Parco delle Madonie** (www.parcodellemadonie.it) Official site.

➡ **Cefalù-sicily.it** (www.cefalu-sicily.it) A map of Cefalù and other info.

➡ **Milazzo Info** (www.milazzo.info) Info about Milazzo.

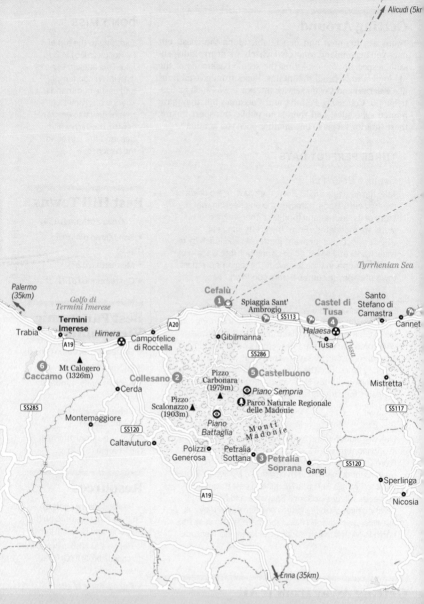

Alicudi (5km)

Tyrrhenian Sea

Palermo
(35km)

*Golfo di
Termini Imerese*

Cefalù
1

Spiaggia Sant'
Ambrogio
SS113

**Castel di
Tusa**

Santo
Stefano di
Camastra

Cannet

Termini
Imerese

Trabia

A19

Himera

Campofelice
di Roccella

A20

Gibilmanna

Halaesa

Tusa

Tusa

SS286

6
Caccamo

Mt Calogero
(1326m)

Cerda

Collesano **2**

Pizzo
Carbonara
(1979m)

5 **Castelbuono**

Piano Sempria

Mistretta

Parco Naturale Regionale
delle Madonie

SS117

Montemaggiore

SS285

Pizzo
Scalonazzo
(1903m)

*Piano
Battaglia*

M o n t i
M a d o n i e

Caltavuturo

Polizzi
Generosa

Petralia
Sottana

3 **Petralia
Soprana**

Gangi

SS120

Sperlinga

A19

Nicosia

Enna (35km)

Tyrrhenian Coast Highlights

1 Choose the glitter that
suits you best – the sparkling
gold mosaics of the Duomo at
Cefalù (p116), or the fashion-
conscious beach scene a few
paces away.

2 Relive the glory days of
Italy's greatest road race at
the Museo Targa Florio in
Collesano (p125).

3 While away a chilly
mountain evening by the

blazing fire in a **Petralia
Soprana** (p123) pizzeria.

4 Celebrate the summer
solstice at the hilltop pyramid
in **Castel di Tusa** (p127),
the newest installation in its

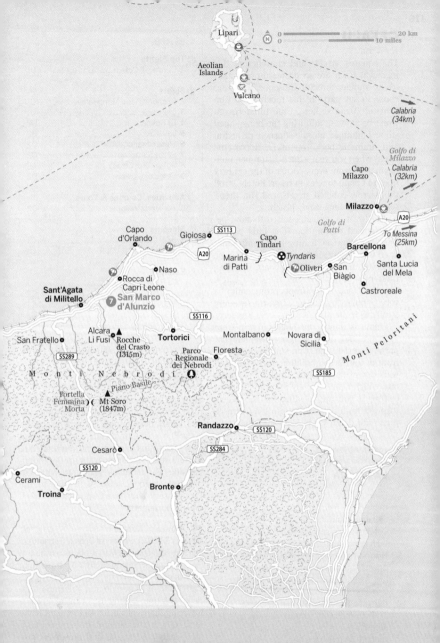

innovative Fiumara d'Arte project.

5 Try a sweet taste of manna, an ancient delicacy made from the sap of local ash trees, at a bakery in **Castelbuono** (p121).

6 Enjoy bird's-eye views of rugged hills and the distant Tyrrhenian from the Norman castle at **Caccamo** (p120).

7 See if you can count all the churches in **San Marco d'Alunzio** (p126) without running out of fingers and toes (hint: there are 22 of them!).

CEFALÙ

POP 14,330

The squares, streets and churches of this medieval town are so postcard-pretty that it's no wonder director Giuseppe Tornatore chose to set parts of his much-loved film *Cinema Paradiso* here. Unfortunately, you won't be alone in admiring the honey-hued stone buildings, mosaic-adorned cathedral and dramatic backdrop of La Rocca (the Rock) when you visit – during summer, holidaymakers from every corner of the country flock to Cefalù to relax in resort hotels, stroll the narrow cobbled streets and sun themselves on the long sandy beach.

The town is perfectly suited to slow, pedestrianised exploration. The little port is lined with narrow fishing boats and populated with local fishermen who can often be observed maintaining their boats, mending their nets and discussing the day's catch. The *lungomare* (seafront promenade) is very popular for the *passeggiata* (evening stroll), as is the main street, Corso Ruggero.

Cefalù is only a one-hour rail trip from Palermo, and there is also convenient car parking next to the train station. From the front of the station building, turn right and walk down Via Gramsci to reach Via Matteotti, which heads directly into the old town centre. If you are heading for the beach, turn left from the station into Via Gramsci, turn right down Via N Martoglio, then take

Via Vazzano, which will bring you to the western end of the *lungomare*.

⊙ Sights & Activities

Most of Cefalù's sights are found in the historic town centre around Corso Ruggero and Piazza del Duomo. The only exception is La Rocca – to appreciate the magnificent views from this ancient eyrie you'll need to brave a steep half-hour walk up the mountainside. For fabulous sea views with less physical exertion, make your way to the 17th-century **Bastione Capo Marchiafava**, off Via Bordenaro.

★ **Duomo di Cefalù**   CATHEDRAL
(☑ 0921 92 20 21; Piazza del Duomo; ☉ 8am-7pm Apr-Sep, 8am-5pm Oct-Mar) Cefalù's cathedral is one of the jewels in Sicily's Arab-Norman crown, only equalled in magnificence by the Cattedrale di Monreale and Palermo's Cappella Palatina. Filling the central apse, a towering figure of Christ All Powerful is the focal point of the elaborate Byzantine mosaics – Sicily's oldest and best preserved, predating those of Monreale by 20 or 30 years.

In his hand, a compassionate-looking Christ holds an open Bible bearing a Latin and Greek inscription from John 8:12: 'I am the light of the world; he who follows me shall not walk in darkness.' Other mosaic

---

DON'T MISS

LA ROCCA

Looming over the town, the craggy mass of **La Rocca** (admission €3; ☉ 9am-6.45pm May-Sep, 9am-4.45pm Oct-Apr) is the site where the Arabs built their citadel, occupying it until the Norman conquest in 1061 forced them down from the mountain to the port below. An enormous staircase, the **Salita Saraceno**, winds up through three tiers of city walls, a 30-minute climb.

The windswept summit appears a suitable home for the race of giants that are said to have been Sicily's first inhabitants. There are stunning views of the town and the sea below, and the ruined 4th-century **Tempio di Diana** (☉ 24hr) provides a quiet and romantic getaway for young lovers.

Cefalù

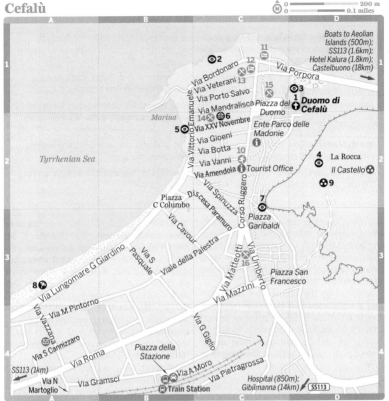

groups include the Virgin with Four Archangels dressed as Byzantine officials.

The 16 interior columns with Roman capitals probably came from the Tempio di Diana on La Rocca.

Legend tells us that the cathedral was built by Roger II in the 12th century to fulfil a vow to God after his fleet was saved during a violent storm off Cefalù. In fact, it was more likely the result of Roger's tempestuous relationship with the Palermitan archbishopric. Eager to curb the growing influence of the papacy in Sicily (with whom the Palermo archbishopric had close ties), Roger thought that building a mighty church so far from Palermo would prove an effective reminder of his power across the island and pose a disincentive to any potential usurpers. It's thus hardly surprising that the cathedral's architecture is distinctly fortress-like.

You can enjoy the view of the cathedral's soaring twin pyramid towers, framed by La Rocca, over a morning coffee or evening aperitif in the Piazza del Duomo.

Cloisters   CLOISTER
(adult/senior/student €3/2/1; ⊙10am-1pm & 3-6pm) To the left of the main entrance are the cathedral's cloisters, which feature ancient columns supporting graceful Arab-Norman arches. The finely carved capitals depict a mix of religious and secular images, all detailed on a free handout available at the ticket desk – among the most interesting are the depictions of acrobats, a pair of crocodiles and Noah's Ark.

Museo Mandralisca   MUSEUM
(☑0921 42 15 47; www.museomandralisca.it; Via Mandralisca 13; adult/child under 6yr/child 6-10yr/child 11-15yr €5/free/1/3; ⊙9am-7pm) This small, privately owned museum showcases a collection amassed by parliamentarian, archaeologist and natural-history buff, Baron Mandralisca (1809–64). The rather faded

TOP TRAVEL THEMES – TYRRHENIAN COAST

Archaeological Sites Abandon your deck chair and umbrella for a few mornings to soak up history rather than the sun while visiting the ruins of ancient settlements such as Tyndaris and Halaesa.

Cathedrals Every town, however small, seems to have a lavishly decorated cathedral gracing its main piazza. Start a survey of the best at the magnificent Duomo di Cefalù.

Fabulous Fortresses This coast has been fortified against possible invaders for millennia. Check out some of its sensationally sited strongholds, including the Norman castle at Caccamo.

Monti Madonie Take our driving tour through the Madonie mountains, visiting historic hilltop villages and dining in acclaimed restaurants along the way.

Slow Food Discover the delights of local food products, dishes and traditions when eating your way through the Madonie and Nebrodi regional parks.

displays of Greek ceramics and Arab pottery are of marginal interest compared to Antonello da Messina's splendid *Ritratto di un uomo ignoto* (Portrait of an Unknown Man; 1465), considered one of the most distinctive portraits of the Italian Renaissance.

Acquired by the Baron after he discovered it being used as a makeshift cupboard door in Lipari, da Messina's painting depicts a man with an enigmatic smirk, almost as captivating and thought provoking as the Mona Lisa's – albeit without the attendant hype.

Spiaggia di Cefalù BEACH

Cefalù's crescent-shaped beach is one of the most popular along the whole coast. In summer it is packed, so be sure to arrive early to get a good spot. Though some sections require a ticket, the area closest to the old town is public and you can hire a beach umbrella and deck chair for approximately €15 per day.

Lavatoio HISTORIC SITE

(Via Vittorio Emanuele) FREE Descend the curving stone steps to this picturesque cluster of 16th-century wash basins, built over a spring that was well known in antiquity.

✗ Eating

Despite being packed with restaurants, Cefalù is one of the only major towns on the island to be totally ignored by both the *Gambero Rosso* and *Osteria D'Italia* (Slow Food Movement) restaurant guides – a damning but deserved indictment. If all you're after is a passable meal with a great view, you'll find plenty of seafront terrace restaurants along Via Bordonaro in the old town centre.

★ Ti Vitti SICILIAN €€

(www.ristorantetivitti.com; Via Umberto I 34; meals €30-40) At this up-and-coming eatery named after a Sicilian card game, talented young chef Vincenzo Collaro whips up divine pasta, fresh-from-the-market fish dishes and some of the best *cannoli* you'll find anywhere in Sicily. His insistence on using only the freshest ingredients means no swordfish out of season, and special locally sourced treats such as basilisco mushrooms from the Monte Madonie.

In winter, the menu gets stripped down to three *antipasti*, three *primi* and three *secondi*, all super-fresh based on what's available at the market that morning.

La Botte SICILIAN €€

(🌐 0921 42 43 15; www.labottecefalu.com; Via Veterani 20; meals €30-35; ⏲12.30-2.30pm & 7.30-10.30pm Tue-Sun) This small, family-run restaurant just off Corso Ruggero serves a good choice of antipasti, seasonally driven pasta dishes and seafood-dominated mains. The fixed menu of three fish courses plus a side dish offers good value.

La Galleria SICILIAN, CAFE €€

(🌐 0921 42 02 11; www.lagalleriacefalu.it; Via Mandralisca 23; meals €25-40; ⏲closed Thu year-round & Mon in winter) This is about as hip as Cefalù gets. Functioning as a restaurant, cafe, internet point, bookshop and occasional gallery space, La Galleria has an informal vibe, an elegant internal garden and an innovative menu that mixes standard *primi* and *secondi* with a range of all-in-one dishes (€12 to €15) designed to be meals in themselves.

Ostaria del Duomo
SICILIAN €€

(☑ 0921 42 18 38; www.ostariadelduomo.it; Via Seminario 5; meals €30; ☺ noon-midnight) For full-on views of the cathedral and the Rocca while you dine, nothing compares to this touristy spot with outdoor tables facing the cathedral. Its reputation for serving fresh dishes utilising locally sourced produce makes it a safe choice. Try the house speciality of *carpaccio de pesce* (raw, thinly sliced fish), accompanied by your selection from the extensive wine list.

ℹ Information

EMERGENCIES
Ambulance (☑ 0921 42 45 44, 118)
Hospital (☑ 0921 92 01 11; Contrada Pietra-pollastra) On the main road out of town in the direction of Palermo.
Questura (☑ 0921 92 60 11; Via Roma 15)

TOURIST INFORMATION
Ente Parco delle Madonie (☑ 0921 92 33 27; www.parcodellemadonie.it; Corso Ruggero 116; ☺ 8am-8pm daily May-Sep, 8am-6pm Mon-Sat Oct-Apr) Knowledgeable and friendly staff supply information about the Parco Naturale Regionale delle Madonie.
Tourist Office (☑ 0921 42 10 50; strcefalu@ regione.sicilia.it; Corso Ruggero 77; ☺ 9am-1pm & 3-7.30pm Mon-Sat) English-speaking staff, lots of leaflets and good maps.

WEBSITES
Lonely Planet (www.lonelyplanet.com/italy/sicily/cefalu) Planning advice, author recommendations, traveller reviews and insider tips.

ℹ Getting There & Around

BOAT
From May to September, **SMIV** (Società Marittima Italiana Veloce; www.smiv.it) runs daily boat trips between Cefalù and the Aeolian Islands. Their 8am boat serves Lipari and Vulcano (one-way/return €30/60), returning to Cefalù at 6.45pm. A second boat serves Panarea and Stromboli (one-way/return €40/80), leaving at 11am and returning to Cefalù around 11.45pm. Rates include free pick up at any Cefalù hotel. Tickets are available at **Turismez Viaggi** (☑ 0921 42 12 64; www.turismezviaggi.it; Corso Ruggero 83) next door to the tourist office.

BUS
Buses depart from outside the train station regularly from Monday to Saturday, with occasional Sunday services. **SAIS** (www.saistrasporti.it) travels to Palermo (€5.70, one hour, five Monday to Friday, four Saturday) and Castelbuono

(€2.60, 40 minutes, six Monday to Saturday, one Sunday). **Lombardo & Glorioso** (☑ 0921 92 36 48; www.lombardoeglorioso.it) also operates one daily bus to/from Castelbuono. **Sommatinese** (☑ 0921 42 43 01; www.sommatinese.it) operates a local service to Gibilmanna (25 minutes, 13 Monday to Saturday, four Sunday).

CAR & MOTORCYCLE
Cefalù is situated just off the A20-E90 toll road that travels between Messina and Palermo. To hire a bike, Vespa or motorbike, try **Scooter for Rent** (☑ 0921 42 04 96; www.scooterforrent.it; Via Vittorio Emanuele 57; per day/week 50cc Vespa €35/175, mountain bike €10/45).

PARKING
Finding a car park can be a nightmarish challenge in summer. Try the convenient car parking next to the train station (€2 for the first two hours and €1 every extra hour) or on the *lungomare*.

TRAIN
Regular services go to Palermo (from €5.15, 45 minutes to 1¼ hours, 15 Monday to Saturday, 11 on Sunday) and virtually every other town on the coast.

AROUND CEFALÙ

Termini Imerese

The Romans discovered the therapeutic value of Termini Imerese's mineral-laden waters way back in 252 BC, and the town has been a popular thermal spa centre ever since. These days, all the spa action occurs at the Grand Hotel delle Terme (☑ 091 811 35 57; www.grandhoteldelleterme.it; Piazza delle Terme 2; per person with breakfast €85-120, with half board €120-130; P ❄ ☀), a large Liberty-style building dating from 1890. Built on the site of the original Roman baths, the hotel's natural steam baths and bathing pools are popular with Italians seeking treatment for conditions such as obesity, rheumatism, psoriasis and bronchial problems. The complex also includes a 'beauty farm' offering cosmetic and relaxation treatments.

From the Grand Hotel delle Terme, in the lower town, you can walk to the upper town to visit a clutch of churches, including the 17th-century cathedral and Chiesa di Santa Maria della Misericordia (Church of Our Lady of Mercy) and the 14th-century Chiesa di Santa Caterina (Church of Saint Catherine), which has lovely 15th-century frescoes by local artists Nicolo and Giacomo

BEST BEACHES

Stake a claim to a sandy patch of paradise at the following resorts and throw yourself into the swing of the Sicilian summer scene.

Cefalù This wildly popular resort town balances magnificent cultural attractions with a beach scene that is as renowned as Taormina's.

Oliveri This sandy stretch of beach beneath the ancient settlement of Tyndaris hosts fewer holidaymakers than many of its neighbours.

Sant'Agata di Militello A garish funfair, *gelato* vendors, gentle waves and a seafront promenade just perfect for the *passeggiata* (evening stroll) make this boisterous resort a popular choice for families.

Graffeo illustrating the life of the saint. Unfortunately, the coast surrounding the town is blighted with an ugly commercial port.

Trains travel regularly from Termini Imerese to Cefalù (€3.45, 30 minutes, 10 daily) and Palermo (€3.45, 25 to 45 minutes, every 20 minutes). AST (☏ 840 000323; www.aziendasicilianatrasporti.it) also operates buses to/from Palermo (€3.90, one hour, three daily). The train station is southeast of the town centre along the coast; all buses arrive and depart just in front of the train station.

Caccamo

Lorded over by its imposing Castello di Caccamo (☏ 0918 14 92 52; adult/reduced €4/free; ☉ 9am-1pm & 3-7pm Sat-Mon, 8.30am-1.30pm & 3-8pm Tue-Fri), this hilltop town is a popular day trip from both Cefalù and Palermo. Though the area was settled in ancient times, Caccamo was officially founded in 1093, when the Normans began building their fortress on a rocky spur of Monte San Calogero. The castle was enlarged by the noble Chiaramonte family in the 14th century and is now one of Italy's largest and most impressive, with walls and fortifications that originally included ingenious traps for any intruder who might have breached the outer perimeter.

Beyond the castle's first gate, a ramp leads to a broad courtyard that gives access to several monumental, sparsely decorated rooms, from which you can enjoy magnificent views of the surrounding countryside.

Nestled in the shadow of the castle, accessed downhill from Corso Umberto I, is the picturesque Piazza Duomo. It's home to an 11th-century cathedral known as the Chiesa Madre, which is dedicated to St George. Remodelled twice (in 1477 and 1614), the cathedral's sacristy has some lovely carvings of the *Madonna con bambino e angeli* (Madonna with Child and Angels) and *Santi Pietro e Paolo* (Sts Peter and Paul), both by Francesco Laurana.

For lunch, make your way to the Slow Food–celebrated A Castellana (☏ 091 814 86 67; www.castellana.it; Piazza dei Caduti 4; set menus €22-25; ☉ noon-2.30pm & 7-10pm Tue-Sun), located in the grain stores of the castle. It has a panoramic terrace for summer dining and is renowned for its assured treatment of classic Sicilian dishes. You can order à la carte or opt for an excellent-value set menu comprising four courses plus coffee.

Caccamo is on the SS285 between Palermo and Agrigento. Randazzo (☏ 091 814 82 35; www.autobusrandazzo.altervista.it) buses travel to/from Cefalù (€4.40, 70 minutes, one daily), Palermo (€4.60, 70 minutes, three daily) and Termini Imerese (€2.50, 30 minutes, six to nine daily). There are no Sunday services.

Himera

Founded in 648 BC by Greeks from Zankle (now Messina), this usually deserted archaeological site (☏ 091 814 01 28; adult €2, EU citizen 18-25yr €1, under 18 or 65+ free; ☉ 9am-4pm Mon-Sat, 9am-1.30pm Sun) was named after the river Imera, which flows nearby. It was the first Greek settlement on this part of the island and was a strategic outpost on the border of the Carthaginian-controlled west. In 480 BC the town was the scene of a decisive battle, with the combined armies of Theron of Agrigento and Gelon of Syracuse defeating a sizable Carthaginian army led by Hamilcar, who threw himself on the funeral pyre of the Carthaginian dead in a heroic act of self-immolation. The Carthaginians had intended to take Himera and then wrest control of the island from Greek hands, but the Greek victory put an end to all that. In 409 BC, Himera paid the price for Carthage's defeat, when Hamilcar's nephew Hannibal destroyed the town in revenge for his uncle's death.

Unfortunately, the remains here are disappointing when compared with other Greek sites around the island. The only recognisable ruin is the Tempio della Vittoria (Temple of Victory), a Doric structure supposedly built to commemorate the defeat of the Carthaginians. Whatever its origin, Hannibal did a good job of destroying it.

Some artefacts recovered from the site are kept in a small antiquarium about 100m west of the site's entrance (it's up a small lane off the other side of the main road). Although the more impressive pieces are in Palermo's Museo Archeologico Regionale, you can still see well-sculpted lionhead spouts that were used to drain water off the temple's roof.

Nancini & Saso (www.nancinisaso.com) buses travel between Termini Imerese and Villaura, stopping at Himera en route (€2.50, 15 minutes, three daily Monday to Saturday).

PARCO NATURALE REGIONALE DELLE MADONIE

Travellers making their way between Palermo and Cefalù have the option of visiting two very different destinations within the space of a few days. After spending time jostling with armies of sun-seeking holidaymakers on the overdeveloped coast, savvy visitors inevitably choose to abandon their deckchairs and head to the hills to savour the spectacular scenery and tranquil surrounds of the 400-sq-km Madonie regional park (www.parcodellemadonie.it).

The Monti Madonie (Madonie mountains) are crowned by Pizzo Carbonara – at 1979m the highest mountain in Sicily after Mt Etna – and the regional park takes in farms, hilltop towns and ski resorts.

Here, the seasons are distinct: spring sees spectacular spreads of wildflowers carpeting the mountain slopes; autumn brings with it wild mushrooms and the rich hues of forest foliage; winter prompts downhill action on the ski slopes; and June and July offer blissfully cool temperatures and an escape from the coastal crowds.

This is an area where people live and work, not just a nature reserve, meaning that you can combine hiking with visits to historic hilltop towns and meals in some of Sicily's best restaurants. It's perfectly suited to slow, culturally rich travel.

Park offices in Petralia Sottana and Cefalù offer details about several one-day walks, as well as information about transport and accommodation. They also stock the 1:50,000 *Madonie/Carta dei Sentieri e del Paesaggio* map (€3), which highlights the region's walking trails.

Getting There & Away

The best way to explore the Madonie Regional Park is by car, but it's also possible to access the major towns by bus from the coast.

BY CAR

To access the park from Palermo and other points west, head east along the coastal SS113 to Campofelice di Roccella and then turn off for Collesano, 13km inland. From Cefalù it is even easier: just follow the directions for the Santuario di Gibilmanna (Sanctuary of Gibilmanna), 14km to the south on the SP54bis.

BY BUS

From Palermo, SAIS Trasporti (p79) operates services to Castelbuono (€8.30, 1¾ hours, three Monday to Saturday, one Sunday), as well as two to three buses per day to Petralia Soprana (€9.90, two hours), stopping en route at Polizzi Generosa (€8.90, 1¼ hours) and Petralia Sottana (€9.90, 1¾ hours). AST (p79) also runs three buses Monday through Saturday from Palermo to Castelbuono (€6.60, 2½ hours) via Collesano (€5.40, 1¾ hours).

From Cefalù, SAIS (p119) operates services to Castelbuono (€2.60, 40 minutes, six daily Monday to Saturday, one Sunday).

Castelbuono

POP 9152 / ELEV 423M

The charming capital of the Madonie is set amid ancient manna ash and chestnut forests. It owes much of its building stock and character to the Ventimiglias, a powerful noble family who ruled the town between the 14th and 16th centuries.

Sights & Activities

Castello dei Ventimiglia   CASTLE
(☎0921 67 12 11; Piazza Castello; adult/reduced €4/2; ☉9.30am-1pm & 3.30-7pm Tue-Sun) Originally known as the *Castello del Buon Aere* (Castle of Good Air), the enormous castle that soars above Castelbuono's golden patchwork of houses gave the town its name and is its most distinctive landmark. Built by Francesco I Ventimiglia in 1316, it features displays on local archaeology and Castelbuono's history.

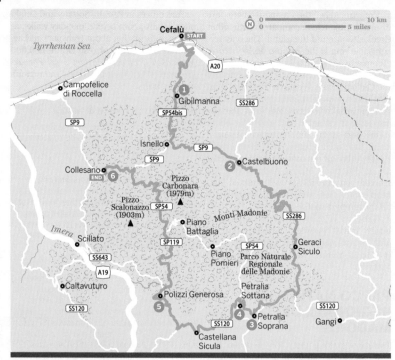

Driving Tour
Monti Madonie

START CEFALÙ
END COLLESANO
LENGTH 113KM; ONE TO THREE DAYS

This tour takes in the most picturesque towns in the Madonie mountains and rewards leisurely exploration; to see everything in one day is possible, but will be tiring.

From Cefalù, follow the winding SP54bis for approximately 15km to the ❶ **Santuario di Gibilmanna**, spectacularly perched 800m above sea level on the slopes of Pizzo Sant'Angelo (1081m). Here, in the 17th century, the Virgin Mary reputedly restored sight to two blind worshippers and speech to a mute. The miracle was later confirmed by the Vatican, and the church has since become one of Sicily's most important shrines. The views over the Madonie from the belvedere out front are spectacular.

From Gibilmanna, head 18km southeast on the SP9 to ❷ **Castelbuono**, presided over by its magnificent 14th-century castle, then take the winding SS286 to the picturesque mountain town of ❸ **Petralia Soprana**. The road, intermittently fringed by dense forest, is relentlessly sinuous but offers wonderful views over the valleys.

After lunching in Petralia Soprana or its pretty sister town of ❹ **Petralia Sottana**, follow the SS120 for 19km to ❺ **Polizzi Generosa**, nestled at the entrance to the Imera Valley. Named *generosa* (generous) by Frederick II in the 1230s, the town is now best known as a trekking base for the Madonie, and is riddled with churches that are often shrouded in mist. It's also home to a pastry known as the *sfoglio*: sweet dough filled with artisanal sheep's milk cheese, cinnamon, chocolate and sugar.

Your last stop is medieval ❻ **Collesano**, 26km northwest on the SP119 and SP54 (or take the SS643 and SP54; both routes afford splendid mountain views). Don't miss the Targa Florio museum, which celebrates the history of the Madonie's now-defunct mountain road race, and make sure to stick around town for a hearty mountain dinner at delightful Casale Drinzi (p125).

Popular legend has it that the castle is haunted by the 14th-century Queen Constance Chiaramonte, who is said to run along the corridors, regular as clockwork, on the first Tuesday of the month. At the heart of the fortress is the Cappella di Sant'Anna (Chapel of St Anne), which dates from 1683 and is decorated with marvellous stuccowork from the school of renowned Sicilian sculptor Giacomo Serpotta. It houses the supposed skull of the saint in a silver urn.

Museo Naturalistico Francesco Minà Palumbo   MUSEUM
(☑0921 67 71 74; www.museominapalumbo.it; Via Roma 72; adult €2, under10yr or 65+ €1; ◷9am-1pm & 3.30-7.30pm) Named after the naturalist Francesco Min à Palumbo (1837–99), this unassuming museum is housed in the former convent of Santa Venera. It's home to a collection of artefacts that gives an exhaustive insight into the botany, natural history, minerals and archaeology of the Madonie mountains.

✖ Eating

Castelbuono's rustic regional cuisine showcases fruits of the Madonie such as *funghi di bosco* (forest mushrooms) and *cinghiale* (wild boar).

Fiasconaro   PASTRIES & CAKES €
(☑0921 67 12 31; www.fiasconaro.com; Piazza Margherita 10; pastries from €1; ◷6.30am-midnight Thu-Tue) Home of the local speciality, *mannetto* (manna cake), this much-loved *pasticceria* on the main road leading to the castle is also packed with treats such as buttery *cornetti* (croissants), decadently sweet *cassata siciliana* (sponge cake with cream, marzipan, chocolate and candied fruit) and the unusual *testa di Turco* (Turk's head; blancmange with puff pastry in the middle). Its home-made *gelato* is also very good.

The *pasticceria* is on one side of the road and the Fiasconaro cafe is opposite – it's perfectly acceptable to purchase your sweet treat at the *pasticceria* and take it to the cafe.

A Rua Fera   PIZZERIA, SICILIAN €
(☑0921 67 67 23; Via Roma 71; pizzas €4-8, meals €20-28; ◷12.30-3pm & 7-11pm Wed-Mon) His use of gourmet local ingredients make Antonio Marannano's pizzas a cut above the competition. His pasta dishes are also delicious, with tempting choices such as *pappardelle fresche con funghi di stagione* (fresh pappardelle noodles with seasonal mushrooms). Stone walls, beamed ceilings, tile floors and delightful smoky aromas all contribute to the rustic atmosphere.

★Nangalarruni   SICILIAN €€
(☑0921 67 14 28; www.hostarianangalarruni.it; Via delle Confraternite 10; fixed menus €23-32; ◷12.30-3pm & 7-10pm, closed Wed in winter) Famous throughout Sicily for its delicious dishes featuring forest mushrooms and wild boar, Giuseppe Carollo's eatery deserves equal renown for its splendid Sicilian wine selection, displayed on the shelves of the cosy wood-beamed dining room. Spike your appetite with an array of local cheeses, then move on to mains featuring fresh ricotta, locally sourced vegetables and roast meats.

Romitaggio   SICILIAN €€
(☑0921 67 13 23; www.romitaggio.it; Contrada da San Guglielmo; meals €24-29; ◷noon-3pm & 8-10pm Thu-Tue) Climb the hill to this ancient Benedictine monastery, 4km from Castelbuono in San Guglielmo, to sample traditional Madonita dishes including antipasto with *salsicce secche* (dried sausage), *ricotta fresca* (fresh ricotta), *provola della madonie* (local provolone cheese) and homepreserved olives. Slow Food–acclaimed delights include stewed rabbit or kid and *filetto di maiale al pistacchio* (pork fillet with pistachios).

❶ Information

The **Pro Loco** (☑389 6893810, 0921 67 11 24; prolococastelbuono@libero.it; Piazza Castello; ◷9.30am-1pm) office adjacent to the castle offers information on Castelbuono and the Madonie in general.

Petralia Soprana

POP 3431 / ELEV 1147M

Beautifully positioned at the top of a hill above a tree line of pines, Petralia Soprana (from the Italian word *sopra*, meaning 'above') is one of the best-preserved small towns in north-central Sicily, full of picturesque stone houses and curling wrought-iron balconies brimming with geraniums. It's also the highest village in the Madonie. There's not much for visitors to do except wander around the narrow cobbled lanes, visit a couple of churches and have lunch at Da Salvatore.

TYRRHENIAN COAST PETRALIA SOPRANA

◉ Sights & Activities

**Chiesa di Santa Maria
di Loreto** CHURCH

(Via Loreto) The most beautiful of Petralia Soprana's many churches is the 18th-century Chiesa di Santa Maria di Loreto, at the end of Via Loreto, off the main square, Piazza del Popolo (follow the signs to Da Salvatore). Inside is an altarpiece by Gagini and a Madonna by Giacomo Mancini. To the right of the church through an arch is the town's belvedere, with views across the valley and to Etna on a clear day.

Chiesa Santi Pietro e Paolo CATHEDRAL

(off Piazza dei Quattro Cannoli) The town's cathedral, located on Piazza del Popolo, off Piazza dei Quattro Cannoli, was consecrated in 1497 and has an elegant 18th-century portico and a 15th-century campanile (bell tower). It is dedicated to Sts Peter and Paul.

✗ Eating

★ Da Salvatore TRATTORIA, PIZZERIA €

(☑ 0921 68 01 69; Piazza San Michele 3; pizzas €4-8, meals €15-23; ⊙ closed Tue except in summer, dinner in winter, 2 weeks in Jul & 2 weeks in Sep) Salvatore Ruvutuso, his wife Maria and two children run this Slow Food–acclaimed trattoria with its summertime sidewalk seating and wonderfully cosy interior dining room. Kick off with a delicious selection of antipasti including frittata, superb *caponata* and pungent *provola delle madonie*, then choose from a daily menu that usually features a rustic pasta, vegetable soup or fragrant stew.

Pizzas are only served in the evening. The restaurant is tucked into a little square near the Chiesa di Santa Maria di Loreto – just follow the signs. Note: no credit cards.

✈ Getting There & Around

CAR & MOTORCYCLE

To reach Petralia Soprana from Petralia Sottana, drive up Corso Paolo Agliata to Piazza Umberto and follow the winding narrow road leading uphill through the arch at the right-hand side of the Chiesa Madre, veering right at the first fork.

PARKING

There is limited free car parking in Piazza del Popolo. Alternatively, park on the side of the road leading uphill into town.

Petralia Sottana

POP 2960 / ELEV 1000M

Below Petralia Soprana, the town of Petralia Sottana (from the Italian *sotto,* meaning 'under') is the gateway to the regional park and the headquarters of the Ente Parco delle Madonie (☑ 0921 68 40 11; Corso Paolo Agliata 16; ⊙ 8am-2pm & 3-7pm Mon-Fri, 3-7pm Sat, 10.30am-1pm & 4.30-7pm Sun). The park office, located in the foyer of the Museo Civico Antonio Collisani, supplies maps and walking itineraries for the Madonie along with brochures and information about Petralia Sottana itself.

◉ Sights & Activities

Petralia Sottana is dominated by its main street, Corso Paolo Agliata, which is a popular shopping strip during the day and hosts the town's surprisingly busy *passeggiata* (evening stroll) in the early evening. Like Petralia Soprana, the town possesses a number of handsome churches, including the baroque Chiesa di San Francesco on the Corso and the 17th-century Chiesa Madre at the end of the Corso on Piazza Umberto. The *campanile* of the latter is the town's major landmark. On the road leading to Petralia Soprana is the Chiesa di Santissima Trinità alla Badia, which has a handsome marble altarpiece carved by Giandomenico Gagini.

Museo Civico Antonio Collisani MUSEUM

(☑ 0921 64 18 11; www.comune.petraliasottana. pa.it; Corso Paolo Agliata 100; adult/reduced €2/1; ⊙ 8am-2pm & 3-7pm Mon-Fri, 3-7pm Sat, 10.30am-1pm & 4.30-7pm Sun) Focusing on the archaeology and geology of the Madonie, this small but interesting museum has an impressive display of fossils found in the area and is worth a short visit. There's also an excellent education centre for young children (resources in Italian only).

✗ Eating

★ Petrae Lejum SICILIAN €

(☑ 0921 64 19 47; Corso Paolo Agliata 113; meals €18-27; ⊙ closed Fri dinner except in Aug) This down-to-earth, Slow Food–acclaimed eatery on Petralia's main street is beloved for its warm welcome, generous portions and bargain prices. The house speciality is *pasta con sugo di cinghiale e funghi* (pasta with wild boar and mushrooms); other *primi* incorporate classic Sicilian ingredients such as ricotta, pistachios, almonds and wild fennel. Serious aficionados will appreciate the multicourse wild boar menu.

ⓘ Getting There & Around

PARKING

There is a car park overlooking the valley directly opposite the junction of the SS120 and Corso Paolo Agliata (Petralia's main street). You'll find a second car park around the back side of the Chiesa Madre – drive through the arch just above the church, take the first left-hand fork and look for it on the left-hand side.

Piano Battaglia

More Swiss than Sicilian, the little ski resort at Piano Battaglia (www.piano battaglia.it) is dotted with chalets that play host to an ever-growing number of Sicilian downhill skiers in winter.

The Mufara (northern slopes) skiing complex goes up to heights of 1840m and serves 3.5km of runs, while the Mufaretta (southwest slopes) reaches 1680m, with a run about 500m long. There are two ski lifts up to the ski runs. You can also do cross-country and alpine skiing.

With the advent of spring, Piano Battaglia becomes an equally good walking and mountain-biking area, with plenty of signposted paths and a profusion of wildflowers. One popular walk starts at the Rifugio Piero Merlino in Piano Battaglia and heads north–northwest, taking in Pizzo Scalonazzo (1903m) and Pizzo Carbonara to end in an area of oak woodland at Piano Sempria (1300m). The *rifugio* can help you with itineraries and guides.

From Petralia Sottana, it's a twisty 16km climb along the SP54 to Piano Battaglia.

Collesano

POP 4072 / ELEV 917M

The upper reaches of this charming medieval town are dominated by the pink-and-cream Basilica San Pietro on Corso Vittorio Emanuele and the weathered remains of a nearby Norman castle. Like Castelbuono, the town was once governed by the Ventimiglias and retains an aristocratic air.

◉ Sights & Activities

There are a number of churches worthy of a visit, including the frescoed 15th-century Duomo (aka Santa Maria la Nuova), the 12th-century Chiesa di St Maria la Vecchia, the 17th-century Chiesa di St Maria del Gesù and the early-16th century Chiesa di St Giacomo.

Museo Targa Florio   MUSEUM
(☎0921 66 46 84; www.museotargaflorio.it; Corso Vittorio Emanuele 3; adult/over 65yr €2/1; ⊙9.30am-12.30pm & 3.30-7pm, closed Mon & Thu afternoons) This unique little museum displays photographs and memorabilia documenting the Targa Florio, the world's oldest sports-car racing event. Established by wealthy automobile enthusiast Vincenzo Florio in 1906, then discontinued in 1977 due to safety concerns, the 72km-race along the Monti Madonie's treacherous narrow roads was intensely challenging, with countless hairpin bends testing both the driver's skill and the car's performance.

A plaque in the museum's first room chronicles the names and car models of all the winners throughout the event's seven-decade history (in case you're wondering, Porsche won the most times, followed closely by Alfa Romeo).

✗ Eating

★Casale Drinzi   SICILIAN €
(☎0921 66 40 27; www.casaledrinzi.it; Contrada Drinzi, SP9; pizzas €3.50-7, meals €17-22; ⊙closed most of Feb) This wooden chalet in the hills immediately above Collesano is one of the Madonie's absolute gems – one whiff of the delicious aromas emanating from the kitchen and you'll know you've come to the right place. The menu features hearty mountain specialities such as stewed pork with artichokes and smoked ham alongside other rustic favourites featuring Slow Food–recognised regional ingredients.

Items not to be missed when available include the *degustazione di antipasti* (a plate of stuffed zucchini flowers, deep-fried ricotta, lardo-topped bruschetta and chargrilled local onions), *pappardelle al sugo di selvaggina* (home-made pasta ribbons with a game sauce) and *fagiolo Badda Nera* (beans grown in the area around Polizzi Generosa). Pizzas are added to the menu at night – a good reason to book into the on-site B&B (singles/doubles €30/60).

PARCO REGIONALE DEI NEBRODI

The Nebrodi Regional Park (www.parco-deinebrodi.it) was established in 1993 and constitutes the single largest forested area in Sicily. In fact, this is Sicilian author Gesualdo Bufalino's real 'island within an island', dotted with remote and traditional villages that host few visitors.

The forest ranges in altitude from 1200m to 1500m, and is an undulating landscape of beech, oak, elm, ash, cork, maple and yew trees that shelter the remnants of Sicily's wildlife: porcupines, San Fratello horses and wildcats, as well as a healthy population of birds of prey such as golden eagles, lanner and peregrine falcons and griffon vultures. The high pastures have always been home to hard-working agricultural communities that harvest delicious mushrooms and hazelnuts, churn out creamy ricotta and graze cows, sheep, horses, goats and pigs.

The highest peak in the park is Monte Soro (1847m), and the Lago di Biviere is a lovely natural lake supporting herons and stilts.

There are visitor centres in Alcara Li Fusi (094179 39 04; Via Ugo Foscolo 1), Bronte (338 2993077; Castello di Nelson), Cesarò (095 773 20 61; Via Bellini 79), Mistretta (Via Aversa 26) and Randazzo (095 799 16 11;

Corso Umberto 197) and smaller information points in several other towns including Floresta (Via Umberto I), but all keep irregular hours and most staff speak Italian only. For more information, see www.parks.it/parco.nebrodi or www.parcodeinebrodi.it.

San Marco D'Alunzio

POP 2078 / ELEV 550M

This spectacularly situated hilltop town, 9km from the coast, was founded by the Greeks in the 5th century BC and then occupied by the Romans, who named it Aluntium and built structures such as the Tempio di Ercole (Temple of Hercules) at the town's entrance. A Norman church, now roofless, was subsequently built on the temple's red marble base.

Southeast of the town is the trekking base, Longi, and southwest is Alcara Li Fusi, a small village situated beneath the impressive Rocche del Crasto (1315m), a nesting site of the golden eagle.

Sights & Activities

Virtually all of San Marco d'Alunzio's older buildings and its 22 churches were made using locally quarried marble. At the top of the hill are the scant remains of the first castle built by the Normans in Sicily.

ⓘ GETTING TO THE NEBRODI REGIONAL PARK

The best way to explore the park is by car, as bus services are few and far between.

By Car

The SS116 starts at Capo d'Orlando on the coast and climbs to Floresta (1275m), the highest village in the park, where you can stop for local olives, cheeses and meats at Alimentari Giuseppe Calabrese on the main square. From here, the road makes a spectacular descent to Randazzo, with unforgettable views of Mt Etna.

Cutting through the heart of the park is the enchanting SS289, which links Sant'Agata di Militello with Cesarò in the interior. Along the route is San Fratello, a typical Nebrodi town originally founded by Roger I's third wife, Adelaide di Monferrato, for her Lombard cousins (hence the strange local dialect).

If you're coming from the Monti Madonie, a pretty highland route into the Nebrodi is the SS120. Starting from Petralia Sottana, head east through the gorgeous hill towns of Gangi, Sperlinga and Nicosia, then turn north on the SS117 to Mistretta. The landscape is especially picturesque in springtime, when the high rolling hills are covered in wildflowers. On clear days, there are good distant views of Mt Etna to the southeast.

By Bus

Interbus (0935 2 24 60; www.interbus.it) operates buses from Messina to Cesarò (€8.90, three hours, one daily Monday to Saturday), Mistretta (€9.20, 2¼ hours, one daily Monday to Friday) and Randazzo (€6.70, two hours, one daily Monday to Saturday). It also offers service between the coastal town of Santo Stefano di Camastra and Mistretta (35 minutes, four daily Monday to Friday, two daily on weekends).

Chiesa di Santa Maria delle Grazie CHURCH

The most impressive of San Marco d' Alunzio's churches is the Chiesa di Santa Maria delle Grazie, where there's a Domenico Gagini statue of the *Madonna con bambino e San Giovanni* (Madonna with Child and St John) from 1481.

Museo della Cultura e delle Arti Figurative Bizantine e Normanne MUSEUM

(Museum of Byzantine & Norman Culture & Figurative Art; ☑ 0941 79 77 19; Badia Nica, Via Ferraloro; admission €1.55; ☺ 9am-1pm & 3-7pm) Next to the 16th-century Chiesa di San Teodoro, in a restored 16th-century Benedictine monastery, is a lovely space showing fresco fragments from the town's churches and a somewhat motley collection of columns, capitals and other bits and pieces from the Greek, Roman, Byzantine and Norman periods, most of them excavated in the surrounding area.

ℹ Information

Tourist Information Office (☑ 0941 79 73 39; www.sanmarco-turismo.it; Via Aluntia; ☺ 9am-1pm year-round, plus 3-7pm Oct-Apr, 3.30-7.30pm May & Sep, 4-8pm Jun-Aug) Opposite the Chiesa Madre.

Mistretta

Located on the western border of Nebrodi Regional Park, and accessed via the SS117 from Santo Stefano di Camastra, is the charming hilltop time capsule of Mistretta. The streets here have hardly changed over the past 300 years, and most of the locals look as if they've been around for almost as long. Little disturbs the mountain quietude – the only action occurs at the Gran Bar, an old-fashioned bar/pasticceria housed in a building dating from 1660. Its homemade biscuits are delicious; be sure to sample a few.

COASTAL RESORT VILLAGES

The 83km stretch of coastline between Cefalù and Capo d'Orlando to the east is dotted with little coves, relatively clean beaches and family-friendly resort villages. Beyond Capo d'Orlando the coast becomes more developed and industrialised the closer you get to Milazzo, the main point of departure for the Aeolian Islands.

Castel di Tusa

Named after the castle that now lies in ruins 600m above it, this small coastal resort about 25km east of Cefalù is best known for the controversial Fiumara d'Arte, an open-air sculpture park featuring a collection of contemporary artworks scattered along the *fiumara* (riverbed) of the Tusa River. The most recent, and most impressive, installation is the Piramide 38° Parallelo, a gleaming rust-coloured steel pyramid high on a hilltop above the sea, unveiled in March 2010 and now a regular gathering point for solstice celebrations.

From Castel di Tusa's beach, a small road leads inland to the parent village of Tusa. Between the coastal resort and the village, about 3km up from the coast, you'll see a signpost for Halaesa (☑ 0921 33 45 31; ☺ 9am-1hr before sunset) FREE, a Greek city founded in the 5th century BC. Beautifully positioned on a hill, and accessed through a small olive grove, it commands fine views of the surrounding countryside and – on a clear day – the Aeolian Islands. The most conspicuous ruins are those of its agora and its massive, rusticated walls. Downhill, at the entrance to the site, are the remains of a Colombarium, a 2nd-century Roman necropolis with some well-preserved stonework.

Castel di Tusa is serviced by trains from Milazzo (€7.25, 1½ to 1¾ hours, eight daily) and Palermo (€6.35, 1¼ to 1½ hours, eight daily). The station is at Tusa.

Sant'Agata di Militello

This popular resort town grew up around the Torre della Marina, a coastal watchtower erected in the 13th century. In summer it's usually crammed with Italians eager to make the most of the long stretch of pebbled beach. There are few cultural sites other than the much-modified Castello Gallego in the town centre.

Sant'Agata is a gateway for the Parco Regionale dei Nebrodi, and if you are going to head into the park, it may be worth starting your trip with a quick visit to the Museo Etno-Antropologico dei Nebrodi (☑ 0941 72 23 08; Via Cosenz 70; admission free; ☺ 8.30am-1.30pm Mon-Sat), which has displays on traditional mountain life.

There are frequent trains to Milazzo (from €5.15, 45 minutes to one hour, 18 daily) and Palermo (from €8, 1¾ to two hours, 14 daily).

Capo d'Orlando

The busiest resort town on the coast after Cefalù, Capo d'Orlando was founded – legend tells us – when one of Charlemagne's generals, a chap called Orlando, stood on the headland and declared it a fine place to build a castle. The ruins of this structure are still visible. In 1299 Frederick II of Aragon was defeated here by the rebellious baron Roger of Lauria, backed up by the joint forces of Catalonia and Anjou. More-recent rebels include the town's shopkeepers and traders, who made a name for themselves in the 1990s with their stand against the Mafia's demands for *pizzo* (protection money).

Visitors come here for the beaches, both sandy and rocky, that are on either side of town. The best swimming is to the east.

The best restaurant in town is La Tartaruga (☎0941 95 50 12; www.hoteltartaruga.it; Via Lido San Gregorio 41; meals €35; ⊗closed Mon & Nov) in the seafront hotel of the same name. The town's tourist office (☎0941 91 53 18; www.turismocapodorlando.it; Palazzo Satellite, Contrada Muscale; ⊗8.30am-2pm Mon-Fri,

plus 3-6pm Tue & Thu) is 2km west of here, several blocks inland from the point.

The best way to get here is by train from Milazzo (from €4.65, 35 to 50 minutes, 18 daily) or Palermo (from €8.30, 1¾ to 2¼ hours, 13 daily).

MILAZZO

POP 32,092

Hardly Sicily's prettiest town, Milazzo is hemmed in on its eastern perimeter by industrial development that can make even the most open-minded visitor run for the nearest hydrofoil. Indeed, the prime reason for setting foot in this town is to get to the Aeolian Islands. But, away from the refineries and busy dock, Milazzo has a pretty *Borgo Antico* (Old Town), and the isthmus that juts out to the north is an area of great natural beauty dotted with rocky coves.

⊙ Sights & Activities

★Il Castello   CASTLE
(www.compagniadelcastellomilazzo.it; Salita Castello; ⊗8.30am-1pm & 3.30-8pm Tue-Sun) FREE
Milazzo's enormous castle was built by Frederick II in 1239 and added to by Charles V of Aragon. It was originally the site of a Greek acropolis, then that of an Arab-Norman citadel. The whole of Milazzo once fit within its

WORTH A TRIP

TYNDARIS

At Capo Tindari, just off the autostrada between Milazzo and Cefalù, a historic church and an ancient Greco-Roman site make an interesting detour. Coming from the east, turn off the autostrada at Oliveri and follow signs for Tindari/Tyndaris. If you're coming from the west, the site is 12km from Marina di Patti on the SS113.

The enormous Santuario della Madonna del Tindari (Sanctuary of the Madonna of Tindari; ☎0941 36 90 03; www.santuariotindari.it; ⊗6.45am-12.30pm & 2.30-7pm Mon-Sat, 6.45am-12.45pm & 2.30-8pm Sun) can be seen from miles around: it sits right on the cape, its dome glistening in the sun. A sanctuary was built here in the 16th century to house the icon of the *Bruna Madonnina del Tindari* (Black Madonna of Tindari), but the current garishly decorated building mainly dates from the 20th century. The inscription underneath the icon reads *Nigra sum, sed hermosa* (I am black, but beautiful).

From the sanctuary, a path leads to the entrance of a more ancient holy place, Tyndaris (☎0941 36 90 23; adult €4, EU student 18-25yr €2, EU citizen under 18 or 65+ free; ⊗9am-1hr before sunset), founded by Dionysis of Syracuse after his victory over the Carthaginians in 396 BC. The secluded ruins (a basilica, agora, Roman house and Greek theatre) are set on the cliff edge amid prickly pears, olives and cypress trees. In summer you can clearly see the Aeolian Islands and the lovely Oliveri lagoon in the bay below. There's also a small museum displaying artefacts excavated at the site.

Drivers must park in the paid lot at the foot of the hill, then walk (15 minutes) or take the shuttle bus (€0.80 return, five minutes) up to the sanctuary and the ruins.

huge walls. In 1860, Garibaldi's troops successfully stormed the castle, which was at that time manned by Bourbon soldiers.

The castle grounds contain the city's Duomo Vecchio (old cathedral) and the ruins of the Palazzo dei Giurati (the old town hall). It's a lovely site to clamber around, full of flowers and crumbling walls. To get here, climb the Salita Castello, which rises up through the atmospheric Old Town. Note that at the time of research, the castle's medieval core was closed to visitors due to ongoing restoration work, but the outer perimeter remained open, including the Benedictine monastery and cloisters, the Duomo, and the Aragonese outer walls, which command dreamy views of the bay and the Aeolians.

Antiquarium di Milazzo   MUSEUM
(☑090 922 34 71; Via Impallomeni; ⊙9am-2pm Mon, 9am-7pm Tue-Sat, 2-7pm Sun) **FREE** Housed just below the castle in the 16th-century Quartiere degli Spagnoli defensive barracks, Milazzo's newest museum displays treasures dating from Neolithic times to the Byzantine era, amassed over seven decades of local archaeological digs. The collection is strong on household ceramics and funerary urns, with an emphasis on the Greek and prehistoric periods.

Capo Milazzo   WATERFRONT
If you have a car, don't miss the scenic drive north along **Strada Panoramica** to see the gorgeous, rugged coastline of **Capo Milazzo**. At the end of the isthmus is a lighthouse; park in the nearby lot, from where short walks lead to the Santuario Rupestre di San Antonio da Padova (p129) and the Piscina di Venere (p129).

Alternatively, you can arrange a boat trip (ask at the tourist office) around the rocky cape to Baia del Tonno on the western side of the isthmus.

**Santuario Rupestre di
San Antonio da Padova**   RUIN
(⊙9am-7pm) The evocative remains of this 13th-century church sit astride a hillside overlooking Capo Milazzo's crystal-clear waters. It was here that San Antonio da Padova famously sought refuge after a January 1221 shipwreck. Between the 16th and 18th centuries the original church was significantly spruced up with new altars and marble bas-reliefs, before falling into its current ruined state.

VENUS' SWIMMING POOL

Out at the very tip of Capo Milazzo, the gorgeous rock-fringed **Piscina di Venere** (Venus' Pool) makes an idyllic spot for swimming and sunbathing. Accessed by a 15-minute walk from the Capo Milazzo parking lot through a landscape of olive groves, cactus and stone walls, its tranquil turquoise waters are separated by a small ring of rocks from the ultramarine Mediterranean just beyond.

✖ Eating

★**Al Bagatto**   SICILIAN €€
(☑090 922 42 12; www.albagatto.com; Via Massimiliano Regis 11; meals €30; ⊙closed lunch, all day Sun & 2 weeks in Sep) Pass through the frosted-glass doors of this bustling *enoteca* (wine bar) and you'll quickly discover you've made the right choice. Mellow jazz, even mellower lighting, a fabulous wine list and a genial host complement the menu of local, Slow Food–celebrated dishes such as *costolette di maialino nero in salsa di senape all'antica* (cutlet of black pork in a mustard-fruit sauce).

There are only seven tables, so book ahead – if you don't score a table, you can join the local bohemian set and prop yourself at the bar to enjoy a delicious plate of antipasto with a glass of wine.

Salamone E Mare   SEAFOOD €€
(☑090 928 12 33; Strada Panoramica 36; meals €28-38; ⊙noon-3pm & 7.30pm-midnight Tue-Sun, plus Mon Jul & Aug) North along the isthmus, this restaurant has a terrace that juts out over the water, endowing it with wonderful views that are perfectly complemented by a menu dominated by locally caught seafood, simply but expertly prepared. Trademark dishes include *carpaccio di pescespada* (thinly sliced raw swordfish), *spaghetti ai gamberi* (spaghetti with prawns) and giant triangular ravioli stuffed with fresh fish.

❶ Information

EMERGENCIES
Ambulance (☑118)
Hospital (☑090 9 29 01; Villaggio Grazia)
Questura (☑090 923 03 00; Via Municipio 1)

MOVING ON?

For tips, recommendations and reviews, head to shop.lonelyplanet.com to purchase a downloadable PDF of the Puglia, Basilicata & Calabria chapter from Lonely Planet's *Italy* guide.

TOURIST INFORMATION

Pro Loco Milazzo (Molo Marullo 3; ⊗8.30am-1.30pm & 3.30-7.30pm) Milazzo's brand-new tourist office opened on the waterfront in summer 2013, a stone's throw from the hydrofoil dock.

❶ Getting There & Around

BOAT

Milazzo is the primary point of departure for ferries and hydrofoils to the Aeolian Islands, with three companies providing year-round service. The main operators – **Ustica Lines** (www.ustica-lines.it), Siremar (p313) and **NGI** (www.ngi-spa.it) – all have ticket offices along Via dei Mille opposite the port.

CAR & MOTORCYCLE

Milazzo is situated just off the A20-E90 toll road that travels between Messina and Palermo.

INTERCITY BUS

Buses depart from Piazza della Repubblica near the port. **Giuntabus** (☑ 090 67 57 49; www.giuntabustrasporti.com) runs frequently to/from Messina (€4.10, 50 minutes, 18 daily Monday to Friday, 15 on Saturday, three on Sunday).

LOCAL BUS

AST buses 4 and 5 run between the train station and port (€1.10, 10 minutes) roughly once an hour between 6.45am and 7.50pm. Bus 6 runs between the port and Capo Milazzo (€1.10, 15 minutes) six times daily between 7.50am and 5.10pm. Note that buses above operate Monday through Saturday only; Sunday and holiday service had been indefinitely suspended at the time of research. Tickets (valid for two hours) can be bought inside the train station or at the shop opposite the quayside bus stop with the AST sign.

PARKING

If you want to leave your car here while you island-hop, private garages charge approximately €12 per day. For a list of garages, see www.milazzo.info/it/garage.html. Short-term street parking (€0.35 per 30 minutes) is also available in spaces marked with blue lines.

TAXI

A taxi from the station to the port will cost approximately €10 to €12.

TRAIN

Regular services travel to Palermo (from €10.40, 2¼ to 3½ hours, 13 daily) and Messina (€3.45, 25 to 40 minutes, hourly).

Aeolian Islands

Best Places to Eat

➡ A Cannata (p147)

➡ Ristorante Villa Carla (p147)

➡ La Sirena (p156)

➡ Le Macine (p140)

➡ Trattoria da Paolino (p149)

Best Places to Stay

➡ Hotel Signum (p259)

➡ Hotel Raya (p260)

➡ Casa del Sole (p260)

➡ Diana Brown (p258)

➡ Capofaro (p259)

Why Go?

Rising out of the cobalt blue seas off Sicily's northeastern coast, the Unesco-protected Aeolian Islands (Lipari, Vulcano, Salina, Panarea, Stromboli, Filicudi and Alicudi) are a little piece of paradise, a magical outdoor playground offering thrills and spills at every turn. Stunning waters provide sport for swimmers, sailors and divers while trekkers can climb hissing volcanoes and gourmets can sup on honey-sweet Malvasia wine. The obvious base is Lipari, the largest and liveliest of the seven islands, but it's by no means the only option. Salina boasts excellent accommodation and good transport links, while Stromboli and Vulcano entertain nature lovers with awe-inspiring volcanic shenanigans and black-sand beaches. Ultrachic Panarea offers luxurious living at lower prices in the off-season, while Filicudi and Alicudi have an end-of-the-line appeal that's irresistible for fans of off-the-beaten-track adventure.

Road/Sea Distances (KM)

	Lipari	Messina	Milazzo	Santa Maria Salina
Messina	50			
Milazzo	35	40		
Santa Maria Salina	20	80	65	
Stromboli	45	75	70	45

DON'T MISS

The scenic boat ride back from Spiaggia Valle i Muria to Lipari at sunset, passing by the awe-inspiring sea-rock formations of Lipari's western shore.

Best Hikes

➡ Stromboli Crater (p151)

➡ Pianoconte to Quattropani (p138)

➡ Zucco Grande (p156)

➡ Filo dell'Arpa (p157)

➡ Punta del Corvo (p149)

Best Views

➡ Quattrocchi (p138)

➡ Capo Grillo (p143)

➡ Fossa delle Felci (p145)

➡ Sciara del Fuoco (p153)

➡ Pollara (p146)

Resources

➡ **Eolie Booking** (www.eoliebooking.com) Book a shuttle bus from Catania Airport to Milazzo.

➡ **Estate Eolie** (www.estateolie.net/en) English-language news and practical tips on all seven islands.

➡ **Eolnet** (www.eolnet.it/eng) A grab bag of Aeolian resources, including weather reports, Aeolian recipes and more.

Getting Around

Transport in the Aeolians means settling into a slower rhythm. Siremar and Ustica Lines run frequent hydrofoils connecting all seven islands; ferries ply the same routes, costing less but taking twice as long. Lipari, Vulcano and Salina are the only islands with significant road networks; here, rental scooters and local buses are your best means of locomotion; rental cars are available but pricey. Walking is a joy on all seven islands, thanks to scenic footpaths and limited traffic.

THREE PERFECT DAYS

Pamper Yourself on Salina

The Aeolians' greenest island struts its stuff at mealtimes with garden-fresh produce, abundant seafood and locally grown Malvasia wine. Hotels here are among the islands' cushiest too. Wake up late to cappuccino with an ocean view, indulge in a *ciclo benessere* (spa treatment) at Hotel Signum (p259) in Malfa, pack a picnic to photogenic Pollara (p146) or visit one of the local vineyards, then dine at Villa Carla (p147), A Cannata (p147) or any of the island's other standout restaurants.

Scale a Pair of Active Volcanoes

It's not every day you can climb two active volcanoes in less than 24 hours. Here's how: catch the 7:50am hydrofoil from Lipari to Vulcano, and reach the island's steam-belching summit by midmorning, before the heat and the hordes of day trippers arrive. Return to Lipari's Marina Corta (p136) for lunch, then hop on a tour boat to Stromboli in time to join your trekking party in the late afternoon. By sunset, you'll be oohing and ahing over the stunning fireworks of Europe's most active volcano. Trek back down for pizza in the piazza, then ride a boat home to your familiar Lipari bed.

Island-Hop Till You Drop

No matter what island you wake up on, a boat tour can expand your horizons in a hurry. Local operators typically offer tours to multiple islands in a single day, offering a taste of the Aeolians' varied personalities even to those with limited time.

Getting Away from It All

➡ **Stay on Stromboli's forgotten western shore** Far from the tourist bustle, tiny Ginostra village has just enough infrastructure to save you from sleeping on lava rocks.

➡ **Flee to Filicudi** This gorgeous island rarely gets very busy, even in peak season.

➡ **Sail out to Alicudi** For sheer solitude, nothing trumps Alicudi, one of the Mediterranean's most isolated spots.

❶ Getting There & Away

AIR

The only way to reach the Aeolians by air is to take a helicopter. Panarea-based **Air Panarea** (☑ 090 983 44 28; www.airpanarea.com) operates transfers to the Aeolians year-round from points in Sicily, including Catania, Palermo and Taormina, and from the Italian mainland (Rome, Naples, Salerno, Reggio di Calabria). Prices cover the entire six-seat helicopter and vary according to departure point and destination; for details, contact Air Panarea via its online form.

BOAT

The main point of departure for the Aeolians is Milazzo, from where there are regular year-round car ferries and hydrofoils. Lipari is the Aeolians' main point of arrival and its transport hub, with connections to all the other islands. Services are most frequent between June and September and much reduced in winter, when heavy seas can affect schedules. Ferries are cheaper, less frequent and much slower than hydrofoils, although they are less vulnerable to bad weather. The main operating companies are **Ustica Lines** (www.usticalines.it), which operates hydrofoils only; **Siremar** (www.siremar.it), which has hydrofoils and ferries; and **NGI** (☑ 090 928 40 91; www.ngi-spa.it), which runs ferries only. Note that the information listed below refers to high-season crossings and is not comprehensive; check the respective company websites for more detailed information. From Milazzo, there are hydrofoils to Vulcano (€15, 45 minutes, 15 daily), Lipari (€15.80, one hour, 16 daily), Salina (€17.55, 1¾ hours, 10 daily), Panarea (€17.80, 2¼ to 2½ hours, five daily), Stromboli (€20.95, 2¾ to three hours, five daily), Filicudi (€22.25, 2¾ hours, two daily) and Alicudi (€27.70, 3¼ hours, two daily). Get tickets from the sales offices on Via dei Mille.

Other year-round services include Ustica Lines hydrofoils from Messina to Lipari (€22.90, 1½ to 3½ hours, five daily summer, one daily winter) and Siremar ferries from Naples to Lipari (€59, 13½ hours, twice weekly) and the other islands. In summer only, Ustica Lines also offers a daily service from Palermo that makes stops on all seven islands.

BUS

Travellers arriving at Catania's Fontanarossa airport can reach the Aeolians fairly easily, thanks to regular shuttle bus services. **Giuntabus** (☑ 090 67 37 82; www.giuntabus.com) runs a twice-daily shuttle (one way/return €13/24, 1¾ hours) between Fontanarossa airport and Milazzo's hydrofoil dock, leaving the airport at 11.50am and 4.45pm, returning from Milazzo at 9.15am and 2pm daily. Tickets are available on the bus. **Eoliebooking** (www.eoliebooking.com)

offers a more frequent but pricier year-round shuttle service (€25 to €35 per person, minimum two people, up to five departures daily) along the same route.

CAR & MOTORCYCLE

Only Lipari, Vulcano, Salina and Filicudi have roads suitable for automobile traffic. Scooter- and car-rental outlets are readily available on the first three, and both Lipari and Salina have good local bus systems. Bringing your own car over to the islands is expensive: from Milazzo to Lipari or Vulcano, the minimum cost is €55 each way; to Salina or Filicudi, it's €70 each way. If you're only visiting the islands for a couple of days, you're generally better off leaving your car in a garage in Milazzo (from €12 per day); for a list of garages, see www.milazzo.info/it/garage.html. For longer trips, bringing your own vehicle can still work out cheaper than hiring one, but note that restrictions apply – between July and September you can only take a car if you have booked accommodation for at least seven days.

LIPARI

POP 11,700

Lipari is the largest, busiest and most accessible of the Aeolian Islands. Visitors arriving from the mainland will likely experience it as a relaxing introduction to island life; on the other hand, if you've just come from the outer Aeolians, it may feel a bit like the big city!

The main focus is Lipari Town, the archipelago's principal transport hub and the nearest thing that islanders have to a capital city. A busy little port with a pretty, pastel-coloured seafront and plenty of accommodation, it makes the most convenient base for island-hopping. Away from the town, Lipari reveals a rugged and typically Mediterranean landscape of low-lying *macchia* (dense shrubland), silent, windswept highlands, precipitous cliffs and dreamy blue waters.

Named after Liparus, the father-in-law of Aeolus (the Greek god of the winds), Lipari was settled in the 4th millennium BC by the Stentillenians, Sicily's first known inhabitants. These early islanders developed a flourishing economy based on obsidian, a glassy volcanic rock used to make primitive tools.

Commerce continued under the Greeks, but the arrival of the Romans in the 3rd century BC signalled the end of the islanders' good fortunes. The Roman authorities were in a vengeful mood after the islanders had

Aeolian Islands Highlights

1 Dig through five millennia of island history at the archaeological museum in **Lipari** (p135).

2 Savour local wine and capers in the tranquil vineyard-clad interior of **Salina** (p145), the Aeolians' lushest island.

3 Watch **Stromboli** (p148) erupt at sunset, then relish the magic of the return hike, with the moonlit Tyrrhenian glowing far below your feet.

4 Lounge poolside on a sunny whitewashed terrace in **Panarea** (p148), or explore its constellation of five offshore islands on a day trip.

5 Dive in search of sunken Greek and Roman ships off Capo Graziano on **Filicudi.**

6 Hold your nose and cover your body with sulphurous ooze in the other-worldly mud baths of **Vulcano** (p142).

7 Escape to **Alicudi** (p157), where fishermen still run the show and donkeys sometimes seem to outnumber tourists.

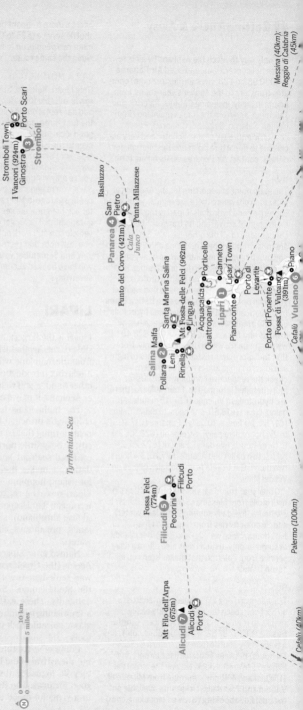

Tyrrhenian Sea

Stromboli Town
I Vancori (924m) ▲ Porto Scari
Ginostra ● **3**
Stromboli

Panarea **4** San
Pietro ●   ● Basiluzzo
Punto del Corvo (421m) ▲ *Cala*
Junco ● Ponta Milazzese

Salina Malfa
Pollara ●   ● Santa Marina Salina
Leni ●   ● Lingua
Rinella ● Mt Fossa delle Felci (962m) ▲
Salina 2

Acquacalda ●
Quattropani ● ● Porticello
● Canneto
Pianoconte ● ● Lipari Town
Lipari 1
Porto di
Levante ●
Porto di Ponente ● ● Piano
Fossa di Vulcano
(391m) ▲
Cefalù **Vulcano 6**

Fossa Felci
(774m) ▲
Pecorini ● ● Filicudi
Filicudi 5 Porto

Mt Filo dell'Arpa
(675m) ▲
Alicudi ●
Alicudi 7 Porto

Palermo (100km)

Cefalù (40km)

Messina (40km);
Reggio di Calabria
(45km)

0 —— 10 km
0 —— 5 miles

sided against them in the First Punic War, and reduced the island to a state of poverty through punitive taxation.

Over the ensuing centuries, volcanic eruptions and pirate attacks – most famously in 1544, when Barbarossa burnt Lipari Town to the ground and took off with most of its female population – kept the islanders in a state of constant fear.

Unremitting poverty ensured large-scale emigration, which continued until well into the 20th century, leaving the island remote and unwanted. During Italy's fascist period in the 1930s, Mussolini used Lipari Town's castle to imprison his political opponents. Things gradually started to improve with the onset of tourism in the 1950s, and now Lipari sits at the heart of one of Sicily's most revered holiday destinations.

⊙ Sights

Lipari's main sights, such as they are, are in Lipari Town. However, to find the best swimming and hiking spots and enjoy some sensational views, you'll need to head into the island's rugged hinterland.

⊙ Lipari Town

Although it's the main tourist centre in the Aeolians, Lipari Town hasn't yet sold its soul, and it retains a charming, laid-back island vibe. There are few sights beyond the soaring clifftop citadel and archaeological museum, but it's lovely to stroll the labyrinthine alleyways with the sun on your face and nothing to do but enjoy the relaxed atmosphere. The best approach to the citadel is Via del Concordato, a stairway that leads up from Via Garibaldi to the Cattedrale di San Bartolomeo.

★Museo Archeologico
Regionale Eoliano   MUSEUM
(☑090 988 01 74; www.regione.sicilia.it/beniculturali/museolipari; Castello di Lipari; adult/18-25 yr/EU citizen under 18 yr & over 65 yr €6/3/free; ⊙9am-1pm & 3-6pm Mon-Sat, 9am-1pm Sun) A must-see for lovers of Mediterranean history, Lipari's archaeological museum boasts one of Europe's finest collections of ancient finds. Especially worthwhile are the Sezione Preistorica, devoted to locally discovered artefacts from the Neolithic and Bronze Ages to the Greco-Roman era, and the Sezione Classica, highlights of which include

ancient shipwreck cargoes and the world's largest collection of Greek theatrical masks.

The museum is divided into several sections, each housed in a separate building. Start in the Sezione Preistorica in the Palazzo Vescovile (Bishop's Palace) next to the Cattedrale. A plethora of artefacts displayed in chronological order provides a fascinating insight into the development of the island's earliest cultures. Among the first items on display are finely sculpted tools made from the obsidian on which Lipari's early economy was based – telling evidence of the relative sophistication of the island's prehistoric civilisation. Prehistoric finds from the other islands are housed in a small pavilion directly in front of the Palazzo Vescovile.

On the other side of the cathedral is the Sezione Classica. Highlights here include finds from Lipari's 11th-century-BC necropolis, including a sizeable collection of burial urns. There's also a staggering array of amphorae salvaged from shipwrecks off the coasts of Panarea, Filicudi and Lipari itself. Upstairs are impressive displays of decorated vases and the museum's treasured collection of Greek theatrical masks. On this same floor you'll find a number of statuettes – the one of *Andromeda con bambino* (Andromeda with Child) is particularly beautiful – along with some elegant jewellery and a collection of polychromatic vases decorated by an artist simply known as Il Pittore Liparoto (the Lipari Painter; 300–270 BC).

Other sections worth a quick look are the Sezione Epigrafica (Epigraphic Section), across the road from the Sezione Preistorica, which has a small garden littered with engraved stones and a room of Greek and Roman tombs; and the Sezione Vulcanologica (Vulcanology Section), which illustrates the Aeolians' volcanic geology.

AEOLIAN ISLANDS LIPARI

Lipari Town

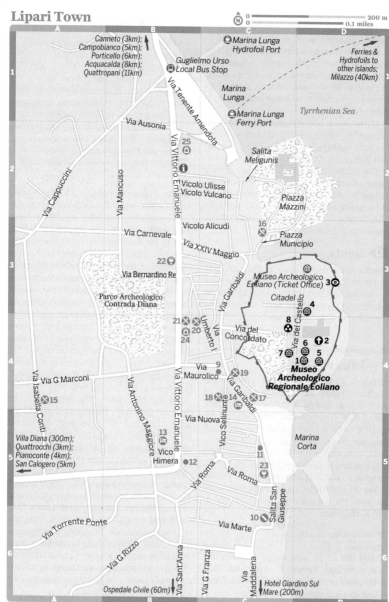

AEOLIAN ISLANDS LIPARI

0   200 m
0   0.1 miles

Canneto (3km);
Campobianco (5km);
Porticello (6km);
Acquacalda (8km);
Quattropani (11km)

Marina Lunga
Hydrofoil Port

Ferries &
Hydrofoils to
other islands;
Milazzo (40km)

Guglielmo Urso
Local Bus Stop

Via Tenente Amendola

Via Ausonia

Marina
Lunga

Marina Lunga
Ferry Port

Tyrrhenian Sea

Via Vittorio Emanuele

25

Salita
Meligunis

Via Cappuccini

Via Mancuso

Vicolo Ulisse
Vicolo Vulcano

Piazza
Mazzini

Via Carnevale

Vicolo Alicudi

Via XXIV Maggio

16

Piazza
Municipio

22

Via Bernardino Re

Via Garibaldi

Museo Archeologico
Eoliano (Ticket Office) 3

Parco Archeologico
Contrada Diana

Citadel

4

21   20
24

Via Umberto I

8

Via del
Concordato

Via del Castello

6

7   1

2

5

Museo
Archeologico
Regionale Eoliano

Via Isabella Conti

Via G Marconi

Via Maurolico

9

19

Via Vittorio Emanuele

Via Antonino Maggiore

15

18   14

17

Via Nuova

Vico Selinunte

Villa Diana (300m);
Quattrocchi (3km);
Pianoconte (4km);
San Calogero (5km)

13

Vico
Himera

12

11

Marina
Corta

Via Roma

23

Via Roma

Via Torrente Ponte

Via G Rizzo

Via Sant'Anna

Via G Franza

10

Via Marte

Salita San
Giuseppe

Ospedale Civile (60m)

Via Maddalena

Hotel Giardino Sul
Mare (200m)

Town Centre

PROMENADE

One of Lipari Town's great pleasures is
simply wandering its streets, lapping up
the laid-back island atmosphere. Lipari's
liveliest street is **Via Vittorio Emanuele**, a
cheerful thoroughfare lined with bars, cafes,

restaurants and delis. The street really comes
into its own in the early evening, when it's
closed to traffic and the locals come out for
their *passeggiata* (evening stroll).

Another atmospheric area is **Marina
Corta**, down at the end of Via Garibaldi,

Lipari Town

a pretty little marina ringed by popular bars and restaurants.

Citadel
CITADEL

After the pirate Barbarossa rampaged through in 1544, murdering most of Lipari's men and enslaving the women, the island's Spanish overlords fortified Lipari by constructing a citadel (also known as the castle) around the town centre. The town has since moved downhill but much of the citadel's impregnable wall structure survives; it's an impressive sight, especially when seen from below.

Parco Archeologico
RUIN

In the sunken area opposite Lipari's cathedral, you can see the remains of a series of circular huts, the oldest of which date to the 17th century BC. Nearby, at the southern end of the citadel, you'll find some Greek sarcophagi adjacent to an open-air amphitheatre that was built in 1978.

Cattedrale di San Bartolomeo
CHURCH

A fine example of 17th-century baroque architecture, this church was built to replace the original Norman cathedral destroyed by Barbarossa. Little remains of the 12th-century original except a section of Benedictine cloister to the right of the main entrance. The interior features a silver statue of St Bartholomew (1728), Lipari's patron saint, with his flayed skin tucked under his arm.

◉ Around Lipari

Although Lipari Town is so self-contained that you could easily spend your entire holiday there, the rest of the island is well worth checking out, especially if you want to find the best swimming and hiking spots. The island is small enough that a grand tour only takes about an hour by car. If you've got more time on your hands, you can also make your way around on public buses.

★ Spiaggia Valle i Muria
BEACH

This dark, pebbly beach on the southwestern shore, lapped by clean waters and surrounded by dramatic cliffs, is one of Lipari's best swimming and sunbathing spots. The turn-off, about 3km west of Lipari Town, is easily reachable by car, scooter or local bus; follow the road towards Pianoconte until you see signs. From here, it's a steep 15-minute downhill walk.

The route down to the beach starts as a paved road, but eventually narrows to a dirt trail, passing through an idyllic landscape of long grass, flowers and cacti. Slogging back up the hill is a real workout, so come prepared for the day with water, sunscreen and a picnic lunch.

In good weather, Lipari resident Barni (☑ 339 8221583, 349 1839555) serves food and drinks from his rustic cavelike bar on the beach, and also provides boat transfers to

Lipari Island

Salina (10km); Filicudi (35km); Alicudi (50km)
La Parete dei Gabbiani
Punta Castagna
Acquacalda
Porticello
Rocche
Mt Pilato   Rosse
(476m)   Spiaggia della Papesca
Quattropani
Mt Chìrica
(602m)   Campobianco
Old Kaolin   Spiaggia Bianca
Mine
Pietra   Canneto
del Bagno   Mt San Angelo
(594m)
Secca del   Pianoconte
Bagno   San   Panarea (20km); Stromboli (40km)
Calogero
Lipari Town
Quattrocchi
Spiaggia Valle   Milazzo
i Muria   (40km)
Tyrrhenian
Sea
Pietra Menalda
Bocche di Vulcano   Vulcano (6km)

and from Marina Corta in Lipari (€5/10 one way/return). This is an especially nice way to get home after a long day on the beach. Navigating through the *faraglioni* (rock spires) of Lipari's western shore at sunset, with Vulcano's crater smoking on the horizon, is an unforgettable experience.

★ **Quattrocchi** VIEW POINT

Lipari's best views are from a celebrated viewpoint known as Quattrocchi (Four Eyes), 3km west of town. Follow the road for Pianoconte and look on your left about 300m beyond the turn-off for Spiaggia Valle i Muria. You'll know you're in the right place when you see a sensational coastal panorama unfold in front of you.

Stretching off to the south, great, grey cliffs plunge into the sea, while in the distance plumes of sinister smoke rise from the dark heights of neighbouring Vulcano.

Spiaggia Bianca BEACH

About 4km north of Lipari Town, this is the most popular beach on the island, its name a reference to the layers of pumice dust that once covered it. These have been slowly washed away by the rough winter seas, leaving it a dark shade of grey.

Canneto BEACH

The nearest beach to Lipari Town is the long, pebbly strip at Canneto, 3km north of town on the other side of a jutting headland.

Campobianco MINE

A few kilometres north of the beach at Canneto lies the Campobianco quarry, where huge gashes of white rock streak down the green hillside. These are the result of extensive pumice quarrying, which was an important local industry until 2000, when Unesco called for curtailment of mining operations as a condition for granting World Heritage status to the Aeolians.

Spiaggia della Papesca BEACH

Beyond Campobianco at Porticello, this pebble beach is dusted white by the fine pumice that gives the sea its limpid turquoise colour.

🏃 Activities

Hiking

Away from the more obvious coastal pleasures, there's some lovely hiking on Lipari, especially along the rugged northern and western coastlines. Most walks involve fairly steep slopes, although the summer heat is as likely to wear you down as the terrain. Take all the usual precautions: a hat, sunblock, plenty of water, and try to avoid the midday sun.

★ **Pianoconte to Quattropani** HIKING

This three- to four-hour hike starts from Pianoconte's school (5km west of Lipari Town), descending towards the sea along a paved road, which eventually narrows to a trail. Levelling out along the coastal bluffs, a relatively flat section skirts Lipari's western shoreline, affording fabulous views of Salina, Vulcano, Filicudi and Alicudi, before climbing steeply to the town of Quattropani.

As you descend from Pianoconte, you'll pass the old Roman baths of San Calogero, famous in antiquity for the thermal spring that flowed at a constant temperature of 60°C. Climbing back to Quattropani, you'll also pass the old Kaolin Mine, where the hillside is still visibly scarred. The trail can just as easily be hiked in the opposite direction, starting just south of the town of Quattropani. Either way, the strenuous climbs and steep descents are rewarded with spectacular coastal scenery. Both ends of the trail can be reached by local bus: on the way there, ask the driver to let you off at the trailhead; returning, look for the official bus stop in either Pianoconte or Quattropani.

Quattropani to Acquacalda

The pleasant hour-long downhill stroll from Quattropani to Acquacalda follows a paved but lightly travelled road hugging Lipari's north shore, affording spectacular views of Salina and a distant Stromboli. Take the bus to Quattropani (€1.90), then simply proceed downhill on the main road 5km to Acquacalda, where you can catch the bus (€1.55) back to Lipari.

Monte Pilato
HIKING

At Lipari's northeastern corner, Monte Pilato is a mountain of pumice and obsidian formed by a volcanic explosion in AD 700. A 2km trail leads to its summit (476m), starting from Ristorante Da Lauro in the town of Acquacalda. Up top, there's a nice view of the fields of solidified obsidian known as Rocche Rosse (Red Rocks).

Nesos
WALKING

(☑090 981 48 38; www.nesos.org; Via Vittorio Emanuele 24) ✐ Run by conservation biologist Pietro Lo Cascio, this recommended local environmental organisation leads guided walks on Lipari and throughout the Aeolians (€10, plus boat fare if travelling beyond Lipari). It also publishes the excellent hiking guide *15 Walks in the Aeolian Islands* (available in English, German, French and Italian).

Diving

Lipari's crystalline waters provide plenty of sport for snorkellers and scuba divers.

Diving Center La Gorgonia
DIVING

(☑090 981 26 16; www.lagorgoniadiving.it; Salita San Giuseppe) This outfit offers courses, boat transport, equipment hire and general information about scuba diving and snorkelling around Lipari. A single dive costs €30 if you have your own kit or €50 with rental equipment. Courses range from €55 for the basic Discover Scuba Diving class to €750 for an Assistant Instructor course. See the website for a complete price list.

☞ Tours

A boat tour around Lipari is a good way of seeing the island, and the only way of getting to some of the more inaccessible swimming spots. Lipari's high concentration of tour operators also makes it a great base from which to embark on day trips to the outer Aeolian Islands.

Numerous agencies in town offer tours. Prices vary depending on the season, but as a rough guide allow €20 for a tour of Lipari and Vulcano, €45 to visit Filicudi and Alicudi, €45 for a day trip to Panarea and Stromboli, or €80 for a late-afternoon trip to Stromboli with a guided trip up the mountain at sunset and a late-night return to Lipari. Tour companies generally operate from March to October.

Da Massimo/Dolce Vita
BOAT TOUR

(☑090 981 30 86; www.damassimo.it; Via Maurolico 2) One of Lipari's best established agencies, well positioned on a side street between Via Vittorio Emanuele and Via Garibaldi. Specialises in sunset hikes to the top of Stromboli, returning by boat to Lipari the same evening. It also hires out boats and dinghies.

★ Festivals & Events

Easter Celebrations
RELIGIOUS

Heartfelt and theatrical, Lipari's traditional Easter celebrations kick off on Palm Sunday with the Via Crucis, a costumed candlelit

---

DON'T MISS

DIVING SPOTS AROUND LIPARI

Lipari's got some spectacular spots for divers to explore. The folks at Diving Center La Gorgonia can point you to the spots below and many more:

➡ **Punta Castagna** (difficult; depth 10m to 40m) A spectacular dive with a 10m white pumice platform interrupted by multicoloured channels.

➡ **Secca del Bagno** (difficult; depth 40m to 45m) A breathtaking collection of colourful walls that are swathed with schools of technicolor fish.

➡ **Pietra Menalda** (medium; depth 18m to 40m) See the homes of octopuses, eel, groupers and other sea critters on the southern side of the island.

➡ **Pietra del Bagno** (all levels; 20m to 40m) Circumnavigate the Bagno rock while witnessing colourful rock surfaces and sea life.

➡ **La Parete dei Gabbiani** (medium; 20m to 45m) A black-and-white dive: black lava rock streaked with white pumice stone, hiding cracks that are home to lobsters.

procession from Piazza Mazzini up to the citadel, culminating in a reenactment of the crucifixion. The mood is similarly sombre on Good Friday, when groups of barefoot penitents accompany statues of Christ around town in an atmosphere of funereal silence.

Easter Day is more light-hearted, with two processions, one headed by the resurrected Jesus and the other by the Virgin Mary, meeting in Marina Corta to fireworks and noisy rejoicing.

✖ Eating

The waters of the archipelago abound with fish, including tuna, mullet, cuttlefish and sole, all of which end up on restaurant tables. Swordfish is a particular favourite, although you'll only find fresh swordfish between May and July; outside of that period it will almost certainly be frozen. Another island staple is *pasta all'eoliana*, a simple blend of capers, olive oil and basil. The local wine is Malvasia, which has a DOC *(Denominazione di origine controllata)* accreditation and a sweet taste of honey.

Many restaurants close during the winter season between late October and Easter.

Gilberto e Vera SANDWICHES €
(www.gilbertoevera.it; Via Garibaldi 22-24; sandwiches €5; ⊙ 7.30am-3pm & 4pm-midnight) This rather touristy place near Marina Corta is a convenient spot to pick up sandwiches for a day of hiking or beach-hopping. There are over two dozen varieties on the menu, with Sicilian ingredients like capers, olives, eggplant and tuna making frequent appearances. Unconventional hours also make it a good choice for a mid-afternoon snack or glass of wine.

Pasticceria Subba PASTRIES & CAKES €
(☑ 090 981 13 52; Via Vittorio Emanuele 92; sweets from €1; ⊙ 7am-10pm) One of Lipari's great indulgences is a cake from this famous *pasticceria* (pastry shop). In business since 1930, the main shop fronts Via Vittorio Emanuele but behind is a lovely outdoor seating area where you can linger over a coffee and fabulous pastries and cakes.

La Piazzetta PIZZERIA €
(☑ 090 981 25 22; Via San Vincenzo; pizzas €6-10; ⊙ 7-11pm, closed Thu Sep-Jun) A lively pizzeria with vine-draped outdoor seating that has served the likes of Audrey Hepburn; it's one block east of Via Vittorio Emanuele.

★ **Le Macine** SICILIAN €€
(☑ 090 982 23 87; www.lemacine.org; Via Stradale 9, Pianoconte; meals €27-36; ⊙ 12.30-3pm & 7-10pm daily May-Sep, Sat & Sun Oct-Apr) This country restaurant in Pianoconte, 4.5km from Lipari Town, comes into its own in summer, when meals are served on the terrace. Seafood and fresh vegetables star in dishes such as swordfish cakes with artichokes, shrimp-filled ravioli or fish in *ghiotta* sauce (with olive oil, capers, tomatoes, garlic and basil). Reservations are advised, as is the free shuttle service.

Kasbah MODERN SICILIAN, PIZZERIA €€
(☑ 090 981 10 75; Vico Selinunte 41; pizzas €5-9, meals €28-33; ⊙ 7-11pm Mar-Oct) This perennial local favourite is hidden down narrow Vico Selinunte. Food runs from high-quality wood-fired pizzas to exquisite pastas, fish dishes and wild cards like stewed lamb with veggies or couscous-crusted anchovy fritters. The casual-chic dining room is all minimalist white decor juxtaposed against grey linen tablecloths and stone walls; out back there's a candlelit garden.

La Cambusa TRATTORIA €€
(☑ 349 4766061; www.lacambusalipari.it; Via Garibaldi 72; meals €25-27; ⊙ 12.30-3pm & 7.30-10pm Easter-Oct) Old seafaring prints and a menu of traditional fish staples give this little trattoria the cosy air of a retired fisherman's house. Locals and visitors crowd the sidewalk tables and squeeze into the tiny interior for unpretentious classics such as spaghetti *ai gamberetti* (with prawns) and *sarde a beccafico* (lightly fried sardines stuffed with breadcrumbs, raisins, pine nuts and parsley).

E Pulera MODERN SICILIAN €€€
(☑ 090 981 11 58; www.pulera.it; Via Isabella Conti; meals €35-50; ⊙ 7.30-10pm May-Oct) With its serene garden setting, low lighting, artsy tile-topped tables and exquisite food, E Pulera makes an upscale but relaxed choice for a romantic dinner. Start with a carpaccio of tuna with blood oranges and capers, choose from a vast array of Aeolian and Sicilian meat and fish dishes, then finish with *cassata* or biscotti with sweet Malvasia wine.

Filippino SICILIAN €€€
(☑ 090 981 10 02; www.filippino.it; Piazza Municipio; meals €35-50; ⊙ closed Mon Oct-Mar) In business for over a century, Filippino is a mainstay of Lipari's culinary scene, considered by many the island's finest restaurant.

AEOLIAN ISLANDS LIPARI

AEOLIAN ACCOMMODATION

Aeolian accommodation is largely seasonal, with most places opening between Easter and October. Hotels tend to be three-star and above, with prices and standards universally high. There's also a burgeoning crop of B&Bs, offering lower prices with a homier atmosphere. Lipari, Stromboli and Salina offer the most choice. Here are a few great options to get you started.

➡ A magnificent retreat, Salina's Hotel Signum (p259) has the lot: an infinity pool, tasteful rooms, a spa complex and a terrace restaurant.

➡ With a range of rooms in the heart of Lipari Town, Diana Brown (p258) offers value for money, location and a portside welcome.

➡ Modest, difficult to get to, and cut off from the world, Filicudi's Pensione La Sirena (p260) offers sunny rooms in a quiet corner of paradise.

➡ Let out all the stops at Hotel Raya (p260), a decadent honeycomb of whitewashed rooms and terraces with its own spring-fed pool and waterfront restaurant.

➡ Relax on the sunny citrus-scented patio at family-run Casa del Sole (p260), one of Stromboli's oldest homes, now converted to a low-key guesthouse.

Housed in an elegant glass pavilion adjacent to the citadel, its army of white-coated waiters serves a dizzying array of Sicilian classics and homegrown innovations, from savory fish stews to jasmine mousse for dessert. Dress appropriately and book ahead.

🍷 Drinking

Bar La Precchia   BAR
(☑090 981 13 03; Via Vittorio Emanuele 191) If you fancy a late-night drink or simply want a prime people-watching perch during the *passeggiata* (evening stroll), pull up a chair at this hugely popular bar. It has an enormous menu of drinks, from *cafe frappe* and fruit milkshakes to cocktails and wine, and stays open until the small hours. Occasional live music adds to the party atmosphere.

Il Gabbiano   BAR
(☑090 981 14 71; Marina Corta) One of several bars, cafes and restaurants at Marina Corta, Il Gabbiano has tables laid out on a pretty piazza. Like everywhere on the island, it's touristy, but it's a scenic spot to chill out over a cool drink, an ice cream cone or a more substantial afternoon snack.

Shopping

La Formagella   FOOD & DRINK
(Via Vittorio Emanuele 250; ☺9am-1pm & 4-7pm) You simply can't leave the Aeolian Islands without a small pot of capers and a bottle of sweet Malvasia wine. You can get both, along with meats, cheeses and other delicious goodies, at this gourmet grocery-deli just around the corner from the hydrofoil dock.

Fratelli Laise   FOOD & DRINK
(www.fratellilaise.com; Via Vittorio Emanuele 118; ☺9am-1pm & 4-7pm) About two-thirds of the way down from Marina Lunga to Marina Corta, a lush, technicolor fruit display announces the presence of this traditional greengrocer, piled high with wines, sweets, *anis* (aniseed) biscuits, pâtés, capers and olive oils. It's an excellent place to find food gifts to bring home – or simply to stock up on picnic provisions.

ℹ Orientation

Hydrofoils and ferries dock at Marina Lunga, one of two ports at Lipari Town; the other, used by tour boats, is Marina Corta on the other side of the clifftop citadel. The seafront road circles the entire island, a journey of about 30km.

ℹ Information

Ambulance (☑090 988 54 67)
Farmacia Sparacino (☑090 981 13 92; Via Vittorio Emanuele 174; ☺10am-1pm & 5-9pm)
Ospedale Civile (☑090 988 51 11; Via Sant'Anna) Operates a first-aid service.
Police (☑090 981 13 33; Via Marconi)
Tourist office (☑090 988 00 95; Via Vittorio Emanuele 202; ☺9am-1pm & 4.30-7pm Mon, Wed & Fri, 9am-1pm Tue & Thu) Lipari's office provides information covering all of the Aeolian Islands.

ⓘ Getting There & Around

BOAT

The main port is Marina Lunga, where you'll find a joint ticket office for the two main companies serving the island – **Siremar** (☑ 090 981 12 20; www.siremar.it) and **Ustica Lines** (☑ 090 981 24 48; www.usticalines.it) – and a kiosk for the smaller ferry operator **NGI** (☑ 090 928 40 91; www.ngi-spa.it). Timetable information is displayed at the ticket office and is also available at the tourist office. Adjacent to the ticket offices is a **left-luggage office** (☑ 347 997 35 45; per piece for 12hr €3, plus €5 if left overnight; ☉ 8am-5pm). From Lipari you can catch ferries and hydrofoils to all the other islands: Vulcano (ferry/hydrofoil €4.70/5.80, 25/10 minutes), Santa Marina Salina (ferry/hydrofoil €6.70/9.60, 50/25 minutes), Panarea (ferry/hydrofoil €7.50/9.80, two hours/one hour), Stromboli (ferry/hydrofoil €12.40/17.80, 3½/1½ hours), Filicudi (ferry/hydrofoil €11.10/15.80, 2¾/1¼ hours) and Alicudi (ferry/hydrofoil €13.95/18.85, four/two hours). Services also run to Milazzo and ports on the Sicilian and Italian mainland.

BUS

Island bus services are run by **Autobus Guglielmo Urso** (☑ 090 981 10 26; www.ursobus.com/orariursobus.pdf). Opposite the Esso petrol station at Marina Lunga is the bus stop. One main route serves the island's eastern shore, from Lipari Town to Canneto (five minutes) and Acquacalda (20 minutes), with 12 buses Monday to Saturday, seven on Sunday. Another route runs from Lipari Town to the western highland settlements of Quattrocchi, Pianoconte and Quattropani. Individual tickets range in price from €1.50 to €1.90. If you plan on using the bus a lot, you'll save money by buying a ticket booklet (six/10/20 tickets for €7/10.50/20.50).

CAR & MOTORCYCLE

Lipari is not big – only 38 sq km – but to explore it in depth it can be helpful to have your own wheels. There are various outfits opposite the hydrofoil dock at Marina Lunga where you can hire bikes, scooters and cars, including **Da Marcello** (☑ 090 981 12 34; www.noleggiodamarcello.com; Via Tenente Amendola) and **Da Luigi** (☑ 090 988 05 40; www.noleggiolipari.it; Marina Lunga). Allow about €10 per day for a bike, between €15 and €40 per day for a scooter, and from €30 to €70 per day for a small car.

VULCANO

POP 715

Approaching Vulcano, it's difficult not to feel a slight shiver down your spine as you spot the white trails of smoke rising from the island's ominous peaks. However, any

sense of disquiet is quickly supplanted by a more earthy reaction as you get your first whiff of the vile sulphurous gases that infuse the air. Vulcano's volcanic nature has long been impressing visitors – the ancient Romans believed it to be the chimney of the fire god Vulcan's workshop – and the island is today celebrated for its therapeutic mud baths and hot springs. The main drawcard, however, remains the Fossa di Vulcano, or Gran Cratere (Large Crater), the steaming volcano that towers over the island's northeastern shores.

There's no sightseeing as such on Vulcano, but it's a great place to spend a day or two, swimming off the dark volcanic beaches, sailing the wild coast or climbing up to the smoking crater. Most of the action is centred on touristy Porto di Levante and the black beaches at Porto di Ponente, but once you get away from these places, the landscape takes on a quiet, rural aspect with vegetable gardens, birdsong and a surprising amount of greenery.

◉ Sights & Activities

★ **Fossa di Vulcano**   WALKING
(admission €3) Vulcano's top attraction is the straightforward trek up its 391m volcano (no guide required). Start early if possible

and bring a hat, sunscreen and water. Follow the signs south along Strada Provinciale, then turn left onto the zigzag gravel track that leads to the summit. It's about an hour's scramble to the lowest point of the crater's edge (290m).

From here, the sight of the steaming crater encrusted with red and yellow crystals is reward enough, but it's well worth lingering up top for a while. You can descend steeply to the crater floor or, better yet, continue climbing around the rim for stunning views of all the islands lined up to the north.

Laghetto di Fanghi   MUD BATHS
(admission €2, incl visit to faraglione €2.50, shower €1, towel €2.60; ⊙7am-11pm summer, 8.30am-5pm winter) Backed by a *faraglione* (rocky spire) and stinking of rotten eggs, Vulcano's harbourside pool of thick, coffee-coloured sulphurous gloop isn't exactly a five-star beauty farm. But the warm mud has long been considered an excellent treatment for rheumatic pains and skin diseases, and if you don't mind smelling funny for a few days, rolling around in the mud can be fun.

Once you have had time to relax in the muddy water, get some soft clay from the bottom of the pool and apply it to your body and face. Don't let any of the mud get in your eyes as the sulphur is acidic and can damage the retina (keep your hair mud-free too). Wait for the clay mask to dry, wash it off in the pool, then run to the natural spa around the corner, where there are hot, bubbling springs in a small, natural seawater pool.

Spiaggia Sabbia Nera   BEACH
Vulcano's beach scene is centred on this smooth strip of black sand at Porto di Ponente, about 10 minutes' walk beyond the mud pools on the western side of the peninsula. One of the few sandy beaches in the Aeolians, it's a scenic spot, curving around a bay of limpid, glassy waters out of which rise jutting *faraglioni*.

From the beach, a road traverses a small isthmus to Vulcanello (123m), a bulb of land that was spewed out by a volcanic eruption in 183 BC. Here you'll find the famous Valle dei Mostri (Valley of the Monsters), a group of wind-eroded dark rocks that have formed grotesque shapes.

★Capo Grillo   VIEW POINT
For spectacular views without the physical exertion of climbing Fossa di Vulcano, you can drive out to Capo Grillo, about 3km northeast from the midisland settlement of Piano. From here you'll get breathtaking perspectives on Lipari and Salina, with Panarea, Stromboli and Filicudi off in the distance.

Gelso   BEACH
On the island's southern coast, Gelso is a picturesque little port with a family-run restaurant and a couple of black-sand beaches that rarely get very crowded. In summer there's a bus service to get there, but you'll be much better off hiring a car or scooter, as services are limited and it's a 15km walk back if you get stranded.

There's not much to Gelso itself, but before you get to the village, a steep dirt track (pedestrians only) branches off to Spiaggia dell'Asina (Donkey Beach), a crescent of black sand giving onto inviting waters. A second beach, Spiaggia Cannitello, is surrounded by lush, almost tropical greenery. Both beaches have a rudimentary bar/cafe, where you can hire sun lounges and umbrellas.

Boat Tours   BOAT TOUR
In summer you can take boat tours of the island from the port – local operators set up in kiosks – for about €15 per person. Highlights to look out for include the Grotta del Cavallo, a sea cave known for its light effects, and the Piscina di Venere, a natural swimming pool set in its own rocky amphitheatre.

> ## ⓘ MUD-BATH TIPS
>
> ➡ Don't stay in longer than 10 or 15 minutes – the water/mud is slightly radioactive. Pregnant women should avoid it altogether.
>
> ➡ Don't use your favourite fluffy towel or one you've 'borrowed' from a hotel – most hotels will provide a special *fanghi* (mud bath) towel on request.
>
> ➡ If you have a sulphite allergy, stay away.
>
> ➡ Remember to remove watches and jewellery.
>
> ➡ Take flip-flops or sandals – there are hot air vents that can scald your feet.
>
> ➡ Wear a swimsuit you don't mind destroying: once the smell gets in, it's easier to buy a new one than to get rid of the pong.

AEOLIAN ISLANDS VULCANO

Diving Centre Saracen DIVING
(☎ 347 7283341; www.divingcentersaracen.com/
vulcano; Via Porto di Ponente; ☺ Easter–Oct) This
local dive centre offers a range of dives
(from €50, equipment included), plus
snorkelling excursions (€35) that focus on
Vulcano's many marine caves and subterra-
nean hot springs. It also sponsors the **Vulcano Dive Festival** (www.festivalmaresicilia.it)
in late June.

Sicily in Kayak KAYAKING
(☎ 329 5381229; www.sicilyinkayak.com) This
outfit offers kayaking tours around Vulcano
and the other Aeolians, ranging in length
from half a day to an entire week.

Centro Nautica Baia di Levante BOATING
(☎ 339 3372795; www.baialevante.it; ☺ Apr–Oct)
If you prefer to explore Vulcano's waters
on your own, you can rent boats from this
shack to the left of the hydrofoil dock. As
a rough guide, allow for anything between
€60 and €120 per day for a four-person
boat.

✖ Eating

Vulcano's restaurants tend to be overpriced
tourist traps, but there are some welcome
exceptions.

Ritrovo Remigio CAFE, BAR €
(☎ 090 985 20 85; Porto di Levante; cannoli €2.50;
☺ 6am–11.30pm) This bar directly opposite
the hydrofoil dock makes a great place to
grab a *cannolo* (tube of biscuity pastry filled
with sweetened ricotta) while waiting for
your boat. It's also got a good selection of ice
cream.

★ La Forgia Maurizio SICILIAN, INDIAN €€
(☎ 339 1379107; Strada Provinciale 45, Porto di
Levante; meals €30–40; ☺ noon–3pm & 7–11pm)
The owner of this devilishly good restaurant
spent 20 winters in Goa, India; Eastern influences sneak into a menu of Sicilian specialities, all prepared and presented with
flair. Don't miss the *liquore di kumquat e
cardamom*, Maurizio's homemade answer
to *limoncello*. The tasting menu is a good
deal at €30 including wine and dessert.

Maria Tindara SICILIAN €€
(☎ 090 985 30 04; Via Provinciale 38, Piano; meals
€25–35) Amid the fields and vineyards of
Vulcano's fertile central plateau, 7km south
of the port, this cosy family-run restaurant
serves excellent caponata and delicious
homemade pasta with traditional Sicilian in-

gredients alongside mountain specialties like
grilled lamb. With local regulars hanging out
at the bar up front, it makes a pleasant antidote to the tourist-thronged eateries in Porto
di Levante.

Trattoria Maniaci Pina SEAFOOD €€
(☎ 368 668555; Gelso; meals €25–30; ☺ May–mid-
Oct) On the south side of the island, beside
a black-sand beach, this atmospheric, down-
to-earth trattoria serves hefty portions of
fresh-caught fish at affordable prices. Two
local men do the fishing, and their mothers
do the cooking.

❶ Orientation

Boats dock at the Porto di Levante. From here
it's a short walk – bear right as you exit the
harbour area – to the *fanghi* (mud baths), hidden behind a small hillock of rocks. Continuing
beyond the mud pools, the road leads to Porto
di Ponente, where you'll find a number of hotels
and Spiaggia Sabbia Nera (Black Sand Beach), a
long stretch of black sand. For the Fossa di Vulcano, bear left as you disembark and continue
approximately 1km along the base of the volcano
until you see the '*escursioni cratere*' sign on your
left indicating the way up.

❶ Information

Emergency Doctor (☎ 090 985 22 20; Via
Favaloro, Porto di Levante)
Farmacia Bonarrigo (☎ 090 985 22 44; Via
Favaloro 1, Porto di Levante)
Police (☎ 090 985 21 10)

❶ Getting There & Around

BICYCLE
Bikes can be hired from Sprint da Luigi, which
can also organise island tours.

BOAT
Vulcano is an intermediate stop between Milazzo
(ferry/hydrofoil €10.80/13.90, two hours/45
minutes) and Lipari (ferry/hydrofoil €4.70/5.80,
25/10 minutes), with regular services in both
directions. Ticket offices are near the dock at
Porto di Levante.

BUS
Between mid-June and mid-September, **Bus Vul-
cania Tour di Scaffidi** (☎ 090 985 30 73) runs
buses across the island, from Porto di Levante
to Porto di Ponente (€1.55), Piano and Capo
Grillo (€2, 20 minutes, approximately seven daily
Monday to Saturday, two Sunday) and to Gelso
(€2.30, 40 minutes, approximately three daily).
There's a timetable posted at the beginning of Via
Provinciale, near Ritrovo Remigio. Buy tickets on

the bus. If you're going to the beaches at Gelso, ask the driver to let you off at the dirt track.

CAR & MOTORCYCLE

Sprint da Luigi (☎ 090 985 22 08; Via Provinciale, Porto di Levante) Scooters (per day from €20), bicycles (from €5) and cars (from €40) are available from this friendly outfit near the port (follow the signs or just ask for Luigi). Multilingual owners Luigi and Nidra speak English, French and German and offer a wealth of tips for exploring the island. They also rent out an apartment (€40 to €70) in Vulcano's tranquil interior.

TAXI

Santi (☎ 366 3028712) provides taxi service as well as guided trips around the island. Call ahead to negotiate rates.

Salina

SALINA

POP 2600

In stark contrast to the exposed volcanic terrain of the other Aeolian Islands, Salina boasts a lush, verdant landscape. Woodlands, wildflowers, thick yellow gorse bushes and serried ranks of grapevines carpet its hillsides in vibrant colours and cool greens, while high coastal cliffs plunge into the breaking waters below. The island – the second largest in the archipelago – is the only one to enjoy natural freshwater springs and it's these, combined with the volcanic soil, that make it so fertile. The Aeolians' famous Malvasia wine is produced here, and Salina's fat, juicy capers flavour many local dishes.

Although named after the *saline* (salt works) of Lingua, Salina is shaped by two extinct volcanoes, Monte dei Porri (860m) and Monte Fossa delle Felci (962m), the Aeolians' two highest peaks. These rise in the centre of the island, forming a natural barrier between the main settlements and ensuring that the sleepy villages retain their own individual atmosphere. Tourism has encroached on island life, particularly in Santa Marina Salina and nearby Lingua, but away from these, there's a distinct feeling of remoteness – a sense that the rest of the world really is a very long way away. If that sounds good, you'll love Salina.

◎ Sights & Activities

★ **Monte Fossa delle Felci**   MOUNTAIN

For jaw-dropping views, climb to the Aeolians' highest point, Monte Fossa delle Felci (962m). The two-hour ascent starts from the **Santuario della Madonna del Terzito**, an imposing 19th-century church at Valdichiesa, in the valley separating the island's two volcanoes. Up top, gorgeous perspectives unfold on the symmetrically arrayed volcanic cones of Monte dei Porri, Filicudi and a distant Alicudi.

From the sanctuary – an important place of pilgrimage for islanders, particularly around the Feast of the Assumption on 15 August – you can follow a signposted track up through pine and chestnut woodlands and fields of ferns, all the way to the top. Along the way you'll see plenty of colourful flora, including wild violets, asparagus and a plant known locally as *cipudazza* (Latin *Urginea marittima*), which was sold to the Calabrians to make soap but is used locally as mouse poison!

Once you've reached the summit (the last 100m are particularly tough), the views are breathtaking, particularly looking west towards Filicudi and Alicudi, and also from the southeast ridge where you can look down over the Lingua salt lagoon and over to Lipari and Vulcano. To get to the trailhead by public transport take the bus from Santa Marina Salina to Malfa, then change for a Rinella-bound bus and ask the driver to let you off at the sanctuary.

Santa Marina Salina   TOWN

Salina's main port, Santa Marina is a typical island settlement with steeply stacked whitewashed houses rising up the hillside. The principal street is **Via Risorgimento**, a lively pedestrian-only strip lined by cafes and boutiques. It's not a big place, and there are no specific sights, but it makes an ideal base for exploring the rest of the island.

Lingua TOWN

Three kilometres south of Santa Marina Salina, the tiny village of Lingua is a popular summer hang-out, with a couple of hotels, a few trattorias and a small beach. Its main feature is the salt lagoon, which sits under an old lighthouse at the end of the village. The centre of the summer scene is seafront Piazza Marina Garibaldi.

Until quite recently the salt works were an important local employer, but now the lagoon only provides sustenance for the migrating birds that pass through in spring and autumn en route to and from Africa. Lingua's most famous business venture these days is Da Alfredo, a bar/gelateria famous across Sicily for its flavourful *granite*.

Malfa TOWN

Tumbling down the hillside to a small shingle beach, this settlement on Salina's north coast is the island's largest, though you'd never guess it from the tranquil atmosphere. About halfway between the town entrance and the sea is the main church square, focal point of Malfa's laid-back social life, from which sloping lanes fan up and down the hillsides.

Pollara TOWN

Don't miss a trip to sleepy Pollara, sandwiched dramatically between the sea and the steep slopes of an extinct volcanic crater on Salina's western edge. The gorgeous beach here was used as a location in the 1994 film *Il Postino*, although the land access route to the beach has since been closed due to landslide danger.

You can still descend the steep stone steps at the northwest end of town and swim across to the beach, or simply admire the spectacular view, with its backdrop of volcanic cliffs.

Rinella TOWN

This tiny hamlet on the south coast is Salina's second port, regularly served by hydrofoils and ferries. Pastel-coloured houses huddle around the waterfront, and there are a couple of decent swimming spots nearby. If the sandy beach by the village centre gets too cramped, follow the path to Punta Megna, from where you can access the pebbly Spiaggia Pra Venezia.

Museo dell'Emigrazione Eoliana MUSEUM

(Emigration Museum; ☏ 392 2694313; Palazzo Marchetti, Via Conti, Malfa; ◷ 5-8pm Jul-Sep, by appointment Oct-Jun) FREE This museum in Palazzo Marchetti near the top of Malfa gives visitors a sobering perspective on the scale and effect of emigration from the Aeolian Islands.

★ Salus Per Aquam SPA

(Wellness Center; ☏ 090 984 42 22; www.hotelsignum.it; Via Scalo 15, Malfa; admission €45, treatments extra; ◷ Oct-Mar) Enjoy a revitalising hot-spring soak or a cleansing sweat in a traditional adobe-walled steam house at Hotel Signum's fabulous spa. The complex includes several stylish jacuzzis on a pretty flagstoned patio, and blissful spaces where you can immerse your body in salt crystals, get a massage or pamper yourself with natural essences of citrus, malvasia and capers.

Wineries WINE TASTING

Outside Malfa there are numerous wineries where you can try the local Malvasia wine. Signposted off the main road, Fenech (☏ 090 984 40 41; www.fenech.it; Via Fratelli Mirabilo 41) is

---

MALVASIA

Salina's good fortune is its freshwater springs. It is the only island of the Aeolians with natural water sources, the result of which is the startling greenery. The islanders have put this to good use, producing their own style of wine, Malvasia. It is thought that the Greeks brought the grapes to the islands in 588 BC, and the name is derived from Monenvasìa, a Greek city.

The wine is still produced according to traditional techniques using the Malvasia grape and the now-rare red Corinthian grape. The harvest generally occurs in the second week of September when the grapes are picked and laid out to dry on woven cane mats. The drying process is crucial: the grapes must dry out enough to concentrate the sweet flavour but not too much, which would caramelise them.

The result is a dark-golden or light-amber wine that tastes, some say, of honey. It is usually drunk in very small glasses and goes well with cheese, sweet biscuits and almond pastries.

an acclaimed producer; their 2012 Malvasia won awards at five international competitions. Another important Malvasia is produced at the luxurious Capofaro (p259) resort on the 13-acre Tasca d'Almerita estate between Malfa and Santa Marina.

Boat Tours
BOAT TOUR

Some of the best swimming spots in the area are only accessible by sea, so you'll need to sign up for a boat tour or hire a boat for yourself. **Salina Relax Boats** (☑345 216 23 08; www.salinarelaxboats.com; Via Roma 86, Santa Marina Salina) offers various tours of Salina and the other islands, costing between €60 and €70 per person; it also hires out boats and runs a water-taxi service.

✖ Eating

Salina is arguably the best place to eat in all of the Aeolians, thanks in part to the prevalence of fresh produce from local gardens.

★ Da Alfredo
SANDWICHES €

(Piazza Marina Garibaldi, Lingua; granite €2.60, sandwiches €8-12) Salina's most atmospheric option for an affordable snack, Alfredo's place is renowned all over Sicily for its *granite:* ices made with coffee, fresh fruit or locally grown pistachios and almonds. It's also worth a visit for its *pane cunzato* – open-faced sandwiches piled high with tuna, ricotta, eggplant, tomatoes, capers and olives; split one with a friend – they're huge!

Al Cappero
SICILIAN €

(☑090 984 39 68; www.alcappero.it; Pollara; meals €21-25; ⊙lunch Easter-May, lunch & dinner Jun–mid-Sep) This family-run place in Pollara with a sprawling outdoor terrace specialises in old-fashioned Sicilian home cooking, including several vegetarian options. It also sells home-grown capers and rents out simple rooms down the street (€20 to €35 per person).

Il Fornaio
BAKERY €

(Via Risorgimento 150, Santa Marina Salina; snacks from €1) Assuage those midmorning and midafternoon hunger pangs by following your nose to this fabulous bakery, where you'll find delicious *cornetti* (Italian croissants), *sfincione palermitana* (Palermitan spongy pizza topped by onion and tomato) and other fresh-baked treats.

DON'T MISS

TOP EATING & DRINKING EXPERIENCES

➡ People come from far and wide for Alfredo's historic *granite* (ice drinks flavoured with ground almonds or fresh fruit) at Da Alfredo.

➡ Dine alfresco on superb country cuisine at Le Macine (p140), an *agriturismo* (farm-stay) in the hills above Lipari.

➡ Grapes cultivated on the volcanic slopes of Salina are used to make the Aeolians' acclaimed Malvasia wine.

➡ The pizzas at L'Osservatorio (p154) are fine, but the main event here is the view up to Stromboli's smoking flanks.

★ Ristorante Villa Carla
SICILIAN €€

(☑090 980 90 13; Via S Lucia, Leni; meals €30-35; ⊙7-10pm Jun-Aug, by arrangement rest of year) At their home in the hills above Rinella, Carla Rando and Carmelo Princiotta serve unforgettable meals featuring specialities such as homemade tagliatelle with pistachio and oranges, or fresh-caught fish broiled in a crust of parsley, basil, mint and citrus zest. Two outdoor terraces framed by roses and cactus offer pretty views across the water to the surrounding islands. Reservations required.

★ A Cannata
SICILIAN €€

(☑090 984 31 61; Via Umberto I 13, Lingua; meals €32; ⊙12.30-2.30pm & 7.30-10pm) Delectable home-cooked seafood meals, accompanied by local vegetables, are served in a sun-filled seafront pavilion at this unassuming but exceptional restaurant, run by the same family for nearly four decades. Start with the house speciality, *maccheroni* with eggplant, pine nuts, mozzarella and ricotta, before moving onto a second course of *calamaretti* (baby squid) cooked with Salina's showpiece Malvasia wine.

'nni Lausta
MODERN SICILIAN €€

(☑090 984 34 86; www.isolasalina.com; Via Risorgimento, Santa Marina Salina; meals €25-40; ⊙noon-11pm Easter-Oct) This stylish modern eatery with its cute lobster logo serves superb food based on fresh local ingredients, with 80% of the produce originating in its own garden. The downstairs bar is popular for aperitifs and late-night drinking. At lunchtime it offers a fixed-price three-course menu including a glass of wine for €25, and takeaway gourmet sandwiches for €5.

Orientation

Most boats dock at Santa Marina Salina, the island's biggest settlement. The town's main street, Via Risorgimento, runs parallel to the seafront one block back from the port. Salina's other main settlements are: Lingua, 3km south of Santa Marina Salina; Malfa, on the northern coast; inland Leni; and Rinella, a tiny fishing hamlet on the southern coast. Note that many hydrofoils stop in at Rinella as well as Santa Marina Salina.

ⓘ Information

Emergency Doctor (☎ 090 984 40 05)
Farmacia Comunale (☎ 090 984 30 89; Via Risorgimento, Santa Marina Salina)
Police (☎ 090 984 30 19; Via Lungomare, Santa Marina Salina)

ⓘ Getting There & Around

BICYCLE

Hire mountain bikes from Antonio Bongiorno, one block uphill from Santa Marina's hydrofoil dock.

BOAT

Siremar (www.siremar.it) and **Ustica Lines** (www.usticalines.it) run hydrofoils to Santa Marina Salina from Lipari (€10.10, 20 to 40 minutes, 12 to 16 daily), Vulcano (€11.90, 40 to 45 minutes, five daily) and Milazzo (€19.05, 1½ to 1¾ hours, 12 to 16 daily). Less frequent services connect Santa Marina with Stromboli, Panarea, Filicudi and Alicudi. Ustica Lines also offers daily sailings to/from Messina (€27, 1¾ to 2¾ hours, three daily in summer, one in winter). Many of the above services call at Rinella en route. Siremar and Ustica share a **ticket office** (☎ 090 984 30 03; Piazza Santa Marina, Santa Marina Salina).

BUS

Citis (☎ 090 984 41 50; www.trasportisalina. it) provides dependable local bus service year-round. There are bus stops near the ports in Santa Marina and Rinella, and timetables are posted around the island.

Buses run nine times Monday to Saturday and five times Sunday from Santa Marina to Lingua (€1.80, five to 10 minutes) and Malfa (€1.80, 15 to 20 minutes), There are also two direct buses daily (one on Sunday) from Santa Marina to Valdichiesa (€2.20, 25 minutes), Leni (€2.50, 30 minutes) and Rinella (€2.50, 40 minutes). Several other buses to these latter three destinations require a change in Malfa, which adds as much

as 45 minutes to the journey. From Santa Marina to Pollara (€2.20, 25 minutes to 1½ hours), a change of buses in Malfa is always required; several buses make good connections Monday to Saturday, but on Sunday the schedules are frustratingly out of synch.

CAR & MOTORCYCLE

Antonio Bongiorno (☎ 090 984 34 09; www. rentbongiorno.it; Via Risorgimento 222, Santa Marina Salina) hires out scooters (from €20 per day) and cars (from €50 per day).

PANAREA

POP 240

Exclusive and expensive, Panarea is the smallest and most fashionable of the Aeolians, attracting the international jet-setters and Milanese fashionistas for a taste of *dolce far niente* (sweet nothing). In summer luxury yachts fill the tiny harbour and flocks of day trippers traipse around the car-free whitewashed streets of San Pietro, the port and principal settlement. Panarea is a strictly summer-only destination with very little going on outside the tourist season – in fact, arrive between November and Easter and you'll find most places closed.

◉ Sights & Activities

Panarea offers a nice mix of activities, both on the mainland and offshore. Its largely traffic-free streets and small network of trails make it an appealing walking destination in spring and autumn. All the sights following are within easy striking distance of San Pietro. North of town lie the tiny community of Ditella and the rocky beach at Spiaggia Fumarola. South is the village of Drauto, followed by sandy Spiaggetta Zimmari, the prehistoric village and the crystal-clear waters of Cala Junco.

Offshore Islands   ISLAND

Five islets off Panarea's eastern shore can be toured by boat. Nearest to Panarea is **Dattilo**, which has a pretty little beach called Le Guglie. The isle of **Lisca Bianca** also offers good swimming on a small white beach. North of Dattilo, **Basiluzzo** is the largest of the five islets, given over to the cultivation of capers.

The remaining islands are **Lisca Nera** and **Bottaro**, the latter actually nothing more than a protruding rock. On the seabed beneath the narrow channel between Lisca Bianca and Bottaro lies the **wreck** of a 19th-century English ship. Divers can hire scuba equipment and organise dives at Amphibia (☑335 1245332; www.amphibia.it; Via Comunale San Pietro) in San Pietro.

To reach the islands, you'll need to hire a boat – ask at the seafront kiosks at San Pietro or try Nautilus (☑333 4233161; www.panarea.com/nautilus; Via Drautto) at Drautto, south of San Pietro; prices range from €50 to €70 per day.

★ **Cala Junco** BEACH
Near Panarea's prehistoric village, about 30 minutes south of San Pietro, steps lead down to this gorgeous little cove with a rock-strewn beach and dreamy aquamarine waters.

Villaggio Preistorico ARCHAEOLOGICAL SITE
Thirty minutes' walk south of San Pietro, dramatically sited on Punta Milazzese, an elevated headland surrounded by the sea, these 23 stone huts with round foundations are remnants of a prehistoric village dating back to the 14th century BC. Pottery found here shows distinctly Minoan influences, lending credence to the theory that the islanders maintained trading ties with the Cretans.

To get here, climb the steep series of steps south from Spiaggetta Zimmari, then follow the signs.

Spiaggetta Zimmari BEACH
This small stretch of brown sand backed by a steep dune, about 20 minutes south of San Pietro, is Panarea's only sandy beach and gets packed in summer.

Spiaggia Fumarola BEACH
To the north of San Pietro, this stone beach with full-on views of Stromboli is reached via a steep, winding descent north of Ditella. Outside peak months this is an isolated spot ideal for a quiet swim, but in July and August, the sun-seekers move in en masse and the ringing of mobile phones becomes incessant.

Punta del Corvo HIKING
At 421m, this rocky outcropping is Panarea's highest point and a popular day-hiking destination. Two trails (marked 1 and 2 on local maps) converge here, and can be combined into a scenic full-island circuit. Allow about four hours for the full round trip, and be ready for some steep climbs and descents.

From up top, there are spectacular views of all six of the neighboring Aeolian Islands.

THE AEOLIANS' TOP SWIMMING SPOTS

Sandy beaches are few and far between, but the islands offer some breathtaking spots to take a dip:

Forgia Vecchia The best of Stromboli's black volcanic beaches (p154), sandwiched between limpid waters and green mountain slopes.

Piscina di Venere Transparent turquoise waters (p143) in a natural rock amphitheatre.

Pollara A tiny, rocky beach (p146) backing onto a volcanic crater, made famous by the film *Il Postino*.

Spiaggia Valle i Muria Dwarfed by dark plunging cliffs, this pebbly beach (p137) is Lipari's best.

Cala Junco A crystalline cove backed by dramatic headlands and the ruins of a Bronze Age village.

🍴 Eating

★ **Trattoria da Paolino** SICILIAN €€
(☑090 98 30 08; Via Iditella 75; meals €30-40; ⏰12.30-3pm & 7.30-10pm Easter–mid-Oct) For four decades, Paolino has been serving an ever-changing menu of top-quality, home-style Aeolian specialities on his breezy blue-and-white terrace overlooking the sea, a 10-minute walk north from the harbour. Tuna figures prominently on the menu (smoked, *sott'olio*, or mixed with pine nuts and wild fennel in *pasta magna magna*) alongside plenty of other superb fish, pasta and vegetable dishes.

Da Francesco SICILIAN €€
(☑090 98 30 23; Via San Pietro; meals €25-28; ⏰Mar-Nov) Up a short flight of stairs from the port (follow the signs), Da Francesco is as close as you'll get to a value-for-money eatery on Panarea. It's a laid-back trattoria with an outdoor terrace, fine sea views over to Stromboli, and a straightforward menu of pastas and fish dishes. Try the restaurant speciality: spaghetti *alla disgraziata* (with tomatoes, aubergines, chilli, capers, olives and ricotta). Simple rooms are also available (single €30 to €50, double €50 to €150).

ℹ Getting There & Around

BOAT

In summer **Siremar** (☎ 090 98 30 07; www.siremar.it) and **Ustica Lines** (☎ 090 98 33 44; www.usticalines.it) run up to eight hydrofoils daily to/from Stromboli (€11.10, 30 to 45 minutes), Lipari (€10.40, 25 minutes to one hour) and Milazzo (€18.80, 1½ to 2¼ hours). In winter, there are fewer services. Siremar also runs ferries to all destinations above; ferries cost about 30% less than the hydrofoil, but take about twice as long. Ticket offices for both companies are at the port in San Pietro.

CAR & MOTORCYCLE

Cars are not allowed on Panarea, but you won't need one as the island is small enough to get around on foot. The preferred mode of transport is golf carts. To arrange a taxi contact **Pantaxi** (☎ 333 3138610).

STROMBOLI

POP 400

Emerging out of the blue haze like a menacing maritime pyramid, Stromboli's smoking silhouette conforms perfectly to one's childhood idea of a volcano. In fact, the island of Stromboli is just the tip of a vast underwater volcano that rises from the seabed 1476m below. The most captivating of the Aeolian Islands, it's a hugely popular day-trip destination as well as the summer favourite of designers Dolce and Gabbana, who have a holiday home here. But to best appreciate its primordial beauty, languid pace and the romance that lured Roberto Rossellini and his lover Ingrid Bergman here in 1949, you'll need to give it a few days.

Volcanic activity has scarred and blackened much of the island but the northeastern corner is inhabited and it's here that you'll find the island's famous black beaches (some very good, with excellent sand) and the main settlement sprawled attractively along the volcano's lower slopes. Despite the picture-postcard appearance, life here is tough: food and drinking water have to be ferried in, there are no roads across the island, and until relatively recently there was no electricity in Ginostra, the island's second settlement on the west coast. If the weather turns rough and the sea goes wild, ferries and hydrofoils are cancelled and the island is completely cut off. And if all that isn't enough, there's still the constant possibility of the volcano blowing its top, as it did in February 2007, although fortunately without any harmful consequences.

◉ Sights & Activities

To climb to the top of Stromboli you'll need to hire a guide or go on an organised trek. Maximum group size is 20 people, and while there are usually multiple groups on the mountain, spaces can still fill up. To avoid disappointment, book early – if possible a

STROMBOLI FACTS

➡ Stromboli is Europe's only permanently active volcano and is the youngest in the Aeolian archipelago.

➡ The island has been inhabited since Neolithic times but the volcano has never destroyed Stromboli town.

➡ Stromboli was used to control important trade routes in the Tyrrhenian Sea, as it overlooks the other Aeolian Islands, the Italian mainland and the Straits of Messina. Because of this and its exploding crater, it was known as the 'Lighthouse of the Mediterranean'.

➡ The pinnacle of rock known as Strombolicchio, which can be seen just off the coast near Ficogrande, is the remnant of the original volcano that collapsed into the sea. Strombolicchio is what is left of the central cylinder (the neck) of the volcano, in which the lava solidified.

➡ The word 'sciara' comes from the Arabic sharia (meaning 'street'), thus the Sciara del Fuoco is a 'Street of Fire'.

➡ On 30 December 2002, landslides caused by volcanic activity provoked two tidal waves between 5m and 10m high. Stromboli town and Ginostra were both hit.

➡ The 2002–2003 eruptions increased the crater size from 35m to 125m.

➡ The 2007 eruption opened two new craters on the summit.

Stromboli

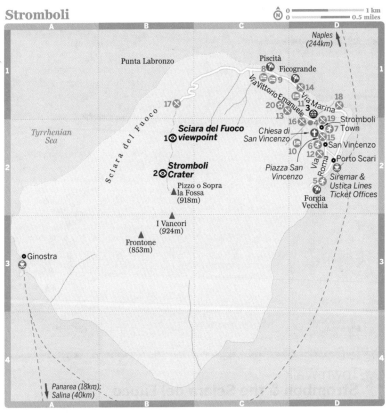

Stromboli

week or more before you want to climb. The standard fee for group climbs is €25 per person, plus tax (at the time of research the tax was €3 but expected to rise to €5).

★ **Stromboli Crater**   VOLCANO

For nature lovers, climbing Stromboli is one of Sicily's not-to-be-missed experiences. Since 2005 access has been strictly

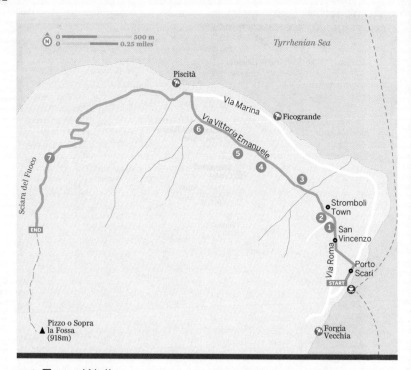

Town Walk
Stromboli & the Sciara del Fuoco

START STROMBOLI HYDROFOIL PORT
END SCIARA DEL FUOCO
LENGTH 4KM; TWO HOURS ONE WAY

You're allowed to hike this trail unaccompanied, as the viewpoint sits below the 400m 'restricted' level.

Leave the port two to three hours before sundown. This allows you to arrive at the viewpoint around sunset and watch the volcano's fireworks juxtaposed against the darkening sky. Make sure to bring a torch (flashlight); it's absolutely essential for the return hike.

From the port, walk up Via Roma towards Stromboli's main square, stopping in for homemade ice cream at **1 Lapillo Gelato** (p154). After passing Stromboli's main church, **2 Chiesa San Vincenzo**, continue downhill to the **3 Red House** (p154), site of Ingrid Bergman and Roberto Rossellini's torrid love affair while filming *Stromboli: Terra di Dio* in 1949.

A few hundred metres further on, as the main road jogs briefly left, look for **4 Bottega del Marano** (p154), a neighbourhood grocery with a great deli where you can pick up trail snacks and water. Soon thereafter you'll pass **5 La Libreria sull'Isola** (p155), a bookstore that doubles as a movie theatre in summer.

About 2km from your starting point, pass **6 Chiesa di Piscità** on your left, then descend briefly to a left-hand turn-off with signs for L'Osservatorio. Start climbing gradually, paralleling the sea at first, then following a series of switchbacks to **7 L'Osservatorio** (p154) pizzeria.

From the pizzeria to the viewpoint the climb is much steeper. Arriving at the Sciara del Fuoco viewpoint, prepare to be amazed! The sight of the volcano's eruptions, followed by cascades of molten rock crashing down the lava-blackened mountainside into the sea is stunning. Linger past nightfall, as the volcano's orange glow becomes more dramatic with the waning light.

ANOTHER ANGLE ON STROMBOLI'S FIREWORKS

For fabulous views of the volcano's eruptions without climbing to the summit (and without spending a single euro-cent), hike the comparatively easy trail to the viewpoint over Sciara del Fuoco (Street of Fire), the blackened laval scar that runs down the mountain's northern flank. Because the viewpoint sits just below 400m, you're allowed to go here on your own, but do bring a torch if you're walking at night.

The explosions usually occur every 20 minutes or so and are preceded by a loud belly-roar as gases force the magma into the air. After each eruption, you can watch as red-hot rocks tumble down the seemingly endless slope, creating visible and audible splashes as they plop into the sea. It's all incredibly exciting. For best viewing, come on a on a still night, when the livid red Sciara and exploding cone are dramatically visible.

Arriving here around sunset will allow you to hike one direction in daylight, then stop for pizza and more volcano-gawking at L'Osservatorio (p154) on the way back down. Making the trek just before dawn is also a memorable experience, as you'll likely have the whole mountain to yourself.

The trail to the viewpoint starts in Piscità, about 2km west of Stromboli's port. From here it takes about 30 minutes to get to L'Osservatorio, and another half hour to reach the viewpoint. Bring plenty of water – the climb gets steep towards the end.

regulated: you can walk freely to 400m, but need a guide to continue any higher. Organised treks depart daily (between 3.30pm and 6pm, depending on season), timed to reach the summit (924m) at sunset and to allow 45 minutes to observe the crater's fireworks.

The youngest of the Aeolian volcanoes, Stromboli was formed only 40,000 years ago and its gases continue to send up an almost constant spray of liquid magma, a process defined by vulcanologists as *attività stromboliana* (Strombolian activity).

The most recent major eruptions took place on 27 February 2007. Two new summit craters were formed and lava flowed down the mountain's western flank but little real harm was done. Previously, an eruption in April 2003 showered the village of Ginostra with rocks, and activity in December 2002 produced a tsunami, causing damage to Stromboli town, injuring six people and closing the island to visitors for a few months.

The climb itself takes 2½ to three hours, while the descent back to Piazza San Vincenzo is shorter (1½ to two hours). All told, it's a demanding five- to six-hour trek up to the top and back; you'll need to have proper walking shoes, a backpack that allows free movement of both arms, clothing for cold and wet weather, a change of T-shirt, a handkerchief to protect against dust (wear glasses not contact lenses), a torch (flashlight), several litres of water and some food. If you haven't got any of these, Totem Trekking (090 986 57 52; www.totemtrekking

stromboli.com; Piazza San Vincenzo 4; 9.30am-1pm & 3.30-7pm) hires out all the necessary equipment, including boots (€6), backpacks (€5), hiking poles (€4), torches (€3) and windbreakers (€5).

Magmatrek   CLIMBING
(090 986 57 68; www.magmatrek.it; Via Vittorio Emanuele) Has experienced, multilingual (English-, German- and French-speaking) guides that lead daily treks up the volcano (maximum group size of 20 people). It can also put together tailor-made treks for individuals or groups.

Stromboli Guide   CLIMBING
(Il Vulcano ai Piedi; 090 98 61 44; www.stromboliguide.it; Via Roma) A reputable outfit led by Stromboli native Nino Zerilli, a guide affiliated with the Associazione Guide Alpine Italiane.

Stromboli Adventures   CLIMBING
(090 98 62 64; www.stromboliadventures.it; Via Vittorio Emanuele) To the right of the church, this smaller agency, staffed by year-round residents, has been around for over 30 years.

Boat Tours   BOAT TOUR
One of the most popular ways of viewing Stromboli's nocturnal fireworks is to take a boat tour of the island. Società Navigazione Pippo (090 98 61 35; pipponav.stromboli@libero.it; Porto Scari) and Antonio Cacetta (090 98 60 23; Vico Salina 10) are among the numerous outfits running boat tours out of Porto Scari. The two most popular itineraries

STROMBOLI'S SLEEPIER SIDE

To see Stromboli's less touristy side, hop off the ferry at Ginostra, a tiny village on the island's western shore. There are only 30 year-round residents here, but you can sleep overnight at **B&B Luna Rossa** (☑ 090 988 00 49; www.ginostra-stromboli.it/bed-breakfast. php; r per person from €20) and eat at L'Incontro (☑ 090 981 23 05; www.ginostraincontro. it; meals €25-30), which also rents out simple rooms.

It's possible to climb from Ginostra to Stromboli's crater, but this is a physically demanding approach and you'll need a private guide, making it more costly than the standard tourist trek. At the time of research, Magmatrek (p153) was also contemplating the possibility of starting regular tours from the Ginostra side – contact them for up-to-the-minute details.

Siremar (p156) runs occasional boats from Stromboli's main port to Ginostra (€7.80, 10 minutes). Outside peak summer season (mid-June to mid-September), you can also get here by Ustica Lines (p156) hydrofoil from any of the surrounding islands, including Lipari (€16.80, 1½ hours) and Panarea (€10.40, 20 minutes).

are a three-hour round-the-island daytime cruise (€25), including an hour of free time to explore Ginostra and a swimming break at Strombolicchio (the rock islet jutting out of the water off the north coast), and a 1½-hour sunset excursion (€20) to watch the Sciara del Fuoco explosions from the sea.

Beaches   BEACH

Stromboli's black sandy beaches are the best in the Aeolian archipelago. The most accessible and popular swimming and sunbathing is at Ficogrande, a strip of rocks and black volcanic sand about a 10-minute walk northwest of the hydrofoil dock. Further-flung beaches worth exploring are at Piscità to the west and Forgia Vecchia, about 300m south of the port, a long stretch of black pebbles curving around a tranquil bay and backed by the volcano's green slopes.

Red House   HISTORIC BUILDING

(Via Vittorio Emanuele 22) This rusty-red house is where Ingrid Bergman and Roberto Rossellini lived together while filming *Stromboli, Terra di Dio* in 1949. Their liaison provoked a scandal in the film world, as both were married to other people at the time. Descending from San Vincenzo church on Stromboli's main square, look for a plaque marking the house on the right-hand side.

You can't actually go inside, but it's interesting to see the scene of such a famous romance.

La Sirenetta Diving   DIVING

(☑ 338 8919675, 347 5961499; www.lasirenetta diving.it; Via Marina 33; ⊙ Jun–mid-Sep) Opposite the beach at La Sirenetta Park Hotel,

La Sirenetta offers diving courses as well as accompanied dives.

🍴 Eating & Drinking

Eating out in Stromboli is an expensive business as most food items have to be shipped in. Seafood is ubiquitous but pizza provides a good alternative.

★ L'Osservatorio   PIZZERIA €

(☑ 090 98 63 60; pizzas €6.50-10.50; ⊙ 10.30am-late) Sure, you could eat a pizza in town, but come on – you're on Stromboli! Make the 45-minute uphill trek to this pizzeria and you'll be rewarded with exceptional volcano views from the newly expanded panoramic terrace, best after sundown.

La Bottega del Marano   DELI €

(Via Vittorio Emanuele; snacks from €2; ⊙ 8.30am-1pm & 4.30-7.30pm Mon-Sat) The perfect source for volcano-climbing provisions or a self-catering lunch, this reasonably priced neighbourhood grocery, five minutes west of the trekking-agency offices, has a well-stocked deli case full of meats, cheeses, olives, artichokes and sun-dried tomatoes, plus shelves full of wine and awesomely tasty mini-focaccias (€2).

Lapillo Gelato   ICE CREAM €

(Via Roma; ice creams from €2.50; ⊙ 10am-1pm & 3.30pm-midnight Jun–mid-Sep, 3.30-9pm mid-Sep–May) On the main street between the port and the church, this artisanal *gelateria* is a great place to fuel up with homemade ice cream before making the big climb. The pistachio flavour is pure creamy bliss.

Ritrovo Ingrid CAFE, PIZZERIA €
(☑090 98 63 85; Piazza San Vincenzo; pizzas from €6.50; ⊙8am-1am, to 3am Jul & Aug) A Stromboli institution, the panoramic terrace of this all-purpose cafe/gelateria/pizzeria is busy throughout the day as islanders come for their morning cappuccino, tourists pop in for an ice cream and trekkers compare notes over an evening pizza.

Punta Lena SICILIAN €€
(☑090 98 62 04; Via Marina 8; meals €35-40; ⊙mid-May–mid-Oct) There's nothing flash about this family-run restaurant with its waterfront terrace – decoration is limited to fresh flowers and soothing seascapes over Strombolicchio – but the food is as good as you'll get anywhere on the island. Signature dishes include *gamberetti marinati* (marinated prawns) and spaghetti *alla stromboliana* (with wild fennel, cherry tomatoes and breadcrumbs).

Ai Gechi SEAFOOD €€
(☑090 98 62 13; Vico Salina 12, Porto Scari; meals €31-35; ⊙noon-3pm & 7-11pm Easter–mid-Oct) Follow the trail of painted lizards to this great hideaway, down an alley off Via Roma. Flanked by a towering cactus, the shaded verandah of a whitewashed Aeolian house serves as the dining area, eclectically decorated with ship lamps and a whale skeleton the owner discovered nearby. Gorgeous traditional seafood is served with a slightly modern twist, backed by an excellent local wine list.

Locanda del Barbablù SEAFOOD €€
(☑090 98 61 18; www.barbablu.it; Via Vittorio Emanuele 17; mains from €25; ⊙dinner mid-Jun–mid-Sep) This dusky pink Aeolian inn houses the island's classiest restaurant, with the same owner and staff since 1984. It's a fashionable port of call for the August aperitif set, with a lively bar and rustic-chic decor. The three daily offerings are all built around fresh-caught local seafood: a seafood antipasto, a fish-with-pasta dish, and a grilled fish special with vegetables. There's also an excellent list of Sicilian wines.

★La Tartana Club SICILIAN, BAR €€€
(☑090 98 60 25; Via Marina; meals from €35; ⊙June–mid-Sep) Break bread with Dolce and Gabbana and the president of Italy at this chic restaurant-bar, a long-standing favourite of Stromboli's beautiful people. Lunch is a casual buffet on the seafront terrace, while the evening scene is more refined, with ape-

ritifs and cocktails at the piano bar and diners romancing over candlelit tables.

Regulars also flock here to read the morning paper over coffee at breakfast time or indulge in La Tartana's trademark dessert, *coppa Stromboli*, a volcano-shaped mass of chocolate, sweet cream and hazelnut ice cream studded with candied cherries and doused in a lava flow of strawberry syrup.

☆ Entertainment

La Libreria sull'Isola CINEMA
(⊙10.30am-1pm & 5-7.30pm Easter-Sep, to 10pm Jul & Aug) This sweet little bookstore doubles as a cinema during the summer months, showing films nightly in its open-air courtyard, including a once-weekly screening of Rossellini and Bergman's *Stromboli*. At the time of research it was just ramping up to add yoga classes and a teahouse on its cosy outdoor patio.

❶ Orientation

Boats arrive at Porto Scari, downhill from the main town. Most accommodation, as well as the meeting point for guided hikes, is a short walk up the Scalo Scari on Via Roma. At the top of Via Roma is the central square, Piazza San Vincenzo, from where Via Vittorio Emanuele continues westwards. To reach the path for the Sciara del Fuoco, follow Via Vittorio Emanuele until you see signs for L'Osservatorio off to the left. Note that there is no street lighting on Stromboli except in a couple of main streets and on Piazza San Vincenzo, so bring a torch/flashlight.

❶ Information

Emergency Doctor (☑090 98 60 97; Via Vittorio Emanuele)
Police (☑090 98 60 21; Via Roma) On the left as you walk up Via Roma.

❶ Getting There & Around

There are no cars on Stromboli, just scooters, electric carts and three-wheeler vehicles known locally as *ape*. Most hotels will provide free transport to and from the dock if you call ahead. Walking on the island is easy and pleasant.

BOAT
Stromboli is the easternmost of the Aeolians. Hydrofoils connect the island with Panarea (€11.10, 30 minutes), Salina (€17.80, one to 1¼ hours), Lipari (€17.80, one to two hours) and Milazzo (€21.45, 2¼ to three hours). There are up to eight daily services in summer, but this falls to two a day in winter.

Siremar also runs car ferries from Stromboli to Naples (€44, 10½ hours) and Milazzo (€15.25, six hours), as well as to Lipari (€12.40, 3½ hours) and the other Aeolians. In bad weather the service is often disrupted or cancelled altogether, as Stromboli's dock is smaller than others on the Aeolians. Ticket offices for **Ustica Lines** (☑ 090 98 60 03; www.usticalines.it) and **Siremar** (☑ 090 98 60 16; www.siremar.it) are at the port.

CAR & MOTORCYCLE

You can hire scooters from **Motonautica Mandarano** (☑ 090 98 62 12; Via Marina; per day about €20). From the port follow the road to your left; you'll find it after about 300m.

TAXI

For taxi service, call **Sabbia Nera Taxi** (☑ 090 98 63 90; sabbianerastromboli.com).

FILICUDI

POP 235

Among the prettiest and least developed of the Aeolian Islands, Filicudi is also one of the oldest, dating back to tectonic activity 700,000 years ago. Shaped like a snail when seen from some angles, the island entices visitors with a its rugged coastline lapped by crystal-clear waters and pitted by deep grottoes. The island has just a few small villages. The best food and accommodation options are found just above the port or at Pecorini Mare, a tiny fishing hamlet clustered around a small pebble beach, about 3km further west.

☉ Sights & Activities

Attractions include the dazzling Grotta del Bue Marino on the island's western edge and Scoglio della Canna (Cane Reef), a dramatic 71m *faraglione* off Filicudi's northwestern shore. Offshore from Capo Graziano lies the Museo Archeologico Sottomarino area, where the sunken wrecks of nine ancient Greek and Roman ships provide fabulous diving opportunities.There's also a small network of hiking trails, including the multihour climb to Fossa Felci (774m) at the centre of the island.

Prehistoric Village   ARCHAEOLOGICAL SITE

(☉24hr) Follow the main road 10 minutes southeast of the port towards Capo Graziano, where a marked trail branches east to this smattering of Bronze Age huts on a terraced hillside. Discovered in 1952, they date to 1800 BC, four hundred years

before Panarea's Punta Milazzese. Though poorly maintained, it remains an evocative spot, with lovely sea and island views.

From the village you can descend to Filicudi's only real beach, a stony affair that offers the easiest swimming on the island – if you want to take a dip elsewhere, you'll have to clamber down some jagged rocks or rent a boat.

Zucco Grande   HIKING

A beautiful 60- to 90-minute uphill hike from the port leads to Zucco Grande, a village on Filicudi's northeast flank that's been largely abandoned, though a few enterprising villagers have recently begun renovating some of the ruined homes. The trail winds along flower-covered hillsides high above the sea, with spectacular views back to Capo Graziano and the port.

I Delfini   OUTDOORS

(☑ 340 1484645, 090 988 90 77; www.idelfinifilicudi.it; Pecorini) At this all-purpose agency, Nino Terrano organises dives, rents out diving equipment (€35 per day) and scooters (€25 per day) and offers boat trips around the island (€15 per person), pointing out local attractions along the way. He can usually be found at Pecorini's small marina.

Apogon Diving Center   DIVING

(☑347 3307185; www.apogon.it; Filicudi Porto; dives from €35) This local dive center provides everything you need to explore Filicudi's watery depths.

✗ Eating

★La Sirena Restaurant   SEAFOOD €€

(☑090 988 99 97; www.pensionelasirena.it; meals €27-37) Nothing beats dining on La Sirena's pretty tiled terrace in tiny seaside Pecorini Mare. Pull up a straw-seated chair at a little wooden table, admire the front-row view of colourful boats, rocky beach and sparkling Mediterranean and feast on fresh local seafood preceded by appetisers like tuna and neonata fritters or *carbonara di pesce* (spaghetti with fish-based carbonara sauce) .

★Ristorante La Canna   SEAFOOD €€

(☑090 988 99 56; www.lacannahotel.it; meals €28; ☉1-3pm & 8-10pm) Delicious traditional Sicilian seafood is accompanied by fresh produce from the surrounding gardens at this hillside restaurant, adjacent to the hotel of the same name. It's up a steep set of steps from the harbour. Non-hotel guests should reserve ahead.

ℹ Getting There & Around

Siremar (year-round) and Ustica Lines (summer only) run hydrofoils from Filicudi to Lipari (€15.80, 1¼ hours), Santa Marina Salina (€13.70, 45 minutes), Rinella (€11.40, 30 minutes) and Alicudi (€11.10, 30 minutes). Service is considerably less frequent than elsewhere in the archipelago. Siremar also runs occasional car ferries to/from Filicudi.

ALICUDI

If your goal is to *really* get away from it all, Alicudi just might be your dream destination. As isolated a place as you'll find in the entire Mediterranean basin, its main settlement has minimal facilities and no roads. The chief forms of transportation here are boat and mule – you'll see the latter hauling goods up and down the steep stone steps from the port the minute you disembark.

Outside summer season, when the town's lone hotel, Ericusa (p261), opens for four months, this is the kind of place where you have to ask around for rooms, and where the evening's chief entertainment is watching fishermen congregating by the port at midnight to unload and clean fish. By day it's a great place for off-the-beaten-track hiking – indeed, walkers and curiosity-seekers are about the only tourists you'll see here outside peak summer season.

Aside from strolling the streets around the port or climbing the island's central peak, there isn't much else to do save potter around and find a peaceful place to sunbathe – the best spots are to the south of the port, where you will have to clamber over boulders to reach the sea. As you would expect, the waters are crystal clear and there's nothing to disturb you save the occasional hum of a fishing boat.

A two-hour trek up a relentlessly steep but pretty series of stone staircases leads to Monte Filo dell'Arpa (675m) at the top of the island; simply follow the blue arrows painted on the walls. A pretty church, Chiesa di San Bartolo, marks the hike's midpoint. Up top you can circle the crater of the extinct volcano or follow cattle trails to the dramatic cliffs on Alicudi's western edge.

Near the summit you'll also find the Timpone delle Femmine, huge fissures where women are said to have taken refuge during pirate raids. Be sure to wear sturdy shoes and bring plenty of water as there is virtually no shade along the way.

Siremar (year-round) and Ustica Lines (summer only) run hydrofoils from Alicudi to Lipari (€18.85, two hours), Santa Marina Salina (€18.80, 1½ hours), Rinella (€16.80, 1¼ hours) and Filicudi (€11.10, 30 minutes).

Ionian Coast

Why Go?

The Ionian Coast is dotted with Sicily's superlatives – the island's highest volcano, Mt Etna, is here; the queen of all resorts, Taormina, perches on a clifftop; and it's home to Sicily's second-largest city, Catania. Catania is the region's centre, a wonderful and shabby city with a great pulse and active street- and nightlife. Its fish market, La Pescheria, is one of Sicily's greatest sights, and the baroque architecture of the city's historic centre is beautiful, if somewhat battered. Halfway up a rocky mountainside, regal Taormina is sophisticated and exclusive, a favourite of holidaying VIPs and day-tripping tourists. Brooding menacingly on the city's doorstep, Mt Etna offers unforgettable hiking, both to the summit craters and around the woods that carpet its lower slopes. Etna is also a wine area and, with a car, it's fun to tour the mountain in search of the perfect vintage.

Best Places to Eat

➡ Cutilisci (p177)

➡ Trattoria di De Fiore (p176)

➡ Locanda Cerami (p176)

➡ Me Cumpari Turridu (p177)

➡ Al Duomo (p169)

Best Places to Stay

➡ B&B Crociferi (p262)

➡ UNA Hotel Palace (p263)

➡ Hotel Villa Belvedere (p261)

➡ Isoco Guest House (p261)

➡ Il Principe (p262)

Road Distances (KM)

	Acireale	Catania	Messina	Nicolosi
Catania	15			
Messina	85	95		
Nicolosi	20	15	100	
Taormina	40	50	50	60

Getting Around

Driving around the Ionian Coast and inland provides for some wonderful scenery. Take the SS114 from Catania down the Riviera dei Ciclopi and wind through the town streets and taking a peak at the beaches, towards Taormina. Several buses take this route from Catania throughout the day. There are decent roads surrounding Etna.

THREE PERFECT DAYS

King of the Ionian Resorts

Wake up in Taormina, where you can admire the stunning setting of the Teatro Greco (p167) and its memorable views to Mt Etna. Spend the rest of the morning exploring the town's medieval streets, browsing among the delis on Corso Umberto I (p167) and thrilling to the verdant delights of Villa Comunale (p168). After lunch head down to Isola Bella (p168) for some seaside fun.

Mount Etna

You'll have seen it looming in the distance and now is the time to explore Mt Etna. You can take a tour from Taormina or Catania or, better still, pick up a car and go it alone. The easiest approach is the southern ascent via Rifugio Sapienza (p185) and a cable car, which takes you up to 2500m. From there you can follow with a guide or venture into the black wilderness on your own. Once back safely, decamp to Nicolosi for a comfortable and convenient overnight stay.

Catania

Head to Catania for a shot of urban energy and gastronomic exercise. Start off by admiring the baroque churches on Via Crociferi (p175) and the grand *palazzi* (palaces or mansions) of Piazza del Duomo (p171) before ducking down to La Pescheria (p174) fish market and an unforgettable seafood lunch at Osteria Antica Marina (p178). Set the rest of the day aside for strolling along Via Etnea (p174) followed by a night out around Piazza Bellini.

Getting Away from It All

➡ **Savoca** Hidden away in the hills north of Taormina is this atmospheric village (p165), used as a film location for *The Godfather*.

➡ **Santa Maria la Scala** Turn your back on the crowds and head to this tiny fishing hamlet (p181) for a seafood lunch.

➡ **Pineta Ragabo** On Mt Etna's quieter northern slopes is a huge wood (p185) that makes a lovely place for a picnic under the pines.

DON'T MISS

Climbing up to Etna's craters and tasting wine and honey that is grown from the soil of the great volcano.

Best Trattorias

➡ Trattoria Di De Fiore (p176)

➡ Trattoria La Grotta (p182)

➡ Antico Orto Dei Limono (p186)

➡ Osteria Antica Marina (p178)

➡ Le Tre Bocche (p178)

Best Sights

➡ Etna's Craters (p183)

➡ Teatro Greco (p167)

➡ La Pescheria market (p174)

➡ Acireale's Historic Centre (p181)

➡ Catania's baroque along Via Crociferi (p171)

Resources

➡ **Parks.it** (www.parks.it/parco.etna) A good introduction to the Parco dell'Etna and environs.

➡ **Comune di Catania** (www.comune.catania.it) Extensive listings, suggested itineraries and transport info.

➡ **Taormina Tourist Office** (www.gate2taormina.com) General comprehensive website with historical background and practical details.

➡ **Trasporti sullo Stretto** (www.trasporti sullostretto.it) Up-to-date timetables of Messina ferry crossings.

IONIAN COAST

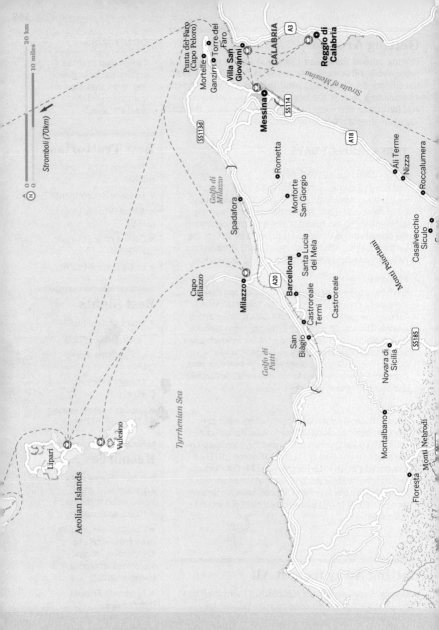

Ionian Coast Highlights

1 Hiking up to the craters of **Mt Etna** (p183) and enjoying honey and wine tastings atop the mountain.

2 Getting up early and seeing fisherfolk unload their offerings at **La Pescheria** (p174), Catania's famous fish market, before exploring the city's baroque architecture and vivacious nightlife.

3 Strolling around Taormina's **Teatro Greco** (p167) and taking in the views of the coast and the grand volcano.

4 Having a swim at Taormina's **Isola Bella** (p168).

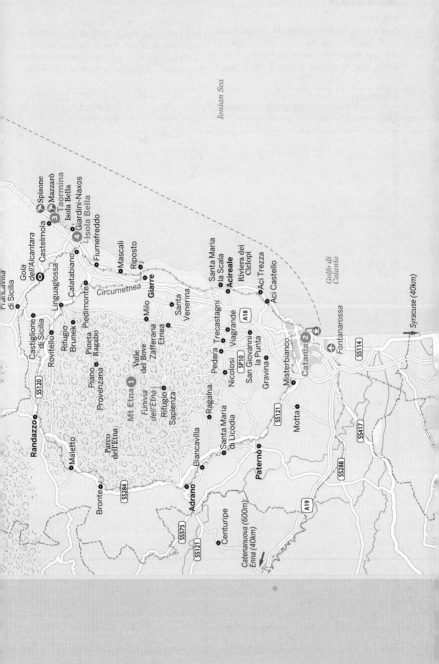

Ionian Sea

Spisone
Mazzarò
Taormina
Isola Bella
Giardini-Naxos
Isola Bella
Castelmola
Fiumefreddo
Mascali
Riposto
Gola
dell'Alcantara
Linguaglossa
Calatabiano
Circumetnea
Milo **Giarre**
Santa Maria
la Scala
Acireale
Riviera dei
Ciclopi
Castiglione
di Sicilia
Rovitello
Rifugio
Brunek
Pineta Piedimonte
Ragabo
Santa
Venerina
Aci Trezza
Aci Castello
Golfo di
Catania
Piano
Provenzana
Zafferana
Etnea
Pedara
Trecastagni
Viagrande
A18
Mt Etna
Valle
del Bove
Ragalna
Nicolosi
San Giovanni
la Punta
SP10
Catania
Fontanarossa
Funivia
dell'Etna
Rifugio
Sapienza
Gravina
Misterbianco
Maletto
Parco
dell'Etna
Santa Maria
di Licodia
SS121
Motta
SS114
Syracuse (40km)
Biancavilla
Randazzo
SS120
Bronte
SS284
Adrano
SS417
SS575
SS121
Centuripe
SS288
Catenanuova (600m)
Enna (40km)
A19

Francavilla
di Sicilia

MESSINA

POP 243,380

Just a few kilometres from the Italian mainland, Messina sits on a curved harbour at the northernmost point of Sicily's Ionian Coast. For centuries it has been a major transport hub and today it's an important gateway to and from the island. A big, busy, traffic-clogged city, it is unlikely to waylay you long, but if you do find yourself passing through, there are a few sights worth checking out. Its impressive centre has wide boulevards and elegant turn-of-the-century

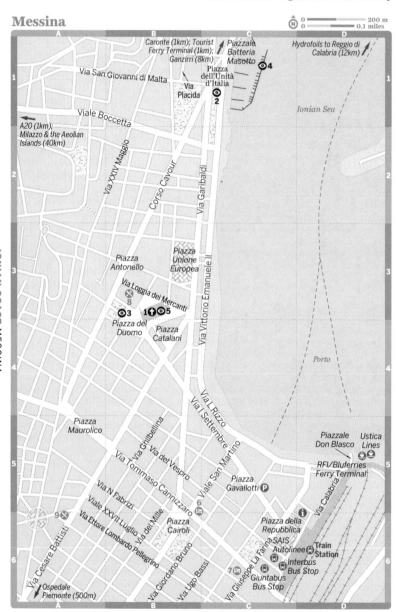

Messina

buildings, its cathedral is one of Sicily's finest, and the local swordfish is celebrated by gourmets across the island. Historical monuments are thin on the ground, though, as the city was virtually razed by an earthquake in 1908 and then devastated by mass bombing in WWII.

Messina is, and always has been, about the strait, the impossibly narrow stretch of water that divides Sicily from the Italian peninsula. The Greeks mythologised the strait's clashing currents as the twin monsters of Charybdis (the whirlpool) and Scylla (the six-headed monster), and swimming there is still dangerous. The currents are not the only danger, though. Beneath the choppy sea is a geological fault line that poses a constant threat. In 1908 it provoked a devastating earthquake – Europe's deadliest ever – which sank the shore by half a metre and killed between 84,000 and 200,000 people.

Modern seismologists worry about what effect it could have on a bridge built across the channel. Plans to construct the world's largest suspension bridge over the strait – which have been on the drawing board for years – are still a bone of contention, with successive national governments regularly giving them the go-ahead, then cancelling them.

◉ Sights & Activities

Duomo   CATHEDRAL
(Piazza del Duomo; ⊙7am-7pm Mon-Sat, 7.30am-1pm & 4-7.30pm Sun) Messina's one great sight is the Norman Duomo, one of Sicily's finest cathedrals, or at least a faithful replica of one of Sicily's finest cathedrals. It holds an impressive carved altar and a huge inlaid organ, the third largest in Europe. The original

cathedral was built in the 12th century and accidentally burnt to the ground in 1254. It was rebuilt several times.

The earthquakes of 1783 and 1908 destroyed it, and the structure was ruined again when a WWII incendiary bomb reduced it to rubble in 1943. Very little remains of the original structure, except for the stripy marble inlay, the tracery of the facade and the fantastic Catalan Gothic portal. Treasures such as the famous Manta d'Oro (Golden Mantle), used to 'cloak' holy pictures during religious celebrations, are kept in the Museo della Cattedrale.

Piazza Del Duomo   SQUARE
Outside the Duomo, you can't miss the 60m *campanile* (bell tower) and its incongruous astronomical clock, said to be the world's largest. Built in Strasbourg in 1733, it strikes at noon, setting in motion a procession of bronze automata that sets off a comical roaring lion and crowing cockerel. Climb the tower to see the enormous figures up close.

Facing the tower, the marble **Fontana di Orione** (1553) commemorates Orion, the mythical founder of Messina, while nearby on Piazza Catalani, the 12th-century **Chiesa della Santissima Annunziata dei Catalani** is a fine example of Arab-Norman construction.

Museo Regionale   MUSEUM
(⊡090 36 12 92; Viale della Libertà 465; adult/reduced €5/3; ⊙9am-1.30pm Mon-Fri, 4.30-7pm Tue, Thu & Sat, 9am-12.30pm Sun) Messina's considerable art collection is held here. The most famous work is the *San Gregorio* (St Gregory) polyptych by local boy Antonello da Messina (1430–79). Although in pretty shabby condition, its five panels are wonderfully figurative. There are also two splendid works by Caravaggio (1571–1610): *L'Adorazione dei pastori* (Adoration of the Shepherds) and *Risurrezione di Lazzaro* (Resurrection of Lazarus).

Another highlight is *Madonna con bambino e santi* (Virgin with Child and Saints), by Antonello da Messina.

To get here, pick up a tram at Piazza Cairoli and take a ride up the sickle-shaped harbour. Halfway along, you'll see the 16th-century **Fontana del Nettuno** (Neptune's Fountain) in the middle of two busy roads, and the colossal golden statue, the **Madonnino del Porto**, towering over the port. Carry on to the end of the line for the Museo Regionale.

✕ Eating

Messina is famous for its quality *pesce spada* (swordfish), which is typically served *agghiotta,* with pine nuts, sultanas, garlic, basil and tomatoes.

Trattoria Dudù   TRATTORIA €

(☑ 090 67 43 93; Via Cesare Battisti 122-124; meals €22; ☉ Mon-Sat) This is a homey, family-run trattoria, ideal for a hearty lunch. It's not a smart place, its interior a cheerful jumble of fading family photos, *presepi* (nativity scene) figures, puppets and assorted bric-a-brac, but the food is good, and excellent value. The delicious swordfish more than lives up to its reputation.

Osteria Del Campanile   SICILIAN €€

(☑ 090 71 14 18; Via Loggia dei Mercanti 9; piz-zas €6, meals €25; ☉ Mon-Sat) With its warm wooden interior and prime location – just behind the Duomo – this cosy hostelry is a good bet for classic coastal cuisine. The menu features all the usual suspects – pizza, pasta with seafood, grilled meat and fish – as well as a few novelties such as *risotto gam-beri e curry* (prawn and curry risotto).

In summer, tables flood the outside area, creating a buzzing street-side atmosphere.

❶ Orientation

Driving in Messina is not an especially pleas-ant experience, although once you've made it through to the city centre, the grid system makes navigation a bit easier. The main things to know are that the principal streets, Via Garibaldi and Via Vittorio Emanuele II, run parallel to the sea, and that the main transport hub is Piazza della Repubblica, at the southern end of the waterfront. Here you'll find the train station and intercity bus stops; Bluferries also dock near here. To get to the city centre from Piazza della Repubblica, turn left into Via Giuseppe La Farina and take the first right into Via Tommaso Canniz-zaro to reach Piazza Cairoli.

❶ Information

EMERGENCIES

Ospedale Piemonte (☑ 090 22 21; Viale Europa) Has a casualty service.
Police Station (☑ 0903 6611; Via Placida 2)

TOURIST INFORMATION

Tourist Office (☑ 090 67 29 44; infotur@ comune.messina.it; Piazza Repubblica 44; ☉ 9am-1.30pm Mon-Fri, 3-5pm Tue & Thu) Friendly English-speaking staff with good information about Messina. To the left as you face the train station.

❶ Getting There & Around

BOAT

Messina is the main point of arrival for ferries and hydrofoils from the Italian mainland. De-tailed timetable information is available online at www.trasportisul lostretto.it. **Caronte & Tourist** (☑ 800 627414; www.carontetourist.it) serves Villa San Giovanni (passenger/car €2.50/37, 25 minutes). **RFI/Bluferries** (www.rfi.it; Porto di Messina, Piazzale Don Blasco) operates frequent passenger-only ferries to/from Reggio di Calabria (€4, 35 minutes) and car ferries to/from Villa San Giovanni (passenger/car €2/28, 35 minutes). **Ustica Lines** (☑ 090 36 40 44; www.usticalines.it; Via Vittorio Emanuele II) runs hydrofoils to/from Reggio di Calabria (€3.50, 30 minutes, six to 11 daily summer) and Lipari (€24.20, 1½ hours, five daily summer, once daily winter).

BUS & TRAM

Giuntabus (☑ 090 67 57 49; Piazza della Re-pubblica) runs a service to Milazzo (€4, 50 min-utes, 15 daily Monday to Saturday, three Sunday) for connections to the Aeolian Islands. **Interbus** (☑ 090 66 17 54; www.interbus.it; Piazza della Repubblica 6) runs a regular service to Taormina (€4.20, 1½ hours, hourly Monday to Saturday, twice Sunday), while **SAIS Autolinee** (☑ 090 77 19 14; www.saisautolinee.it; Piazza della Repub-blica 6) serves Palermo (€15.80, 2¾ hours, at least four daily Monday to Saturday, three Sun-day), Catania (€8.30, 1½ hours, hourly Monday to Saturday, 10 Sunday) and Catania airport (€9.10, two hours, at least nine daily Monday to Saturday, six Sunday). In town, an electric tram runs from Piazza Cairoli via the train station up to the Museo Regionale. Buy tickets (single €1.30) from *tabacchi* (tobacco shops).

CAR & MOTORCYCLE

For Palermo, Milazzo (connections to the Aeolian Islands), Taormina, Catania and Syracuse, turn right from the docks and follow Via Vittorio Emanuele II along the waterfront up to Piazza dell'Unità d'Italia. Here, double back on Corso Cavour and turn right into Viale Boccetta, follow-ing the green A20 autostrada (motorway) signs. Car hire is available at **Hertz** (☑ 090 34 44 24; www.hertz.it; Via Vittorio Emanuele II 113) and **Sicilcar** (☑ 0904 6942; www.sicilcar.net; Via Garibaldi 187).

PARKING

If you have no luck parking on the street (blue lines denote pay-and-display meter parking), there's a useful multistorey car park, **Parcheg-gio Cavallotti** (Via I Settembre; ☉ 5am-11.30pm Mon-Sat), near Piazza Cairoli.

➡ **Etna Touring** (☏ 095 791 80 00; www.etnatouring.com; Via Roma 1, Nicolosi) You can explore Mt Etna on your own, but going with a guide ensures that you won't miss anything or accidentally stumble into a fuming crater.

➡ **Gola Dell'Alcantara (p170)** A renowned beauty spot, this deep rocky canyon is bisected by the freezing Alcantara river. In summer you can wade through the waters, sunbathe or walk along the surrounding nature trails.

Sail ahoy Take a boat tour to explore the caves and black volcanic rocks of the Riviera dei Ciclopi, the popular stretch of coastline north of Catania. Inquire at Catania's Tourist Office for more information.

➡ **Isola Bella (p168)** This picture-perfect bay offers the best swimming near Taormina, as well as excellent diving courtesy of Nike Diving Centre.

➡ **Ferrovia Circumetnea (p186)** If you prefer to keep distance between yourself and Etna's volatile craters, jump on a train and tour the small towns that circle the volcano's base.

TRAIN

As a rule buses are a better bet than trains, particularly to Milazzo and Taormina, but there are several daily trains to Catania (€6.90, 1½ to two hours), Syracuse (€10.20 to €20.50, 2½ to three hours) and Palermo (€13, 3½ hours).

AROUND MESSINA

Ganzirri

From Messina the coast curves around to Sicily's most northeasterly point, **Punta del Faro** (also called Capo Peloro), just 3km across the water from the Italian mainland. South of the cape is the lakeside town of Ganzirri, a popular summer hang-out and pretty setting for a fish dinner. Mussels are the local speciality – they're cultivated in the salty lake waters – and **La Napoletana** (☏ 090 39 10 32; Via Lago Grande 29; meals €30-35; ⊙ Thu-Tue) is a good place to try them. A family-run restaurant housed in a neoclassical villa, it specialises in local seafood, so expect plenty of mussels, clams, swordfish and *stoccafisso* (stockfish).

On the other side of the cape, **Mortelle** is the area's most popular summer resort, where the Messinese go to sunbathe and hang out.

Savoca

Sandwiched between the Peloritani mountains and the sea, the SS114 hugs the coast as it heads south towards Taormina. It's a slow drive, past never-ending towns that merge one into another, but with the sparkling blue sea to keep you company it's not unpleasant. (You can cover the same ground much more quickly on the elevated A18 autostrada.) For a change of scene take a detour to the tiny, trapped-in-time village of Savoca, high in the hills 4km inland from Santa Teresa di Riva.

Surrounded by encroaching green peaks, the village seems unchanged since medieval times, with its gated walls, rustic stone cottages and haunting churches. It even has its own **catacombs** (admission by donation; ⊙ 9am-noon Tue-Sat, 3-7pm Tue-Sun), beneath a Cappucini monastery, where the macabre bodies of a few mummified bigwigs stand in a series of wall niches.

The village's main claim to fame is its association with *The Godfather* film – Michael Corleone's marriage to Apollonia was filmed here. One of the locations used was **Bar Vitelli**, a rustic bar located by the village entrance and a lovely spot for a cool lemon *granita* (crushed-ice drink). For more information about the village, ask at the small **tourist office** (☏ 0942 76 11 25; http://turismo.comune.savoca.me.it; Via San Michele; ⊙ 9.40am-1pm & 3-6.20pm Tue-Sun).

TAORMINA

POP 11,095 / ELEV 204M

Spectacularly perched on the side of a mountain, Taormina is Sicily's most popular summer destination, a chic resort town beloved of holidaying high-rollers and visiting celebs. And while it is unashamedly touristy and has a main street lined with high-end

Taormina

N

0 — 200 m
0 — 0.1 miles

Bar Turrisi (1.3km);
Castelmola (1.3km)

Via Rotabile per Castelmola

Mt Tauro
(378m)

Ospedale San Vincenzo (2km);
Via Pietro Rizzo; Piazza San
Giardini-Naxos (5km);
Mt Etna (45km)

Via Dionisio Primo

Via Cuseni

Via Diodoro Siculo

Piazza Sant'
Antonio Abate

Corso Umberto I

Via Rotabile per Castelmola

Mazzarò (950m);
Isola Bella (1.1km);
Nike Diving Centre (1.1km);
Spisone (1.1km)

Via Guardio la Vecchia

Interbus (110m);
(4km)

A18 (500m);
Savoca (28km)

Via San Pancrazio

Via Luigi Pirandello

Porta
Messina

Chiesa dei
Cappuccini

Via Cappuccini

Hotel Condor (160m);
Isoco Guest House (200m)

Via Timeo

Piazza
Santa
Caterina

Via Teatro Greco

Via Timoleone

Via Ginnasio

Parco Duchi di Cesarò
(Villa Comunale)

Via Bagnoli Croce

Piazzetta
Filea

Via Giardinazzo

Via Naumachie

Corso Umberto I

Via A. Marziani

Via Roma

Vico la
Floresta

Via Circonvallazione

Piazza
IX Aprile

Porta di
Mezzo e Torre
dell'Orologio

Via
Paladini

Piazza
Garibaldi

Piazza
Paladini

Via Santa Maria
dei Greci

Piazza San
Domenico

Vico
Ebrei

Piazza del
Duomo

Taormina

designer shops, the town remains an achingly beautiful spot with gorgeous medieval churches, a stunning Greek theatre and sweeping views over the Gulf of Naxos and Mt Etna.

Founded in the 4th century BC, it enjoyed great prosperity under the Greek ruler Gelon II and later under the Romans, but fell into quiet obscurity after being conquered by the Normans in 1087. Its modern reincarnation as a tourist destination dates to the 18th century, when it was discovered by northern Europeans on the Grand Tour. Goethe was an early fan, as was DH Lawrence, who lived

here between 1920 and 1923, and over the years it has seduced a whole army of writers, artists, aristocrats and royals.

Note that it gets extremely busy in July and August and virtually shuts down between November and Easter. The best time to visit is either side of high season, April to May or September to October.

⊙ Sights & Activities

Teatro Greco AMPHITHEATRE
(☑094 22 32 20; Via Teatro Greco; adult/reduced/ EU under 18 & over 65 €10/5/free; ⊙9am-1hr before sunset) Taormina's premier attraction is this perfect horseshoe-shaped theatre, suspended between sea and sky, with Mt Etna looming on the southern horizon. Built in the 3rd century BC, it's the most dramatically situated Greek theatre in the world and the second largest in Sicily (after Syracuse). In summer the theatre is used as the venue for international arts and film festivals.

In peak season the site is best explored early in the morning to avoid the crowds.

Corso Umberto STREET
One of the chief delights of Taormina is wandering along its pedestrian-friendly medieval main avenue, Corso Umberto I, lined with antique and jewellery shops, delis and designer boutiques. Midway down, pause to revel in the stunning panoramic views of Mt Etna and the seacoast from Piazza IX Aprile and pop your head into the charming rococo church, Chiesa San Giuseppe (Piazza IX Aprile; ⊙9am-7pm).

Continue west through the 12th-century clock tower, Torre dell'Orologio, into the Borgo Medievale, the oldest quarter of town. A few blocks further along is Piazza del Duomo, where teenagers congregate around the ornate baroque fountain (built 1635), which sports a two-legged centaur with the bust of an angel, the symbol of Taormina. On the eastern side of this piazza is the 13th-century cathedral. It survived much of the Renaissance-style remodelling undertaken throughout the town by the Spanish aristocracy in the 15th century. The Renaissance influence is better illustrated in various palaces along the Corso, including Palazzo Duca di Santo Stefano with its Norman-Gothic windows, Palazzo Corvaja (Largo Santa) (the tourist office) and Palazzo Ciampoli (now the Hotel El Jebel).

IONIAN COAST TAORMINA

Villa Comunale
PARK

(Parco Duchi di Cesarò; Via Bagnoli Croce; ⊙9am-midnight summer, 9am-sunset winter) To escape the crowds, wander down to these stunningly sited public gardens. Created by Englishwoman Florence Trevelyan, they're a lush paradise of tropical plants and delicate flowers. There's also a children's play area.

Monte Tauro
VIEW POINT

The short 20-minute climb to the top of Monte Tauro (378m) is not exactly Himalayan but it is steep and the final steps are quite hard work. Your reward is a massive panoramic view over Taormina's rooftops, the Teatro Greco and, beyond, to the coast.

From Via Circonvallazione, a signposted path leads up past the Santuario Madonna della Rocca, and beyond towards the windswept ruins of a Saracen castello (castle). You can't actually get to the castle – a locked gate blocks the path – but it's the views rather than the sights that are the real appeal.

Castelmola
HILLTOP VILLAGE

For eye-popping views of the coastline, head 5km up Via Leonardo da Vinci to this hilltop village crowned by a ruined castle. The walk will take around an hour and is along a well-paved route. Alternatively, Interbus runs an hourly service (one way/return €1.70/2.80) up the hill.

Beaches
SWIMMING

The nearest beach to Taormina is at Mazzarò, accessible by funivia (cable car; 1 way/return €3/3.50; ⊙9am-8.15pm Oct-Mar, 9am-1am Apr-Sep) from Via Luigi Pirandello. It's a popular pebbly beach well serviced with umbrellas and deck chairs for hire (from about €8 per day). To the south of the beach, and an easy walk past the Sant'Andrea hotel, is Isola Bella, a tiny island set in a stunning cove.

Isola Bella was once home to Florence Trevelyan and it is her house that sits in silent solitude on top of the rocky islet.

There's wonderful snorkelling in the crystalline waters or you can hire a boat and pootle around the rocky bays. If you prefer your adventures underwater, Nike Diving Centre (☑339 1961559; www.diveniketaormina. com; single dive incl kite hire from €45) offers a range of packages from its base at the northern end of the beach.

For a real sandy beach you will have to go to Spisone, just beneath the autostrada exit – turn left from the cable-car station and it's about a 10-minute walk.

☞ Tours

If you're based in Taormina and want to explore further afield without having to hire a car or deal with public transport, a day trip is well worth considering. SAT (☑094 22 46 53; www.satgroup.it; Corso Umberto I 73) is one of a number of agencies that organises day trips to Mt Etna and the nearby beauty spot, Gola dell'Alcantara (€45), as well as to Syracuse (€45), Palermo and Cefalù (€55), and Agrigento (€55). Saistours (☑0942 62 06 71; www.saistours.com; Corso Umberto I 222) offers a range of more sporty tours, such as quad-bike (€92) and mountain-bike (€89) tours of Etna.

✖ Festivals & Events

Taormina Arte
PERFORMING ARTS

(www.taormina-arte.com) In July and August, this festival features opera, dance, theatre and music concerts with an impressive list of international names.

Taormina FilmFest
FILM

(www.taorminafilmfest.it) Hollywood big shots arrive in mid-June for a week of film screenings, premieres and press conferences at the Teatro Greco.

✖ Eating

There's no getting around it – eating in Taormina is expensive. Prices are universally higher here than in the rest of Sicily and service is not always what it should be. That said, there are some excellent restaurants and as long as you avoid the obvious tourist traps you can eat well. Note that reservations are essential at the more exclusive places.

La Piazzetta
SICILIAN €€

(☑0942 62 63 17; Via Paladini 5; meals €25; ⊙closed Mon in winter) Tucked in the corner of the very picturesque Piazza Paladini, this place has all the classics, such as *pasta alla Norma* and a variety of fresh fish. The wine list has some good local reds and whites. Recommended.

Il Baccanale
TRATTORIA €€

(☑0942 62 53 90; Piazzetta Filea 1; meals €25-30) Resembling a Sicilian theme park with old black-and-white photos, gaudy paintings and a kitsch Caltagirone ceramic panel depicting a Bacchanalian banquet scene, this colourful trattoria knows how to impress. Thankfully, the food is less ostentatious. There's classic *insalata caprese* (tomato and mozzarella salad) and *pasta alla Norma* (pasta with aubergine, tomato and ricotta).

Don't miss the long list of fishy mains, and a complimentary almond liqueur to round things off.

Tiramisù PIZZERIA, SICILIAN €€
(094 22 48 03; Via Cappuccini 1; pizzas €7-14, meals €35; Wed-Mon) This stylish place near Porta Messina makes fabulous meals, from *linguine cozze, menta e zucchine* (pasta with mussels, mint and zucchini) to old favourites such as *scaloppine al limone e panna* (veal escalope in lemon-cream sauce). When dessert rolls around, don't miss the trademark tiramisu, a perfect ending to any meal here.

Al Duomo SICILIAN €€€
(0942 62 56 56; Vico Ebrei 11; meals €55; lunch & dinner Tue-Sun Nov-Mar) This highly acclaimed restaurant with a romantic terrace overlooking the cathedral puts a modern spin on Sicilian classics like *pesce alla messinese* (fish fillets with tomatoes, capers and olives) and *agnello n'grassatu* (lamb stew with potatoes). For a splurge, indulge in the chef's six-course tasting menu (€60).

Casa Grugno GASTRONOMIC €€€
(094 22 12 08; www.casagrugno.it; Via Santa Maria dei Greci; meals €70-80; dinner Mon-Sat) With a walled-in terrace surrounded by plants, Taormina's most fashionable restaurant specialises in sublime modern Sicilian cuisine, under the direction of new chef David Tamburini. Multilingual waiters describe the origins of each ultra-fresh local ingredient as they serve dishes such as red mullet fillets with grilled fennel, orange and saffron or risotto with green peas, candied ginger and marjoram.

La Giara MODERN SICILIAN €€€
(094 22 33 60; Vico la Floresta 1; meals €60) A meal on the rooftop terrace at La Giara is a Taormina classic. This is one of the best-looking restaurants in town, with a smooth art deco interior and a piano bar worthy of Bogart in *Casablanca*. The food is modern but grounded in island tradition, with dishes such as risotto with wild herbs, and squid served in a Marsala reduction. Bookings are essential.

Drinking & Nightlife

Taormina's nightlife revolves around the town's numerous bars and cafes, most of which have outdoor seating.

Shatulle BAR
(Piazza Paladini 4; Tue-Sun) An intimate square just off Corso Umberto, Piazza Paladini is a perennial favourite with Taormina's young, well-dressed night owls. One of the best, and most popular, of the square-side bars is this hip, gay-friendly spot with outdoor seating, an inviting vibe and a fine selection of cocktails (from €5.50).

Wunderbar Caffè CAFE
(0942 62 50 32; Piazza IX Aprile 7) A Taormina landmark since the *dolce vita* 1960s, this glamorous and achingly expensive cafe has served them all – Tennessee Williams, who liked to watch 'the squares go by', Greta Garbo, Richard Burton and Elizabeth Taylor. With tables spread over the vibrant piazza and white-jacketed waiters taking the orders, it is still very much the quintessential Taormina watering hole.

Shopping

Shopping is a popular pastime in Taormina, particularly on Corso Umberto I. Here you'll find inviting delis and attractive boutiques selling high-quality ceramic goods, lace and linen tableware, antique furniture and jewellery.

Carlo Mirella Panarello CERAMICS
(Via Antonio Marziani) Sicily has a long tradition of ceramic production and this is a good bet for original ceramic designs. The workshop is on Via A Marzani (ring the bell for admission), while around the corner on Corso Umberto I, the shop sells more traditional jewellery, bags and hats.

La Torinese FOOD, WINE
(Corso Umberto 59) This is a fantastic place to stock up on local olive oil, capers, marmalade, honey and wine. Smash-proof bubble wrapping helps to bring everything home in one piece.

Information

EMERGENCIES
Police Station (0942 61 02 01; Corso Umberto 219)

MEDICAL SERVICES
Ospedale San Vincenzo (0942 57 92 97; Contrada Sirina) Downhill, 2km from the centre.

TOURIST INFORMATION
Tourist Office (094 22 32 43; www.gate 2taormina.com; Piazza Santa Caterina, off Corso Umberto I; 8.30am-2.30pm &

GOLA DELL'ALCANTARA

Located 15km inland from Giardini-Naxos, the Gola dell'Alcantara (www.terralcantara. it/en; admission €8; ☉8am-sunset) is a vertiginous 25m-high natural gorge bisected by the freezing waters of the Alcantara river (the name is derived from the Arabic *al qantara*, meaning bridge). Characterised by its weirdly symmetrical rock formations – created when a red-hot lava flow hit the water and splintered the basalt into lava prisms – it's a spectacular sight well worth searching out.

The gorge is now part of the Parco Botanico e Geologico Terralcantara, which is within the Parco Fluviale dell'Alcantara regional park. It's out of bounds between November and March due to the risk of flash flooding, but is open during the rest of the year. To get to the bottom there's a lift near the car park or a 224-step staircase some 200m or so uphill from the lift. Once down by the river, you can hire waders to splash around in the icy waters or simply sunbathe on the surrounding banks. There are also 3.5km of nature trails in the area. For further details contact the park office (☎094 298 50 10).

3.30-7pm Mon-Fri year-round, 9am-1pm & 4-6.30pm Sat Apr-Oct) Has helpful multilingual staff and plenty of practical information.

ℹ Getting There & Around

BUS

The bus is the best way to reach Taormina. The bus station is on Via Luigi Pirandello, a 400m walk from Porta Messina, the northeastern entrance to the old town. **Etna Trasporti** (☎095 53 27 16; www.etnatrasporti.it) runs direct to/ from Catania airport (€7.90, 1½ hours, six daily Monday to Saturday, four Sunday). **Interbus** (☎0942 62 53 01; Via Luigi Pirandello) services run to/from Messina (€4.20, 1½ hours, hourly Monday to Saturday, twice Sunday), Catania (€4.80, 1½ hours, 14 daily Monday to Saturday, eight Sunday) and Castelmola (€1.80, 15 minutes, at least seven daily).

CAR & MOTORCYCLE

Taormina is on the A18 autostrada and the SS114. The historic centre is closed to nonresident traffic and Corso Umberto I is closed to all traffic. You can hire cars and scooters at **California Car Rental** (☎094 22 37 69; www.california rentcar.com; Via Bagnoli Croce 86; Vespa per day/week €35/224, Fiat Panda €64/300) near Villa Comunale. Reckon on €30/60 per day for a Vespa/Fiat Panda.

Some top-end hotels offer limited parking, otherwise you'll have to leave your car in one of the two car parks outside the historic centre: Porta Catania or Lumbi. Both are within walking distance of Corso Umberto I.

TRAIN

Taormina's train station is 2km downhill from the main town, making the train a last resort. If you do arrive this way – there are direct trains to/ from Catania and Messina – catch the Interbus

service (one-way €1.50) up to town. It runs roughly every 30 to 90 minutes, less often on Sunday.

AROUND TAORMINA

Giardini-Naxos

POP 9560

The unpretentious resort of Giardini-Naxos is a popular alternative to more expensive Taormina. Action is centred on a long parade of hotels, bars, pizzerias and souvenir shops strung along the beach. It heaves in summer but outside of the high season (Easter to October) there's nothing going on and you won't miss much if you pass it by.

◉ Sights & Activities

Beach BEACH

Giardini's long beach (mainly sand and coarse grey pebbles) curves around the crescent-shaped bay between Capo Taormina and Capo Schisò, a lick of prehistoric lava at the southern end. There is a small *spiaggia libera* (free beach), but most of it is given over to lidos (private beach clubs).

You will pay around €2.50 for entry, €5 for a sun lounge and €3 for an umbrella. If you fancy a bit of exercise, canoes can be hired for about €7 per hour.

Greek Ruins ARCHAEOLOGICAL SITE

You'd never know it to look at it, but Giardini-Naxos is the oldest Greek settlement in Sicily; its origins date to 735 BC. You can visit the rather scant remains of the original settlement – a 300m stretch of wall, a small temple and a couple of other structures – at the southern end of the seafront road.

There's also a small museum (☑094 25 10 01; Via Schisò; adult/reduced €2/1; ⊗9am-7pm), with bits and bobs uncovered during the excavation.

✖ Eating

Ristorante Pizzeria Royale

PIZZA/SEAFOOD €€

(☑0942 36 68; Lungomare Schisò 34; pizzas from €5, meals €25; ⊗Thu-Tue) Of the restaurants that line the seafront, Ristorante Pizzeria Royale is an excellent midrange option. Like everywhere in Giardini it's touristy, but the food is decent and the atmosphere friendly. There is a range of seafood pastas and grilled meat and fish, but it's the pizzas that really stand out – served bubbling hot straight from the wood-fired oven.

❶ Information

Tourist Office (☑0942 25 10 10; Via Tysandros 54; ⊗9am-1pm Mon-Fri, 3.30-6.30pm Mon-Thu) Can provide accommodation lists and handy maps.

❶ Getting There & Around

BUS

Interbus (☑0942 62 53 01; www.interbus.it) Regular services run between Giardini-Naxos and Taormina's bus station, stopping at the train station en route.

TRAIN

Giardini shares its train station with Taormina. It's situated at the northern end of the seafront, about 10 minutes' walk from the town centre.

CATANIA

POP 296,470

For all its noise, chaos and scruffiness that hit the visitor at first glance, Catania has energy to sell and a beautiful, Unesco-listed historic centre. Grandiose black-and-white *palazzi* tower over baroque piazzas and the city has one of the most vibrant fish markets on the island, together with hundreds of bars, clubs and eateries that cater to the city's fun-loving (largely student) population. All the while, Mt Etna broods on the horizon, its powerful presence adding a thrilling edge – and a beautiful backdrop – to Sicily's second-largest city.

Catania, or Katane as it was once called, was originally founded by the Chalcidians in 729 BC, growing to become a major regional power in the 4th and 5th centuries BC. In subsequent centuries it was ruled by a succession of foreign powers, first the Romans, then the Byzantines, Saracens and Normans, but by the mid-17th century it had once again become a prosperous commercial centre. Then, in the late 1600s, disaster struck. Twice. First, Mt Etna erupted in 1669, engulfing the city in boiling lava and killing 12,000 people. Then, in 1693, a huge earthquake hit leaving a further 20,000 people dead. But out of the ashes arose the city that stands today. Under the supervision of architects Giovanni Vaccarini and Stefano Ittar, a new street grid was created incorporating spacious squares and streets of differing widths, all designed to provide escape routes and greater shelter in case of another eruption. Grandiose *palazzi* and churches were built in baroque style out of the black volcanic rock that Etna had rained on the city.

In modern times, years of neglect left many of the city's great buildings on the verge of decay but renovations in the early 2000s restored many of them to their former glory.

⊙ Sights & Activities

Piazza del Duomo

SQUARE

A Unesco World Heritage Site, Catania's central square is a set piece of sinuous buildings and a grand cathedral, all built in the unique local baroque style, with its contrasting lava and limestone. In the centre of the piazza is Catania's most memorable monument, and a symbol of the city, the smiling Fontana dell'Elefante (Piazza del Duomo) built in 1736.

The naive black-lava elephant, dating from the Roman period, is surmounted by an improbable Egyptian obelisk. Legend has it that it belonged to the 8th-century magician Eliodorus, who reputedly made his living by turning people into animals. The obelisk is believed to possess magical powers that help calm Mt Etna's restless activity. At the piazza's southwest corner, the Fontana dell'Amenano fountain marks the entrance to Catania's fish market and commemorates the Amenano River, which once ran above ground and on whose banks the Greeks first founded the city of Katáne.

Catania

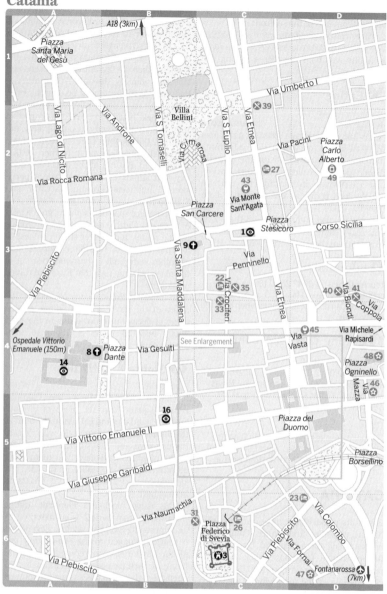

IONIAN COAST CATANIA

Cattedrale di Sant'Agata   CATHEDRAL
(095 32 00 44; Piazza del Duomo; 8am-noon
& 4-7pm) Inside the cool, vaulted interior of
this cathedral, beyond its impressive marble
facade sporting two orders of columns taken

from the Roman amphitheatre, lie the relics
of the city's patron saint.

The young virgin Agata resisted the ad-
vances of the nefarious Quintian (AD 250)
and was horribly mutilated (her breasts

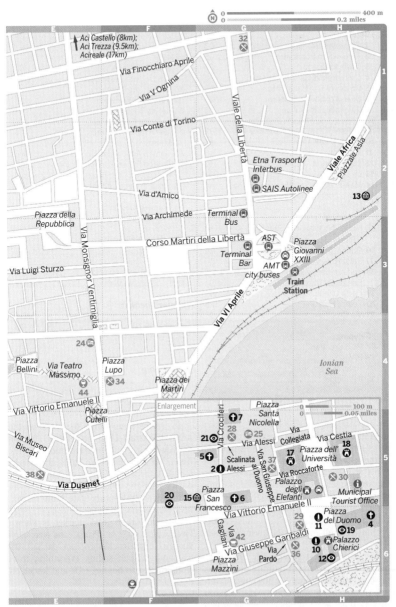

were hacked off and her body rolled in hot coals). You can actually visit the dungeons where these atrocities were committed under the **Chiesa di Sant'Agata al Carcere** (Piazza San Carcere; ◷ 8.30am-1pm & 3-8pm Tue-Sat) behind the Roman amphitheatre on Piazza Stesicoro. The saint's jewel-drenched effigy is ecstatically venerated on 5 February in one of Sicily's largest festivals.

Catania

Street Markets   MARKET

Catania's great markets are street theatre at its most thrilling. The best show in town is the raucous fish market, **La Pescheria** (Via Pardo; ⊘7am-2pm), which takes over the streets behind Piazza del Duomo every workday morning. Tables groan under the weight of decapitated swordfish, ruby-pink prawns and trays full of clams, mussels, sea urchins and all manner of mysterious sea life.

Fishmongers gut silvery fish, and high-heeled housewives step daintily over pools of blood-stained water. It's absolutely riveting. If you fancy a taste of the exotic ware on display, there are a number of excellent fish restaurants down here.

Carcasses of meat, skinned sheep's heads, strings of sausages, huge wheels of cheese and mountains of luscious fruit and veg are all rolled together in a few jam-packed alleyways.

To get here, go down the steps at the south of Piazza del Duomo near the Fontana dell'Amenano, a commemoration of the Amenano river on whose banks the Greeks founded the city of Katane. Alternatively, duck under the adjacent **Porta Uzeda**, an impressive 17th-century gate built to connect Via Etnea with the port.

Catania's other great market is known locally as **La Fiera** (Piazza Carlo Alberto, off Via Etna; ⊘8am-1pm Mon-Fri, 8am-7pm Sat). It's a chaotic kasbah selling everything from fruit and veg to bootleg CDs and knock-off designer bags.

Via Etnea   STREET

It's not difficult to see how Catania's main shopping street got its name – on a clear day you can see Mt Etna rising menacingly at the end of it. Via Etnea runs straight from Piazza del Duomo up to the foothills below Etna. Lined with modern department stores, bars and pavement cafes, it's busy at most times but heaves on Saturday afternoons, when shoppers pile in from the suburbs to hang out and update their wardrobes.

At its southern end, Piazza dell'Università is a great place to take stock over a coffee and cake. On the other side of the square is Palazzo dell'Università, the Vaccarini-designed building that houses the city university. On the eastern flank is another Vaccarini edifice, Palazzo Sangiuliano.

To escape the madding crowds, continue up to the lovely Villa Bellini (⊗8am-8pm) gardens where you can relax on a shady bench and admire views up to Etna.

Museo Belliniano   MUSEUM
(🖉095 715 05 35; Piazza San Francesco 3; ⊗9am-1pm Mon-Sat) FREE One of Italy's great opera composers, Vincenzo Bellini was born in Catania in 1801. The house has since been converted into this museum, which boasts an interesting collection of Bellini memorabilia, including original scores, photographs and his death mask.

In his short life (he died aged 34), Bellini composed 10 operas, including the famous trio: *La sonnambula* (The Sleepwalker), *I puritani* (The Puritans) and *Norma*, which has since been immortalised as the name of Sicily's most famous pasta dish – *pasta alla Norma*.

Via Crociferi   STREET
A lovely, tranquil spot for a morning stroll, Via Crociferi is one of Catania's most attractive streets, famous for its exuberant baroque churches and imposing 18th-century *palazzi*.

The Arco di San Benedetto (Via Crociferi), an arch built by the Benedictines in 1704, marks the beginning of Via Crociferi. According to legend, the arch was built in a single night to defy a city ordinance against its construction on the grounds that it was a seismic liability.

Chiesa di San Francesco   CHURCH
(Piazza San Francesco; ⊗8.30am-noon & 4-7.30pm) The piazza is lorded over by this church, which houses six of the 11 giant candelabras that are paraded around town during the Festa di Sant'Agata.

Chiesa di San Benedetto   CHURCH
(Via Crociferi; ⊗7am-noon & 3.30-6pm Thu, 10am-noon Sun) Inside this church, built between 1704 and 1713, is some splendid stucco and marble work, as well as a rather graphic

fresco of a woman being tortured in front of a curious sultan.

Chiesa di San Giuliano   CHURCH
(Via Crociferi) This church, about halfway up Via Crociferi on the right-hand side, is famous for its convex facade designed by Vaccarini between 1738 and 1751.

Chiesa di San Nicolò all'Arena   CHURCH
(Via Gesuiti; ⊗9am-1pm) Sicily's largest church is the monumentally ugly Chiesa di San Nicolò all'Arena. The church was commissioned in 1687 but building was interrupted by the earthquake of 1693 and then by problems with its size – it measures 105m long, 48m wide and 62m high – and it was never actually finished.

Much more impressive than the church is the adjoining Monastero di San Nicolò all'Arena, Europe's second-largest monastery. Built in 1703 and now part of the city university, it boasts a grand internal cloister and one of Sicily's most important libraries. You can't actually enter the cloisters but you see them from the surrounding corridors.

Roman Ruins   ARCHAEOLOGICAL SITE
Little remains of the prosperous Roman city that Catania once was, but you can walk among the sunken ruins of the Anfiteatro Romano (Roman Amphitheatre; Piazza Stesicoro; admission free; ⊗9am-1.30pm & 2.30-6pm). It doesn't look like much today, but in its 2nd-century-BC heyday it was vast, extending as far south as Via Penninello and seating up to 16,000 spectators.

Go down to the vaults and you'll get an inkling of just how complex a structure it must have been.

There are more theatrical ruins on Via Vittorio Emanuele II, where you can visit the 2nd-century remains of a Teatro Romano (Via Vittorio Emanuele II) (Roman Theatre) and its small rehearsal theatre, the Odeon (Via Vittorio Emanuele II 266; theatre & odeon €3; ⊗9am-1pm & 2.30-6pm Mon-Sat, 9am-1.30pm Sun).

Castello Ursino   CASTLE
Catania's foreboding castle, the 13th-century Castello Ursino, once guarded the city from atop a seafront cliff. However, the 1693 earthquake changed the landscape and the whole area to the south was reclaimed by the lava, leaving the castle completely landlocked. The castle now houses the Museo Civico (🖉095 34 58 30; Piazza Federico II di

HAVE A SELTZ

Heaven on a hot day, or at any other time for that matter, is a €1 *seltz* from one of the kiosks on Via Dusmet down by La Pescheria (p174). A *seltz* is a nonalcoholic mix of fizzy water (on draft at the kiosks), freshly squeezed lemon juice and natural fruit syrup. There are various flavours but the *seltz mandarino* (with mandarin orange) is our favourite.

Svevia; ⊙9am-1pm & 3-7pm Mon-Sat, 8.30am-1.30pm Sun) and its valuable archaeological collection.

Put together by Catania's most important aristocratic family, the Biscaris, the collection features some colossal classical sculpture, as well as a number of Greek vases and fine mosaics.

Le Ciminiere MUSEUM
(☑095 734 99 11) Catania's answer to London's Tate Modern, Le Ciminiere is a modern museum complex housed in a converted sulphur refinery. There are two museums and two permanent exhibitions, one dedicated to old radios and the other displaying a fascinating collection of historic maps, as well as a cafe-restaurant and performance spaces.

Of the museums, the most interesting is the **Museo Storico dello Sbarco in Sicilia** (☑095 53 35 40; admission €4; ⊙9am-12.30pm Tue-Sun, 3-5pm Tue & Thu), which illustrates the history of the WWII Allied landings in Sicily. The other museum, the **Museo del Cinema**, takes a specialist look at Catania's early-20th-century film industry. Check with the municipal tourist office for details of temporary exhibitions.

★☆ Festivals & Events

Festa di Sant'Agata RELIGIOUS
In Catania's biggest religious festival (3 to 5 February), one million Catanians follow the Fercolo (a silver reliquary bust of Saint Agata) along the main street of the city accompanied by spectacular fireworks.

Etnafest ARTS
From July through December, this arts festival brings classical music, puppet shows and a varied program of rock, pop, blues, reggae and jazz concerts to Le Ciminiere.

Sicily Jazz and More JAZZ FESTIVAL
Italian and international jazz stars perform at Le Ciminiere in November.

Eating

Eating out in Catania is a real pleasure. There's a huge choice of snack bars, trattorias and restaurants, and the city's street food is superb. Be sure not to miss the savoury *arancini* (fried rice balls), *cartocciate* (bread stuffed with ham, mozzarella, olives and tomato) and *pasta alla Norma*, which originated here.

Trattoria di De Fiore TRATTORIA €
(☑095 31 62 83; Via Coppola 24/26; meals €15-25; ⊙from 1pm Tue-Sun) This neighbourhood trattoria is presided over by septuagenarian chef Mamma Rosanna, who uses organic flour and fresh, local ingredients to re-create her great-grandmother's recipes, including the best *pasta alla Norma* you'll taste anywhere in Sicily. Service can be excruciatingly slow and the door doesn't always open promptly at 1pm, but food like this is well worth waiting for.

Rosanna says her grandmother called *pasta alla Norma* Mungibeddu – Sicilian dialect for Mt Etna – in honour of Catania's famous volcano: tomatoes were the red lava, aubergine the black cinders, ricotta the snow and basil leaves the mountain vegetation. Don't miss the *zeppoline di ricotta* (sweet ricotta fritters dusted with powdered sugar), a dessert invented by Rosanna herself.

Locanda Cerami PIZZERIA €
(☑095 224 67 82; www.locandacerami.com; Via Crociferi 69; pizza €5.50-11) This gorgeous pizzeria has an excellent setting – in the summer months, the tables are on the steps of one of the many baroque churches – and some of the most innovative pizza you'll find anywhere on the island, plus an excellent wine list. Try the *principessa* pizza, with aromatic speck and pistacchio nuts.

Traditional pizzas are also available and just as great.

Il Borgo Di Federico BARBECUE €
(☑095 67 98 19; Piazza Federico di Svevia 100; pizzas from €5, meals €18) The restaurants around Castello Ursino are known for their meat, particularly barbecued meat, and Il Borgo di Federico is no exception. A modest, unpretentious outfit with a bustling, TV-on-in-the-corner atmosphere, it's a good place

for a filling antipasto buffet – olives, fried croquettes, frittata, cured meats, octopus salad – followed by a no-nonsense plate of *polpette* (meat balls).

Spinella   PASTRIES & CAKES €
(☑ 095 32 72 47; Via Etnea 300; snacks from €1.80)
The Slow Food movement especially recommends Spinella's traditional sweets – try the *frutta martorana* (marzipan sweets shaped like fruits and vegetables) and *olivette di sant'Agata* (olive-shaped sweets typically made only in January and February, for the festival of St Agatha). If you don't fancy a sit-down lunch but want something tasty on the hoof, Spinella also serves the best *arancini* in town.

Grand Café Tabbacco   PASTRIES & CAKES €
(Via Etnea 28; ☷ 7am-midnight) Of the number of cafes on Piazza dell'Università, pride of place goes to this elegant old-school *pasticceria* (pastry shop) with outdoor seating and a devilish selection of *dolci* (sweets), fresh-fruit tarts and cakes.

★**Cutilisci**   MODERN SICILIAN €€
(☑ 095 37 25 58; www.cutilisci.it; Via San Giovanni li Cuti 67-69; meals €30-35; ☷ lunch & dinner Wed-Mon, dinner Tue) One of the loveliest lunch and/or dinner experiences in Catania is to be had at this seafront restaurant, in the small harbour of San Giovanni li Cuti. When the weather is good, the tables are out on the small pavement terrace overlooking the sea, and the fish, meat and vegetarian dishes are prepared with sophistication, originality and imagination.

Fish and seafood lovers should try the swordfish steak with an orange and fennel salad, or the seafood cous cous, both wonderful with a local white wine. Vegetarians can opt for a variety of pasta dishes or the excellent barley and vegetable tabbouleh.

★**Me Cumpari Turridu**   SICILIAN €€
(☑ 095 715 01 42; Via Ventimiglia 15; meals €35-40; ☷ Mon-Sat) A quirky little spot that mixes tradition and modernity both in food and decor, this place is a real discovery. There's fresh pasta to be savoured – try the ricotta and marjoram ravioli in a pork sauce, or the cannellini with donkey-meat ragu. Vegetarians can opt for the Ustica lentil stew, with broad beans and fennel. It's Slow Food–recommended.

Meat eaters are spoilt with a variety of barbecued meat, and there is a wealth of Sicilian cheeses on offer.

48 HOURS IN CATANIA

Gourmet Traveller

Catania provides plenty of opportunities for enthusiastic gourmets. Whet your appetite at La Pescheria (p174) fish market before adjourning for a languid seafood lunch at a market-side restaurant. After a well-deserved pause pick yourself up with a late afternoon coffee and *dolci* (sweets) at Grand Café Tabbacco (p177). On your second day, head up to San Giovani Li Cuti harbour, and eat at Cutilisci (p177), Catania's best fish restaurant. Tables are on a charming *piazzetta* overlooking the sea and a small pier. At dinner time, try *pasta alla Norma*, the city's signature dish, at Trattoria di De Fiore (p176).

Trace the City's History

Already a major power when the Romans barged in during the 3rd century BC, Catania retains little of its classical past, but you can sniff around the sunken ruins of what was once a vast Roman amphitheatre, the Anfiteatro Romano (p175), and visit a 2nd-century Roman theatre, the Teatro Romano (p175). More evident are Catania's baroque treasures – the soaring Cattedrale di Sant'Agata (p172) takes pride of place, but also impressive are the *palazzi* around Piazza del Duomo (p171) and the churches of Via Crociferi (p175).

A Volcanic Excursion

Leaning menacingly over the city, Mt Etna is a thrilling sight, a far-from-extinct volcano that could go off at any time. Just hope it doesn't erupt as you head up on a day trip from Catania. Recover on day two, exploring the vineyards and woods that carpet the mountain's lower slopes.

LOCAL SPECIALITIES

Swordfish, Messina You'll find *pesce spada* (swordfish) on menus across Sicily, but the best are caught in the Strait of Messina between May and July.

Pasta alla Norma, Catania Named after a Bellini opera, this is a classic Catania dish of fried aubergine (eggplant), tomato and salted ricotta.

Honey, Zafferana Etnea This small town on Etna's eastern slopes is celebrated for its honey, made from a range of local flowers.

Wine, Mt Etna Grapes grown on Etna go into Etna DOC, one of Sicily's best-known wines.

Mussels, Ganzirri Diners head up here from Messina to dine on *cozze* (mussels) cultivated in a salt lake.

Le Tre Bocche
TRATTORIA €€

(☑095 53 87 38; Via Mario Sangiorgi 7; meals €35-45; ☺Tue-Sun) A fantastic Slow Food–recommended trattoria that takes pride in the freshest seafood and fish – so much so, they have a stand at La Pescheria market. Short pasta comes with wonderful sauces such as bottarga (fish roe) and artichoke, spaghetti are soaked in sea urchins or squid ink, and risotto is mixed with courgette and king prawns.

The antipasti buffet has fish carpaccios and marinated prawns, and the *secondi* are best for indulging in *ricciola* (yellowtail) baked with potatoes or sea bream cooked in sea water.

Al Cortile Alessi
PIZZERIA €

(☑095 31 54 44; Via Alessi 28; pizzas €6-9, mains €8-12; ☺8pm-1am Tue-Sun) Catanians of all ages – but especially students – flock here on weekend evenings, drawn by the excellent pizzas and a good selection of Sicilian dishes – try their *zuppa di pesce* (fish soup), a fantastic stew of different fish in a thick tomato sauce. The draft beer, cocktails and a relaxed atmosphere are at the outdoor courtyard shaded by banana trees.

Metró
MODERN SICILIAN €€

(☑095 32 20 98; www.ristorantemetro.it; Via Crociferi 76; meals €30-37; ☺lunch & dinner Mon-Fri, lunch Sat) A delightful restaurant with outdoor seating, Metró ticks all the right boxes. The look is simple, with bright lighting and wine bottles on the walls but the menu is altogether more ambitious, featuring a fabulous carpaccio starter and some excellent tuna dishes – try the *tagliata* or the tuna steak with caramelised onions.

Also great are the *lasagnette con ricotta infornata e pinoli* (lasagne with baked ricotta and pine nuts). The wine list is imaginative though heavily biased towards regional producers.

Trattoria Casalinga
TRATTORIA €€

(☑095 31 13 19; Via Biondi 19; meals €25-30; ☺Mon-Sat) This is one of Catania's best-known and best-loved trattorias. A homey, family-run eatery presided over by patron Nino, it does a thriving business feeding lunching office workers and hungry theatregoers – Teatro Massimo Bellini is not far away. The onus is on earthy regional food, so roll up for salami and cheese starters, pasta with seasonal veggies and juicy grilled meats/fish.

Creamy *cannoli* (pastry shells stuffed with sweet ricotta) will have you smiling as you leave.

Sicilia In Bocca
Alla Marinara
SEAFOOD €€

(☑095 250 02 08; Via Dusmet 35; meals €30-35; ☺lunch Tue-Sat, dinner daily) Catania's 14th-century sea walls provide the suggestive setting for this popular restaurant. With the smell of the sea breezing in, seafood is the obvious choice – it does a delicious swordfish carpaccio with citrus fruit dressing. Sit in the lively brick-arched dining hall or enjoy views of the Duomo from the upstairs terrace.

Osteria Antica Marina
SEAFOOD €€

(☑095 34 81 97; Via Pardo 29; meals €35-45; ☺Thu-Tue) This rustic but classy trattoria behind the fish market is *the* place to come for seafood. A variety of tasting menus showcases everything from swordfish to scampi, cuttlefish to calamari. Decor-wise think solid wooden tables and rough stone walls. Reservations are essential.

Osteria Pizzeria Antica Sicilia SICILIAN €€

(☏095 715 10 75; Via Roccaforte 15; pizzas €6-8, meals €30-35) With its gaudy frescoes, stark white lights and busy workaday atmosphere, this bustling trattoria is no place for a romantic tête-à-tête. But if you're after a decent, value-for-money dinner, it will do very nicely, thank you. Seafood is the star, with staples such as *linguine ai ricci* (thin pasta ribbons with sea urchins) and *calamari arrosto* (roast squid).

Ambasciata Del Mare SEAFOOD €€

(☏095 34 10 03; www.ambasciatadelmare.it; Piazza Duomo 6; meals €35-40; ☺Tue-Sun) Overlooking the fish market, La Pescheria, this refined restaurant has built a strong local reputation by serving creative seafood. And while the standard is high – the oysters and stylish antipasti are superb – the pastas don't always hit the mark. Ditto the wine-red dining hall, which looks good but gets very cramped when full. Bookings are recommended. Quality of service can vary.

🍸 Drinking & Nightlife

Not surprisingly for a busy university town, Catania has a great nightlife. There are dozens of cafes, bars and live-music venues across town but hubs include Piazza Bellini (a student favourite), Via Montesano and Via Penninello. Opening hours are generally from around 9pm to 2am, although things often don't hot up until around midnight.

To see what's going on pick up a copy of *Lapis* at the tourist office.

Da Vincenzo CAFE

(Piazza Mazzini 19) This is a beautiful cafe on the corner of the sunny piazza, and the perfect place for a breakfast of coffee, croissant and freshly squeezed Sicilian oranges in the sunshine. The interior is all high ceilings, antique marble-topped tables and rustic chairs, and the atmosphere is wonderfully relaxed. Snacks, drinks and gorgeous *granitas* are available too.

Energie Cafe BAR, CAFE

(Via Monte Sant'Agata 10) A favourite with Catania's stylish aperitivo set, Energie Café is a slick urban bar with kaleidoscopic '70s-inspired decor, streetside seating and laid-back jazz-infused tunes. If you're at a loose end on a Sunday afternoon, Fashion Aperitif is a mellow happy hour with a rich buffet and live DJ set.

Heaven BAR

(Via Teatro Massimo 39; ☺9pm-2am) Pedestrianised Via Teatro Massimo heaves late at night as crowds swill outside the many bars. One of the best-known addresses is Heaven, a trendy lounge bar sporting kooky black-and-white designs and a 12m-long LED-lit bar. Outside, where most people end up, there's seating on massive black leather sofas. DJs up the ante on Wednesday, Friday and Saturday nights.

Perbacco Wine Bar WINE BAR

(☏095 250 34 78; Via Vasta 12-14; ☺8am-late) This is one of Catania's most popular wine bars. Locals of all ages crowd the sofas and wicker chairs under the burgundy canopies to chat, sip and snack until the wee hours. There's a warm, laid-back buzz and a good selection of cocktails, wines (mainly Sicilian and Italian) and rum.

☆ Entertainment

Enola Jazz Club JAZZ CLUB

(☏095 32 62 47; Via Mazza 14) The godfather of Catania's jazz scene, the Enola Jazz Club attracts big-name Italian and international artists to its pocket-sized stage, while also trumpeting new and emerging local talent. Like all self-respecting jazz clubs it's a tight squeeze with a fairly nondescript decor, but that in no way diminishes the hot, steamy atmosphere.

La Lomax CULTURAL CENTRE

(☏095 286 28 12; www.lalomax.it; Via Fornai 44) This multipurpose cultural centre hosts all sorts of events – club nights, folk-music festivals, modern art exhibitions – as well as housing a song and dance school and running a range of courses. It's up near Castello Urbino, hidden away in a small street off Via Plebiscito. Check *Lapis* or the centre's website for upcoming events.

Teatro Massimo Bellini OPERA HOUSE

(☏095 730 61 11; www.teatromassimobellini.it; Via Perrotta 12; ☺Nov-Jun) Catania's premier theatre is named after the city's most famous son, composer Vincenzo Bellini. Sporting the full red-and-gold-gilt look, it stages a year-round season of opera and an eight-month program of classical music from November to June. Tickets, which are available online, start at around €13 and rise to €84 for a first-night front-row seat.

ADVANCE PLANNING

➡ Festa di Sant'Agata (p176) Catania grinds to a halt between 3 and 5 February as millions take to the streets to celebrate the city's patron saint. Accommodation must be booked well in advance.

➡ Carnevale (p181) Plan to be in Acireale in February. The town's spectacular carnival celebrations are among the most popular in Sicily, with great parades of huge papier mâché figures.

➡ Taormina Arte (p168) Get in early with reservations and ticket requests for Taormina's film, music and theatre festival held over July and August.

Zò   CULTURAL CENTRE

(☑ 095 53 38 71; www.zoculture.it; Piazzale Asia 6) Part of Le Ciminiere complex, Zò is dedicated to promoting contemporary art and performance. It hosts an eclectic program of events that ranges from club nights, concerts and film screenings to art exhibitions, dance performances, installations and theatre workshops. Check out its website for upcoming events, many of which are free of charge.

ℹ Information

EMERGENCIES

Police Station (☑ 095 736 71 11; Piazza Santa Nicolella)

MEDICAL SERVICES

Ospedale Vittorio Emanuele (☑ 091 743 54 52; Via Plebiscito 628) Has a 24-hour emergency doctor.

TOURIST INFORMATION

Airport Tourist Office (☑ 095 093 70 23; ⊙9am-9pm)

Municipal Tourist Office (☑ 095 742 55 73; www.comune.catania.it; Via Vittorio Emanuele II 172; ⊙ 8.15am-7.15pm Mon-Fri, to 12.15pm Sat)

WEBSITE

Lonely Planet (www.lonelyplanet.com/italy/sicily/catania) Planning advice, author recommendations, traveller reviews and insider tips.

ℹ Getting There & Around

AIR

Catania's **Fontanarossa airport** (CTA; www.aeroporto.catania.it) is 7km southwest of the city centre. **AMT** (☑ 095 751 96 11; www.amt.ct.it) Alibus 457 runs to the airport from the train station (€1, 30 minutes, every 20 minutes). A taxi for four people plus luggage costs about €28.

BOAT

From the **ferry terminal** on the southeastern edge of the historic centre, there are ferries to/from Naples. **TTT Lines** (☑ 095 34 85 86, 800 91 53 65; www.tttlines.it) operates the daily Naples ferry. Fares per person for a *poltrona* (airline-type armchair) in low/high season are €38/60.

BUS

There are two main bus terminuses in Catania: Interbus, Etna and SAIS Autolinee run to/from the **Terminal Bus** (Via Archimede). As a rule buses are quicker than trains for most destinations. **AST** (☑ 095 723 05 35; www.aziendasicilianatrasporti.it) runs to many provincial towns around Catania, including Nicolosi (€2.40, one hour, half-hourly). Tickets are available at the **Terminal Bar** over the road from the bus stops. **Interbus – Etna Trasporti** (☑ 095 53 03 96; www.interbus.it) has buses to Syracuse (€6, 1¼ hours, hourly Monday to Saturday, six Sunday) and Taormina (€4.90, 1½ hours, 14 daily Monday to Saturday, eight Sunday), while **SAIS Autolinee** (☑ 095 53 61 68; www.saistrasporti.it; Via d'Amico 181) serves Palermo (€14.90, 2½ hours, 13 daily Monday to Saturday, nine Sunday) and Messina (€8.10, 1½ hours, half-hourly Monday to Saturday, eight Sunday).

In town, the 1-4 local bus runs from the train station to Via Etnea, and the 4-7 local bus runs to Piazza del Duomo. Tickets, from *tabacchi*, cost €1 and last 90 minutes.

CAR & MOTORCYCLE

Catania is easily reached from Messina on the A18 autostrada as well as from Palermo on the A19. From the autostrada, signs for the city centre direct you to Via Etnea. Choosing to drive in town means you will have to deal with the city's complicated one-way system – for example, you can only drive along Via Vittorio Emanuele II from west to east, while the parallel Via Giuseppe Garibaldi runs from east to west.

Parking is extremely difficult in the city centre. If you're bringing your own car, consider staying at a hotel/B&B with parking facilities; if you're hiring a car, the advice is to pick up the car as you leave town and return it when you re-enter.

For a taxi, call **CST** (☑ 095 33 09 66). There are taxi ranks at the train station and on Piazza del Duomo.

TRAIN
Frequent, but very slow, trains connect Catania with Messina (€7 to €10.50 , 1½ to two hours) and Syracuse (€6.35 to €9.50, 1¼ hours), while there are one or two direct services to Palermo (€12.50 to €15.30) and Agrigento (€10.40 to €14.50).

RIVIERA DEI CICLOPI

Extending north of Catania, the Riviera dei Ciclopi is an attractive stretch of coastline that makes a good, value-for-money alternative to Taormina. Until quite recently it was a desperately poor area of isolated fishing villages, but tourism has given it a much needed impetus and it is now a lively summer stomping ground. There are few sandy beaches but the swimming is excellent, and there are plenty of hotels, restaurants and bars. The coast owes its name to a Homeric legend according to which the towering black rocks that rise out of the sea – actually great hunks of solidified lava – were thrown by the blinded Cyclops, Polyphemus, in a desperate attempt to stop Odysseus escaping.

Acireale

POP 52,855
The main town on the Riviera, Acireale is set on a series of lava terraces that drop to the sea about 17km north of Catania. Although it's not exactly undiscovered, it remains largely tourist free, which is a mystery because it's a great-looking town with a stately baroque centre and a number of imposing public buildings. Downhill 2km is the small fishing village of Santa Maria la Scala, a perfect port of call for a seafood lunch.

Acireale has long been known for its thermal waters but its modern claim to fame is its spectacular Carnevale festivities.

◉ Sights & Activities

Historic Centre   NEIGHBOURHOOD
To see Acireale's stunning architecture, start at Piazza Duomo, a grandiose piazza surrounded on three sides by monumental buildings. On the western flank is the cathedral (◷8am-12.30pm & 3.30-8pm), built in the early 1600s and topped by towering conical-capped spires. Inside, the echoing vaults and chapels are richly frescoed.

Next to the cathedral, the Basilica dei Santi Pietro e Paolo (◷8am-12.30pm & 3.30-8pm) displays a typically elaborate 18th-century facade, while over the road Palazzo Municipale impresses with its wrought-iron balconies and imposing central portal.

From the piazza, Via Ruggero Settimo leads south to Piazza Lionardo Vigo and the gorgeous Basilica di San Sebastiano (◷8am-12.30pm & 3.30-8pm), one of the town's finest baroque buildings. Behind the majestic facade, itself preceded by a grand balustrade and statues of Old Testament characters, the interior features some fine, if rather faded, frescoes recounting episodes from the life of St Sebastian.

Nearby, the streets around Piazza Marconi host Acireale's noisy *pescheria* (fish market).

Puppet Theatres   THEATRE
Acireale has a long tradition of puppet theatre and there are a couple of places where you can learn all about it: L'Antico Teatro dei Pupi (www.teatropu pimacri.it; Via Alessi 5; admission free; ◷9.30am-12.30pm & 4.30-7.30pm), which has a collection of puppets and theatrical paraphernalia, and the Teatro-Museo dell'Opera dei Pupi (☑095 764 80 35; www.operadeipupi.com; Via Nazionale 195; ◷9am-noon & 6-9pm Wed, Sat & Sun summer, 9am-noon & 3-6pm winter).

Santa Maria La Scala   VILLAGE
There are two reasons to make the 2km downhill walk to this minute fishing village. One is the walk itself which, once you've crossed the main road, is a lovely country stroll with gorgeous coastal views. The other is to eat seafood at one of the delightful trattorias.

To get to the village, which consists of little more than a tiny harbour, a church, some houses and a black beach, follow Via Romeo down from Piazza Duomo, cross the main road and keep going.

☆ Festivals & Events

Carnevale   CARNIVAL
(www.carnevaleacireale.com) The best time to visit Acireale is during February's Carnevale when the town puts on one of the best spectacles in Sicily. The stars of the show are the

elaborately decorated floats, some bedecked in technicolour flower displays, others carrying huge papier mâché caricatures of local celebrities. All around bands play, costumed dancers leap about and confetti rains.

The exact dates vary each year but you can get details on the event's comprehensive website. And if you miss it first time round, don't worry, there's a rerun, albeit on a smaller scale, in early August.

✗ Eating

La Taverna TRATTORIA **€€**
(☑ 095 60 12 61; Via Ercole 4, Acireale; pizzas from €5, meals €25-30) La Taverna is a straight-up trattoria, serving traditional Sicilian food at honest prices. Given its location in the midst of the fish market, it's at its best at lunch when hungry locals pop in for grilled catch of the day or *calamari arrosto* (roast squid). Seafood is the obvious choice, but it also does some fine nonfish dishes.

Try the *pasta con funghi porcini* (pasta with porcini mushrooms) and all the usual pizzas.

L'Oste Scuro SEAFOOD **€€**
(☑ 095 763 40 01; Piazza Lionardo Vigo 5-6, Acireale; meals €30-35) With the shouts of the nearby fish market ringing in the air and views to the Basilica di San Sebastiano, this is a fine setting for a filling fish meal. Tuck into the seafood classic *pasta con gamberi, zucchini e zafferano* (pasta with prawns, courgettes and saffron) followed by a towering sauté of mussels and clams.

Trattoria La Grotta TRATTORIA **€€**
(☑ 095 764 81 53; Via Scalo Grande 46, Santa Maria la Scala; meals €30; ⊘ Wed-Mon) Eating at La Grotta, the best of the Santa Maria la Scala restaurants, is a memorable experience. As you enter you pass the fish counter where your order is picked out and weighed before going in the pot. The dining area is atmospherically set in the body of a cave. When it comes to it, the food is superb.

MOVING ON?

For tips, recommendations and reviews, head to shop.lonelyplanet.com to purchase a downloadable PDF of the Puglia, Basilicata & Calabria chapter from Lonely Planet's *Italy* guide.

The house speciality is *insalata di mare* (seafood salad), a mouth-watering mix of prawns, calamari and octopus, and the grilled fish is quite sensational.

❶ Information

Tourist Office (☑ 095 89 52 49; Via Romeo 2; ⊘ 8am-2pm & 3-9pm)

Aci Trezza

A few kilometres south of Acireale, Aci Trezza is a small fishing village with a lively seafront and a number of good restaurants. Offshore, a series of surreal, jagged basalt rocks, the Scogli dei Ciclopi, rise out of the sea. These are the mythical missiles that the blinded Cyclops, Polyphemus (who lived in Etna), is supposed to have thrown at the fleeing Odysseus. Aci Trezza is also celebrated as the setting of *I Malavoglia*, Giovanni Verga's 19th-century literary masterpiece of life in a poor, isolated fishing community.

◉ Sights & Activities

Seafront NEIGHBOURHOOD
The principal activity in Aci Trezza is hanging out on the seafront, sunbathing in the day – wooden platforms are set up over the black volcanic rocks – and waltzing up and down after dark. You can enjoy the spectacle from one of the *lungomare* (seafront promenade) bars.

The **Café de Mar** (Lungomare Ciclopi; ⊘ 8pm-late), next to Grand Hotel i Faraglioni, is ideal with its white sofas and armchairs scattered across a palm-shaded garden.

To explore the coast's caves, coves and bays, there are a number of operators at the port offering boat tours. One such, **Vaporetto Polifemo** (☑ 095 27 73 70; www.vaporetto polifemo.it) runs daily excursions along the coast from €12.

La Casa del Nespolo MUSEUM
(☑ 095 711 66 38; www.museocasadelnespolo. info; Via Arciprete De Maria 15; admission €1.55; ⊘ 9.30am-1pm & 5-9pm Jul-Aug, reduced hr Sep-Jun) A typical 19th-century house, La Casa del Nespolo is a small museum celebrating Giovanni Verga's great novel *I Malavoglia* and Luchino Visconti's 1948 film adaptation of it, *La Terra Trema*. The collection includes a selection of 19th-century household objects and work tools but the most

Time your visit The best time for walking is between April and May, and September and October. It gets very busy, and very hot, in high summer.

Bring the right kit Even when it's boiling hot at lower altitudes, it's windy up top and temperatures can fall below freezing. You'll need proper walking boots/shoes, a wind jacket, warm headgear and gloves. If you don't have your own, you can hire a kit at Rifugio Sapienza. In summer pack sunscreen, sunglasses and a hat, and make sure you have enough bottled water. If you usually wear contact lenses, bring glasses as there's usually a lot of dust swirling around.

Get a decent map The best is Selca's 1:25,000 *Mt Etna*, otherwise pick up the free *Mt Etna and Mother Nature* map from tourist offices.

Bring a mobile phone and a compass If walking independently, a mobile phone is an excellent safety precaution, though it may not work in certain locations. Also take a compass as fog is not uncommon.

Cash or credit card? The *funivia* (cable car) ticket office accepts both.

interesting exhibits are the photos that Verga himself took of Aci Trezza.

Eating

Trattoria Verga Da Gaetano   TRATTORIA
(☑ 095 27 63 42; Via Provinciale 119; meals €30-35)
One of many restaurants in the port area, this trattoria has an excellent local reputation. It's situated right in the heart of town – overlooking a terrace above ranks of moored fishing boats – and decorated with hundreds of framed pictures, photos and posters. The menu is typical, proposing, among other fish dishes, marinated anchovies, linguine with scampi and delicious prawn kebabs.

Aci Castello

POP 18.195

Marking the beginning, or end, of the Riviera dei Ciclopi, Aci Castello is only 9km from Catania's city centre, making it an easy day trip from the city, even by public transport (take bus 534 from Piazza Borsellino). There's swimming and sunbathing off the volcanic rocks, otherwise the main attraction is the *castello* set atop a vast black rock. La Rocca di Acicastello, as the rock is known, is apparently something of a vulcanological rarity, having emerged from an underwater fissure. Grafted onto its top is a dark, brooding **Norman castle** (adult/reduced €1.50/free-0.50; ☺ 9am-1pm & 3-8pm May-Sep, 9am-1pm & 3-5pm Oct-Apr), built in the 13th century on top of an earlier Arab fortification. It's in

surprisingly good shape considering its age, and hosts a small **museum** with a collection of geological rock samples and bizarre prehistoric skulls.

MOUNT ETNA

ELEV 3329M

Dominating the landscape of eastern Sicily, Mt Etna is a massive brooding presence. At 3329m it is Italy's highest mountain south of the Alps and the largest active volcano in Europe. It's in an almost constant state of activity and eruptions occur frequently, most spectacularly from the four summit craters, but more often, and more dangerously, from the fissures and old craters on the mountain's flanks. This activity, which is closely monitored by 120 seismic activity stations and satellites, means that it is occasionally closed to visitors.

The volcano, known locally as Mongibello (derived from the Latin (*mons*) and Arabic (*gibel*) words for mountain), emerged out of volcanic activity about 35,000 years ago. Not surprisingly, the ancients viewed it with awe. The Greeks believed that Vulcan, god of fire and metalwork, had his workshop here, and that Polyphemus, the one-eyed Cyclops, lived in a cave on its slopes. Another legend held that Typhon, a 100-headed monster, was trapped under the mountain by Zeus and has been spitting out flames ever since.

The first recorded eruption took place in about 1500 BC; since then it has erupted

IONIAN COAST MOUNT ETNA

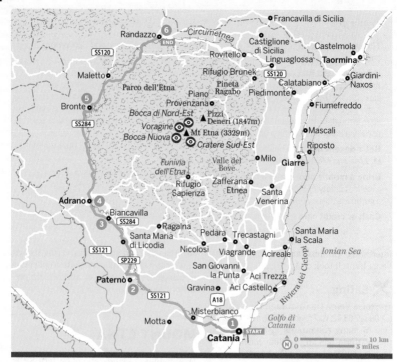

 ## Driving Tour
Etna's Western Flank

START CATANIA
FINISH RANDAZZO
LENGTH 78KM/ONE DAY

The five small towns on the western side of the Parco dell'Etna offer a wonderful escape. Tourism has largely passed by these towns and each has a unique character.

Heading west out of ❶ **Catania** on the SS121 brings you to ❷ **Paternò**, a scruffy workaday town built around an 11th-century Norman castello. Built in 1072 as a defence against the Saracens, the castle has been rebuilt over the centuries and now all that remains is the keep. But most impressive are the sweeping views up to Etna.

Continuing on the SP229 you'll pass huge *fichi d'india* (prickly pears) and orange groves (and piles of litter) on the way to ❸ **Biancavilla**, a small town founded by Albanian refugees in 1480 but now typically Sicilian with many baroque churches. The market town of ❹ **Adrano**, 3km further, boasts a robust Norman castello rising from a huge fortified base, commissioned by Count Roger II in the late 11th century. It now houses a small museum. Nearby, on Via Catania, you can see the remains of Adranon, a 4th-century-BC Greek settlement.

The SS284 heads directly north through acres of nut groves to ❺ **Bronte**, famous throughout Italy for its pistachios (make sure to try a pistachio ice cream from the main strip, Corso Umberto). Beyond Bronte, the road leads through an increasingly rugged landscape, interspersed with chunks of lava flow, as it heads up to ❻ **Randazzo**, the most interesting of Etna's towns.

Heavy bombing in WWII meant that much of the town's grey medieval centre had to be reconstructed. The main sights are the three crenellated churches – the Cattedrale di Santa Maria, the Chiesa di San Nicolò and the Chiesa di San Martino – which in the 16th century took turns to act as the town cathedral. Round off the day with dinner at San Giorgio e Il Drago, a Slow Food–recommended trattoria with outdoor seating in the historic centre.

more than 200 times. The most devastating eruption was in 1669 when a massive river of lava poured down the southern slope, destroying 16 towns, engulfing a good part of Catania and killing up to 12,000 people. More recently, spectacular eruptions in 2002 caused immense damage to the infrastructure on the southern side of the mountain and a violent eruption in September 2007 threw up a 400m-high cloud of ash causing the temporary closure of Catania airport.

Since 1987 the volcano and its slopes have been part of a national park, the Parco dell'Etna. Encompassing 590 sq km and some 21 towns, the park's varied landscape ranges from the severe, snowcapped mountaintop to lunar deserts of barren black lava, beech woods and lush vineyards where the area's highly rated DOC wine is produced.

◉ Sights & Activities

Guided Tours   GUIDED TOUR
There are many operators offering guided tours up to the craters and elsewhere on the mountain, and even if your natural inclination is to avoid them, they are well worth considering. The guides know the mountain inside out, and are able to direct you to the most spectacular points, as well as explain what you're looking at. They also offer a valuable safety precaution. Tours typically involve some walking and 4WD transport.

Recommended reliable operators are **Acquaterra** (☏095 50 30 20; www.acquaterra. com), which also offers snow-shoe excursions and canoeing on the Alcantara river, **Etna Experience** (☏095 723 29 24; www. etnaexperience.com), **Etna Sicily Touring** (☏392 509 02 98; www.etnasicilytouring.com), **Gruppo Guide Alpine Etna Nord** (☏095 777 45 02; www.guidetnanord.com) and **Gruppo Guide Alpine Etna Sud** (☏095 791 47 55; www.etnaguide.com).

Prices vary depending on the tour you take but you should bank on from €45 per person for a half-day tour (usually morning or sunset) and about €65 for a full day.

Rifugio Sapienza   VILLAGE
Whether driving yourself or coming by public transport, the starting point for the southern ascent is Rifugio Sapienza (1923m), a small cluster of souvenir shops and bars based around a mountain refuge. From here there are various options for getting up to the crater area.

The easiest is to take the **Funivia dell'Etna** (☏095 91 41 41; www.funiviaetna.com; one-way/ return €14.50/27, incl bus & guide €51; ☉9am-4.30pm) up to 2500m and then a minibus to the Torre del Filosfo at 2920m. Alternatively, you can forego the minibus and walk from the upper cable-car station. It's quite a steep 2km walk and you should allow yourself up to four hours to get back in time for the return cable car. Another option is to walk all the way from Rifugio Sapienza, but this is a strenuous climb that will take about four hours (less on the way down). Note that in windy weather the cable-car service is suspended and replaced by a minibus.

There are four craters at the top: Bocca di Nord-Est (northeast crater), Voragine, Bocca Nuova and Cratere Sud-Est (southeast crater). The two you're most likely to see are Cratere Sud-Est, a perfect black cone and one of the most active, and Bocca Nuova, the youngest of the four. How close you can get will depend on the level of volcanic activity. If you're hiking without a guide, always err on the side of caution as the dangers around the craters are very real. To the east of the crater area, the Valle del Bove, a massive depression formed after a cone collapsed several thousand years ago, falls away in a precipitous 1000m drop, smoke billowing up from its blackened depths.

Piano Provenzana   WALKING TRAILS
The gateway to Etna's quieter and more picturesque northern slopes is Piano Provenzana (1800m), a small ski station about 16km up from Linguaglossa. From here, **STAR** (☏347 495 70 91; www.funiviaetna.com/star_etna_nord.html) runs jeep tours up the slopes between May and October. You can do two tours: to Pizzi Deneri and the Volcanic Observatory at 2800m, or up to the main crater at 3200m.

The Pizzi Deneri and Volcanic Observatory trip is a two-hour affair, while the main crater excursion is longer, at three hours. Both involve some walking and afford spectacular views of the Peloritani, Nebrodi and Madonie mountain ranges and the Valle del Bove. Further down, there's lovely summer walking in the pine, birch and larch trees of the **Pineta Ragabo**, a vast wood accessible from the Mareneve road between Linguaglossa and Milo.

Note that you'll need your own car to get to Piano Provenzana and the Pineta Ragabo, as no public transport passes this way.

Wine & Honey Tasting WINE TASTING

Mt Etna is an important wine area, producing Etna DOC, one of 22 Sicilian wines to carry the *Denominazione di Origine Controllata* denomination. There are numerous wineries in the area where you can taste the local *vino*, including Gambino (☑095 227 26 78; www.vinigambino.it; Contrada Petto Dragone; ☺8.30am-5.30pm, reservations preferred) near Linguaglossa. The Linguaglossa tourist office can provide further names and addresses.

Another gastronomic treat is the honey produced in Zafferana Etnea. This small town on Etna's eastern slopes has a long tradition of apiculture and apparently produces up to 35% of Italy's honey. To see what's so special about it visit Oro d'Etna, where you can try honey made from orange blossom, chestnuts and lemons.

Skiing & Cycling SKIING, CYCLING

Sicily is an unlikely skiing destination but you can do both downhill and cross-country here between December and March. The state of the slopes and how many lifts are working depends on the latest volcanic activity – check the current situation at www.etnasci.it.

In decent conditions there are five pistes on the southern side of the mountain and three on the northern side. A daily ski pass costs €25 in Nicolosi (south) and €17 in Linguaglossa (north).

If cycling is your thing, there are some fine (albeit tough) trails around the mountain; you can hire bikes from Etna Touring (p165) in Nicolosi for €15 per day. It can also organise guided rides on request.

Ferrovia Circumetnea TOURIST TRAIN

(FCE; ☑095 54 12 50; www.circumetnea.it) A good way to enjoy armchair views of Etna is to jump on the Ferrovia Etnea train. Operating out of Catania, this slow train follows a 114km trail around the base of the volcano, stopping off at a number of small towns on the way and affording great views.

From Catania it takes two hours to reach Randazzo (one way/return €5/8) in the mountain's northern reaches.

To get to the FCE station in Catania catch the metro from the main train station to the FCE station at Via Caronda (metro stop: Borgo) or take bus 429 or 432 up Via Etnea and ask to be let off at the 'Borgo' metro stop.

Eating

Agriturismo San Marco AGRITURISMO €

(☑38 94 23 72 94; www.agriturismosanmarco.com; meals €23) Find your way to this welcoming *agriturismo* (farm stay) near Rovitello for authentic farmhouse food in a lovely bucolic setting. Kick off with a selection of cured meats and local cheeses, before tucking into a bowl of fresh pasta with meaty *ragú* and a *secondo* (second course) of succulent grilled meat. Bookings are required, but you'll need to call for directions anyway.

Antico Orto Dei Limono SICILIAN €€

(☑095 91 08 08; Via Grotte 4; pizzas from €5, set menu €26; ☺Wed-Mon) There can be few better ways of rounding off a day in the mountains than with a meal at this delightful Nicolosi restaurant. Tastefully housed in a converted wine and oil press, it specialises in delicious tried-and-tested country fare. It's all good but the abundant house antipasto (a mix of creamy ricotta, salami and marinated vegetables) is a knockout.

Also try the excellent pasta with *ragù*, peas and mushrooms. If you're really hungry, go for the pharaonic set menu, which at €28 is excellent value.

Orientation

The two main approaches to Etna are from the north and south. The southern route, signposted as Etna Sud, is via Nicolosi and Rifugio Sapienza, 18km further up the mountain. The northern approach, Etna Nord, is through Piano Provenzana, 16km southwest of Linguaglossa.

Information

EMERGENCIES

Soccorso Alpino della Guardia di Finanza (☑095 53 17 77) Mountain rescue.

TOURIST INFORMATION

Proloco Linguaglossa (☑095 64 30 94; www.prolocolinguaglossa.it; Piazza Annunziata 5; ☺9am-1pm & 4-7pm Mon-Sat, 9am-noon Sun) On Etna's northern side.

Nicolosi Tourist Office (☑095 91 44 88; www.aast-nicolosi.it; Piazza Vittorio Emanuele, Nicolosi; ☺9am-1pm Mon-Fri, 4-6pm Mon, Tue & Thu)

Parco dell'Etna (☑095 82 11 11; www.parcoetna.ct.it; Via del Convento 45; ☺9am-2pm & 4-7.30pm) About 1km from the centre of Nicolosi.

IONIAN COAST MOUNT ETNA

❶ Getting There & Around

BUS

AST (☎ 095 723 05 35; www.aziendasiciliana trasporti.it) runs a daily bus from Catania to Rifugio Sapienza (return €5.60) via Nicolosi, departing at 8.15am and returning at 4.30pm. Between 15 June and 15 September there's a second departure, leaving Catania at 11.20pm. **Ferrovia Circumetnea** (☎ 095 54 12 50; www. circumetnea.it) operates infrequent weekday buses between Catania and Linguaglossa (€4.40, 1¼ hours).

CAR & MOTORCYCLE

Nicolosi is about 17km northwest of Catania on the SP10. From Nicolosi it's a further 18km up to Rifugio Sapienza. For Linguaglossa take the A18 autostrada from Catania, exit at Fiumefreddo and follow the SS120 towards Randazzo.

Syracuse & the Southeast

Why Go?

With its outstanding classical ruins, beautiful baroque towns and sandy beaches, this is Sicily's top draw. The temptation is to stay in Syracuse, hanging out in the piazzas and sunning yourself on the seafront, but drag yourself away and you'll be rewarded with some of Sicily's most charming towns. Noto, Modica and Ragusa are the star performers with their baroque treasures and gastronomic delights – ice cream in Noto, chocolate in Modica and one of Sicily's finest restaurants in Ragusa – but the countryside is also worth exploring. Prehistoric tombs stud huge rocky ravines while birdwatchers and seekers of peaceful beaches can find paradise at the Riserva Naturale Oasi Faunistica di Vendicari.

Best Places to Eat

➡ Ristorante Duomo (p215)
➡ Don Camillo (p200)
➡ Le Vin De L'Assasin Bistrot (p198)
➡ Il Liberty (p207)
➡ Trattoria del Crocifisso da Baglieri (p207)

Best Places to Sleep

➡ Villa dei Papiri (p265)
➡ Hotel Gutkowski (p264)
➡ B&B dei Viaggiatori, Viandanti e Sognatori (p264)
➡ La Corte del Sole (p265)
➡ Villa Quartarella (p265)

Road Distances (KM)

	Modica	Noto	Pachino	Ragusa
Noto	40			
Pachino	40	25		
Ragusa	15	50	55	
Syracuse	75	40	55	85

Getting Around

Public transport for this area is pretty poor, so it's best if you have your own wheels. There are good train connections between Syracuse and Noto. It's hard to generalise about buses, which can be convenient or very slow, depending on where you are.

THREE PERFECT DAYS

Classical to Baroque

Before the sun gets too hot head up to the Parco Archeologico della Neapolis (p193) to explore Syracuse's superb classical ruins. Afterwards, visit the Museo Archeologico Paolo Orsi (p195), one of Sicily's top archaeological museums, and then lunch in Ortygia. Spend the afternoon strolling Ortygia's baroque lanes, before winding down with a drink on Piazza del Duomo (p192) and a late seafood dinner.

Heading South

Pick up a car and head south to search out Sicily's great baroque towns. First stop is Noto and its unforgettable main street, Corso Vittorio Emanuele. Whilst here make sure to get an ice cream from Corrado Costanzo (p208), arguably Sicily's best gelateria (ice-cream shop). From Noto push on to Modica, where you can lunch with the locals at the Osteria dei Sapori Perduti (p210). The last leg leads to Ragusa, or more specifically Ragusa Ibla (p213). The stunning cathedral here is a masterclass in baroque architecture.

Coasting

Take the time to explore the area's lovely, low-key coastline. You could spend a very pleasant day birdwatching, walking and sunbathing at the Riserva Naturale Oasi Faunistica di Vendicari (p209), but if you want to see a bit more continue south to the Cape Area's Marzamemi, a good spot for a seafood lunch and a drop of local wine. The end of the road, literally, is Portopalo di Capo Passero, a summer resort with beautifully transparent waters.

Getting Away from It All

➡ **Akrai** Little known and little publicised, the remains of classical Akrai (p203) sit in grassy solitude overlooking Palazzolo Acreide.

➡ **Cava d'Ispica** Explore the rocky catacombs and cave dwellings of Cava d'Ispica (p212).

➡ **Necropoli di Pantalica** You're sure to find peace walking among the Bronze Age tombs at the Necropoli di Pantalica (p203).

DON'T MISS

Ortygia, Syracuse's historical centre, is one of Sicily's finest places to get lost in, and find yourself again at the magnificent Piazza Duomo.

Best Foodie Nibbles

➡ Dolceria Bonajuto (p210)

➡ Caffè Sicilia (p208)

➡ Cantina Rudinì (p209)

Best Baroque Treasures

➡ Chiesa di San Giorgio (p209), Modica

➡ Corso Vittorio Emanuele, Noto (p205)

➡ Duomo (p192), Syracuse

➡ Piazza Duomo (p213), Ragusa

Resources

➡ **Istituto Nazionale Dramma Antico** (www.indafondazione.org) For details of Syracuse's classical-drama season.

➡ **Modica Comune** (www.comune.modica.rg.it) Accommodation and restaurant listings.

➡ **Noto Comune** (www.comune.noto.sr.it) Info about monuments, events and transport.

➡ **Ragusa Comune** (www.comune.ragusa.it) Comprehensive information on Ragusa and its environs.

➡ **Syracuse Comune** (www.comune.siracusa.it/essereturista/turismo/home.htm) Listings, transport information and details of the main sights.

Syracuse & the Southeast Highlights

1 Wandering Ortygia, Syracuse's historic centre, and its magnificent **Piazza del Duomo** (p192), before exploring Syracuse's fantastic classical ruins, the Parco Archeologico della Neapolis.

2 Admiring the stunning baroque centre of **Noto** (p189), with its cathedral and manicured main street.

3 Tasting a unique take on chocolate in **Modica** (p209) and delighting in the town's beautiful, lived-in baroque centre.

4 Descending into the centre of **Ragusa** (p212), packed with whirling baroque beauty.

5 Relaxing on the beaches and walking around the **Riserva Naturale Oasi Faunistica di Vendicari** (p209).

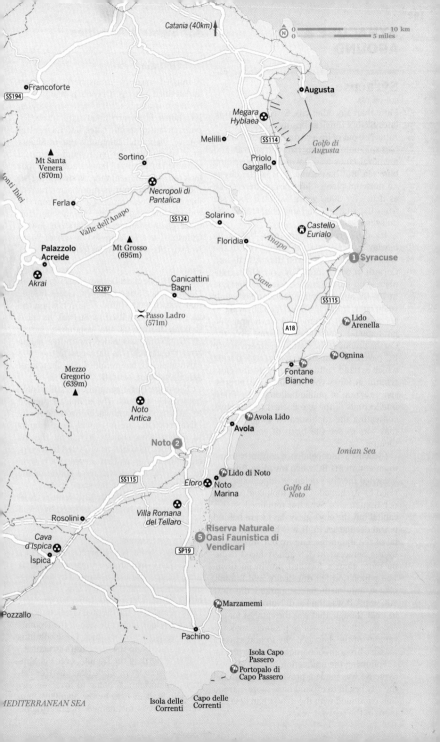

Catania (40km)

Francoforte
SS194

Mt Santa
Venera
(870m)

Monti Iblei

Sortino

Ferla

Necropoli di
Pantalica

Valle dell'Anapo

SS124

Palazzolo
Acreide

Mt Grosso
(695m)

Akrai

SS287

Passo Ladro
(571m)

Mezzo
Gregorio
(639m)

Noto
Antica

Noto 2

SS115

Eloro
Noto
Marina

Rosolini

Villa Romana
del Tellaro

Cava
d'Ispica
Ispica

SP19

Pozzallo

Augusta

Megara
Hyblaea

Melilli

Priolo
Gargallo

SS114

Golfo di
Augusta

Solarino

Floridia

Castello
Eurialo

Anapo

1 Syracuse

Canicattini
Bagni

Ciane

SS115

Lido
Arenella

A18

Ognina

Fontane
Bianche

Avola Lido

Avola

Ionian Sea

Lido di Noto

Golfo di
Noto

Riserva Naturale
5 Oasi Faunistica di
Vendicari

Marzamemi

Pachino

Isola Capo
Passero
Portopalo di
Capo Passero

MEDITERRANEAN SEA

Isola delle
Correnti

Capo delle
Correnti

N
0   10 km
0   5 miles

SYRACUSE & AROUND

Syracuse

POP 124,085

More than any other city, Syracuse encapsulates Sicily's timeless beauty. Ancient Greek ruins rise out of lush citrus orchards, cafe tables spill onto dazzling baroque piazzas, and medieval lanes lead down to the sparkling blue sea. But handsome as it is, the city is no museum piece – life goes on here much as it has for 3000 years, as you'll soon see from the snarling mid-morning traffic and noisy markets.

It's difficult to imagine now but in its heyday Syracuse was the largest city in the ancient world, bigger even than Athens and Corinth. It was founded by Corinthian colonists, who landed on the island of Ortygia in 734 BC and set up the mainland city four years later. It quickly flourished, growing to become a rich commercial town and major regional powerhouse. Victory over the Carthaginians at the Battle of Himera in 480 BC paved the way for a golden age, during which art and culture thrived and the city's tyrannical kings commissioned an impressive program of public building. The finest intellectuals of the age flocked to Syracuse, cultivating the sophisticated urban culture that was to see the birth of comic Greek theatre.

Syracuse's independence abruptly came to an end in 211 BC when invading Romans breached the city's defences, ingeniously devised by Archimedes, and took control. Under Roman rule Syracuse remained Sicily's capital but the city's glory days were behind it and decline set in. It was briefly the capital of the Byzantine Empire but was sacked by the Saracens in 878 and reduced to little more than a fortified provincial town. The population fell drastically, and famine, plague and earthquakes marked the next 800 years. It was the Val di Noto earthquake in 1693, though, that was the catalyst for energetic urban renewal as planners took advantage of the damaged city to undertake a massive program of baroque reconstruction.

Following the unification of Italy in 1865, Syracuse was made a provincial capital and the city began to expand once more, a trend that continued with the ugly urban development of the postwar years.

◉ Sights & Activities

◉ Ortygia

A tangled maze of atmospheric alleyways and refined piazzas, Ortygia is really what Syracuse is all about. It is a joy to wander. Its skinny lanes are lined with attractive *palazzi*, trattorias and cafes, and the central square, Piazza del Duomo, is one of Sicily's most spectacular. The entire mini-peninsula is framed by beautiful houses and walls that look out onto the sea; there is swimming off the rocks in the summer months and incredible views all year round. Get away from the tourist crowds and explore the mesmerising maze of La Giudecca, Ortygia's old Jewish Quarter. The area, accessed by way of Ponte Nuovo, is best explored on foot.

Duomo CATHEDRAL
(Map p194; Piazza del Duomo; ⊙8am-7pm) The Duomo was a 5th-century BC Greek temple that was converted into a church when the island was evangelised by St Paul. Its most striking feature is the columned facade (1728–53) that was added by Andrea Palma after the church was damaged in the 1693 earthquake. It barely hides the Temple of Athena skeleton beneath.

The huge Doric columns are still visible both inside and out. The temple, dedicated to Athena, was renowned throughout the Mediterranean, in no small part thanks to Cicero, who visited Ortygia in the 1st century BC. Its roof was crowned by a golden statue of Athena that served as a beacon to sailors at sea; nowadays a statue of the Virgin Mary stands in the same spot.

Inside, look out for a 13th-century Norman font in the baptistry, adorned by seven bronze lions.

Piazza del Duomo PIAZZA
(Map p194) Syracuse's showpiece square is a masterpiece in baroque town planning. A long, rectangular piazza flanked by flamboyant *palazzi*, it sits on what was once Syracuse's ancient acropolis (fortified citadel). Little remains of the original Greek building but if you look along the side of the Duomo, you'll see a number of thick Doric columns incorporated into the cathedral's structure.

To the north of the Duomo, over Via Minerva, Palazzo Municipale (Map p194) (or Palazzo Senatoriale), is home to Syracuse city council. Built in 1629 by the Spaniard Juan Vermexio, it is nicknamed 'Il Lucertolone' (the Lizard) after the architect's signature – a small lizard carved into a stone on the left corner of the cornice. On the other side of the Duomo, the elegant, 17th-century Palazzo Arcivescovile (Map p194; ☑ 093 16 79 68) (Archbishop's Palace) is home to the Biblioteca Alagoniana and some rare 13th-century manuscripts.

Over the square, in the northwestern corner, is the Palazzo Beneventano del Bosco (Map p194), which has a pretty 18th-century facade, while at its southern end is the Chiesa di Santa Lucia alla Badia (Map p194), dedicated to St Lucy, the city's patron saint.

Legendary Fountains   FOUNTAIN

Fresh water has been bubbling up at the Fontana Aretusa (Map p194) since ancient times when it was the city's main water supply. The fountain, now the place to hang out on summer evenings, is a monumental affair set around a pond full of papyrus plants and grey mullets.

Legend has it that the mythical goddess of hunting, Artemis, transformed her beautiful handmaiden Aretusa into the spring to protect her from the unwelcome attention of the river god Alpheus. In her watery guise, Aretusa fled from Arcadia under the sea, hotly pursued by Alpheus, their waters mingling as she came to the surface in Ortygia.

Artemis is the star turn of the 19th-century fountain (Map p194; Piazza Archimede) that's the highlight of Piazza Archimede, a handsome square circled by imposing Catalan Gothic *palazzi*, including Palazzo Lanza (Map p194; Piazza Archimede) and Palazzo Platamone (Map p194), now home to the Banca d'Italia.

Miqwe   JEWISH

(Ritual bath; Map p194; ☑ 093 12 22 55; Via Alagona 52; hourly tours €5; ☺11am & noon daily, 4pm, 5pm & 6pm Mon-Sat) In the old Jewish ghetto, known as the Giudecca, you can visit an ancient Jewish *miqwe* that lies buried 20m beneath the Alla Giudecca hotel. The baths were once connected to a synagogue, but were blocked by members of the Jewish community when they were expelled from the island in 1492.

It's a fascinating sight – the three deep pools intended for total immersion constantly bubble with fresh water, which now has to be pumped out of the chamber to prevent flooding. There is a separate, private pool that was for the sole use of the rabbi.

Galleria Regionale di Palazzo Bellomo   ART GALLERY

(Map p194; ☑ 093 16 95 11; www.regione.sicilia.it/beniculturali/palazzobellomo; Via Capodieci 16; adult/reduced €8/4; ☺9am-7pm Tue-Sat, 9am-1pm Sun) Just up from the fountain is this art museum, housed in a 13th-century Catalan-Gothic palace. The eclectic collection ranges from early Byzantine and Norman stonework to 19th-century Caltagirone ceramics; in between, there's a good range of medieval religious paintings and sculpture.

Lido Maniace   BEACH

(Map p194; www.lidomaniace.it; 2 people €10) If you want something glam (though also a bit squashed), rent a pew on Syracuse's tiny Lido Maniace – a rocky platform of sun beds and shades where you can dip into the water. Otherwise, swim off one of the wooden platforms near the Giudecca.

Biblios Cafe   LANGUAGE COURSE

(Map p194; ☑ 093 12 14 91; www.biblios-cafe.it; Via del Consiglio Reginale 11) Right in the heart of the Ortygia action, Biblios Cafe is a well-known cafe-cum-bookshop that organises a whole range of cultural activities, including visits to local vineyards, art classes and language courses. Italian lessons, which emphasise everyday conversational language, can be organised on an individual basis (€25 per hour) or as part of a course lasting from a week to a month (per one/four weeks €220/700).

◉ Mainland Syracuse

Although not as picturesque as Ortygia, the mainland city boasts a number of fascinating archaeological sights. The most compelling is the Parco Archeologico della Neapolis to the north of the city centre, but you'll also find plenty of interest at the city's renowned archaeological museum, the Museo Archeologico Paolo Orsi. Underground, an extensive network of catacombs dates from the Roman era.

Parco Archeologico della Neapolis   ARCHAEOLOGICAL SITE

(Map p196; ☑ 093 16 50 68; Viale Paradiso; adult/reduced €10/free-€5; ☺9am-6pm Apr-Oct, 9am-4pm Nov-Mar) For the classicist, Syracuse's real attraction is this archaeological park, with its pearly white, 5th-century-BC Teatro Greco (Map p196; Parco Archeologico della Neapolis), hewn out of the rock above the city. This theatre saw the last tragedies of

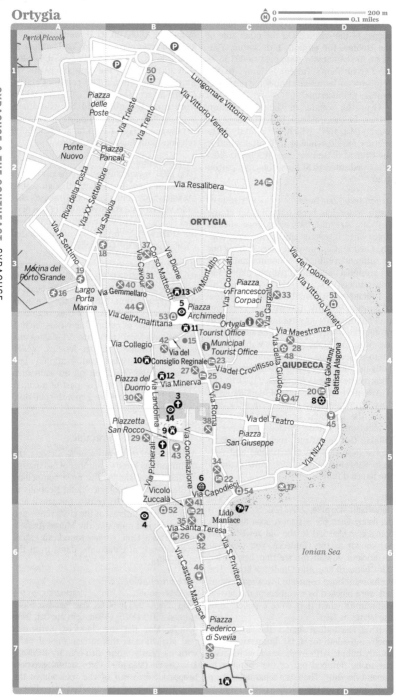

Ortygia

SYRACUSE & THE SOUTHEAST SYRACUSE

Ortygia

Aeschylus (including *The Persians*), which were first performed here in his presence. In late spring it is brought to life again with an annual season of classical theatre.

Just beside the theatre is the mysterious **Latomia del Paradiso** (Map p196; Parco Archeologico della Neapolis), deep, precipitous limestone quarries out of which the stone for the ancient city was extracted. These quarries, riddled with catacombs and filled with citrus and magnolia trees, are where the 7000 survivors of the war between Syracuse and Athens in 413 BC were imprisoned. The **Orecchio di Dionisio** (Ear of Dionysius; Map p196; Parco Archeologico della Neapolis, Latomia del Paradiso), a grotto 23m by 3m deep, was named by Caravaggio after the tyrant, who is said to have used the almost perfect acoustics of the quarry to eavesdrop on his prisoners.

Back outside this area you'll find the entrance to the 2nd-century **Anfiteatro Romano** (Map p196), originally used for gladiatorial combats and horse races. The Spaniards, little interested in archaeology, largely destroyed the site in the 16th century, using it as a quarry to build Ortygia's city walls. West of the amphitheatre is the 3rd-century-BC **Ara di Gerone II** (Map p196; Parco Archeologico della Neapolis), a monolithic sacrificial altar to Heron II where up to 450 oxen could be killed at one time.

To reach the park, take bus 1, 3 or 12 from Ortygia's Piazza Pancali and get off at the corner of Corso Gelone and Viale Teocrito. Alternatively, the walk from Ortygia will take about 30 minutes. If driving, you can park along Viale Augusto (tickets available at the nearby souvenir kiosks).

Museo Archeologico Paolo Orsi MUSEUM
(Map p196; ☎ 0931 46 40 22; Viale Teocrito; adult/reduced €8/4; ⊙9am-6pm Tue-Sat, 9am-1pm Sun) In the grounds of Villa Landolina, about

Syracuse

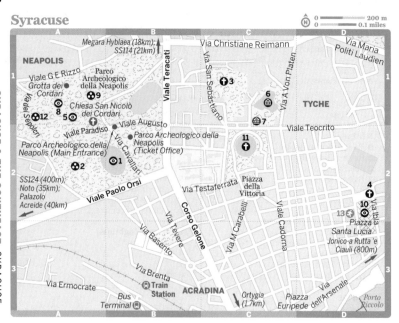

500m east of the archaeological park, this wheelchair-accessible museum contains one of Sicily's largest, best organised and most interesting archaeological collections. Allow plenty of time to get through the museum's four distinct sectors; serious archaeology buffs may even want to consider splitting their visit into two days.

Basilica di Santa Lucia al Sepolcro
CHURCH, CATACOMBS

(Map p196; www.basilicasantalucia.com; Piazza Santa Lucia) The northern end of one of the city's biggest squares, Piazza Santa Lucia (Map p196), is dominated by the Basilica di Santa Lucia al Sepolcro. The 17th-century church is built on the spot where the city's patron saint, Lucia, an aristocratic girl who devoted herself to saintliness after being blessed by St Agatha, was martyred in 304.

It's an impressive sight with its columned portico, Norman tower and 18th-century octagonal chapel known as the Sepolcro. But the main drawcard is Caravaggio's *Seppellimento di Santa Lucia* (The Burial of Saint Lucy, 1609), which after a lengthy restoration at Palazzo Bellomo has been returned to its rightful place over the basilica's main altar. Beneath the church is an impressive network of catacombs, used by the early Christians for burials.

According to Roman law, Christians were not allowed to bury their dead within the city limits (which during the Roman occupation did not extend beyond Ortygia), so the early Christians used the outlying district of Tyche for burials, accessing underground aqueducts unused since Greek times. New tunnels were carved out, and the result was a labyrinthine network of burial chambers.

Basilica di San Giovanni
CHURCH, CATACOMBS

(Map p196; Via San Sebastiano; ☺ 9.30am-12.30pm & 2.30-5.30pm Tue-Sun) The city's most extensive catacombs (Map p196) lie beneath the Basilica di San Giovanni, itself a pretty, truncated church that served as the city's cathedral in the 17th century. It is dedicated to the city's first bishop, St Marcian, who was tied to one of its pillars and flogged to death in 254. The catacombs, visitable by guided tour only, are dank and spooky.

Thousands of little niches line the walls, and tunnels lead off from the main chamber (*decumanus maximus*) into *rotonde,* round chambers used by the faithful for praying. All of the treasures that accompanied the dead on their spiritual journey fell victim to tomb robbers over the centuries bar one: a sarcophagus unearthed in 1872 and now on exhibition in the Museo Archeologico Paolo Orsi.

Museo del Papiro
MUSEUM

(Map p196; ☎ 093 16 16 16; www.museodelpapiro .it; Viale Teocrito 66; ☺ 9am-1pm Tue-Sun) FREE This small museum includes papyrus documents and products, boats and an English-language film about the history of papyrus. The plant grows in abundance around the Ciane River, near Syracuse, and was used to make paper in the 18th century.

Santuario della Madonna delle Lacrime
CHURCH

(Sanctuary of Our Lady of the Tears; Map p196; www. madonnadellelacrime.it; Viale Teocrito; ☺ 8am-noon & 4-7pm) FREE Supposedly modelled on the shape of a tear drop, the 102m-high spire of this church dominates Syracuse's skyline. The modern church beneath it houses a statue of the Virgin Mary that allegedly wept for five days in 1953 and bestowed more than 300 miraculous cures. To learn more, head to the Museo delle Lacrimazione (Museum of the Lacrymation; Map p196; admission €1.55; ☺ 9am-12.30pm & 4-6pm) on the sanctuary's lower floor.

Beaches
BEACH

When the heat of the summer kicks in, the sparkling blue waters that surround Ortygia's sea walls look very tempting. The best swimming in town is off the rocks at Forte Vigliena (Map p194), although beach bunnies would do better to make the short trip south to the sandy blue-flag beaches at Lido Arenella. Be warned, though, that it gets very busy here, particularly on summer weekends.

Further south, there's good swimming at rocky Ognina and the popular Fontane Bianche beach.

Boat Tours
CRUISES

There are a number of outfits offering cruises along the coast. Between March and October, Compagnia del Selene (Map p194; ☎ 340 0558769; www.compagniadelselene.it; Via Malta 63; 50-minute tour per person €10) runs boat tours around Ortygia, offering great views of the historic centre and Castello Maniace (Map p194), a robust 13th-century castle.

For something more romantic, book a berth on one of the four yachts run by Sailing Team (Map p194; ☎ 093 16 08 08; www.sailingteam.biz; Via Savoia 14; day trip up to 12 people €350) and set off down the southern coast to explore beaches and uncontaminated nature reserves. It also runs trips to the Aeolian Islands and sailing courses; see its website for details.

Guided Tours
TOUR

Syracuse has a host of professional guides offering tours of the city and environs. They generally escort groups so prices are steep, ranging from €150 for half a day to €235 for a whole day (groups of up to 18 people). The tourist office can put you in touch with authorised operators, otherwise contact Syrako Tourist Services (Map p194; ☎ 093 12 41 33; www.syrako.it; Largo Porta Marina), which can arrange guides on your behalf.

To explore the local countryside, Natura Sicula (Map p196; ☎ 328 8857092; www.naturasicula.it; Piazza Santa Lucia 24/C) is a local association that runs excursions and guided nature walks (about €6 to €8 per person).

Ente Fauna Siciliana
TOUR

(☎ 338 4888822; www.entefaunasiciliana.it; Viale Montedoro 79; per person mountain-bike trip to Cava Cardinale €10, trekking on Etna €6) Landlubbers should consider an excursion with Ente Fauna Siciliana. Itineraries include short hikes along the coastline (€5 per person) and archaeological and botanical itineraries. A *calendario attività* (activities calendar) with booking numbers and departure points can be downloaded from the website. Most of the tours are in Italian only.

Festivals & Events

Cycle of Classical Plays THEATRE
(☑ 800 542644, 0931 48 72 48; www.indafondazione.org; tickets from €15) Classical Greek drama returns to Syracuse's ancient Teatro Greco. Two plays are produced each year with performances (in Italian) held in May and June. Programs and ticket information are available on the website.

Festa di Santa Lucia RELIGIOUS
On 13 December, the enormous silver statue of the city's patron saint wends its way from the cathedral to Piazza Santa Lucia accompanied by fireworks.

✕ Eating

Ortygia is the best place to eat. Its narrow lanes are chock-full of trattorias, restaurants, cafes and bars, and while some are obvious tourist traps, many are not, and you'll have no trouble finding somewhere to suit your style. Most places specialise in seafood so expect plenty of fishy pasta and grilled catches-of-the-day.

Solaria Vini & Liquori SICILIAN €
(Map p194; ☑ 0931 46 30 07; www.enotecasolaria.com; Via Roma 86) This small, rustic *enoteca* (wine shop) is wonderfully old school, with rows of rough wooden tables and dark bottles lined up on floor-to-ceiling shelves. But it's not just a shop, you can stop by for a glass of wine and a bite to eat – think platters of cheese, olives, prosciutto, anchovies and sardines.

The wine list is extensive (see the website) and, though biased towards Italian and Sicilian labels, includes a number of French vintages and some Champagnes.

Sicilia in Tavola SICILIAN €
(Map p194; ☑ 392 461 08 89; Via Cavour 28; pasta €7-12; ☺ Tue-Sun) One of a number of popular eateries on Via Cavour, this snug hole-in-the-wall trattoria has built a strong local reputation on the back of its homemade pasta and fresh seafood. To taste for yourself try the prawn ravioli, which is served with small cherry tomatoes and chopped mint, or the delicious *fettuccine allo scoglio* (with seafood sauce).

Adding to the fun is a bustling atmosphere and the clutter that adorns the wooden walls. Reservations are recommended.

Osteria Da Mariano SICILIAN €
(Map p194; ☑ 093 16 74 44; Vicolo Zuccolà 9; meals €20; ☺ Tue-Sun) Any restaurant that is full on a Monday night in February is doing something right. Old-timer waiters squeeze past tightly packed tables, dishing out earthy country food to legions of boisterous diners. Antipasti of bruschetta, ricotta, salami and marinated vegetables are followed by simple pastas of *penne* (pasta tubes) in meaty sausage sauce, and *dolci* (sweets) of sesame biscuits and candied ginger.

Caffè Minerva BAKERY €
(Map p194; Via Roma 58) A popular, people-watching cafe serving a good range of Sicilian cakes and pastries, the best cup of tea on the island and a nice, frothy cappuccino.

Gelati Bianca GELATO €
(Map p194; Via Pompeo Picherali 2; cone/cup from €1.80; ☺ daily) It's not just the location off Piazza del Duomo that's the attraction – the house-made gelato is pretty good too.

Pasticceria Tipica Catanese PASTRIES & CAKES €
(Corso Umberto 46; pastries from €1) If you want a good cafe on the mainland, this is a great option.

★ Le Vin De L'Assasin Bistrot MEDITERRANEAN €€
(Map p194; ☑ 093 16 61 59; Via Roma 15; meals €30-45; ☺ dinner Tue-Sun, lunch Sun) A refreshing and stylish restaurant with excellent food that takes an original French twist on Sicilian ingredients – the tuna steak topped with hazelnuts and honey is unforgettable. The owner, Saro, is friendly and generous with his time and offers advice on the menu and, having spent years in Paris, brings a sophisticated touch to the Ortygia dining scene.

The ceilings are tall and the walls painted in bright colours, though the little tables on the narrow Via Roma are wonderful in the evening breeze. Offerings scrawled on the chalkboard include French classics like *quiche lorraine* and *croque-monsieur*, Breton oysters, salads with impeccable vinaigrette dressing, a host of meat and fish mains and a splendid *millefoglie* of eggplant and sweet red peppers. It's also a perfect late-night stop for wine by the glass or one of its homemade, over-the-top creamy and chocolatey desserts. The wine list is extensive, with Sicilian, Italian and French offerings, and you can order by the glass. There is no *coperto* (cover charge). Reservations are recommended on weekend evenings.

Taberna Sveva
SICILIAN €€

(Map p194; ☑ 093 12 46 63; Piazza Federico di Svevia; meals €25-35; ☺ Thu-Tue) Away from the main tourist maelstrom, the charming Taberna Sveva is tucked away in a quiet corner of Ortygia. On warm summer evenings the outdoor terrace is the place to sit, with alfresco tables set out on a tranquil cobbled square in front of Syracuse's 13th-century castle. The food is traditional Sicilian, so expect plenty of tuna and swordfish and some wonderful pasta.

Particularly good are the *gnocchi al pistacchio* (with olive oil, parmesan, pepper, garlic and grated pistachio nuts). Slow Food recommended.

Osteria Vite e Vitello
MEAT €€

(Map p194; ☑ 0931 46 42 69; Piazza Francesco Corpaci 1; meals €33; ☺ Mon-Sat) Bucking the trend for seafood, this cheerful Ortygia trattoria flies the flag for meat-eaters (and how). Delicious *involtini* (meat rolls) are stuffed with prosciutto, cheese and onion; pork steaks are cased in crusts of green Sicilian pistachios; ricotta ravioli is served in a rich pork *ragù* (meat sauce). It's all delightfully decadent.

Portions are encyclopaedic in size and the wine list is long enough to satisfy most amateur aficionados.

La Gazza Ladra
SICILIAN €€

(Map p194; ☑ 340 0602428; Via Cavour 8; meals €25-30; ☺ Tue-Sun Sep-Jun) Great food served in welcoming surroundings at honest prices: the recipe for success sounds simple but few manage it as well as this friendly, pocket-sized osteria. Run by a husband-and-wife team, it's a bright, laid-back place with colourful photos on white walls, iron-and-glass tables and an open kitchen.

The food? Hearty, filling fare made with ripe local ingredients – try the *pasta alla Norma* (with creamy aubergines), fresh seafood and homemade puddings. Slow Food recommended.

La Medusa
SICILIAN €€

(Map p194; ☑ 093 16 14 03; Via S Teresa 21-23; meals €25-30; ☺ Tue-Sun) This is one of the best known and most popular restaurants in Ortygia. It made its name serving delicious couscous, but chef-owner Kamel also knows his way around a fish – the *antipasto del mare* (seafood starter) and *fritto misto*

(mixed fish fry) come highly recommended. But beware, helpings are enormous so be careful not to over-order. Service is friendly and accommodating.

You will need to book ahead.

Le Baronie
SICILIAN €€

(Map p194; ☑ 093 16 88 84; www.ristorantelebaronie.com; Via Gargallo 26; meals €25-30; ☺ Tue-Sun) Offering a boisterous atmosphere in an old Catalan-Gothic mansion, Le Baronie prides itself on traditional cuisine with a twist, such as swordfish with a pepper-and-brandy sauce. There is also a pleasant garden dotted with sarcophagi.

Jonico-a Rutta 'e Ciauli
SICILIAN €€

(☑ 093 16 55 40; Riviera Dionisio il Grande 194; pizzas €4-7, meals €25-35; ☺ Wed-Mon Jun-Sep) It's a long and not particularly enticing hike to this seafront restaurant, but once you're there you'll appreciate the effort. Inside it's all exposed brickwork and rusty farm tools; outside on the terrace it's pure bliss, with the sun in your face, a cooling sea breeze and dreamy views. Not surprisingly, fish features heavily on the menu.

Try the *spaghetti alla palermitana* (with sardines and fennel) and *orata c'aranci* (sea bream cooked in orange juice). Alternatives include grilled steaks and evening pizzas.

Trattoria Pescomare
TRATTORIA €€

(Map p194; ☑ 093 12 10 75; Via Landolina 6; meals €25-30) Near the cathedral, the Pescomare serves a good selection of local fish dishes and a wide range of pizza. Grab a spot in the vine-covered courtyard and feast on the *spaghetti alle cozze* (spaghetti with mussels).

Trattoria Archimede
TRATTORIA €€

(Map p194; ☑ 093 16 97 01; Via Gemmellaro 8; set menus €13-18, meals €28; ☺ Mon-Sat) Although this Ortygia eatery serves its fair share of tourists, there's no denying its historic credentials – it has been in business since 1938. But while times change, the restaurant's loyalty to local seafood remains entrenched and the menu is distinctly fishy, with such crowd-pleasers as *tagliolini al nero di seppie* (string-like pasta with cuttlefish ink) and *pesce all'acqua pazza* (fish cooked with garlic, tomatoes, capers and olives).

Trattoria la Foglia
TRATTORIA €€

(Map p194; ☑ 093 16 62 33; www.lafoglia.it; Via Capodieci 21; meals €30-35; ☺ Wed-Mon Apr-Oct) Sporting a bizarre look that's half Edwardian country house, half boho chic, this is one

SYRACUSE & THE SOUTHEAST SYRACUSE

TOP TOURS & COURSES

Guided nature walks Join the locals on a guided walk in the Syracuse countryside courtesy of the Natura Sicula (p197) association.

Italian cookery classes Brush up your cooking skills with a three-hour lesson at La Corte del Sole (p209) hotel, near Lido di Noto.

Learn the language In Syracuse, Biblios Cafe (p193) runs language courses enlivened by shopping trips to the local market, cooking lessons and visits to local wine producers.

Montalbano tour Follow in the footsteps of TV detective Salvo Montalbano on an Allakatalla (p206) or Echoes Events (www.echoesevents.com) tour of the series' locations: Palazzolo Acreide, Noto, Pantalica, Modica, Scicli, Donnafugata and Ragusa.

Take to the sea Draw anchor in Syracuse and sail down the southern coast on one of the yachts of Sailing Team (p197), stopping to explore sandy beaches and protected wetlands.

Syracuse restaurant where the decor is as memorable as the food. Classical music is piped into the brocaded dining room as diners sit down to a menu that matches heartwarming starters with homemade pasta and seafood staples such as grilled *pesce spada* (swordfish) and *polpette di tonno* (tuna meatballs).

Gran Caffè del Duomo CAFE €
(Map p194; ☑093 12 15 44; Piazza del Duomo 18) You'd normally avoid a place like this, thinking it screams 'location plus expense', but a reasonable tourist menu and prime position in this beautiful square makes it a viable option.

It's the best vantage point on the square: the perfect people-watching perch and a great place to enjoy a languid glass of wine.

Piano B PIZZERIA €
(☑0931 6 68 51; Via Cairoli 18; pizza €5-9.50, salads €5.50-15, grilled meat €15-22; ☺closed Mon) Brisk, friendly service complements the trendy, casual atmosphere at this eatery just west of Ortygia. It's popular with young Syracusans for its pizzas, grilled meat and extensive salad menu.

★**Don Camillo** MODERN SICILIAN €€€
(Map p194; ☑093 16 71 33; www.ristorantedon-camillosiracusa.it; Via Maestranza 96; meals €55; ☺lunch & dinner Mon-Sat) An elegant restaurant with an impressive kitchen, top service and a classy atmosphere. Try the starter of 'black' king prawns in a thick almond cream soup, and lick your lips over the *tagliata di pesce spada* (grilled and sliced swordfish) in a tomato sauce, or the red snapper with fig and lemon. The tuna *tagliata* with a red pepper 'marmalade' is also divine.

Finish with a blood-orange ice cream. Slow Food recommended.

🍷 Drinking & Nightlife

A vibrant university town, Syracuse has a lively cafe culture, with many bars and cafes spilling over Ortygia's pretty streets. Piazzetta San Rocco is a popular spot, as is the seafront around Fontana Aretusa.

Tinkité BAR
(Map p194; ☑093 11 85 59 36; Via Mario Minniti 3; ☺8.30am-10.30pm) A cool and cute bar in the labyrinth of narrow streets of La Giudecca, Tinkité is popular with Syracuse's cool crowd at *aperitivo* time. There are cakes, coffee and a ton of different teas that you can enjoy whilst admiring the surrounding *palazzi*. Some tables sit outside, while the interior is a cool indigo.

Peter Pan WINE BAR
(Map p194; ☑0931 46 89 37; Via Castello Maniace 46/48; glass of wine €4-7; ☺10am-2.30pm & 7.30pm-2am) Brunch, beer, books, cocktails and live music make this tiny bar an excellent place to while away some time. It also serves a limited menu of cheese and charcuterie to soak up those huge glasses of wine.

Bar San Rocco BAR
(Map p194; Piazzetta San Rocco) Hip about-towners head to San Rocco, the smoothest of the bars on Piazzetta San Rocco, for early evening *aperitivi* (complete with bountiful bar snacks) and cocktails late into the night. Inside, it's a narrow, stone-vaulted affair, but the main action is outside on the vivacious *piazzetta* where summer crowds gather un-

til the early hours. Occasional live music and DJ sets fuel the laid-back vibe.

Café Giufá   BAR
(Map p194; ☎0931 46 53 95; Via Cavour 25; ☺closed Mon in winter) A fun bar that spreads onto the tiny square at the back, the Giufá has some good DJs who like reggae, jungle and dub beats, and the crowd – including the bar staff – are jolly and friendly. Beer's the name of the game here.

Il Blu   WINE BAR
(Map p194; Via Nizza) A superb wine bar with a cosy front porch near the waterfront, this is a great place to take in the sun in between dips in the sea.

☆ Entertainment

Piccolo Teatro dei Pupi   PUPPET THEATRE
(Map p194; ☎0931 46 55 40; www.pupari.com; Via della Giudecca 17) Syracuse's thriving puppet theatre hosts regular performances; see its website for a calendar. You can also buy puppets at its workshop next door.

🛍 Shopping

Browsing Ortygia's quirky boutiques is great fun. Good buys include papyrus paper, ceramics and handmade jewellery.

Antico Mercato   MARKET
(Map p194; ☺8am-1pm Mon-Sat) Syracuse's produce market is near the harbour, where red-canopied stalls overflow with piles of mussels, oysters, octopus and shellfish. You can also find good bread and local pastries, vegetables and fruit – all perfect if you're self catering.

Untitled   CLOTHING
(Map p194; ☎093 16 45 74; www.untitled-trendwear.com; Via Serafino Privitera 39; ☺10.30am-2.30pm & 4.30-8.30pm) You could describe this boutique in a snippet: clothes to die for and prices to give you a heart attack. But if you've got several hundred euros to spend on a beautifully crafted, quality, simple and timeless garment, bag, shoes or hat, this is the place for you. It stocks pieces by Italian and international designers.

Galleria Bellomo   ARTISANAL
(Map p194; www.bellomogalleria.com; Via Capodieci 15) Papyrus paper is the reason to come to this Ortygia gallery near Fontana Aretusa. Here you'll find a range of papery products, including greeting cards, bookmarks and writing paper, as well as a series of water-

colour landscapes. Prices start at around €3 for a postcard, rising to hundreds of euros for original works of art.

Massimo Izzo   JEWELLERY
(Map p194; www.massimoizzo.com; Piazza Archimede 25) The flamboyant jewellery of Messina-born Massimo Izzo is not for the faint-hearted. Featuring bold idiosyncratic designs and made with Sciacca coral, gold and precious stones, his handmade pieces are often inspired by themes close to the Sicilian heart: the sea, theatre and classical antiquity.

a 'nacalora   CHILDREN'S CLOTHING, TOYS
(Map p194; ☎093 11 88 74 44; Via Roma 37; ☺10am-1pm & 4-8pm) A gorgeous little boutique that sells small French, Spanish, Scandinavian and Italian designer clothes and toys. There are the quirky and charming Bobo Choses clothes, sewn Danish toys (a fabric castle or spaceship kit is just wonderful), wooden toys, party outfits - everything is carefully chosen, tasteful and just beautiful.

Circo Fortuna   CERAMICS
(Map p194; www.circofortuna.it; Via dei Tolomei 20) Produces whimsical ceramics.

ℹ Orientation

Syracuse's main sights are concentrated in two areas: Ortygia, and 2km across town at the Parco Archeologico della Neapolis. Ortygia, Syracuse's historic centre and most atmospheric neighbourhood, is an island joined to the mainland by a couple of bridges. It is well signposted and has a useful car park (Parcheggio Talete). If coming by bus, you'll be dropped off at the bus terminal in front of the train station. From here it's about a 1km walk to Ortygia – head straight down Corso Umberto. Alternatively, a free shuttle bus connects the station with Piazza Archimede in Ortygia. Via Roma is Ortygia's main thoroughfare.

ℹ Information

EMERGENCIES
Police Station (☎093 16 51 76; Piazza S Giuseppe)

MEDICAL SERVICES
Ospedale Umberto I (☎0931 72 40 33; Via Testaferrata 1)

TOURIST INFORMATION
Municipal Tourist Office (Map p194; ☎800 555000; Via Roma 31; ☺9am-1pm & 2-5.30pm Mon-Fri, 9am-noon Sat)

BEST ANCIENT SITES

→ Teatro Greco (p193), Syracuse – the highlight of Syracuse's ancient ruins is this dramatic Greek amphitheatre.

→ Akrai (p203), Palazzolo Acreide – walk among the grassy ruins of what was once a thriving Greek colony.

→ Villa Romana del Tellaro (p209), the Noto Coast – expressive mosaics depict mythical scenes at this ancient Roman villa.

→ Megara Hyblaea (below), near Syracuse – the remnants of a 4th-century-BC city resist the encroaching onslaught of modern industry.

→ Eloro (p209), the Noto Coast – as much as the ruins, it's the dreamy coastal setting that's the main draw.

Ortygia Tourist Office (Map p194; ☏ 093 146 42 55; Via Maestranza 33; ⊗8am-2pm & 2.30-5.30pm Mon-Fri, 8am-2pm Sat)

WEBSITES

Lonely Planet (www.lonelyplanet.com/italy/sicily/syracuse) Planning advice, author recommendations, traveller reviews and insider tips.

ⓘ Getting There & Around

BUS

Buses are generally faster and more convenient than trains. From the terminal on Corso Umberto near the train station, **Interbus** (☏ 093 16 67 10; www.interbus.it) runs buses to Noto (€3.40, one hour, two to four daily Monday to Saturday, two Sunday), Catania (€6, 1½ hours, hourly Monday to Saturday, six Sunday) and its airport, and Palermo (€12, 3¼ hours, three daily). You can buy tickets at the kiosk by the bus stops. **AST** (☏ 840 000323; www.aziendasicilianatrasporti.it) runs services to Piazza Armerina (€8.80, four hours, one daily) and Ragusa (€6.90, 2¼ hours, four daily Monday to Saturday, two Sunday). Tickets are available at the train station bar.

Free (white) shuttle buses connect the train station with Ortygia and the main car parks, while local bus 12 runs between Ortygia and Parco Archeologico della Neapolis. A two-hour city bus ticket costs €1.10.

CAR

The dual-carriageway SS114 heads north from Syracuse to Catania, while the SS115 runs south to Noto and Modica. While the approach roads to Syracuse are rarely very busy, traffic gets increasingly heavy as you enter town and can be pretty bad in the city centre.

If you're staying in Ortygia, the best place to park is Parcheggio Talete (free 5am to 9pm, and €1 9pm to 5am) on Via Vittorio Veneto. Nearby, there's also parking on Piazza delle Poste but here you'll pay €0.60 per hour. Note that most of Ortygia is a limited traffic zone, restricted to residents and those with special permission. On-street parking is hard to find during the week, less so on Sunday when it's often free.

TRAIN

Up to 10 trains depart daily for Messina (InterCity/regional €18.50/9.75, 2½ to three hours) and Catania (InterCity/regional €9.50/6.35, 1¼ hours). Some go on to Rome, Turin, Milan and other long-distance destinations. There are also slow trains to Noto (€3.45, 35 minutes, eight Monday to Saturday, one Sunday) and Ragusa (€7.65, 2¼ hours, three daily).

Around Syracuse

The area around Syracuse is not always especially attractive, particularly north of town where the coast is blighted by ugly oil refineries and heavy industry, but there are a few sights that reward exploration.

Seven kilometres west of town in the outlying quarter of Epipolae is the Castello Eurialo (☏ 093 171 17 73; adult/reduced €4/2; ⊗9am-6pm daily summer, 9am-3pm Mon-Sat & 9am-1pm Sun winter), the stronghold of Syracuse's Greek defensive works. Built during the reign of Hieron II, it was adapted and fortified by Archimedes and was considered impregnable. Unfortunately for Syracuse, the castle was taken by the Romans without a fight. The views back to Syracuse make it worth the trip.

If you can find them in the midst of the surrounding industrial sprawl, the ruins of ancient Megara Hyblaea (adult/reduced €4/2; ⊗9am-1hr before sunset) are well worth a detour. The city, founded in 728 BC by Greeks from Megara, prospered until 483 BC when it was razed by the Syracuse dictator Gelon. It was then rebuilt in 340 BC only to be destroyed a second time by the Romans in 213 BC. Most of the ruins you see today date to the 4th-century city. You'll need your own car to get here – it's 20km north of Syracuse, signposted off the SS114.

A popular diversion between May and September is a boat trip (per person €10) up the Ciane, a mythical river dedicated to the nymph Ciane, who tried to thwart the abduction of Persephone by Hades. A spring,

2km upriver, is said to have been formed by her mother. The river habitat – a tangle of lush papyrus – is the only place outside North Africa where papyrus grows wild. Along the way, you can check out the ruins of the Olympeion, a temple from the 6th century BC.

The embarkation point for the boats is 5km outside Syracuse on the SS115 – from town follow signs to Palazzolo Acreide.

THE SOUTHEAST

Dominated by the Monti Iblei hills, Sicily's southeast harbours some of the island's most beautiful towns. In particular, Unesco-listed Noto, Modica and Ragusa stand out for their sumptuous baroque architecture and stunning historic centres. And while these places are not exactly undiscovered they are not yet on the main tourist radar, and outside of peak periods are largely free of visitors. Elsewhere, the region is quietly rural, its gently rugged landscape characterised by weathered limestone cliffs and deep rocky gorges.

Valle Dell'Anapo & Around

For some beautifully wild and unspoilt countryside, take the SS124 northwest from Syracuse towards Palazzolo Acreide. After about 36km, turn off right towards Ferla. The signposted road plunges steeply to the floor of the Valle dell'Anapo (Anapo Valley), a deep limestone gorge. Once at the bottom you can leave your car by the Forestry Commission hut and walk through the woodlands on foot. It's pretty gentle walking, although paths marked 'B' are slightly more challenging.

Continuing about 5km up from the valley floor you come to Ferla, a small town with an attractive baroque centre, and another 11km beyond that the Necropoli di Pantalica FREE, an important Iron Age and Bronze Age necropolis. Situated on a huge plateau, it's an extensive, isolated area of limestone rocks honeycombed by more than 5000 tombs. The site's origins date to between the 13th and 8th centuries BC, and although no one is absolutely sure, it is thought that this was the Siculi capital of Hybla. There's no ticket office or main entrance, but there's a car park at the end of the long, winding road down from Ferla.

Palazzolo Acreide

POP 9085 / ELEV 670M

Few people make it up to Palazzolo Acreide, but those who do find a charming, laid-back town with a wealth of baroque architecture and some of the area's finest (and least publicised) ancient ruins. The original medieval town was abandoned after the 1693 earthquake, after which a new Palazzolo was built in the shadow of the Greek settlement of Akrai.

◉ Sights & Activities

Historic Centre NEIGHBOURHOOD
The town's central focus is Piazza del Popolo, which is a striking square dominated by the ornate bulk of the Chiesa di San Sebastiano and Palazzo Municipale, Palazzolo's impressive town hall. From here you can take a short walk north that will bring you to Piazza Moro as well as two other exquisite baroque churches, the Chiesa Madre and Chiesa di San Paolo.

These two churches, the first on the square's northern flank and the second on the southern side, form a theatrical ensemble of columns, gargoyles and fleurs-de-lis. At the top of Via Annunziata (the main road leading right out of Piazza Moro) is the fourth of the town's baroque treasures, the Chiesa dell'Annunziata, with a richly adorned portal of twirling columns.

Casa-Museo di Antonino Uccello MUSEUM
(☑093 188 14 99; www.antoninouccello.it; Via Machiavelli 19; ☺9am-1pm & 2.30-7pm) FREE Off Piazza del Popolo is the former home of the poet and scholar Antonino Uccello (1922–79), a museum since 1984. Uccello devoted himself to preserving what he feared was disappearing from Sicilian life, so this is the place to go if you want to see what 18th-century farmers would have worn or how they ground olives to make oil.

The museum houses a traditional stable, bedroom and living quarters. Only 10 people are allowed in at a time, and a custodian will escort you. Ring the doorbell to gain admission.

Akrai ARCHAEOLOGICAL SITE
(☑0931 88 14 99; Colle dell'Acromonte; admission €4; ☺9am-7pm Mon-Sat, 9am-5pm Sun Apr-Oct, 9am-4pm Mon-Sat Nov-Mar) A 20-minute uphill walk from Piazza del Popolo, the archaeological park of Akrai is one of the area's best-kept secrets. The city of Akrai,

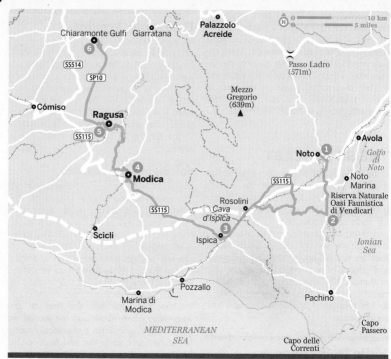

Driving Tour
Baroque Towns

START NOTO
END CHIARAMONTE GULFI
LENGTH 71KM/TWO DAYS

A land of remote rocky gorges, sweeping views and silent valleys, Sicily's southeastern corner is home to the 'baroque triangle', an area of Unesco-listed hilltop towns famous for their lavish baroque architecture. This tour takes in some of the finest, all within easy driving distance of each other.

Just over 35km south of Syracuse, **1 Noto** is home to what is arguably Sicily's most beautiful street – Corso Vittorio Emanuele, a pedestrianised boulevard lined with golden baroque *palazzi*. From Noto, pop into the **2 Riserva Naturale Oasi Faunistica di Vendicari** (p209), ideal for walking around and swimming off its beaches. Continue on to Ispica, a hilltop town overlooking a huge canyon, the **3 Cava d'Ispica** (p212), riddled with prehistoric tombs. Follow the

SS115 for a further 18km brings you to **4 Modica**, a bustling town set in a deep rocky gorge. There's excellent accommodation and a wealth of great restaurants, so this makes a good place to stay overnight. The best of the baroque sights are up in Modica Alta, the high part of town, but make sure you have energy left for the *passeggiata* (evening stroll) on Corso Umberto I and dinner at Osteria dei Sapori Perduti.

Next morning, a short, winding, up-and-down drive through rock-littered hilltops leads to **5 Ragusa**, one of Sicily's nine provincial capitals. The town is divided in two – it's Ragusa Ibla that you want, a claustrophobic warren of grey stone houses and elegant *palazzi* that opens up onto Piazza Duomo, a superb example of 18th-century town planning. Although you can eat well in Ragusa, consider lunching in **6 Chiaramonte Gulfi**, a tranquil hilltop town some 20km to the north along the SP10, famous for its olive oil and delicious pork.

Syracuse's first inland colony, was established to defend the overland trading route to other Greek settlements. Nowadays, its ruins are an evocative sight, even if the lack of explanatory signs means that you're often not sure what you're looking at.

The most impressive (and obvious) ruin is the Greek theatre, built at the end of the 3rd century BC but later altered by the Romans. A perfect semi-circle, it once had a capacity of 600. Behind the theatre are two *latomie* (quarries), which were later converted into Christian burial chambers. The larger of the two, the Intagliata, has catacombs and altars cut into its sides, while the narrower one, the Intagliatella, has a wonderful relief of a large banquet cut into the rock face.

South of the archaeological zone are a series of 3rd-century-BC stone sculptures known as the Santoni (Holy Men). It's a 15-minute walk down to the statues, but you'll need to go with a guide as the area around the statues is closed to the general public.

✖ Eating

Pasticceria Caprice   PASTRIES & CAKES €
(Map p172; ☎ 093 188 28 46; Corso Vittorio Emanuele 21; snacks from €1.50; ⊘ daily) This popular cafe-cum-cake shop is a great spot for a quick bite of lunch or a mid-afternoon pick-me-up. There's a daily selection of pastas and simple meat dishes, which you can follow up with something from the tempting display of cakes, biscuits and ice cream. Seating is in a grand back room with vaulted ceiling and chandeliers or on a thin streetside terrace.

Il Portico   SICILIAN €€
(☎ 093 188 15 32; Via Orologio 6; pizzas from €4, meals €25, tasting menus €35-45; ⊘ Wed-Mon) Just back from Via Carlo Alberto, this formal little restaurant has swagged rose curtains, high-backed chairs and florid painted ceilings. The food focuses on local Iblean mountain dishes, so expect plenty of grilled meats, mushrooms and cheeses. Typical of the house style is the *ravioli casarecci di ricotta al sugo di maiale* (homemade ricotta ravioli with pork *ragù*) and cheese platter.

ℹ Information

Tourist office (☎ 093 147 21 81; www.comune. palazzolo.acreide.sr.it; Piazza del Popolo 7; ⊘ 9am-1pm & 3-7pm)

ℹ Getting There & Around

BUS
Regular AST buses connect with Syracuse (€4, 1¼ hours).

CAR
Palazzolo is 40km west of Syracuse via the scenic SS124.

Noto

POP 23,765 / ELEV 160M

Located less than 40km south of Syracuse, Noto boasts one of Sicily's most beautiful historic centres. The *pièce de résistance* is Corso Vittorio Emanuele, an elegantly manicured walkway flanked by thrilling baroque *palazzi* and churches. Stunning at any time of the day, it is especially fabulous in the early evening when the lovely red-gold buildings seem to glow with a soft inner light.

Although a town called Noto or Netum has existed here for many centuries, the Noto that you see today dates to the early 18th century, when it was almost entirely rebuilt in the wake of the devastating 1693 earthquake. Creator of many of the finest buildings was Rosario Gagliardi, a local architect whose extroverted style also graces churches in Modica and Ragusa.

◎ Sights & Activities

Piazza Municipio   PIAZZA
About halfway along Corso Vittorio Emanuele is the graceful Piazza Municipio, flanked by Noto's most dramatic buildings. To the north, sitting in stately pomp at the head of Paolo Labisi's monumental staircase is the Cattedrale di San Nicolò, surrounded by a series of elegant palaces. To the left (west) is Palazzo Landolina, once home to the powerful Sant'Alfano family.

Over the road Palazzo Ducezio has a lovely columned facade interspersed with round arches. Designed in 1746 by Vincenzo Sinatra, it now houses Noto's Town Hall.

★ Cattedrale di San Nicolò   CATHEDRAL
(www.cattedralenoto.it; Piazza Municipio; ⊘ 9am-1pm & 3-8pm) Pride of place in Noto goes to the renovated San Nicolò Cathedral. Following its dome's collapse and subsequent restructuring, the cathedral was scrubbed of centuries of dust and dirt and reopened in June 2007, once again gleaming in its peachy glow.

Noto

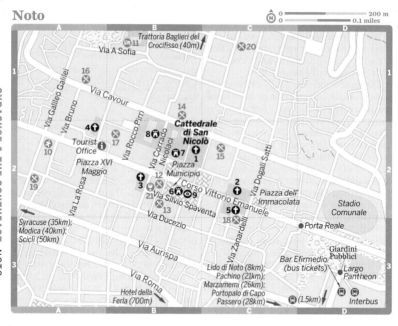

The re-opening was a major event in town, with the inhabitants keen to see the cathedral looking brand new.

Palazzo Nicolaci di Villadorata PALACE
(☑ 320 5568038; www.palazzonicolaci.it; Via Nicolaci; adult/reduced €4/2; ☺ 10am-1pm & 3-7.30pm)
In the Palazzo Villadorata, the wrought-iron balconies are supported by a pantomime of grotesque figures. Although empty of furnishings, the brocaded walls and frescoed ceilings of the *palazzo* give an idea of the sumptuous lifestyle of Sicilian nobles, as re-created in the Giuseppe Tomasi di Lampedusa novel *Il Gattopardo* (The Leopard).

Chiesa del Santissimo Salvatore CHURCH
(Corso Vittorio Emanuele) Situated towards the grand Porta Reale is the Chiesa del Santissimo Salvatore with its adjoining nunnery, which was reserved for the daughters of local nobility. The interior is the most impressive in Noto, but unfortunately it is closed to the public. The fountain suspended on a wall next to it remained after Noto's streets were lowered in 1840 to facilitate the movement of carriages.

Chiesa di Santa Chiara CHURCH
(Corso Vittorio Emanuele; admission €2; ☺ 9.30am-1pm & 3-7pm) Offering great views of the cath-

edral, this church was built by the baroque maestro Rosario Gagliardi between 1745 and 1758. The oval-plan interior is typically lavish, although the main drawcard is the panoramic view from the rooftop terrace.

Chiesa di San Carlo al Corso CHURCH
(Corso Vittorio Emanuele; admission €2; ☺ 9am-12.30pm & 4-7pm) For an alternative viewing platform, head down the road to the Chiesa di San Carlo al Corso where you can climb to the top of the *campanile* (belltower). If you suffer from vertigo, stick to admiring the handsome concave facade with its three orders of rising columns.

Other Churches CHURCH
Towering over the tourist office on Piazza XVI Maggio are the Chiesa di San Domenico and the extraordinary Dominican Monastery, both designed by Rosario Gagliardi.

Allakatalla TOURS
(☑ 093 157 40 80; www.allakatalla.it; Corso Vittorio Emanuele 47) If you want to join an organised tour, Allakatalla offers a wide range of packages, ranging from guided excursions to Syracuse to week-long jaunts around Mt Etna's vineyards and the locations used in the *Inspector Montalbano* TV series.

Noto

🎊 Festivals & Events

Infiorata STREET CARNIVAL

Noto's big annual jamboree is the Infiorata, held around the third Sunday in May. The highlight of the festival is the decoration of Via Corrada Nicolaci, with works of art made entirely from flower petals.

🍴 Eating

There are a number of restaurants in the historical centre, but pride of place goes to a cafe, famous for its *granite* (crushed-ice drinks), and a gelateria that churns out fabulous ice cream.

Trattoria del Carmine TRATTORIA €

(☑093 183 87 05; Via Ducezio 1; meals €18; ☺Tue-Sun) Much loved by locals and visiting celebs – look for the photo of Maria Grazia Cucinotta (Beatrice from the film *Il Postino*) on the wall – this is a modest family-run trattoria

that serves honest, down-to-earth Sicilian food. Expect antipasti of ricotta, olives and sliced salami, pasta with meat *ragù, involtini* and straightforward roast meats.

Trattoria Al Buco SICILIAN €

(☑093 183 81 42; Via Zanardelli 1; ☺Tue-Sun) This bustling, popular place is a good cheap option in Noto, and locals like it too. There are several vegetarian options and the fish is fresh and delicious.

⭐**Il Liberty** MODERN SICILIAN €€

(☑093 157 32 26; www.illiberty.com; Via Cavour 40; meals €27-35; ☺Tue-Sun) The vaulted dining room makes an atmospheric place to sample Milan-trained chef Giuseppe Angelino's contemporary spin on Sicilian cookery. An excellent local wine list supplements the inspired menu, which moves from superb appetisers like *millefoglie* – wafer-thin layers of crusty cheese and ground pistachios layered with minty sweet-and-sour vegetables – straight through to desserts like warm cinnamon-ricotta cake with homemade orange compote.

⭐**Trattoria del Crocifisso da Baglieri** TRATTORIA €€

(☑093 157 11 51; www.ristorantecrocifisso.it; Via Principe Umberto 48; meals €30-35) High up the many stairs of Noto Alta, this Slow Food–acclaimed trattoria with an extensive wine list is a Noto favourite. The rustic antipasto is rich in creamy aubergine, fried fennel, olives, cheeses and so on, and this is a great place to taste a Sicilian classic, in season – *macco di fave* (broad bean puree) with ricotta and toasted breadcrumbs.

More high-quality Sicilian classics are to be enjoyed, such as *pasta con le sarde* (pasta with sardines) and *caserecce* (short handmade pasta) *alla Norma*. Meat eaters will be pleased with the juicy roast lamb or pork belly, while fish and seafood lovers can feast on stuffed squid and sea bass baked in salt.

I Sapori del Val di Noto MODERN SICILIAN €€

(☑093 183 93 22; Ronco Bernardo Leanti 9; meals €30; ☺lunch & dinner Tue-Sun) A wonderful family-run restaurant that bridges the traditional and the modern with ease and sophistication. Try the *caserecce* with a pistachio cream, or couscous with swordfish and *caponata* (pepper and tomato stew). Finish with a wonderful almond, lemon and chocolate cake. Slow Food recommended.

ICE CREAM & GRANITE

It's a heady claim, but some say Noto has the two best *gelaterie* (ice-cream shops) in the world. Facing off for the honours are the **Caffè Sicilia** (☑093 183 50 13; Corso Vittorio Emanuele 125; desserts from €2) and, just around the corner, Corrado Costanzo (p208). Of the two, Corrado has the better ice cream – try a lick of pistachio or *amaro* (dark liqueur) flavour – but Caffè Sicilia is famous for its *granite* (drinks made of crushed ice with fruit juice). Depending on the season, you could go for *fragolini* (tiny wild strawberries) or *gelsi* (mulberry) flavours, or stick to the classic *caffè* (coffee) or *mandorla* (almond).

Both places make superb *cassata* (made with ricotta cheese, chocolate and candied fruit), *dolci di mandorle* (almond cakes and sweets) and *torrone* (nougat).

Ristorante
Il Cantuccio   MODERN SICILIAN **€€**
(☑093 183 74 64; www.ristoranteilcantuccio.it; Via Cavour 12; meals €30-35; ⊘dinner Tue-Sun, lunch Sun) Chef Valentina presents a seasonally changing menu that combines familiar Sicilian ingredients in exciting new ways. Try her exquisite *gnocchi al pesto del Cantuccio* (ricotta-potato dumplings with basil, parsley, mint, capers, almonds and cherry tomatoes), then move on to memorable main courses such as lemon-stuffed bass with orange-fennel salad.

Ristorante Neas   SICILIAN **€€**
(☑093 157 35 38; Via Rocco Pirri 30; ⊘Tue-Sun) You'll find a high standard of both food and service at this place, which opens its terrace in summer. Try the *linguine allo scoglio* (with mixed seafood), or the legendary fish soup.

Dolceria Corrado
Costanzo   PASTRIES & CAKES **€**
(☑093 183 52 43; Via Silvio Spaventa 9) Just around the corner from Caffè Sicilia (p208), Costanzo is famous for its gelati, *torrone*, *dolci di mandorla* (almond sweets) and *cassata* (with ricotta, chocolate and candied fruit).

Drinking

Anche gli Angeli   LOUNGE BAR
(☑093 157 60 23; www.anchegliangeli.com; Via A da Brescia 2) A lounge bar, 'concept store', restaurant and live-music venue, this is an incredible space in a small town such as Noto. Sitting inside several vaulted rooms with exposed brick walls, it stocks books and clothes and numerous Sicilian delicacies and serves food, but it's best for a snack, several drinks and listening to the live music or DJ sets.

❶ Information

EMERGENCIES
Police station (☑093 183 52 02; Via Brindisi 1)

TOURIST INFORMATION
Tourist office (☑093 157 37 79; www.comune. noto.sr.it; Piazza XVI Maggio; ⊘9am-1pm & 3-8pm)

❶ Getting There & Around

BUS
Regular **AST** (☑840 000323; www.azienda-sicilianatrasporti.it) and **Interbus** (☑093 52 24 60; www.interbus.it) services run to/from Syracuse (€3.40, one hour) and Catania (€8.10, 1½ hours). Buy tickets at **Bar Efirmedio** (Via di Piemonte 6) near the bus station on Largo Pantheon. Local year-round buses also connect with Noto Marina.

CAR
The SS115 connects Noto with Syracuse, about 36km to the northeast.

TRAIN
Regular trains run from Syracuse (€3.45, 35 minutes, eight Monday to Saturday, one Sunday), but the station is located about 1.5km south of the historic centre.

The Noto Coast

Noto's coastal satellite is **Lido di Noto**, a typical beach town of holiday villas and resort hotels that's practically deserted for 10 months of the year.

Further down, at Sicily's southeastern point, the cape offers little in the way of excitement, but its electric colours, laid-back atmosphere and relative lack of development make it a relaxing stopoff. The main centre is **Pachino**, a busy market town surrounded by fertile vineyards, while Marzamemi, 5km away, is a quiet fishing town that doubles as a low-key summer resort.

On the road between the two, Cantina Rudinì (☑093 159 53 33; www.vinirudini.it; Contrada Camporeale) is a good place to stock up on the local Nero d'Avola wine. Once in Marzamemi, a fish meal at Ristorante Giramapao (☑093 184 11 49; Via Marzamemi 77; meals €38; ☺Tue-Sun) does wonders for the soul, especially if it's grilled catch-of-the-day accompanied by a carafe of local wine.

From Marzamemi the road follows the coast south to Portopalo di Capo Passero, a popular summer hang-out. The small island off the coast is Isola Capo Passero, with a castle and nature reserve.

In between Noto and the cape are several sights worth stopping at.

Eloro
ARCHAEOLOGICAL SITE

(☺9am-1pm) FREE Just south of Lido di Noto is this archaeological site, where the sparse ruins of the 7th-century-BC Syracusan colony of Helorus lie in lush green grass. It's an attractive setting, even if it's quite hard to make out what you're looking at. In fact, excavations have so far unearthed a portion of the city walls, a small temple dedicated to Demeter and a theatre. On either side of the hill are long, sandy beaches.

Riserva Naturale Oasi Faunistica di Vendicari
PARK

(☑093 16 74 50; ☺7am-8pm Apr-Oct, 7am-5pm Nov-Mar) FREE Butting onto the ruins of Eloro is a wonderful stretch of wild coastline encompassing three separate marshes and a number of sandy beaches. From the main entrance (signposted off the Noto–Pachino road), it's about a 10-minute walk to the nearest beach, where you can pick up a path along the coast.

The reserve, which boasts its own Swabian tower and an abandoned tuna-processing plant, is an important marine environment, providing sanctuary to resident and migratory birds, including the black-winged stilt, the stork, wild goose and flamingo. Observation posts enable you to watch in relative comfort.

Villa Romana del Tellaro
ROMAN SITE

(☑338 9733084; www.villaromanadeltellaro.com; adult/reduced €6/3; ☺9am-7pm) Going south towards Pachino on the main SP19 brings you to this Roman villa harbouring some fascinating mosaics. The villa was largely destroyed by fire in the 4th century, but painstaking excavation has brought to light fragments of the original floor mosaics, which depict hunting scenes and episodes from Greek mythology.

La Corte del Sole Cooking Lessons
COOKING COURSE

(☑320 820210; www.lacortedelsole.it; Contrada Bucachemi; per person €55-126) Overlooking the green fields of Eloro is this stylish hotel housed in a traditional Sicilian *masseria* (fortified farmhouse). A delightful place to stay, it also offers a range of activities including cooking lessons (from three hours €55) run by the hotel chef and, in winter, tours to study the 80 or so types of wild orchids found in the area.

Modica

POP 54,720 / ELEV 296M

With its steeply stacked medieval centre and spectacular baroque cathedral, Modica is one of southern Sicily's most atmospheric towns. But unlike some of the other Unesco-listed cities in the area, it doesn't package its treasures into a single easy-to-see street or central piazza: rather, they are spread around the town and take some discovering. It can take a little while to orientate yourself in Modica but once you've got the measure of the bustling streets and steep staircases you'll find a warm, genuine town with a welcoming vibe and a strong sense of pride.

An important Greek and Roman city, Modica's heyday came in the 14th century when, as the personal fiefdom of the Chiaramonte family, it was one of the most powerful cities in Sicily.

⊙ Sights & Activities

Chiesa di San Giorgio & Modica Alta
CHURCH

(Corso San Giorgio; ☺8am-1pm & 3.30-7.30pm) The high point of a trip to Modica – quite literally as it's up in Modica Alta – is the Chiesa di San Giorgio, one of Sicily's most extraordinary baroque churches. Considered Rosario Gagliardi's great masterpiece, it stands in isolated splendour at the top of a majestic 250-step staircase, its sumptuous three-tiered facade towering above the medieval alleyways of the historic centre.

The glitzy interior, a sun-lit kaleidoscope of silvers, golds and egg-shell blues, displays all the hallmarks of early-18th-century Sicilian baroque.

Chiesa di San Giovanni Evangelista
CHURCH

(off Piazza San Giovanni) Marking the top of Modica Alta is this grand baroque church, prefaced by a sweeping staircase. Nearby, located at the end of Via Pizzo, a viewing balcony offers great panoramas over the old town.

Corso Umberto I
STREET

Bisecting Modica Bassa, Corso Umberto I is the place to lap up the lively local atmosphere. A wide avenue flanked by graceful palaces, churches, restaurants, bars and boutiques, it is where the locals come to parade during the evening *passeggiata*. Originally a raging river ran through town, but after major flood damage in 1902 it was dammed and Corso Umberto was built over it.

Obvious landmarks include the **Cattedrale di San Pietro** (Corso Umberto I), an impressive church atop a rippling staircase lined with life-sized statues of the apostles; and the **Chiesa Santa Maria del Carmine** (Piazza Matteoti; ⊙ 9am-1pm & 4-7.30pm), also known as Santa Maria dell'Annunziata.

For a break from baroque, head off the *corso* to Via Grimaldi where the **Chiesa Rupestre di San Nicolò Inferiore** (Piazzetta Grimaldi; admission €2; ⊙ 10am-1pm Mon-Sat, 4-7pm daily) boasts some rich Byzantine frescoes. Ring the bell for admission.

Back on the main street, next to the tourist office in Palazzo della Cultura, the **Museo Civico** (Corso Umberto I 149; admission €3; ⊙ 10am-1pm & 4-7pm Tue-Sun) houses Modica's collection of archaeological finds from Modica and Cava d'Ispica, dating back to the Neolithic period.

Eating

Taverna Nicastro
SICILIAN €

(☑ 093 294 58 84; Via S Antonino 28; meals €14-20; ⊙ dinner Tue-Sat) With over 60 years of history and a long-standing Slow Food recommendation, this is one of the upper town's most authentic and atmospheric restaurants, and a bargain to boot. The carnivore-friendly menu includes grilled meat, boiled veal, lamb stew and pasta specialities such as ricotta ravioli with pork *ragù*.

La Rusticana
TRATTORIA €

(☑ 093 294 29 50; Viale Medaglie d'Oro 34; meals €25; ⊙ dinner daily, lunch Sun) A rustic trattoria in Modica Bassa, close to the railway station, where you can try hearty country fare from the region, such as *focaccia* stuffed with potato and onion, or ricotta and sausage, and bean and vegetable minestrone. Mains range from roast rabbit to lamb, though there is fish on the menu too. It's cheap and charming, and Slow Food recommended.

Dolceria Bonajuto
CHOCOLATE €

(☑ 093 294 12 25; www.bonajuto.it; Corso Umberto I 159; ⊙ 9am-1.30pm Mon-Sat, 4.30-8.30pm daily) Sicily's oldest chocolate factory is the perfect place to taste Modica's famous chocolate. Flavoured with cinnamon, vanilla, orange peel and even hot peppers, it's a legacy of the town's Spanish overlords who imported cocoa from their South American colonies.

Osteria dei Sapori Perduti
SICILIAN €

(☑ 093 294 42 47; Corso Umberto I 228-230; meals €15-21; ⊙ Wed-Mon) On Modica's main drag, this attractive restaurant mixes rustic decor, elegantly dressed waiters, and very reasonable prices on Sicilian specialities like *cunigghju â stimpirata* (sweet and sour rabbit).

Fattoria delle Torri
SEAFOOD €€

(☑ 093 275 12 86; Vico Napolitano 14, Modica Alta; meals from €35; ⊙ closed Sun evening & Mon) This is one of Modica's smartest restaurants. Housed in an elegant 18th-century *palazzo*, it has a beautiful dining area with tables set under stone arches and bay windows looking onto a small internal garden. The seafood is particularly gorgeous, especially when combined with a crisp, dry white wine such as Cerasuolo di Vittoria.

BEST PIAZZAS

➡ Piazza del Duomo (p192) – Syracuse's refined outdoor drawing room is set around the city's triumphal Duomo.

➡ Piazza Municipio (p205) – Noto's golden baroque architecture surrounds this graceful square.

➡ Piazza Duomo (p213) – sloping down from Ragusa's fairy-tale cathedral, this is an open-air masterpiece.

➡ Piazza del Popolo (p203) – an impressive baroque square in the charming and oft-overlooked country town of Palazzolo Acreide.

➡ Corso Umberto I (above) – OK, so it's not a piazza, but Modica's lively central street cuts a dashing swath.

CHIARAMONTE GULFI

Some 20km north of Ragusa, Chiaramonte Gulfi is a delightful hilltop town with a gastronomic reputation. It produces a highly rated olive oil accredited with the *Denominazione d'Origine Protetta* (DOP) quality rating and is famed for its pork products.

The place to buy ham, and indeed to lunch on superb pork, is **Ristorante Majore** (☑093 292 80 19; www.majore.it; Via dei Martiri Ungheresi 12; meals €20-25; ☺Tue-Sun), a much-acclaimed trattoria just off central Piazza Duomo. It's unpretentious and old-school, and the menu is unapologetically meaty, with signature dishes *risotto alla majore* (with pork *ragù* and local cheese) and *falsomagro alla siciliana* (pork meatballs stuffed with salami, cheese, eggs and carrot).

To build up an appetite, wander the knot of old medieval streets in the historic centre and crow over the vast views. There are also eight museums in town, the most interesting of which is the **Museo dell'Olio** (Olive Oil Museum; ☑093 271 11 11; www.comune.chiaramonte.rg.it; admission €1; ☺8.30am-1.30pm Mon-Fri, 9.30am-1pm & 3-6pm Sat & Sun) in Palazzo Montesanto. The highlight is an olive press from 1614, but there's also a collection of old farming tools and other curios relating to rural life.

To get to Chiaramonte Gulfi from Ragusa, the shortest and most scenic drive is via the SP10.

La Locanda del Colonnello SICILIAN €€ (☑093 275 24 23; Vico Biscari 6; meals €25-30; ☺lunch & dinner Wed-Mon) This Slow Food restaurant is a fantastic place to try Sicilian specialities with an original twist – the *macco di fave* with roasted octopus is a winner. Also try the ravioli stuffed with ricotta and marjoram in a pork sauce. A real feast is roast lamb with potatoes. Finish it all off with a smooth *gelo di limone* (lemon jelly).

🛈 Orientation

Modica is divided into two parts: Modica Alta (Upper Modica) and Modica Bassa (Lower Modica). Whether driving or coming by public transport you'll arrive in Modica Bassa. The main street here, Corso Umberto I, forms the bottom of the V-shaped wedge on which the historic centre sits. Most hotels and restaurants are in Modica Bassa, within easy walking distance of Corso Umberto, although the cathedral and a number of churches are in the high town. It's a fairly tough climb to the top.

🛈 Information

EMERGENCIES
Police station (☑093 276 92 11; Via del Campo Sportivo 48)

TOURIST INFORMATION
Tourist office (☑093 275 96 34; www.comune.modica.rg.it; Corso Umberto I 141; ☺9am-1pm & 3.30-7.30pm Mon-Sat, 10am-1pm Sun)

🛈 Getting There & Around

BUS
Modica's bus station is at Piazzale Falcone-Borsellino at the top end of Corso Umberto I. From here buses run to/from Syracuse (€6, 2½ hours, nine daily Monday to Saturday, four Sunday), Noto (€3.90, 1½ hours, three daily Monday to Saturday, one Sunday) and Ragusa (€2.40, 25 minutes, hourly Monday to Saturday, four Sunday).

CAR
From Noto to Modica it's about 40km along the SS115.

Parking can be a problem, particularly if you arrive mid-morning. A good place to try is Corso Garibaldi (turn right at the Cattedrale di San Pietro).

TRAIN
There are trains to Ragusa (€2.25, 20 minutes, four to five Monday to Saturday) and Syracuse (€7, 1¾ hours, four Monday to Saturday).

South of Modica

Scicli

About 10km southwest of Modica, Scicli is a pleasant country town with a charming baroque centre and a pretty, palm-fringed central piazza. Overlooking everything is a rocky peak topped by an abandoned church, the **Chiesa di San Matteo**. It's not too hard

Ragusa

a walk up to the church to admire the views over town – simply follow the yellow sign up from Palazzo Beneventano and keep going for about 10 minutes.

Cava d'Ispica

Stretching for some 13km between Modica and Ispica, the Cava d'Ispica (☎ 0932 95 11 33; admission €2; ☺ 9am-1.30pm Mon-Sat) is a verdant gorge studded with thousands of natural caves and grottoes. Evidence of human habitation dates to about 2000 BC, and over the millennia the caves have served as Neolithic tombs, early Christian catacombs and medieval dwellings. A number of rock churches also survive from the Byzantine period. The canyon, accessible from the Noto side of Ispica (it's signposted off the main Noto–Ispica SS115), is not always open so check ahead with the Modica tourist office.

Ragusa

POP 72,755 / ELEV 502M

Set amidst the rocky peaks northwest of Modica, Ragusa is a town of two faces. Sitting on the top of the hill is Ragusa Superiore, a busy workaday town with sensible grid-pattern streets and all the trappings of a modern provincial capital, while etched into the hillside further down is Ragusa Ibla. This sloping area of tangled alleyways, grey stone houses and baroque *palazzi* is effectively Ragusa's historic centre and it's quite magnificent.

Like every other town in the region, Ragusa Ibla (the old town) collapsed after the 1693 earthquake and a new town, Ragusa Superiore, was built on a high plateau above. But the old aristocracy was loath to leave the tottering *palazzi* and rebuilt Ragusa Ibla on exactly the same spot. The two towns were merged in 1927.

◉ Sights & Activities

Cattedrale di San Giorgio   CATHEDRAL
(Piazza Duomo; ☺ 10am-12.30pm & 4-6.30pm) At the top end of the sloping Piazza Duomo is the town's pride and joy, the mid-18th century cathedral with its magnificent neoclassical dome and stained-glass windows. It's set high above a grand staircase behind a palatial iron gate (the entrance is up the stairs to the left of the church). One of Rosario Gagliardi's finest accomplishments, its extravagant convex facade rises like a three-tiered wedding cake, supported by gradually narrowing Corinthian columns and punctuated by jutting cornices. The interior is not

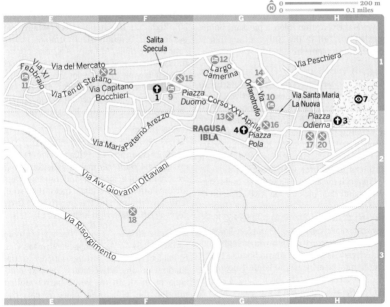

quite as sumptuous, although there are two paintings by Dario Guerci and a statue of St George on horseback.

Ragusa Ibla   HISTORIC CENTRE

Ragusa Ibla is a joy to wander, its labyrinthine lanes weaving through rock-grey *palazzi* to open onto beautiful, sun-drenched piazzas. It's easy to get lost but you can never go too far wrong, and sooner or later you'll end up at **Piazza Duomo**, Ragusa's sublime central square.

East of the piazza, Corso XXV Aprile leads down to a second eye-catching Gagliardi church, **Chiesa di San Giuseppe** (Piazza Pola), with an elliptical interior topped by a cupola decorated with a fresco of the Gloria di San Benedetto (Glory of St Benedict, 1793) by Sebastiano Lo Monaco. Further downhill, to the right of the entrance of the Giardino Ibleo, you can see the Catalan Gothic portal of what was once the large **Chiesa di San Giorgio Vecchio**, but is now mostly ruined. In the lunette there is an interesting bas-relief of St George killing the dragon.

At the other end of Ragusa Ibla, the **Chiesa del Purgatorio** (Piazza della Repubblica) is one of the few churches in town to have survived the great 1693 earthquake.

Ragusa

Giardino Ibleo GARDENS

(⏰8am-8pm) At the eastern end of the old town is the Giardino Ibleo, a pleasant public garden laid out in the 19th century that is perfect for a picnic lunch.

Ragusa Superiore NEIGHBOURHOOD

One of the best reasons for heading up to Ragusa's modern and less-attractive half is to walk down again. It takes about half an hour to descend the *Salita Commendatore*, a winding pass of stairs and narrow archways that leads down to Ragusa Ibla past the Chiesa di Santa Maria delle Scale, a 15th-century church with great views.

To reach the Salita, follow Corso Italia eastwards and then pick up Via XXIV Maggio.

The main attraction up top is the Duomo di San Giovanni Battista (☎093 262 16 58; www.cattedralesangiovanni.it; Piazza San Giovanni), a vast 19th-century church whose highly ornate facade is set off by Mario Spada's pretty campanile. Nearby, below Ponte Nuovo, the Museo Archeologico Ibleo (☎093 262 29 63; Via Natalelli; admission €3; ⏰9am-1.30pm & 4-7.30pm) houses finds from the 6th-century-BC Greek settlement of Kamarina on the coast.

🍴 Eating

Ragusa has a good selection of eateries ranging from luxury fine-dining restaurants to cheerful neighbourhood trattorias. Most of the best are in Ragusa Ibla.

Il Barocco TRADITIONAL ITALIAN €

(☎093 265 23 97; Via Orfanotrofio 29; meals €17-30) This beloved traditional restaurant has an evocative setting in an old stable block, the troughs now filled with wine bottles instead of water. At the *enoteca* (wine bar) next door, you can taste cheeses and olive oil and purchase other exquisite Sicilian edibles.

Quattro Gatti SICILIAN €

(☎093 224 56 12; Via Valverde 95; meals €18; ⏰dinner, closed Mon Oct-May & Sun Jun-Sep) This fabulous Sicilian-Slovak-run eatery near the Giardini Iblei serves an amazing four-course fixed-price menu bursting with fresh, local flavours. The antipasti spread is especially memorable, as are the seasonally changing specials scribbled on the blackboard up front. Slovak-inspired offerings such as goulash and apple strudel round out a menu of Sicilian classics.

Ai Lumi Trattoria SICILIAN €

(☎093 262 12 24; Corso XXV Aprile 16; €25-30) Right on the main street, where the *passeggiata* (evening stroll) unfolds before your dining table, Ai Lumi is a great opportunity to eat well in elegant surroundings without having to pay a lot for the experience. The fish soup is a favourite, and the fish and meat menus offer local delicacies. Enjoy some wine too and watch Ragusa stroll.

Gelati DiVini GELATO €

(☎093 222 89 89; www.gelatidivini.it; Piazza Duomo 20; ice cream from €2; ⏰10am-midnight) This exceptional *gelateria* makes wine-flavoured ice creams like marsala and muscat, plus unconventional offerings including rose, fennel, wild mint and the surprisingly tasty *gocce verdi*, made with local olive oil.

Cucina e Vino MODERN SICILIAN €€

(☎093 268 64 47; Via Orfanotrofio 91; meals €33; ⏰Thu-Tue) Whether sitting outside in the shadow of the 18th-century Palazzo Battaglia or inside in the white barrel-vaulted interior, this is a lovely place to eat. The menu – in fact there are two, one for fish and one for meat – is more ambitious than most in this price bracket, with adventurous antipasti and unusual mains such as *cernia* (grouper) served with onion marmalade.

Friendly service and a decent wine list round off the evening. It's Slow Food recommended.

La Rusticana TRATTORIA €€

(☎093 222 79 81; Corso XXV Aprile 68; meals €25; ⏰Wed-Mon) Fans of the *Montalbano* TV series will want to eat here, as it's where scenes set in the fictional Trattoria San Calogero were filmed. In reality, it's a cheerful, boisterous trattoria whose generous portions and relaxed vine-covered terrace ensure a loyal clientele. The food is defiantly *casareccia* (home-style), so expect no-frills pasta and uncomplicated cuts of grilled meat. Slow Food recommended.

Orfeo SICILIAN €€

(☎093 262 10 35; Via Sant'Anna 117; meals €25-30; ⏰Mon-Sat) Up in Ragusa Superiore, this is a long-standing Ragusa address. The setting is not the most beautiful in town, but the traditional cuisine continues to find favour with locals and visiting business people who come for classics like *polpette con piselli* (meatballs with peas) or gnocchi *radiccio e provola al fumo* (with red chicory and smoked cheese).

★ **Ristorante Duomo** MODERN SICILIAN €€€
(☑ 093 265 12 65; Via Capitano Bocchieri 31; meals €90-100, tasting menus €135-140) This is generally regarded as one of Sicily's best restaurants. Behind the stained-glass door, small rooms are outfitted like private parlours, ensuring a suitably romantic ambience for Chef Ciccio Sultano's refined creations. These combine ingredients in an imaginative and unconventional way while making constant use of classic Sicilian ingredients such as pistachios, fennel, almonds and Nero d'Avola wine. Booking is essential.

Locanda Don Serafino SICILIAN €€€
(☑ 093 224 87 78; Via Giovanni Ottaviano; tasting menu €78; ☺ Wed-Mon) This memorable restaurant might be housed in a series of rocky caves, but the look is elegant yet understated, with warm lighting, starched-white tables and bare rock walls. The food is traditional with a modern twist: try the lasagnette with cocoa and ricotta cheese, or rabbit with bacon and Sicilian pistachio nuts. Reservations recommended.

Orientation

If you're driving, follow signs to Ragusa Ibla, where the main sights, hotels and restaurants are. Leave your car in one of the signposted car parks and walk into town. From the car park under Piazza della Repubblica it's a 10-minute walk or so to the central Piazza Duomo – follow Via Del Mercato, then Via XI Febbraio; go left up Via Ten Di Stefano then along its continuation, Via Capitano Bocchieri. If taking public transport you will arrive in Ragusa Superiore, whose main streets are Via Roma and Corso Italia. From the upper town a local bus runs down to Giardino Ibleo in Ragusa Ibla.

ⓘ Information

Police Station (☑ 093 262 49 22; Via Mario Rapisardi)

ⓘ Getting There & Around

BUS

AST (www.aziendasicilianatrasporti.it) and **Interbus-Etna Trasporti** (www.etnatrasporti.it) buses serve the bus station at Via Zama in Ragusa Superiore. There are regular connections to Catania (€8.30, one hour and 50 minutes), Syracuse (€6.90, 2¼ hours) and Modica (€2.40, 25 minutes). City buses 1 and 3 run from Piazza del Popolo in the upper town to Piazza Pola and the Giardino Ibleo in Ragusa Ibla.

CAR

If coming from Modica 15km away, or Syracuse some 90km to the northeast, take the SS115.

Unless your hotel has parking or can advise you on where to park, your best bet is to leave your car at the car park below Piazza della Repubblica in Ragusa Ibla; much of the old town is closed to nonresidential traffic.

TAXI

Call ☑ 093 224 41 09.

TRAIN

Trains run to Modica (€2.25, 20 minutes, five to six Monday to Saturday) and Syracuse (€7.65, two hours, two Monday to Saturday).

Central Sicily

Best Places to Eat

➡ Coria (p230)
➡ Amici Miei (p225)
➡ Il Locandiere (p230)
➡ Vicolo Duomo (p232)
➡ Antica Hostaria (p222)

Best Places to Sleep

➡ Tre Metri Sopra Il Cielo (p267)
➡ Suite d'Autore (p267)
➡ Azienda Agrituristica Gigliotto (p267)
➡ Baglio San Pietro (p266)
➡ Baglio Pollicarini (p266)

Why Go?

Sicily's wild and empty interior is a beautiful, uncompromising land, a timeless landscape of silent, sunburnt peaks, grey stone villages and forgotten valleys. Traditions live on and life is lived at a gentle, rural pace. It's an area that encourages the simple pleasures – long lunches of earthy country food, meandering through hilltop towns, enjoying the scenery.

The newly reopened Villa Romana del Casale, in Piazza Armerina, is a must-see, and the handsome town of Caltagirone has some stunning ceramics and an awesome staircase. Enna, a busy provincial capital, boasts a striking medieval centre and some great hilltop views of the surrounding mountainous region. Northeast of Enna, a string of hilltop towns make for excellent touring.

Road Distances (KM)

	Caltagirone	Caltanissetta	Enna	Nicosia
Caltanissetta	85			
Enna	60	30		
Nicosia	100	65	50	
Piazza Armerina	30	50	35	70

Getting Around

Central Sicily is best explored by car – there are bus connections between the towns, but for dipping into hidden villages and taking in the mountain views, your own wheels are priceless.

THREE PERFECT DAYS

Start in the Past

Make an early start in Piazza Armerina and beat the coach parties to the recently reopened Villa Romana del Casale (p226). Once you've applauded the villa's extraordinary Roman mosaics, head out to Morgantina (p229) to investigate the ruins of an ancient Greek city. Spend the late afternoon exploring Piazza Armerina's historic centre, making sure to head up the hill to the landmark cathedral (p224). Round the day off with a relaxed trattoria meal at Amici Miei (p225) or a more formal dinner at Al Fogher (p225).

Explore Caltagirone

Make your way to Caltagirone, a delightful hilltop town known for its ceramics. Get into the swing of things by climbing the Scalinata di Santa Maria del Monte (p229) and inspecting the Museo della Ceramica (p230). Clear your head with a wander around the Giardino Pubblico (p230), a pretty shaded park with views over to Mt Etna, then while away the rest of the day admiring the attractive old town and its fancy baroque churches.

Hilltop Hoods

Lording it over the hills and valleys of central Sicily, Enna is the king of the area's hilltop towns. Visit its impregnable Castello di Lombardia (p220) and the impressive Duomo (p221) before heading over the valley to Calascibetta. Afterwards push on to Nicosia, another handsome hilltop town, with a grand central square and 14th-century cathedral.

Getting Away from It All

→ **Morgantina** Head out to the these ancient ruins, spread over two windswept hills.

→ **Regaleali** One of Sicily's most important wine estates, this is about as remote as it gets.

→ **Lago di Pozzillo** Stock up on picnic provisions and head out to this picturesque lake in the hills between Agira and Regalbuto.

DON'T MISS

Ogle bikini-clad girls and mythical macho men at the thrilling mosaics in Villa Romana del Casale (p226), depicting episodes from ancient mythology, hunting scenes and groups of lasses working out with weights.

Best Hilltop Towns

→ Caltagirone (p229)

→ Enna (p220)

→ Calascibetta (p223)

→ Nicosia (p223)

Best Lookouts

→ Castello Di Lombardia (p220)

→ Centuripe

→ Scalinata di Santa Maria del Monte (p229)

→ Piazza Armerina's cathedral (p224)

→ Aidone (p227)

Resources

→ **Turismo Enna** (www.turismoenna.it) Info on sights, monuments and transport in Enna and its environs.

→ **Piazza Net** (www.piazzanet.it) Inspirational rather than practical info on Piazza Armerina, its history, monuments and events.

→ **Comune di Caltagirone** (www.comune.caltagirone.ct.it) Difficult to navigate but has listings, transport and historical background.

Central Sicily Highlights

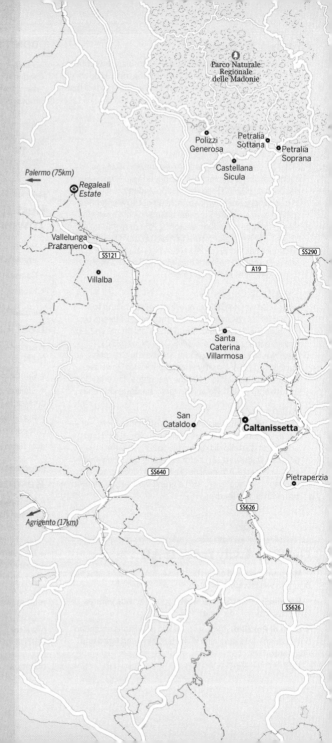

1 Visit the newly reopened **Villa Romana del Casale** (p226), in Piazza Armerina, with its magnificent mosaics.

2 Be facinated by **Morgantina** (p229), the remains of an ancient Greek city.

3 Check out Piazza Armerina's historic centre and **cathedral** (p224).

4 Climb Caltagirone's **Scalinata di Santa Maria del Monte** (p229), the most spectacular staircase you're ever likely to see.

5 Visit the beautiful hilltop towns of **Enna** (p220) and **Nicosia** (p223).

Parco Naturale Regionale delle Madonie

Polizzi Generosa

Petralia Sottana

Petralia Soprana

Castellana Sicula

Palermo (75km)

Regaleali Estate

Vallelunga Pratameno

SS121

SS290

A19

Villalba

Santa Caterina Villarmosa

San Cataldo

Caltanissetta

SS640

Pietraperzia

Agrigento (17km)

SS626

SS626

ENNA

POP 28,100 / ELEV 931M

Italy's highest provincial capital, Enna stands above the hills and valleys of central Sicily. The town is a dramatic sight, seemingly impregnable atop a precipitous mountain. Inside you'll discover a calm working centre with a handsome medieval core and, cloud cover permitting, some fabulous views. There's not enough to warrant an extended stay but it is a great place to escape the tourist pack and enjoy some cool mountain air, particularly in summer when the sun bakes everything around to a yellow crisp.

The city has a long and varied history. In ancient times it was famous as the centre of a cult of Demeter, but its strategic position meant that it was often fought over, and successive waves of colonising forces conquered it, including the Carthaginians, Romans, Byzantines and Arabs. In 1087 the Normans wrested it from the Arabs and turned it into an important fortified town. Throughout much of its history, it remained an important agricultural centre, supplying far-flung places with grain, wheat, cotton and cane, a tradition that continues today, albeit on a far smaller scale.

The Museo Alessi houses the valuable contents of the cathedral's treasury. It was unfortunately closed in April 2007 due to a lack of funds, and locals and visitors are still eagerly awaiting its reopening – if it has reopened when you visit, check out the museum's collection, originally the property of Canon Giuseppe Alessi (1774–1837), who left it to his brother with the intention that he then donate it to the Church.

The town of Enna is split in two: the hilltop historic centre, Enna Alta, and the modern town, Enna Bassa, below. Everything of interest is up in Enna Alta.

⊙ Sights & Activities

Castello Di Lombardia   CASTLE
(☎ 093 550 09 62; ⊙ 9am-8pm summer, to 4pm winter) **FREE** One of Sicily's most formidable castles guards Enna's highest point, at the easternmost edge of the historic centre. The original castle was built by the Saracens and later reinforced by the Normans; Frederick II of Hohenstaufen ordered that a powerful curtain wall be built with towers on every side.

The wall is still intact but only six of the original 20 towers remain, of which the tallest is the Torre Pisano (Castello di Lombardia, Piazza Mazzini; ⊙ 9am-8pm) **FREE**, which you can climb from the Cortile dei Cavalieri, one of the castle's well-preserved inner courtyards. From the top, there are fabulous views over the valley to the town of Calascibetta and to Mt Etna in the northeast.

Torre di Federico II   TOWER
(Via Torre di Federico; ⊙ 8am-6pm) **FREE** Secret passageways once led to this octagonal tower, which now stands in Enna's public gardens. Once part of the town's old defence system, it stands nearly 24m high.

Rocca Di Cerere   TEMPLE
Just below the entrance to the castle is a huge rock, which was once home to Enna's Temple of Demeter (Ceres to the Romans), goddess of fertility and agriculture. The temple, built in 480 BC by the tyrant Gelon,

Enna

is supposed to have featured a statue of King Triptolemus, the only mortal to witness the rape of Demeter's daughter Persephone.

There's not much left of the temple now, but the rocky platform, accessible by a series of steep steps, is a great place for a picnic or to take in the sunset.

Duomo CATHEDRAL
(Via Roma; ☺ 9am-1pm & 4-7pm) The Duomo is the most impressive of the historic buildings that line Via Roma, Enna's showpiece street. Built over 200 years after the original Gothic cathedral burnt down in 1446, it boasts an imposing facade, complete with a square 17th-century belltower, and a truly sumptuous interior.

Traces remain of the original church, including the transept and polygonal apses, but the rest is pure baroque, including an ornamental coffered wood ceiling, hanging chandeliers and a dramatic, scene-stealing altar. Other points of interest include the bases of the grey basalt columns, decorated with grotesque carvings of snakes with human heads; the pulpit and stoup, both set on Greco-Roman remains from the Temple of Demeter; 17th-century presbytery paintings by Filippo Paladino; and the altarpieces by Guglielmo Borremans.

**Museo Archeologico di
Palazzo Varisano** MUSEUM
(☎ 093 5507 6304; Piazza Mazzini 8; ☺ 9am-1pm Mon-Fri) FREE This museum reopened in 2011 after years of closure. It has a good collection of local artefacts (labelled in Italian) excavated from throughout the region, as well as objects borrowed from Syracuse's and Agrigento's archaeological museums. Of particular interest is the Attic-style red-and-black *krater* (drinking vase) found in the town itself.

Palazzo Pollicarini PALACE
(Via Roma) On the southwestern side of Piazza Colaianni next to the Grande Albergo Sicilia, is this Catalan-Gothic *palazzo*, one of Enna's most handsome buildings. Although it has been converted into private apartments, you can still nip in to take a peek at the medieval staircase in the central courtyard.

Piazzas PIAZZA
As you continue down Via Roma, you eventually come to Piazza Vittorio Emanuele II, Enna's main square. Forming much of the piazza's northern flank is the sombre bulk of the Chiesa di San Francesco d'Assisi and its 15th-century belltower. Just off the piazza is another small square, Piazza F Crispi, which commands sweeping views over the valley to Calascibetta.

In the centre of the piazza, graffiti emblazons the Fontana del Ratto di Prosperina, a monumental fountain commemorating Enna's most enduring legend (see p222).

Lago Di Pergusa SWIMMING
Surrounded by woodland about 9km south of town is one of Sicily's few natural lakes. It's a popular summer hang-out with some sandy beaches, a number of big resort-style hotels and an unlikely motor-racing circuit,

Enna

◉ Sights

THE MYTH OF PERSEPHONE

The tale of Hades' capture of Demeter's daughter Persephone (also known as Proserpina) is one of the most famous Greek myths. According to Homeric legend, Hades (god of the underworld) emerged from his lair and abducted Persephone while she was gathering flowers around Lago di Pergusa (p221). Not knowing where her daughter had disappeared to, Demeter (goddess of the harvest) forbade the earth to bear fruit as she wandered the world looking for her. Eventually, she turned to Zeus, threatening that if he didn't return her daughter she would inflict eternal famine on the world. Zeus submitted to her threat and ordered Hades to release Persephone, though stipulating that every year she should spend six months in the underworld with Hades and six months in Sicily with her mother. Demeter still mourns during Persephone's time in the underworld, bringing winter to the world; her joy at her daughter's return is heralded by the blossoms of springtime.

but out of season it's a rather forlorn place offering little reason to linger.

Certainly, there is nothing to connect it to the mythical tale of Persephone, for which it's so famous.

To get to the lake, take local bus 5 from the bus stop on Via Pergusa. By car it's signposted along the SS561.

⭐ Festivals & Events

Holy Week RELIGIOUS

The week building up to Easter is marked by solemn religious celebrations, during which the city's religious confraternities parade around in creepy capes and white hoods. The main events are on Palm Sunday, Good Friday and Easter Sunday.

Festa di Maria Santissima della Visitazione STREET CARNIVAL

Fireworks and scantily clad farmers mark the town's patron saint's day on 2 July. The farmers, dressed in white sheets, drag an effigy of the Madonna of the Visitation through town on a cart called La Nave d'Oro (Golden Ship).

🍴 Eating

Unlike the coast, the staple here is meat, and local dishes usually involve lamb or beef and a tasty array of mushrooms and grilled vegetables. Specialities include *castrato* (charcoal-grilled castrated ram) and *polpettone* (stuffed lamb or meatballs). Soups and sausages are also a feature.

La Fontana TRATTORIA €

(☑ 093 52 54 65; Via Volturno 6; meals €23; ☻ Tue-Sun) A long-standing trattoria opposite Piazza F Crispi, this is a relaxed spot for some filling Sicilian country fare, like *minestrone*

di verdura (vegetable minestrone) followed by grilled chicken or *fegato arrosto* (roast liver). There's seating in the cheerful interior or, in summer, on the panoramic piazza.

Antica Hostaria SICILIAN €€

(☑ 093 52 25 21; Via Castagna 9; meals €33; ☻ Wed-Mon) Housed in the stable block of an 18th-century *palazzo*, this is one of Enna's best restaurants. There's nothing especially memorable about the rustic decor but the food is another matter. The menu is seasonal, and past successes have included wild-asparagus risotto, fava-bean purée and roast pork with almonds. The wine list is also a cut above average with some fine Sicilian labels.

La Trinacria SICILIAN €€

(☑ 093 550 20 22; Viale Caterina Savoca 20; meals €30; ☻ Mon-Sat) A great restaurant on the scenic road down from the castle. Diners are met with a big welcoming smile and then plied with huge helpings of fabulous country food. Antipasti of ham, salami, fried croquettes, cheese, olives and marinated vegetables are followed by pharaonic pasta dishes and juicy cuts of roast meat.

It's a popular spot, which ensures a warm, boisterous atmosphere.

Ristorante Centrale SICILIAN €€

(☑ 093 550 09 63; www.ristorantecentrale.net; Piazza VI Dicembre 9; meals €25; ☻ Sun-Fri) This historic family-run restaurant has hosted a roll call of famous diners, including Italy's last king, Vittorio Emanuele III, and opera maestro Placido Domingo. Yet there's nothing fancy about the place, neither in look nor culinary style, with the onus on tried-and-tested dishes based on delicious local ingredients such as sausages, mushrooms and seasonal veggies.

ℹ Information

EMERGENCIES

Police (☎ 093 552 21 11; Via San Giovanni 2)

MEDICAL SERVICES

Ospedale Umberto I (☎ 093 551 61 11; Contrada Ferrante, Enna Bassa)

TOURIST INFORMATION

Tourist Information Point (☎ 093 556 15 34; Castello di Lombardia; ☉ 10am-6pm Mar-Oct) In the car park next to the castle.

ℹ Getting There & Around

BUS

The bus is the best way to reach Enna by public transport. Enna's **bus station** (Viale Diaz) is in the upper town: to get to the town centre from there, turn right and follow Viale Diaz to Corso Sicilia, turn right again and follow it to Via Sant'Agata, which leads to Via Roma, Enna Alta's main street. Service is more frequent from the stop in Enna Bassa, 3km downhill. Hourly local buses connect Enna Bassa with the upper town, except on Sundays when it's every two hours.

SAIS (☎ 093 550 09 02; www.saisautolinee. it) runs services to Catania (€7.50, 1¼ hours, 10 daily Monday to Friday, seven Saturday) and Palermo (€10, 1¾ hours, up to seven daily Monday to Friday, four Saturday). For Agrigento change at Caltanissetta (€4.20, one hour, six daily Monday to Friday, four Saturday). Regular buses also run to Piazza Armerina (€3.30, 30 minutes, nine daily Monday to Friday, five Saturday). Services to all destinations are drastically reduced on Sundays.

CAR

Enna is on the main Catania–Palermo A19 autostrada, about 83km from Catania, 135km from Palermo.

NORTH OF ENNA

Calascibetta

A densely packed maze of narrow streets set above a sheer precipice, Calascibetta was originally built by the Saracens during their siege of Enna in 951 and was later strengthened by the Norman king Roger I. The most impressive sight is the 14th-century Chiesa Madre (☉ 9am-1pm & 3-7pm), Calascibetta's landmark cathedral. Northwest 3km, the Necropoli di Realmese FREE is worth investigating, with some 300 rock tombs dating from 850 BC.

Nicosia

Set on four hills, this ancient town was once the most important of a chain of fortified Norman towns stretching from Palermo to Messina. Modern times have been tougher, and between 1950 and 1970 nearly half the town's population emigrated.

The centre of action is Piazza Garibaldi, a handsome square dominated by the elegant 14th-century facade and Catalan-Gothic campanile of the Cattedrale di San Nicolò. From the piazza, Via Salamone leads past crumbling Franco-Lombard *palazzi* to the Chiesa di Santa Maria Maggiore, a reconstruction of a 13th-century church destroyed by a landslide in 1757. Inside is a lovely marble polyptych by Gagini. From the terrace the ruins of a Norman castle are visible on a rocky crag above town.

Near the entrance to Nicosia, Baglio San Pietro (p266) has comfortable guest rooms and delicious wood-fired *porchetta* (suckling pig) on the restaurant menu; bookings are necessary.

SOUTH OF ENNA

South of Enna, the landscape becomes less dramatic, flattening out and taking on a more rural aspect as rugged mountain scenery gives way to gentle cultivated fields dotted with busy agricultural towns. The two main attractions are Piazza Armerina, celebrated for its Roman mosaics, and Caltagirone, a centre of traditional ceramic production. Both towns have decent accommodation and interesting historic centres. The remains of the Greek city of Morgantina, northeast of Aidone, are considerable and worth more than the trickle of visitors they receive.

Piazza Armerina

POP 20,900 / ELEV 697M

Set amid fertile farming country, this charming market town takes its name from the Colle Armerino, one of the three hills on which it is built. It is actually two towns in one: the original Piazza was founded by the Saracens in the 10th century on the slope of the Colle Armerino, while a 15th-century expansion to the southeast was redefined by an urban grid established in the 17th century.

Piazza Armerina

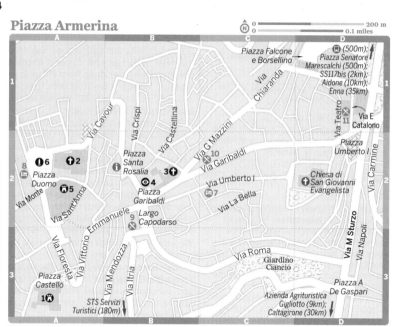

Piazza Armerina

You can easily spend a day or two pottering about its labyrinthine streets and visiting the extraordinary mosaics at the nearby Villa Romana del Casale. With the addition of some pleasant accommodation and tasty restaurants, Piazza Armerina becomes an unexpected treat.

◉ Sights & Activities

Historic Centre   HISTORIC QUARTER

Often overlooked by people rushing to the Villa Romana del Casale, Piazza's hilltop medieval centre is worth more than the passing glance that many people give it. The highpoint is the hilltop **cathedral** (Piazza Duomo; ☉8am-noon & 3.30-7pm). A landmark for miles around – the towering dome rises 66m – it's a huge, bulky affair with a severe 18th-century facade and an airy blue-and-white interior.

Of note is the altar painting, a copy of the Byzantine painting *Madonna delle Vittorie* (Virgin of the Victories), which was supposedly presented to Count Roger I by Pope Nicholas II. To the side of the main church, the 44m-high bell tower is a leftover from an earlier 14th-century church.

The handsome square in front of the cathedral affords splendid views of the surrounding countryside and is flanked by **Palazzo Trigona**, a baronial palace that has been earmarked to house a new archaeological museum. In the centre of the square, the **statue** is of Baron Marco Trigona, the aristocrat who financed the cathedral's construction.

Off Piazza Duomo is **Via Monte**, the arterial road of the 13th-century city, with its warren of tiny alleys fanning like the ribs of a fishbone. This is the town's most picturesque quarter. Alternatively, take Via Floresta, beside Palazzo Trigona, to arrive at the ruins of the 14th-century Castello Aragonese.

From the cathedral, Via Cavour hairpins down to Piazza Garibaldi, the elegant heart of the old town. Overlooking the square is Palazzo di Città, Piazza's refined town hall (closed to the public), and the Chiesa di San Rocco (known as the Fundrò), next to which there's a pretty internal courtyard.

✪ Festivals & Events

Palio Dei Normanni   STREET CARNIVAL
Piazza Armerina bursts into life on 13 and 14 August for its great annual event – a medieval pageant celebrating Count Roger's capture of the town from the Moors in 1087. Events kick off on the 13th with costumed parades and a reenactment of Count Roger being presented with the city keys.

The highlight on the 14th is the great joust, known as the *quintana*, between the four districts of the city – Monte, Canali, Castellina and Casalotto. At the end of the day the winning district is presented with a standard depicting Our Lady of the Victories.

✗ Eating

Da Totò   TRATTORIA €
(☑ 093 568 01 53; Via G Mazzini 27; meals €23; ⊘ Tue-Sun) Don't let the stark white lights and bland decor put you off, this popular trattoria serves excellent value-for-money food. Antipasti are of the ham, cheese and grilled veg variety, while pastas are paired with earthy sauces of porcini mushrooms or ripe local vegetables. Main courses are similarly unpretentious with peppered grilled steak a menu mainstay.

Service is friendly and the laid-back atmosphere conducive to a nice, relaxed meal.

★ Amici Miei   TRATTORIA €€
(☑ 093 568 35 41; Largo Capodarso 5; pizzas from €4.50, meals €25-30; ⊘ Fri-Wed) With its exposed stone walls, low wooden ceiling, wine racks and wood-fired pizza oven, this friendly trattoria perfectly looks the part. It's not just looks, though – the food is spot on. The pizzas are great – locals come here for takeaway – and the pastas hale and hearty.

Special mention should also go to the *antipasto della casa,* a fabulous platter of frittata, sliced pancetta, cheese, caponata, and ricotta with balsamic vinegar.

Ristorante Teatro   TRATTORIA €€
(☑ 093 58 56 62; Via Teatro 1; meals €25; ⊘ Thu-Tue) Dine in the shadow of Piazza Armerina's local theatre at this welcoming family-run trattoria. The theatre theme translates to framed theatre bills on the white walls and a showy roof fresco – better than the outside terrace – but the food is far from stagey. There are excellent pizzas, filling pastas and a huge range of meat dishes.

Al Fogher   MODERN SICILIAN €€€
(☑ 093 568 41 23; www.alfogher.net; Contrada Bellia SS117bis; meals €50; ⊘ closed Sun evening & Mon) This is one of central Sicily's top restaurants, serving sophisticated modern cuisine to a demanding and appreciative clientele. It's about 3km out of town, but your journey is rewarded with dishes such as suckling pig with tuna egg sauce and asparagus, or mullet served with yellow capsicum, wild rice and pistachio. Equal attention is given to the wine list, which contains up to 400 labels. Reservations required.

❶ Orientation

Orientate yourself from the large area comprising Piazza Generale A Cascino and Piazza Falcone e Borsellino, just off the main road through town. From here Via Mazzini leads down to Piazza Garibaldi, the old town's focal square. Most of the town's sights are an easy walk from here, including the cathedral at the top of Via Cavour.

❶ Information

Municipal Tourist Office (☑ 093 568 30 49; www.comune.piazzaarmerina.en.it; Piazza Santa Rosalia; ⊘ 9am-1pm & 3.30-7pm Mon-Fri)

❶ Getting There & Around

BUS
Interbus (www.interbus.it) runs a service to Catania (€8.90, 1¾ hours, two to four daily). **SAIS** (☑ 093 568 01 19; www.saisautolinee.it) buses connect Piazza Armerina with Enna (€3.40, 30 minutes, nine daily Monday to Friday, five Saturday).

CAR
The SS117bis links Piazza Armerina with Enna 33km to the north.

CENTRAL SICILY PIAZZA ARMERINA

Villa Romana del Casale

The Unesco-listed Villa Romana del Casale (☏093 568 00 36; www.villaromanadelcasale.it; adult/reduced €10/5; ☺9am-6pm summer, to 4pm winter) is central Sicily's biggest attraction, and it reopened in spring 2013 after years of reconstruction. It is decorated with the finest Roman floor mosaics in existence. The mosaics cover almost the entire floor of the villa and are considered unique for their natural, narrative style, the range of their subject matter and variety of colour.

Situated in a wooded valley 5km southwest of the town centre, the villa, sumptuous even by decadent Roman standards, is thought to have been the country retreat of Marcus Aurelius Maximianus, Rome's co-emperor during the reign of Diocletian (AD 286–305). Certainly, the size of the complex – four interconnected groups of buildings spread over the hillside – and the 3535 sq metres of multicoloured floor mosaics suggests a palace of imperial standing.

Following a landslide in the 12th century, the villa lay under 10m of mud for some 700 years, and was thus protected from the damaging effects of air, wind and rain. It was only when serious excavation work began in the 1950s that the mosaics were brought back to light.

The recent restoration covered almost the entire complex with a wooden roof, to protect the mosaics from the elements. There is an elevated walkway that allows visitors to view the mosaics and the structure in its entirety. Architects report a dissatisfaction with the structure for the lack of light, and the shadows that obscure the colours and vivacity of the mosaics, but the condition of the mosaics has been much improved. The challenge of further deterioration of the entire villa remains to be battled, but it's a pleasure to be able to enjoy this marvellous site once again.

If you want to arrange a guide, contact the Comune di Piazza Armerina (☏093 598 22 46) or STS Servizi Turistici (☏093 568 70 27; www.guardalasicilia.it; Via Scarpello 2-4); otherwise you can organise one directly at the site.

◎ Sights

Thermae   ROMAN SITE
To the north of the villa's main entrance, which leads through the remnants of a triumphal arch into an elegant atrium (forecourt), is the villa's baths complex. Accessible via the palaestra (gymnasium), which has a

Villa Romana del Casale

⊛N 0 — 100 m
0 — 0.05 miles

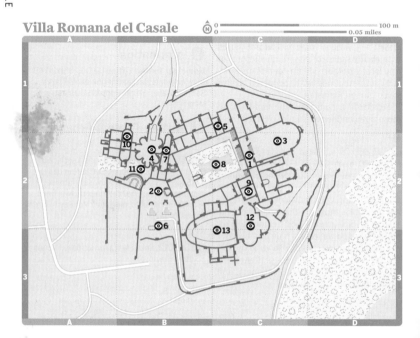

splendid mosaic depicting a chariot race at the Circus Maximus in Rome (the room is also known as the Salone del Circo or Circus Room), is the octagonal frigidarium (cold room), where the radiating apses contained cold plunge pools, and a tepidarium (warm room), where you can now see the exposed brickwork and vents that allowed hot steam into the room.

Peristyle & Great Hunt
ROMAN SITE

The main part of the villa is centred on the peristyle, a vast covered courtyard lined with amusing animal heads. This is where guests would have been received before being taken through to the basilica (throne room). Of the rooms on the northern side of the peristyle, the most interesting is a dining room featuring a hunting mosaic called the Little Hunt – 'little' because the big hunt is over on the eastern flank of the peristyle in the Ambulacrodella Scena della Grande Caccia (Corridor of the Great Hunt). This 64m-long corridor is emblazoned with dramatic hunting scenes of tigers, leopards, elephants, antelopes, ostriches and a rhino – animals that the Romans eventually hunted to extinction in North Africa. The first figure is resplendent in a Byzantine cape and is flanked by two soldiers, most likely Maximianus himself and two members of his personal guard.

Bikini Girls
MOSAIC

Just off the southern end of the Ambulacro della Scena della Grande Caccia, in the Sala delle Dieci Ragazze (Room of the 10 Girls), is the villa's most famous mosaic. It depicts nine (originally there were 10) bikini-clad girls working out with weights and dinky dumbbells, in preparation for the Olympic games.

Mythical Trials
APARTMENTS

On one side of the Ambulacro is a series of apartments where the floor illustrations reproduce scenes from Homer and other mythical episodes. Of particular interest is the triclinium (banquet hall), with a splendid depiction of the labours of Hercules, where the tortured monsters are ensnared by a smirking Odysseus.

To view the xystus (elliptical courtyard), which you can see from the triclinium, you have to exit the building and walk around the apse.

❶ Getting There & Away

If driving to Villa Romana del Casale, follow signs along the SP15 from Piazza Armerina's town centre. By public transport it's harder but not impossible. Between May and September CTS Autolinee runs seven daily buses to the site, departing from Piazza Senatore Marescalchi on the hour (9am to noon and 4pm to 7pm) and returning from the villa on the half-hour.

Outside summer you will have to walk – it's downhill, not too strenuous, and takes about an hour. The walk back is only steep for the last part. Taxis will take you there, wait for an hour, and drive you back to town for about €25; to book one, call ☎ 093 568 05 01.

Aidone

Heading northeast from Piazza Armerina, the road leads past attractive woodland and rocky grass banks to the sleepy hilltop village of Aidone. Although a nice enough place – check out the grandstand views over the surrounding valley – the one reason to stop off is to visit the Museo Archeologico (☎093 58 73 07; www.regione.sicilia.it/beni culturali/deadimorgantina; adult/reduced €6/3; ☺9am-7pm). This small museum whets the appetite for the Greek ruins at Morgantina with a small collection of artefacts from the site, and displays chronicling life in ancient times and the recent excavation work. In 2011, amid great fanfare, the museum welcomed back to its rightful home in central Sicily the long-lost Dea di Morgantina, an ancient statue of Venus. For over two decades the statue had been on display at the Getty Museum in Los Angeles, California, but when authorities discovered that the statue had been smuggled out of Italy with help from grave robbers the Italian government initiated moves to repatriate it.

Villa Romana del Casale

◎ Sights

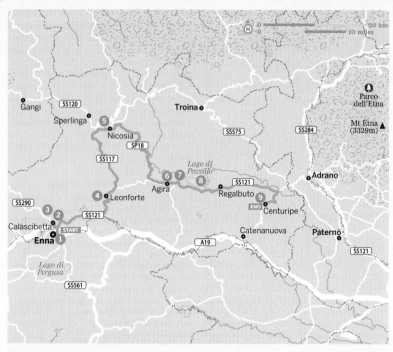

Driving Tour
Enna to Etna

START ENNA
END CENTURIPE
LENGTH 115KM; ONE OR TWO DAYS

From ① **Enna** cross the valley and climb the 2km or so to ② **Calascibetta**. The most impressive sight is the 14th-century Chiesa Madre, Calascibetta's landmark cathedral. Northwest 3km is the ③ **Necropoli di Realmese** (p223), with some 300 rock tombs dating from 850 BC.

Continuing on the SS121 from Calascibetta, the road winds and weaves 20km up to ④ **Leonforte**, an attractive baroque town once famous for horse breeding. The town's most imposing building is the Palazzo Baronale but the drawcard is the lavish Granfonte fountain. Built in 1651 by Nicolò Branciforte, it's made up of 24 separate jets against a sculpted facade.

The next leg takes you 30km up the SS117 through dramatic scenery to ⑤ **Nicosia**. Set on four hills, the centre of action is Piazza Garibaldi. Check out the Cattedrale di San Nicolò, the Franco-Lombard *palazzi* and the Chiesa di Santa Maria Maggiore. Near the entrance to Nicosia, Baglio San Pietro is great for a meal break or even an overnight stop.

Push southwards along the SP18 to ⑥ **Agira**, another sloping hillside town capped by a medieval Norman castle. A couple of kilometres out of Agira on the SS121 the well-tended ⑦ **Canadian Military Cemetery** houses the graves of 490 soldiers killed in July 1943. Further on the SS121, ⑧ **Lago di Pozzillo** is a scenic stretch of water surrounded by hills and groves of almond trees, ideal for a picnic.

Some 13km east of Regalbuto, there's a turn-off for ⑨ **Centuripe**, a small town whose grandstand views of Mt Etna have earned it the nickname the Balcone di Sicilia (Balcony of Sicily). Unfortunately, its strategic position has also brought bloodshed and the town has often been fought over. In 1943 the Allies captured the town and the Germans, realising that their foothold in Sicily had slipped, retreated to the Italian mainland.

Morgantina

At the end of a paved track, 4km downhill from Aidone, are the noteworthy remains of Morgantina (adult/reduced €6/3; ☺9am-1hr before sunset), an ancient Greek settlement spread across two hills and the connecting valley. Morgeti, an early Sicilian settlement, was founded in 850 BC on Cittadella hill, but this town was destroyed in 459 BC and a new one was built on a second hill, Serra Orlando. It was an important trading post during the reign of the Syracusan tyrant Hieron II (269–215 BC) but slipped into decline after defeat by the Romans in 211 BC and was eventually abandoned. In 1955 archaeologists identified the site and began its excavation, which continues to this day.

The centre of town is the two-storey agora (marketplace), the trapezoidal stairway of which was used as seating during public meetings. The upper level had a market and you can still see the walls that divided one shop from the next. The lower level was the site of the 1000-capacity theatre, which was originally built in the 3rd century BC but later altered by the Romans. It remains in excellent condition.

To the northeast are the city's residential quarters, where the town's well-off lived, as testified by the ornate wall decorations and handsome mosaics in the inner rooms. Another residential quarter has been found behind the theatre and its considerable ruins are well worth checking out.

To get to the site you'll need your own transport as no buses stop nearby.

Caltagirone

POP 39,500 / ELEV 608M

Caltagirone, an attractive hilltop town, is renowned throughout Sicily for its ceramics. The area's high-quality clay has supported production for more than 1000 years and still today the industry is an important money-spinner. The town's earliest settlers worked with terracotta but it was the Arabs, arriving in the 10th century, who kickstarted the industry by introducing glazed polychromatic colours, particularly the yellows and blues that have distinguished the local ceramics ever since. Everywhere you go in Caltagirone you're reminded of its ceramic traditions, most emphatically at the Scalinata di Santa Maria del Monte, the town's celebrated ceramic-inlaid staircase.

Traditional celebrations are heartfelt in these parts and watching them is an unforgettable experience. You won't need to book tickets but it pays to think ahead about accommodation.

➡ Holy Week (p222) – Plan to be in Enna for one of the town's sinister Holy Week processions, the best of which is on Good Friday.

➡ Festa di San Giacomo (p229) – Book ahead for Caltagirone's annual shindig on 24 and 25 July. The highlight is the spectacular illumination of the town's famous staircase.

➡ Palio Dei Normanni (p225) – Accommodation is at a premium in Piazza Armerina on 13 and 14 August as crowds gather for the annual medieval pageant.

Caltagirone's history dates to pre-Greek times but the town's name is Arabic in origin, a derivation of the words *kalat* and *gerun*, meaning 'castle' and 'cave'. Little remains of the town's early incarnations as it was almost entirely destroyed by the earthquake in 1693 and subsequently rebuilt in the baroque style so typical of Sicily's southeast.

◉ Sights & Activities

Scalinata di Santa Maria
Del Monte   HISTORIC STAIRCASE

Caltagirone's most evocative sight is this monumental staircase, known locally as the Scalinata di Santa Maria del Monte, which rises from Piazza Municipio to the Chiesa di Santa Maria del Monte, at the top of the town. Built in the early 17th century to connect the old hilltop centre with newer developments around Piazza Municipio, it was originally divided into several flights of steps separated by small squares.

These were eventually unified in the 1880s to create the 142-step flight that stands today. The hand-painted maiolica tiles were a relatively recent addition, only being added in 1956. It's all very impressive, although by the time you get to the top, you'll probably be more interested in having a sit-down than admiring the tilework. Fortunately, the huge views will quickly restore your will to move. The steps, lined with colourful ceramic shops, are at their finest during Caltagirone's annual celebration, the **Festa di San Giacomo** (Feast of St James) on 24 and 25 July, when the entire staircase is lit by more than 4000 oil lamps.

At the bottom of the staircase, **Piazza Municipio** is overshadowed by a number of grand buildings, including the **Galleria Luigi Sturzo**. Named after a revered former mayor, Luigi Sturzo (1871–1959), and housed in Palazzo Senatorio, where once the town senate sat, the gallery hosts temporary exhibitions and the tourist information desk.

Museo della Ceramica MUSEUM
(Regional Ceramics Museum; ☑ 093 35 84 18; Via Roma; adult/reduced €3/2; ☺ 9am-6pm) Down from the main historic centre, the Museo della Ceramica is the place to learn about the Sicilian ceramics industry. Exhibits, which include Greek terracotta works, medieval kitchenware and some excessively elaborate 18th-century maiolica statuettes, chronicle developments from prehistoric times to the 19th century.

Museo d'Arte Contemporanea Caltagirone MUSEUM
(☑ 093 32 10 83; Viale Regina Elena 10; ☺ 9.30am-1.30pm Mon, Tue & Thu-Sat, 9am-12.30pm Sun, 4-7pm Tue & Fri-Sun) FREE This small museum has a contemporary collection, including works by the renowned local artist Gianni Ballarò.

Giardino Pubblico GARDENS
Next to the Museo della Ceramica, the Giardino Pubblico is a lovely place to see out the late afternoon, perhaps with an ice cream or a glass of something cool at the park bar. Manicured avenues lead down to a central space where ceramic-tiled benches look onto an art nouveau pavilion.

Look the other way for views stretching into the distance – on a clear day, as far as Mt Etna.

Chiesa di San Francesco d'Assisi CHURCH
(Piazza San Francesco d'Assisi) Caltagirone has an extraordinary number of churches, almost 30 in the historic centre alone. Most are baroque, dating to the building boom of the early 18th century, although some have earlier origins. One such, the Chiesa di San Francesco d'Assisi dates to the 13th century but now displays an extraordinarily flamboyant baroque facade.

Near the church, the 17th-century **Ponte San Francesco** (San Francesco Bridge) is worth a close look for its ceramic floral embellishments.

Chiesa del Carmine CHURCH
(Piazza del Carmine; ☺ 10.30am-1pm & 3.30-6.30pm) Higher up in the old town, down a side street off the *scalinata*, the Chiesa del Carmine is worth a quick look for its huge terracotta *presepe* (nativity scene – *presepi* are a Caltagirone tradition) covering 72 sq metres.

✖ Eating

Il Locandiere SEAFOOD €€
(☑ 093 35 82 92; Via Luigi Sturzo 55-59; meals €30; ☺ Tue-Sun) Those in the know head to this smart little restaurant for top-quality seafood and impeccable service. What exactly you'll eat depends on the day's catch, but the fish couscous is superb and the *casarecce con ragù di tonno* (pasta fingers with tuna sauce) a sure-fire hit. *Dolci* (sweet) showstoppers include delicious *connoli a cucchiao* (*cannoli* with fig cream).

The wine list is long enough to please most palates.

Il Palazzo Dei Marchesi Di Santa Barbara SICILIAN €€
(☑ 093 32 24 06; Via San Bonaventura 22; pizzas from €4, meals €30; ☺ Tue-Sun) A baronial staircase takes you to the 1st floor of an aristocratic palace, and onto this smart, friendly restaurant, known for its excellent seasonal cuisine. The onus is on meat – the *straccetti di manzo con cuori di carciofo in crema di asparagi selvatici* (pork with artichoke hearts in a wild asparagus sauce) is a standout.

La Piazzetta SICILIAN €€
(☑ 093 32 41 78; Via Vespri 20; pizzas from €4.50, meals €25; ☺ Fri-Wed) For many locals Saturday night means a slap-up meal at La Piazzetta, a much-loved *centro storico* (historic city centre) restaurant. That might mean a pizza and beer or something more substantial like fresh pasta with pistachio pesto followed by a mountainous mixed grill. It's not haute cuisine but the food is tasty, the atmosphere is convivial and prices are honest.

Coria MODERN SICILIAN €€€
(☑ 093 32 65 96; www.ristorantecoria.it; Via Infermeria 24; meals from €40; ☺ closed Mon winter, Wed summer) Caltagirone's top restaurant is

an established address on the island's fine-dining circuit. Its reputation rides on innovative regional cuisine, as exemplified in reworked classics such as *spaghetti con sarde in crema di finocchietto* (spaghetti with sardines in a fennel sauce) and *biscotto con crema di arance e gelatino di cioccolato e menta* (biscuit with orange cream and chocolate and mint jelly). Reservations required.

Shopping

Ceramic Caltagirone CERAMICS

If you're in the market for a souvenir, there are about 120 ceramics shops in town. Two recommended stores are Le Maioliche (☑ 093 35 31 39; www.varsallona.it; Discesa Collegio 1), where local artist Ricardo Varsallona exhibits his traditional and modern works, and Ceramiche Failla (☑ 093 33 40 00; Scalinata di Santa Maria del Monte 45) on the main *scalinata*.

Orientation

Caltagirone is divided into an upper and lower town, with everything of interest in the upper town. Orientate yourself around Piazza Municipio, the upper town's focal square. From here, the Scalinata di Santa Maria del Monte rises to the northeast, while shop-lined Via Vittorio Emanuele heads off west and Via Luigi Sturzo runs northeast to Viale Regina Elena, a ring road with useful parking. Just south of Piazza Municipio, Piazza Umberto connects with Via Roma, which runs down to the Giardino Pubblico. Buses stop in Piazza Umberto.

Information

Tourist information desk (☑ 093 34 13 65; www.comune.caltagirone.ct.it; Galleria Luigi Sforzo, Piazza Municipio; ☺ 9am-7pm Mon-Sat) Near the bottom of the Scalinata di Santa Maria del Monte.

Getting There & Around

BUS

There are **AST** (☑ 840 000323; www.azienda sicilianatrasporti.it) buses to/from Piazza Armerina (€4, 1½ hours, seven daily Monday to Saturday) and Syracuse (€10.20, three hours, one daily Monday to Saturday) and an **SAIS** (☑ 093 550 09 02; www.saisautolinee.it) service to/from Enna (€6.20, 1¼ hours, daily).

CAR

Caltagirone is just off the SS417, the road that connects Gela on the south coast with Catania in the east. From Piazza Armerina, follow SS117bis south and then cut across country on the SS124.

If you're staying in the upper town, there's useful parking on Viale Regina Elena.

THE WESTERN INTERIOR

Bearing the scars of a history of neglect and poverty, Sicily's western interior is a bleached landscape of rolling hills and small, isolated towns. For centuries the area was divided into large *latifondi* (landed estates) owned by absentee landlords, and still today the area seems remote and largely cut off from the rest of the world. It's a tough area to travel without your own car, although interest is mainly limited to the main city Caltanissetta and the large Regaleali wine estate.

Caltanissetta

POP 60,300 / ELEV 568M

One of Sicily's nine provincial capitals, Caltanissetta is the largest city in the area, a scruffy, workaday place with little obvious appeal. But if you do find yourself passing through, there's a fine central piazza and, in the suburbs, a mildly interesting archaeological museum.

WORTH A TRIP

WINE TASTING & COOKING COURSES

The area west of Caltanissetta is wild and remote. But if you want to get away from everything, head to the beautiful Regaleali estate (☑ 092 154 40 11; www.tascadalmerita. it) near the village of Vallelunga. One of five wine-producing estates owned by the Tasca d'Almerita family, it has some 400 hectares of vineyards, a high-tech winery and a residential cooking school (☑ 093 481 46 54; www.annatascalanza.com) run by Anna Tasca Lanza. Visits to the winery are limited to guided tours (with optional tastings) for between eight and 25 people, which must be booked ahead. Cooking courses range from three- to five-day packages (€1000–€2000 per person including accommodation) to a day-long lesson and lunch (€150). Further details are available on the website.

The city, originally founded by the Greeks, enjoyed prosperity in the first half of the 20th century as capital of the Sicilian sulphur-mining industry and is today an important agricultural centre.

◉ Sights & Activities

Piazza Garibaldi   HISTORIC QUARTER
Caltanissetta's historic centre converges on Piazza Garibaldi, which is a handsome pedestrian-only piazza flanked by the Duomo, the town hall and the baroque Chiesa di San Sebastiano. The Duomo has a late-Renaissance appearance, but substantial alterations made in the 19th century have ruined the overall effect. Inside, if you find the church open, are frescoes by the 18th-century Flemish artist Guglielmo Borremans.

Museo Archeologico   MUSEUM
(☑093 456 70 62; Contrada Santo Spirito; adult/reduced €2/1; ☉9am-1pm & 3.30-7pm, closed last Mon of month) In the suburbs, sporadically signposted from the city centre, the Museo Archeologico displays a collection of prehistoric finds from all over Sicily, including vases, tools, early Sicilian ceramics and rare terracotta figurines from the Bronze Age. The church you'll see near the museum car park is the 12th-century Abbazia di Santo Spirito, one of the few surviving relics from the city's Norman period.

Eating

Vicolo Duomo   TRATTORIA
(☑093 458 23 31; Vicolo Neviera 1; meals €30; ☉closed Sun & lunch Mon) Hidden away in a tiny alleyway just off Piazza Garibaldi, this is the place to eat in town. A colourful trattoria, it specialises in earthy country fare such as pasta with spring peas and fava beans, and pork shin in Nero d'Avola wine.

❶ Information

Tourist office (☑093 42 10 89; Viale Conte Testasecca 20; ☉9am-1pm Mon-Fri, 4-6pm Wed)

❶ Getting There & Around

BUS

From the bus station on Via Colaianni, **SAIS Autolinee** (☑800 211020; www.saisautolinee. it) runs to Enna (€4.10, one hour) at least four times daily, while **SAIS Trasporti** (☑093 456 40 72; www.saistrasporti.it) operates up to 10 daily buses to/from Agrigento (€6.20, 1¼ hours).

CAR

If coming from Enna or the north take the A19 autostrada to join the SS640, which passes through Caltanissetta en route to Agrigento.

Mediterranean Coast

Best Places to Eat

➡ Ristorante La Madia (p248)
➡ La Lampara (p245)
➡ Hostaria Del Vicolo (p246)
➡ Trattoria Al Faro (p245)
➡ M.A.T.E.S (p246)
➡ Kalòs (p240)

Best Places to Sleep

➡ Camere a Sud (p267)
➡ Villa Athena (p267)
➡ Al Moro (p268)
➡ Vecchia Masseria (p268)
➡ B&B Da Lulo e Gagà (p268)

Why Go?

Sicily's Mediterranean coast is a mixed bag. The main attraction of the area, the spectacular ruins of the Valley of the Temples – unparalleled across the island for their significance, expanse and beauty – are overlooked by ranks of unsightly tower blocks, giving the city of Agrigento an odd air. West of Agrigento, the development soon peters out and the landscape takes on a wilder, less contaminated aspect. Here you'll find some wonderful sandy beaches, particularly at the Riserva Naturale Torre Salsa and Eraclea Minoa, and tracts of beautiful, unspoilt countryside. The chalk hills of the Scala dei Turchi are a spectacular sight and there's a great beach too. Further west, the pretty spa town of Sciacca is well worth a day or two for its excellent seafood restaurants and handsome historic streets. Don't miss Favara's art neighbourhood, Farm Cultural Park, an innovative and vibrant art project that has revived a town.

Road Distances (KM)

	Agrigento	Caltabellotta	Gela	Licata
Caltabellota	60			
Gela	75	130		
Licata	45	100	30	
Sciacca	60	20	130	100

DON'T MISS

Retrace the glories of Sicily's Greek past at Agrigento's Valley of the Temples. The temples, the best outside Greece, are what's left of ancient Akragas, once the Western world's fourth-largest city.

Best Beaches

➡ Spiaggia dei Conigli (p248)

➡ Torre Salsa (p243)

➡ Scala dei Turchi (p243)

➡ Eraclea Minoa (p243)

➡ Falconara (p248)

Best Museums

➡ Museo Archeologico (p239), Agrigento

➡ Museo Archeologico (p249), Gela

Resources

➡ **Grand Hotel delle Terme** (www.grandhoteldelleterme.com) Details on the spa treatments (plus costs) available in Sciacca.

➡ **Servizio Turistico Regionale Sciacca** (www.servizioturisticoregionalesciacca.it) Sciacca carnival programs, accommodation listings, histories and itineraries.

➡ **Valle dei Templi** (www.lavalledeitempli.it) Up-to-date information on the Valley of the Temples' guides, opening hours etc.

Getting Around

You can get around from Agrigento to the Valley of the Temples on public transport quite easily, and there are buses between most of the main towns in the region, but to fully explore the beaches and the coast in general, you'll need your own wheels.

THREE PERFECT DAYS

Valley of the Temples

Sicily's most popular archaeological site, Agrigento's Valley of the Temples is well worth an entire day – in fact, nothing less does it the justice it deserves. Start in the eastern zone (p235) where you'll find the two most famous temples, the Tempio di Hera and the outstanding Tempio della Concordia, before crossing to the western zone (p238)and a picnic lunch in the Giardino della Kolymbetra (p238). Afterwards, if you have any strength left, head up to the Museo Archeologico (p239).

Sciacca

Sciacca is a spa town famous for its carnival celebrations. Treat yourself to a massage and mudpack at the Nuovo Stabilimento Termale (p245) and a fish feast at the port, then head out to the Castello Incantato (p245) to pore over its collection of weird sculpted heads. Spend the rest of the day strolling through the attractive historic centre and perusing the characteristic ceramic shops.

Beach Beauties

The coastal stretch between Agrigento and Sciacca offers great swimming and pockets of unspoilt nature. Join the local sunseekers at the Scala dei Turchi, a celebrated beauty spot near Realmonte, or push on to the lovely sandy beach at the Riserva Naturale Torre Salsa (p243), where there's also some fine coastal walking. Further west, you can explore the ruins of Eraclea Minoa (p243) before heading down to the beach, one of the best on this stretch of the coast.

Getting Away from It All

➡ **Riserva Naturale Macalube di Aragona** This reserve is famous for its pint-size mud volcanoes.

➡ **Caltabellotta** The towering hilltop town of Caltabellotta commands huge panoramic views.

➡ **Mazzarino** Visit the baroque churches in sleepy Mazzarino, many of which are decorated by the Tuscan artist Filippino Paladino.

AGRIGENTO

POP 59,135

At one time the fourth-largest city in the known world, Agrigento, or Akragas as it was then known, is home to Sicily's most impressive Greek ruins. Situated about 3km below the ugly modern city, the Unesco-listed Valley of the Temples is one of the most mesmerising sites in the Mediterranean, boasting the best-preserved Doric temples outside Greece. On the travel radar since Goethe sang their praises in the 18th century, they are now Sicily's single biggest tourist site, with more than 600,000 visitors a year.

Up the hill, modern Agrigento is not an immediately appealing prospect. Huge motorway elevations converge on a ragged hilltop centre scarred by brutish tower blocks and riddled with choking traffic. However, hidden behind this depressing outer ring is an attractive medieval kernel with some fine accommodation and a lively evening buzz.

Ancient Akragas was founded by settlers from Gela and Rhodes in 581 BC. The presence of a ready water supply ensured its rapid growth and by the 5th century BC it had become one of the Mediterranean's great cities, with a population of 200,000 and a reputation as a party hot spot. The Greek poet Pindar described it as 'the most beautiful (city) of those inhabited by mortals' and wrote that its citizens 'feasted as if there were no tomorrow'.

Its good fortunes began to waver in the 4th and 3rd centuries BC as it passed successively between Greek, Carthaginian and Roman hands. The Romans, who took the city in 210 BC, renamed it Agrigentum and encouraged farming and trade, thus laying the foundations for its future as an important Byzantine commercial centre.

In the 7th century most of the city's residents moved up the hill to the site of the present-day city, virtually abandoning the old town. Experts don't know exactly why, but the most credible theories suggest it was to escape the threat of the North African Saracens. As a defence policy it worked for close to 200 years until the city fell to the Saracens at the start of the 9th century.

Agrigento didn't change much until the 19th century, when the western half of the city was built. Allied bombing in WWII forced a second wave of development in the post-war years, culminating in a bout of construction in the '60s and '70s. Many of the tower blocks that overshadow the Valley of the Temples date to this period.

The centre of the town's lively, medieval core is Via Atenea, an attractive strip lined with smart shops, trattorias and bars. Narrow alleyways wind upwards off the main street, through tightly packed *palazzi*.

◉ Sights & Activities

★ Valley of the Temples
(Valle dei Templi) ARCHAEOLOGICAL SITE
(☑ 092 262 16 11; www.parcovalledeitempli.it; adult/ EU under 18yr & over 65yr/EU 18-25yr incl Quartiere Ellenistico-Romano €10/free/5, incl Museo Archeologico €13.50/free/7) One of southern Europe's most compelling archaeological sites, the 13 sq km Parco Valle dei Templi encompasses the ruins of the ancient city of Akragas. The highlight is the stunning Tempio della Concordia, one of the best-preserved Greek temples in existence and one of a series built on a ridge to act as beacons for homecoming sailors.

The park is split into two areas: the eastern zone, with the most spectacular temples, and over the road the western zone. There are two ticket offices, one at the park's eastern edge by the Tempio di Hera and another at Piazza Alexander Hardcastle on the main SS118 road between the two zones. The car park is by the eastern entrance.

Eastern Zone ARCHAEOLOGICAL SITE
(⊙ 8.30am-7pm summer, 9am-5pm winter, plus 7.30-9.30pm Mon-Fri, 7.30-11.30pm Sat & Sun Julearly Sep) If you only have time to explore part of the Parco Valle dei Templi, make it the eastern zone, where you'll find the park's three best-preserved temples. Overlooking the eastern ticket office, the 5th-century-BC **Tempio di Hera** (Temple of Hera; Map p240), also known as the Tempio di Giunone (Temple of Juno), is perched on the edge of a ridge. Though partly destroyed by an earthquake in the Middle Ages, much of the colonnade remains intact as does a long altar, originally used for sacrifices. The traces of red are the result of fire damage, most likely during the Carthaginian invasion of 406 BC.

From here, the path continues westwards, past a gnarled 800-year-old olive tree and a series of Byzantine tombs built into the city walls, to the **Tempio della Concordia** (Temple of Concord; Map p240). This remarkable edifice, the model for Unesco's logo, has survived almost entirely intact since it was constructed in 430 BC. There are several

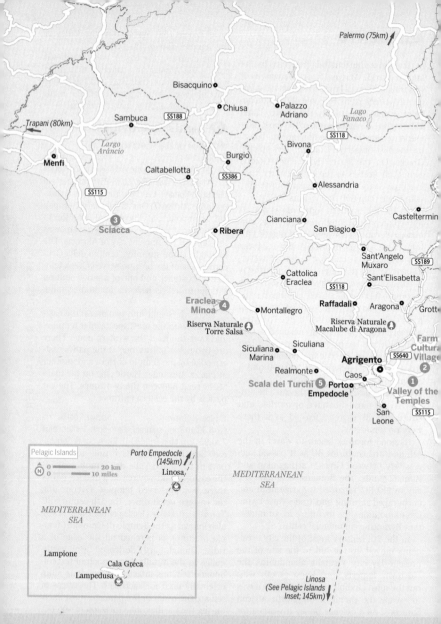

Mediterranean Coast Highlights

1 Agrigento's **Valley of the Temples** (p235) has no competition in Sicily – it is simply spectacular.

2 The innovative, orginal art 'neighbourhood' **Farm Cultural Park** (p249) in Favara is unmissable.

3 **Sciacca**'s (p243) carnival and spa treatments are great energy rechargers.

Catania
(60km)

Mussomeli

Campofranco

Bompensiere   San Cataldo

Montedoro

Racalmuto

SS640

Canicattì
Castrofilippo

Delia

SS190   Sommatino

Naro

SS576

Camastra

Ravanusa

Campobello
di Licata

SS123

SS626d

Palma di
Montechiaro

Licata   Falconara

Gela

Enna

Caltanissetta

Pietraperzia

Barrafranca

SS191

Riesi   Mazzarino

San
Michele

SS626   SS190

Butera

SP8

Il Castelluccio   SS117bis   Niscemi

SS115

Ragusa (50km);
Mòdica (65km)

4 Greek ruins and natural
mud scrubs are to be had at
Eraclea Minoa (p243).

5 Enjoy sunset views from
the stunning **Scala dei Turchi**
(p243).

Agrigento

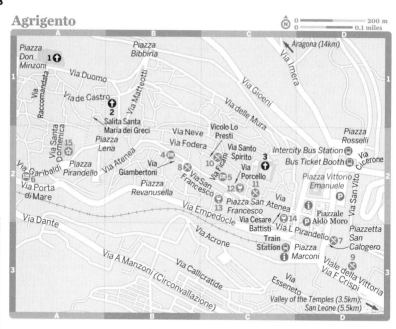

reasons why it has survived while other temples have not, one being that it was converted into a Christian basilica in the 6th century and the main structure was reinforced. The principle reason, though, is more down to earth. Beneath the hard rock on which the temple stands is a layer of soft clay that acts as a kind of natural shock absorber, protecting it from earthquake tremors. Whether the Greek engineers knew this when they built the temple is the subject of debate but modern scholars tend to think they did. In 1748 the temple was restored to its original form and given the name it's now known by. The last of the zone's temples, the **Tempio di Ercole** (Temple of Hercules; Map p240), is the oldest, dating from the end of 6 BC. Eight of its 38 columns have been raised and you can wander around the remains of the rest. Down from the main temples, you can see a little temple set on a high base. This is known as the **Tomba di Terone** (Tomb of Theron; Map p240), although it dates to 75 BC, about 500 years after the death of Theron, Agrigento's Greek tyrant.

Western Zone ARCHAEOLOGICAL SITE
(☉9am-7pm summer, 9am-5pm winter) The main feature of the park's western zone is the crumbled ruin of the **Tempio di Giove** (Temple of Olympian Zeus; Map p240). Covering an area of 112m by 56m with columns 20m high, this would have been the largest Doric temple ever built had its construction not been interrupted by the Carthaginians sacking Akragas. The incomplete temple was later destroyed by an earthquake. Lying flat on his back amid the rubble is an 8m-tall *telamon* (a sculpted figure of a man with arms raised), originally intended to support the temple's weight. It's actually a copy of the original, which is in the Museo Archeologico. A short hop away, four columns mark the **Tempio dei Dioscuri** (Temple of Castor and Pollux; Map p240), a 5th-century-BC temple that was destroyed by earthquake and partially rebuilt in the 19th century. Just behind is a complex of altars and small buildings believed to be part of the 6th-century-BC **Santuario delle Divine Chthoniche** (Sanctuary of the Chthonic Deities; Map p240). In a natural cleft near the sanctuary is the **Giardino della Kolymbetra** (Map p240; adult/reduced €2/1; ☉10am-6pm Apr-Jun, 10am-7pm Jul-Sep), a lush garden with more than 300 (labelled) species of plants and some welcome picnic tables. It's a steep climb down to the garden, best avoided if you've got dicky knees.

Agrigento

Museo Archeologico　　　　　　　MUSEUM
(Map p240; ☑092 24 01 11; Contrada San Nicola; admission incl Valley of the Temples adult/reduced €13.50/7; ⊙9am-7pm Tue-Sat, 9am-1pm Sun & Mon) North of the temples, this wheelchair-accessible museum is one of Sicily's finest, with a huge collection of clearly labelled artefacts from the excavated site. Noteworthy are the dazzling displays of Greek painted ceramics and the awe-inspiring reconstructed *telamone*, a colossal statue recovered from the nearby Tempio di Giove.

Cathedral　　　　　　　　　　　CATHEDRAL
(Map p238; Via Duomo; ⊙9.30am-12.30pm & 4-6pm) The city's magnificent and striking 11th-century cathedral has been much altered over the centuries. It boasts a wonderful Norman ceiling and a mysterious letter from the Devil.

Old Nick is reputed to have tried to seduce the Virgin of Agrigento by writing to her promising her all the treasure in the world. The Virgin was having none of it, though, and she dobbed him in to the priest, who still holds this mysterious missive.

**Chiesa di Santa Maria
dei Greci**　　　　　　　　　　　　CHURCH
(Salita Santa Maria dei Greci; Map p238; ⊙9am-12.30pm & 4-6pm Mon-Sat) Downhill from the cathedral, this small church stands on the site of a 5th-century Doric temple dedicated to Athena. Inside are some badly damaged Byzantine frescoes and the remains of the original Norman ceiling.

Monastero di Santo Spirito　　CONVENT
(Map p238) Back towards Piazzale Aldo Moro, at the top of a set of steps off Via Atenea, is the Monastero di Santo Spirito, founded by Cistercian nuns around 1290. A handsome Gothic portal leads inside, where the nuns are still in residence, praying, meditating and baking heavenly pastries, including *dolci di mandorla* (almond pastries), pistachio *cuscusu* and *bucellati* (rolled sweet dough with figs). To buy some, press the doorbell, say *'Vorrei comprare qualche dolce'* ('I'd like to buy a few cakes') and see how you go.

Upstairs, the small **Museo Civico** (Map p238; ☑092 240 14 50; admission €2.50; ⊙9am-1pm & 3-6pm Mon-Fri, 9am-1pm Sat) is worth a quick visit as much for the views over the Valley of the Temples as its poorly labelled miscellany of objects.

 Festivals & Events

Sagra del Mandorlo in Fiore　　CULTURE
A huge folk festival held on the first Sunday in February, when the Valley of the Temples is cloaked in almond blossom.

Festa di San Calògero　　　　RELIGIOUS
During this week-long festival centred on the first Sunday in July, the statue of St Calògero (who saved Agrigento from the plague) is carried through town while spectators throw spiced loaves at it.

✖ Eating

There are a few good trattorias up in Agrigento's historic centre but many of the smarter restaurants are dotted around the area between the Valley of the Temples and San Leone, on the sea. Agrigento itself is

---

SHH! WE'RE IN A CHURCH

A remarkable acoustic phenomenon known as *il portavoce* (the carrying voice) means even the faintest sound carries in Agrigento's cathedral, but this only seems to work in the favour of the priest standing in the apse. Should parishioners whisper in the back row near the cathedral door, the priest can hear their every word even though he's standing some 85m away!

Valley of the Temples

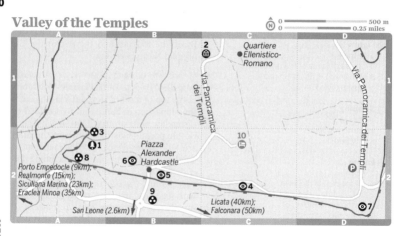

N 0 ——— 500 m
0 ——— 0.25 miles

Quartiere
• Ellenistico-
Romano

Piazza
Alexander
Hardcastle

Porto Empedocle (9km);
Realmonte (15km);
Siciliana Marina (23km);
Eraclea Minoa (35km);

San Leone (2.6km)

Licata (40km);
Falconara (50km)

Valley of the Temples

⦿ Sights

1 Giardino della Kolymbetra A2
2 Museo Archeologico C1
3 Sanctuary of the Chthonic
    Deities A2
4 Tempio della Concordia C2
5 Tempio di Ercole B2
6 Tempio di Giove B2
7 Tempio di Hera D2
8 Temple dei Dioscuri A2
9 Tomba di Therone B2

⌂ Sleeping

10 Villa Athena...C2

famous for the unctuous Arab sweet *cuscu-su* (looks like semolina couscous but is made of almonds and pistachio).

✕ Town Centre

Le Cuspidi   GELATO €
(Map p238; ☑ 092 259 59 14; Viale della Vittoria; ice cream from €1; ☺ 9am-late) This fabulous gelateria is the perfect antidote to Agrigento's oppressive heat. Especially scrumptious is the pistachio, flecked with nuts and super creamy.

Trattoria Concordia   TRATTORIA €
(Map p238; ☑ 092 22 26 68; Via Porcello 8; meals €18-30; ☺ lunch & dinner) Tucked up a side alley, this rustic trattoria with exposed stone and stucco walls specialises in grilled fish along with Sicilian *primi* like *casarecce con pesce spada, melanzane e menta* (pasta with swordfish, eggplant and mint).

Ristorante Per Bacco   SICILIAN €
(Map p238; ☑ 092 255 33 69; Vicolo Lo Presti 2; meals from €17; ☺ dinner Tue-Sun) The food may not quite live up to the charm of the setting – under stone and brick arches and beamed ceilings – but the service is friendly, and the set menus for under €20 are good value at this restaurant just above Via Atenea.

★ Kalòs   MODERN SICILIAN €€
(Map p238; ☑ 092 22 63 89; www.ristorantekalos.it; Piazzetta San Calogero; meals €30-40; ☺ lunch & dinner) A classically 'smart' restaurant with a couple of cute tables on the tiny balcony and excellent food. There is home-made pasta – try the *spaghetti all'agrigentina*, a simple primo of fresh tomatoes, basil and pistachio, and follow up with a *spada gratinata* – the fish is baked and covered in bread crumbs. Combine with a local white wine and finish with an almond *semifreddo*.

L'Ambasciata di Sicilia   SICILIAN €€
(Map p238; ☑ 092 22 05 26; Via Giambertoni 2; meals €22-33; ☺ Mon-Sat) At the 'Sicilian Embassy', they do everything they can to improve foreign relations, plying tourists with tasty plates of traditional Sicilian fare and good seafood. Order an octopus and it arrives so fresh it feels as if it's staring you in the eyes. Try to get a table on the small outdoor terrace, which has splendid views.

✕ Valley of the Temples

Kokalos   PIZZERIA €
(☑ 092 260 64 27; Via Magazzeni 3; pizzas €5-11, meals €17-30; ☺ lunch & dinner) This eatery, resembling a Wild West ranch, is the perfect

place to enjoy wood-fired pizza on the summer terrace while gazing out over the temples. You will need a car to get here – it's up a dusty track 2km southeast of town.

Leon d'Oro   SICILIAN €€
(☑ 092 241 44 00; Viale Emporium 102; meals €35; ☺ Tue-Sun) A much-lauded local favourite, Leon d'Oro specialises in the fish and fowl that typify Agrigento's cuisine. The menu is in local dialect, in keeping with the rustic ambience. Dishes to look out for include *baccalà* (salted cod) with potatoes and *calamari su agrumi* (cuttlefish served with local citrus fruits).

Owner Totò also keeps an exceptional cellar and is more than happy to advise on wine choices.

Le Caprice   MODERN SICILIAN €€
(☑ 092 241 13 64; Via Cavaleri Magazzeni; meals €30-35; ☺ Tue-Sun) Long considered one of Agrigento's better restaurants, Le Caprice is set in its own park complete with pool and swans. It's a big place – it can cater to around 500 people – and is renowned for its swimmingly fresh seafood. Start with a plate from the lush antipasto buffet before diving into the restaurant's signature dish, mixed seafood grill. A glass of cool local white is the perfect accompaniment.

Il Déhors   MODERN SICILIAN €€
(☑ 092 251 10 61; Contrada Maddalusa; meals €40; ☺ Tue-Sun) The restaurant of the Foresteria Baglio della Luna is an elegant fine-dining establishment offering innovative Sicilian cuisine and views over the Valley of the Temples. Fresh local seafood appears in sophisticated creations such as sea bream with *pecorino* cheese and aubergine tartare, or grilled tuna with mint couscous and pepper sauce. Reservations required.

☕ Drinking & Nightlife

QOC   BAR
(Map p238; ☑ 092 22 71 07; www.qoc.me; Via Cesare Battisti 8; ☺ Tue-Sun) A trendy little place just off Via Atenea, QOC bills itself as an 'Outfit, Restaurant, Bar', but it does 'bar' best, with good, themed *aperitivo* (happy hour) and late-night cocktails. There is a good-looking restaurant upstairs and a fixed-menu lunch (€10), but the food is average. The owner and staff are friendly and it's a great place to hang out among young *agrigentini*.

Café Girasole   WINE BAR
(Map p238; Via Atenea 68-70; ☺ Mon-Sat) By day this popular cafe-cum-wine-bar does brisk business serving coffee and *panini* to working locals. By evening it morphs into a trendy hangout for the 30-something *aperitivo* set, who stop by for cocktails and table snacks. Good atmosphere and outdoor seating.

Teatro Pirandello   THEATRE
(Map p238; ☑ 092 22 50 19; www.teatroluigipirandello.it; Piazza Pirandello; tickets €18-23) This city-run theatre is Sicily's third largest, after Palermo's Teatro Massimo and Catania's Teatro Massimo Bellini. Works by local hero Luigi Pirandello figure prominently. The program runs from November to April.

Mojo Wine Bar   WINE BAR
(Map p238; ☑ 092 246 30 13; www.mojo4music.it; Piazza San Francesco 11-13; ☺ Mon-Sat) A trendy *enoteca* (wine bar) in a pretty piazza. Enjoy a cool white Inzolia, and munch on olives and spicy salami, as you listen to some laid-back jazz.

❶ Orientation

There are two centres of interest in Agrigento: the historic centre and the Valley of the Temples.

MEDITERRANEAN COAST AGRIGENTO

ADVANCE PLANNING

There are several top experiences that you'd do well to book in advance.

➡ A guide at the Valley of the Temples – You don't need a guide for the temples but if you want one, you can organise it before arriving.

➡ Spa treatment at Sciacca – Sciacca's thermal waters are big business, so it pays to arrange an appointment if you want to pamper yourself.

➡ Sciacca's carnival – One of Sicily's top events, Sciacca's carnival celebrations attract huge crowds, putting pressure on the town's limited accommodation. Get in early to avoid disappointment.

➡ Ristorante La Madia (p248) – Licata's acclaimed restaurant is one of Sicily's finest, so make reservations.

VULCANELLI DI MACALUBE

Some 15km north of Agrigento, near the town of Aragona, the Vulcanelli di Macalube are a bizarre and fascinating sight. A series of metre-high mud volcanoes rising out of a barren expanse of cracked mud, they are the result of a rare geological phenomenon known as sedimentary volcanism. This is a process by which pressurised natural gas, in this case methane, forces underground soil to explode through the earth's surface. Once on the surface, the bubbling mud dries in the sun, thus creating the pint-sized volcanoes.

The *vulcanelli* are now part of the Riserva Naturale Macalube di Aragona (☑092 269 92 10; www.macalife.it; ⊘9am-7pm) FREE, managed by Legambiente, Italy's main environmental organisation. To get to the site you will need your own transport – the buses from Agrigento to Aragona leave you 4km short of the reserve.

The historic centre's main street is Via Atenea, which runs westwards from Piazzale Aldo Moro to Piazza Pirandello. The intercity bus station is on Piazza Rosselli, just north of Piazzale Aldo Moro, while the train station is to the south, on Piazza Marconi. The Valley of the Temples is about 3km below the modern town: from Piazza Marconi take Via Francesco Crispi and Via Panoramica Valle dei Templi for the valley's eastern entrance and car park.

ℹ️ Information

EMERGENCIES

Police Station (☑092 248 31 11; Piazza Vittorio Emanuele 2)

MEDICAL SERVICES

Ospedale San Giovanni di Dio (☑092 244 21 11; Contrada da Consolida) North of the centre.

TOURIST INFORMATION

Tourist Office (Map p238; ☑800 236837; www.comune.agrigento.it; Piazzale Aldo Moro 1; ⊘8am-2pm Mon-Fri, 8am-1pm Sat) Inside the Provincia building; offers information on the city and province.

Tourist Information Point (Map p238; train station; ⊘8am-8pm Mon-Fri, 8am-2pm Sat)

ℹ️ Getting There & Around

BUS

From most destinations, the bus is the easiest way to get to Agrigento. The intercity bus station and ticket booths are on Piazza Rosselli, just off Piazza Vittorio Emanuele. **Cuffaro** (☑091 616 15 10; www.cuffaro.info) runs services to Palermo (€8.70, two hours, nine daily Monday to Saturday, three Sunday). **SAIS Trasporti** (☑092 22 93 24; www.saistrasporti.it) runs buses to Catania and Catania airport (€12.40, three hours, at least 10 daily) and Caltanissetta (€5.80, 1¼ hours, at least 10 daily). **SAL** (☑092 240 13 60; www.autolineesal.it) serves Palermo's Falcone-Borsellino airport (€12.10, 2½ hours).

CAR

Agrigento is easily accessible by road from all of Sicily's main towns. The SS189 and SS121 connect with Palermo, while the SS115 runs along the coast. For Enna, take the SS640 via Caltanissetta.

In town, Via Atenea, the main street in the historic centre, is closed to traffic from 9am to 8pm, with a short break during lunchtime when cars can pass through the centre (for loading luggage, for example). Parking is a nightmare in Agrigento. There's metered parking at Piazza Vittorio Emanuele and on the streets around Piazzale Aldo Moro, although you'll have to arrive early to find a space.

TRAIN

Trains run regularly to/from Palermo (€8, 2½ hours, 11 daily). There are also two daily direct trains to/from Catania (€12, four hours). The train station has left-luggage lockers (per 12 hours €2.50).

WEST OF AGRIGENTO

The main SS115 road follows the coast westwards from Agrigento, passing through some fine countryside as it runs on to the historic spa town of Sciacca. En route you'll pass a number of excellent sandy beaches, a nature reserve and what is left of an ancient Greek town that was supposedly founded by the Cretan king Minos, the man behind the Minotaur myth.

Casa Natale di Pirandello

Southwest of Agrigento in the suburb of Caos, about 2km along the SS115 to Porto Empedocle, is this house (☑092 251 18 26; admission €2; ⊘9am-1pm & 3-7pm), the birthplace of Luigi Pirandello (1867–1936). One of the giants of modern Italian literature, and winner of the 1934 Nobel Prize for Literature,

Pirandello started his career writing short stories and novels, but is best known as a playwright, author of masterpieces such as *Sei personaggi in ricerca di un autore* (Six Characters in Search of an Author) and *Enrico IV* (Henry IV).

He left Agrigento as a young man but returned most summers to spend time at the family villa, which is now a small museum, stacked full of first editions, photographs, reviews and theatre bills. Pirandello's ashes are kept in an urn buried at the foot of a pine tree in the garden.

Just a few kilometres down the road, Porto Empedocle, the main port for ferries to the Pelagic Islands, has its own literary claim to fame. Andrea Camilleri, Italy's most popular living author and creator of Inspector Montalbano, was born here in 1925.

Beaches & Beauty Spots

The nearest beach to Agrigento is at San Leone, the town's vivacious seafront satellite. However, with your own wheels you'll find some stunning spots further west along the SS115.

One of the most beautiful, and least publicised, sights in the Agrigento area is the Scala dei Turchi. This is a blindingly white rock shaped like a giant staircase that juts out into the sea near the small town of Realmonte, 15km west of Agrigento. Named after the Arab and Turkish pirates who used to hide out from stormy weather here, it's a popular spot with local sunseekers who come to sunbathe on the milky-smooth rock and swim in the indigo sea. Take a picnic to make a full day of it, otherwise you can lunch at the Lido Scala dei Turchi at the top of the steps down to the beach.

A further 5km west of Realmonte, there's a great sandy beach at Siculiana Marina and lovely walking at the WWF-administered Riserva Naturale Torre Salsa (www.wwftorresalsa.it), where well-marked trails offer panoramic views of the surrounding mountains and coast. A good place to cool off is the beautiful Torre Salsa beach, accessed from the reserve's northern entrance.

Eraclea Minoa

Nowadays a small summer resort – empty for most of the year, packed in July and August – Eraclea Minoa was an important Greek settlement in ancient times. According to legend it was originally founded by the Cretan king Minos who came to Sicily in pursuit of Daedalus, a former favourite who had fallen out of grace and escaped from Crete. Historical evidence suggests the city was established by Greek colonists in the 6th century BC and went on to flourish in the 4th and 5th centuries. The scant remains of the city can now be seen at the archaeological park (admission €4.50; ⊙9am-1hr before sunset Mon-Sat) on a headland back from the main seafront village. The ruins are relatively scarce – the crumbling remains of the soft sandstone theatre are covered with protective plastic – but the views and singing scrub are gorgeous.

Once you've done the history, head down to the beach, a wonderful, photogenic strip of golden sand backed by willowy eucalyptus trees, cypress groves and chalk cliffs. Here you can indulge in a refreshing facial massage. There's a natural mud rock at the western end of the beach, which you can scrape off and rub onto your skin – you'll see all the locals doing the same. Dry off in the sun then rinse in the sea and you'll have removed 10 years in 10 minutes.

Sciacca

POP 40,930

Famous for its historic spas and flamboyant carnival celebrations, Sciacca is the main town on this stretch of the coast. It was founded in the 5th century BC as a thermal resort for nearby Selinunte and later flourished under the Saracens, who arrived in the 9th century and named it *Xacca* (meaning 'water' in Arabic), and the Normans. Its healing waters continue to be the big drawcard, attracting coachloads of Italian tourists who come to treat their assorted ailments in the sulphurous vapours and mineral-rich mud. Spas and thermal cures apart, it's a laid-back town with an attractive medieval core and some excellent seafood restaurants.

Sciacca retains much of its medieval layout, which divided the town into quarters, each laid out on a strip of rock descending towards the sea. Today interest is focused on the main artery, Corso Vittorio Emanuele, and the historic centre above it. About halfway along the street, Piazza Scandaliato is a popular hang-out, with views (and stairs) to the fishing harbour below.

Sciacca

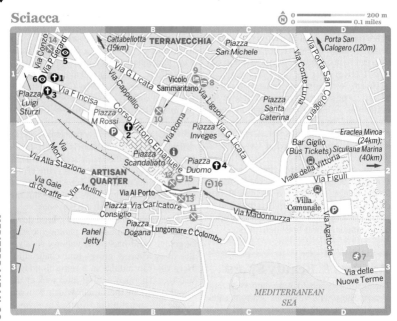

Sciacca

⊙ Sights & Activities

Historic Centre   NEIGHBOURHOOD

The place to start is Sciacca's main street, Corso Vittorio Emanuele, an attractive strip lined with impressive *palazzi*, ceramic shops and some interesting churches. At the western end, Palazzo Steripinto (Corso Vittorio Emanuele) is an imposing example of 16th-century Catalan Gothic architecture, recognisable by its ashlar rustication and twin-mullioned windows.

Just to the south, near Porta San Salvatore, are two interesting churches: the 14th-century Chiesa di Santa Margherita, which features a superb Renaissance portal and a rather chipped baroque interior; and the Chiesa del Carmine, whose odd-looking 13th-century rose window predates the majolica-tiled dome by some 600 years.

Continuing east along Corso Vittorio Emanuele brings you to Piazza Scandaliato, the sloping piazza opposite the tourist office. Here you can hang out with the locals, perhaps over a coffee or lemon *granita* (crushed-ice drink), at the Gran Caffè Scandaglia (☑092 52 10 82; Piazza Scandaliato 5-6), watching the world go by and discussing the events of the day. The square's western end is formed by the Chiesa di San Domenico, an 18th-century reconstruction of a 16th-century church.

Further east, Piazza Duomo is home to Sciacca's handsome Chiesa Madre (☺8am-noon & 4.30-7.30pm). First built in 1108, it was rebuilt in 1656, incorporating three apses from the original Norman structure and adding an uncompleted facade.

Castello Incantato
PUBLIC ART
(Enchanted Castle; ☑092 599 30 44; admission €3.50; ☺9am-1pm & 4-8pm Tue-Sat summer, 9am-1pm & 3-5pm Tue-Sun winter) About 3km east of town, the Castello Incantato is actually a large park festooned with thousands of sculpted heads. The man behind this bizarre collection was Filippo Bentivegna (1888–1967), a local artist who used sculpture to exorcise the memories of an unhappy sojourn in the USA – each head is supposed to represent one of his memories.

His eccentricities were legion and still today people enjoy recalling them. Apparently, he regarded his work as a sexual act and demanded to be addressed as 'Eccellenza' (Your Excellency).

Spa Treatments
SPA
(treatments €34-200) The place to take the waters in town is the Nuovo Stabilimento Termale (☑092 596 11 11; www.grandhoteldelle terme.com; Via Agatocle 2), a thermal-baths complex next door to the Grand Hotel delle Terme. Here you can indulge in a vast range of treatments, including shiatsu massage, mudpacks and hydrotherapy in a 32°C pool. Prices range from €34 for a straightforward facial to €200 for an uplifting 50-minute breast-toning treatment.

With your own car you could also head up to Monte Cronio, 7km out of town, to breathe the natural cave vapours of the Stufe di San Calogero (☑092 52 61 53).

 Eating

Sciacca has an active fishing port which makes it an excellent place to eat fish and seafood. The best fish restaurants are down by the port.

Trattoria Al Faro
SEAFOOD €
(☑092 52 53 49; Via Al Porto 25; set menu €17.50-25; ☺Mon-Sat) If the idea of budget seafood usually sets alarm bells ringing, think again. This welcoming portside trattoria is one of the few places you can feast on delicious

fresh fish and still get change from €20. What's served depends on what the boats have brought in.

Tasty staples to look out for include *pasta con le sarde* (with sardines, fennel, breadcrumbs and raisins) and grilled calamari.

Ristorante Miramare
SICILIAN €
(☑092 52 60 50; Piazza Scandaliato 6; meals €25) Popular with local elderly folk, this restaurant and pizzeria sits on the corner of Sciacca's lovely belvedere. It's a place with simple traditional dishes, such as pasta with tomatoes and seafood, good fresh fish and decent pizza. The harbour views are lovely and it's best to get here for an early evening supper as the sun goes down.

Trattoria La Vecchia Conza
TRATTORIA €€
(☑092 52 53 85; Via Gerardi 39; meals €25-30; ☺Tue-Sun) Near the medieval Porta San Salvatore, this laid-back eatery is popular with lunching locals. It's decked out in typical trattoria style with brick arches and hanging ceramics and serves a predominantly fish-based menu. Follow an antipasto of *polpettine di acciughe* (anchovy balls) with *risotto alla marinara in salsa zafferano* (risotto with seafood in a saffron sauce).

La Lampara
SEAFOOD €€
(☑092 58 50 85; Via Caricatore 33; meals €35; ☺Tue-Sun) In contrast to the scruffy portside streets, La Lampara is a contemporary

SCIACCA CARNIVAL

Sciacca's carnival is famous for its flamboyance and fabulous party atmosphere. Held between the last Thursday before Lent and Shrove Tuesday, and repeated in mid-May, it features an amazing parade of huge papier mâché figures mounted on floats.

The festival opens with carnival king Peppi Nappa receiving the city's keys. The technicolour floats are then released into the streets with their bizarre cast of grotesque caricatures: the figures are handmade each year using traditional methods and are modelled on political and social personalities. The floats wind through the streets of the Old Town, while masked revellers dance to locally composed music and satirical poetry is read aloud.

restaurant serving a modern, creative fish menu. Highly recommended is the tuna steak, cooked in sesame seeds and served with balsamic vinegar, and the chocolate cake with pistachio ice cream.

Hostaria Del Vicolo   MODERN SICILIAN €€€
(☑092 52 30 71; www.hostariadelvicolo.it; Vicolo Sammaritano 10; meals €45-55; ☺closed Sun evening & Mon) Tucked away in a tiny alley in the Old Town, this formal restaurant is a culinary tour de force: heavy tablecloths, noiseless service and an ample wine list. The menu is traditional Sicilian with modern twists, and the fresh pasta is great. Slow Food recommended.

For a *primo* (first course) try the *taglioni al nero di seppia e ricotta salata* (flat strings of pasta with cuttlefish ink and salted ricotta), while *merluzzo ai fichi secchi* (cod with dried figs) makes for a superb main course.

🛍 Shopping

Ceramiche Gaspare Patti   CERAMICS
(☑092 599 32 98; Corso Vittorio Emanuele 95) Sciacca has a long-standing tradition of ceramic production and there are numerous shops selling brightly coloured crockery. For something more original look up this Aladdin's cave of a shop in front of the Chiesa Madre. Gaspare Patti prides himself on his idiosyncratic style and his shop is packed with strange and original creations, well worth a look even if you're not going to buy.

ℹ Information

EMERGENCIES
Police Station (☑092 596 50 11; Via Jacopo Ruffini 12)

MEDICAL SERVICES
Hospital (☑092 596 21 11; Via Pompei)

TOURIST INFORMATION
Tourist Office (☑092 52 27 44; www.servizio-turisticoregionalesciacca.it; Corso Vittorio Emanuele 84; ☺9am-2pm Mon-Fri, 3.30-6.30pm Wed) On the main strip, with helpful English-speaking staff.

ℹ Getting There & Around

BUS
Lumia (☑092 22 04 14; www.autolineelumia. it) serves Agrigento (€6.20, 1¾ hours, 11 daily Monday to Saturday, two Sunday) and Trapani (€8.50, four hours, three daily Monday to Saturday, one Sunday). All buses arrive at the Villa Comunale on Via Figuli and leave from Via Agatocle. Buy your tickets at Bar Giglio at Viale della Vittoria 22.

CAR
Sciacca is about 60km from Agrigento along the SS115. There's parking on Via Agatocle near the Nuovo Stabilimento Termale and on the unnamed piazza beneath Piazza Scandaliato.

Caltabellotta

It's quite a drive up to Caltabellotta. Not so much because of the distances involved – it's only 19km northeast of Sciacca – but because the road rises almost vertically as it winds its way to the hilltop village at 949m above sea level. But make it to the top and you're rewarded with some amazing panoramic views of 21 (apparently) surrounding villages. The highest vantage point is the ruined **Norman castle** at the top of the village, where a peace treaty was signed in 1302 ending the Sicilian Vespers. Viewed from here, the town's terracotta roofs and grey houses appear to cling to the cliffside like a perfect mosaic. The town was originally named Kal'at Bellut by the Arabs, meaning 'oak rock'. Below the castle, the restored **Chiesa Madre** retains an original Gothic portal and pointed arches. On the edge of the village lies the derelict monastery of **San Pellegrino**, from where you can see caves that were used as tombs as far back as prehistoric times.

There is a great, Slow Food recommended restaurant, **M.A.T.E.S.** (☑092 595 23 27; Vicolo Storto 3, Caltabellotta; meals €30; ☺closed Sun dinner & 2 weeks in Oct), in the historic centre, where you can eat some traditional Sicilian fare, such as tagliatelle with broad bean puree and sausage, vegetable risotto, or juicy, falling-off-the-bone roast pork and lamb. Finish with their fantastic *cannoli*.

If you're without a car, Lumia buses serve Caltabellotta from Sciacca (€2.90, 50 minutes, four daily Monday to Friday).

EAST OF AGRIGENTO

The area east of Agrigento is one of marked contrasts. Travel a few kilometres inland from the industrial horror show that surrounds Gela and you'll find a silent, rural world of green fields, hills and sleepy medieval towns. The coast is free of tourist development and with your own transport you'll find some wild, unspoilt beaches.

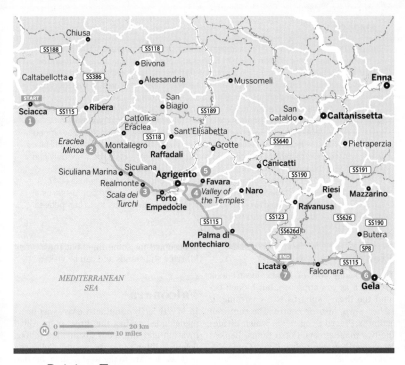

Driving Tour
Temples, Art & Beaches

START SCIACCA
END LICATA
LENGTH 150KM/THREE TO FOUR DAYS

Start in the lovely seaside town of
1 Sciacca. After exploring the centre's
many elegant *palazzi*, descend to the working
port for a lunch of fresh fish. Later, opt for a
spa treatment or a stroll around the Castello
Incantato, where you'll see eccentric local art
in natural surroundings. Some 30km east,
at **2 Eraclea Minoa**, dip your toes first into
ancient history at the archaeological park and
then into seawater at the eponymous beach.
Follow the green-coloured people and smoth-
er your self with rejuvenating clay at the mud
rock. Further is the spectacular **3 Scala dei
Turchi**, a starchy-white rock formation in the
shape of a giant staircase. It's a great place to
watch the sunset and have a picnic dinner.

The peak of the tour is Agrigento's
4 Valley of the Temples (p235), Sicily's

greatest site. Take an entire day to wander
the expansive park. At the end, dine at one of
the restaurants overlooking the temples, lit
by night lights and beaming over the valley.
Don't miss the spectacular **5 Farm Cultural
Park** (p249) at Favara, 14km northeast of
Agrigento – this local art project has taken
over an entire part of the historic centre of
the dilapidated town and injected vibrancy
into the local community. Explore the beaches east of Agrigento and take the slow road
towards Gela, heading for the wild and unspoilt expanses along the Gela Riviera. Avoid
the town of Gela but, if you want some more
ancient art, check out **6 Capo Soprano**
(p250) at its western edge, where you'll find
the town's ancient Greek fortifications and
the ruins of Sicily's only surviving Greek
baths. Double back on the SS115 to end your
tour at **7 Licata**, where the Michelin-starred
restaurant Ristorante La Madia awaits – considered one of Sicily's finest, it makes a great
finale for the journey.

LAMPEDUSA

Lampedusa, the largest of the three Pelagic Islands (the other two are Linosa and Lampione), lies about 200km south of Sicily, closer to Tunisia than Italy. Surrounded by stunning aquamarine waters, it's a popular summer holiday destination whose year-round population of 6100 more than trebles in July and August. In winter transport connections are cut back and almost every hotel and restaurant shuts up shop.

The island's single main attraction is its beaches, which are strung along the 11km south coast. The most famous, and one of the Mediterranean's most beautiful, is Spiaggia dei Conigli (aka Rabbit Beach) at Isola dei Conigli, a dreamy secluded bay lapped by shallow, turquoise waters. The beach is part of a unique nature reserve, the only place in Italy where *Caretta caretta* (loggerhead sea turtles) lay their eggs (between July and August). Other beaches include Cala Francese, Cala Galera and Cala Greca.

Siremar (☎ 89 21 23; www.siremar.it) runs year-round ferries to Lampedusa (€47.10, 9½ hours) from Porto Empedocle. Between late June and early September, Ustica Lines (p78) runs six weekly hydrofoils (€55.40, 4¼ hours). You can fly directly to Lampedusa from Palermo and, in summer, from Rome.

Licata

The workaday port of Licata doesn't look like much as you approach, but hidden behind the dreary suburbs is a charming, if rather worn, historic centre. The centre of action is Piazza Progresso, which divides the two main streets, Corso Roma, flanked by elegant baroque *palazzi,* and Corso Vittorio Emanuele.

At the top of town, a 16th-century castle affords views down to the harbour. As pleasant as it is wandering along Licata's bustling streets, the main reason to stop here is to eat. For a memorable fine-dining experience, Ristorante La Madia (☎ 092 277 14 43; www.ristorantelamadia.it; Via Filippo Re Capriata 22; meals €60; ⊙ Wed-Mon) is Michelin-starred and considered one of Sicily's finest. A labour of love for local-born chef Pino Cuttaia, it serves modern Sicilian dishes based on authentic Mediterranean ingredients, such as *merluzzo* (cod) smoked over pine cones or cuttlefish served with fennel cream. For something simpler, head to the Hostaria L'Oste e il Sacrestano (☎ 092 277 47 36; Via Sant'Andrea 19; meals €30; ⊙ closed Sun dinner & Mon), a Slow Food Movement recommended eatery just off Corso Vittorio Emanuele, where you can feast on local meat and freshly fished seafood.

Beyond Licata, the unexceptional town of Palma di Montechiaro is the ancestral seat of the princes of Lampedusa, made famous by Giuseppe Tomasi di Lampedusa, author of *Il Gattopardo* (The Leopard). The family's 17th-century ancestral palace has been unoccupied for some time, but the Chiesa Matrice still stands and can be visited.

Falconara

In WWII Sicily's southern coast was heavily defended against the threat of an Allied invasion and still today abandoned pillbox defences litter the area around Gela. The best beaches are to the west of town beyond the so-called Gela Riviera, and are wild and unspoilt. At Falconara, 20km west of Gela, you can lay your towel out at a superb sandy beach overlooked by an impressive 14th-century castle, the Castello di Falconara. This is not open to the public as it's privately owned by an aristocratic family, but you can stay by booking through I Castelli (☎ 095 779 30 97; www.icastelli.net).

Gela

POP 77,115

Despite a distinguished past as one of Sicily's great ancient cities, modern Gela is a disappointment, a chaotic industrial city with a reputation as a mafia hot spot. Little remains of its heyday as the economic engine room of the great Greek colony that eventually founded Akragas, Eraclea Minoa and Selinunte. The city was sacked by Carthage in 405 BC and then razed by forces from Agrigento in 282 BC. More recently it was the first Italian town to be liberated by the Allies in WWII (in July 1943), but not before it had been bombed to rubble in the build-up to the invasion. Post-war development saw the construction of the vast petrochemical refineries that still blight the city along with swathes of cheap housing blocks. Other than a fascinating archaeology museum and remains of the city's ancient fortifications, there are few reasons to stop by.

◉ Sights & Activities

Museo Archeologico MUSEUM
(☑ 093 391 26 26; Corso Vittorio Emanuele; adult/reduced incl acropoli & Capo Soprano €3/1.50; ⊙ 9am-6pm, closed last Mon of month) The Museo Archeologico is the only place offering an insight into Gela's great artistic past. It contains artefacts from the city's ancient acropolis and is rightly famed for its staggering collection of red-and-black *kraters* (vases used to mix wine and water), the largest such collection in the world.

These terracotta vases were a local speciality between the 7th and 4th centuries BC, admired throughout the Greek world for the delicacy of their designs and superb figurative work.

Other treasures include Italy's most important collection of ancient vases dating from the 8th to the 6th centuries, and some 600 silver coins minted in Agrigento, Gela, Syracuse, Messina and Athens. At one time the collection numbered more than 1000 coins, but it was stolen in 1976 and only about half of it was ever recovered. More

---

FAVARA: FARM CULTURAL PARK

It's one of the great joys of travel, and indeed life, to come across something so unexpected and mind-bendingly wonderful in the midst of what appears to be the bleakest of places, that one's ideas of what's possible change entirely.

This is the case with Favara, a town that sits a mere 14km from Agrigento's Valley of the Temples but falls off any tourist's map. Favara is known mainly for two things: having one of Italy's highest rates of unemployment and many ugly buildings.

But things changed when, back in 2010, married couple Andrea Bartoli and Favara-born Florinda Saieva bought several abandoned buildings in the town's dilapidated centre and set up a neighbourhood for art, the fantastic **Farm Cultural Park** (www.farm-culturalpark.com; Cortile Bentivegna; ⊙ 10am-1pm & 4-8pm Tue-Fri, 11am-1pm & 4-10pm Sat & Sun) **FREE**. The project brought in international artists, media and visitors, and a whole new breath of life to Favara and its inhabitants – several elderly local women, who had clung to their homes in the semi-abandoned town centre, now live amongst the exhibition spaces. They are happy to have company and to once again reside in a neighbourhood that is safe and alive. 'We wanted to do something that would make Favara a good place for its inhabitants, for our kids. A place where people wanted to live and contribute to', says Bartoli. 'And art is the best way to bring people together and make something worthwhile.' And indeed, once you've spent a few hours wandering around the spaces, and talking to Bartoli, Favara is transformed into one of the most exciting places in Sicily.

The structures that make the farm are areas for exhibitions by international and local artists, and there is a shop, a little garden bar, and a kitchen that is rented out to groups to host dinner parties. There are cultural events, talks, screenings, workshops, shows and, of course, exhibitions, going on at all times. Building walls serve as giant canvases for paintings and sculptures, while courtyards are full of practical installations such as plant-pot chairs and brick fountains; Farm also holds the world's biggest collection of Terry Richardson's provocative fashion photography. Everything is beautifully designed, and the energy of innovation and originality simply oozes out of the space.

Bartoli and Saieva have even managed to incorporate the local castle, the Castello dei Chiaramonte, a largely unused 13th-century building, into his project, hosting various workshops. The number of young local people who come to volunteer at the farm rises each year, and many now see a point in remaining in Favara, rather than looking for work elsewhere. Don't miss this fascinating, inspiring place.

To stay in Favara, try the renovated **Belmonte Hotel** (www.belmontehotel.com; Via Sottotenente Saieva 4-10, off Piazza Cavour; s €60-70, d €90-110) and its good on-site restaurant, Le Traveggole. Farm Cultural Park has an entire masseria, **FARM** (☑ 093 434 66 00; www.farm-ospitalitadicampagna.it; 1 week from €600; **P**✱✦), near the village of Butera, but this is rented out only in its entirety. Still, if you're looking for a gorgeous place to host a big party, look no further.

recently, the city has acquired three unusual terracotta altars. These were found in 2003 in a 5th-century-BC warehouse, which had been buried under 6m of sand.

Outside the museum a gate leads to a small **acropoli** (Acropolis; ⊙ 9am-1hr before sunset), where you can see the scant remains of the ancient Greek acropolis. Adding little to the atmosphere are the belching chimneys of a nearby petrochemical plant.

Capo Soprano · HISTORIC SITE

At the western edge of town, 4km west of the museum, you will find the remains of Gela's ancient **Greek fortifications** (adult/reduced incl acropoli & Museo Archeological €3/1.50; ⊙ 9am-1hr before sunset). Built by the tyrant of Syracuse, Timoleon, in 333 BC, they are in a remarkable state of preservation, most likely the result of being covered by sand dunes for thousands of years until they were discovered in 1948.

The 8m-high walls were built to prevent sand being blown into the city by the blustery sea wind. Today many of the walls are in ruins and the authorities have planted trees to act as a buffer against the encroaching sand. It makes for a pretty site, planted with mimosa and eucalyptus trees, perfect for a picnic. Some 500m from the walls, next to the hospital, are the ruins of Sicily's only surviving **Greek baths** (Via Europa; ⊙ daily), which date to the 4th century BC.

⊙ Getting There & Around

BUS

From Piazza Stazione, in front of the train station, regular buses run to Agrigento and nearby towns, as well as Syracuse and Caltanissetta.

CAR

Gela is well connected by road: the SS115 leads westwards to Agrigento and east to Ragusa and Modica, while the SS117bis connects with Caltagirone (via the SS417) and Piazza Armerina. Follow the signs for the town centre and museum, which is at the eastern end of Corso Vittorio Emanuele, the town's principal east–west street.

Hilltop Towns

From Gela, it's an easy 20km drive along the SP8 up to the lovely hilltop village of **Butera**. Prosperous and content under the Spanish rule of the Branciforte family, Butera lacks the down-at-heel atmosphere of many rural towns in the interior, even if its location ensures an air of self-sufficient isolation. It has a lovely town church, the **Chiesa Madre**, with some modest treasures, a Renaissance triptych and a painting of the Madonna by Filippino Paladino, but the main sight is the panorama that unfolds beneath you from the hilltop **Norman castle**.

Continuing northwards, winding through kilometres of deserted farmland, passing the occasional tractor, the SS190 leads up to **Mazzarino**, the historic seat of the Branciforte clan. Now a small, sleepy town, it's definitely worth a quick look for its clutch of baroque churches, many of which boast works of art by the Tuscan 16th-century artist Filippino Paladino, and the ostentatious funerary monuments of the Branciforte princes. Many of the churches are closed to the public, but you can get into them by asking at the super-helpful **tourist office** (☑ 093 438 49 84; Corso Vittorio Emanuele 410; ⊙ 9am-1pm & 4-8pm summer, 9am-1pm & 3-7pm winter) on the main street.

Accommodation

Best Places to Stay

➡ Hotel Signum (p259)

➡ Pensione Tranchina (p254)

➡ Villa Athena (p267)

➡ Hotel Villa Belvedere (p261)

Best Agriturismi

➡ Agriturismo San Marco (p264)

➡ Villa Quartarella (p265)

➡ Green Manors Country Hotel (p258)

➡ Villa dei Papiri (p265)

Best B&Bs

➡ Il Profumo del Sale (p256)

➡ Palazzo Pantaleo (p252)

➡ Isoco Guest House (p261)

➡ B&B Crociferi (p262)

Where to Stay

There's no shortage of alluring accommodation options in Sicily. At the budget end of the price spectrum you can opt for a *pensione* (guesthouse) or a B&B, both of which will generally be of one- to three-star standard. *Alberghi* (hotels), which may range from one star to five stars, are more expensive. *Locande* (inns) and *affittacamere* (rooms for rent) are not included in the star classification system; they are usually the cheapest options on offer, although in some areas (such as the Aeolian Islands) the standard can be very high and prices are adjusted accordingly.

Around Etna and Piano Battaglia in the Parco Naturale Regionale delle Madonie there are a number of *rifugi* (mountain chalets), most of which are open all year. Many are operated by Club Alpino Siciliano.

Agriturismi (working farms and country houses that offer rooms to visitors on holiday) are becoming more common and are well worth considering, as is the small but slowly growing number of boutique hotels on the island.

Pricing

Unless otherwise indicated, prices quoted in our reviews are for a double room with private bathroom, expressed as a range from low-season to high-season rates. Low-season rates usually apply from October to Easter (with the exception of the Christmas holidays). July, August and Christmas are generally considered high season, while mid-season rates apply the remainder of the year.

Note that each accommodation is assigned a price category (€, €€ or €€€) based on its high-season price.

CATEGORY	COST
€	< €110
€€	€110 to €200
€€€	> €200

PALERMO

In recent years Palermo has seen a dramatic increase in its supply of B&Bs, providing an alternative to the city's more established hotels. The fact that this is a big, busy city means that most hotel rooms come complete with street noise. It's also worth noting that many options occupy floors in historic *palazzi*, where stairs rather than lifts provide the only access.

Palazzo Pantaleo
B&B €

(Map p64; ☑ 091 32 54 71; www.palazzopantaleo. it; Via Ruggero Settimo 74h; s/d/ste €80/100/140; ℗ 🐀) Offering unbeatable comfort and convenient location, Giuseppe Scaccianoce's cheerful B&B occupies the top floor of an old *palazzo* half a block from Piazza Politeama, hidden from the busy street in a quiet courtyard with free parking. The five rooms feature high ceilings, marble, tile or wooden floors, soundproof windows and modern bathroom fixtures. There's also one spacious suite.

B&B Amélie
B&B €

(Map p64; ☑ 091 33 59 20; www.bb-amelie.it; Via Prinicipe di Belmonte 94; s €40-60, d €60-80, tr €90-100; ❀ @ 🐀) On a pedestrianised New City street a stone's throw from Teatro Politeama, the affable, multilingual Angela has converted her grandmother's spacious 6th floor flat into a cheery B&B. Rooms are colourfully decorated, and the corner triple has a sunny terrace. Angela, a native Palermitan, generously shares her local knowledge and serves a tasty breakfast featuring homemade cakes and jams.

People with allergies needn't worry about the cat on the logo; the place is spotless, with no pets or fur in sight!

Butera 28
APARTMENT €

(Map p58; ☑ 333 3165432; www.butera28.it; Via Butera 28; apt per day €60-180, per week €380-1150; ❀ 🐀) Delightful multilingual owner Nicoletta rents 11 comfortable apartments in her elegant *palazzo* near Piazza della Kalsa. Units range in size from 30 to 180 sq metres, most sleeping a family of four or more. Four apartments face the sea (No 9 is especially nice), most have laundry facilities and all have well-equipped kitchens. Nicoletta also offers fabulous cooking classes.

Hotel Orientale
HOTEL €

(Map p58; ☑ 091 616 57 27; www.albergoorientale.191.it; Via Maqueda 26; s €30, d €40-50, tr €50-60; ❀ 🐀) This *palazzo*'s grand marble stairway and arcaded courtyard, complete with rusty bicycles, stray cats and strung-up washing, is an evocative introduction to one of Palermo's most atmospherically faded budget hotels. Breakfast is served under the lovely frescoed ceiling in the library. Room 8 overlooks the tail end of the Ballaró market, close enough to hear vendors singing in the morning.

B&B Novecento
B&B €

(Map p58; ☑ 091 976 11 94; www.bed-breakfast-palermo.com; Via Roma 62; s €45-65, d €50-100; ❀ 🐀) Convenient to the train station, this welcoming B&B on the 5th floor of a Via Roma *palazzo* wins guests over with the warm hospitality of owners Elisa and Dario and a breakfast emphasizing homemade bread and organic ingredients. Each room has its own private exterior bathroom just across the hall.

A Casa di Amici
HOSTEL €

(Map p54; ☑ 091 58 48 84; www.acasadiamici.com; Via Volturno 6; dm €19-23, d €65, without bathroom d €40; ❀ @ 🐀) In a renovated 19th-century *palazzo*, this artsy, hostel-type place behind Teatro Massimo has four colourful rooms sleeping two to four, with shared bathrooms and a guest kitchen. Two annexes, including one on Via Dante (opened in 2013), offer additional rooms, including one family-friendly unit with private bathroom and terrace. Multilingual owner Claudia provides helpful maps, information displays and advice.

Ai Cartari
B&B €

(Map p58; ☑ 091 611 63 72; www.aicartari.com; Via Alessandro Paternostro 62; d €80-120; ❀ 🐀) Live like a Palermitan in one of these two nicely decorated suites (each of which sleeps up to five people). Your front door opens on to the cute Piazza San Francesco d'Assisi, and Palermo's most famous *focacceria*, Antica Focacceria di San Francesco, is just on your doorstep. Minimum two-night stay.

BB22
B&B €€

(Map p58; ☑ 335 790 87 33; www.bb22.it; Largo Cavalieri di Malta 22; s €100-140, d €140-210; ❀ @ 🐀) A B&B in name only, Palermo's most gorgeous small hotel is a little palace of luxury, with welcoming hosts, elegant and stylish rooms, silky quilts, quirky designer lamps, plasma TVs and firm beds. It's all tucked away on a tiny back street in the midst of the Vucciria neighbourhood.

As good as the regular rooms are, it's the suite that wins our undying affection. The

ACCOMMODATION PRICING

free-standing bath is placed conveniently in front of the luscious bed, the room is beautified with antique furniture and gorgeous wooden floors, you get your own walk-in wardrobe and you can pop open your champagne in the designer kitchenette. Pure honeymoon material!

Grand Hotel Piazza Borsa HOTEL €€
(Map p58; ☑ 091 32 00 75; www.piazzaborsa.com; Via dei Cartari 18; s €119-189, d €160-208, ste €350-790; P ❋ @ ☎) Opened in 2010 in Palermo's former stock exchange, this grand four-star hotel encompasses three separate buildings housing 127 rooms. Nicest are the high-ceilinged suites with Jaccuzis and windows facing Piazza San Francesco. Parking costs €18 per 24-hour period.

Quintocanto Hotel & Spa HOTEL €€
(Map p54; ☑ 091 58 49 13; www.quintocantohotel.com; Corso Vittoria Emanuele 310; s €125-135, d €145-195, ste €254; ❋ ☎) Housed in a modernised 16th-century *palazzo*, Quintocanto woos visitors with its prime city-centre location and a wellness centre where guests enjoy free access to the sauna, Turkish bath and whirlpool tub (additional spa services including massages cost extra). Book ahead for rooms 319 and 420, which have terraces with superb views of San Giuseppe dei Teatini church next door.

The hotel's excellent restaurant is operated by the team from Mondello's acclaimed Bye Bye Blues.

Hotel Principe di Villafranca BOUTIQUE HOTEL €€
(Map p64; ☑ 091 611 85 23; www.principedivillafranca.it; Via Turrisi Colonna 4; d €108-297; P ❋ @ ☎) Furnished with fine linens and antiques, this sophisticated hotel is just west of Viale della Libertá in one of Palermo's most peaceful, exclusive neighbourhoods. Public spaces include a cosy sitting area with library, fireplace and displays of local designers' work; among the comfortable, high-ceilinged rooms, junior suite 105 stands out, decorated with artwork loaned by Palermo's modern art museum.

Hotel Ucciardhome HOTEL €€
(Map p64; ☑ 091 34 84 26; www.hotelucciardhome.com; Via Enrico Albanese, 34; r €65-150, ste €130-280; ❋ ☎) 'Become a prisoner of relaxation!' – so reads the marketing spiel at this boutiquey business hotel opposite Palermo's notorious Ucciardone prison. Large rooms with ultra-comfortable beds are decorated in an

elegant minimalist style, and there's also a wine bar for relaxing after a day spent exploring the city. Rates fluctuate widely based on demand; check online for last-minute deals.

Grand Hotel et des Palmes HOTEL €€
(Map p64; ☑ 091 602 81 11; www.grandhotel-et-des-palmes.com; Via Roma 398; s €95-165, d €105-260, ste €245-385; P ❋ @ ☎) Dating from 1874, this is one of Palermo's most historically fascinating hotels. Like a royal court, it's been the scene of intrigue, liaisons and double-dealings. The grand salons still impress with their chandeliers and gigantic mirrors, while the rooms feature high ceilings and marble-clad bathrooms. Rates drop considerably during slow periods; look online for the best deals.

Around Palermo

Ustica

Le Terrazze APARTMENTS €
(☑ 091 844 99 01; www.leterrazzeustica.it; Via C Colombo 3; d apt €40-99; ❋ ☎) The lovely Carmen presides over this family-run cluster of apartments, all with kitchens and – as the name would imply – terraces with harbour views. Rooms number 1 through 8 sleep two to three people, with sea views improving as the numbers increase. There's also a family unit (number 9), sleeping four, with its own private terrace.

Hotel Clelia HOTEL €
(☑ 091 844 90 39; www.hotelclelia.it; Via Sindaco I 29, Ustica; s €29-95, d €48-158; ❋ @ ☎) Especially good value in the off-season, this centrally located three-star hotel with attached restaurant also rents out holiday houses sleeping two to four people. Staff can help organise scooter and boat hire, diving and snorkelling tours and guided walks.

Hotel Diana

HOTEL €

(☑091 844 91 09; www.hoteldiana-ustica.com; Contrada San Paolo; r per person €40-60, with half board €55-80; ☺Easter-Oct; ⓐⓦ) High on a hillside 1km south of town, this odd-looking cylindrical hotel has been run by the same family since 1964. Despite the rather dated atmosphere, there are plenty of positives here: friendly staff, a pool with panoramic terrace, a seaside swimming platform (accessed by a long steep staircase), and home-cooked meals featuring produce from the surrounding fields.

Ficuzza

Antica Stazione Ferrovia di Ficuzza

HOTEL €

(☑091 846 00 00; www.anticastazione.it; Ficuzza; per person €35, with half-board €55; ⓦ ⓐ) Off the SS118, between Palermo and Corleone, this restaurant and hotel offers a truly unique accommodation option, occupying a de-commissioned 19th-century train station in the middle of thick woods where Bourbon princes once hunted game. Rooms are simple but comfortable and the restaurant is a real highlight. Staff can assist you with outdoor activities in the nearby national park, including horse-riding, hiking and mountain-bike riding.

The hotel hosts two annual live jazz and blues events: the Ficuzza J & B Summerfest in August and the Ficuzza J & B Winter Club in late February/early March.

WESTERN SICILY

Castellammare del Golfo

Hotel Cala Marina

HOTEL €€

(☑0924 53 18 41; www.hotelcalamarina.it; Via Zangara 1; s €4w0-90, d €65-160; ℗@ⓐ) Only a 30-minute drive from Falcone-Borsolino airport, this small hotel overlooking Castellammare's harbour is known for its helpful staff and clean, comfortable rooms. It's worth paying a bit extra for an executive room as these come with balconies overlooking the sea. On-site garage parking costs €5, or you can park free on nearby streets.

Scopello

★Pensione Tranchina

PENSION €

(☑0924 54 10 99; www.pensionetranchina.com; Via Diaz 7; B&B per person €36-46, half-board per person €55-72; ⓦⓐ) Wonderful home-cooked meals, a prime location in the centre of Scopello, and the friendly welcome of hosts Marisin and Salvatore make this one of western Sicily's most beloved *pensioni*. Rooms are modern, with the best enjoying balconies with distant sea views. On chilly evenings, guests share stories around the blazing fire downstairs.

Tonnara di Scopello

APARTMENT €€

(☑339 307 19 70; www.tonnaradiscopello.com; Largo Tonnara Scopello; apt per week €560-2100; ℗) The accommodation is basic (no TV, air-con or breakfast), but this will quickly be forgiven once you set eyes on this historic *tonnara* (former tuna-processing plant) in a small cove on the water's edge, with its own pebbled swimming beach and seafront terrace. The 13 kitchen-equipped apartments sleep two to six, with a minimum seven-day stay required in summer.

Pricing varies wildly according to availability, the season and the number of guests.

Riserva Naturale dello Zingaro

Baglio La Luna

B&B €

(☑335 836 28 56; www.bagliolaluna.com; s €70-100, d €70-130; ☺Apr-Oct; ℗) Perched high on a hillside 2km outside the northern entrance to Riserva Naturale dello Zingaro, this B&B is a great place to get away from it all. The converted old farmhouse houses five rooms, the best of which have sea views (worth the €10 surcharge). Breakfast is served on a stone terrace under the trees, with birds singing all around.

Trapani

Ai Lumi B&B

B&B €

(Map p93; ☑0923 54 09 22; www.ailumi.it; Corso Vittorio Emanuele 71; s €40-70, d €70-100, tr €90-125, q €100-150; ⓦⓐ) Housed in an 18th-century *palazzo,* this centrally located B&B offers 13 rooms of varying size. Best are the spacious apartments (numbers 33, 34 and 35), with kitchenettes and balconies overlooking Trapani's most elegant pedestrian street. Upstairs apartment 23 is also lovely, with a private balcony reached by a spiral staircase. Guests get discounts at the hotel's atmospheric restaurant next door.

Albergo Maccotta HOTEL €
(Map p93; ☑ 0923 2 84 18; www.albergomaccotta. it; Via degli Argentieri 4; s €30-40, d without breakfast €60-75; ✳ @ 🕲) This unassuming hotel in the centre of the Old Town offers clean and neat rooms. There's no atmosphere to speak of, but prices are extremely reasonable, the location is quiet and there are features including satellite TV in every room. The optional breakfast costs extra (€5 per couple, or €3 for individuals).

Le Chiavi di San Francesco HOTEL €
(Map p93; ☑ 0923 43 80 13; www.lechiavidisanfrancesco.com; Via Tartaglia 18; d €80-110, ste €140; ✳ 🕲) Opposite the Chiesa di San Francesco, this popular hotel has 16 rooms featuring cheerful colour schemes and small but clean bathrooms. Angle for one of the superior rooms up front, which offer more space, better light and optional kitchen facilities.

Erice

Note that temperatures in Erice can plummet in winter, and hotels tend to skimp on heating when there aren't many guests.

Baglio Santa Croce HOTEL €€
(☑ 0923 89 11 11; www.bagliosantacroce.it; SS 187, km 12.3, Contrada Ragosia da Santa Croce, Valderice; per person B&B €54-65, half board €70-82, full board €85-98; P ✳ 🕲 ✖) This converted 17th-century baglio is located 9km east of Erice in Valderice. Set amid citrus groves and lush gardens, the original stone building and its less attractive modern extension offer 67 rooms, some with exposed stone walls and wooden ceiling beams. There's a restaurant, and the swimming pool, with its stupendous views, is a great addition in summer.

Hotel Elimo HOTEL €€
(Map p97; ☑ 0923 86 93 77; www.hotelelimo.it; Via Vittorio Emanuele 23; s €80-110, d €90-130, ste €150-170; P @ 🕲) Communal spaces at this atmospheric historic house are filled with tiled beams, marble fireplaces, intriguing art, knick-knacks and antiques. The bedrooms are more mainstream, although many (along with the hotel terrace and restaurant) have breathtaking vistas south and

west towards the Saline di Trapani, the Egadi Islands and the shimmering sea.

Hotel San Domenico HOTEL €€
(Map p97; ☑ 0923 86 01 28; www.hotel-sandomenico.it; Via Tommaso Guarrasi 26; s €65-100, d €75-145; ✳ 🕲) The most comfortable rooms in town are on offer at this immaculately kept, family-run hotel. The best of the bunch, room 301, has its own panoramic terrace, but all offer modern conveniences including minibars, LCD TVs and updated bathrooms. The delicious breakfast features fresh pastries.

Egadi Islands

Favignana

★ Cas'almare BOUTIQUE HOTEL €€€
(☑ 0923 92 15 76; www.casalmarefavignana.com; Strada Comunale Frascia; d €200-300; ⊙ late May-early Oct; P ✳) This stylish resort right at the water's edge has only five rooms, all converted from an old fisherman's house, with lovely views of the sea and the striking rock formations just offshore, which shelter natural warm pools for guests to soak in. The nicest two rooms upstairs have splendid bathtubs and can be joined together into a family suite.

Il Giardino delle Aloe AGRITURISMO €
(☑ 348 412 30 40; www.ilgiardinodellealoe.it; 2-person apt € 50-150, 3-person apt €70-170, 4-person apt €80-180; ♿) Only 200m by footpath from Grotta Perciata beach, this family-friendly agriturismo is beautifully landscaped, with lush green lawns, herb gardens and desert plants, including several aloe species. Each of the seven apartments (including one built into a tufa cave) comes with full kitchen, there's an onsite restaurant and free bikes are provided for the easy 3km commute into Favignana town.

Albergo Egadi HOTEL €€
(☑ 0923 92 12 32; www.albergoegadi.it; Via Colombo 17, Favignana town; s €65-115, d €100-200; ✳ 🕲) The classiest of several in-town hotel options, Albergo Egadi is a real treat. The stylish rooms feature attractive colour schemes and excellent bathrooms; the two on the top floor share a panoramic terrace. The hotel also has a restaurant, which offers a seafood-dominated tasting menu that changes each night.

Cas'almare shares a beach club with its equally chic sister resort Casa Favonio, on the west side of the island with olive groves, vegetable gardens and sunset views over neighbouring Marettimo.

Levanzo

Albergo Paradiso   HOTEL €€

(☑ 0923 92 40 80; www.albergoparadiso.eu; Via Lungomare; per person with half board €50-85, with full board €70-100; ☺ closed Nov-Mar; ☀) Levanzo's most attractive accommodation option has 15 rooms and a pretty geranium-clad terrace where you can eat well (meals €30 to €40). Rooms are simply furnished, but have sea views.

Marettimo

★Marettimo Residence   APARTMENT €€

(☑ 0923 92 32 02; www.marettimoresidence.it; Via Telegrafo 3; d with breakfast €75-165, weekly apt without breakfast d €360-1200, q €600-1700, plus cleaning charge of €40-60; @ 🕿 ☀ ♿) Lovingly landscaped with bougainvillea, palms and herbs, this hillside complex south of the port is ideal for families or anyone wishing to linger a while on Marettimo. Each of the 44 apartments comes with a kitchen and porch. It has a small swimming pool, a pair of Jacuzzis, a kids' playground, a cafe, a barbecue area and a multilingual library.

One night a week, Bolognese owner Fausto hosts a dinner in which local fishermen and their families provide the food and guests pay the fishermen directly. The residence is open year-round.

Marsala

★Il Profumo del Sale   B&B €

(Map p104; ☑ 0923 189 04 72; www.ilprofumodelsale.it; Via Vaccari 8; s €35, d €50-60; 🕿) A dream B&B in every imaginable way, Profumo del Sale has a perfect city-centre location and three attractive rooms – including a palatial front unit with cathedral views from its small balcony – all enhanced by welcoming touches such as almond cookies and fine soaps. Sophisticated owner Celsa is full of great tips about Marsala and the local area.

Hotel Carmine   HOTEL €€

(Map p104; ☑ 0923 71 19 07; www.hotelcarmine.it; Piazza Carmine 16; s €70-105, d €100-130; 🅿 ☀ @ 🕿) This lovely hotel in a 16th-century monastery has elegant rooms (especially

numbers 7 and 30), with original blue-and-gold majolica tiles, stone walls, antique furniture and lofty beamed ceilings. Enjoy your cornflakes in the baronial-style breakfast room with its historic frescoes and over-the-top chandelier, or sip your drink by the roaring fireplace in winter. Modern perks include a rooftop solarium.

Selinunte

The hotels in Marinella di Selinunte are sorely lacking in charm. Be warned that the smell from the marina can be a bit whiffy.

★Sicilia Cuore Mio   B&B €

(Map p109; ☑ 0924 4 60 77; www.siciliacuoremio.it; Via della Cittadella 44; d €68-95; 🕿 ♿) An absolute no-brainer for anyone staying overnight in Selinunte, this lovely B&B is smack between the ruins and the sea, with an upstairs terrace overlooking both. Alba Centonze rents out five rooms, including an ultra-family-friendly seven-person apartment, in her grandparents' remodelled 19th-century home. Guests enjoy breakfast (including homemade jams, cannoli and more) on a shady patio bordered by olive trees.

TYRRHENIAN COAST

Cefalù

B&B Casanova   B&B €

(Map p117; ☑ 0921 92 30 65; www.casanovabb.it; Via Porpora 3; s €40-70, d €55-100, q €80-140; ☀ 🕿) This B&B on the waterfront has rooms of varying size, from a cramped single with one minuscule window to the Ruggero room, a palatial space sleeping up to four, with a vaulted frescoed ceiling, decorative tile floors and French doors offering grand views of Cefalù's medieval centre. All guests share access to a small terrace overlooking the sea.

La Plumeria   HOTEL €€

(Map p117; ☑ 0921 92 58 97; www.laplumeriahotel.it; Corso Ruggero 185; d €129-209; 🅿 ☀ 🕿) Opened in 2010, this hotel's big selling point is its perfect location between the *duomo* and the waterfront, with free parking a few minutes away. Rooms are unexceptional, but clean and well-appointed. Room 301 on the top floor is the sweetest of the lot, a cosy eyrie with checkerboard tile floors and a small terrace looking up to the *duomo*.

Hotel Kalura
HOTEL €€

(☎ 0921 42 13 54; www.hotel-kalura.com; Via Vincenzo Cavallaro 13; d €89-179; P ❀ @ ☀) East of town on a rocky outcrop, this German-run, family-oriented hotel has its own pebbly beach, restaurant and fabulous pool. Most rooms have sea views, and the hotel arranges loads of activities, including mountain biking, hiking, canoeing, pedalos, diving and dance nights. It's a 20-minute walk into town.

Castelbuono

Relais Santa Anastasia
HOTEL €€

(☎ 0921 67 22 33; www.santa-anastasia-relais.it; Contrada Santa Anastasia; s €80-190, d €125-245) Set amid the picturesque vineyards of a highly regarded wine estate, this converted 12th-century abbey boasts extremely comfortable rooms, a sensational pool terrace with views of the Aeolian Islands and two restaurants serving food and wine from the estate. You'll find it 9km from Castelbuono in the direction of Cefalù.

Piano Battaglia

Rifugio Piero Merlino
HOSTEL €

(☎ 0921 64 99 95; www.rifugiopieromerlino.it; r per person €35, with half board/full board €50/65) Run by the Club Alpino Siciliano, this simple chalet with wood-panelled rooms sleeping two or four and is open year-round. There are eating and drinking areas, and staff can provide information on skiing, cycling and walking.

Petralia Sottana

★ Albergo Il Castello
HOTEL €

(☎ 0921 64 12 50; www.il-castello.net; Via Generale di Maria 27; s/d €40/70; ❀) Tucked into a back street above Petralia Sottana's Duomo, this pretty-as-a-picture inn has immaculate rooms and three-star amenities. Its restaurant specialises in pizza (weekends only) and top-notch mountain cuisine featuring local mushrooms and truffles. Driving up the narrow winding streets to the hotel calls for Schumacher-standard driving skills; you're better off parking in the free public lot three blocks below.

Polizzi Generosa

Antico Feudo San Giorgio
AGRITURISMO €

(☎ 0921 60 06 90; www.feudosangiorgio.it; SS120, km 46, Contrada San Giorgio; r per person with breakfast €40-50, with half board €55-70; ☀ ♨) At the foot of the Madonie, just 4km from the autostrada (motorway), owners Fabiola and Giancorado have converted this 300-hectare *fattoria* (fortified country estate) into an *agriturismo* producing organic olives, grain, beef and wine. Rooms are simple (no aircon, no TV), encouraging guests to appreciate the divine setting: steep, rolling hills and ancient trees planted with the dowry money of Giancarlo's grandmother.

Meals featuring local produce are served downstairs in a large dining room with vaulted ceilings. In late summer they still make homemade tomato sauce in a giant copper cauldron.

Castel di Tusa

★ Atelier Sul Mare
BOUTIQUE HOTEL €€

(☎ 0921 33 42 95; www.ateliersulmare.com; Via Battisti 4; s €85-95, d €120-140, art rooms s €105-115, d €160-180; P ❀ @) Founded by Antonio Presti, the entrepreneur and art collector behind the town's Fiumara d'Arte project, this utterly whimsical hotel at the water's edge has 22 'art rooms' conceptualised and realised by Italian and international artists between 1990 and 2013. There are also 18 standard rooms, all with original artworks and many with sea views. Check the website for special offers.

The entire hotel is treated like an art project, with tours offered Saturdays and Sundays at noon (free for guests, €5 for nonguests). Guests who stay longer than one night are invited to change rooms as often as they like to get an intimate perspective on multiple artists' work.

Parco Regionale dei Nebrodi

Agriturismo Pardo
AGRITURISMO €

(☎ 0941 66 40 03; www.agriturismopardo.it; Contrada Pardo, Ucria; half board per person €50; P) Run by an octogenarian retired vascular surgeon, this *agriturismo* in Ucria (on the road to Floresta) offers high-ceilinged rooms with sweeping sea and valley views in an old stone building surrounded by hazelnut orchards. The fabulous dinners feature locally sourced seasonal treats such as battered and delicately fried sage leaves, wild asparagus risotto or pasta with hazelnuts, bacon and anchovies.

San Marco d'Alunzio

B&B La Tela di Penelope B&B €
(☑ 0941 79 77 34; www.lateladipenelope-vacanze. com; Via Aluntina 48; s €35-45, d €50-70; ❈ ☎) Attached to a traditional weaving studio, this three-room B&B is perfectly placed in the heart of picturesque San Marco d'Alunzio. Rooms (two with private balconies) enjoy views of the historic centre or the distant Aeolian Islands, and all guests share a small kitchen. Owners can arrange tours of the weaving studio, the town and the nearby Parco Regionale dei Nebrodi.

Milazzo

B&B L'Alberghetto B&B €
(☑ 393 9633705; www.lalberghettobeb.it; Via Umberto I 142; d €65-100, 3-person apt €85-130, 4-person apt €100-150; ❈ ☎) Run by the superfriendly Stefano and Barbara, this B&B halfway between the port and the castle has been lovingly remodelled, retaining historical details while incorporating brand-new fixtures throughout. There are three rooms in the main house, but families will want to look across the street at the pair of comfortable apartments with clean white walls, exposed stone-and-brick arches and full kitchens.

Petit Hotel HOTEL €€
(☑ 090 928 67 84; www.petithotel.it; Via dei Mille; s €65-104, d €89-129; ❈ ☎) Right opposite the hydrofoil dock, the Petit Hotel makes much of its ecofriendly credentials, featuring renewable energy sources, biodegradable paint, organic cotton sheets and delicious, organically sourced breakfasts. Rooms are spic and span, with lovely Caltagirone tile floors; front-facing units enjoy ferry-port views, as does the 2nd-floor terrace.

Around Milazzo

Green Manors Country Hotel AGRITURISMO €€
(☑ 090 974 65 15; www.greenmanors.it; Via Porticato, Castroreale; d incl breakfast & dinner €140-200; P ❈ @ ☎) Family-run and absolutely gorgeous, Green Manors is set in 7 acres of gardens and offers everything guests look

for in a good *agriturismo:* attentive and friendly service, large pool, tranquil rural atmosphere and excellent food. There are nine individually decorated rooms, two of which have private terraces. Shuttle service is available from Milazzo (€25, 30 minutes) or Taormina (€70, 50 minutes).

AEOLIAN ISLANDS

Lipari

★**Diana Brown** B&B €
(Map p136; ☑ 090 981 25 84; www.dianabrown. it; Vico Himera 3; s €30-90, d €40-100, tr €50-130; ❈ ☎) Tucked down a narrow alley, South African Diana's delightful rooms sport tile floors, abundant hot water and welcome extras such as kettles, fridges, clothes-drying racks and satellite TV. Units downstairs are darker but have built-in kitchenettes. There's a sunny breakfast terrace and solarium with deck chairs, plus book exchange and laundry service. Optional breakfast costs €5 extra per person.

Enzo Il Negro GUESTHOUSE €
(Map p136; ☑ 090 981 31 63; www.enzoilnegro.com; Via Garibaldi 29; s €40-50, d €60-90; ❈ ☎) Run by an older couple, this simple guesthouse near Marina Corta offers spacious, tiled, pine-furnished rooms with fridges. Two panoramic terraces overlook the rooftops, the harbour and the castle walls.

Casajanca BOUTIQUE HOTEL €€
(☑ 090 988 02 22; www.casajanca.it; Via Marina Garibaldi 115, Canneto; d €80-200; ❈) A stone's throw from the beach at Canneto, this is a charming little hotel with 10 rooms, all decorated with polished antique furniture and impeccable taste. The dappled courtyard, a relaxing place to enjoy breakfast, boasts an inviting natural thermal water pool. Pets are welcome, and transfers from Lipari's port are included in the price.

Villa Diana HOTEL €€
(☑ 090 981 14 03; www.villadiana.com; Via Edwin Hunziker 1; s €45-80, d €67-145; ⊙ closed Nov-Mar; P ❈ ☎) Swiss artist Edwin Hunziker converted this Aeolian house into a bohemian-spirited hotel in the 1950s. It stands above Lipari town in a garden of citrus trees and olives and offers panoramic views from the terrace. Amenities include free private parking and use of the tennis court.

Hotel Giardino Sul Mare   HOTEL €€
(⌨ 090 981 10 04; www.giardinosulmare.it; Via Maddalena 65; d €80-230; ☺ Apr-Oct; ❋ ✉) This family-run hotel's top attraction is its superb seaside location, a few blocks south of Marina Corta. The pool terrace on the cliff edge is fabulous, but if you prefer to swim in the sea there's also direct access to a rocky platform below. Most rooms have terraces and high ceilings; they're a bit tired and bland otherwise.

Vulcano

Casa Arcada   B&B, APARTMENT €
(⌨ 347 6497633; www.casaarcada.it; Via Sotto Cratere; B&B per person €27-55, d apt per week €350-790; ❋) Conveniently located at the foot of the volcano, 20m back from the main road between the port and the crater path, this sweet whitewashed complex offers bed and breakfast in five simple rooms with air-con and minifridges, along with weekly rental apartments. The communal upstairs terrace affords lovely views up to the volcano and across the water to Lipari.

Casa delle Stelle   B&B €
(⌨ 347 9063689; www.bblacasadellestelle.blogspot.it; Contrada Gelso; per person €25-30; Ⓟ) This lovely hideaway, high in the hills above the island's south shore, is run by former Gelso lighthouse keeper Sauro and his wife Maria. The two guest rooms share a living room, fully equipped kitchen and panoramic terrace with spectacular views of the Mediterranean and a distant Mt Etna. In summer, local buses will drop you at the gate.

Salina

A Cannata   PENSION €€
(⌨ 090 984 31 61; www.acannata.it; Via Umberto, Lingua; r per person incl breakfast €40-90, incl half-board €65-115; ☎) Near Lingua's waterfront, this long-established family-run *pensione* offers three simple rooms above its superb Slow Food-acclaimed restaurant, but its best accommodations are in the cheerful orange and blue annexe down the street, completely remodeled in 2013. Here you'll find 25 spacious units gleaming with hand-painted tiles, many overlooking Lingua's picturesque salt lagoon. Half-board is optional year-round, but highly recommended.

Hotel Mamma Santina   BOUTIQUE HOTEL €€
(⌨ 090 984 30 54; www.mammasantina.it; Via Sanità 40, Santa Marina Salina; d €110-250; ☺ Apr-Oct; ❋ @ ☎ ✉) A labour of love for its architect owner, this boutique hotel has inviting rooms decorated with pretty tiles in traditional Aeolian designs. Many of the sea-view terraces come equipped with hammocks, and on warm evenings the attached restaurant (meals €35 to €40) has outdoor seating overlooking the glowing blue pool and landscaped garden.

La Locanda del Postino   HOTEL €€
(⌨ 090 984 39 58; www.lalocandadelpostino.it; Via Picone 10, Pollara; €100-240; ❋) This whitewashed 10-room hotel's main claim to fame is its peaceful end-of-the-line location in the hills above Pollara. The large shared terrace with Aeolian-style columns and sea views is pleasant for lounging, though value for money is not as great as at other places around Salina.

★ **Hotel Signum**   BOUTIQUE HOTEL €€
(⌨ 090 984 42 22; www.hotelsignum.it; Via Scalo 15, Malfa; d €160-500; ❋ ☎ ✉) Hidden in Malfa's hillside lanes and gleaming with recent renovations is this alluring labyrinth of antique-clad rooms, peach-coloured stucco walls, tall blue windows and vine-covered terraces with full-on views of Stromboli. The attached wellness centre, a stunning pool and one of the island's best-regarded restaurants make this the perfect place to unwind for a few days in utter comfort.

Capofaro   BOUTIQUE HOTEL €€€
(⌨ 090 984 43 30; www.capofaro.it; Via Faro 3, Malfa; d €230-440, ste €370-640; ☺ late Apr–early Oct; ❋ @ ☎ ✉) Immerse yourself in luxury at this five-star boutique resort halfway between Santa Marina and Malfa, surrounded by well-tended Malvasia vineyards and a picturesque lighthouse. The 20 rooms all have sharp white decor and terraces looking straight out to smoking Stromboli. Tennis courts, poolside massages, wine tasting, vineyard visits and occasional cooking courses complete this perfect vision of island chic.

Panarea

Pippo & Maria Soldino   RENTAL ROOMS €
(⌨ 333 137 25 44, 090 98 30 61; Via Iditella; s €30-60, d €60-120) Escape Panarea's crowds and high prices at this family-run oasis in

Ditella, a 15-minute walk north of the port. Backed by a rugged hillside, a cluster of terracotta orange buildings with blue doors holds 10 clean white rooms with pretty tiled terraces. There's also a rental house with full kitchen and private terrace, sleeping up to six (€350 per night).

★**Hotel Raya**   BOUTIQUE HOTEL €€€
([☎] 090 98 30 13; www.hotelraya.it; Via San Pietro; d €180-540; ☉ late Apr–Sep; [❋][@][❋]) Experience Panarea's chic allure to the fullest at this honeycomb of exquisite white adobe-walled rooms tucked up against a flower-bedecked volcanic hillside. Seductive details abound, including batik bedspreads, Mediterranean landscaping, picture-perfect terraces looking out to Stromboli, and a Jacuzzi filled with mineral water from the island's natural hot springs. It also offers a restaurant, a summer disco and a fabulous pool.

Quartara   HOTEL €€€
([☎] 090 98 30 27; www.quartarahotel.com; Via San Pietro 15; s €120-280, d €200-480) In the heart of town and run by the same family for nearly four decades, Quartara offers 13 comfortable, tile-floored rooms, the best four of which come with private sea-view terraces. All guests have access to the upstairs solarium and Jacuzzi, and a telescope for night-time stargazing. The attached Broccia restaurant serves excellent Aeolian cuisine.

Stromboli

★**Casa del Sole**   GUESTHOUSE €
(Map p151; [☎] 090 98 63 00; www.casadelsolestromboli.it; Via Cincotta; dm €25-30, s €30-50, d €60-100) This cheerful Aeolian-style guesthouse is only 100m from a sweet black-sand beach in Piscità, the tranquil neighbourhood at the west end of town. Dorms, private doubles and a guest kitchen all surround a sunny patio, overhung with vines, fragrant with lemon blossoms, and decorated with the masks and stone carvings of sculptor-owner Tano Russo. Call for free pickup (low season only) or take a taxi (€10) from the port 2km away.

Albergo Brasile   PENSION €
(Map p151; [☎] 090 98 60 08; www.strombolialbergobrasile.it; Via Soldato Cincotta; d €70-90, half-board per person €70-90; ☉ Easter-Oct; [❋]) A great budget option, this laid-back *pensione* has cool, white rooms, a pretty entrance courtyard with lemon and olive trees and a multilingual paperback library

for guests' reading pleasure. The roof terrace commands views of the sea one side and the volcano the other. Two larger rooms with air-con cost extra. Half-board is compulsory in July and August.

Il Giardino Segreto   B&B €€
(Map p151; [☎] 347 560 1347; www.giardinosegretobb.it; Via Francesco Natoli; d €72-134; [❋][☎]) In a 'secret garden' framed by picturesque rows of cypresses, this six-room B&B is five minutes' walk above the church on the way to the volcano. Downstairs units include breakfast on the rooftop terrace but are rather gloomy and cave-like; those further up the hill are nicer, with breezy semi-private terraces and kitchenettes (but no breakfast).

La Sirenetta Park Hotel   HOTEL €€€
(Map p151; [☎] 090 98 60 25; www.lasirenetta.it; Via Marina 33; s €90-150, d €120-300; ☉ late Apr–late Oct; [❋][❋]) A lovely terraced complex on the beach at Ficogrande, this was Stromboli's first-ever hotel – the current owner's father counted Ingrid Bergman as an early guest. It's a laid-back place with white, summery rooms, a large swimming pool, a first-class restaurant and its own amphitheatre used to screen films and stage theatrical performances.

Filicudi

Hotel La Canna   HOTEL €€
([☎] 090 988 99 56; Via Rosa 43; d €70-150, half-board per person €80-150) Perched like a private paradise high above the port, this delightful hotel features rooms with beams, terracotta tiles and panoramic terraces with a seagull's eye view of the harbor sparkling below. Delicious traditional meals at the attached restaurant feature produce from the adjacent gardens.

Pensione La Sirena   PENSION €€
([☎] 090 988 99 97; www.pensionelasirena.it; Via Pecorini Mare; d €120-160, half-board per person €90-130; ☉ May-Sep; [❋]) La Sirena is the ideal place to relax into the laid-back Aeolian lifestyle. A wonderful *pensione* in the tiny fishing village of Pecorini Mare, it has traditional, high-ceilinged rooms with French doors opening onto beach views and a superb seafood restaurant (meals €27 to €37). There are also several houses spread across the village, sleeping between two and 12 people.

Alicudi

Silvio Taranto
RENTAL ROOMS €

(☑ 090 988 99 22; r per person €25, dinner per person €20) Numbering among Alicudi's four dozen year-round residents are this local fisherman and his lovely wife Gabriella, who can arrange room rentals and delicious home-cooked meals any time of year. They're just a block south and a block uphill from the boat dock, and can come meet you if you call ahead.

Ericusa
HOTEL €€

(☑ 090 988 99 02; www.alicudihotel.it; Via Regina Elena; r per person with half-board €75-95, with full-board €100-120; ⊘ Jun-Sep) Alicudi's lone hotel, just south of the port, opens only from June through September, when its 12 rooms fill up quickly. There's a pleasant terrace restaurant overlooking the sea; half-board is obligatory for hotel guests.

IONIAN COAST

Messina

Hotel Cairoli
HOTEL €

(Map p162; ☑ 090 67 37 55; www.hotelcairoli.it; Viale San Martino 63; s/d €45/80) Just off Piazza Cairoli, this is a convenient and comfortable budget hotel in Messina, though the decor is pretty nondescript. The owner is friendly, the beds hard and some rooms have sweet pieces of antique-style furniture.

Royal Palace Hotel
HOTEL €€

(Map p162; ☑ 090 65 03; www.framonhotels.com; Via Tommaso Cannizzaro 3; s €60-125, d €95-165; P ✴) An unfortunate city-centre landmark, this grey concrete monster is easy to find, has parking (€11 per night, a definite plus) and offers comfortable, corporate-style rooms. The decor is a throwback to the dark days of the 1970s with dated, dizzying patterned carpets, low sofas and plenty of brown and orange.

Taormina

★ Isoco Guest House
B&B €

(Map p166; ☑ 094 22 36 79; www.isoco.it; Via Salita Branco 2; s €65-120, d €85-120; ⊘ Mar-Nov; P ✴ @) Every room in this exceptionally welcoming, gay-friendly B&B is dedicated to an artist – from Botticelli to the sculpted buttocks and pant-popping thighs on the walls of the Herb Ritts room. The excellent breakfast, free internet access, sundecks and outdoor Jacuzzi are great as well. Multi-course dinners are available on the terrace (€25 per person including drinks) in summer. German and English spoken.

B&B Le Sibille
B&B €

(Map p166; ☑ 349 7262862; www.lesibille.net; Corso Umberto 187a; d €60-110, apt per week without breakfast €400-620; ⊘ Apr-Oct; @ ☎) This B&B wins points for its prime location on Taormina's pedestrian thoroughfare, its rooftop breakfast terrace and its cheerful, artistically tiled self-catering apartments. Light sleepers beware: Corso Umberto can get noisy with holidaymakers!

Hostel Taormina
HOSTEL €

(Map p166; ☑ 349 1026161, 094 262 55 05; www.hosteltaormina.com; Via Circonvallazione 13; dm €17-23, d €58-80; ✴ @ ☎) The town's only hostel is open year-round and occupies a house with a roof terrace commanding panoramic sea views. It's small (only 23 beds in three dorms and one private room) and facilities are basic, but manager Francesco is a helpful and friendly guy, beds are comfortable and there's a communal kitchen. No breakfast.

Le 4 Fontane
B&B €

(Map p166; ☑ 094 262 55 20; www.le4fontane.it; Corso Umberto 231; s €40-70, d €60-110) Another excellent budget B&B, on the top floor of an old palazzo, Le 4 Fontane is run by a friendly couple and has three spacious, well-equipped rooms, two of which have views of Piazza del Duomo.

★ Hotel Villa Belvedere
HOTEL €€

(Map p166; ☑ 094 22 37 91; www.villabelvedere.it; Via Bagnoli Croce 79; s €70-190, d €80-280, ste €120-450; ⊘ Mar-late Nov; ✴ @ ☎ ☲) Built in 1902, the jaw-droppingly pretty Villa Belvedere was one of the original grand hotels, well-positioned with fabulous views and luxurious gardens, which are a particular highlight. There is also a swimming pool with a 100-year-old palm tree rising from a small island in the middle.

Hotel del Corso
HOTEL €€

(Map p166; ☑ 0942 62 86 98; www.hoteldelcorsotaormina.com; Corso Umberto I 238; s €49-89, d €79-140; ✴) Boasting a prime position on the main drag, this welcoming hotel is one of the few located in the Borgo Medioevale and one of the few to remain open year-round. It's a modest affair with bright, unfussy rooms and a small breakfast terrace overlooking the crenellated Palazzo Duca di Santo Stefano.

Pensione Svizzera
B&B €€

(Map p166; ☑ 094 22 37 90; www.pensionesvizzera.com; Via Luigi Pirandello 26; s €60-100, d €80-125) A very popular B&B teetering on the edge of a cliff with views over Mazzarò bay. Many of the rooms have balconies. The hotel can also organise tennis and diving.

Hotel Condor
HOTEL €€

(☑ 094 22 31 24; www.condorhotel.com; Via Cappuccini 25; d €70-120; ☺ Mar–mid-Nov; P ✱) Just outside the pedestrianised centre is this cordial, family-run hotel. Rooms are bright and airy with minimal decor and plain, functional furniture. The best have small sea-view terraces (for which you pay slightly more). Breakfast is served on the panoramic rooftop terrace and parking is available (€10).

Casa Turchetti
B&B €€€

(Map p166; ☑ 094 262 50 13; www.casaturchetti.com; Salita dei Gracchi 18/20; d €200-250, jr ste €350; ✱ ☎) Every detail is perfect in this painstakingly restored former music school, recently converted to a luxurious B&B on a back alley just above Corso Umberto. Vintage furniture and fixtures, handcrafted woodwork, fine homespun sheets and modern bathrooms all contribute to the elegant feel; the spacious rooftop terrace is just icing on the cake.

Giardini-Naxos

Hotel La Riva
HOTEL €€

(☑ 094 25 13 29; www.hotellariva.com; Via Tysandros 52; s €55-77, d €70-120; P ✱) Right on the seafront, next to the tourist office, this is a lovely family-run hotel with 40 rooms, all individually decorated with traditional Sicilian furnishings and marvellous inlaid wood bedsteads. There's nothing flash about the place, but it's got character and the graceful owners extend a warm welcome.

Catania

★ B&B Crociferi
B&B €

(Map p172; ☑ 095 715 22 66; www.bbcrociferi.it; Via Crociferi 81; d €75-85, tr €100-110, 4-bed apt €120; ✱ ☎) Affording easy access to the animated nightlife of Catania's historic centre, this B&B in a beautifully decorated family home is Catania's most delightful place to stay. Rooms are spacious, with high ceilings, antique tiles, frescoes and artistic accoutrements from the owners' travels in India. There are three rooms and two glorious apartments, which all fill up fast, so book ahead.

Each room has its own private bathroom across the hall. The upstairs apartments are spacious, elegant and light, and the four-bed apartment boasts a marvellous roof terrace, perfect for moonlit glasses of wine.

Marco (who speaks French) offers tours of the coastline in his private boat, while Teresa (who speaks German and English) makes a delicious, varied breakfast in her floral kitchen.

BAD
B&B €

(Map p172; ☑ 095 34 69 03; www.badcatania.com; Via Colombo 24; s €40-55, d €60-80, apt €70-120; ✱ ☎) An uninhibitedly colourful, modern sense of style prevails at this trendy B&B. All rooms feature local art work and TVs with DVD players. The two-level upstairs apartment with full kitchen and private terrace is a fab option for self-caterers, especially since the fish and vegetable markets are right around the corner. The staff is great about suggesting cultural goings-on about town.

Palazzu Stidda
APARTMENT €

(Map p172; ☑ 095 34 88 26; www.palazzu-stidda.com; Vicolo della Lanterna 5; d €70-100, q €120-140; ☎ ✎) A great option for families, these three delightful apartments on a peaceful dead-end alley have all the comforts of home plus a host of whimsical touches. Each has a flowery mini-balcony, and all are decorated with the owners' art work, handmade furniture, family heirlooms and vintage finds from local antiques markets. French and English spoken.

Apartments 2 and 3 each come with a washing machine, kitchen, high chair and stroller, and ample space for a family of four. Apartment 1 is smaller and costs €10 to €20 less. Check the website for the season-varied pricing.

Il Principe
HOTEL €€

(Map p172; ☑ 095 250 03 45; www.ilprincipehotel.com; Via Alessi 24; d €109-189, ste €129-209; ✱ @ ☎) This boutique-style hotel in an 18th-century building features luxurious rooms on one of the liveliest nightlife streets in town (thank goodness for double glazing!).

Perks include international cable TV, free wi-fi, and fluffy bathrobes to wear on your way to the Turkish steam bath. Check online for regularly updated special rates.

Forty new rooms were added in 2012. A whole new wing of the hotel, adjacent to the original building, and a wellness centre and solarium are planned. More expensive suites have spiral staircases leading to a second level and marble bathrooms with Jaccuzis. Some of the rooms have little natural light, so check before committing.

Hotel Novecento HOTEL €€
(Map p172; ☑ 095 31 04 88; www.hotelnovecento-catania.it; Via Monsignor Ventimiglia 37; d €70-120) An elegant hotel at very reasonable prices. Inside, the art nouveau interior gives it a classy feel and bedrooms are decorated with turn-of-the-century furnishings. There is no restaurant but breakfast is served in the hotel cafe.

UNA Hotel Palace HOTEL €€
(Map p172; ☑ 095 250 51 11; www.unahotels.it; Via Etnea 218; s €99-125, d €125-175, ste €201-329) A top-end hotel in a city that's badly in need of some seriously upmarket options, UNA brings a bit of city slick to Catania. Part of an Italy-wide chain, this hotel has a gleaming white interior, polished service and good rooms. The top draw are the views of Etna from the 7th floor rooftop garden bar that serves cocktails and aperitifs at sunset.

The six ivory-coloured floors lead onto equally sleek white rooms, with contrasting black-frame beds and gold lamps, and the white-black-gold combination is repeated across the four-star hotel. It has a gym and a Turkish bath, though sadly no pool. The views of the smoking cone of Etna from the rooftop terrace are mesmerising, so make sure you grab a few drinks and enjoy. It's posh all right, but prices drop significantly in winter.

Riviera Dei Ciclopi

Acireale

Epos B&B B&B €
(☑ 392 4848113; www.bbepos.it; Via Provinciale 262; s €45, d €60; ❋) About five minutes' walk from the seafront, this charming B&B is in an early-1900s house. Its five rooms, each named after a character from Homer's Odyssey, sport bold orange, red and yellow, and

antique-style furniture. Guests have use of a kitchen, complete with a barbecue, and access to a small terrace.

Al Duomo B&B €
(Map p166; ☑ 347 9078323; www.alduomo.org; Via Calì 5; s/d/tr/q €60/80/110/140; ❋) The pick of Acireale's accommodation is this four-room apartment in a restored 19th-century *palazzo*. Just off Piazza Duomo, it's colourful and stylish, each room individually coloured with attractive vaulted ceilings and balcony views towards the town's baroque centre.

Aci Trezza

Grand Hotel I Faraglioni HOTEL €€
(☑ 095 093 04 64; www.grandhotelfaraglioni.com; Lungomare Ciclopi 115; s €95-110, d €105-130; ❋ @) This drumlike four-star is a landmark on the Aci Trezza seafront. Inside, rooms are gleaming white with mod-cons and views over the Faraglioni (sea rock towers). There's sunbathing on a seaside sundeck and a popular restaurant, La Terrazza, where locals and visitors head for pizza and aperitifs.

Mt Etna

South

Hotel Alle Pendici HOTEL €
(☑ 095 791 43 10; www.hotelallependici.com; Viale della Regione 18, Nicolosi; s €50-70, d €65-90, t €85-115) In Nicolosi, just off the main route up to the cable-car station, this country-style hotel offers excellent value for money. Its rooms are tasteful, combining exposed brickwork with rustic wood furniture and the occasional hanging chandelier. Some have views up Etna's southern slopes.

B&B Massalargia B&B €
(☑ 095 791 45 86; www.massalargia.it; Via Manzoni 19; s €38-45, d €55-78) An amiable owner runs this pleasant place, 2km from Nicolosi en route to Catania. The rooms are large with lots of thoughtful, homey touches and there's a sitting room for the use of guests.

B&B La Giara B&B €
(☑ 095 791 90 22; www.giara.it; Viale della Regione 12a; s €35-50, d €55-80; ☎) The rooms here are washed in bright colours and sport wrought-iron beds, rattan furniture, colourful prints and large balconies. There's free wi-fi, and your friendly, English-speaking hostess Patrizia can help with excursions,

bike rental and transfers from the Catania airport (€40).

Rifugio Sapienza
MOUNTAIN CHALET €€

(☑095 91 53 21; www.rifugiosapienza.com; Piazzale Funivia; per person B&B/half-board/full board €55/75/90) As close to the summit as you can get, this place adjacent to the cable car offers comfortable accommodation with a good restaurant.

North

Agriturismo San Marco
AGRITURISMO €

(☑389 4237294; www.agriturismosanmarco.com; per person B&B/half-board/full board €35/53/68; ✦🐾) Get back to basics at this delightful *agriturismo* near Rovitello. Run by a jovial elderly couple, it's a bit off the beaten track but the bucolic setting, rustic rooms and superb country cooking more than compensate. It also has a swimming pool and a kids' play area complete with swing and slides. Call ahead for directions.

SYRACUSE & THE SOUTHEAST

Syracuse

★B&B dei Viaggiatori, Viandanti e Sognatori
B&B €

(Map p194; ☑0931 2 47 81; www.bedandbreakfastsicily.it; Via Roma 156, Ortigia; s €35-50, d €55-70, tr €75-80; ✦🐾) Decorated with verve and boasting a prime location in Ortygia, this is Syracuse's best B&B. There's a lovely bohemian feel, with books and pieces of antique furniture juxtaposed against bright walls. In an old *palazzo* at the end of Via Roma, it's run by the super-friendly Simone and Alessandra. The sunny roof terrace with sweeping sea views makes a perfect breakfast spot.

B&B L'Acanto
B&B €

(Map p194; ☑0931 46 11 29; www.bebsicily.com; Via Roma 15; s €35-50, d €55-85, tr €75-85, q €100) The recently refurbished L'Acanto remains a very popular, value-for-money B&B, now with a more modern, stylish feel. Rooms have been lifted out of the tired and traditional with several charming vintage furniture pieces and murals – check out the beautiful Sicilian carriages and puppets gracing the walls. It's set around a pretty internal courtyard.

The B&B is run by the same family as the B&B dei Viaggiatori, Viandanti e Sognatori.

Palazzo del Sale
B&B €

(Map p194; ☑0931 6 59 58; www.palazzodelsale. com; Via Santa Teresa 25, Ortigia; s €75-95, d €90-115, d with terrace €100-125; ✦@🐾) The six rooms at this designer B&B are hot property in summer, so be sure to book ahead. All are well sized, with high ceilings and good beds. Coffee and tea are always available in the comfortable communal lounge. The owners operate a second property right on the beach near Porto Piccolo (www.giuggiulena. it).

B&B Aretusa
APARTMENTS €

(Map p194; ☑0931 48 34 84; www.aretusavacanze. com; Vicolo Zuccalà 1; d €59-90, tr €70-120, q €105-147; P✦@🐾) This great budget option, elbowed into a tiny pedestrian street in a 17th-century building, has large rooms and apartments with kitchenettes, computers, wi-fi, satellite TV and small balconies from where you can shake hands with your neighbour across the way.

★Hotel Gutkowski
HOTEL €€

(Map p194; ☑0931 46 58 61; www.guthotel.it; Lungomare Vittorini 26; s €60-80, d €75-130; ✦@🐾) Book well in advance for one of the sea-view rooms at this calmly stylish hotel on the Ortygia waterfront, at the edge of la Giudecca neighbourhood. Rooms are divided between two buildings, both with pretty tiled floors, walls in teals, greys, blues and browns, and with a minimal style and a mix of vintage and industrial details.

You'll also find a nice sun terrace with sea views, and a cosy internet area with fireplace for those without their own computer, though there is free wi-fi in most of the hotel.

Alla Giudecca
HOTEL €€

(Map p194; ☑0931 2 22 55; www.allagiudecca.it; Via Alagona 52; s €60-100, d €80-120; ✦@🐾) Located in the old Jewish quarter, this charming hotel boasts 23 suites with warm terracotta-tiled floors, exposed wood beams and lashings of heavy white linen. The communal areas are a warren of vaulted rooms full of museum-quality antiques and enormous tapestries, and feature cosy sofas gathered around huge fireplaces.

Hotel Roma
HOTEL €€

(Map p194; ☑0931 46 56 26; www.hotelroma-siracusa.it; Via Roma 66; s €75-105, d €105-149;

P ❄ @ 🛜) Within steps of Piazza del Duomo, this *palazzo* has rooms with parquet floors, oriental rugs, wood-beam ceilings and tasteful artwork, plus free bike use, a gym and a sauna.

Around Syracuse

Villa dei Papiri — AGRITURISMO €€
(📞 0931 72 13 21; www.villadeipapiri.it; Contrada Cozzo Pantano; d €50-132, 2-person ste €105-154, 4-person ste €140-208; P ❄ @ 🛜) Immersed in an Eden of orange groves and papyrus reeds 8km outside Syracuse, this lovely *agriturismo* sits next to the Fonte Ciana spring immortalised in Ovid's *Metamorphosis*. Eight family suites are housed in a beautifully converted 19th-century farmhouse, with double rooms dotted around the lush grounds. Breakfast is served in a baronial stone-walled hall.

There are plenty of other perks to keep guests in a holiday mood, including river excursions, bike rentals and an open-door policy towards pets.

Palazzola Acreide

B&B Attiko — B&B €
(📞 0931 87 53 94; www.attiko.it; Ronco Corridore 10; s €35-40, d €60-70; ❄) This unpretentious B&B makes for a lovely overnight stay. The convivial owner extends a hearty welcome to his family home, which has five guest rooms, some decorated in traditional style, others with more colourful ethnic furnishings. Topping everything is a panoramic rooftop terrace.

Noto

B&B Montandòn — B&B €
(Map p206; 📞 0931 83 63 89; www.b-bmontandon.it; Via Sofia 50; s €40-50, d €60-80; ❄) Accessed via an imposing vaulted hallway, this snug B&B is in a crumbling *palazzo* near the top of town. A cheerfully cluttered hall leads onto three light-filled rooms, each with its own small balcony, wrought-iron bed and elegant furnishings.

Hotel della Ferla — HOTEL €€
(📞 0931 57 60 07; www.hoteldellaferla.it; Via Gramsci; s €48-78, d €84-120; P ❄ 🛜) This friendly family-run hotel in a residential area near the train station offers large, bright rooms with pine furnishings and small balconies, plus free parking.

The Noto Coast

La Corte del Sole — RURAL INN €€
(📞 320 820210; www.lacortedelsole.it; Contrada Bucachemi; per person €55-126; P ❄ @ 🛜 ☀) Overlooking the green fields of Eloro is this stylish hotel housed in a traditional Sicilian *masseria* (fortified farmhouse). A delightful place to stay, it also offers a range of activities including cooking lessons (p209) run by the hotel chef and, in winter, tours to study the 80 or so types of wild orchids found in the area.

Modica

★ Villa Quartarella — AGRITURISMO €
(📞 360 654829; www.quartarella.com; Contrada Quartarella; s €40, d €75-80) Spacious rooms and welcoming hosts make this converted villa in the countryside south of Modica the obvious choice for anyone travelling by car. Owners Francesco and Francesca are generous in sharing their love and encyclopaedic knowledge of local history, flora and fauna and can suggest a multitude of driving itineraries in the surrounding area.

The delicious, ample breakfasts include everything from home-raised eggs to intriguing Modican sweets.

B&B Il Cavaliere — B&B €
(📞 0932 94 72 19; www.palazzoilcavaliere.it; Corso Umberto I 259; s €39-59, d €65-80, ste €95-130; ❄ 🛜) Stay in aristocratic style at this classy B&B in a 19th-century *palazzo*, just down from the bus station on Modica's main strip. Standard rooms have less character than the beautiful front suite and the large, high-ceilinged common rooms, which retain original tiled floors and frescoed ceilings. The elegant breakfast room has lovely views of Chiesa di San Giorgio church.

Hotel Relais Modica — HOTEL €
(📞 0932 75 44 51; www.hotelrelaismodica.it; Via Campailla; d €85-110; ❄ @) Guests are assured a warm welcome at this inviting old-school hotel. Housed in a converted *palazzo* just off Corso Umberto I, it's an attractive hostelry with 10 bright, cheery rooms, each slightly different but all spacious and quietly elegant. It has free internet in reception and satellite TV in the rooms.

Hotel Demohàc HOTEL €

(✍ 0932 75 41 30; www.hoteldemohac.it; Via Campailla 15; s €55-65, d €85-110; ✻) Taking inspiration from Modica's literary legacy – poet and Nobel Prize–winner Salvatore Quasimodo was born here in 1901 – the 10 rooms in this dapper hotel are each named after a writer. And in keeping with the bookish theme, they are decked out with good-looking antiques, chaise longues and writing tables.

Albergo I Tetti di Siciliando GUESTHOUSE €

(✍ 0932 94 28 43; www.siciliando.it; Via Cannata 24; d €58-70, without bathroom €48-58; ✻✻🛜) This is a wonderful guesthouse in the old town, just off central Corso Umberto. The rooms are simple, spacious and airy, and many have views of Modica's steeply stacked houses. Extras include bike hire (per day/ week €15/80).

Ragusa

Risveglio Ibleo B&B €

(Map p212; ✍ 0932 24 78 11; www.risveglioibleo. com; Largo Camerina 3; r per person €42.50; 🅿🛜) Housed in an 18th-century Liberty-style villa, this welcoming place has spacious, high-ceilinged rooms, walls hung with family portraits and a flower-flanked terrace overlooking the rooftops. The older couple who run the place go out of their way to share local culture, including their own homemade culinary delights.

Caelum Hyblae B&B €€

(Map p212; ✍ 0932 22 04 02; www.bbcaelumhyblae.it; Salita Specula 11, Ragusa Ibla; d €100-120) With its book-lined reception and crisp white decor, this stylish, family-run B&B exudes quiet sophistication. Each of the seven rooms has views over the cathedral, and while they're not the biggest, they're immaculately turned out with unadorned walls, pristine beds and functional modern furniture.

Il Barocco HOTEL €€

(Map p212; ✍ 0932 66 31 05; www.ilbarocco.it; Via Santa Maria La Nuova; s €55-80, d €90-125; ✻) An easy five-minute walk from central Piazza Duomo, this is a friendly three-star. Its distinctive salmon-pink facade complements a traditional interior of antique-style furniture, polished wood and baked floor tiles, while rooms, accessible via a twisting iron staircase, are comfortable and decent-sized.

Locanda Don Serafino INN €€

(Map p212; ✍ 0932 22 00 65; www.locandadonserafino.it; Via XI Febbraio 15; s €80-138, d €90-168; ✻@) This historic inn near the *duomo* has beautiful rooms, some with original vaulted stone ceilings, plus a well-regarded restaurant nearby. For €9 extra, guests get access to the Lido Azzurro beach at Marina di Ragusa, 25km away.

CENTRAL SICILY

Enna

Accommodation is in short supply in Enna, but there are plenty of hotels and *agriturismi* around Lago di Pergusa, 9km south of town.

Baglio Pollicarini AGRITURISMO €€

(✍ 0935 54 19 82; www.bagliopollicarini.it; Contrada Pollicarini; s €45-95, d €75-180, campsite per person/tent €7/9; 🅿) This splendid *agriturismo* is housed in a 17th-century convent near the Lago di Pergusa. The monks' cells have long since been converted into comfortable guest rooms, but the thick stone walls, vaulted ceilings and fading frescoes leave a historical imprint. There's also a dedicated camping area and an in-house restaurant (meals from €25).

Grande Albergo Sicilia HOTEL €€

(Map p220; ✍ 0935 50 08 50; www.hotelsiciliaenna.it; Piazza Napoleone Colaianni 7; s €60-75, d €90-102; 🅿✻) Up in the historic centre, Enna's best hotel hides its lights behind a crude concrete facade. Once inside, you'll find a panoramic breakfast terrace and cheery, comfortable rooms with kitsch gold-framed Botticelli prints and wrought-iron bedsteads.

Nicosia

Baglio San Pietro AGRITURISMO €€

(✍ 0935 64 05 29; www.bagliosanpietro.com; Contrada San Pietro; per person B&B €45, half/ full board €62/75; 🅿✻) Near the entrance to Nicosia (on the SS117 to Agira), this is an *agriturismo* in the true sense of the word, a working farm with 10 comfortable, rustic-style rooms and a restaurant specialising in earthy country food. You can go horse-riding (one hour/half-day €18/50), organise an excursion or simply relax by the pool.

Piazza Armerina

B&B Umberto 33
B&B €

(Map p224; ☑ 0935 68 33 44; www.umberto33.
com; Via Umberto 33; r per person €30; ❋) Run
by superfriendly Giovanni, this modest B&B
is a real home away from home. It has few
frills, but the three guest rooms are clean as
a pin, there's a kitchen for guest use, and the
location, right in the heart of the historic
centre, is ideal. Guests are also treated to a
complimentary bottle of wine from Giovanni's *enoteca* (wine bar).

Azienda Agrituristica
Gigliotto
AGRITURISMO €

(☑ 0933 97 08 98; www.gigliotto.com; Contrada
Gigliotto, SS117; s €60-80, d €80-100; ℗ ❋) An
ancient *masseria* (manor farm) dating
to the 14th century, Gigliotto is set in rolling Tuscan-style countryside 9km south
of Piazza Armerina. The homestead has 14
rural-styled rooms and a farmhouse restaurant with a picturesque outdoor terrace. It
produces its own wine: visits to the in-house
winery and wine tastings can be arranged.

★ Suite d'Autore
BOUTIQUE HOTEL €€

(Map p224; ☑ 0935 68 85 53; www.suitedautore.it;
Via Monte I; d €100-140; ❋) With lime-green pol-
ystyrene furniture, 19th-century frescoes and
a giant circular bed floating in a floor of liquid tiles, this unique design hotel is one of Piazza Armerina's great sights. Each of its seven
rooms is themed after a period in design, and
everything you see – and that includes works
of contemporary art – is for sale.

The owner, Ettore, is a great source of
local information and a guide around the
newly restored Villa Romana del Casale.

Caltagirone

★ B&B Tre Metri Sopra Il Cielo
B&B €

(☑ 0933 193 51 06; www.bbtremetrisopraficelo.it;
Via Bongiovanni 72; d €60-80; ❋) Just off Caltagirone's famous staircase, this is a fantastic B&B run by a friendly and enthusiastic
young couple. The decor varies between
the six rooms but is universally tasteful and
there can be few finer places to breakfast
than on the spectacular balcony overlooking
Caltagirone's rooftops and the hills beyond.

La Pilozza Infiorata
B&B €

(☑ 0933 2 21 62; www.lapilozzainfiorata.com; Via
SS Salvatore 97; s €35-45, d €70, q €100-110; ❋)
Graceful rooms await at this smart B&B in

the historic centre. Against a white and sky-
blue colour scheme, sloping wood-beamed
ceilings, antique furniture and displays of
backlit ceramics combine to give the interior
a low-key, elegant look. Breakfast is served
on the sweet terrace in the warmer months.
There are newly added two- to four-person
apartments.

MEDITERRANEAN COAST

Agrigento

Town Centre

Camere a Sud
B&B €

(Map p238; ☑ 349 6384424; www.camereasud.it;
Via Ficani 6; r €60-70; ❋ @ 🛜) A lovely B&B in
the centre of Agrigento, Camere a Sud has
three guest rooms decorated with style and
taste – traditional decor and contemporary
textiles are matched with bright colours and
modern art. The sumptuous breakfast is
served on the terrace in the warmer months.

Atenea 191
B&B €

(Map p238; ☑ 349 595594; www.atenea191.com;
Via Atenea 191; s €45-60, d €65-85; ❋ 🛜) New
owner Pompeo runs this friendly B&B on
Agrigento's main shopping thoroughfare.
The breakfast terrace has sweeping views
over the valley, as do some rooms.

City Bed
B&B €

(Map p238; ☑ 0922 40 30 91; www.citybed.it; Via
Garibaldi 61; s €40-60, d €49-69; ❋) An urbane
pied-à-terre, City Bed offers great value for
money, a warm welcome and classy rooms.
Cool white tones and a black-and-white
chessboard floor set the tone for the spacious entrance halls, while frescoed ceilings
cap the cool, modern rooms. Breakfast is
served in a bar on nearby Piazza Pirandello.

Valley of the Temples

★ Villa Athena
LUXURY HOTEL €€€

(Map p240; ☑ 0922 59 62 88; www.hotelvillaath-
ena.it; Via Passeggiata Archeologica 33; s €130-190,
d €150-350, ste €240-890; ℗ ❋ @ 🛜 ❋) With
the Tempio della Concordia lit up in the
near distance and palm trees lending an exotic *Arabian Nights* feel, the views from this
historic five-star are magnificent. Housed in
an aristocratic 18th-century villa, the hotel's
interior, gleaming after a recent makeover, is
a picture of white, ceramic cool.

The Villa Suite – with two cavernous rooms floored in antique tiles, a freestanding Jaccuzi and a vast terrace looking straight at the temples – vies for the title of coolest hotel room in Sicily.

Foresteria Baglio della Luna HOTEL €€€
(☑0922 51 10 61; www.bagliodellaluna.com; Contrada Maddalusa; s €140-210, d €170-250) This handsome converted *baglio* (manor house) has rooms that are somewhat old and tired, though the location and the magnificent garden make up for what's lacking in freshness. Il Déhors, the hotel restaurant, is rated as one of the best in Sicily. It is a little tricky to find, but check the website for exact directions.

Sciacca

B&B Da Lulo e Gagà B&B €
(Map p244; ☑349 6140880; www.bedbreakfast lulogaga.com; Vicolo Muscarnera 9; d €60; ❋) Kooky, fun and original, Lulo's works of art set this great B&B apart. Owls made of multicoloured pebbles, mosaic-framed mirrors and painted ceramics adorn the sunny little apartment, while cacti and Egyptian hieroglyphics brighten the pint-sized terrace.

Al Moro B&B €
(Map p244; ☑0925 8 67 56; www.almoro.com; Via Liguori 44; s €55-65, d €80-100, ste €100-160; ❋) Cool 21st-century decor combines with 13th-century architecture in Sciacca's historic centre. Al Moro is a slick, good-looking boutique B&B, with rooms revealing a clean, white colour scheme, exposed girders and jazzy mosaic-tiled bathrooms. The abundant breakfast is served downstairs in a vaulted stone hall just off a small courtyard.

Villa Palocla HOTEL €€
(☑0925 90 28 12; www.villapalo cla.it; Contrada Raganella; d/tr/q €115/140/180; P ❋ @ ☀) This charming hotel is an oasis of tranquillity just outside Sciacca. Housed in an 18th-century villa, and surrounded by orange groves, it retains a baronial feel with a cobbled courtyard and wrought-iron balconies. The interior is pure country house with lots of floral fabrics, ceramic tiles and dark wood.

East of Agrigento

Vecchia Masseria AGRITURISMO €€
(☑0935 68 40 03; www.vecchiamasseria.com; Contrada Cutuminello; s €50-90, d €70-160; P ❋ ☀) It takes some getting to, but once you've found this *agriturismo* about 20km northeast of Gela, you won't want to leave. With elegant, soothing rooms, a highly reputed restaurant, a swimming pool and a long list of services, it's ideally set up as a rural hideaway. No credit cards.

Understand
Sicily

Sicily Today

These are tough times for Sicily. The same economic woes that have crippled Italy's Mediterranean neighbours in recent years are now hitting southern Italy with full force. While there are some hopeful signs – community groups continue to chip away at the Mafia's influence in Sicilian society, and the 2012 election of anti-Mafia politicians Rosario Crocetta and Leoluca Orlando has been widely well-received – the next couple of years will likely be challenging, as Sicilians struggle to regain their economic bearings.

Best on Film

Nuovo Cinema Paradiso (Cinema Paradiso, 1988) Semi-autobiographical tale of small-town life from Sicilian director Giuseppe Tornatore.

Il Postino (The Postman, 1994) On the gorgeous island of Salina, Pablo Neruda philosophises with a humble Sicilian postman.

Stromboli, Terra di Dio (Stromboli, Land of God, 1950) Bergman and Rossellini's explosive tale of romance, with Stromboli's volcanic fireworks as a backdrop.

Best in Print

The Leopard (Giuseppe Tomasi di Lampedusa, 1958) Sicily's greatest novel, examining the Risorgimento's impact on Sicilian culture through the eyes of an ageing aristocrat.

Seeking Sicily (John Keahey, 2011) Engaging Sicilian travelogue, touching on many aspects of the island's culture and history, by a veteran American journalist.

Midnight in Sicily (Peter Robb, 1996) Disturbing but fascinating portrait of postwar Sicily, from an Australian expatriate living in Naples.

La Crisi

As of mid-2013, it's hard to go anywhere in Sicily without hearing about *la crisi* (the crisis), shorthand for the severe financial downturn currently affecting Italy. While recent economic conditions have not been great anywhere in Italy, the impact of the crisis has been especially devastating to Sicily and its southern Italian neighbours. Sicilian unemployment for the first quarter of 2013 was over 20%, compared to 12% nationally. Meanwhile, youth employment had surged to 52%, leaving Sicily second only to Calabria among Italian regions and creating hand-wringing responses in even the most sanguine of observers. This is a frightening day-to-day reality for Sicilians, particularly those aged between 16 and 25.

Fuelling these bad numbers in part was Fiat's December 2011 closure of its factory in Termini Imerese, just east of Palermo, after 41 years in business – a move that deprived over 2000 local residents of steady manufacturing jobs. Other noteworthy casualties of the economic downturn include Palermo's venerable Flaccovio bookstore, Guadagna shopping centre and Grande Mig-liore department store.

The crisis is also having a serious impact on the tourism sector. Ask hoteliers and they'll tell you that visitor numbers are down, both among foreign and domestic travellers. Even the Italians who are still travelling are cutting back on their spending, with the result that prices for tourist basics such as restaurant meals and accommodation have had to be frozen at 2011 levels due to lack of demand. While lower costs may be a welcome surprise for foreign visitors, they're bad news for Sicilians who depend on tourist dollars to pay the bills. A sobering reminder of the grim toll these numbers were taking were the suicides of two hotel owners on the Aeolian Islands in the days surrounding Easter 2013, driven in part by feelings of financial desperation.

Throughout Sicily, funding cutbacks prompted by the crisis have also led to a shortening of business hours and the potential closure of some smaller museums and archaeological sites, though the major tourist sites remain largely unaffected.

The Impact of Immigration

Another issue that Sicilians are grappling with is the impact of immigration. Being so close to North Africa, the island has always been a crossroads, but recent political turmoil in Libya and Tunisia has increased the flow of newcomers. While many Sicilians welcome new immigrants as a vibrant component of regional culture, others are unhappy with Sicily's status as an unofficial gateway into Europe, viewing immigrants primarily as competitors for jobs and strains on the island's already inadequate housing and infrastructure.

Traditional immigration for economic motives has recently been supplemented by a massive upsurge in refugees seeking political asylum. Many asylum-seekers arrive first on the Sicilian island of Lampedusa, whose close proximity to northern Africa makes it a popular destination for boat traffic. In March 2011, reacting to overcrowded conditions at Lampedusa, the Berlusconi government opened a brand-new immigrant detention centre at Mineo, in Catania province. The centre has provoked backlash both from Sicilians who object to receiving so many refugees on Sicilian soil, and from human-rights groups, who have been scathing in their condemnation of living conditions at the centre. As this book goes to press, over 2800 refugees are still being held at Mineo, awaiting word on their asylum requests with no clear plans for their release; meanwhile, violent protests among detainees within the centre are on the rise.

Bridge to Nowhere?

In the aftermath of Silvio Berlusconi's recent fall from grace, it appears that Sicily's grandiose Straits of Messina bridge project may finally be headed for the dustheap. The bridge, intended to link Messina with Reggio di Calabria on the Italian mainland, had been touted by Berlusconi as a crucial new land connection between Sicily and the rest of Italy. However, the project was always controversial. While some in Sicily welcomed the prospect of increased economic activity based on the anticipated flood of new arrivals from mainland Italy, others raised serious concerns about the project's environmental impact, seismic safety implications, and high cost, especially the diversion of resources away from other more pressing regional infrastructure projects. As this book goes to press, the Italian government has placed a two-year hold on the bridge project pending further study.

POPULATION: **5 MILLION**

AREA: **25,711 SQ KM**

UNEMPLOYMENT: **20.7%**

PER CAPITA GDP: **€16,600**

if Sicily were 100 people

97 would be Italian
3 would be foreign citizens

religious participation
(% of population)

58
attend services
once a month

30
attend services
once a year

12
never attend
services

population per sq km

SICILY   ITALY   UK

≈ 195 people

History

Over the millennia, Sicily's strategic position in the middle of the Mediterranean has lured culture after culture to its shores, resulting in one of Europe's richest and most remarkable histories. Disputed for centuries by a steady parade of ancient peoples including the Greeks, Carthaginians and Romans, the island saw subsequent rule by invading forces of Byzantines, Saracens, Normans, Germans, Angevins, Spanish and others before finally claiming its pivotal role within a unified Italy in the early 1860s.

Some of Sicily's earliest population centres grew up around Lipari, in the Aeolian Islands. Thanks to Lipari's volcanic origins, it was a prime source of obsidian, valued by Bronze Age peoples as an ideal material for making cutting tools. Obsidian mined in Lipari during the 2nd millennium BC has been found throughout the Mediterranean.

Early Settlement

The first evidence of an organised settlement on Sicily belongs to the Stentillenians, who came from the Middle East and settled on the island's eastern shores sometime between 4000 and 3000 BC. But it was the settlers from the middle of the 2nd millennium BC who radically defined the island's character and whose early presence helps us understand Sicily's complexities. Thucydides (c 460–404 BC) records three major tribes: the Sicanians, who originated either in Spain or North Africa and settled in the north and west (giving these areas their Eastern flavour); the Elymians from Greece, who settled in the south; and the Siculians (or Sikels), who came from the Calabrian peninsula and spread out along the Ionian Coast.

Greeks & Phoenicians

The acquisition of Sicily was an obvious step for the ever-expanding Greek city-states. Following the earlier lead of the Elymians, the Chalcidians landed on Sicily's Ionian Coast in 735 BC and founded a small settlement at Naxos. They were followed a year later by the Corinthians, who built their colony on the southeastern island of Ortygia, calling it Syracoussai (Syracuse). The Chalcidians went further south from their own fort and founded a second town called Katane (Catania) in 729 BC, and the two carried on stitching towns and settlements together until three-quarters of the island was in Hellenic hands.

TIMELINE	1250–850 BC	735–580 BC	480 BC
	Settlers found small colonies at Stentinello, Megara Hyblaea and Lipari. They begin the lucrative business of trading obsidian.	Greek cities are founded at Naxos in 735 BC, Syracuse in 734 BC, Megara Hyblaea in 728 BC, Gela in 689 BC, and Selinunte and Messina in 628 BC. Agrigento is established in 581 BC.	Commanding a vast army of mercenaries, the Carthaginian general Hamilcar seeks to wrest control of Himera from the Greeks, but is soundly defeated by the Greek tyrant Gelon.

The growing Greek power in the south and east created tensions with the Phoenicians, who had settled on the western side of the island around 850 BC; in turn, the Phoenicians' alliance with the powerful city-state of Carthage (in modern-day Tunisia) was of serious concern to the Greeks. By 480 BC the Carthaginians were mustering a huge invading force of some 300,000 mercenaries. Commanded by one of their great generals, Hamilcar, the force landed on Sicily and besieged Himera (near Termini Imerese), but the vast army was defeated by the crafty Greek tyrant Gelon, whose troops breached Hamilcar's lines by pretending to be Carthaginian reinforcements.

A much-needed period of peace followed in Sicily. The Greek colonies had lucrative trade deals thanks to the island's rich resources, and the remains of their cities testify to their wealth and sophistication.

With the advent of the Peloponnesian Wars, Syracuse decided to challenge the hegemony of mainland Greece. Athens, infuriated by the Sicilian 'upstart', decided to attack Syracuse in 415 BC, mounting the 'Great Expedition' – the largest fleet ever assembled. Despite the fleet's size and Athens' confidence, Syracuse fought back and the mainland Greek army suffered a humiliating defeat.

Though Syracuse was celebrating its victory, the rest of Sicily was in a constant state of civil war. This provided the perfect opportunity for Carthage to seek its revenge for Himera, and in 409 BC a new army led by Hamilcar's bitter but brilliant nephew Hannibal wreaked havoc in the Sicilian countryside, completely destroying Selinunte, Himera, Agrigento and Gela. The Syracusans were eventually forced to surrender everything except the city of Syracuse itself to Carthage.

The Romans

The First Punic War (264–241 BC) saw Rome challenge Carthage for possession of Sicily, and at the end of the war the victorious Romans claimed the island as their first province outside the Italian mainland. Under the Romans, the majority of Sicilians lived in horrifyingly reduced circumstances; native inhabitants were refused the right to citizenship and forced into indentured slavery on *latifondi* – huge landed estates that were to cause so many of the island's woes in later years. Not surprisingly, Rome's less-than-enlightened rule led to a revolt by slaves in 135 BC and the Second Servile War in 104–101 BC.

A Byzantine Interlude

After Rome fell to the Visigoths in AD 470, Sicily was occupied by Vandals from North Africa, but their tenure was relatively brief. In 535 the Byzantine general Belisarius landed an army and was welcomed by a

Best Prehistoric Sites

Necropoli di Pantalica, near Syracuse

Capo Graziano, Filicudi, Aeolian Islands

Punta Milazzese, Panarea, Aeolian Islands

415 BC	409 BC	241 BC	241 BC–AD 470
An emboldened Syracuse seeks to assert its independence from Greece, provoking a massive backlash from Athens. The Great Expedition, an Athenian fleet of unprecedented size, is defeated by Syracusan troops.	Hannibal's army wreaks havoc on Selinunte, Agrigento, Himera and Gela, forcing the Syracusans to surrender their western Sicilian territories to Carthage and retreat to Syracuse.	Sandwiched between the superpowers of Carthage and Rome, Sicily becomes the battleground for a war whose outcome is to place it firmly within the Roman Empire.	As Rome's first colony, Sicily suffers the worst of Roman rule: native inhabitants are refused the right of citizenship and forced into indentured slavery.

population that, despite over 700 years of Roman occupation, was still largely Greek, both in language and custom. The Byzantines were eager to use Sicily as a launching pad for the retaking of lands owned by the combined forces of Arabs, Berbers and Spanish Muslims (collectively known as the Saracens), but their dreams were not to be realised.

Enter Islam

In AD 827, the Saracen army landed at Mazara del Vallo. Palermo fell in 831, followed by Syracuse in 878. Under the Arabs, churches were converted to mosques and Arabic was made the common language. At the same time, much-needed land reforms were introduced and trade, agriculture and mining were fostered. New crops were introduced, including citrus trees, date palms and sugar cane, and a system of water supply and irrigation was developed.

Palermo became the capital of the new emirate and, over the next 200 years, it became one of the most splendid cities in the Arab world, a haven of culture and commerce rivalled only by Córdoba in Spain.

The Kingdom of the Sun

The Arabs called the Normans 'wolves' because of their barbarous ferocity and the terrifying speed with which they were mopping up territory on the mainland. By 1053, after six years of mercenary activity, Robert Guiscard (c 1015–85), the Norman conquistador, had comprehensively defeated the combined forces of the Calabrian Byzantines, the Lombards and the papal forces at the Battle of Civitate.

Having established his supremacy, Robert turned his attentions to expanding the territories under his control. To achieve this, he had to deal with the Vatican. In return for being invested with the titles of duke of Puglia and Calabria in 1059, Robert agreed to chase the Saracens out of Sicily and restore Christianity to the island. He delegated this task – and promised the island – to his younger brother Roger I (1031–1101), who landed his troops at Messina in 1061, capturing the port by surprise. In 1064 Roger tried to take Palermo but was repulsed by a well-organised Saracen army; it wasn't until Robert arrived in 1072 with substantial reinforcements that the city fell into Norman hands.

Impressed by the island's cultured Arab lifestyle, Roger shamelessly borrowed and improved on it, spending vast amounts of money on palaces and churches and encouraging a cosmopolitan atmosphere in his court. He also wisely opted for a policy of reconciliation with the indigenous people; Arabic and Greek continued to be spoken along with French, and Arab engineers, bureaucrats and architects continued to be employed by the court. He was succeeded by his widow, Adelasia (Adelaide), who ruled until 1130 when Roger II (1095–1154) was crowned king.

Sunken ships litter the sea floor around Sicily. Discoveries from these shipwrecks are displayed at museums throughout the region. Three of the most extraordinary are the remains of a Carthaginian warship in Marsala, the statue of a dancing satyr in Mazara del Vallo and the collection of ancient amphorae in Lipari.

535	827–965	1059–72	1072–1101
Keen to use the island as a launching pad for retaking Saracen lands, the Byzantines conquer Sicily; Syracuse temporarily becomes the empire's capital in 663.	The Saracens land at Mazara del Vallo. Sicily is united under Arab rule and Palermo is the second-largest city in the world after Constantinople.	The Norman conquistador Robert Guiscard vows to expel the Saracens from Sicily. With the help of his younger brother, Roger I, he seizes Palermo in 1072.	Sicily's brightest period in history ensues under Roger I, with a cosmopolitan and multicultural court. Many significant palaces and churches are built during this time.

The Enlightened Leader

Roger II was a keen intellectual whose court was unrivalled for its exotic splendour and learning. His rule was remarkable for his patronage of the arts, and also for his achievement in building an efficient and multicultural civil service that was the envy of Europe. He also enlarged the kingdom to include Malta, most of southern Italy and even parts of North Africa.

The Setting Sun

Roger's son and successor, William I (1108–66), inherited the kingdom upon his father's death in 1154. Nicknamed 'William the Bad', he was a vain and corrupt ruler.

The appointment of Walter of the Mill (Gualtiero Offamiglia) as archbishop of Palermo at the connivance of the pope was to create a dangerous power struggle between church and throne for the next 20 years – a challenge that was taken up by William II (1152–89) when he ordered the creation of a second archbishopric at Monreale.

William II's premature death at the age of 36 led to a power tussle, and an assembly of barons elected Roger II's illegitimate grandson Tancred (c 1130–94) to the throne. His accession was immediately contested by the German (or Swabian) king Henry VI (1165–97), head of the House of Hohenstaufen, who laid claim to the throne by virtue of his marriage to Roger II's daughter, Constance.

Tancred died in 1194, and no sooner had his young son, William III, been installed as king than the Hohenstaufen fleet docked in Messina. On Christmas Day of that year Henry VI declared himself king and young William was imprisoned in the castle at Caltabellotta in southern Sicily, where he eventually died (in 1198).

Best Classical Sites

Valle dei Templi, Agrigento

Selinunte

Segesta

Parco Archeologico della Neapolis, Syracuse

Teatro Greco, Taormina

Wonder of the World

Henry paid scant attention to his Sicilian kingdom, and died of malaria in 1197. He was succeeded by his young heir Frederick (1194–1250), known as both Frederick I of Sicily and Frederick II of Hohenstaufen.

Frederick was a keen intellectual with a penchant for political manoeuvring, but he was also a totalitarian despot who fortified the eastern seaboard from Messina to Syracuse and sacked rebellious Catania in 1232. Under his rule, Sicily became a centralised state playing a key commercial and cultural role in European affairs, and Palermo gained a reputation as the continent's most important city. In the latter years of his reign Frederick became known as Stupor Mundi, 'Wonder of the World', in recognition of his successful rule.

When Frederick died in 1250, he was succeeded by his son Conrad IV of Germany (1228–54), but the island was initially ruled by his younger

1130–1154	1145	1154–91	1198–1250
Roger II builds one of the most efficient civil services in Europe. His court is responsible for the creation of the first written legal code in Sicilian history.	El Idrisi's planisphere (a large, silver global map) – an important medieval geographical work that accurately maps Europe, North Africa and western Asia – is completed for Roger II.	William I inherits the kingdom, triggering a power struggle between church and throne. Walter of the Mill is appointed Palermo's archbishop. The great cathedrals of Monreale and Palermo are built.	Under Frederick I, Palermo is considered Europe's most important city and Sicily is a key player in Europe. But Frederick imposes heavy taxes and restrictions on free trade.

and illegitimate son, Manfred (1232–66). Conrad arrived in Sicily in 1252 to take control but died of malaria after only two years. Manfred again took the reins, first as regent to Conrad's infant son Conradin and then, after forging an alliance with the Saracens, in his own right in 1258.

The Sicilian Vespers

In 1266 the Angevin army, led by Charles of Anjou, brother of the French King Louis IX, defeated and killed Manfred at Benevento on the Italian mainland. Two years later, Manfred's 15-year-old nephew and heir, Conradin, was defeated at Tagliacozzo, captured by the Angevins and publicly beheaded in Naples.

After such a bloody start, the Angevins were hated and feared. Sicily was weighed down by onerous taxes, religious persecution was the order of the day and Norman fiefdoms were removed and awarded to French aristocrats.

On Easter Monday 1282, the city of Palermo exploded in rebellion. Incited by the alleged rape of a local girl by a gang of French troops, peasants lynched every French soldier they could get their hands on. The revolt spread to the countryside and was supported by the barons, who had formed an alliance with Peter of Aragon, who landed at Trapani with a large army and was proclaimed king. For the next 20 years, the Aragonese and the Angevins were engaged in the War of the Sicilian Vespers – a war that was eventually won by the Spanish.

Five Hundred Years of Solitude

By the end of the 14th century Sicily had been thoroughly marginalised. The eastern Mediterranean was sealed off by the Ottoman Turks, while the Italian mainland was off-limits on account of Sicily's political ties with Spain. As a result the Renaissance passed the island by, reinforcing the oppressive effects of poverty and ignorance. Even Spain lost interest in its colony, choosing to rule through viceroys.

By the end of the 15th century, the viceroy's court was a den of corruption, and the most influential body on the island became the Catholic Church (whose archbishops and bishops were mostly Spaniards). The church exercised draconian powers through a network of Holy Office tribunals, otherwise known as the Inquisition.

Reeling under the weight of state oppression, ordinary Sicilians demanded reform. But Spanish monarchs were preoccupied by the wars of the Spanish succession and Sicily was subsequently passed around from European power to European power like an unwanted Christmas present. Eventually the Spanish reclaimed the island in 1734, this time under the Bourbon king Charles I of Sicily (1734–59).

Best Norman Sites

Palazzo dei Normanni, Palermo

Cappella Palatina, Palermo

Cattedrale di Palermo, Palermo

Cattedrale di Monreale, Monreale

San Giovanni degli Eremiti, Palermo

Duomo di Cefalù, Cefalù

Castello di Caccamo, Caccamo

Castello di Lombardia, Enna

1266–82 ⟩	1282 ⟩	1487 ⟩	1669 ⟩
Charles of Anjou is crowned king in 1266, leading to a brief and unpopular period of French rule, characterised by high taxes and transfer of land ownership to the Angevin aristocracy.	The Sicilian Vespers, a violent uprising in Palermo, sparks countrywide revolt against the Angevin troops. Peter of Aragon rushes in to fill the vacuum, initiating 500 years of Spanish rule.	The end of religious tolerance is cemented by the expulsion of Jews from all Spanish territories. The Spanish Inquisition terrorises Sicily with nearly three centuries of imprisonment, torture and killings.	The worst eruption in Etna's history levels Catania and the east-coast towns. It's preceded by a three-day earthquake. The eruption lasts four months, flooding the city with rivers of lava.

Under the reign of Charles I's successor, Ferdinand IV, the landed gentry vetoed any attempts at liberalisation. Large exports of grain continued to enrich the aristocracy while normal Sicilians died of starvation.

Exit Feudalism

Although Napoleon never occupied Sicily, his capture of Naples in 1799 forced Ferdinand to move to Sicily. The Bourbon king's ridiculous tax demands were soon met with open revolt by the peasantry and the more far-sighted nobles, who believed that the only way to maintain the status quo was to usher in limited reforms. After strong pressure, Ferdinand reluctantly agreed in 1812 to the drawing up of a constitution whereby a two-chamber parliament was formed and feudal privileges were abolished.

The Risorgimento

With the final defeat of Napoleon in 1815, Ferdinand once again united Naples and Sicily as the 'Kingdom of the Two Sicilies', taking the title Ferdinand I. For the next 12 years the island was divided between a minority who sought an independent Sicily, and a majority who believed that the island's survival could only be assured as part of a unified Italy, an ideal being promoted on the mainland as part of the political and social movement known as the Risorgimento (reunification period).

On 4 April 1860 the revolutionary committees of Palermo gave orders for a revolt against the tottering Bourbon state. The news reached Giuseppe Garibaldi, who decided this was the moment to begin his campaign for the unification of Italy. He landed in Marsala on 11 May 1860 with about 1000 soldiers – the famous *mille* – and defeated a Bourbon army of 15,000 at Calatafimi on 15 May, taking Palermo two weeks later.

Despite his revolutionary fervour, Garibaldi was not a reformer in the social sense, and his soldiers blocked every attempt at a land grab on the part of the ordinary worker. On 21 October a referendum was held that saw a staggering 99% of eligible Sicilian voters opt for unification with the Piedmontese House of Savoy, which controlled most of Northern and Central Italy. Its head, King Victor Emmanuel II, aspired to rule a united Italy and had supported Garibaldi's expedition to Sicily. He was to become the first king of a unified Italy on 17 March 1861.

Fascism, Conservatism & WWII

Sicily struggled to adapt to the Savoys. The old aristocracy by and large maintained their privileges, and hopes of social reform soon dwindled.

What the island really needed was a far-reaching policy of agrarian reform, including a redistribution of land. The partial break-up of large

Best Archaeological Museums

Museo Archeologico Regionale, Palermo

Museo Archeologico, Agrigento

Museo Archeologico Eoliano, Lipari

Museo Archeologico Paolo Orsi, Syracuse

Sicilian History in Print & Podcast

The Leopard by Giuseppe Tomasi di Lampedusa

Seeking Sicily by John Keahey

Norman Centuries (podcast) by Lars Brownworth

1693	1799–1815	1820–48	1860–61
A devastating earthquake and associated tsunamis destroy dozens of communities in southeastern Sicily, leading to the eventual reconstruction of Noto, Ragusa, Modica and several other cities in baroque style.	Napoleon takes control of Naples, leading to a weakening of Bourbon powers and the drafting of an 1812 constitution that establishes a two-chamber parliament and abolishes feudal privileges.	The first uprising against the Bourbons occurs in Palermo. It is followed by others in Syracuse in 1837 and Palermo in 1848.	Garibaldi lands in Marsala and defeats the Bourbon army, taking Palermo two weeks later. King Victor Emmanuel II becomes the first king of a unified Italy on 17 March 1861.

UNCONVENTIONAL HISTORY MUSEUMS

Mixed in with all of Sicily's fabulous archaeological museums and ancient sites are a couple of off-the-beaten-track treasures that shine a light on the island's more recent history.

➡ The brand-new Museo dell'Inquisizione (p62) looks at the history and impact of the Inquisition on Sicily. Housed in the historic prisons of Palermo's Palazzo Chiaromonte Steri, it features cell after cell filled with prisoners' graffiti and artwork. Guided tours (in English upon request) provide fascinating historical context.

➡ CIDMA (p82), south of Palermo in Corleone, brings you face to face with the sordid history of the Sicilian Mafia, as well as the powerful resistance movement that's sprung up on the island in recent years. Photos powerfully document the tragic consequences of Mafia violence, while bilingual tour guides – actively engaged in the museum's anti-Mafia mission – offer a voice of hope for the future.

estates after the abolition of feudalism still only benefited the *gabellotti* (agricultural middlemen who policed the peasants on behalf of the aristocracy), who leased the land from the owners only to then charge prohibitive ground rents to the peasants who lived and worked on it.

To assist them with their rent collections the bailiffs enlisted the help of local gangs, who acted as intermediaries between the tenant and the owner, sorting out disputes and regulating affairs in the absence of an effective judicial system. These individuals were called *mafiosi* and were organised into small territorial gangs drawn up along family lines. They effectively filled the vacuum that existed between the people and the state, slotting in to the role of local power brokers.

In 1922, Benito Mussolini took power in Rome. With the growing influence of the Mafia dons threatening his dominance in Sicily, Mussolini dispatched Cesare Mori to Palermo with orders to crush lawlessness and insurrection in Sicily. Mori did this by ordering the round-up of individuals suspected of involvement in 'illegal organisations'.

By the 1930s, Mussolini had bigger fish to fry – his sights were set on the colonisation of Libya as Italy's Fourth Shore, ultimately dragging Sicily into WWII. Chosen as the springboard for the recapture of mainland Italy, Sicily suffered greatly from heavy Allied bombing. Ironically, the war presented the Mafia with the perfect opportunity to get back at Mussolini and it collaborated with the Allied forces, assisting in the capture of the island in 1943.

1860–94	1922–43	1943–44	1951–75
The emergence of the *mafiosi* fills the vacuum between the people and the state. The need for social reform strengthens the growing trade union, the *fasci*.	Benito Mussolini brings Fascism and almost succeeds in stamping out the Mafia. He drags Sicily into WWII by colonising Libya. Sicily suffers greatly from Allied bombing.	The Mafia collaborates with the Allied forces, assisting in the capture of the island. Sicily is taken in 39 days. Mafia Don Calogero Vizzini is appointed as the island's administrator.	Sicily's petrochemical, citrus and fishing industries collapse, leading to widespread unemployment. One million Sicilians emigrate to northern Europe.

Postwar Woes & Mani Pulite

The most powerful force in Sicilian politics in the latter half of the 20th century was the Democrazia Cristiana (DC; Christian Democrats), a centre-right Catholic party that appealed to the island's traditional conservatism. Allied closely with the Church, the DC promised wide-ranging reforms while at the same time demanding vigilance against godless communism. It was greatly aided in its efforts by the Mafia, which ensured that the local DC mayor would always top the poll. The Mafia's reward was *clientelismo* (political patronage) that ensured it was granted favourable contracts.

This constant interference by the Mafia in the island's economy did much to nullify the efforts of Rome to reduce the gap between the prosperous north and the poor south. The well-intentioned Cassa del Mezzogiorno (Southern Italy Development Fund), set up in 1950, was aimed at kick-starting the pitiful economy of the south, and Sicily was one of its main beneficiaries, receiving state and European Communities (EC) money for all kinds of projects. However, the disappearance of large amounts of cash eventually led the central government to scrap the fund in 1992, leaving the island to fend for itself.

In the same year, the huge Tangentopoli (Bribesville) scandal (the institutionalisation of kickbacks and bribes, which had been the country's modus operandi since WWII) made headline news. Although it was largely focused on the industrial north of Italy, the repercussions of the widespread investigation into graft (known as *Mani Pulite*, or Clean Hands) were inevitably felt in Sicily, a region where politics, business and the Mafia were long-time bedfellows. The scandal eventually brought about the demise of the DC party.

In the meantime, things were changing in regard to how the Sicilians viewed the Mafia, thanks to the investigating magistrates Paolo Borsellino and Giovanni Falcone. They contributed greatly to turning the climate of opinion against the Mafia on both sides of the Atlantic, and made it possible for ordinary Sicilians to speak about and against the Mafia more freely. When they were tragically murdered in the summer of 1992, it was a great loss for Italy and Sicily, but it was these deaths that finally broke the Mafia's code of *omertà* (silence), which had ruled the island for so long. A series of high-profile arrests have followed in the two decades since, including the apprehensions of legendary Mafia kingpins Salvatore 'Totò' Riina in 1993, Leoluca Bagarella in 1995, Bernardo 'the Tractor' Provenzano in 2006, Salvatore Lo Piccolo in 2007 and Domenico 'the Veterinarian' Raccuglia in 2009.

1992	1995–99	2006	2013
Sicilian anti-Mafia magistrates Giovanni Falcone and Paolo Borsellino are murdered within two months of each other. Their deaths provoke widespread outrage and strengthen popular resistance to the Mafia.	Giulio Andreotti, the former Italian prime minister, is charged with Mafia association, and goes on trial. He is acquitted due to lack of evidence in 1999.	The Sicilian Godfather, Bernardo Provenzano, is arrested after 40 years on the run. His arrest marks an important milestone in the fight against the Mafia.	Sicily continues to grapple economically, with early 2013 figures presenting a harsh reality: overall unemployment at 20.71% and youth unemployment at 52%.

The Sicilian Table

'Leave the gun. Take the cannoli.' Sicily's food is so good that even the mobsters in *The Godfather* turned to it for comfort. And indeed, in this nation where food is at the centre of existence and where there are so many delicious regional variations, the cuisine of Sicily is considered one of Italy's best. A huge part of anyone's visit here will be taken up with eating and drinking. Prepare to have your taste buds pampered!

Land of Timeless Culinary Traditions

While it's perfectly normal to order 'a *biscotti*' or 'a *cannoli*' back home in London or New York, note that these are actually plural forms in Italian; use the singular form '*un biscotto*' or '*un cannolo*' while in Sicily – unless of course you truly want a pile of them!

Sicily's kitchen is packed with fresh ingredients, unexpected flavours and delectable combinations. The island's rich pantry has evolved over a long period, shaped by successive waves of invaders but always finding its roots in Sicily's abundant soil and surrounding waters. Over the centuries, many traditional recipes have taken hold, surviving to the present day. Fish and shellfish from the Mediterranean form one of the lasting foundations of the island's cuisine. The abundance of fruit and vegetables has also been evident since the times of the ancient Greeks – Homer famously said of the island, 'Here luxuriant trees are always in their prime, pomegranates and pears, and apples glowing red, succulent figs and olives swelling sleek and dark', and wrote about wild fennel and caper bushes growing on the hills. But it wasn't until the Arabs came to the island that the cuisine really took shape. The Saracens brought the ever-present aubergine (eggplant), as well as citrus fruits, and they are believed to have introduced pasta to the island. They also spiced things up with saffron and sultanas, and contrasted the dishes' delicate flavours with the crunch of almonds and pistachios. In fact, the Arabs were so influential that couscous is present on every menu in western Sicily. And, on top of this, the Saracens brought sugar cane to these shores, helping Sicily develop all those fantastic sweets.

What's really impressive about Sicily's cuisine is that most of these amazing tastes came out of poverty and deprivation. The extravagant recipes of the *monsù* (chefs; from the French *monsieur le chef*) employed by the island's aristocrats were adapted to fit the budget and means of the less fortunate. Ordinary Sicilians applied the principle of preserving the freshness of the ingredients and, most importantly, never letting one taste overpower another. And that's the crunch of it, so to speak, the key to all of Sicily's dishes: simplicity.

Three Colours

Sicily's favourite ingredients can be grouped according to the *tricolore* – the three colours of the Italian flag. The following are the basics that will be found in the pantry of any Sicilian; through these you can get to the core of the island's cuisine.

Red

You may think red is the colour of passion, but when it comes to Sicilian cooking, it's also the colour of the most important ingredient of all: the tomato. *Il pomodoro* or *il pomodorino* (cherry tomato) is at the foundation of most sauces, whether it's cooked, blanched or simply scattered fresh over a heap of pasta. Sicilian tomatoes are renowned throughout Italy for their sweet flavour, especially the *pomodoro di Pachino,* a special variety that's cultivated in southeastern Sicily. You'll often see tomatoes hanging in bunches outside houses (especially on the island of Salina, where the locals claim it's the best way to keep them fresh). Sun-dried tomatoes are another way of preserving tomatoes, and many Sicilians use this version in the winter months, when fresh tomatoes aren't easy to find.

Peppers are another must-have vegetable for Sicilians, and you'll find both the bell-shaped version and the long, pointy type in many starters and antipasti. A favourite dish involving red, green and yellow peppers is *peperonata in agridolce,* where peppers are stewed with onions, pine nuts, raisins and capers.

White

Garlic is, of course, a major ingredient in Sicilian cooking. It is added to around 80% of savoury recipes, and it sometimes forms the main component of a sauce, as in *spaghetti aglio olio* (spaghetti with garlic and oil) – simple and delicious. Sicilians use crushed fresh cloves, most commonly on grilled or baked fish, or fry it thinly sliced to flavour the oil.

'White' is also for cheese. Sicilians like to sprinkle liberal helpings of a strong cheese called *caciocavallo* on their pasta dishes (despite the word *cavallo,* which means 'horse', the cheese is actually made from cow's milk). Parmesan has only recently found its way onto the menu, and Sicilians will shriek with horror if you sprinkle it on the wrong sauce. Ricotta cheese, both dried and fresh, often features on Sicilian menus. Eaten really fresh (less than 24 hours old), it tastes like heaven. *Pecorino* cheese is another favourite. Made of sheep's milk, it has a strong aroma and is often added to sauces; the most distinctive *pecorini* come from the Madonie and Nebrodi mountains, and are highlighted as important but endangered by the Slow Food Foundation for Biodiversity.

Mandorle (almonds) usually come blanched. They are widely cultivated throughout Sicily and they add a wonderful crunch to many a dish.

Almost all restaurants in Sicily charge €2 to €3 per person for *pane e coperto* (bread and cover charge). Theoretically this pays for the basket of bread that's brought out while you wait for the rest of your meal to arrive. If the waiter forgets, just ask!

THE SICILIAN TABLE THREE COLOURS

SICILIAN IGP & DOP VARIETIES

A number of Sicilian food specialities have earned special recognition under Italy's national DOP (protected origin) program and the European Union's IGP (protected geographical indication) program. These designations help promote and safeguard the reputations of quality agricultural products throughout the island. Some of the most famous DOP and IGP products are listed below, each followed by the name of the region where it's cultivated.

➡ **Pistacchi Verdi di Bronte DOP** Green pistachios from Bronte, on Mt Etna's western slopes (Ionian Coast).

➡ **Pomodori di Pachino IGP** Cherry tomatoes from Ragusa and Syracuse (Southeastern Sicily).

➡ **Fichidindia dell'Etna DOP** Prickly pear cactus fruit from Mt Etna (Ionian Coast).

➡ **Limoni di Siracusa IGP** Lemons from Syracuse (Southeastern Sicily).

➡ **Arance Rosse di Sicilia IGP** Sicilian red oranges (Syracuse and the Southeast, Ionian Coast, Central Sicily).

➡ **Pesche di Leonforte IGP** Peaches from the Enna region (Central Sicily).

➡ **Pecorino Siciliano DOP** Sheep's milk cheese, available island-wide.

➡ **Ragusano DOP** Cow's milk cheese from Ragusa (Southeastern Sicily).

➡ **Capperi di Pantelleria IGP** Capers from the island of Pantelleria, off Sicily's southwestern coast.

➡ **Nocellara del Belice DOP** Olives from the Belice valley (Western Sicily).

Almonds are also used to make one of the most common *granite* (flavoured crushed ice), as well as wonderful biscuits. The Sicilians have invented *latte di mandorla,* a delicious cold drink that is basically almond pulp and water; it is drunk mostly in the west, where you can also buy it in supermarkets, and it's freshly made in many bars.

Cappuccino and caffè latte are served everywhere at breakfast time, but you'll stick out like a sore thumb if you ask for milk in your coffee after noon – at lunch and dinner time, Sicilians only drink it black.

Green

Good olive oil is one of the prime delicacies of Sicilian cuisine, and several traditional olive varieties have been grown on the island for centuries. The main types are *biancolilla* (southwestern Sicily), *nocellara* and *ogliarola messinese* (northeast), *cerasuola* (between Sciacca and Paceco) and *nocellara del Belice* (Trapani province).

You'll detect the smell of *basilico* (basil) wafting from most Sicilian kitchens. While the herb is used in northern Italy mainly for making pesto, the Sicilians have taken this a step further, making *pesto alla Trapanese* with its fragrant leaves. In this dish, basil is combined with blanched and peeled tomatoes, grated *pecorino* cheese, a healthy clove or two of garlic and some crushed almonds. The ingredients are bashed together with a pestle and mortar, some good olive oil is added, and the sauce is mixed with short pasta.

Pistachios are hugely popular in Sicily. Brought to Sicily by the Arabs and cultivated on the fertile volcanic-soil plains of the island, the nut is used in both savoury and sweet recipes – some of the best ice cream is made from pistachios. And the good news is that, if eaten regularly, the pistachio can significantly reduce cholesterol (although that unfortunately does not apply when eaten in ice-cream form!).

Sicilian Classics: Antipasti

Sarde a beccafico
Rolled, stuffed sardines.

Arancinette
Savoury fried rice balls.

Caponata *Sweet-and-sour mix of aubergines, capers and olives.*

Staples

Bread, pasta, antipasti, fish, meat...with so many delicious staples in Sicilian cuisine, you'll be spoilt for choice. You'll also find loads of traditional regional specialities to sample, many made with products showcased by the **Fondazione Slow Food** (www.fondazioneslowfood.com) organisation.

Bread

Bread has always been a staple food for the Sicilian peasant. Made from durum wheat, Sicilian bread is coarse and golden, fashioned into myriad ritualistic and regional shapes, from braids to rings to flowers. Baked bread is treated with the greatest respect and in the past only the head of the family had the privilege of slicing the loaf.

Periods of dire poverty and starvation no doubt gave rise to the common use of breadcrumbs, which served to stretch meagre ingredients and fill up hungry stomachs. Such economy lives on in famous dishes such as *involtini,* in which slices of meat or fish are wrapped around a sometimes-spicy breadcrumb stuffing and then pan-fried or grilled. Breadcrumbs (rather than grated cheese) are also sprinkled on some pasta dishes, such as *pasta con le sarde.* Some other popular dishes made with a bread-dough base include *sfincione* (local form of pizza made with tomatoes, onions and sometimes anchovies), *impanata* (bread-dough snacks stuffed with meat, vegetables or cheese) and *scaccie* (discs of bread dough spread with a filling and rolled up into a pancake).

Sicilian Classics: First Courses

Pasta alla norma (Catania)

Pasta con le sarde (Palermo)

Couscous alla trapanese (Trapani)

Pasta all'eoliana (Aeolian Islands)

Antipasti

Sicilians' love of strong flavours and unusual combinations lends itself well to the antipasto (literally 'before the meal', or appetiser) platter. Helping yourself to a selection of antipasti from the buffet is a great way to explore some of Sicily's wonderful flavours, ranging from marinated sardines and slivers of raw herring to fruity cheeses and a whole range of marinated, baked and fresh vegetables, including artichokes, peppers, sun-dried tomatoes, eggplant and the most famous of all – *caponata* (cooked vegetable salad made with tomatoes, aubergines, celery, capers, olives and onions). In mountainous regions, the antipasto selection tends to shift more towards sausages, cheeses, mushrooms or hearty *arancinette*, fried balls of rice stuffed with meat and tomato sauce. If you're lucky, you'll also find rare treats such as delicately breaded and fried sage leaves or squash blossoms.

Pasta

Pasta is possibly Italy's (and Sicily's) most famous export. While fresh pasta *(pasta fresca)* is now common on most Sicilian restaurant menus, it is dry pasta that has always been the staple of Sicily and southern Italy – mainly because dry pasta is more economical.

The most famous of all Sicilian pasta dishes is *pasta con le sarde* (pasta with sardines). It is a heavy dish, but the liberal use of wild mountain fennel (unique to Sicily), onions, pine nuts and raisins gives the sardines a wonderfully exotic flavour. Other famous dishes include Catania's *pasta alla Norma,* with its rich combination of tomatoes, aubergines and salted ricotta, the Aeolian Islands' *pasta all'eoliana*, made with local olives, capers, cherry tomatoes, olive oil and basil, the ever-popular *spaghetti ai ricci* (with sea urchins) and *pasta al pesce spada e menta*, made with fresh swordfish and mint. In the interior you will often find sauces made from meat and game (including wild boar, rabbit and beef) as well as *pasta alle nocciole*, with a sauce based on the hazelnuts of the Nebrodi and Madonie mountains. Baroque Modica is where the island's best lasagne *(lasagne cacate)* is made; in this version, two kinds of cheese – ricotta and *pecorino* – are added to minced beef and sausage, and spread between layers of homemade pasta squares.

Fish

The extensive development of fishing and – until recent years – the widespread presence of fish such as sardines, tuna and mackerel off the island's shores have ensured that fish is a staple food.

A Palermitan favourite is *sarde a beccafico alla Palermitana* (sardines stuffed with anchovies, pine nuts, currants and parsley), served either as an appetiser or a second course. However, the filet mignon of the marine world is the *pesce spada* (swordfish), served either grilled with lemon, olive oil and oregano, or as *involtini* (slices of swordfish rolled around a spicy filling of onions, currants, pine nuts and breadcrumbs).

The best swordfish is caught in Messina, where they serve the classic *agghiotta di pesce spada* (also called *pesce spada alla Messinese*), a mouthwatering dish flavoured with pine nuts, sultanas, garlic, basil and tomatoes. The Egadi Islands are home to two splendid fish dishes: *tonno 'nfurnatu* (oven-baked tuna with tomatoes, capers and green olives) and *alalunga di Favignana al ragù* (fried albacore served in a spicy sauce of tomatoes, red chilli peppers and garlic). It is not uncommon to see the latter sauce also appear as part of your pasta dish.

Shellfish are popular throughout the island, especially calamari or *calamaretti* (baby squid), which is prepared in a variety of ways, including stuffed, fried or cooked in a tomato sauce. You'll also find plenty of *cozze* (mussels), *vongole* (clams) and *gamberi* (shrimp). Another popular and ubiquitous treat is *frittura mista* (sometimes called *fritto misto*), a blend of lightly breaded and fried shrimp, squid and/or fish.

Meat

Although you can find a limited number of meat dishes along the coast, you won't taste the best until you move further inland. The province of Ragusa is renowned for its imaginative and varied uses of meat, particularly mutton, beef, pork and rabbit. Its most famous dish is *falsomagro*, a stuffed roll of minced beef, sausages, bacon, egg and *pecorino* cheese.

In Palermo, it's not uncommon to compliment a woman by calling her bella come una cassata (lovely as a cassata).

THE SICILIAN TABLE STAPLES

Sicilian restaurants typically open for lunch between noon and 1pm, closing between 2.30pm and 3pm. Places reopen for dinner between 7pm and 8pm, but most Sicilians don't show up until 9pm or later, especially in summertime.

Sicilian Classics: Second Courses

Scaloppine al marsala *Veal cutlets with Marsala wine.*

Involtini di pesce spada *Swordfish roll-ups with raisins, pine nuts and bread crumbs.*

Frittura mista *Fried squid, shrimp and other seafood.*

Another local speciality is *coniglio all'agrodolce* (sweet-and-sour rabbit), which is marinated in a sauce of red wine flavoured with onions, olive oil, bay leaves and rosemary. The Nebrodi mountains are famous for a variety of pork products derived from the indigenous *Nero dei Nebrodi*, also known as *suino nero* (literally, black pig). In the neighbouring Madonie mountains, the town of Castelbuono is the home of *capretto in umido* (stewed kid) and *agnello al forno alla Madonita* (Madonie-style roast lamb). Locally caught *cinghiale* (wild boar) is served in stews, sauces and sausages. Don't be put off if goat or kid dishes are described on the menu as *castrato* – it means the goat was castrated, giving the meat a tender quality. Thankfully, it doesn't refer to what's on your plate.

As any Sicilian can tell you, *cannoli* are meant to be eaten with your fingers, even in a fancy restaurant. Leave the knife and fork behind, grasp that little sugary beauty between thumb and forefinger, and crunch away to your heart's content!

Sweets

Sicily's extraordinary pastries are rich in colour and elaborately designed. The queen of Sicilian desserts, the *cassata,* is made with ricotta, sugar, vanilla, diced chocolate and candied fruits. The equally famous *cannoli,* pastry tubes filled with sweetened ricotta and sometimes finished off with candied fruit, chocolate pieces or crumbled pistachios, are found pretty much everywhere. Another ubiquitous treat is *frutta di Martorana,* named after the church in Palermo that first began producing them. These marzipan confections, shaped to resemble fruits (or whatever takes the creator's fancy), are part of a Sicilian tradition that dates back to the Middle Ages. In late October they're sold in stalls around Palermo in anticipation of Ognissanti (All Souls' Day), but they're also commonly available year-round in painted souvenir boxes throughout Sicily.

Other Sicilian sweets worth sampling are *paste di mandorle* (almond cookies), *gelo di melone* (something like watermelon jelly), *biscotti regina* (sesame-coated biscuits that originated in Palermo but are now widely available throughout the island), *cassatelle* (pouches of dough stuffed with sweetened ricotta and chocolate, originally from Trapani province), *cuccia* (an Arab cake made with grain, honey and ricotta, sold in western Sicily) and *sfogli polizzani* (a speciality of Polizzi Generosa in the Madonie mountains, made with chocolate, cinnamon and fresh sheep's milk cheese).

Plenty of seasonal treats are prepared in conjunction with religious festivals. These include the cute little *pecorelle di marzapane* (marzipan lambs) that start appearing in pastry shop windows around Easter Week, *pupe* (sugar dolls made to celebrate All Souls' Day on 1 November), *ucchiuzzi* (biscuits shaped like eyes, made for the Festa di Santa Lucia on 13 December) and *buccellati* (dough rings stuffed with minced figs, raisins, almonds, candied fruit and/or orange peel, especially popular around Christmas).

Looking for something a little more daring? A good place to start is the southeastern town of Modica, where you can try chocolate laced with spicy peppers (prepared from an Aztec recipe brought here directly from Mexico when Sicily was under Spanish rule) or *'mpanatigghi* (Modican pastries stuffed with minced meat, almonds, chocolate, cloves and cinnamon).

Ever wonder where Sicily's two favourite desserts got their names? *Cassata* comes from the Arabic word *qas'ah*, referring to the terracotta bowl used to shape the cake; *cannolo* comes from *canna* (cane, as in sugar cane).

Any decent *pasticceria* (pastry shop) will have an enormous spread of freshly made cakes and pastries. It is very common for Sicilians to have their meal in a restaurant and then go to a pastry shop, where they have a coffee and cake while standing at the bar.

Gelati & Granite

Despite Etna's belly of fire, its peak is a natural freezer, and snow that falls on Etna lasts well into the searing summer, insulated by a fine blanket of volcanic ash. The Romans and Greeks treasured the snow, using it to chill their wine, but it was the Arabs who first started the Sicilian mania for all things icy – *granita* (flavoured crushed ice), gelato (ice cream) and *semifreddo* (literally 'semi-frozen'; a cold, creamy dessert).

The origins of ice cream lie in the Arab *sarbat* (sherbet), a concoction of sweet fruit syrups chilled with iced water, which was then developed into *granita* (where crushed ice was mixed with fruit juice, coffee, almond milk and so on) and *cremolata* (fruit syrups chilled with iced milk), the forerunner to gelato.

Home-made gelato *(gelato artigianale)* is sold at cafes and bars across the island, and is truly delicious. You should try it like a Sicilian – first thing in the morning in a brioche!

Granite are sometimes topped with fresh whipped cream, and are often eaten with a brioche. Favourite flavours include coffee and almond, though lemon is great in summer. During July, August and September, try a *granita di gelsi* (mulberry), a delicious seasonal offering.

Wine

Sicily's vineyards cover nearly 120,000 hectares, making it the second-largest wine-producing region in Italy. But while grapes have always been grown here, Sicilian wine is for the most part not well known outside the island.

The most common varietal is Nero d'Avola, a robust red similar to syrah or shiraz. Vintages are produced by numerous Sicilian wineries, including **Planeta** (www.planeta.it), which has four estates around the island; **Donnafugata** (www.donnafugata.it) in Western Sicily; **Azienda Agricola COS** (www.cosvittoria.it) near Mt Etna; and **Azienda Agricola G Milazzo** (www.milazzovini.com) near Agrigento. Try Planeta's Plumbago and Santa Cecilia labels, Donnafugata's Mille e una Notte, COS' Nero di Lupo and Milazzo's Maria Costanza and Terre della Baronia Rosso.

Local cabernet sauvignons are less common but worth sampling; the version produced by **Tasca d'Almerita** (www.tascadalmerita.it) at its Regaleali estate in Caltanissetta province is particularly highly regarded (the estate also produces an excellent Nero d'Avola under its Rosso del Conte label).

The sangiovese-like Nerello Mascalese and Nerello Cappuccio are used in the popular Etna Rosso DOC; try the Contrada Porcaria and Contrada Sciaranuova vintages produced by the **Passopisciaro** (www.passopisciaro. com) estate or the Serra della Contessa, Rovittello and Pietramarina produced by **Vinicola Benanti** (www.vinicolabenanti.it).

Cerasuolo di Vittoria, a blend of Nero d'Avola and Frappato grapes, is Sicily's only DOCG *(denominazione d'origine controllata e garantita)* wine. The more restrictive DOCG classification indicates that Cerasuolo is routinely analysed and tasted by government inspectors before bottling, and sealed with an official label to prevent tampering. Look for Planeta's vintages, which are produced at its estate in Dorilli, and those by COS.

Though the local reds are good, the region is probably best known for its white wines, including those produced at **Abbazia Santa Anastasia** (www.abbaziasantanastasia.it) near Castelbuono, and **Fazio Wines** (www. faziowines.it) near Erice, Tasca d'Almerita and Passopisciaro.

Common white varietals include Carricante, Chardonnay, Grillo, Inzolia, Cataratto, Inzolia, Cataratto, Grecanico and Corinto. Look out for Tasca d'Almerita's Nozze d'Oro Inzolia blend, Fazio's Catarratto Chardonnay, Abbazia Santa Anastasia's chardonnay blends, and Passopisciaro's Guardiola Chardonnay.

Most wines are fairly cheap, though (as for any wine) prices vary according to the vintage. In a restaurant a bottle of decent wine should cost you around €15 to €25, with a table wine *(vino da tavola)* at around €10.

Sicilian dessert wines are excellent, and are well worth buying to take home. Top of the list is Marsala's sweet wine; the best (and most widely known) labels are Florio (p105) and **Pellegrino** (www.carlopellegrino.it). Sweet Malvasia (from the Aeolian island of Salina) is a honey-sweet wine

---

THE SICILIAN TABLE WINE

Sweet tooths take note: in Sicily it's perfectly acceptable to eat ice cream first thing in the morning. Two of the island's most popular summertime breakfasts are *gelato e brioche* (a roll filled with ice cream) or *granita con panna* (flavored crushed ice topped with whipped cream)!

In late afternoon, just before dinnertime, Sicilians go to local bars to socialize over *aperitivi* - glasses of wine and alcohol, often accompanied by free snacks. This ritual is a great way to mingle with Italians, and it can even serve as a light dinner if you're not particularly hungry.

whose best producers include **Carlo Hauner** (www.hauner.it), **Capofaro** (capofaro.it/en/malvasia) and Fenech (p146) – just look for one of these names on the bottle and you'll know you have a good drop. Italy's most famous Moscato (Muscat), made from *zibibbo* grapes, is the Passito di Pantelleria from the island of the same name; it has a deep-amber colour and an extraordinary taste of apricots and vanilla.

The subscription-based **Gambero Rosso Wine Guide** (www.gambero-rosso.it) is generally considered to be the bible of Italian wines and offers plenty of information about Sicilian wines and wineries.

Food Glossary

eacciughe	a•choo•ge	anchovies
aceto	a•*che*•to	vinegar
acqua	a•kwa	water
aglio	a•lyo	garlic
agnello	a•*nye*•lo	lamb
aragosta	a•ra•*go*•sta	lobster
arancia	a•*ran*•cha	orange
arrosto/a	a•*ros*•to/ a	roasted
asparagi	as•*pa*•ra•jee	asparagus
bicchiere	bee•*kye*•re	glass
birra	*bee*•ra	beer
bistecca	bi•*ste*•ka	steak
burro	*boo*•ro	butter
caffè	ka•*fe*	coffee
cameriere/a	ka•mer•*ye*•re/a	waiter (m/f)
capretto	kap•*re*•to	kid (goat)
carciofi	kar•*chyo*•fee	artichokes
carota	ka•*ro*•ta	carrot
carta dei vini	*kar*•ta dey•*vee*•nee	wine list
cavolo	*ka*•vo•lo	cabbage
cena	*che*•na	dinner
ciliegia	chee•*lye*•ja	cherry
cipolle	chee•*po*•le	onions
coltello	kol•*te*•lo	knife
coniglio	ko•*nee*•lyo	rabbit
conto	*kon*•to	bill/cheque
cozze	*ko*•tse	mussels
cucchiaio	koo•*kya*•yo	spoon
enoteca	e•no•*te*•ka	wine bar
fagiolini	fa•jo•*lee*•nee	green beans
fegato	fe•*ga*•to	liver
fico	*fee*•ko	fig
finocchio	fee•*no*•kyo	fennel
forchetta	for•*ke*•ta	fork
formaggio	for•*ma*•jo	cheese
fragole	*fra*•go•le	strawberries
friggitoria	free•jee•to•*ree*•a	fried-food stand
frutti di mare	*froo*•tee dee *ma*•re	seafood
funghi	*foon*•gee	mushrooms
gamberoni	gam•be•*ro*•nee	prawns

granchio	*gran*•kyo	crab
insalata	een•sa•*la*•ta	salad
lampone	lam•*po*•ne	raspberry
latte	*la*•te	milk
limone	lee•*mo*•ne	lemon
manzo	*man*•dzo	beef
mela	*me*•la	apple
melanzane	me•lan•*dza*•ne	aubergine
melone	me•*lo*•ne	cantaloupe; rock melon
merluzzo	mer•*loo*•tso	cod
miele	*mye*•le	honey
olio	o•*lyo*	oil
oliva	o•*lee*•va	olive
osteria	os•te•*ree*•a	informal restaurant
ostriche	os•*tree*•ke	oysters
pane	*pa*•ne	bread
panna	*pa*•na	cream
pasticceria	pas•tee•che•*ree*•a	patisserie
patate	pa•*ta*•te	potatoes
pepe	*pe*•pe	pepper
peperoncino	pe•pe•ron•*chee*•no	chilli
peperoni	pe•pe•*ro*•nee	capsicum
pera	*pe*•re	pear
pesca	*pes*•ka	peach
pesce spada	*pe*•she *spa*•da	swordfish
pollo	*po*•lo	chicken
pomodori	po•mo•*do*•ree	tomatoes
pranzo	*pran*•dzo	lunch
prima colazione	*pree*•ma ko•la•*tsyo*•ne	breakfast
riso	*ree*•so	rice
ristorante	ree•sto•*ran*•te	restaurant
rucola	*roo*•ko•la	rocket; arugula
sale	*sa*•le	salt
salsiccia	sal•*see*•cha	sausage
sarde	*sar*•de	sardines
sgombro	*sgom*•bro	mackerel
spinaci	spee•*na*•chee	spinach
spuntino	spoon•*tee*•no	snack
tartufo	tar•*too*•fo	truffle
tè	te	tea
tonno	*to*•no	tuna
tovagliolo	to•va•*lyo*•lo	napkin
trattoria	tra•to•*ree*•a	informal restaurant
trippa	*tree*•pa	tripe
uva	*oo*•va	grapes
vegetaliano/a	ve•je•ta•*lya*•no/a	vegan (m/f)
vegetariano/a	ve•je•ta•*rya*•no/a	vegetarian (m/f)
vino bianco	*vee*•no *byan*•ko	white wine
vino rosso	*vee*•no *ro*•so	red wine

The Sicilian Way of Life

When asked to name their nationality, most locals will say 'Sicilian' rather than 'Italian', reinforcing a generally held Italian belief that the Sicilian culture and character are markedly different to those of the rest of the country. Though sharing many traits with fellow residents of the Mezzogiorno (the part of southern Italy comprising Sicily, Abruzzo, Basilica, Campania, Calabria, Apulia, Molise and Sardinia), Sicilians have a dialect and civil society that are as distinctive as they are fascinating.

Identity

Ogni beni di la campagna veni. All good things come from the countryside.

The uniqueness of the Sicilian experience is perhaps summed up best by author Giuseppe Tomasi di Lampedusa in Sicily's most famous novel, *Il Gattopardo* (The Leopard). In one memorable passage, his protagonist the Prince of Salina tries to explain the Sicilian character to a Piedmontese representative of the new Kingdom of Italy as follows: 'This violence of landscape, this cruelty of climate, this continual tension in everything, and even these monuments of the past, magnificent yet incomprehensible because not built by us and yet standing round us like lovely mute ghosts... All these things have formed our character, which is thus conditioned by events outside our control as well as by a terrifying insularity of mind.'

In modern Sicily, the prevailing stereotype is that Palermo and Catania stand at opposite ends of the island's character. 'In Palermo, we're more traditional, more conservative', says Massimo, a Palermo shopkeeper. 'The Catanians are more outward looking, and better at commerce.' Some ascribe the Palermitans' conservative character to their Arab predecessors, while the Greeks get all the credit for the Catanians' democratic outlook, their sense of commerce and their alleged cunning. Beyond this divide, Sicilians are generally thought of as conservative and suspicious (usually by mainland Italians), stoical and spiritual, confident and gregarious, and as the possessors of a rich and dark sense of humour.

Colonised for centuries, Sicilians have absorbed myriad traits – indeed, writer Gesualdo Bufalino believed Sicilians suffered from an 'excess of identity', at the core of which was the islanders' conviction that Sicilian culture stands at the centre of the world. This can make the visitor feel terribly excluded, as there is still an awful lot of Sicily that is beyond the prying eyes of the tourist.

SICILIAN PROVERBS

Sicilian culture is big on proverbs. Even as Sicilians embrace many aspects of modern life, their everyday speech is laced with traditional sayings whose roots go back several centuries. Spoken in Sicilian (a language in its own right and quite distinct from Italian), these proverbs often require translation even for other Italians. See the sidebars in this chapter for a representative sampling, with loose translations into English.

TIDES OF CHANGE

For all of its supposed conservatism, modern-day Sicily has recently been at the centre of some major cultural shifts. Two of these are the growing acceptance of gays in Italian society and the repudiation of Mafia control. Both of these threads converge in the story of Rosario Crocetta, who was elected Sicily's new governor in 2012.

Back in 2003, Mr Crocetta became the first openly gay Italian politician to win a mayoral election, though he had to fight the Mafia to get there. The original vote tally showed him losing by a narrow margin, but after Crocetta discovered evidence of Mafia tampering, he managed to convince a court to overturn the results. Since then he's ridden a wave of public popularity all the way to the governor's office, ending over six decades of right-wing rule. Along the way, despite three Mafia attempts on his life, he has remained an outspoken critic of organised crime.

That said, it is difficult to make blanket assertions about Sicilian culture, if only because there are huge differences between the more modern-minded city dwellers and those from the traditionally conservative countryside. It is certain, however, that modern attitudes are changing conservative traditions. In the larger university cities such as Palermo, Catania, Syracuse and Messina, you will find a vibrant youth culture and a liberal lifestyle.

Public vs Private

Family is the bedrock of Sicilian life, and loyalty to family and friends is one of the most important qualities you can possess. As Luigi Barzini (1908–84), author of *The Italians,* noted, 'A happy private life helps tolerate an appalling public life.' This chasm between the private arena and public forum is a noticeable aspect of Sicilian life, and has evolved over years of intrusive foreign domination.

A megghiu parola e chidda ca unsi rici. The best word is the one that remains unspoken.

Maintaining a *bella figura* (beautiful image) is very important to the average Sicilian, and striving to appear better off than you really are (known as *spagnolismo*) is a regional pastime. Though not confined to Sicily, *spagnolismo* on the island has its roots in the excesses of the Spanish-ruled 18th century, when the race for status was so competitive that the king considered outlawing extravagance. In this climate, how you and your family appeared to the outside world was (and still is) a matter of honour, respectability and pride. In a social context, keeping up appearances extends to dressing well, behaving modestly, performing religious and social duties and fulfilling all essential family obligations; in the context of the extended family, where gossip is rife, a good image protects one's privacy.

In this heavily patriarchal society, 'manliness' is a man's prime concern. The main role of the 'head of the family' is to take care of his family, oil the wheels of personal influence and facilitate the upward mobility of family members. Women, on the other hand, are traditionally the repository of the family's honour, and even though unmarried couples commonly live together nowadays, there are still young couples who undertake lengthy engagements for the appearance of respectability.

Cu sparti avi a megghiu parti. The one who divides things up gets the better share.

Traditionally, personal wealth is closely and jealously guarded. Family money can support many individuals, while emigrant remittances have vastly improved the lot of many villagers.

A Woman's Place

'In Sicily, women are more dangerous than shotguns', said Fabrizio (Angelo Infanti) in *The Godfather.* 'A woman at the window is a woman to be shunned', proclaimed the writer Giovanni Verga in the 19th century. And

'Women are too stupid to be involved in the complex world of finance', decided a judge when faced with a female Mafia suspect in the 1990s. As in many places in the Mediterranean, a woman's position in Sicily has always been a difficult one.

Sparagna la farina mentre la coffa e' china; quannu lu furnu pari, servi a nenti lu sparag- nari. Save flour while the bag is full; when you can see the bottom, there's nothing left to save.

A Sicilian mother and wife commands the utmost respect within the home, and is expected to act as the moral and emotional compass for her family. Although, or perhaps because, male sexuality holds an almost mythical status, women's modesty – which includes being quiet and feminine, staying indoors and remaining a virgin until married – has had to be ferociously guarded. To this day the worst insult that can be directed to a Sicilian man is *cornuto,* meaning that his wife has been unfaithful.

But things are changing for Sicilian women. More and more unmarried women live with their partners, especially in the cities, and enjoy the liberal lifestyle of many other Western countries. Improvements in educational opportunities and changing attitudes mean that the number of women with successful careers is growing, although a 2012 Global Gender Gap Index published by the World Economic Forum still placed Italy near the bottom of the list of European nations when it comes to closing the gap between the sexes in terms of political, professional and economic parity.

Agneddu e sucu e finiu u vattiu. When the lamb's all gone, the baptism is over. (When the food's all gone, the party's over.)

Sicily and Italy also have traditionally had some of the lowest percentages in Europe of women in government. The situation is slowly improving: in 2013, seven ministers out of 21 ((up from four in 2009) and 295 of of 952 parliamentarians (up from 193) were female, although a number of those women are alleged to have attained their positions because former prime minister Silvio Berlusconi found them attractive. It's a situation that feminist organisations such as Sicily's **Arcidonna** (www.arcidonna.org) are working to change.

Saints & Sinners

Religion is a big deal in Sicily. With the exception of the small Muslim communities of Palermo and the larger Tunisian Muslim community in Mazara del Vallo, the overwhelming majority of Sicilians consider themselves practising Roman Catholics. Even before the 1929 Lateran Treaty between the Vatican and Italy, when Roman Catholicism became the official religion of the country, Sicily was incontrovertibly Catholic, mostly due to 500 years of Spanish domination. In 1985 the treaty was renegotiated, so that Catholicism was no longer the state religion and religious education was no longer compulsory, but this only reflected the reality of mainland Italy north of Rome; in Sicily, the Catholic Church remains strong and extremely popular.

BRIDGING THE CULTURAL DIVIDE

Maria Sanciolo-Bell was born in Sicily, lives in Australia and spends much of her time forging cultural links between the island and the rest of the world. A director of **Echoes Events** (www.echoesevents.com), a cultural tourism and events company with offices in Melbourne and Catania, she and her Sicilian business associate Gaetano Failla are passionate about Sicilian culture and run a huge range of programs celebrating it. Whether it be running opera masterclasses with Sicilian maestros, conducting regional cookery courses, sponsoring international art exchanges or taking international visitors on tours of the locations used in the *Inspector Montalbano* TV series and *Godfather* films, Echoes plays an important role in raising the cultural profile of Sicily and highlighting its attractions on the world stage. As she says: 'Many people only know of Sicily in relation to the Mafia. We are committed to raising awareness of its incredibly rich and diverse heritage and to making people aware of the cultural interrelationships – rather than the cultural divides – between Sicily and the rest of the world.'

In the small communities of the interior you will find that the mix of faith and superstition that for centuries dictated Sicilian behaviour is still strong. The younger, more cosmopolitan sections of society living in the cities tend to dismiss their elders' deepest expressions of religious devotion, but most people still maintain an air of respect.

Pilgrimages remain a central part of the religious ritual, with thousands of Sicilians travelling to places such as Santuario della Madonna at Tindari or Santuario di Gibilmanna in the Madonie mountains. The depth of religious feeling associated with these sanctuaries is underscored by the large number of *ex votos* (votive offerings) brought to both places by worshippers seeking divine intervention or giving thanks for a miracle attributed to the Madonna.

Annual feast days of patron saints are also enthusiastically celebrated throughout the island, morphing into massive city-wide events in the larger urban areas. Palermo's mid-July Festa di Santa Rosalia spans three solid days, with the patroness paraded down Corso Vittorio Emanuele from the cathedral to the waterfront in a grandiose *carro triunfale* (triumphal carriage), flanked by adoring crowds. In Catania, the Festa di Sant'Agata in early February also lasts for three days, with over a million devotees pouring into the streets to follow a silver reliquary bust of the saint. Syracuse's mid-December Festa di Santa Lucia, while smaller, is celebrated with similar fervor. All three festivals are accompanied by spectacular fireworks.

Easter celebrations mark the high point in Sicily's religious calendar. Settimana Santa (Holy Week) is traditionally a time for Sicilians to take time off from work, get together with their families and participate in religious observances. Many places around the island celebrate Holy Week with elaborate processions. The most famous of these is Trapani's I Misteri, a four-day event in which 20 life-sized statues representing different moments in Christ's Passion are carried through the streets by members of the city's traditional guilds. Other cities covered in this guide that have noteworthy Easter processions include Caltanissetta, Lipari and Enna.

Immigration & Emigration

Immigration and emigration are among the most pressing contemporary issues, and Sicily is no stranger to the subject. Since the end of the 19th century the island has suffered an enormous drain of human resources through emigration. Between 1880 and 1910, over 1.5 million Sicilians left for the US, and in 1900 the island was the world's main area of emigration. In the 20th century, tens of thousands of Sicilians moved away in search of a better life in Northern Italy, North America, Australia and other countries. Today, huge numbers of young Sicilians – often the most educated – continue to leave the island. This brain-drain epidemic is largely the result of the grim unemployment rate and the entrenched system of patronage and nepotism, which makes it difficult for young people to get well-paid jobs without having the right connections.

Also, the fact that Sicily is one of the favoured ports of call for the thousands of *extracomunitari* (immigrants from outside the EU) who have flooded into Italy, some of them illegally, has led to extra strain being placed on housing and infrastructure as well as increased competition for jobs. Even so, Sicilians as a general rule have shown themselves to be hospitable to these newcomers and understanding of the difficulties faced by political and economic refugees from neighbouring countries that have recently suffered social upheavals, most notably Libya and Tunisia.

Testa c'un parra si chiama cucuzza. A head that doesn't speak is called a pumpkin. (If something's on your mind, don't keep it to yourself!)

Cu mancia fa muddica. He who eats leaves breadcrumbs. (If you do something wrong, people will find out.)

Cu si voli 'mbriacari, di vino bonu l'avi a fare. He who wants to get drunk should do it with good wine.

THE SICILIAN WAY OF LIFE IMMIGRATION & EMIGRATION

Sicily on Page & Screen

Writers and film-makers have long been inspired by Sicily's harsh landscape, rich history and complex society. They have rarely seen the island through rose-tinted glasses – endemic poverty and corruption are hard to romanticise or whitewash – and their words, images and narratives offer an invaluable insight into the local culture and society.

Sicily in Print

Dogged by centuries of isolation, and divided into an illiterate peasantry and a decadent aristocracy, Sicily prior to the 19th century suffered from a complete absence of notable literature.

With such a context it is interesting to learn that the first official literature in Italian was written in Palermo in the 13th century at the School of Poetry, patronised by Frederick II. But such high-minded works were irrelevant to the peasants, whose main pleasure was the regular celebration of saints' days and religious occasions and, later, the popular theatre of the *opera dei pupi* (puppet theatre).

Local Voices

The political upheaval of the 19th and 20th centuries finally broke the silence of the Sicilian pen, and the literary colossus Giovanni Verga (1840–1922) emerged onto the scene. Living through some of the most intense historical vicissitudes of modern Italy – the unification of Italy, WWI and the rise of Fascism – his work was to have a major impact on Italian literature. His greatest novel, *I Malavoglia* (The Malavoglia Family; 1881), essentially a story about a family's struggle for survival through desperate times in Sicily, is still a permanent fixture on every Sicilian schoolchild's reading list.

Since then Sicilian writers have produced fiction to rival the best contemporary European works. Playwright and novelist Luigi Pirandello (1867–1936) was awarded the Nobel Prize for Literature in 1934 for a

THE LEOPARD

Written by Giuseppe Tomasi di Lampedusa and published posthumously in 1958, *Il Gattopardo* (The Leopard) is generally considered to be the greatest Sicilian novel ever written. The story of an ageing aristocrat grappling with the political and sociological changes that are being brought to the island by the Risorgimento (reunification period), it is set in an era and milieu that Lampedusa, the last of a long line of minor princes in Sicily, evokes magnificently. Faced with choosing between tradition and modernity, the book's central character takes the only honourable path (for him) and opts for tradition, thus signing the warrant for his family's loss of wealth, power and influence. Unusually, the 1963 cinematic version by director Luchino Visconti – himself a member of the Italian aristocracy – is as critically acclaimed as the novel.

LITERARY SETTINGS

➡ Aci Trezza – Giovanni Verga's *I Malavoglia* is set in this fishing village on the Ionian Coast.

➡ Palazzo dei Normanni (p55) – much of Barry Unsworth's *The Ruby in Her Navel* is set in this Norman fortress near Palermo.

➡ Palma di Montechiaro, near Agrigento – thought to be Giuseppe di Lampedusa's inspiration for the town of Donnafugata in his novel *Il Gattopardo* (The Leopard).

➡ Porto Empedocle – features in Luigi Pirandello's early novels and is the inspiration for Andrea Camilleri's fictional town of Vigatà.

➡ Syracuse – the setting for Elio Vittorini's *Conversazione in Sicilia*.

substantial body of work, which included the play *Sei Personaggi in Ricerca di un Autore* (Six Characters in Search of an Author; 1921). Poet Salvatore Quasimodo (1901–68) won the award in 1959 for his exquisite lyric verse, which included delightful translations of works by Shakespeare and Pab-lo Neruda. Elio Vittorini (1908–66) captured the essence of the Sicilian migration north in his masterpiece *Conversazione in Sicilia* (1941), the story of a man's return to the roots of his personal, historical and cultural identity.

Sicily's most famous novel was a one-off by an aristocrat whose intent was to chronicle the social upheaval caused by the end of the old regime and the unification of Italy. Giuseppe Tomasi di Lampedusa (1896–1957) published *Il Gattopardo* (The Leopard) in 1958 to immediate critical acclaim. Though a period novel, its enduring relevance lies in the minutely accurate observations of what it means to be Sicilian.

Much of Sicily's 20th-century literature is more political than literary. None is more so than the work of Danilo Dolci (1924–97), a social activist commonly known as the 'Sicilian Gandhi'. His *Report from Palermo* (1959) and subsequent *Sicilian Lives* (1981), both detailing the squalid living conditions of many of Sicily's poorest inhabitants, earned him the enduring animosity of the authorities and the Church. (Cardinal Ernesto Ruffini publicly denounced him for 'defaming' all Sicilians.) He, too, was nominated for the Nobel Prize and was awarded the Lenin Peace Prize in 1958.

The other great subject for modern Sicilian writers is, of course, the Mafia. For a masterful insight into the island's destructive relationship with organised crime, search out the work of Leonardo Sciascia (1921–89), whose novel *Il Giorno della Civetta* (The Day of the Owl; 1961) was the first Italian novel to take the Mafia as its subject. Throughout his career, Sciascia probed the topic, practically inventing a genre of his own. His protégé Gesualdo Bufalino (1920–96) won the prestigious Strega Prize in 1988 for his novel *Le Menzogne della Notte* (Night's Lies), the tale of four condemned men who spend the eve of their execution recounting the most memorable moments of their lives. Bufalino went on to become one of Italy's finest writers, mastering a style akin to literary baroque – intense, tortured and surreal. His haunting novel *La Diceria dell'Untore* (The Plague Sower; 1981), which won Italy's Campiello Prize, is the story of a tuberculosis patient at a Palermo sanatorium in the late 1940s. Guiding the reader through a landscape of doom, Bufalino invokes the horrors of wartime and the hopelessness of the patients who come to know each other 'before our lead-sealed freight car arrives at the depot of its destination'.

INSPECTOR MONTALBANO

Crime-fiction writer Michael Dibdin once wrote that there are three hardship postings that no Italian cop wants: Sicily, Sardinia and the Alto Adige. We're pretty sure that Inspector Salvo Montalbano, the much-loved protagonist in Andrea Camilleri's Montalbano books (www.andreacamilleri.net), would indignantly deny that this was the case. When not using his boundless stores of intuition and charm to solve crimes in the fictional town of Vigàta (based on Camilleri's birthplace of Porto Empedocle near Agrigento), this proudly Sicilian sleuth divides his time between gastronomy (only local dishes) and his long-suffering girlfriend, Livia. Our favourite excerpt of dialogue would have to be this: Waiter: 'What can I get for you, Inspector?' Montalbano: 'Everything'.

There are 17 novels and four short-story collections in the Montalbano series, all set in Sicily. Start with the inspector's first outing in *La Forma dell'Acqua* (The Shape of Water; 1994) and you're unlikely to want to stop until you've read them all.

Devotees of the acclaimed TV adaptation, starring Luca Zingaretti, can book an Inspector Montalbano tour with Echoes Events (p291) or Allakatalla (p206). Both these tours visit Ragusa, where the series is filmed, and Echoes can organise for you to eat at Don Calogero's trattoria or stay overnight in the Inspector's beachside house in Scicli.

Well-known feminist novelist and playwright Dacia Maraini (born 1936) has written a number of novels set in Sicily, including the award-winning historical romance *La Lunga Vita di Marianna Ucrìa* (The Silent Duchess; 1990), which was made into the film *Marianna Ucrìa* by Italian director Roberto Faenze in 1997.

> Leonardo Sciascia's collection of his top short stories, *The Wine Dark Sea*, explores the complicated world of Sicilian Mafia culture.

Through Foreign Eyes

A number of foreigners or expats have also written about Sicily. Enjoyable but lightweight titles include Peter Moore's humorous travelogue *Vroom by the Sea* (2007), which recounts his adventures exploring the island on a Vespa named Donatella (because it's the same shade of lurid orange as Donatella Versace); Brian P Johnston's *Sicilian Summer: A Story of Honour, Religion and the Perfect Cassata* (2007), which is full of village politics and eccentric personalities; and Marlena de Blasi's *That Summer in Sicily* (2008), a Mills & Boon–ish story about a Sicilian woman's relationship with a much-older member of the Sicilian aristocracy.

Mary Taylor Simeti's *On Persephone's Island* and Peter Robb's *Midnight in Sicily* are much more substantial. Simeti, an American who has been living on the island since 1962, offers fascinating insights into its history, culture and cuisine; and Robb's portrait of the Mezzogiorno is notable for its impeccable research and compelling narrative, especially the sections dealing with the Mafia.

> **Notable Films**
>
> *Kaos* – Paolo and Vittorio Taviani
>
> *La Terra Trema* – Luchino Visconti
>
> *The Godfather* trilogy – Francis Ford Coppola
>
> *Cinema Paradiso* – Giuseppe Tornatore
>
> *Stromboli* – Roberto Rossellini

Historical novels of note include Barry Unsworth's *The Ruby in Her Navel* (2006) and Tariq Ali's *A Sultan in Palermo* (2005). Both are set against the backdrop of the Norman court of Roger II (known to his Arabic subjects as Sultan Rujeri).

And finally, mention should be made of three eminently readable histories: *The Day of Battle: the War in Sicily and Italy 1943–1944* (2008), by Rick Atkinson; *The Normans in Sicily* (2004), by John Julius Norwich; and *The Sicilian Vespers: A History of the Mediterranean World in the Later Thirteenth Century* (1992), by Steven Runciman.

Sicily on Film

The rich emotional, psychological and physical landscapes of Sicily have inspired some of the world's best film-makers.

Visconti's two classics, *La Terra Trema* (The Earth Shook; 1948) and *Il Gattopardo* (The Leopard; 1963), illustrate the breadth of Sicilian tales – the former a story of grinding poverty and misfortune in a benighted fishing family, while the latter oozes the kind of grand decadence that one imagines preceded the French Revolution.

Antonioni's enigmatic mystery *L'Avventura* (The Adventure; 1960) focuses on the disappearance of one member of a group of bored and spoiled Roman socialites on a cruise around the Aeolian Islands, and though its existentialist plot has been described by many critics as impenetrable and pretentious, its stunning visuals are universally admired.

In Rossellini's *Stromboli: Terra di Dio* (Stromboli: Land of God; 1950), the explosive love affair between a Lithuanian refugee and a local fisherman is aptly viewed against the backdrop of the erupting volcano, while the hypnotic beauty of Michael Radford's *Il Postino* (The Postman; 1994) seduces viewers into a false sense of security, which is shattered by the film's tragic denouement.

However, it is Francis Ford Coppola's modern masterpiece, *The Godfather* trilogy (Part I, 1972; Part II, 1974; Part III, 1990), that really succeeds in marrying the psychological landscape of the characters with their physical environment. The varying intensities of light and dark superbly mirror the constant undercurrent of quivering emotion and black betrayal. The *coup de grâce* is the final scene of Part III, where Mascagni's opera, *Cavalleria Rusticana,* a foreboding story of love and betrayal, is interspersed with scenes of Michael Corleone's final acts of murder that ultimately lead to the death of the person he loves most, his daughter.

Other directors who have worked here include the Taviani brothers, who filmed *Kaos* in 1984, seeking to reproduce the mad logic of Sicilian-born author Luigi Pirandello's universe. The aptly named film is a series of tales about loss, lust, love, emigration and death played out through fantastical story lines. The film's title comes from the village near Agrigento where Pirandello was born (although it is spelled with a 'C').

Sicilians enjoy a good guffaw, and Pietor Germi's *Divorzio all'Italiana* (Divorce, Italian Style), set on the island, was a big hit here when it was released in 1961. More recent comedies include Roberto Benigni's *Il Piccolo Diavolo* (The Little Devil; 1988) and *Johnny Stecchino* (Johnny Toothpick; 1991).

Other films set in Sicily include Wim Wender's *Palermo Shooting* (2008), lambasted by most critics as pretentious and boring; and *Sicilia!* (1999), a film version of Elio Vittorini's acclaimed novel *Conversazione in Sicilia*, directed by Danièle Huillet and Jean-Marie Straub.

Sicily itself has produced few directors of note, with the best-known exception being Giuseppe Tornatore (born 1956). Tornatore followed up on the incredible success of his semi-autobiographical film *Nuovo Cinema Paradiso* (Cinema Paradiso; 1988) with films including *Malèna* (2000), starring Monica Bellucci in a coming-of-age story set in Sicily in the 1940s; *L'Uomo delle Stele* (The Star Maker; 1995), also set in rural Sicily in the 1940s; and *Baarìa – La Porta del Vento* (Baarìa – Door of the Wind; 2009), the story of three generations of a local family between 1920 and 1980. Two versions of *Baarìa* were made: the first in the local Sicilian dialect of Baariotu and the second dubbed in Italian.

Like Tornatore, Roman-born Emanuele Crialese has made Sicily his muse. Two of his films, *Respiro* (2002) and *Nuovomondo* (The Golden Door; 2006), are set here. *Respiro* is about a woman whose unorthodox behaviour challenges her family and islander neighbours, while *Nuovomondo* is a dreamy record of a Sicilian family's emigration to New York at the turn of the 20th century. Crialese's 2011 film *Terraferma* deals with the very contemporary issue of illegal immigration on the island of Linosa through a story of a fisherman's family.

See a careful study of 21st-century Sicily in Emanuele Crialese's film *Terraferma*, dealing with illegal immigration.

The Mafia

For many people, the word 'Mafia' is synonymous with Sicily, thanks to the country's infamous historical relationship with the organisation and the many films made about the Cosa Nostra – namely, and most famously, *The Godfather* trilogy. Starting life all the way back in the 18th century, the Mafia has shaped today's Sicily both through its criminal activities and, more recently, the brave and crucial anti-Mafia movement, which has involved a gradual resistance from all levels of Sicilian society.

Origins

The origins of the word 'mafia' are said to derive from the Arabic words 'mu'afah' or 'place of refuge', or 'mahjas', meaning 'boasting'.

The word 'mafia' was in common usage for more than 110 years before it was officially acknowledged as referring to an actual organisation. Although formally recorded by the Palermitan prefecture in 1865, the term was not included in the Italian penal code until 1982.

The origins of the word have been much debated. The author Norman Lewis has suggested that it derives from the Arabic *mu'afah* or 'place of refuge'. Nineteenth-century etymologists proposed *mahjas,* the Arabic word for 'boasting'. Whatever the origin, the term *mafioso* existed long before the organisation known as the Mafia, and was used to describe a character who was elegant and proud, with an independent vitality and spirit.

The concept of the *mafioso* goes all the way back to the late 15th century when commercial opportunities were so restricted that even the overprivileged feudal nobles were forced to make changes in order to survive. They introduced a policy of resettlement that forced thousands of farmers off the land and into new towns; the idea was to streamline crop growth, but it also destroyed the lives of the peasants in the process. Many of the aristocrats moved to big cities such as Palermo and Messina, leaving their estates in the hands of *gabellotti* (bailiffs), who were charged with collecting ground rents. They, in turn, employed the early *mafiosi* – who were small gangs of armed peasants – to help them solve any 'problems' that came up on the way. The *mafiosi* were soon robbing large estates and generally causing mayhem, but the local authorities were inept at dealing with them as they would quickly disappear into the brush.

The bandits struck a mixture of fear and admiration into the peasantry, who were happy to support any efforts to destabilise the feudal system. They became willing accomplices in protecting the outlaws, and although it would be another 400 years before crime became 'organised', the 16th and 17th centuries witnessed a substantial increase in the activities of brigand bands. The bands were referred to as Mafia, while the peasants' loyalty to their own people resulted in the name Cosa Nostra (Our Thing). The early-day Mafia's way of protecting itself from prosecution was to become the modern Mafia's most important weapon: the code of silence, or *omertà.*

The 'New' Mafia

Up until WWII the Mafia had operated almost exclusively in the countryside, but with the end of the conflict Cosa Nostra began its expansion into the cities. It took over the construction industry, channelling funds into its bank accounts and creating a network of kickbacks that were factored into every project undertaken. In 1953 a one-off meeting between representatives of the US and Sicilian Mafias resulted in the creation of the first Sicilian Commission, which had representatives of the six main Mafia families (or *cosche,* literally meaning 'artichoke') to efficiently run its next expansion into the extremely lucrative world of narcotics. At the head of the commission was Luciano Liggio from Corleone, whose 'family' had played a vital role in developing US–Sicilian relations.

Throughout the 1960s and '70s the Mafia earned billions of dollars from the drug trade. Inevitably, the raised stakes made the different Mafia families greedy for a greater share and from the late 1960s onwards Sicily was awash with vicious feuds that left hundreds dead.

The most sensational assassination was that of the chief prefect of police, General Carlo Alberto Dalla Chiesa, whom the national government had sent to Sicily to direct anti-Mafia activities. Dalla Chiesa was ambushed in Palermo in 1982, and his brutal murder led to prosecutors and magistrates being granted wider powers of investigation.

The first real insight into the 'New Mafia' came with the arrest of *mafioso* Tommaso Buscetta, also in 1982. After nearly four years of interrogation, headed by the courageous Palermitan investigating magistrate Giovanni Falcone, Buscetta broke the code of silence. His revelations shocked and fascinated the Italian nation, as he revealed the innermost workings of La Società Onorata (the Honoured Society; the Mafia's chosen name for itself). Tragically, Falcone was assassinated in 1992, as was another courageous anti-Mafia magistrate, Paolo Borsellino.

In 1986, 500 top *mafiosi* were put on trial in the first *maxiprocesso* (supertrial) in a specially constructed bunker near Palermo's Ucciardone prison. The trial resulted in 347 convictions, of which 19 were life imprisonments and the others jail terms totalling a staggering 2665 years.

In January 1993, the authorities arrested the infamous *capo di tutti capi* (boss of bosses), Salvatore (Totò) Riina, the most wanted man in Europe. He was charged with a host of murders, including those of magistrates Falcone and Borsellino, and sentenced to life imprisonment.

The residents of Corleone once petitioned to change the town's name in order to get away from its criminal connotations.

The Anti-Mafia Movement

The anti-Mafia movement is alive and kicking in Sicily, tracing its roots back to the beginning of today's Mafia. According to historians, the movement first appeared in the late 19th century, and lasted in its first incarnation until the 1950s. The movement strove for agrarian reform, targeting the Mafia, conservative political elites and the *latifondisti* (big landowners), but its efforts were shattered when the lack of economic prospects in the postwar era drove thousands of young Sicilians to emigrate in search of work and a better life.

During the 1960s and 1970s, the anti-Mafia movement was headed by political radicals, mainly members of the left-wing groups disenchanted with the Socialist and Communist parties. Giuseppe 'Peppino' Impastato became famous during this period; the son of a *mafioso,* Impastato mocked individual *mafiosi* on his popular underground radio show. He was assassinated in 1978. Things were at their worst for the anti-Mafia movement in the 1980s, when the Mafia was particularly intolerant of

THE MAFIA ON SCREEN

Il Capo dei Capi (The Boss of all Bosses) Italian TV miniseries (2007) about Salvatore Riina.

Dimenticare Palermo (To Forget Palermo) Italian political thriller (1989) directed by Francesco Rosi and co-written by Gore Vidal.

Excellent Cadavers Alexander Stille's 1995 book about Giovanni Falcone was made into a TV movie directed by Ricky Tognazzi in 1999 and a documentary directed by Marco Turco in 2005.

Il Giorno della Civetta (The Day of the Owl) Damiano Damiani's 1968 film was based on Leonardo Sciascia's novel.

The Godfather Trilogy Francis Ford Coppola's 1972–90 masterwork.

In Nome della Legge (In the Name of the Law) Pietro Germi's 1949 Italian neorealist film was co-written by Federico Fellini.

La Piovra (The Octopus) Hugely popular 1984–2001 Italian TV miniseries.

Salvatore Giuliano Francesco Rosi's 1962 neorealist film.

anyone perceived as a potential threat. The assassination in 1982 of General Dalla Chiesa is now seen as one of the major elements in sparking a new wave in the anti-Mafia movement, with Sicilians from all sections of society – from educators and students to political activists and parish priests – becoming involved.

The reformist Christian Democrat Leoluca Orlando, who was elected mayor of Palermo during the 1980s, also helped to increase anti-Mafia sentiment. He led an alliance of left-wing movements and parties to create Palermo Spring, which invalidated the public-sector contracts previously given to Mafia families, restored and reopened public buildings, and aided in the arrests of leading *mafiosi*. During the 1990s, Orlando left the Christian Democrats and set up the anticorruption movement La Rete (the Network), bringing together a broad collection of anti-Mafia individuals and reform organisations. (The party was eventually absorbed by Romano Prodi's Democrat Party in 1999.)

The anti-*pizzo* movement was inspired by the defiance of a shopkeeper called Libero Grassi, whose anonymous letter to an extortionist was featured on the front page of a local newspaper in 1991. Grassi was murdered three weeks later.

Civilian efforts saw housewives hanging sheets daubed with anti-Mafia slogans from their windows, shopkeepers and small entrepreneurs forming associations to oppose extortion, and the formation of groups such as **Libera** (www.libera.it), cofounded in 1994 by Rita Borsellino, the sister of the murdered judge Paolo Borsellino. Libera managed to get the Italian parliament to permit its member organisations to legally acquire properties that had been seized from the Mafia by the government, establishing agricultural cooperatives, *agriturismi* and other legitimate enterprises on these lands (see www.liberaterra.it). Even the Catholic Church, long silent on the Mafia's crimes, finally began to have outspoken anti-Mafia members. The best known was Giuseppe Puglisi, who organised local residents to oppose the Mafia, and who was murdered in 1993.

The Mafia Today

Since Salvatore Riina's conviction, other top *mafiosi* have followed him behind bars, most notably his successor Leoluca Bagarella, arrested in 1995; the Sicilian 'Godfather', Bernardo Provenzano, caught in 2006 after 20 years on the run; Salvatore Lo Piccolo, Provenzano's successor, arrested in 2007; and Domenico Raccuglia (aka 'the Veterinarian'), number two in the organisation, arrested in 2009 after 15 years on the run.

The year 2013 was an eventful one for the anti-Mafia movement. April of that year saw the biggest ever seizure of Mafia-related assets, from businessman Vito Nicastri, who is alleged to have been a front man for the Cosa Nostra. In May, more than 50,000 people attend the beatification of Don Giuseppe Puglisi, the Catholic priest shot by a Mafia hitman in 1993. Puglisi will be the first Mafia victim to be officially declared a martyr by the Roman Catholic Church, a powerful statement for the anti-Mafia movement. The same month, Italy's former head politicians were on trial alongside Mafia bosses such as Salvatore Riina, for involvement with the Mafia in Sicily. Among the accused politicians was Nicola Mancino, the former interior minister.

No one would be so foolish to suggest that the power of the Mafia is a thing of the past, but these events have meant that the powerful core of the organisation is being weakened and that the silence, which for so many years has made progress difficult, is finally being broken.

Today's Mafia has infiltrated daily life, becoming intertwined with legal society: its collaborators and their children are now 'respectable' and influential citizens. Whatever the business activity, the Mafia will often have a hand in it; for example, a legitimate business might secure a building contract, but the Mafia will then tell it where to buy cement or where to hire machinery. Critics call this 'the Invisible Mafia', and point out that a large number of Sicilian business owners still pay some kind of *pizzo* (protection money).

Providing a bright note amid all this is the organisation **Addiopizzo** (www.addiopizzo.org), which campaigns against these iniquitous payments, urging consumers to support businesses that have said 'no' to paying *pizzo*. Its motto, 'A people who pay the *pizzo* are a people without dignity', seems to have struck a chord across the island and a number of tourism businesses – among others – are actively supporting the campaign, devising tours that support restaurants, shops and hotels that have said no to this Mafia extortion (see www.addiopizzotravel.it).

The first mafia 'supertrial' happened in a bunker near Palermo in 1986, where 500 top *mafiosi* were prosecuted; there were 347 convictions, with 19 life imprisonments and overall sentences totalling 2665 years.

Art & Architecture

Centuries of foreign domination have left Sicily with a lavish artistic and architectural legacy. Ancient Greek temples litter the long southern coast while blazing mosaics adorn Roman villas and Byzantine churches, and forbidding Norman castles guard remote hilltop towns. Arriving later, Sicily's baroque maestros took the style to new, mind-bending heights.

Prehistoric Art

Prehistoric art enthusiasts will find rock paintings and graffiti all over Sicily.

The Museo Archeologico Eoliano (p135), in Lipari, showcases a fascinating collection of prehistoric and ancient finds from early Mediterranean times; you can see the charming ceramics and terracotta produced by the first Neolithic indigenous cultures in the region.

The Upper Palaeolithic wall paintings and Neolithic incised drawings at the Grotta del Genovese (p101) were accidentally discovered in 1949 by the painter Francesca Minellono. Between 6000 and 10,000 years old, the images mostly feature animals, such as deer and horses, though you can spot tuna too, a fish traditionally found in the waters off Sicily.

See a stunning collection of prehistoric finds at Lipari's Museo Archeologico Eoliano.

The Greeks & Romans

The Greeks settled in the 8th century BC and left the most enduring architectural legacy on the island. Sicily has some of the most impressive Doric temples in the Western world – the most enchanting are those at the Valle dei Templi (p235) (Valley of the Temples) in Agrigento. Other magnificent remains are at Selinunte, followed by those at the Parco Archaeologico della Neapolis (p193) at Syracuse. The remains of the city of Segesta (p88) form one of the world's most magical ancient sites with a theatre high on the mountain and a never-completed Doric temple dating from around 430 BC. The Teatro Greco (p193) at Syracuse is a masterpiece of classical architecture that could seat 16,000 people, while Taormina's Teatro Greco (p167), built in the 3rd century BC, is the most dramatically situated Greek theatre in the world and the second largest in Sicily, after Syracuse.

TOP ART GALLERIES

➡ Galleria Regionale della Sicilia (p61) – home to works dating from the Middle Ages to the 18th century.

➡ Galleria d'Arte Moderna (p61) – Sicilian paintings and sculptures from the 19th and 20th centuries.

➡ Museo Regionale (p163) – paintings by Caravaggio and home-town boy Antonello da Messina.

➡ Museo Regionale d'Arte Moderna e Contemporanea della Sicilia (Riso) (p57) – a new contemporary art museum hosting temporary exhibitions.

ANTONELLO DA MESSINA

The first – some would say only – great Sicilian painter was Antonello da Messina (1430–79). Originally from Messina, the artist is thought to have painted his first portraits in the late 1460s. They follow a Dutch model, the subject being shown bust-length, against a dark background, full face or in three-quarter view. Most Italian painters had adopted the semiprofile pose for individual portraits up to that point. John Pope-Hennessy described him as 'the first Italian painter for whom the individual portrait was an art form in its own right'. In *The Lives of the Artists* (1550), Vasari described da Messina as 'a man well skilled in his art' and claimed that he was the first Italian painter to use oil paint, a technique Vasari says he had learned in Flanders, though there is no evidence of da Messina having travelled outside Italy.

Only four of his luminous paintings are in Sicily. *Annunziata* (The Virgin Annunciate, 1474–77) is at the Galleria Regionale della Sicilia (p61), in Palermo. His splendid *Ritratto di un uomo ignoto* (Portrait of an Unknown Man, 1465), considered to be one of the most distinctive portraits of the Italian Renaissance, is held at the Museo Mandralisca (p117) in Cefalù. *L'Annunciazione* (Annunciation, 1474) can be seen in Syracuse, and *San Gregorio* (St Gregory, 1473) in Messina.

Sicily's most important Roman sight is the Villa Romana del Casale (p226) in Piazza Armerina. It holds a stunning array of colourful floor mosaics that have been newly restored and date from the 3rd century.

The Normans

The Normans collaborated with Byzantine and Arab architects and artisans, transforming Greek temples into basilicas and building innovative Moorish structures. Norman cathedrals remain some of Sicily's most impressive sights – the Cattedrale di Monreale (p80), the Duomo (p116) in Cefalù, and the Capella Palatina (p55) in Palermo are this period's shining stars.

The Cattedrale di Monreale is considered the finest example of Norman architecture in Sicily; it is covered in stunning mosaics in its entirety, and holds 200 slender columns, incorporating Norman, Arab, Byzantine and classical elements. Cefalù's Duomo is one of the jewels in Sicily's Arab-Norman crown: its elaborate Byzantine mosaics are Sicily's oldest and best preserved.

Palermo's Palazzo dei Normanni (p55) was originally constructed by the Arabs in the 9th century. It was extended by the Normans (namely Roger II) in 1130, and the Cappella Palatina (p55) at its centre is Palermo's prime attraction. Swarming with figures in glittering, dreamy gold, the exquisite, highly sophisticated mosaics were mainly the work of Byzantine Greek artisans brought to Palermo by Roger II in 1140 especially for this project. Other splendid examples from this period are the churches of La Martorana (p53) and San Giovanni degli Eremiti (p56), both in Palermo.

Innovative Sicilian art slowly died out in the 13th century with the arrival of the Hohenstaufen rulers.

The Renaissance: Painting & Sculpture

Although no great architectural heritage remains in Sicily from the Renaissance era, painting and sculpture flourished. Sicily's best-known painter – Antonello da Messina – hails from this time.

The Gagini family were sculptors and architects who founded Sicily's Gagini school, which flourished until the mid-1600s. Domenico Gagini (1420–92), the school's founder, often worked in conjunction with his son, Antonello Gagini (1478–1536). Antonello's most notable work is

Some of the most impressive Doric temples in the Western world are to be found on this island – the best are at Agrigento's Valley of the Temples (Valle dei Templi).

Don't miss the recently reopened Villa Romana del Casale in Piazza Armerina, Sicily's most important Roman sight.

the decorated arch in the Capella della Madonna in Trapani's Santuario dell'Annunziata (p94). He also produced ecclesiastical sculpture in Messina, and a large collection of his works can be seen at the Galleria Regionale della Sicilia (p61) – look out for his statue of the *Madonna del riposo* (1528).

Francesco Laurana (1430–1502), a Dalmatian-born sculptor who is considered both Italian and Croatian (the Croatian version of his name is Frane Vranjanin), spent the period between 1466 and 1471 working in Sicily. Among other works, he produced the tomb of Pietro Speciale in the **Chiesa di San Francesco d'Assisi** (Piazza San Francesco d'Assisi; Map p58; admission free; ☉7am-noon & 4-6pm) in Palermo, and his bust of Eleanor of Aragon, in the Galleria Regionale della Sicilia (p61), is particularly sumptuous.

Baroque Beauties

The Sicilian baroque period was a result of the 1693 earthquake that flattened cities like Catania and left the space for the flourishing of this unique architectural style. Sicily's brand of baroque combined the Spanish baroque with Sicily's own decorative and structural elements. Two architects that dominated during this period were Rosario Gagliardi (1700–70), the designer of the magnificent Cattedrale di San Giorgio (p212) at Ragusa, and Giovanni Battista Vaccarini (1702–69), who spent 30 years re-creating Catania's historical core. Noto's baroque centre is one of Sicily's most powerful examples of this architectural style.

The most important artist from this period was Giacomo Serpotta, born in Palermo in 1656. He specialised in plasterwork decorations on church oratories and you can see one of his masterpieces, Oratorio del Rosario di Santa Cita (p60), in Palermo's church of Santa Cita.

Liberty

Palermo flourished in the art nouveau (or 'Liberty') period. The innovation of architects like Giovan Battista Basile and his son Ernesto, and artists such as Salvatore Gregorietti and Ettore Maria de Begler, who painted the dining room of the **Grand Hotel Villa Igiea** (☎091 54 37 44; www.hotelvillaigieapalermo.com; Salita Belmonte 43) marked this epoch. The two kiosks in front of Palermo's Teatro Massimo (p63) are good examples of Sicily's art nouveau, though the Villa Malfitano (p63) remains the showcase of Liberty architecture. It is most notable for its whimsical interior decoration, which includes a 'Summer Room' with walls painted to resemble a conservatory, and a music room draped with 15th-century tapestries illustrating the *Aeneid*.

Contemporary Sicilian Art

Two artists, Salvatore Fiume (1915–97) and Renato Guttuso (1911–87), mark Sicily's contemporary art scene. Guttuso's masterful 1974 painting of the Vucciria market is one of Sicily's most impressive contemporary art works. The arresting, vibrant colours are the product of the artist's innovative approach – he used crumbled bricks to produce the reds, and burnt wood and candles for the black strokes. It hangs at the Museo dell'Inquisizione (p62) in Palermo.

The best place for a shot in the arm on what's currently going on in Sicily's art world is Favara's Farm Cultural Park (p249), where provocative art and social activism go hand in hand and serve art's great purpose – to try to make a real change.

Were it not for the 1693 earthquake flattening cities like Catania, Sicilian baroque would not have been born.

Survival Guide

Directory
A–Z

Customs Regulations

Duty-free sales within the EU no longer exist. Goods bought in and exported within the EU incur no additional taxes, provided duty has been paid somewhere within the EU and the goods are for personal use.

Travellers entering Italy from outside the EU are allowed to import duty free: 200 cigarettes, 1L of spirits, 2L of wine, 60mL of perfume, 250mL of *eau de toilette*, and other goods up to the value of €175. Anything over this must be declared and the appropriate duty paid.

On leaving the EU, non-EU citizens can reclaim Imposta di Valore Aggiunto (IVA) value-added tax on purchases equal to or over €155. The refund, which is around 12%, only applies to purchases made in affiliated outlets that display a 'Tax Free for Tourists' or similar sign.

Discount Cards

At many state museums and archaeological sites, EU citizens under 18 and over 65 enter free, and those aged between 18 and 25 get a 50% discount. To claim these discounts you'll need a passport, driving licence or ID card. For those under 26, the **Euro<26** (www.euro26.org) card is universally accepted.

Electricity

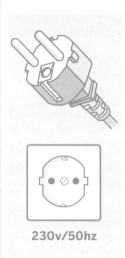

230v/50hz

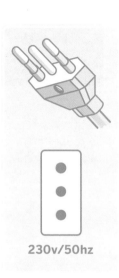

230v/50hz

Embassies & Consulates

For foreign embassies and consulates not listed here, look under 'Ambasciate' or 'Consolati' in the telephone directory. Alternatively, tourist offices might have a list. The German consulate is in Messina; the other listed consulates are all in Palermo.

French Consulate (☎091 58 34 05; www.ambafrance-it.org; Via Principe di Belmonte 101)

German Consulate (☎090 67 17 80; www.rom.diplo.de; Via San Sebastiano 73)

Netherlands Consulate (☎091 630 60 05; www.olanda. it; Via Trapani 1d)

UK Consulate (☎091 32 64 12; www.ukinitaly.fco.gov.uk; Via Cavour 117)

US Consulate (☎091 30 58 57; www.italy.usembassy.gov; Via Vaccarini 1)

Food

In Sicily there are a wide variety of eating establishments. Most of them have a *coperto* (cover charge) of usually €1 to €3 per person; some also include a *servizio* (service charge) of 10% to 15%.

In our listings the following price ranges are quoted for meals, which include a *primo* (first course), *secondo* (second course), *contorno* (side dish) or *dolce* (dessert) and coperto (cover charge).

€ less than €25

€€ €25–€45

€€€ more than €45

Vegetarians & Vegans

Vegetarianism is not specifically catered to in Sicily but the abundance of excellent fruit and veg means that many *antipasti*, pastas and *contorni* feature veg in some form or other. Salads are common and tasty, though you'll need to watch out for the odd anchovy or slice of ham. Similarly, check that your tomato sauce has not been cooked with meat in it. Vegans will be in for a tough time, with many dishes featuring some sort of animal product (butter, eggs or animal stock).

Gay & Lesbian Travellers

Although homosexuality is legal in Sicily, attitudes remain largely conservative and overt displays of affection could attract hostility.

The gay scene is largely centred on Catania and Taormina, and to a lesser extent Palermo. For further information, Italy's largest gay organisation, the Bologna-based **Arcigay** (www.arcigay.it), has branches in both Catania (www.arcigaycatania.it) and Palermo (http://arcigaypalermo.wordpress.com, in Italian). You can also pick up a copy of the free magazine *Clubbing*, which has club and event listings.

Spartacus International Gay Guide, lists male-only venues all over Italy, while online you could try **GuidaGay.**

it (www.gay.it/guida), which has details of gay-friendly bars, clubs, beaches and hotels.

Health

Italy's public-health system is legally bound to provide emergency care to everyone. EU nationals are entitled to reduced-cost, sometimes free, medical care with a European Health Insurance Card (EHIC), available from your home health authority. Non-EU citizens should take out health insurance.

For emergency treatment go to the *pronto soccorso* (casualty) section of an *ospedale* (public hospital), where it's also possible to receive emergency dental treatment. For less serious ailments call the local *guardia medica* (duty doctor); ask at your hotel or nearest tourist office for the number. Pharmacists will fill prescriptions and can provide basic medical advice.

Insurance

Medical Insurance

If you're an EU citizen, an EHIC covers you for free or reduced-cost public medical care but not for emergency repatriation. It is available from health centres in your home country. Citizens from countries outside the EU should find out if there is a reciprocal arrangement for free medical care between their country and Italy (Australia, for example, has such an agreement; carry your Medicare card with you).

US citizens should check whether their health-insurance plan offers coverage for hospital or medical costs abroad – many don't. The US Medicare service provides no coverage outside the US. If you do need health insurance, make sure you get a policy that covers you for the worst possible scenario, such as an accident requiring

We list prices for 'adult/reduced'; the 'reduced' rate refers to the seniors and students discount (in Italy these are almost always the same). Children under seven usually go free, though you can count on heavy discounts until the age of 10.

an emergency flight home. Find out in advance if your insurance plan will make payments directly to providers or reimburse you later for overseas health expenditures abroad.

Travel Insurance

A travel-insurance policy to cover theft, loss and medical problems is highly recommended. It may also cover you for cancellation of and delays in your travel arrangements. Worldwide travel insurance is available at www.lonelyplanet.com/travel_services. You can buy, extend and claim online anytime – even if you're already on the road.

Paying for your ticket with a credit card can often provide limited travel accident insurance, and you may be able to reclaim the payment if the operator doesn't deliver.

Note that some policies specifically exclude 'dangerous activities', which can include scuba diving, motorcycling and even trekking.

Internet Access

Public wi-fi hot spots are increasing in cafes and bars, and many hotels and B&Bs now offer free wi-fi. In accommodation listings the internet icon is used only when there is a computer available for guest use; wi-fi access is indicated with an

WATER

While tap water is reliable and safe throughout the country, most Sicilians prefer to drink *acqua minerale* (bottled mineral water). It will be either *frizzante* (sparkling) or *naturale* (still) and you will be asked in restaurants and bars which you prefer. If you want a glass of tap water, ask for *acqua dal rubinetto*.

icon, though wi-fi is only mentioned in reviews when charges apply.

If you're bringing your own kit, you shouldn't have too many problems hooking up in your room, or at least in the hotel reception or other communal areas. You might need a power transformer (to convert from 110V to 220V if your notebook isn't set up for dual voltage), an RJ-11 phone jack that works with your modem and a plug adapter.

Legal Matters

The most likely reason for a brush with the law is if you have to report a theft. If you do have something stolen and you want to claim it on insurance, you must make a statement to the police; insurance companies won't pay up without proof of a crime.

The Italian police is divided into three main bodies: the black-clad *carabinieri;* the *polizia*, who wear navy blue jackets; and the *guardia di finanza*, who fight tax evasion and drug smuggling. If you run into trouble in Italy, you're likely to end up dealing with either the *polizia* or the *carabinieri*. If, however, you land a parking ticket, you'll need to speak to the *vigili urbani* (traffic wardens).

The legal blood-alcohol limit is 0.05% and random breath tests do occur. Penalties for driving under the influence of alcohol can be severe.

In general, your embassy should be able to provide a list of local lawyers, interpreters and translators.

Maps

City Maps

Our city maps, combined with tourist-office maps, are generally adequate for getting around. More-detailed maps are also available in city bookshops. **Litografia Artistica Cartografica** (LAC; www.globalmap.it) produces detailed maps (costing €7) of a number of Sicilian cities, including Agrigento, Catania, Palermo, Syracuse and Trapani. **Michelin** (www.michelin.it) and **Touring Club Italiano** (TCI; www.touringclubstore.com) also produce decent city maps.

Driving Maps

The best road map is the TCI's *Sicilia* (1:200,000), available at bookshops, airports and motorway cafes in Sicily. The AA's *Road Atlas Italy* (1:250,000), available in the UK, includes Sicily. In Italy, the **Istituto Geografico de Agostini** (www.deagostini.it) publishes the *Carta Stradale Sicilia* (1:200,000; €7.30). Michelin also has a reliable map, *Sicilia*, at a scale of 1:200,000.

Walking Maps

For walking in the Mt Etna area, the 1:25,000 *Mt Etna* map produced by Selca is a good bet. The TCI produces a map of the Parco Regionale dei Nebrodi, at 1:50,000. For exploring the Parco Naturale Regionale delle Madonie, pick up the 1:50,000 *Madonie Carta dei Sentieri e del Paesaggio* from the Palermo tourist office. Alternatively, the tourist offices in the Madonie and Cefalù sell the *Carta dei*

Sentieri del Paesaggio Cefalù (1:50000) for €1.50.

Money

Italy's currency is the euro (€). The euro is divided into 100 cents. Coin denominations are one, two, five, 10, 20 and 50 cents, €1 and €2. The notes are €5, €10, €20, €50, €100, €200 and €500.

For the latest rates check out www.xe.com.

Money can be exchanged in banks, post offices and exchange offices. Banks generally offer the best rates, but shop around as rates fluctuate considerably.

ATMs

Credit and debit cards can be used in ATMs (which are widespread and known locally as *bancomat*) displaying the appropriate sign. Visa and MasterCard are widely recognised, as are Cirrus and Maestro. Remember that every time you withdraw cash there will be fees. Typically you'll be charged a withdrawal fee as well as a conversion charge; if you're using a credit card, you'll also be hit by interest on the cash withdrawn.

If an ATM rejects your card, don't despair. Try a few more ATMs displaying your credit card's logo before assuming the problem lies with your card.

Credit & Debit Cards

Though widely accepted, credit cards are not as ubiquitous in Sicily as they are in the UK or the US, and it's always a good idea to have some cash to hand. Many small guesthouses, trattorias and shops don't take credit cards, and you can't always use them at petrol stations or at motorway ticket barriers.

Major cards such as Visa, MasterCard, Eurocard, Cirrus and Eurocheques are accepted throughout Sicily. Amex is also recognised but it's less common.

Before leaving home, make sure to advise your credit-card holder of your travel plans. Otherwise, you risk having your card blocked – as a security measure, banks block cards when they notice out-of-the-ordinary transactions. Check also any charges you'll incur and what the procedure is if you experience problems or have your card stolen. Most card suppliers will give you an emergency number you can call free of charge for help and advice.

Tipping

You're not expected to tip on top of restaurant service charges, but if you feel the service warrants it, you can leave a little extra, say €1 per person. If there is no service charge, you should consider leaving a 10% tip or rounding the bill up, although it is by no means obligatory. In bars, locals often place a €0.10 or €0.20 coin on the bar when ordering coffee. Tipping taxi drivers is not common practice, but you should tip porters at top-end hotels (€3 to €5).

Opening Hours

Shops Generally open from around 9.30am to 1.30pm and then from around 4pm to 7.30pm Monday to Saturday. Many are closed on Monday morning and some smaller stores also close on Saturday afternoon. Some city department stores and many supermarkets have continuous opening hours from 9am to 8pm Monday to Saturday, with some also opening on Sunday morning, typically until 1pm.

Banks Open from 8.30am to 1.30pm and 2.45pm to 3.45pm Monday to Friday. They are closed on weekends, but it is always possible to find an exchange office open in the larger cities and in major tourist areas.

Post offices Major branches open from 8am to 6.30pm Monday to Friday and also 8am to 12.30pm on Saturday. Smaller post offices generally open from 8am to 1.30pm Monday to Friday and to 12.30pm on Saturday.

Pharmacies (Farmacie) Usually open 9am to 1pm and 3.30pm to 7.30pm. Most shut on Saturday afternoon, Sunday and holidays but a handful remain open on a rotation basis *(farmacie di turno)*. Closed pharmacies display a list of the nearest ones open.

Bars and cafes Generally open 7am to 8pm, although some stay open later and turn into pub-style watering holes. Restaurants typically open from noon to 3pm and 7.30pm to 11pm (later in summer).

Museums, galleries and archaeological sites Hours vary enormously, although many are closed on Monday.

Note also that Sicilian opening hours are not always observed with rigid precision, especially in small towns and outside the busy summer months.

Post

Sicily's postal system, **Poste** (☎803 160; www.poste. it), is never going to win any awards for efficiency but sooner or later letters generally arrive. Delivery is guaranteed to Europe within three days and to the rest of the world within four to eight days.

Stamps *(francobolli)* are available at post offices and authorised tobacconists (look for the official *tabacchi* sign, a big 'T', often white on black) which you'll find in every town and village.

For more important items, use registered mail *(raccomandato)* or insured mail *(assicurato);* the cost depends on the value of the object being sent.

PRACTICALITIES

➡ **Weights & measures** Sicily uses the metric system for weights and measures.

➡ **Electricity** Plugs have two or three round pins, so bring an adapter. The current is 220V, 50Hz.

➡ **Newspapers** Sicily's major regional newspapers are Palermo's *Il Giornale di Sicilia,* Catania's *La Sicilia* and Messina's *La Gazzetta del Sud.* Rome-based *La Repubblica* also has a section dedicated to Sicilian news. English-language newspapers are available, usually one or two days late, in the big cities and major resorts.

➡ **Smoking** Smoking is prohibited in all public spaces, as per EU law.

Public Holidays

Most Sicilians take their annual holiday in August, deserting the cities for the cooler seaside or mountains. This means that many businesses and shops close for at least part of the month, usually around the Feast of the Assumption (Ferragosto) on 15 August. Easter is another busy period, with many resort hotels opening for the season the week before Easter.

Italian schools close for three months in summer, from mid-June to mid-September, for two weeks at Christmas and for a week at Easter.

Individual towns have public holidays to celebrate the feasts of their patron saints. National public holidays in Sicily include the following:

Capodanno (New Year's Day) 1 January

Epifania (Epiphany) 6 January

Pasquetta (Easter Monday) March/April

Giorno della Liberazione (Liberation Day) 25 April

Festa del Lavoro (Labour Day) 1 May

Festa della Repubblica (Republic Day) 2 June

Ferragosto (Feast of the Assumption) 15 August

Festa di Ognisanti (All Saints' Day) 1 November

Festa della Immacolata Concezione (Feast of the Immaculate Conception) 8 December

Natale (Christmas Day) 25 December

Festa di Santo Stefano (Boxing Day) 26 December

Safe Travel

Despite Mafia notoriety, Sicily is not a dangerous place and the biggest threat you face is not from the local *capo* but from faceless pickpockets and bag-snatchers.

Scams

Many scams play on visitors' insecurity with foreign banknotes. One simple con to watch out for is short-changing. A typical scene runs as follows: you pay for a €3 *panino* with a €20 note. The cashier then distractedly gives you a €2 coin and a €5 note before turning away. The trick here is just to wait and chances are that the €10 you're waiting for will appear without a word being said.

Theft

There's no need for paranoia, but be on your guard against pickpockets and bag-snatchers, particularly in crowded markets (Palermo and Catania especially) and when travelling to or from the airports.

A money belt for essentials is a good idea, but avoid delving into it in public by carrying a wallet with a day's worth of cash in it. Don't flaunt watches, cameras and other valuables. If you're carrying a bag or camera, wear the strap across the body and away from the road – moped thieves can swipe a bag and be gone in seconds.

Be careful when you sit down at a streetside cafe or restaurant – never drape your bag over an empty chair by the road or where you can't see it.

Cars, particularly those with foreign number plates or rental-company stickers, are also vulnerable. Never leave valuables in your car and if possible park in a secure parking lot.

Always report theft or loss to the police within 24 hours, and ask for a statement; otherwise, your travel insurance company won't pay out.

Traffic

Sicilian traffic can be a daunting prospect, particularly in Palermo where the only rule seems to be survival of the fastest. However, outside the main urban areas, the situation calms down and the main concern becomes the potholes on the roads and the iffy signposting. As a general rule, traffic is at its quietest between 2pm and 4pm and at lunchtime on Sunday, when few people are out and about.

Drivers are not keen to stop for pedestrians, even at pedestrian crossings. Sicilians simply step off the pavement and walk through the swerving traffic. In the major cities, roads that appear to be for one-way traffic often have special lanes for buses travelling in the opposite direction, so always look both ways before stepping out.

Shopping

Shopping at Sicily's great markets is an experience to remember. Palermo's Mercato del Capo and Catania's La Pescheria fish market are more than just places to shop, they're extraordinary sights in themselves. These are Sicily's two best-known markets but every town worth its salt has at least one.

Sicily's food and wine provide rich shopping opportunities, with any number of local delicacies to choose from. The Aeolian Islands, along with Syracuse, Taormina and Cefalù, have a good number of gourmet delis.

Souvenir hunters are also spoiled for choice. Sicily has a rich tradition of ceramics, with production centred on Caltagirone, Santo Stefano di Camastra and Sciacca. Handmade jewellery is another local tradition, particularly on the west coast in Trapani and Cefalù. Old-fashioned lace and embroidery can be found in Palermo and Taormina, or rural towns like Erice and Caltanissetta.

For the ultimate memento you could always purchase one of Sicily's paladin puppets or a miniature model of the traditional Sicilian cart, the originals of which are now collectors' items.

Telephone

Phone services are provided by a host of companies, including **Telecom Italia** (www.telecomitalia.it), Italy's biggest telecommunications company.

Italian mobile phones operate on the GSM 900/1800 network, which is compatible with the rest of Europe and Australia but not with North American GSM 1900 or the Japanese system (although some GSM 1900/900 phones do work in Italy). If you have a GSM phone that you can unlock (check with your service provider), it can cost as little as €10 to activate a *pre-pagato* (prepaid) SIM card. **TIM** (www.tim.it), **Wind** (www.wind.it) and

Vodafone (www.vodafone. it) all offer SIM cards and all have retail outlets in Sicily. You'll need your passport to open an account. To recharge your card, simply pop into the nearest outlet or buy a *ricarica* (charge card) from a tobacconist.

Mobile call rates range from €0.09 to €0.30 per minute for domestic calls.

Useful Numbers & Codes

Italian area codes all begin with '0' and consist of up to four digits. The area code is followed by a telephone number of anything from four to eight digits. Area codes are an integral part of all telephone numbers in Italy, even if you are calling within a single zone. For example, any number you ring in Palermo will start with 091, even if it's next door. When making domestic and international calls you must always dial the full number including the initial zero. Mobile-phone numbers begin with a three-digit prefix such as 333, 347, 390.

To make an international telephone call from Sicily, dial 00, then the relevant country and area codes followed by the telephone number.

Directory enquiries local ✆1254, international ✆89 24 12

International access code ✆00

International direct-dial code ✆39

International operator ✆170

Time

Sicily is one hour ahead of GMT. Daylight-saving time starts on the last Sunday in March, when clocks are put forward one hour. Clocks go back an hour on the last Sunday in October. Italy operates on the 24-hour clock, so you will see 18.30 rather than 6.30pm on transport timetables.

Toilets

Public toilets are rare in Sicily except at major tourist sites and archaeological parks. Most people use the facilities in bars and cafes – although you might need to buy a coffee first. In many places public loos are pretty grim; try to go armed with some tissues.

Tourist Information

You'll find tourist offices located throughout Sicily. Some are more helpful than others but most are able to provide accommodation lists, rudimentary maps and information on local tourist attractions. Most will also respond to written and telephone requests for information.

Opening hours vary but as a general rule are 8.30am to 12.30pm or 1pm and from 3pm to 7pm Monday to Friday. Hours are usually extended in summer, when some offices also open on Saturday or Sunday. Information booths at major train stations tend to keep similar hours, but in some cases operate only in summer.

Offices in popular destinations such as Palermo, Catania, Taormina, Syracuse and the Aeolian Islands are usually well stocked and staffed by employees with a working knowledge of at least one other language, usually English but also French or German.

Officially, Sicilian tourist offices are known as *Servizi Turistici Regionali* (Regional Tourist Services) but for the sake of simplicity we refer to them as 'tourist offices'. For a full list and other regionwide information, contact Sicily's **Regional Tourist Board** (✆091 707 82 01; www.regione. sicilia.it/turismo; Via Notarbartolo 9, Palermo).

Travellers with Disabilities

Sicily is not an easy island for disabled travellers. Narrow cobbled streets, hair-raising traffic, blocked pavements and tiny lifts make life very difficult for wheelchair users, and those with sight or hearing difficulties.

Under European law, airports are obliged to provide assistance to passengers with reduced mobility, so if you need help en route to Sicily, or on arrival/departure, tell your airline when you book your ticket and they should inform the airport. Facilities are available at both Palermo and Catania airports.

If you are travelling by train, Trenitalia operates a **telephone helpline** (✆199 30 30 60) that has information on the services provided in stations, including provision of wheelchairs, guides and assistance getting on and off trains. Further information is available online at www.trenitalia.com/trenitalia.html under the Other Services link.

If you are driving, the UK blue badge is recognised in Italy, giving you the same parking rights that local disabled drivers have. For more information, go to the **Institute of Advanced Drivers** (www.iam.org.uk) and search for Blue Badge Users.

Two organisations that might be helpful:

Accessible Italy (✆378 94 11 11; www.accessibleitaly. com) A San Marino–based company that specialises in holiday services for the disabled, ranging from tours to the hiring of adapted transport.

Tourism for All (✆in UK 0845 124 99 71; www.tourismforall.org.uk) A British charity that can provide general travelling information – check out the website's very useful FAQ section.

Visas

For up-to-date information on visa requirements, see www.esteri.it/visti.

EU citizens do not need a visa to enter Italy. Nationals of some other countries, including Australia, Canada, Israel, Japan, New Zealand and the USA, do not need visas for stays of up to 90 days in Italy.

Other people wishing to visit Italy have to apply for a Schengen visa, which allows unlimited travel in Italy and 24 other European countries for a 90-day period. You must apply for a Schengen visa in your country of residence and you can not apply for more than two in any 12-month period. They are not renewable inside Italy.

Technically, all foreign visitors to Italy are supposed to register with the local police within eight days of arrival. However, if you're staying in a hotel or hostel you don't need to bother as the hotel will do it for you – this is why they always take your passport details.

Women Travellers

The most common form of discomfort for women travellers is harassment. Local men are not shy about staring and this can be disconcerting, especially if you're on your own. If you feel nervous about travelling solo, dressing smartly and wearing a wedding ring nearly always deters unwanted interest. If you do get hassled, the best response is usually just to ignore it, but if that doesn't work, politely say that you're waiting for your husband (marito) or fiancé (fidanzato) and, if necessary, walk away. Avoid becoming aggressive as this may result in an unpleasant confrontation.

Avoid walking alone on deserted and dark streets, and look for centrally located hotels within easy walking distance of places where you can eat at night. Women should not hitchhike alone.

Transport

GETTING THERE & AWAY

Flights tours, and rail tickets can be booked online at lonelyplanet.com/bookings.

Air

Fares to Sicily fluctuate enormously: tickets are cheapest between November and March and most expensive between June and September. Holidays such as Christmas, New Year and Easter see huge price hikes. Flight schedules are also subject to seasonal variations with the number of flights increasing considerably in summer.

Several low-cost airlines serve Sicily from European destinations, including Ryanair (www.ryanair.com), easyJet (www.easyjet.com), Vueling (www.vueling.com) and TUIFly (www.tuifly.com).

Airports

Sicily's two main airports serve the island's two biggest cities: Palermo and Catania.

Named after two assassinated anti-Mafia judges, Palermo's **Falcone-Borsellino airport** (PMO; Punta Raisi Airport; www.gesap.it) is at Punto Raisi, 30km west of the city. **Alitalia** (www.alitalia.com), blu-express.com and **Meridiana** (www.meridiana.it) operate regular flights to/from most mainland Italian cities; Ryanair, Vueling and **Air Berlin** (www.airberlin.com) are among the low-cost carriers serving London, Barcelona and Berlin.

Just 7km outside Catania, **Fontanarossa airport** (CTA; www.aeroporto.catania.it) is served by up to 31 national and international airlines with connections to 13 Italian cities and destinations across Europe.

Sicily's third-busiest airport, **Vincenzo Florio airport** (TPS; Birgi Airport; www.airgest.it), is 15km south of Trapani at Birgi and is commonly known as Birgi. Ryanair serves three dozen destinations throughout Italy and Europe, including Brussels, London, Manchester, Rome and Stockholm. Other airlines serving domestic Italian destinations from Birgi include Alitalia, **Air One** (flyairone.com) and **Darwin** (www.darwinairline.com), which fly to Rome, Milan and Pantelleria respectively.

Land

Car & Motorcycle

Driving to Sicily is an arduous and expensive task. In terms of budget, you'll need to account for the cost of toll roads and the fact that Italian fuel prices are among the highest in Europe. Your journey time will depend on where you catch the ferry from – Genoa, Civitavecchia, Naples or Villa San Giovanni.

The shortest ferry crossing is between Villa San Giovanni on the toe of the Italian mainland and Messina, but to get to Villa San Giovanni you will need to drive the toll-free A3 autostrada from Salerno.

From the French or Swiss borders you should allow for about 17 hours' driving but only if you keep to the motorways, go flat out (remember that the speed limit in Italy is 130km/h) and avoid traffic, which is something of a vain hope in the summer holiday period (July and August).

Once on Sicily a car or motorbike is a major plus but it is probably easier to hire one than to take your own.

BRINGING YOUR OWN VEHICLE

To bring your own vehicle to Sicily, you will need to have a valid driving licence, proof of vehicle ownership and evidence of third-party insurance. If your vehicle is registered and insured in an EU country, your home-country insurance is sufficient. Theoretically, the International Insurance Certificate, also known as the Carta Verde (Green Card), is no longer required for EU-registered cars, but in case of an accident the police may still ask for it, so consider getting one – your car-insurance company can issue it.

Every vehicle travelling across an international border should display a nationality plate of its country of registration. A warning triangle (to be used in the event of

CLIMATE CHANGE & TRAVEL

Every form of transport that relies on carbon-based fuel generates CO_2, the main cause of human-induced climate change. Modern travel is dependent on aeroplanes, which might use less fuel per kilometre per person than most cars but travel much greater distances. The altitude at which aircraft emit gases (including CO_2) and particles also contributes to their climate change impact. Many websites offer 'carbon calculators' that allow people to estimate the carbon emissions generated by their journey and, for those who wish to do so, to offset the impact of the greenhouse gases emitted with contributions to portfolios of climate-friendly initiatives throughout the world. Lonely Planet offsets the carbon footprint of all staff and author travel.

a breakdown) is compulsory throughout Europe.

DRIVING LICENCES & DOCUMENTATION

When driving in Sicily, always carry your driving licence, the vehicle's registration papers and proof of third-party (liability) insurance. All EU member states' driving licences are recognised in Sicily. If you have a non-EU licence, you'll need to get an International Driving Permit (IDP) to go with your licence. Your national automobile association can issue this and it's valid for 12 months.

Train

If you have the time, getting to Sicily by train is worth considering: it's more environmentally friendly than flying, it's more relaxed and, perhaps best of all, it allows you to break up your journey. Most trains traversing Italy will make a stop off at Rome and Naples, for example.

Italy's national rail company, **Trenitalia** (☑89 20 21; www.trenitalia.com), operates direct trains to Sicily from a number of Italian cities, including Milan, Rome and Naples. If you're travelling from outside the country, you will need to change trains somewhere in Italy, most probably Rome. For detailed info on getting to Sicily from London, check out www.seat61.com.

The *Thomas Cook European Timetable* has Europe-wide train schedules and is available from Thomas Cook

offices worldwide and at www.thomascookpublishing.com.

It is always advisable, and sometimes compulsory, to book seats on international trains. Some of the main international services include transport for private cars – an option worth examining to save wear and tear on your vehicle before it arrives in Sicily. On overnight hauls you can book a *cuccetta* (couchette) for about €20.

Sea

Unless you're flying, arriving in Sicily involves a ferry crossing. Regular car/passenger ferries cross the Strait of Messina (the 3km stretch of water that separates Sicily from the Italian mainland) between Villa San Giovanni and Messina, or Reggio di Calabria and Messina. Ferries also sail to Sicily from Genoa, Civitavecchia, Naples and Cagliari, and from Malta and Tunisia.

Across the Strait of Messina

Caronte & Tourist (☑800 627414; www.carontetourist.it) Car ferries to Messina from Villa San Giovanni.

RFI/Bluferries (www.rfi.it) Car ferries and passenger-only boats to Messina from Villa San Giovanni.

From Italy, Tunisia & Malta

During the high season, all routes are busy and you'll

need to book several weeks in advance. The helpful search engine **Traghetti online** (☑892 112; www.traghettionline.net) provides comprehensive route details and an online booking service.

For Palermo, high-season fares (for an adult and car) start at approximately €120 from Genoa, €81 from Civitavecchia and €35 from Naples. For Catania, you should bank on about €100 from Naples. Crossing the Strait of Messina costs €25 with a small car.

Note that while you do not need to show your passport on internal routes you should keep photo ID handy.

Grandi Navi Veloci (☑010 209 45 91; www.gnv.it) To Palermo from Genoa, Civitavecchia, Naples and Tunis.

Grimaldi (☑081 49 64 44; www.grimaldi-ferries.com) To Palermo from Tunis and Salerno; to Catania from Malta; to Trapani from Tunis.

Tirrenia (☑892 123; www.tirrenia.it) To Palermo from Naples and Cagliari; to Trapani from Cagliari.

TTT Lines (☑800 915365; www.tttlines.it) To Catania from Naples.

Ustica Lines (☑0923 87 38 13; www.usticalines.it) Summer services to Trapani, Ustica and Egadi Islands from Naples.

Virtu Ferries (☑095 53 57 11; www.virtuferries.com) This company runs ferries from Malta to Pozzallo in southeastern Sicily, with onward bus connections from Pozzallo to Catania.

GETTING AROUND

If at all possible, it's preferable to have your own car (or motorbike) in Sicily. Getting around the island on public transport is difficult and time-consuming, although not impossible. Connections between the major cities and coastal resorts are fine, but if you want to venture off the beaten track you could find yourself up against it.

In most cases buses are better than trains, which tend to be very slow. That said, public transport is cheap and it does save you the hassle of dealing with incomprehensible one-way systems, narrow medieval streets and nightmarish parking.

To get to the offshore islands there's an extensive system of hydrofoils and ferries. The frequency of services slows considerably in winter, when many of the islands virtually shut down until the next tourist season.

For Pantelleria and the Pelagic Islands, planes are cheaper and faster than ferries.

Bicycle

There's no great cycling tradition in Sicily, but away from the main cities it can be a great way to see the countryside, particularly during spring (March to May) when it's not too hot and the wildflowers are out in bloom. Cycling is also an excellent way of getting round the smaller offshore islands. Note that much of Sicily is hilly, so you'll need to be in pretty good shape to enjoy the scenery.

There are no special road rules for cyclists, but you would be wise to carry a helmet and lights. If cycling during the summer, make sure you have plenty of water and sunblock as the heat can be exhausting.

Bike hire isn't widespread but it's usually available at coastal resorts and on smaller islands. Some small *pensioni* and *agriturismi* also offer use of bikes to guests. Bank on about €15 per day to hire a bike.

Boat

Sicily's offshore islands are served by *traghetti* (ferries) and *aliscafi* (hydrofoils). To the Aeolian Islands services run from Milazzo; to the Egadi Islands from Trapani; to the Pelagic Islands from Porto Empedocle near Agrigento; and to Ustica from Palermo and Trapani.

Services run year-round, although they are pared back considerably in winter and can be affected by adverse sea conditions.

On overnight services (for example, to the Pelagic Islands or Pantelleria) travellers can choose between cabin accommodation or a *poltrona*, which is an airline-type armchair. Deck class is available only during the summer and only on some ferries, so ask when making your booking. All ferries carry vehicles.

The following serve Sicily's offshore islands:

Navigazione Generale Italiana (NGI; ☎800 250000; www.ngi-spa.it) This company offers a ferry-only service operating out of Milazzo for the Aeolian Islands.

Siremar (www.siremar.it) Siremar operates hydrofoils and/or ferries from Palermo to Ustica, from Milazzo and Naples to the Aeolian Islands, from Trapani to Pantelleria and the Egadi Islands, and from Porto Empedocle to the Pelagic Islands.

Ustica Lines (☎0923 87 38 13; www.usticalines.it) This company runs hydrofoils to Ustica, Pantelleria and the Egadi Islands from Trapani; to the Aeolian Islands from Milazzo and Messina; and to the Pelagic Islands from Porto Empedocle.

Bus

Buses are generally the best way of getting around Sicily. They tend to be faster and more convenient than trains, if a little more expensive, and have the added advantage of dropping you off in town centres (many Sicilian train stations are situated a kilometre or so outside the town they serve). Buses serve just about everywhere on the island, although in rural areas services are often linked to school hours and market opening times, which can mean leaving incredibly early or finding yourself stranded after 2pm. Also watch out for Sundays when services are cut to the bone.

In larger cities, the main intercity bus companies have ticket offices or operate through agencies. In smaller towns and villages, bus tickets are often sold in bars or on the bus.

Sicily's four main bus companies – **AST** (☎840 000323; www.aziendasicilianatrasporti. it), **Interbus** (Map p206; ☎093 52 24 60; www.interbus. it), **SAIS Autolinee** (☎800 211020; www.saisautolinee.it) and **SAIS Trasporti** (www. saistrasporti.it) – cover most island destinations as well as cities on the Italian mainland. Although it is not usually necessary to make reservations on buses, it's best to do so in the high season for overnight or long-haul trips.

Car & Motorcycle

There's no escaping the fact that a car makes getting around Sicily much easier. That said, driving on the island is not exactly stress free, particularly in the big cities where traffic congestion, one-way systems and impossible parking can stretch nerves to the limit. But once on the open road, things calm down considerably and the going is generally pretty good.

314

TRANSPORT CAR & MOTORCYCLE

Roads vary in quality. Some, like the main autostradas (motorways), are good, but small rural roads can be dodgy, especially after heavy rain when axle-breaking potholes appear and landslides lead to road closures.

Sicily has a limited network of motorways, which you'll see prefixed by an A on maps and signs on the island. The main east–west link is the A19, which runs from Catania to Palermo. The A18 runs along the Ionian Coast between Messina and Catania, while the A29 goes from Palermo to the western coast, linking the capital with Trapani and (through the western interior) Mazara del Vallo. The A20 runs from Palermo to Messina. Both the A18 and A20 are toll roads.

After autostrade, the best roads are the *strade statali* (state roads), represented on maps as 'S' or 'SS'. *Strade provinciali* (provincial roads) are sometimes little more than country lanes, but provide access to some of the more beautiful scenery and the small towns and villages. They are represented as 'P' or 'SP' on maps.

Automobile Associations

The Italian automobile association is called the **Automobile Club Italiano** (www.aci. it) or ACI for short. It offers

24-hour roadside assistance (☎803 116 or 800 116800 if calling from a non-Italian mobile phone). You do not have to join but will have to pay a fee of at least €100 if you require roadside help.

Fuel & Spare Parts

Petrol stations are located on the main autostrade and state roads, as well as in cities and towns. The bigger ones are often open 24 hours but smaller stations generally open 7am to 7pm Monday to Saturday with a lunchtime break. Many stations also offer self-service. To use the self-service pumps, you'll need to insert a bill (in denominations of €5, €10, €20 or €50) into a machine and then press the number of the pump you're using.

The cost of fuel in Sicily is high – at the time of research €1.74 for a litre of unleaded petrol (*benzina senza piombo*) and €1.63 for diesel (*gasolio*).

If you have mechanical problems, the nearest petrol station should advise a local mechanic, although few have workshops on-site.

Hire

The major car-rental firms are all represented at Palermo and Catania airports and in major cities. Agencies in seaside resorts also rent out scooters and motorcycles.

Avis (☎06 452 10 83 91; www. avisautonoleggio.it)

Europcar (☎199 30 70 30; www.europcar.it)

Hertz (☎02 694 30 019; www. hertz.it)

Maggiore (☎199 15 11 20; www.maggiore.it)

Sicily by Car (☎800 33 44 40; www.sicilybycar.it)

Sixt (☎06 65 21 11; www. sixt.it)

A small car, for example a Fiat Panda, will cost approximately €65/300 per day/ week; for a scooter bank on about €30 to €35 per day. If possible, try to arrange your rental in advance as you'll get much better rates. Similarly, airport agencies charge more than city-centre branches.

To hire a car, you'll need to be over 21 or more (23 or more for some companies) and have a credit card; for a scooter the minimum age is generally 18. When hiring, always make sure you understand what's covered in the rental agreement (unlimited mileage, tax, insurance, collision-damage waiver and so on) and what your liabilities are. It is also a good idea to get fully comprehensive insurance to cover any untoward bumps or scrapes that are quite likely to happen.

If you are hiring from a reputable company, it will usually give you an emergency number to call in the case of breakdown.

Most hire cars have manual gear transmission.

Parking

Parking in Sicilian towns and cities can be difficult. Blue lines by the side of the road denote pay-and-display parking – buy tickets at the meters or from tobacconists – with rates ranging from €0.50 to €1 per hour. Typically, charges are applied between 8.30am and 1.30pm and then from 3pm and 8pm – outside these

ROAD SIGNS

Most Sicilian road signs are pretty self-explanatory, although it does help to know that *uscita* means exit and that town centres are indicated by the word *centro* and a symbol resembling a circular target. Autostrada signs are in green, main roads in blue, and tourist attractions such as archaeological sites (often referred to as *scavi*, meaning ruins) are in brown or yellow.

One recurring problem is that of the disappearing sign. The big towns are well signposted but off the main roads the situation is not always so clear cut. A typical scenario is that you're heading for a small town X, and spot a sign off to the left; you follow it only to discover that it's the last sign you'll ever see for X. In these situations you'll have to resort to trial and error or satnav.

hours you can leave your car free. You'll also find car parks in the main cities and ports, charging anything from €6 per day. As a general rule, the easiest time to find street parking is the early afternoon between 2pm and 4pm.

Fines for parking violations are applied and you are not safe in a hire car as the rental agency will use your credit card to settle fines.

Road Rules

Contrary to appearances there are road rules in Sicily.

➡ Drive on the right and overtake on the left.

➡ Wear seat belts in the front and back.

➡ Wear a helmet when riding all two-wheeled vehicles.

➡ Carry a warning triangle and fluorescent vest to be worn in the event of an emergency.

➡ Keep your blood-alcohol limit under 0.05% while driving.

➡ Keep your blood-alcohol limit at zero while driving if a new licence holder (those with a licence for less than three years).

➡ Do not use hand-held mobile phones while driving.

➡ Turn on your headlights while driving on roads outside municipalities.

Toll Roads

Sicily's toll roads are the Messina–Palermo A20 autostrada and the Messina–Catania A18. Messina to Palermo costs €11.40; Messina to Catania €4.20. The process is simple: pick up a ticket at the automatic machine as you get on the autostrada and pay a cashier as you exit. Make sure you get into the right lane when you exit – follow the white signs illustrated with a black hand holding bank notes. Credit cards are not always accepted, so have cash on hand.

Taxi

Official taxis are white, metered and expensive. If you need a taxi, you can usually find one in taxi ranks at train and bus stations or by telephoning for one. If you book a taxi by phone, you will be charged for the trip the driver makes to reach you.

Rates vary from city to city, but as a rule the minimum charge is about €5. There's also a baffling array of supplementary charges for night-time/Sunday rides, to/from the airport, extra luggage etc. Reckon on about €10 to €15 for most urban routes.

Train

Travelling by train is an option between Sicily's major towns. Services are limited and slow, although cheap and generally reliable. Trains are all operated by **Trenitalia** (☑89 20 21; www.trenitalia. com), except for those that trundle around the base of Etna, which are run by the private **Ferrovia Circumetnea** (☑095 54 12 50; www. circumetnea.it)

There are several types of train: Intercity (IC) or Intercity Night (ICN) trains are the fastest, stopping only at major stations; *espresso* trains stop at all but the most minor stations, while *regionale* trains are the slowest of all, halting at every stop on the line.

Note that all tickets must be validated *before* you board your train. Simply insert them in the yellow machines installed at the entrance to all train platforms. If you don't validate them you risk a fine. This rule does not apply to tickets purchased outside Italy.

Classes & Costs

There are 1st- and 2nd-class seats on Intercity trains but not on the slower *espresso*

SPEED LIMITS

➡ **Autostrade**
130km/h

➡ **Nonurban highways**
110km/h

➡ **Built-up areas**
50km/h

and *regionale* trains. Travel on Intercity trains means paying a supplement, included in the ticket, determined by the distance you are travelling. If you have a *regionale* ticket and end up hopping on an Intercity train, you'll have to pay the difference on board.

Sample prices for one-way train fares are as follows (return fares are generally double).

FROM	TO	FARE
Catania	Agrigento	€11
Catania	Syracuse	€6.50
Catania	Messina	€7.10
Palermo	Agrigento	€8.30
Palermo	Catania	€15.30
Palermo	Messina	€12.50

Left Luggage

There are left-luggage facilities or lockers at most of the bigger train stations on the island. They are usually open 24 hours or close only for a few hours after midnight. Charges are typically about €4 per day per piece of luggage, although at Palermo it costs €14 for 24 hours.

Reservations

There's no need to reserve tickets for travel within Sicily, but if you're heading up to the Italian mainland on weekends or during holiday periods, it's probably a good idea. A booking fee of about €3 is generally applied. Tickets can be booked at station ticket booths or at most travel agencies.

Language

Standard Italian is Sicily's official language and is spoken almost universally on the island, although most locals speak Sicilian among themselves. Sicilian is referred to as an Italian dialect, but is sufficiently different for some to consider it a language in its own right. Sicilians will readily revert to standard Italian when speaking to anyone from the mainland or abroad, though with the occasional Sicilian word thrown in.

The sounds used in spoken Italian can all be found in English. If you read our coloured pronunciation guides as if they were English, you'll be understood. The stressed syllables are indicated with italics. Note that ai is pronounced as in 'aisle', ay as in 'say', ow as in 'how', dz as the 'ds' in 'lids', and that r is a strong and rolled sound. Keep in mind that Italian consonants can have a stronger, emphatic pronunciation – if the consonant is written as a double letter, it should be pronounced a little stronger, eg *sonno* son·no (sleep) versus *sono* so·no (I am).

BASICS

In this chapter the polite/informal and masculine/feminine options are included where necessary, indicated with 'pol/inf' and 'm/f' respectively.

Hello.	*Buongiorno.*	bwon·jor·no
Goodbye.	*Arrivederci.*	a·ree·ve·der·chee
Yes./No.	*Sì./No.*	see/no

WANT MORE?

For in-depth language information and handy phrases, check out Lonely Planet's *Italian Phrasebook*. You'll find it at **shop.lonelyplanet.com**, or you can buy Lonely Planet's iPhone phrasebooks at the Apple App Store.

Excuse me.	*Mi scusi.* (pol)	mee skoo·zee
	Scusami. (inf)	skoo·za·mee
Sorry.	*Mi dispiace.*	mee dees·pya·che
Please.	*Per favore.*	per fa·vo·re
Thank you.	*Grazie.*	gra·tsye
You're welcome.	*Prego.*	pre·go

How are you?
Come sta/stai? (pol/inf) ko·me sta/stai

Fine. And you?
Bene. E Lei/tu? (pol/inf) be·ne e lay/too

What's your name?
Come si chiama? pol ko·me see kya·ma
Come ti chiami? inf ko·me tee kya·mee

My name is ...
Mi chiamo ... mee kya·mo ...

Do you speak English?
Parla/Parli par·la/par·lee
inglese? (pol/inf) een·gle·ze

I don't understand.
Non capisco. non ka·pee·sko

ACCOMMODATION

Do you have a ... room?	*Avete una camera ...?*	a·ve·te oo·na ka·me·ra ...
double	*doppia con letto matrimoniale*	do·pya kon le·to ma·tree·mo·nya·le
single	*singola*	seen·go·la

How much is it per ...?	*Quanto costa per ...?*	kwan·to kos·ta per ...
night	*una notte*	oo·na no·te
person	*persona*	per·so·na

Is breakfast included?
La colazione è la ko·la·tsyo·ne e
compresa? kom·pre·sa

air-con	aria condizionata	a·rya kon·dee·tsyo·na·ta
bathroom	bagno	ba·nyo
campsite	campeggio	kam·pe·jo
guesthouse	pensione	pen·syo·ne
hotel	albergo	al·ber·go
youth hostel	ostello della gioventù	os·te·lo de·la jo·ven·too
window	finestra	fee·nes·tra

DIRECTIONS

Where's ...?
Dov'è ...? do·ve ...

What's the address?
Qual è l'indirizzo? kwa·le leen·dee·ree·tso

Could you please write it down?
Può scriverlo, per favore? pwo skree·ver·lo per fa·vo·re

Can you show me (on the map)?
Può mostrarmi (sulla pianta)? pwo mos·trar·mee (soo·la pyan·ta)

at the corner	all'angolo	a·lan·go·lo
at the traffic lights	al semaforo	al se·ma·fo·ro
behind	dietro	dye·tro
far	lontano	lon·ta·no
in front of	davanti a	da·van·tee a
left	a sinistra	a see·nee·stra
near	vicino	vee·chee·no
opposite	di fronte a	dee fron·te a
right	a destra	a de·stra
straight ahead	sempre diritto	sem·pre dee·ree·to

EATING & DRINKING

What would you recommend?
Cosa mi consiglia? ko·za mee kon·see·lya

What's in that dish?
Quali ingredienti ci sono in questo piatto? kwa·li een·gre·dyen·tee chee so·no een kwe·sto pya·to

What's the local speciality?
Qual è la specialità di questa regione? kwa·le la spe·cha·lee·ta dee kwe·sta re·jo·ne

That was delicious!
Era squisito! e·ra skwee·zee·to

Cheers!
Salute! sa·loo·te

Please bring the bill.
Mi porta il conto, per favore? mee por·ta eel kon·to per fa·vo·re

KEY PATTERNS

To get by in Italian, mix and match these simple patterns with words of your choice:

When's (the next flight)?
A che ora è (il prossimo volo)? a ke o·ra e (eel pro·see·mo vo·lo)

Where's (the station)?
Dov'è (la stazione)? do·ve (la sta·tsyo·ne)

I'm looking for (a hotel).
Sto cercando (un albergo). sto cher·kan·do (oon al·ber·go)

Do you have (a map)?
Ha (una pianta)? a (oo·na pyan·ta)

Is there (a toilet)?
C'è (un gabinetto)? che (oon ga·bee·ne·to)

I'd like (a coffee).
Vorrei (un caffè). vo·ray (oon ka·fe)

I'd like to (hire a car).
Vorrei (noleggiare una macchina). vo·ray (no·le·ja·re oo·na ma·kee·na)

Can I (enter)?
Posso (entrare)? po·so (en·tra·re)

Could you please (help me)?
Può (aiutarmi), per favore? pwo (a·yoo·tar·mee) per fa·vo·re

Do I have to (book a seat)?
Devo (prenotare un posto)? de·vo (pre·no·ta·re oon po·sto)

I'd like to reserve a table for ...	Vorrei prenotare un tavolo per ...	vo·ray pre·no·ta·re oon ta·vo·lo per ...
(eight) o'clock	le (otto)	le (o·to)
(two) people	(due) persone	(doo·e) per·so·ne

I don't eat ...	Non mangio ...	non man·jo ...
eggs	uova	wo·va
fish	pesce	pe·she
nuts	noci	no·chee
(red) meat	carne (rossa)	kar·ne (ro·sa)

Key Words

| bar | locale | lo·ka·le |
| bottle | bottiglia | bo·tee·lya |

breakfast	prima colazione	pree·ma ko·la·tsyo·ne
cafe	bar	bar
cold	freddo	fre·do
dinner	cena	che·na
drink list	lista delle bevande	lee·sta de·le be·van·de
fork	forchetta	for·ke·ta
glass	bicchiere	bee·kye·re
grocery store	alimentari	a·lee·men·ta·ree
hot	caldo	kal·do
knife	coltello	kol·te·lo
lunch	pranzo	pran·dzo
market	mercato	mer·ka·to
menu	menù	me·noo
plate	piatto	pya·to
restaurant	ristorante	ree·sto·ran·te
spicy	piccante	pee·kan·te
spoon	cucchiaio	koo·kya·yo
vegetarian (food)	vegetariano	ve·je·ta·rya·no
with	con	kon
without	senza	sen·tsa

Meat & Fish

beef	manzo	man·dzo
chicken	pollo	po·lo
duck	anatra	a·na·tra
fish	pesce	pe·she
herring	aringa	a·reen·ga
lamb	agnello	a·nye·lo
lobster	aragosta	a·ra·gos·ta
meat	carne	kar·ne
mussels	cozze	ko·tse
oysters	ostriche	o·stree·ke
pork	maiale	ma·ya·le
prawn	gambero	gam·be·ro
salmon	salmone	sal·mo·ne
scallops	capasante	ka·pa·san·te
seafood	frutti di mare	froo·tee dee ma·re
shrimp	gambero	gam·be·ro
squid	calamari	ka·la·ma·ree
trout	trota	tro·ta
tuna	tonno	to·no
turkey	tacchino	ta·kee·no
veal	vitello	vee·te·lo

Fruit & Vegetables

apple	mela	me·la
beans	fagioli	fa·jo·lee
cabbage	cavolo	ka·vo·lo
capsicum	peperone	pe·pe·ro·ne
carrot	carota	ka·ro·ta
cauliflower	cavolfiore	ka·vol·fyo·re
cucumber	cetriolo	che·tree·o·lo
fruit	frutta	froo·ta
grapes	uva	oo·va
lemon	limone	lee·mo·ne
lentils	lenticchie	len·tee·kye
mushroom	funghi	foon·gee
nuts	noci	no·chee
onions	cipolle	chee·po·le
orange	arancia	a·ran·cha
peach	pesca	pe·ska
peas	piselli	pee·ze·lee
pineapple	ananas	a·na·nas
plum	prugna	proo·nya
potatoes	patate	pa·ta·te
spinach	spinaci	spee·na·chee
tomatoes	pomodori	po·mo·do·ree
vegetables	verdura	ver·doo·ra

Other

bread	pane	pa·ne
butter	burro	boo·ro
cheese	formaggio	for·ma·jo
eggs	uova	wo·va
honey	miele	mye·le
ice	ghiaccio	gya·cho
jam	marmellata	mar·me·la·ta
noodles	pasta	pas·ta
oil	olio	o·lyo

Signs

Aperto	Open
Chiuso	Closed
Donne	Women
Entrata/Ingresso	Entrance
Gabinetti/Servizi	Toilets
Informazioni	Information
Proibito/Vietato	Prohibited
Uomini	Men
Uscita	Exit

pepper	pepe	pe·pe
rice	riso	ree·zo
salt	sale	sa·le
soup	minestra	mee·nes·tra
soy sauce	salsa di soia	sal·sa dee so·ya
sugar	zucchero	tsoo·ke·ro
vinegar	aceto	a·che·to

Drinks

beer	birra	bee·ra
coffee	caffè	ka·fe
(orange) juice	succo (d'arancia)	soo·ko (da·ran·cha)
milk	latte	la·te
red wine	vino rosso	vee·no ro·so
soft drink	bibita	bee·bee·ta
tea	tè	te
(mineral) water	acqua (minerale)	a·kwa (mee·ne·ra·le)
white wine	vino bianco	vee·no byan·ko

EMERGENCIES

Help!
Aiuto! — a·yoo·to

Leave me alone!
Lasciami in pace! — la·sha·mee een pa·che

I'm lost.
Mi sono perso/a. (m/f) — mee so·no per·so/a

Call the police!
Chiami la polizia! — kya·mee la po·lee·tsee·a

Call a doctor!
Chiami un medico! — kya·mee oon me·dee·ko

Where are the toilets?
Dove sono i gabinetti? — do·ve so·no ee ga·bee·ne·tee

I'm sick.
Mi sento male. — mee sen·to ma·le

It hurts here.
Mi fa male qui. — mee fa ma·le kwee

I'm allergic to ...
Sono allergico/a a ... (m/f) — so·no a·ler·jee·ko/a a ...

Question Words
How?	Come?	ko·me
What?	Che cosa?	ke ko·za
When?	Quando?	kwan·do
Where?	Dove?	do·ve
Who?	Chi?	kee
Why?	Perché?	per·ke

SHOPPING & SERVICES

I'd like to buy ...
Vorrei comprare ... — vo·ray kom·pra·re ...

I'm just looking.
Sto solo guardando. — sto so·lo gwar·dan·do

Can I look at it?
Posso dare un'occhiata? — po·so da·re oo·no·kya·ta

How much is this?
Quanto costa questo? — kwan·to kos·ta kwe·sto

It's too expensive.
È troppo caro. — e tro·po ka·ro

Can you lower the price?
Può farmi lo sconto? — pwo far·mee lo skon·to

There's a mistake in the bill.
C'è un errore nel conto. — che oo·ne·ro·re nel kon·to

ATM	Bancomat	ban·ko·mat
credit card	carta di credito	kar·ta dee kre·dee·to
post office	ufficio postale	oo·fee·cho pos·ta·le
tourist office	ufficio del turismo	oo·fee·cho del too·reez·mo

TIME & DATES

What time is it?
Che ora è? — ke o·ra e

It's one o'clock.
È l'una. — e loo·na

It's (two) o'clock.
Sono le (due). — so·no le (doo·e)

Half past (one).
(L'una) e mezza. — (loo·na) e me·dza

in the morning	di mattina	dee ma·tee·na
in the afternoon	di pomeriggio	dee po·me·ree·jo
in the evening	di sera	dee se·ra

yesterday	ieri	ye·ree
today	oggi	o·jee
tomorrow	domani	do·ma·nee

Monday	lunedì	loo·ne·dee
Tuesday	martedì	mar·te·dee
Wednesday	mercoledì	mer·ko·le·dee
Thursday	giovedì	jo·ve·dee
Friday	venerdì	ve·ner·dee
Saturday	sabato	sa·ba·to
Sunday	domenica	do·me·nee·ka

Numbers

1	uno	oo·no
2	due	doo·e
3	tre	tre
4	quattro	kwa·tro
5	cinque	cheen·kwe
6	sei	say
7	sette	se·te
8	otto	o·to
9	nove	no·ve
10	dieci	dye·chee
20	venti	ven·tee
30	trenta	tren·ta
40	quaranta	kwa·ran·ta
50	cinquanta	cheen·kwan·ta
60	sessanta	se·san·ta
70	settanta	se·tan·ta
80	ottanta	o·tan·ta
90	novanta	no·van·ta
100	cento	chen·to
1000	mille	mee·lel

January	gennaio	je·na·yo
February	febbraio	fe·bra·yo
March	marzo	mar·tso
April	aprile	a·pree·le
May	maggio	ma·jo
June	giugno	joo·nyo
July	luglio	loo·lyo
August	agosto	a·gos·to
September	settembre	se·tem·bre
October	ottobre	o·to·bre
November	novembre	no·vem·bre
December	dicembre	dee·chem·bre

TRANSPORT

Public Transport

At what time does the ... leave/arrive?	A che ora parte/ arriva ...?	a ke o·ra par·te/ a·ree·va ...
boat	la nave	la na·ve
bus	l'autobus	low·to·boos
ferry	il traghetto	eel tra·ge·to
plane	l'aereo	la·e·re·o
train	il treno	eel tre·no

... ticket	un biglietto ...	oon bee·lye·to
one-way	di sola andata	dee so·la an·da·ta
return	di andata e ritorno	dee an·da·ta e ree·tor·no

bus stop	fermata dell'autobus	fer·ma·ta del ow·to·boos
platform	binario	bee·na·ryo
ticket office	biglietteria	bee·lye·te·ree·a
timetable	orario	o·ra·ryo
train station	stazione ferroviaria	sta·tsyo·ne fe·ro·vyar·ya

Does it stop at ...?
Si ferma a ...?   see fer·ma a ...

Please tell me when we get to ...
Mi dica per favore   mee dee·ka per fa·vo·re
quando arriviamo a ...   kwan·do a·ree·vya·mo a ...

I want to get off here.
Voglio scendere qui.   vo·lyo shen·de·re kwee

Driving & Cycling

I'd like to hire a/an ...	Vorrei noleggiare un/una ... (m/f)	vo·ray no·le·ja·re oon/oo·na ...
4WD	fuoristrada (m)	fwo·ree·stra·da
bicycle	bicicletta (f)	bee·chee·kle·ta
car	macchina (f)	ma·kee·na
motorbike	moto (f)	mo·to

bicycle pump	pompa della bicicletta	pom·pa de·la bee·chee·kle·ta
child seat	seggiolino	se·jo·lee·no
helmet	casco	kas·ko
mechanic	meccanico	me·ka·nee·ko
petrol/gas	benzina	ben·dzee·na
service station	stazione di servizio	sta·tsyo·ne dee ser·vee·tsyo

Is this the road to ...?
Questa strada porta a ...? kwe·sta stra·da por·ta a ...

(How long) Can I park here?
(Per quanto tempo)   (per kwan·to tem·po)
Posso parcheggiare qui? po·so par·ke·ja·re kwee

The car/motorbike has broken down (at ...).
La macchina/moto si è   la ma·kee·na/mo·to see e
guastata (a ...).   gwas·ta·ta (a ...)

I have a flat tyre.
Ho una gomma bucata.   o oo·na go·ma boo·ka·ta

I've run out of petrol.
Ho esaurito la   o e·zow·ree·to la
benzina.   ben·dzee·na

GLOSSARY

abbazia – abbey

affi ttacamere – rooms for rent

agora – marketplace, meeting place

agriturismo – farm stay

albergo – hotel

alimentari – grocery shop, delicatessen

anfi teatro – amphitheatre

ara – altar

arco – arch

autostrada – motorway, freeway

badia – abbey

baglio – manor house

bancomat – ATM

belvedere – panoramic viewpoint

benzina – petrol

borgo – ancient town or village; sometimes it's used to mean the equivalent of via

cambio – money exchange

campanile – bell tower

campo – fi eld

cannolo – pastry shell stuffed with sweet ricotta

cappella – chapel

carabinieri – police with military and civil duties

Carnevale – carnival period between Epiphany and Lent

casa – house

cava – quarry

centro – centre

chiesa – church

città – town, city

clientelismo – system of political patronage

comune – equivalent to municipality or county; town or city council

contrada – district

corso – main street, avenue

cortile – courtyard

Cosa Nostra – Our Thing; alternative name for the Mafia

diretto – direct; slow train

duomo – cathedral

enoteca – wine bar, wine shop

fangho – mud bath

faraglione – rock tower

ferrovia – train station

festa – festival

fiume – river

fontana – fountain

fossa – pit, hole

funivia – cable car

gola – gorge

golfo – gulf

grotta – cave

guardia medica – emergency doctor service

IC – Intercity; fast train

interregionale – long-distance train that stops frequently

isola – island

lago – lake

largo – small square

latomia – small quarry

lido – beach

locale – slow local train; also called *regionale*

locanda – inn, small hotel

lungomare – seafront road, promenade

mare – sea

mercato – market

molo – wharf

monte – mountain

municipio – town hall, municipal offices

museo – museum

Natale – Christmas

oratorio – oratory

ospedale – hospital

osteria – inn

palazzo – palace, mansion

parco – park

Pasqua – Easter

passeggiata – evening stroll

pensione – small hotel

piazza – square

piazzale – large open square

ponte – bridge

porta – gate, door

questura – police station

reale – royal

regionale – slow local train; also called *locale*

rifugio – mountain hut

riserva naturale – nature reserve

rocca – fortress; rock

sagra – festival, generally dedicated to one food item or theme

sala – room

santuario – sanctuary

scalinata – staircase, steps

spiaggia – beach

stazione – station

strada – street, road

teatro – theatre

tempio – temple

tonnara – tuna-processing plant

torre – tower

traghetto – ferry, boat

treno – train

via – street, road

viale – avenue

vicolo – alley, alleyway

Behind the Scenes

SEND US YOUR FEEDBACK

We love to hear from travellers – your comments keep us on our toes and help make our books better. Our well-travelled team reads every word on what you loved or loathed about this book. Although we cannot reply individually to postal submissions, we always guarantee that your feedback goes straight to the appropriate authors, in time for the next edition. Each person who sends us information is thanked in the next edition – the most useful submissions are rewarded with a selection of digital PDF chapters.

Visit **lonelyplanet.com/contact** to submit your updates and suggestions or to ask for help. Our award-winning website also features inspirational travel stories, news and discussions.

Note: We may edit, reproduce and incorporate your comments in Lonely Planet products such as guidebooks, websites and digital products, so let us know if you don't want your comments reproduced or your name acknowledged. For a copy of our privacy policy visit lonelyplanet.com/privacy.

OUR READERS

Many thanks to the travellers who used the last edition and wrote to us with helpful hints, useful advice and interesting anecdotes:

Alba Martínez, Albert Hassel, Alex Rance, Andrea Amore, Andrea Kraissenger, Anne Falck Nordskar, Ausra Kamicaityte, Bachar Houli, Brandon Ellis, Brett Deledio, Carla Conti, Carlo Costa, Caroline Callow, Charlotte Hendriks, Chris Kyprianou, Christina Judd, Christine Beard, Ciro Spataro, Daniel Schlatter, David Abbott, Dustin Martin, Eleonor Myer, Emanuele Buccheri, Emma Phillips, Emma Ponente, Fidel Gaviola, Gail Lee Saetre, Gary Lopes, Geoff Cole, Giacomo Minaglia, Gianluca Maggiulli, Guido Braschi, Heidi Gabrielsen, Hannu von Hertzen, Ivan Maric, Jack Riewoldt, Jake King, James Williams, Javier Rodríguez, Jeremie Savoir, Joe Parlavecchio, John Rose, Julio Paleta, Julio Sargos, Luciano Baracco, Manfred Mareck, Manuela Arigoni, Marcos Brigans, Marina Poot, Martin Gascoigne, Martin Strothjohann, Mary Oldsiness, Meggy Surimy, Michael Riding, Nelleke Kruijs Voorberge, Nick Vlastuin, Nicola Fiorilla, Pablo Sanchez, Patrick O'Shea, Peter Osburt, Ramon Sonsoz, Richard Bourgoynes, Roger van Founzer, Rolf Grau, Russo Giuseppe, Sarah Poulter, Siegfried Schwab & Ina-Kristin Schlude, Stephanie Schintler, Toby Miller, Trent Cotchin, Tyrone Vickery, Vicki Nicolosi, Victor LaCerva, William & Kathy Leipham

AUTHOR THANKS

Gregor Clark

Grazie mille to all of the kind-hearted Italians who helped make this trip so memorable, especially Angela and Nicoletta in Palermo, the Tagliavia family in Polizzi Generosa, Francesca in Stromboli, Marisin and Salvatore in Scopello, Stefano in Milazzo, and Diana in Lipari. Thanks to Gurty Spam for joining me on the Aeolians and helping me renew my Stromboli obsession. Finally, big hugs to Gaen, Meigan and Chloe, who always make returning home the happiest part of the trip.

Vesna Maric

Thanks, as always, go to Rafael, Frida, my mother and Susana. Big thanks go to Simone, Alessandra, Cesare and baby Arturo, and to Alessandra's mother. *Grazie mille* to Ettore Messina, and Andrea and Florinda in Favara. Thank yous to Joe Bindloss and Gregor Clark – it was a pleasure to work with both of you.

ACKNOWLEDGMENTS

Climate Map Data Climate map data adapted from Peel MC, Finlayson BL & McMahon TA (2007) 'Updated World Map of the Köppen-Geiger Climate Classification', *Hydrology and Earth System Sciences*, 11, 163344.

Cover photograph: Mondello Harbour, Palermo; Alessandro Saffo/4 Corners

THIS BOOK

This sixth edition of Lonely Planet's *Sicily* guidebook was researched and written by Gregor Clark and Vesna Maric. The previous edition was written by Virginia Maxwell and Duncan Garwood, and the 4th edition was written by Vesna Maric. This guidebook was commissioned in Lonely Planet's London office, and produced by the following:
Commissioning Editors Joe Bindloss, Helena Smith

Coordinating Editors Justin Flynn, Simon Williamson
Senior Cartographers Corey Hutchison, Anthony Phelan
Coordinating Layout Designer Clara Monitto
Managing Editors Sasha Baskett, Annelies Mertens
Senior Editor Karyn Noble
Managing Layout Designer Jane Hart
Assisting Editors Kellie Langdon, Charlotte Orr, Kirsten Rawlings
Assisting Cartographers Drishya C, Jackson James,

Nithya Kalyani M, Anoop Shetty
Internal Image Research Kylie McLaughlin
Cover Research Naomi Parker
Language Content Branislava Vladisavljevic

Thanks to Shahara Ahmed, Anita Banh, Ryan Evans, Samantha Forge, Larissa Frost, Chris Girdler, Genesys India, Jouve India, Katie O'Connell, Trent Paton, Martine Power, Angela Tinson, Gerard Walker

Index

NOTES

Map Legend

Sights
- Beach
- Buddhist
- Castle
- Christian
- Hindu
- Islamic
- Jewish
- Monument
- Museum/Gallery
- Ruin
- Winery/Vineyard
- Zoo
- Other Sight

Activities, Courses & Tours
- Diving/Snorkelling
- Canoeing/Kayaking
- Skiing
- Surfing
- Swimming/Pool
- Walking
- Windsurfing
- Other Activity/Course/Tour

Sleeping
- Sleeping
- Camping

Eating
- Eating

Drinking
- Drinking
- Cafe

Entertainment
- Entertainment

Shopping
- Shopping

Information
- Post Office
- Tourist Information

Transport
- Airport
- Border Crossing
- Bus
- Cable Car/Funicular
- Cycling
- Ferry
- Monorail
- Parking
- S-Bahn
- Taxi
- Train/Railway
- Tram
- Tube Station
- U-Bahn
- Underground Train Station
- Other Transport

Routes
- Tollway
- Freeway
- Primary
- Secondary
- Tertiary
- Lane
- Unsealed Road
- Plaza/Mall
- Steps
- Tunnel
- Pedestrian Overpass
- Walking Tour
- Walking Tour Detour
- Path

Boundaries
- International
- State/Province
- Disputed
- Regional/Suburb
- Marine Park
- Cliff
- Wall

Population
- Capital (National)
- Capital (State/Province)
- City/Large Town
- Town/Village

Geographic
- Hut/Shelter
- Lighthouse
- Lookout
- Mountain/Volcano
- Oasis
- Park
- Pass
- Picnic Area
- Waterfall

Hydrography
- River/Creek
- Intermittent River
- Swamp/Mangrove
- Reef
- Canal
- Water
- Dry/Salt/Intermittent Lake
- Glacier

Areas
- Beach/Desert
- Cemetery (Christian)
- Cemetery (Other)
- Park/Forest
- Sportsground
- Sight (Building)
- Top Sight (Building)

OUR STORY

A beat-up old car, a few dollars in the pocket and a sense of adventure. In 1972 that's all Tony and Maureen Wheeler needed for the trip of a lifetime – across Europe and Asia overland to Australia. It took several months, and at the end – broke but inspired – they sat at their kitchen table writing and stapling together their first travel guide, *Across Asia on the Cheap*. Within a week they'd sold 1500 copies. Lonely Planet was born.

Today, Lonely Planet has offices in Melbourne, London, Oakland and Delhi, with more than 600 staff and writers. We share Tony's belief that 'a great guidebook should do three things: inform, educate and amuse'.

OUR WRITERS

Gregor Clark

Coordinating Author, Palermo, Western Sicily, Tyrrhenian Coast, Aeolian Islands

Gregor caught the Italy bug at age 14 during a year in Florence, in which his professor dad trundled the family off to see every fresco, mosaic and museum within a 1000km radius. He's lived in Venice and Le Marche, led Italian bike tours, and huffed and puffed across the Dolomites while researching Lonely Planet's *Cycling Italy*, but his abiding passion is for Sicily, an island he's explored extensively in multiple research trips over the past several years. Highlights of his latest visit include celebrating his birthday atop an erupting Stromboli. A lifelong polyglot with a degree in Romance languages, Gregor writes frequently about Europe and South America for Lonely Planet. He lives with his wife and two daughters in Vermont, USA. Gregor also wrote the Plan Your Trip section (except for Outdoor Activities and Travel with Children), the Sicily Today, History, The Sicilian Table and The Sicilian Way of Life Understand features and the Survival Guide.

Read more about Gregor at:
lonelyplanet.com/members/gregorclark

Vesna Maric

Ionian Coast, Syracuse & the Southeast, Central Sicily, Mediterranean Coast

Vesna has been working for Lonely Planet for nearly a decade and loves writing about the Mediterranean islands. She cherished working on the Sicily guidebook for the second time, and loved revisiting old favourites such as Catania's fish market and the Piazza Duomo at Syracuse. She returned with her three-year-old daughter this time. Vesna also wrote the Outdoor Activities, Travel with Children, Sicily on Page & Screen, The Mafia, and Art & Architecture chapters.

Published by Lonely Planet Publications Pty Ltd
ABN 36 005 607 983
6th edition – January 2014
ISBN 978 1 74220 048 4
© Lonely Planet 2014   Photographs © as indicated 2014
10 9 8 7 6 5 4 3 2
Printed in China